Cost Accounting in Germany and Japan

Münsteraner Schriften zur Internationalen Unternehmensrechnung

Herausgegeben von Peter Kajüter

Band 5

PETER LANG
Frankfurt am Main · Berlin · Bern · Bruxelles · New York · Oxford · Wien

Matthias Moeschler

Cost Accounting in Germany and Japan

A Comparative Analysis

PETER LANG
Internationaler Verlag der Wissenschaften

Bibliographic Information published by the Deutsche Nationalbibliothek
The Deutsche Nationalbibliothek lists this publication in the Deutsche Nationalbibliografie; detailed bibliographic data is available in the internet at http://dnb.d-nb.de.

Zugl.: Münster (Westfalen), Univ., Diss., 2012

D 6
ISSN 1868-7687
ISBN 978-3-631-62389-3

www.peterlang.de

Preface

Today's cost accounting practices have developed over time and have been shaped by various institutional forces, in particular by national culture, education and financial accounting systems. As a consequence, national specifics in cost accounting systems have emerged and still prevail today. These cross-national differences often impede an effective management control in multinational companies. However, companies that try to solve this challenge by standardizing cost accounting systems throughout their subsidiaries might experience resistance by local employees that have different views, habits, and preferences regarding cost accounting. Management accountants in multinational companies should thus be sensitized for cross-national differences in cost accounting so that they can find a suitable trade-off between global standardization and local differentiation. Comparative management accounting research not only contributes in this respect, but can also identify innovative cost accounting systems like ABC and Grenzplankostenrechnung that might be adopted in other countries as well to improve management accounting.

Although empirical research demonstrates that cost and management accounting differs cross-nationally, many arguments from literature are rather anecdotal than empirically verified due to methodological shortcomings. In his dissertation Matthias Moeschler addresses this research deficit. Based on a theoretical framework and a comprehensive analysis of the state of research, he conducted a comprehensive empirical study comparing cost accounting systems between Germany and Japan. Through intensive efforts Matthias Moeschler and his Japanese research partner, Prof. Dr. Shinsuke Wada, obtained a very good response of 626 companies from both countries.

Matthias Moeschler empirically shows that German companies have more complex and more timely cost accounting systems than their Japanese counterparts. He explains these cross-national differences by demonstrating that German cost accountants are more specialized, have more theoretical knowledge, have more comprehensive IT systems and receive more top management support than their Japanese counterparts. Cost accounting objectives on the contrary differ only slightly between both countries. The author furthermore identifies different reasons for German and Japanese companies to install complex and timely cost accounting systems. Based on the responses from Germany and Japan, Matthias Moeschler elaborates several recommendations for practitioners. Graphical analyses, for example, indicate that complexity of cost accounting systems has a positive but diminishing marginal effect upon cost accounting performance in Germany. In Japan, this relationship is identified for both complexity and timeliness of cost accounting systems.

The empirical findings provide comprehensive insights into similarities and differences of cost accounting systems between Germany and Japan. They are highly relevant to both researchers and practitioners. This study furthermore identifies several suggestions how to improve research on comparative management accounting. The study thereby significantly contributes to the research stream of comparative management accounting.

Considering the valuable academic contribution and the practical relevance of Matthias Moeschler's work, I wish his thesis a lot attention by academics and practitioners.

Münster, January 2012 Prof. Dr. Peter Kajüter

Preface

The different developments of accounting systems affect the construct of current cost accounting practices in Japan and Germany. In general, accounting theory and its practices from not only UK/USA but also Germany were introduced into Japan at the early stage of establishing Japanese management systems. The accounting systems from different cultural backgrounds gradually took root, being eventually modified to fit the Japanese cultural and institutional contexts in organizations.

Japanese companies developed a distinct approach to cost accounting. However, cost management tools like target costing were intensively discussed in literature, little is known in Western countries about the particularities of Japanese cost accounting apart from some anecdotal evidence. This lack of research is the starting point for the thesis of Matthias Moeschler. Knowing the particularities of cost accounting in Japan, UK/USA and Germany is valuable to enhance national cost accounting by identifying successful foreign systems and practices as well as to manage multinational companies by sensitizing practitioners about cross-national differences in cost accounting.

There are many comparative management accounting studies so far, however few capture the relationships of culture and cost accounting practices. Matthias Moeschler has carried through a comprehensive study with highly theoretical and practical relevance. His study provides several new empirical findings while considering for methodological particularities in comparative management accounting research. Matthias Moeschler has analyzed 626 responses from Japan and Germany to empirically demonstrate differences in cost accounting between both countries. Utilizing the data from the questionnaire obtained from Japanese and German companies, he further traces these differences back to cross-national variance in education and specialization of management accountants.

Some findings from this research prevail that Japanese cost accounting systems are more simple than German counterparts. Although both countries are in accord with avoiding uncertainty, it does not necessarily mean that two countries use the same tools in cost accounting. Japanese cost accountants acquire knowledge of cost accounting mainly on the job. In this sense, the main functions of Japanese cost accountants are integrated into Japanese management systems.

In fact, comparing Japan and Germany is useful in understanding how cost accounting practices vary and resemble under different cultural, economic, and institutional conditions. It is also noteworthy even in competitive and international concerns to find out the deeper cross-cultural understandings by considering the comprehensive features of cost accounting practices in Japan and Germany.

I have greatly enjoyed working with Matthias Moeschler and Prof. Dr. Peter Kajüter, his supervisor, on this international research project. I would like to thank Matthias Moeschler and Prof. Dr. Kajuter for fruitful discussions.

I wish that this thesis will gain in popularity not only in Germany and Japan but also in Anglophone countries looking for the further development of cost accounting systems.

I wish Matthias Moeschler every success and happiness – both in his career and his private life.

Osaka, January 2012 Associate Prof. Dr. Shinsuke Wada

Acknowledgement

I have written this thesis during my time as a PhD student at the Chair of International Accounting at the University of Münster. This work was accepted as a dissertation by the Münster School of Business and Economics in January 2012.

Writing an ambitious PhD thesis is a great challenge, which I could not have completed on my own. Therefore, I would like to thank all those who have supported me in various ways. I am very gratefully obliged to my academic teacher and supervisor, Prof. Dr. Peter Kajüter, who has welcomed me as a PhD student at his chair and who has encouraged my work and provided many valuable suggestions to improve this study. I would also like to thank him for the numerous opportunities to present my work on conferences. I express my sincere gratitude to Prof. Dr. Shinsuke Wada. Without his help it would not have been possible to collect this large number of Japanese responses. I have further received great motivation for my research project from him and I have obtained valuable insights about Japanese particularities in society, management, and accounting. I would further like to thank Prof. Dr. Wolfgang Berens who reviewed and evaluated my study as a second referee. Sincere thanks are further given to Prof. Dr. van Suntum for being the third referee.

I have further received valuable suggestions for my research project by my dear colleagues and friends at the Chair of International Accounting. In particular, I would like to sincerely thank Dr. Tobias Dickmann and Dr. Simon Esser who have both supported me through my entire time at the chair of International Accounting and who have provided me with valuable advice on my research project. I want also to emphasize Dr. Tobias Dickmann's efforts for proofreading the entire dissertation and Dr. Ann-Marie Nienaber for discussing the challenges of applying PLS. I like further to thank the students working at the chair for their extensive literature and copy work. I owe many thanks in particular to Daniela Peters, who supported me by preparing prior research on comparative management accounting, as well as Sophie Grütering, Aaron von Felbert, Gregor Hagemann, and Patrick Hammel who greatly supported me with the collection of the German data set.

I am indebted to more than 600 management accountants in Germany and Japan who responded to the request for information about their companies' cost accounting systems and I wish to thank the Institute of Management Accountants' Foundation for Applied Research and the Melco Foundation for financial support.

With great pleasure I remember my time in Münster with my dear colleagues and friends at the Chair of International Accounting. First of all, I would like to thank Dr. Kristian Bachert. With great pleasure I remember the unforgettable and entertaining time together with him – both at the chair and on our nightlife trips. The only drawback was that he had sometimes to leave our nightlife rips earlier as intended. I have further appreciated Dr. Martin Merschdorf's characteristic sense of humor and I will never forget our collective "painting projects". Special thanks go further to Dr. Tobias Dickmann and Dr. Simon Esser. Both have enriched my first two years at the chair and I have greatly enjoyed our reunions in Münster and Düsseldorf after they have completed their theses. I would further like to thank my colleagues Christina Voets, Daniel Blaesing, Thomas Poplat, and Moritz Schröder for our entertaining nightlife trips and events. With great pleasure I also remember my time with my dear colleagues Marcel Baki, Christian Reisloh, and Maximilian Saucke. Finally, I like to thank Leila Prousch for her administrative support and our pleasant cooperation.

Finally, I extend my profound appreciation and dedication to my girlfriend, my parents, and my sister who have helped me through the difficult times of my research project. To them I dedicate this thesis. I thank Marlene Kraatz for her love, care, understanding, and patience, my parents Rita and Heinrich Moeschler for their continual love, interest, as well as moral and spiritual support during my entire life, and my sister Christiane Moeschler for her help and company. Christiane, I wish you all the best for the start of your young family!

Münster, January 2012 Matthias Moeschler

Contents overview

Contents

Index of illustrations

Index of tables

Index of appendices

Index of abbreviations

ABC	activity-based costing
N/A	no answer possible
bn.	billion
BSC	balanced scorecard
c.	column
CA	California
cf.	confer, compare
CIMA	Chartered Institute of Management Accountants
DPC	Diagnosis Procedure Combination
DRG	Diagnosis Related Groups
e.g.	examples given
ed(s).	editor(s)
edn.	edition
ERP	enterprise resource planning
et al.	et alii; and others
EU	European Union
EVA	Economic Value Added
f.	and the following
F.R.	Federal Republic
GAAP	Generally Accepted Accounting Principles
GLOBE	Global Leadership and Organizational Behaviour Effectiveness Research Program
GPK	Grenzplankostenrechnung
H	hypothesis
HGB	Handelsgesetzbuch
i.e.	that is
IAS	International Accounting Standards
ICFAR	International Comparative Financial Accounting Research

ICMA	Institute of Certified Management Accountants
IFRS	International Financial Reporting Standards
IMA	Institute of Management Accountants
JIT	just-in-time
KMO	Kaiser-Meyer-Olkin measure of sampling adequacy
Mass.	Massachusetts
max	maximum
mill.	million
min	minimum
MNC	multinational corporations
n.e.c.	not elsewhere classified
N/A	not applicable
p.	page
p	probability
P/L statement	profit and loss statement
PDF	Portable Document Format
PLS	partial least squares
R	reversed
RCA	resource consumption accounting
SEM	structural equation modeling
TQC	total quality control
UK	United Kingdom
US	United States
USA	United States of America
VIF	variance inflation factor
vs.	versus

Index of symbols

Ø	arithmetic mean
σ	standard deviation
*	10%-significance level
**	5%-significance level
***	1%-significance level
R	correlation coefficient
X	variable on the observable level
H	construct on the theoretical level
Υ	correspondence rule
→	path between theoretical constructs and between theoretical constructs and their indicators

1 Groundwork

1.1 Introduction

1.1.1 Motivation

Cost accounting has a long tradition. It is one of the management accounting instruments that has contributed to the emergence of accounting as a discipline. The origins of cost accounting can be traced back to the 14th century. Cost accounting as we know it today, however, has emerged since the beginning of the 19th century. It has developed differently across countries. In particular in the UK, USA, and Germany cost accounting ideas and concepts have developed early. As a consequence, these countries have been most influential in spreading cost accounting ideas and concepts around the world[1] and have thereby contributed to the **development of cost accounting** in other countries. Japan, for example, has absorbed many German and US cost accounting ideas and concepts.[2] In spite of these strong influences, Japan has developed a distinct approach to cost accounting.[3] Japan has adapted the Western ideas and concepts to its specific environment and thus cost accounting systems and practices different from those found in the West have emerged as a result of particularities in culture, education, and financial accounting systems.[4] As these determinants vary also between Western countries, strong differences prevail as well, e.g., between the USA and Germany. These **cross-national differences** impede a uniform and coherent business management in MNC. Standardizing cost accounting systems within MNC can in fact facilitate a uniform and coherent business management, but foreign systems might not be accepted by local employees that have different views, habits, and preferences regarding cost accounting systems. For this reason it is necessary to sensitize practitioners for variance in cost accounting, so that they can find a suitable trade-off between standardization and differentiation. The following descriptions about expected cross-national differences in cost accounting between *Western countries and Japan* as well as between the *USA and Germany* and the expected rationale for these differences shall demonstrate the potential conflicts for MNC that plan to transfer their cost accounting systems abroad.

For Western researchers and practitioners the Japanese practices of, e.g., overhead allocation appear rather simplistic and misguiding at first glance.[5] Japanese cost accounting and

---

1 Germany has mainly had a strong influence on European countries until 1945 and on Japan until the 1960s. Cf. *Yoshikawa* (1994b), p. 279; *Blake et al.* (2000), p. 123; *Näsi/Rohde* (2007). After 1945 until today, the USA became the most dominant country. As a consequence, modern instruments like activity-based costing (ABC) have diffused worldwide. See *Bhimani et al.* (2007).

2 Cf. *Winter* (2005); *Yoshikawa* (2001), p. 269f.

3 "Japanese costing has been considered quite different from that found in the West" (*Yoshikawa* (2001), p. 269).

4 In particular national culture has been discussed in literature as a determinant. See, e.g., *Brewer* (1997); *MacArthur* (2006); *Lere* (2009); *Portz/Lere* (2010). An increase in accuracy, detail, and timeliness of cost information leads to higher costs. The management has therefore to make cost-benefit considerations of cost accounting systems. Cf. *Cooper* (1991), p. 147.

5 Cf. *Hiromoto* (1988), p. 22; *Hutchinson/Liao* (2009), p. 32.

cost management systems, however, are apparently highly sophisticated. Since the 1980s, Western researchers and practitioners seek to implement Japanese instruments like target costing and kaizen costing to obtain competitive advantage.[6] One reason for this controversy is cross-national differences in the *philosophy and believes of 'the right way to do things' in cost accounting* (see Figure 1-1). **Western researchers and practitioners** are supposed to postulate a logical causal relationship between overhead costs and overhead allocation bases to capture the reality of costs as precisely as possible.[7] The **Japanese counterparts** are aware of this perspective, but they are characterized in literature to prefer overhead allocation for influencing decisions and for motivating employees to work in the companies' interests.[8] Japanese managers therefore often allocate overhead costs on a labor-cost base to focus design engineers' attention on increasing productivity through automation. Direct labor, however, is a simplistic and relatively inaccurate allocation base, because labor costs constitute only a small proportion of total costs.[9] Thus, this allocation base is suitable for influencing employees, but it is inappropriate for informing managers about the organization's cost situation. Besides differences in the philosophy and believes in cost accounting, also national institutions like the *education* system are expected to significantly differ between Japan and Western countries. Whereas in Western countries it is believed that efficiency raises when the division of work becomes finer and management enhances specialization, in Japan multi-skilling and "the integrated and cooperative idea and the stratified relationship of cooperation between managers and workers lie at the heart of management."[10] Consequently, the degree of specialization in cost accounting might be lower in Japan than in Western countries. Furthermore, a striking feature of the Japanese education system is that employees are extensively trained in-house and by job rotation, which facilitate a general education of the employees.[11]

Not only between culturally distinctive countries, but also within culture groups sharing a similar philosophy and similar believes of 'the right way to do things', significant differences in cost accounting can exist (see Figure 1-1). In the **USA**, for example, the emphasis on *financial reporting* requirements following the stock market crash of 1929 has constrained the further development of cost accounting for a long time. Cost accounting has mainly served financial accounting purposes. At the end of the 1980s, more companies became *interested to run sophisticated systems* like activity-based costing (ABC).[12] Unlike in the USA, a distinct tradition of cost and management accounting has developed in **Germany** since the early 20th century, because the emphasis on financial reporting was rather low. Before the international harmonization of financial accounting systems, German

6 Cf. *Nishimura* (1995), p. 318; *Jones et al.* (1998), p. 204; *Okano/Suzuki* (2007), p. 1119f.; *Hutchinson/Liao* (2009), p. 32.

7 Cf. *Hiromoto* (1988), p. 22f.; *Hutchinson/Liao* (2009), p. 34. Cf. also *Reich* (1995), p. 77.

8 Cf. *Hiromoto* (1988); *Hutchinson/Liao* (2009).

9 Cf. *Hiromoto* (1988), p. 23; *Merchant/Shields* (1993), p. 80.

10 *Nishimura* (2003), p. 60f.

11 Cf. *Wijewardena/Cooray* (1995); section 2.1.1.

12 For the reasons why companies started to install ABC systems see *Johnson/Kaplan* (1987); *Berens* (1997b), p. 858. Few US companies have already installed sophisticated cost accounting systems earlier. See, e.g., *Jones* (1991).

companies used to run financial and cost accounting systems independently of each other in order to avoid distorting effects of tax regulations and prudent measurement principles on cost and management accounting data.[13] Since then German scholars and practitioners have promoted comprehensive cost accounting systems to support managerial decision making and they have developed a strong emphasis on precise and detailed cost information.[14] The study by *Krumwiede/Suessmair* verifies that German companies have a stronger emphasis on precision and run more complex cost accounting systems than their US counterparts.[15] These differences make it difficult for MNEs to introduce their cost accounting systems in foreign subsidiaries. Daimler, for instance, failed to introduce the German system 'Grenzplankostenrechnung' (GPK) in its US subsidiaries.[16]

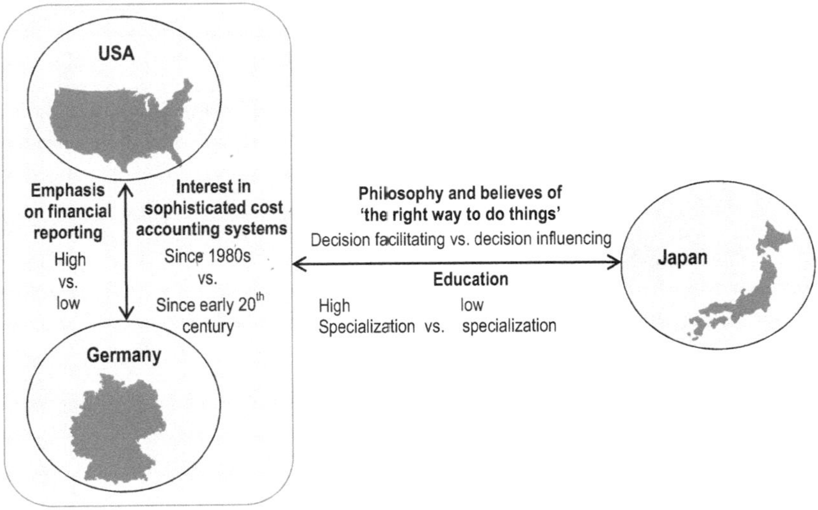

Figure 1-1: Reasons for cross-national differences in cost accounting between USA, Germany, and Japan

13 Cf. *Schildbach* (1997), p. 263. The German financial accounting system was primarily designed to determine tax and dividend payments and to provide information for creditors. Cf. *Nobes/Parker* (2008), p. 29-33.

14 *MacArthur* and *Portz/Lere* explain the strong emphasis on precision and detail by the relatively high degree of uncertainty avoidance in Germany. See *MacArthur* (2006); *Portz/Lere* (2010).

15 Cf. *Krumwiede/Suessmair* (2007a).

16 See *Krumwiede* (2005), p. 31.

The **descriptions** above **are rather anecdotal than empirically proven.**[17] They are mainly based on subjective perceptions of individual researchers and practitioners[18] or on conceptual considerations[19]. Only very few studies have empirically verified the expected differences[20] and even fewer studies have empirically traced differences in cost accounting back to cross-national variance in, e.g., culture and institutions.[21] Whereas management control systems as a management accounting instrument have been investigated 79 times, little attention was paid to comparative research on cost accounting by only 17 studies.[22] These 17 studies are furthermore often limited to the adoption rates of single instruments and they usually suffer methodological deficiencies, wherefore little theoretical and practical contribution has been provided so far. This constitutes an insufficient basis to draw conclusions about cross-national differences in cost accounting.

The lack of knowledge in this research area is surprising, because cost accounting is an essential part of a company's information system. Because of the growing complexity in business, practitioners cannot imagine modern management without cost accounting;[23] it serves as a basis for decision making and provides information for other tasks like cost management to obtain competitive advantage.[24] Although **German and Japanese cost accounting** systems have attracted considerable interest worldwide, only one study superficially compares German and Japanese cost accounting.[25]

More comprehensive knowledge through empirical research is thus required. This study addresses this research gap. The expected strong variance in cost accounting between Germany and Japan and its underlying rationales are the **motivation of this research endeavor.** Knowing about cross-national differences can enhance national cost accounting by introducing foreign systems like ABC. Managers of MNC can furthermore be sensitized to consider country-specifics while aligning local and global cost accounting systems. The insights of this study are not only relevant for German and Japanese scholars and practitioners, but also for their foreign, e.g., US counterparts:[26]

---

17 Also related research areas have been criticized before to provide little knowledge of cross-national differences and that most of the knowledge about cross-national differences is rather anecdotal than empirically verified. Cf. *Holzmüller* (1995), p. 8; *Shields* (1998), p. 506, respectively. Already in 1991 the need for further research in comparative management accounting has been claimed. Cf. *Shields et al.* (1991), p. 62.

18 See, e.g., *Hiromoto* (1988); *Nishimura* (2003); *Hutchinson/Liao* (2009).

19 See, e.g., *MacArthur* (2006); *Portz/Lere* (2010).

20 For an exception see *Krumwiede/Suessmair* (2007a), (2007b).

21 For an exception see *Brewer* (1998). He indicates that high-power-distance / collectivist cultures may generate a higher ABC success than low-power-distance / individualist cultures.

22 Cf. section 1.4.2.

23 Cf. *Weber* (1993), p. 265. Only about 4% of the German companies with more than 100 employees do not apply cost accounting. Cf. *Währisch* (2000), p. 78f.

24 See *Ferrara* (1990). In particular the Japanese instruments target costing and kaizen costing demonstrate the strategic relevance that cost accounting can have.

25 See *Bhimani et al.* (2007).

26 Cf., e.g., *Krumwiede* (2005); *MacArthur* (2006), p. 16; *Hutchinson/Liao* (2009).

> *"[A] dozen years ago European and Japanese managers asked what they could learn from their American counterparts. Perhaps it is time for those American partners to ask what they could learn from their world-class competitors in Europe and Japan."*[27]

As ABC has failed the expectations in Anglophone countries and as the majority of companies there still uses traditional cost accounting systems,[28] German cost accounting systems are discussed in the USA as an alternative solution.[29]

The **research objective** of the study is a *theory-based and empirical comparison of German and Japanese cost accounting*. Similarities and differences are described in more depth and recommendations on how to design effective cost accounting systems in both countries are provided. As many arguments from literature about cross-national differences are rather anecdotal than empirically verified, reasons for cross-national differences in cost accounting are furthermore empirically analyzed.

Prior research on comparative management accounting has already been criticized to be limited in methodology[30] and to generate contradictory results.[31] Due to these shortcomings, little is known about cross-national differences in cost and management accounting and their underlying logic. To assess the state of research, a *catalog of the existing empirical research* on comparative management accounting is compiled. Methodological shortcomings of prior research on cost accounting that influence the explanatory power of the studies are identified including the choice of theoretical perspectives, statistical methods for data analysis, issues in equivalence, and control variables. Based on the findings of the literature review implications are drawn and a *research design* is developed to enable a theoretically and practically relevant survey. The calls from literature and the implications from the literature review are followed while considering the specifics of conducting comparative research. Thereby, this study distinguishes itself from most of the prior comparative studies on cost and management accounting.

In this study *medium-sized companies* from Germany and Japan across three industries (food and beverage, mechanical engineering, and hospitals) are compared via a survey. The following **five research questions** are thereby addressed. The first and the second research question are descriptive, the third and the fourth are explicative, and the fifth is prescriptive.[32]

(1) *Does cost accounting differ between Germany and Japan?*
The study investigates and describes similarities and differences in cost accounting objectives as well as the conceptual design of cost accounting systems between Germany and Japan. Variations are expected to highlight potential conflicts for MNC that plan to transfer their cost accounting systems abroad.

---

27 *Limprecht/Hayes* (1982), p. 137.

28 Cf. *Garg et al.* (2003).

29 See, e.g., *Sharman* (2003a); *Portz/Lere* (2010).

30 Cf. *Harrison/McKinnon* (1999); *Bhimani* (2007).

31 See, e.g., *Chow et al.* (1999b), p. 444f.

32 The characterization of descriptive, explicative, and prescriptive statements is provided in section 1.1.3.1.

(2) *Are differences in cost accounting stronger across countries than across industries?*
Cross-national and cross-industry differences in cost accounting objectives, the conceptual design, and the performance of cost accounting systems are compared to better assess how strong cross-national differences are. Following the call for further research,[33] the relevance of comparative management accounting research is thereby assessed. If cost accounting differs rather across industries than across nations, future research should more intensively compare industries than nations to provide practitioners with recommendations.

(3) *Why does cost accounting differ between Germany and Japan?*
The reasons for cross-national differences in cost accounting objectives, the conceptual design of cost accounting systems, as well as on the relationships between the theoretical constructs are analyzed. Comparative management accounting provides the opportunity to address the impact of further variables (e.g., culture, institutions) on cost accounting that cannot be investigated in a domestic study.

(4) *Which factors influence cost accounting in Germany and Japan? Do these influences differ cross-nationally?*
This study analyses separately for Germany and Japan cause-and-effect relationships between organizational context, cost accounting objectives, and the conceptual design of cost accounting systems. These findings are of theoretical relevance to explain the context dependence of cost accounting systems in both countries. When the relationships differ between both countries, the countries' particularities can be demonstrated. The relationships are also of practical relevance, because practitioners can apply these findings to forecast the characteristics of their cost accounting systems.

(5) *Under which conditions is cost accounting successful in Germany and Japan? Are comprehensive cost accounting systems more successful than simple ones in Germany and in Japan?*
Cause-and-effect relationships are transferred in both countries into recommendations for practitioners by measuring the performance of cost accounting systems. This study thereby identifies the performance of cost accounting systems separately for Germany and Japan considering different organizational contexts and cost accounting objectives. Conceptual designs of cost accounting systems that are successful in one country under a given context and cost accounting objectives might be inefficient in another country. Furthermore, due to national specifics, the relevance of actions to install and maintain cost accounting systems (e.g., investments in IT and top management support) might vary internationally. By highlighting

33 See *Granlund/Lukka* (1998); *Shields* (1998). *Shields* questions the importance of nation as an influence factor. He states that industry-based differences have a higher influence on the demand for and the design and use of, e.g., ABC than nation-based differences. Cf. *Shields* (1998), p. 512. As prior studies have not simultaneously compared the impact of industry and nation in management accounting yet, *Shields*' supposition is still unanswered. Only the study by *Pizam et al.* has compared the impact of nationality and industry cultures upon managerial behavior. See *Pizam et al.* (1997).

these differences, recommendations for practitioners who want to design cost accounting systems in Germany and Japan can be developed.

1.1.2 Outline of the study

This study is divided into four chapters. In the course of the **first chapter**, reflections about methodological aspects in business studies are presented in section 1.1.3. This is necessary to clarify the scientific positioning and the methodology applied in this study to develop the research design. In section 1.1.4 the terms 'management accounting' and 'cost accounting' are defined. A comprehensive understanding of the particularities of comparative management accounting (like issues in equivalence) is required in this study. For this reason, section 1.2 thoroughly describes the fundamentals of comparative management accounting. This knowledge is then applied to assess the state of research, to develop a suitable research design, and to conduct the empirical research. Theoretical perspectives to investigate cross-national differences in cost accounting are described in *section 1.3*. Their comparative advantages and disadvantages are outlined, which provides a basis to determine the most suitable perspectives for this study in section 1.3.8. In *section 1.4* the state of empirical research on comparative management accounting and comparative cost accounting is reviewed. The research gap for this study is thereby defined and implications for this study are drawn. Building upon the prior sections, the research design is derived in *section 1.5*. This includes the determination of the applied research method, the development of the conceptual research framework, the application and specification of the conceptual research framework, as well as actions to ensure cross-national equivalence. Great importance is attached to the construction of the conceptual framework, which aligns and guides chapter 2 and 3.

In **chapter 2** the conceptual framework is specified by conceptualizing and operationalizing its constructs and variables. Context factors (country-specifics, other external context factors, and internal context factors) and the objectives of cost accounting are described in section 2.1 and 2.2. Thereafter, the conceptual design of cost accounting systems is developed in section 2.3. Two dimensions of the system are distinguished: complexity and timeliness. The performance of cost accounting systems is addressed in section 2.4. Hypotheses are developed within the scope of the conceptualization to characterize the relationships between the single variables.

Chapter 3 presents the empirical results. In section 3.1.1 the sample is defined. The data collection process, the quality of the sample, and the preparation of the data are described in section 3.1.2. In section 3.1.3 the fundamentals of the applied statistical methods are explained. Following the arrangements of chapter 2, the results of the empirical analysis are presented thereafter in sections 3.2 to 3.5 (context, cost accounting objectives, cost accounting system, performance). With the help of bi- and multivariate methods the single hypotheses from chapter 2 are tested. The results of multiple regression analyses are verified by structural equation modeling (SEM) in section 3.6. The findings of this chapter are summarized and discussed in section 3.7. Thereby, the practical and theoretical relevance of the findings are described.

Chapter 4 summarizes the main findings of this study by answering the five research questions and describes the contribution of this study. Limitations of this research project are critically discussed and suggestions for further research are provided. The outline of the study is shown in Figure 1-2.

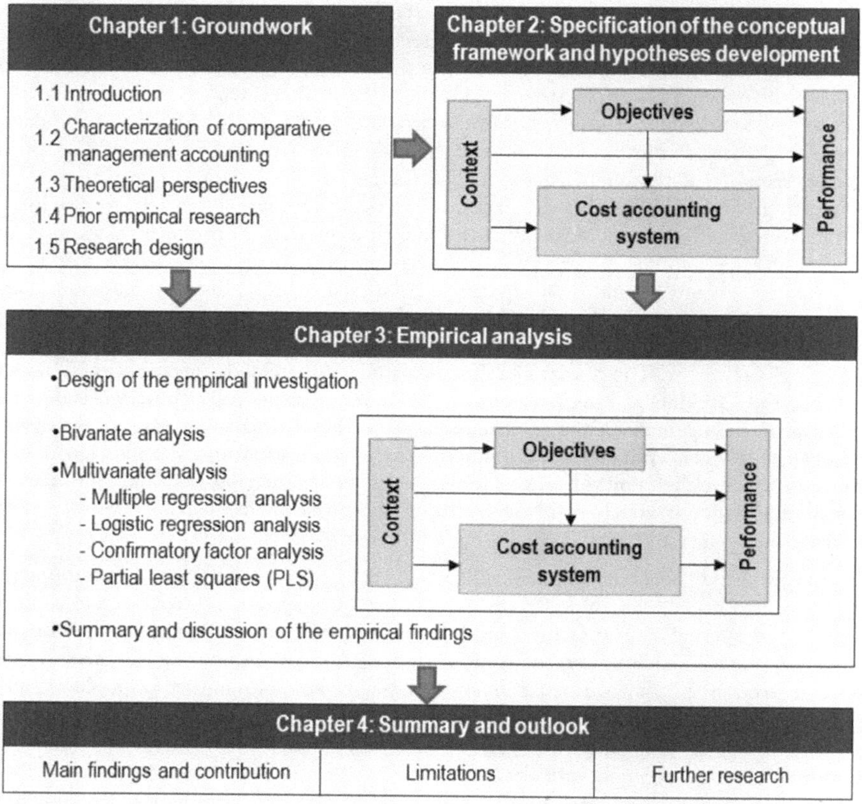

Figure 1-2: Outline of the study

1.1.3 Methodological grounding

Methodology comprises the methods that are appropriate to satisfy research conclusions, like truth claims.[34] Underlying assumptions as well as the methods and theories applied by

34 Cf. *Saudagaran/Diga* (1999), p. 70. Methodology is part of philosophy of science. Philosophy of science is concerned with scientific statements and concepts and it focuses on central problems for science in general that also apply to particular sciences (e.g., physics, chemistry, economics etc.). Hence, philosophy of science can be seen as a meta-scientific discipline. Cf. *Albert* (1976), c. 4674.

researchers may vary fundamentally, in particular within an international context.[35] This pluralism leads to variations in research designs and research results regarding quality, validity, and reliability. Hence, a **reflection of methodology serves** the following **three tasks**: First, it serves the author to critically analyze the practice of science and to highlight occurring difficulties.[36] Thereby, a *fundament for analyzing and evaluating the state of research* is developed (see section 1.4). Especially for comparative management accounting research this is necessary, because it has already been criticized being limited in methodology[37] and generating many contradictory results.[38] Second, it provides a methodological basis to *develop a conceptual framework* contrary to the existing ones, which may be more efficient in addressing the research objectives (see section 1.5.2).[39] Third, the *reader* of this study shall be enabled to classify the study methodologically and to consider its fundamental assumptions while *interpreting the results*. In the following, the objectives and methods of empirical research in business studies are discussed first (section 1.1.3.1 and 1.1.3.2), before the scientific positioning of the study is derived (section 1.1.3.3).

1.1.3.1 Objectives of research in business studies

The aim of every science is to provide a contribution to knowledge,[40] to raise human welfare. The extent to which the scientific outcomes can immediately be practically applied varies. Scientific outcomes can be classified along the **dichotomy of basic research and applied research.**[41] The former aims at theoretical cognition and theory development, the latter provides applicable instruments and methods for practical purposes. As applied and basic research complement each other, they can only be differentiated theoretically.[42] The majority of researchers classify business studies more as an applied than as a basic research

It also encompasses epistemology, because it analyses the way human beings comprehend knowledge. Cf. *Burrell/Morgan* (1979), p. 1.

35 Societies differ in their basic assumptions on the nature of truth and reality. In particular the degree of uncertainty avoidance of societies is expected to have an impact. Whereas in low uncertainty avoiding countries the scientific logic favors induction, in high uncertainty avoiding countries deduction is preferred. Cf. *Hofstede* (2001), p. 178. US researchers, e.g., tend to start off with facts and then work towards a theory (inductive) and the Germans rather prefer to develop theories first and then illustrate them with empirical data (deductive). Cf. *Palazzo* (2002), p. 206-208.

36 Cf. *Raffée/Abel* (1979), p. 1.

37 Cf. *Harrison/McKinnon* (1999); *Bhimani* (2007).

38 See, e.g., *Chow et al.* (1999b), p. 444f.

39 Cf. *Raffée/Abel* (1979), p. 1f.

40 Cf. *Gray* (1983), p. 17.

41 For the differentiation between basic and applied research in business studies see *Stählin* (1973), p. 9-11; *Chmielewicz* (1994), p. 17f.

42 Cf. *v. Keller* (1982), p. 82f. The interrelation between basic and applied research is demonstrated in chapter 1.1.2.

science.[43] Theory building and development should consequently not be carried through for its own sake, but to transfer theory into practically relevant solutions.[44]

In **research** four different types of **statements** are distinguished that follow the dichotomy of basic and applied research.[45] *Descriptive* statements describe an extract from reality to portray it as precisely as possible without any judgments by the researcher(s). Based on a theoretical grounding, an aspect of reality is explained with *explicative* if-then statements. Explicative statements can be converted into *prescriptive* statements to develop recommendations for practitioners: "How can you achieve your objectives?". *Normative* statements are judgments by the researcher(s) that justify certain behavioral patterns.

To derive the four research statements, the researcher has to choose between the following three **research strategies.**[46] The *normative and conceptual strategy* examines complex cause-and-effect relationships and develops recommendations for practitioners mainly based on plausibility. The *formal-analytical strategy* develops and analyzes models, which are simplified and abstract descriptions of problems, to solve them on a theoretical basis. The *empirical strategy* verifies theoretical conclusions by observations or experience. A prerequisite of the normative and conceptual strategy and the formal-analytical strategy is a general understanding of cross-national differences in cost accounting. Only then meaningful recommendations for practitioners can be derived or theoretical models can be set up and solved. However, only little is known about variation in cost accounting across countries so far. The empirical strategy is therefore followed in this study instead of speculating about cross-national differences. The following statements are therefore limited to **empirical research.**

The aim of empirical research is to search for scientific statements that apply to a majority of cases and that support theory building.[47] The development of general statements demands to acquire knowledge by carrying through the **research process** that includes the context of discovery, the context of justification, and the context of application.[48] The conceptual basis of a research process is the conceptual framework (see section 1.5.2). It is developed and specified in the *context of discovery* that comprises conceptual reflections, like the development of hypotheses (see chapter 2). The empirical test of the conceptual framework is carried through in the *context of justification* (see chapter 3). It explains how hypotheses and models are tested against reality.[49] The *context of application* draws conclusions about the application of the scientific work (see section 3.7.3 and chapter 4).[50] The design of the research process may differ regarding how *a general statement is logically derived from reality* and *when statements are constructed.* Researchers in philosophy of science

43 For a debate between basic and applied research among German scholars see *Behrens* (1993), c. 4769.

44 Cf. *Wild* (1966), p. 25.

45 Cf. *Thommen* (1983), p. 34-36; *Sachs/Hauser* (2002), p. 49-53.

46 Cf. *Grochla* (1978), p. 67f.

47 Cf. *Wild* (1976), c. 3890-3896.

48 Cf. *Ulrich/Hill* (1976a), p. 306f.

49 Cf. *Ulrich/Hill* (1976a), p. 306.

50 Cf. *Ulrich/Hill* (1976a), p. 306f.

and researchers in business studies propose different procedures that shape the research process. The two most appropriate methods for this study are described in the following section.[51]

1.1.3.2 Methods of research in business studies

Regarding **how a general statement is logically derived from reality**, advocates of *positivism and empiricism* believe that actual sense experience is the only authentic source of scientific cognition.[52] Accordingly, statements are derived from observed regularities in reality (so-called principle of induction) and are verified empirically. *Critical rationalists* like *Popper* object to this procedure that new statements or theories cannot logically be induced from identified particularities. Hence, knowledge can never be proven as ultimately true. Instead, knowledge is only temporarily true until it is falsified. Theories and hypotheses should be falsifiable so that they can be rationally criticized by empirical testing. By advancing theories through permanently setting up, testing, and rejecting hypotheses, truth is approximated.[53]

Also the second aspect, **when statements are derived**, differs between both methods. Advocates of positivism and empiricism accumulate several observations before hypotheses are derived – as far as it is possible. The critical rationalists condemn this order.[54] They formulate profound hypotheses before testing them against reality.[55]

The underlying assumption of **critical rationalism** to obtain scientific progress through falsification is that theories and laws are stable across time and space.[56] The critical rationalism is assigned and limited to the context of justification of the research process. Due to time and other restrictions, research is often limited to single hypotheses and a narrow formulation of a problem.[57] Those hypotheses can hardly be integrated ex post in a more complex system of research statements. To solve this deficit, the **exploration strategy** has been developed,[58] to shift research from the context of justification towards the context of discovery. This facilitates the construction and development of hypotheses and theories.[59] A **pragmatic interpretation of the critical rationalism** is then required to set up hypotheses that do not always meet the full requirements of the critical rationalism[60] and in this study the tested hypotheses can be characterized as either (preliminary) accepted or reject-

51 Cf. *Behrens* (1993), c. 4764f.

52 Cf. *Kern* (1979), p. 14; *Searcy/Mentzer* (2003), p. 136.

53 Critical rationalists regard the falsification of theories and hypotheses as the main procedure for achieving scientific cognition. Cf. *Ulrich/Hill* (1979), p. 175f.; *Hodgson* (1988), p. 37-39; *Bartel* (1990), p. 58; *Popper/Kiesewetter* (1992), p. 15; *Chmielewicz* (1994), p. 101-104; *Popper* (2002); *Kornmeier* (2007), p. 41.

54 Cf. *Schanz* (1977), p. 69; *Chmielewicz* (1994), p. 143.

55 Cf. Chmielewicz 1994, p. 142f.

56 Cf. *Popper* (1965), p. 81f.; *Popper* (1966), p. 199f.

57 Cf. *Kubicek* (1977), p. 11f.

58 Cf. *Kubicek* (1975); *Kubicek* (1977).

59 Cf. *Kubicek* (1977).

60 Cf. *Wollnik* (1977), p. 58.

ed. By deriving hypotheses deductively and then testing them, more profound hypotheses can gradually be developed. Hence, the exploration strategy connects theory building with theory testing. Research can be described as an iterative learning process, because intellectual assumptions and empirical data are alternately generated to specify and to theoretically develop the research problem.[61] The exploration strategy is subdivided into three main activities.[62]

(1) **Development of a conceptual framework.** The basis of the exploration strategy is the conceptual framework. It highlights unexplored research areas and visualizes the underlying concept of the research process. The researcher's theoretical preconception is clarified by determining theoretical concepts[63] and its relevant features. In addition to that, assumptions about coherences (like cause-and-effect relationships) between functions within the same theoretical concepts and between different theoretical concepts are defined. The conceptual framework enables the researcher to enlarge his preconception and to gain further specific experience.

(2) **Development of a heuristic research design**. In order to gain further specific experience, the researcher has to develop a research design to exploit the heuristic potential of the conceptual framework.

(3) **Empirical exploration**. The gained experience serves to transform the original conceptual framework into a more abstract and formalized theory and to obtain novel research questions, assumptions, and interpretations.[64] In addition to that, the results can constitute a basis for practical recommendations.

1.1.3.3 Scientific positioning of the study

As already described in section 1.1.1, the research objective is to conduct an empirical study to derive descriptive, explicative, and prescriptive statements. The previous section shows that positivism and empiricism focus on theory building, whereas critical rationalism mainly aims at theory testing. The selection of one approach heavily depends upon the state of research. Anticipating some results from section 1.4 it is noticed that prior empirical research has yielded only little new insights. Nevertheless, sufficient knowledge is available in cost accounting research that enables the researchers to set up and test hypotheses. The **exploration strategy** is therefore applied in this study: A conceptual framework and a heuristic research design are developed in section 1.5 and chapter 2. Furthermore, practical recommendations are provided in section 3.7 in the context of empirical exploration. Due to the strict requirements of the critical rationalism, this method is not suitable for following the exploration strategy. Therefore, the **critical rationalism is interpreted pragmatically**: Hypotheses are developed (context of discovery) before theory is tested (context of justification). The conceptual framework and the research design are developed in section 1.5 and single hypotheses are derived in section 2. Empirical explora-

61 Cf. *Kubicek* (1977), p. 14f.

62 Cf. *Kubicek* (1977), p. 15-19.

63 Theoretical concepts are also called conceptual categories. See *Glaser/Strauss* (1967), p. 35-43.

64 Cf. *Wollnik* (1977).

tion follows in chapter 3. Overall, the study applies a pragmatic and applied understanding of science.

Unlike natural sciences, numerous occurrences in business studies seem to be valid only under certain **spatiotemporal conditions**, e.g., because new instruments diffuse across countries and thereby cross-national differences in cost accounting may diminish over time.[65] Hence, it is assumed that for this addressed research area absolute regularity is not given, but there is some degree of regularity in time and space. Hypotheses and theories can only be tested and further developed under certain spatiotemporal conditions in this study. When differences in cost accounting between Germany and Japan are theoretically explained, this cognition is only limited to both countries and only to a certain period of time. In future research, the theories and hypotheses investigated can be enhanced and their area of application can be extended to other countries.[66]

1.1.4 Conceptual delimitation of fundamental terms

In this section the terms 'management accounting' and 'cost accounting' are characterized to circumscribe the research topic and to provide the reader with an understanding of these terms, because within an international context their understanding may vary significantly.

1.1.4.1 Management accounting

As the state of research on comparative management accounting is dominated by American literature,[67] an international, rather Anglo-American characterization of management accounting is followed.[68]

Management accounting, also known as managerial accounting, is the Anglophone pendant to *Controlling*[69] in German-speaking countries and *Kanrikaikei* in Japan. All of them provide managers with information to support their decision making (decision facilitating) or to influence the decisions of subordinate decision makers according to the company's objectives (decision influencing). In spite of these same purposes, variation between management accounting, *Controlling*, and *Kanrikaikei* prevails due to cross-national differences in culture, education, and financial accounting systems. These differences become manifest in the relationship towards financial accounting, the tasks, instruments, and the responsible body for management accounting as well as the role of management accountants and the use of management accounting information.

---

65 Cf. *Wild* (1976), c. 3900.

66 Thereby, the relevant conditions (independent variables) should be investigated that are responsible for the validity or failure of (quasi) theories and hypotheses within or beyond the concerning spatiotemporal conditions. (Quasi) theories and hypotheses should preliminarily be accepted and seen as an important stage to obtain more universal theories. Cf. *Wild* (1976), c. 3901f., with further references. See also *Ulrich/Hill* (1976b), p. 346.

67 See section 1.4.2.

68 This characterization follows *Kajüter/Moeschler* (2011b).

69 Cf. *Sheridan* (1995), p.1; *Ahrens/Chapman* (1999); *Otto* (2000), p. 38; *Becker* (2003), p. 85-87; *Wagenhofer* (2006); *Küpper* (2008), p. 6; *Luther et al.* (2010), p. vii.

Management accounting is differently circumscribed in English-speaking literature. The narrow definition is mainly limited to cost accounting. The broad definition includes also aspects of financial accounting[70] and some even equalize management accounting with accounting.[71] Instead of the broader concept that complicates to demarcate management accounting from financial accounting, a definition is chosen that reflects the contents of Anglo-American textbooks and articles published in management accounting journals. In a literature analysis by *Rosso et al.* each examined Anglo-American textbook treats information support for managers as an important element.[72] Articles published in journals like 'Management Accounting Research' and 'Journal of Management Accounting Research' furthermore do not deal with topics on financial accounting and they are not solely limited to cost accounting. Therefore, the **working definition** by *Horngren* is followed to demarcate management accounting from financial accounting:

> *"Management accounting measures, analyzes, and reports financial and nonfinancial information that helps managers make decisions to fulfill the goals of an organization. Managers use management accounting information to choose, communicate, and implement strategy. They also use management accounting information to coordinate product design, production and marketing decisions. Management accounting focuses on internal reporting."*[73]

To provide managers with relevant information for decision making, management accounting **instruments like cost accounting**, investment appraisal, budgeting, transfer pricing, and balanced scorecards are required.

1.1.4.2 Cost accounting

Cost accounting provides both **management accounting** and **financial accounting** with cost information. For management accounting it serves for solving managerial problems. For financial accounting costs for inventory valuation are generated to meet the requirements of external reporting.[74]

---

70 Cf. *Schoenfeld* (1992), p. 348. In a practice analysis of management accounting, frequently performed work activities in US companies include managing the accounting/finance function, accounting systems and financial reporting, internal consulting, internal auditing, human resources and personnel, computer systems and operations, and investment of funds. Cf. *Siegel* (1996), p. 9.

71 Cf. *Fickert* (1993), p. 204. For instance, *Sweeney* (1983), p. 467f., equalizes management accounting and accounting. The wider definition of management accounting further includes the tasks of financial accounting, treasury, and taxation. Sometimes it even includes insurance management, data processing, and internal audit. Cf. *Stoffel* (1995), p. 155-164.

72 Cf. *Roso et al.* (2003); *Roso et al.* (2005).

73 *Horngren et al.* (2006), p. 2. Whereas this working definition is largely congruent with the German concept of management accounting (cf. *Becker* (2003), p. 86f.; *Küpper* (2008), p. 6), the wider definition of management accounting would be more appropriate for the Japanese one, because in Japan a broader range of tasks including financial accounting is often allocated to *Kanrikaikei* (cf. *Otto* (2000), p. 278-282).

74 Cf., e.g., *Crowningshield/Gorman* (1979), p. 5; *Drury* (2005), p. 20.

Besides inventory valuation, the **cost accounting objectives** planning, decision facilitating, decision influencing, and control can be distinguished following the management process of decision making. Cost accounting furthermore serves operative and strategic objectives.[75] The relevance of the cost accounting objectives is company-specific.

Cost accounting objectives determine the conceptual design of **cost accounting systems**, because these systems should be purposefully designed.[76] Cost accounting systems are a designed set of rules. Different types of cost accounting systems can be distinguished. In literature, they represent theoretical 'ideals' that demonstrate specific ideas about the structure and procedure to accumulate, allocate, and analyze costs. They further serve as a standard to compare them with cost accounting systems applied in practice.[77] Cost accounting systems are often classified by two different dimensions. The first distinguishing feature addresses the degree of cost allocation. According to *full costing* all costs are allocated to cost objects, whereas *variable costing* allocates only variable costs. The other distinguishing feature is the *time reference of costs*[78] differentiating between actual, normal, standard, and target costs. In Anglophone compared to German textbooks, cost accounting is more often systematized according to the *repetition of the production process*. Job costing is recommended for job production and process costing is recommended for continuous production.[79] In Germany and Japan the distinction between *cost type accounting, cost center accounting, and product cost accounting* is widespread both in research and practice. This distinction is geared to the flow of costs starting off with the procurement of resources, followed by the production and the sales of products.[80] As cost accounting systems have to serve different objectives and as they operate under different environments (e.g., industry, company size), they differ between companies, e.g., in terms of the processing effort and the frequency of cost updates.

The objectives and the conceptual design of cost accounting systems determine the **practice of cost accounting**. Whereas systems are defined in this study as theoretical ideas, practice is described as the routine and institutionalized patterns of cost accounting and it includes how cost information is actually used.[81] Whereas cost accounting objectives describe how systems should be applied, practice includes how cost accounting is actually used by the actors. Cost accounting objectives influence practice directly, because they provide guidelines how cost information should be applied, and also indirectly through cost accounting systems. Cost accounting systems determine practice by, e.g., the characteristics of the generated cost information and how this information is provided.

---

75 See section 2.2.

76 Cf., e.g., *Bungenstock* (1995), p. 68f.

77 Cf. *Scapens* (1994), p. 301; *Hummel* (1993), p. 453.

78 Cf., e.g., *Horváth* (2009a), p. 416.

79 Cf., e.g., *Drury* (2008); *Kinney/Raiborn* (2008).

80 Cf. *Friedl et al.* (2009b), p. 39f.

81 Cf. *Scapens* (1994), p. 302f.

1.2 Characterization of comparative management accounting

1.2.1 History and working definition

"A large part of human learning has always occurred through comparison." [82]

Geographic comparison is a form of investigation with a long history traced back to more than 2,000 years. As modern nations arose in the sixteenth century onwards, contrasts across nations were carried through much later.[83] The **first cross-national comparison** dates back to the early eighteenth century, when ten nationalities were described by 17 characteristics in Steiermark (Austria).[84] Whereas, for instance, the Germans were supposed to end their lives in wine, the English are characterized as well-mannered and warm-hearted (see Figure 1-3).

Brief description of types to be found in Europe and their different characteristics

Names	Spanish	French	Belgian	German	English	Swiss	Pole	Hungarian	Muscovite	Turk or Greek
Manners	Haughty	Frivolous	Sly	Open-hearted	Well-mannered	Strong	Peasant	Disloyal	Malicious	Fickle as April weather
Personality	Credulous	Patient and garrulous	Jealous	Passable	Warm-hearted	Cruel	Timid	Inhuman	Quite unlike the slavs	A young devil
Intellect	Clever and wise	Cautious	Sagacious	Witty	Resistant	Ruthless	Disdainful	Still less	No skill whatsoever	Superficially clever
Physical features	Masculine	Childlike	Reluctant	Superior	Effeminate	Ordinary	Medium build	Sanguine	Infinitely rough	Tender, sensitive look
Likes	Flattery and praise	Warfare	Gold	Drink	Voluptuous	Expensive food	The aristocracy	Causing a disturbance	Little figs	Self-love
Pastimes	Games	Intrigue	Chatting	Drinking	Work	Eating	Brawling	Laziness	Sleeping	Being ill
Animal-comparison	An elephant	A fox	A lynx	A lion	A horse	An ox	A bear	A wolf	A donkey	A cat
Life ends	In a boat	In battle	In a monastery	In wine	In water	On the ground	In a manger	By a sword	In the snow	In fraud

Figure 1-3: Excerpt from the table of nations
Source: following *Stanzel* (1997), p. 15

The origins of **comparative management research** date back to the beginning of the 20th century.[85] Not before the 1960s and later than other socio-scientific disciplines,[86] man-

82 *Deutsch* (1996), p. 3.

83 Cf. *Deutsch* (1996), p. 3.

84 These characteristics are based on historical meetings with representatives of the foreign nations as well as on literature like lexica and ethnographic writings. Cf. *Stanzel* (1997), p. 13-36, 44-54; *Stanzel* (1999). See also *Goody* (1977), p. 153-156.

85 *Hatfield* described differences in accounting practices across England, France, Germany, and the USA. Although he wrote his paper in 1911, it was not published until 1966. Cf. *Hatfield* (1966).

agement scholars became increasingly interested in this new research area.[87] Market globalization has witnessed major transformations since then. Globalization provides companies with new opportunities to obtain and secure competitive advantages through investments in foreign countries.[88] It, however, also impedes management, e.g., when different national cultures clash within a company. To secure competitive advantage and to account for country-specifics, multinational corporations (MNC) started to standardize their processes to obtain world-scale efficiency while considering for flexibility and local responsiveness. The challenge of MNC is, among others, to manage the tension between standardization and differentiation and the "ongoing alignment of *local* business processes with *global* corporate strategies"[89]. To account for country-specifics, however, managers have first to be sensitized about cross-national differences through comparative management research. Besides the challenge to manage MNC, the rise of Japan's economic power has brought this research stream forward in the 1980s and has encouraged researchers to discover the reasons for Japan's success. Besides national culture,[90] the Japanese manufacturing and management systems like lean production, just-in-time logistics, and target costing were identified as the main reasons.[91]

More specific research on **comparative management accounting** has suffered a lack of attention in the past. Unlike comparative *financial* accounting, comparative management accounting is youngish.[92] The first examination was published in 1978,[93] but the interest in this field of research did not increase significantly before the 1990s.[94] This development is explained by the rising awareness of management accounting after *Johnson/Kaplan* criticized the state of this discipline in 1987.[95] Although more than 100 empirical studies on comparative management accounting have been carried through so far,[96] only little knowledge of cross-national differences exists. "The research to date has, literally, 'grown like Topsy' (a bit here and a bit there), with no underlying systematic pattern and, hence, with little cumulative addition to our knowledge base."[97] Scholars even see most of this knowledge to be rather anecdotal than empirically verified.[98] *Shields*, for instance, questions cross-cultural differences in management accounting:

86 See, e.g., *Rokkan* (1960); *Frey* (1970).

87 Empirical studies on comparative management have increased over time. See *Roberts* (1970); *Barrett/Bass* (1976); *Boyacigiller/Adler* (1991).

88 Cf. *Kolbe* (1989), p. 4, with further references.

89 *Busco et al.* (2007), p. 65.

90 Cf. *Drucker* (1971); *Vogel* (1979); *Ouchi* (1981); *Pascale/Athos* (1981).

91 Cf., e.g., *Haghirian* (2011), p. 34f.

92 Cf. *Blake et al.* (2003), p. 181.

93 The first study on comparative management accounting is *Horovitz* (1978).

94 For the development of comparative management accounting research see section 1.4.2.

95 Cf. *Miller/Vollmann* (1985); *Johnson/Kaplan* (1987).

96 Cf. section 1.4.2.

97 *Harrison/McKinnon* (1999), p. 502.

98 Cf. *Holzmüller* (1995), p. 8; *Shields* (1998), p. 506. *Shields et al.* have already called in 1991 for further research in comparative management accounting. Cf. *Shields et al.* (1991), p. 62.

> *"I am sometimes left with the feeling that this cultural explanation is supposed to be self-evidently true since little, if any, evidence is offered to support these assertions.* [99]

'Comparative' could mean to compare systems across different time frames, spatial units, as well as across different subjects (e.g., companies, industries, or business functions).[100] In the context of management, however, a limited definition is used: **the study of similarities and differences across countries, societies, or cultures**. Most authors apply the terms 'cross-national', 'cross-societal', and 'cross-cultural' rather in an unreflective way and de facto as a synonym.[101] However, conceptual differences in research between the approaches have already been pointed out in literature.[102]

Bhimani distinguishes between comparative management accounting studies that *describe* and those that *explain* similarities and differences in management accounting (like objectives and systems) across different national settings.[103] Descriptive studies tend to identify differences without seeking to explain the underlying rationales for these differences.[104] Explanatory studies illustrate differences and expressly analyze causal factors for these differences. Describing and explaining similarities and differences are not limited to management accounting objectives and systems – it can also include cause-and-effect relationships, e.g., between management accounting objectives and systems. When cause-and-effect relationships are compared, MNC can further be provided with *recommendations* how they should purposefully design, e.g., management accounting systems of their subsidiaries in different national settings. Hence, the findings of comparative management accounting research can be descriptive, explicative, and prescriptive in nature. The following **working definition** is followed in this study.

---

99 *Shields* (1998), p. 506.

100 Cf. *Boddewyn* (1969), p. 3; *Nath* (1988), p. 1.

101 The reason for that imprecise linguistic usage is the insufficient consideration of the content and the functions of the variable 'culture' in most comparative studies. Cf. *v. Keller* (1982), p. 100. The operationalization of culture by *Hofstede* contributed to this simplification by equalizing cultures and countries. See section 1.3.3. However, cultural borders do not have to correspond to country borders.

102 See *Marsh* (1967), p. 12; *Scheuch* (1967), p. 19; *Boesch/Eckensberger* (1969), p. 516. According to *Scheuch*, the three research areas are demarcated by the content of the explaining variable. "[I]f, in a causal explanation, the relevant feature of the context is political organization, the research is designated cross-national; if it is social organization, cross-societal; or if culture, cross-cultural" (*Scheuch* (1967), p. 19). In this study the emphasis is on cross-national; Germany and Japan are compared. Due to their distinctiveness in social and cultural aspects, this study can also be characterized as cross-social and cross-cultural.

103 Cf. *Bhimani* (2005), p. 250-253.

104 Some descriptive studies, however, provide conjectures and speculations of likely causes for cross-national differences. These conjectures and speculations can be misguiding, when the studies have methodological shortcomings like issues in equivalence and do not consider for control variables. *Groot*, for instance, reports potential conceptual confusion by comparing ABC across the Netherlands and the USA. The Dutch cost center method "is generally the same as activity-based costing, although we use a different name for it" (*Groot* (1999), p. 54). Hence, there are doubts, whether the interviewees are talking about the same instrument due to variation in the meanings of terminology across nations.

Comparative management accounting contrasts management accounting across different national settings. Besides describing similarities and differences, comparative studies can further explain cross-national variance and provide recommendations for practitioners.

The theoretical and practical relevance of comparative management accounting is more comprehensively described in the following.

1.2.2 Theoretical and practical relevance

"Thinking without comparisons is unthinkable. And, in the absence of comparisons, so is all scientific thought and all scientific research." [105]

Every science uses comparisons in one way or another and every step of cognition applies to the results of antecedent comparisons.[106] Comparative management accounting is an instrument for cognition, to raise one's awareness about national and international systems. These insights can be both of theoretical and practical relevance.

Theoretical relevance

In a theoretical view, comparative research offers **new research areas** to enlarge our knowledge base, like investigating the impact of national culture on management accounting. As the international setting offers a much greater variance in context and conditions than an intra-national setting, cross-national research exhibits better conditions to test the robustness of theories and it is more likely to expose their weaknesses.[107] Comparative research thus offers social scientist some kind of **'substitute' for experimental conditions.**[108] By identifying country-specific settings "in which a particular theory or hypothesis does not hold, the researcher has an opportunity to offer modifications to an existing theory or to identify the conditions that must be met for a theory to hold (which is, in effect, a further elaboration of the theory)."[109] Theoretical research is seen as a basis to provide scientifically sound recommendations for practice.[110] Its relevance depends on its usefulness to transfer theory into practically relevant solutions.

105 *Swanson* (1971), p. 145.

106 Cf. *v. Keller* (1982), p. 26. The objectives or phenomena examined are always contrasted with each other regarding certain characteristics that they share. Cf. *Czycholl* (1971), p. 74.

107 Cf. *v. Keller* (1982), p. 42, with further references; *Dyer* (2000), p. 237.

108 "'[C]ontext-embedded' relationships can be empirically tested using societal settings as quasi-experimental sites." *Cheng* (2007), p. 29. See also *Sears* (1961), p. 445f.; *Cheng* (1989). It is a 'substitute' in that sense that the comparison in the social sciences is probably the most adequate technique to the experiment. Cf. *König* (1975), p. 33. However, unlike in an experiment, it is not possible to generate an artificial situation for exploring relationships between variables. Cf. *v. Keller* (1982), p. 42f. It is also hardly possible to analyze two identical objects (e.g. companies) under different conditions. Cf. *Berstecher* (1970), p. 31.

109 *Dyer* (2000), p. 237.

110 Cf. *Wild* (1966), p. 25. See also *Ulrich/Hill* (1976a), p. 306.

Practical relevance

The prevalence of cross-national differences in management accounting has a good and a bad side. The positive aspect is that systems and practices from abroad may demonstrate one efficient way of management that can **enhance national management accounting.**[111] Through comparative research, foreign successful and innovative systems and practices can be identified and their transferability to other countries can be assessed. ABC and the German system 'Grenzplankostenrechnung' (GPK) have turned out as superior management accounting systems that have already been transferred cross-nationally. The first companies that attempt to systematically implement foreign instruments often fail,[112] because they do not adapt these instruments to their environment.[113] This, however, is necessary, because implementing foreign instruments often carry wider social and political implications than companies commonly realize.[114] The US invention ABC has been adapted to the German environment. The conceptual design of the German version, 'Prozesskostenrechnung', differs from its original. As German companies have a higher number of cost centers than their US counterparts,[115] the German version comprises a process hierarchy. Sub-processes are combined first to processes before allocating costs to cost objects.[116] Also GPK has to be adapted to the foreign environment. Some US researchers started this attempt in 2005 by merging GPK with ABC.[117] Comparative research is required to identify foreign successful and innovative systems and practices and

111 Features of successful practices can thereby serve as a recipe to enhance productivity and competitiveness. Cf. *Elger* (1994), p. 2.

112 DaimlerChrysler had difficulties in getting their US subsidiaries to use GPK – mainly due to differences in culture and education. Cf. *Krumwiede* (2005); *MacArthur* (2006); *Krumwiede/Suessmair* (2007a), (2007b). For target costing see *Jones et al.* (1998). Similarly, other Japanese instruments, like just-in-time production or quality circles, were imported in Western companies but struggled in realization. Cf. *Elger* (1994); *Oliver/Wilkinson* (1992). Today, 55% of German and 40% of US manufacturing companies apply target costing. Cf. *Kim et al.* (2002), p. 608; *Kajüter* (2005), p. 91, respectively. One example how target costing has been adapted to the German context is provided by *Tani et al.* Cf. *Tani et al.* (1996).

113 For studies following and studies contrasting this view see *Yu/Zaheer* (2010), p. 478f., with further references.

114 Cf. *Oliver/Wilkinson* (1992), p. 1; *Jamieson* (1982), p. 72. *Jones et al.* believe that a successful adoption of Japanese management accounting practices is mainly prevented by social, not technical differences. The different status of management accountants as well as the lower statuses of cost accounting and team work in Western countries also pose an impressive barrier. Cf. *Jones et al.* (1998).

115 Cf. *Krumwiede/Suessmair* (2007a), p. 6f.; *Krumwiede/Suessmair* (2007b), p. 53f.

116 Cf. *Scheer/Berkau* (1993), p. 116; *Gaiser* (1998), p. 72f. Through the combination of subprocesses to processes, the German version enables a more detailed allocation of costs. 'Prozesskostenrechnung' assigns only the costs of indirect departments, whereas the US version mainly allocates all overhead costs of the production cost centers. Cf. *Kellermanns/Islam* (2004), p. 38. Due to the conceptual differences, the type of use differs between both countries as well. See *Gaiser* (1998), p. 70; *Kellermanns/Islam* (2004), p. 37.

117 See *Clinton/Webber*. (2004); *Webber/Clinton* (2004); *Thomson/Gurowka* (2005), p. 31; *White* (2009). For the necessity to adapt GPK to the US environment see *Portz/Lere* (2010).

to investigate how they are woven into other management systems and the whole society. The conceptual effort of actually adapting management accounting systems to foreign environments, however, is beyond the scope of comparative management accounting research.[118]

The negative aspect of cross-national differences is that it complicates **managing MNC.** To limit the barriers of interaction, some researchers recommend *standardizing systems* within a MNC, to benefit from a uniform and coherent business management.[119] However, standardizing might be inefficient when foreign systems are not accepted, which might thereby constitute barriers for standardization. As demonstrated in section 1.1.1, managers from different countries have different views, habits, and preferences regarding cost accounting systems. This merits *differentiating systems* to meet the country-specific context.[120] By highlighting cross-national differences, practitioners can be sensitized in how far and to what extent they should standardize respectively differentiate their management accounting internationally.[121]

The contribution that comparative management accounting provides depends upon the extent to which management accounting systems and practices vary worldwide. In this context the drivers of convergence and divergence in management accounting as well as their consequences for managing MNC are outlined in the next section.

1.2.3 Convergence and divergence in management accounting

Several scholars state that **variations in management accounting diminish worldwide** due to convergence factors. It is argued that the drivers of convergence are currently dominating those of divergence and that they probably become even stronger in future. Seemingly similar managerial ideas or system designs like ABC become widespread all over the industrialized/post industrial countries.[122] Factors contributing to this development are the internationalization of companies, global competition, IT systems, harmonization of financial reporting standards (IFRS), global research and international education, imita-

---

118 Thus, this conceptual effort has to be carried through by another research area – 'international management accounting'. This research area can fulfill this conceptual effort, but it is based on the basic research findings of comparative research. Excluding the research area 'international management accounting' would mean a decline in relevance for comparative research on management accounting. At the same time, disregarding the results of comparative research on management accounting, international management accounting would lose its most important knowledge base. Cf. *v. Keller* (1982), p. 94. Cf. further *Miller* (1984), p. 77f.; *Shenkar* (2000), p. 109f.

119 Cf. *Perlitz* (2004), p. 570.

120 Cf. *Choi/Mueller* (1978), p. 260. Some researchers even assess that companies understanding and making use of the variety across nations can enhance corporate performance. Cf. *Hoecklin* (1995), p. 15-18. See also *Wilkins/Ouchi* (1983); *Smith* (1992); *Sheridan* (1995), p. 294; *Schneider/Barsoux* (2003); *Portz/Lere* (2010), p. 45.

121 Cf. *Richman* (1965), p. 294. Highlighting cross-national differences can further contribute to sensitize management accountants who want to interpret reports from foreign divisions. Cf. *Amat et al.* (1999a), p. 20; *Kellermanns/Islam* (2004), p. 43, 45f.

122 Cf., e.g., *Bhimani et al.* (2007).

tion of leading companies' practices, and international consultancy firms.[123] *Granlund/Lukka* summarize the drivers of convergence and divergence into economic pressures, coercive pressures, normative pressures, and mimetic processes (see Figure 1-4).

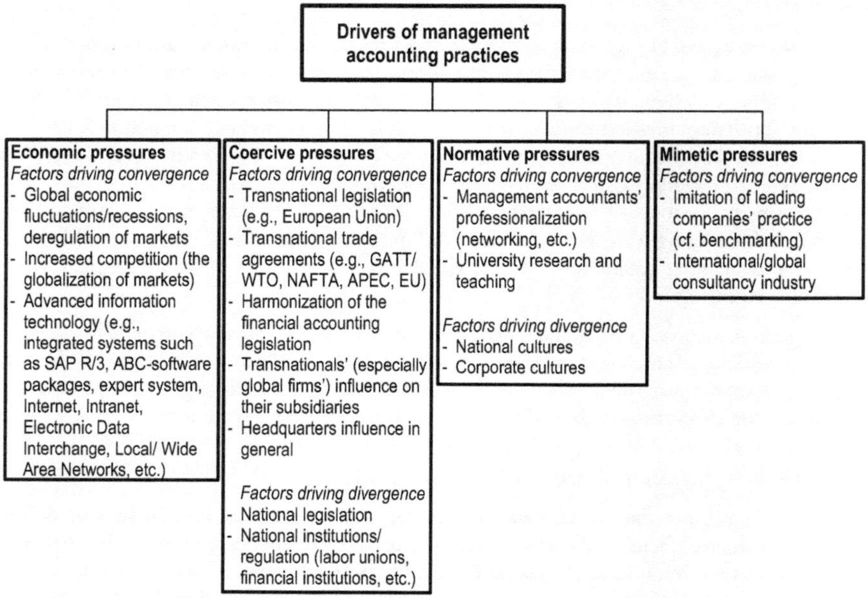

Figure 1-4: Drivers of convergence and divergence of management accounting systems and practices
Source: adopted from *Granlund/Lukka* (1998), p. 157

Drivers that are technical or functional in nature are allocated to the **economic pressures.** IT systems, for example, lead to the standardization of data collection and reporting patterns. Forces that shape the specific national believes in 'good' management accounting include coercive and normative pressures and mimetic processes.[124] **Coercive pressures** stem from formal and informal pressures on organizations. These may be exerted by cultural expectations or may result from organizations on which other organizations are dependent. Due to the harmonization of financial reporting standards, for example, German companies started to abolish imputed costs, which are a particularity of German management accounting.[125] **Normative pressures** generally stem from external sources like formal education and professional networks. They concern social obligations and suitable social procedures in human behavior. An important mechanism that encourages normative isomorphism is the filtering of personnel. Filtering occurs, e.g., through hiring of employees from companies in the same industry. **Mimetic processes** result from uncertainty

123 Cf. *Granlund/Lukka* (1998).

124 Cf. *DiMaggio/Powell* (1983), p. 150-154; *DiMaggio/Powell* (1991b), p. 67-74.

125 Cf. section 2.1.1.2.1.

that encourages imitation of others' successful elements.[126] It encourages homogeneity, because the variety of alternatives that are prevalent or successful are often the ones imitated. Imitating is an effective strategy. When organizations are faced with an ambiguous problem and uncertain solutions, they may select the first alternative that meets acceptable-level goals.[127] As ABC and GPK are considered to be more sophisticated than traditional cost accounting systems, many companies started to implement these systems.[128] Against the background of globalization of the world economy the question arises, which significance country-specifics have for management accounting. As management accounting is likely to converge internationally, but industry-specifics remain, management accounting is expected to differ in future more strongly across industries than across countries.[129] The theoretical and practical relevance of comparative management accounting research would then diminish.

Granlund/Lukka argue that management accounting is mainly **converging on a macro-perspective and diverging on a micro-perspective.**[130] The macro level comprises concepts, ideas, techniques, and system designs, "which form the basis or framework for the micro-level action to take place"[131]. Behavioral patterns and styles of information use are assigned to the micro level.[132] Similarly, *Child* concludes that organizations are becoming more and more alike internationally. However, the behavior of people within organizations is sustaining its cultural specificity.[133]

As a consequence MNC should primarily standardize on a *macro-level*, whereas elements of the *micro-level* should primarily be differentiated to meet national specifics. Parent companies could standardize the basic characteristics of their management accounting systems to create an abstract system devoid of local knowledge.[134] This leaves scope for the subsidiaries to particularize the system according to their national settings as long as management control is still efficient.[135] The parent company could force for example its subsidiaries to implement the basic idea of ABC to allocate overhead costs in a more accurate

126 Cf. *O'Neill et al.* (1998), p. 102f. Higher uncertainty makes decision makers more likely to adopt rule-based behavior. Cf. *Heiner* (1983), p. 570.

127 Cf. *Cyert/March* (1963), p. 120-122. It is therefore expected that organizations rather mimic others in their close environment they are connected to. Cf. *Glaskiewicz/Wasserman* (1989), p. 457.

128 ABC has been implemented by many companies around the world. See, e.g., *Bhimani* (1996); *Groot* (1999); *Rigby* (2001); *Baird et al.* (2004); *Bhimani et al.* (2007). GPK is widespread in German-speaking countries. See *Krumwiede* (2005); *Krumwiede/Suessmair* (2007). GPK is currently discussed in the US literature as an alternative to ABC. See, e.g., *Sharman* (2003a); *Portz/Lere* (2010).

129 See *Granlund/Lukka* (1998); *Shields* (1998).

130 Cf. *Granlund/Lukka* (1998). Cf. further *Winter* (2005), p. 32.

131 *Granlund/Lukka* (1998), p. 153f.

132 Cf. *Granlund/Lukka* (1998), p. 154.

133 He further argues that the majority of the studies supporting the homogenization among organizations focuses on macro level issues, like the structure and technology used by organizations. The majority of the studies concluding divergence among organizations mainly centers on micro level issues, like the behavior of employees within organizations. Cf. *Child* (1981).

134 Cf. *Giddens* (1991).

135 Cf. *Cruz et al.* (2008), p. 2.

way by using cost drivers.[136] The conceptual design of this system can then be specified by the subsidiaries by, e.g., choosing the number of cost drivers and cost pools. Even if management accounting systems were perfectly standardized within a MNC, the actual use of systems still remains different across countries.[137] Hence, behavioral aspects in management accounting cannot perfectly be standardized. Following this distinction, global management accounting systems can be actively reproduced, localized, by the subsidiaries while considering for national specifics. Through the process of differentiation, resistance or irritations can be avoided, which facilitates standardization.[138] Only then *local* business processes can be aligned with *global* corporate strategies, which contributes to the homogenization of systems within a MNC.[139] Hence, **standardization and differentiation are not an antipode.**

Further comparative research is required to provide practitioners an indication of realistic harmonization goals and efforts[140] and to offer scholars a solid basis to investigate the interaction between standardization and differentiation in MNC.[141] Studies addressing this research area can choose between different levels of analysis and different research approaches that are developed in the following two sections.

1.2.4 Framework for analysis

National specifics in management accounting are a complex phenomenon. It therefore makes sense to distinguish different levels of analysis in comparative management accounting research. *Granlund/Lukka* differentiate in this respect between the macro and the micro level (see previous section). This distinction is extended to three levels of analysis (see Table 1-1), because differentiating only between two levels is too unspecific and does not provide enough starting points to arrange a comparative study. This distinction is further valuable to evaluate the state of research on comparative management accounting

---

136 For strategic and operational cost factors that shape ABC cost drivers, see, e.g., *Berens* (1997a), p. 452-454.

137 McDonalds, e.g., offers worldwide standardized food. However, dining at McDonald's in New York means to have a fast meal for a fast buck, whereas in Moscow it is a show of status. Cf. *Trompenaars/Hampden-Turner* (2005), p. 3. "Similarly, social technologies, like matrix structures, reward systems, performance appraisal, empowerment or consultative management, may seem uniform, but will have very different meanings to individuals from different cultures. It all depends on the cultural context" (*Hoecklin* (1995), p. 3).

138 See, e.g., *Busco et al.* (2007).

139 Cf. *Cruz et al.* (2009). See *Beck* (2000). Therefore many management scholars also suggest to consider for national differences (e.g. *Farmer/Richman* (1964); *Graves* (1972); *Triandis* (1982a); *Nishimura* (1995); *Hopper* (1999), p. 58; *Nishimura* (2003), p. 3, 56), "to obtain cross-cultural cooperation in striving for mutually agreed-on goals" (*Graves* (1972), p. 116), or to achieve more effective international operations. For this reason it is often claimed that organizations have to be simultaneously local and global. Cf. *Gernon/Meek* (2001), p. 141f.

140 Cf. *Schweikart* (1985), p. 98.

141 One example of this kind of study is *Cruz et al.* (2009). Several studies also focused on the conditions that facilitate a successful localization. See *Selmer* (2004); *Law et al.* (2004); *Law et al.* (2009).

(section 1.4). On the first two levels, the management accounting objectives and systems are compared with theoretical ideals, whereas the third level brings the routine and institutionalized character of management accounting practice into focus.[142]

Level of analysis	Perspective	Content of analysis	National distinctiveness
Level 1	Macro-perspective	Adoption rate and assessment of systems	Low
Level 2	Mezzo-perspective	Objectives and conceptual design of systems	Middle
Level 3	Micro-perspective	Practice per se	High

Table 1-1: Three levels of analysis in comparative management accounting research
Source: adopted from *Kajüter/Moeschler* (2011a), p. 4

Within the **first level** of analysis (macro-perspective), the *adoption rate* and the *assessment* of management accounting systems like ABC can be compared. The assessment comprises aspects like the perceived usefulness, importance, and difficulties of systems. This level can provide a first impression about cross-national differences in management accounting and their reasons.

Cross-national differences in *objectives* (like the relevance of decision facilitating) and the *conceptual design* of systems (like the complexity of systems) can be determined on the **second level** (mezzo-perspective). This level of analysis provides more insights into national differences and far more explanations can be drawn. Furthermore, relations between objectives and the conceptual design of management accounting systems can be analyzed and compared cross-nationally.

The **third level** (micro-perspective) facilitates to investigate further differences and similarities across nations, because behavioral patterns are additionally addressed. *Practice per se* comprises how practices are embedded in specific contexts and how they are actually applied by the actors – instead of how systems should be applied, which is addressed by management accounting objectives (second level). Assumptions of mainstream economics like the concept of economic rationalists are questioned. Instead, aspects of the new institutionalism theory (see section 1.3.5) are addressed, which stresses the role of organizational rules and routines. Practice per se also includes how management accounting information is actually used. Three different types of use can be distinguished for management accounting.[143] Instrumental use refers to those cases where respondents apply information for decision making or problem-solving purposes, whereas conceptual use refers to influencing a user's awareness, thinking, and comprehension about an issue. Symbolic use prevails, when information is applied to enforce the users own decision or to influence other actors although the decision has already been made.

---

142 Cf. *Scapens* (1994), p. 302f.

143 Cf. *Pelz* (1978), p. 349-357. For an empirical examination of the type of use of cost information in German companies see *Homburg et al.* (1998), p. 36-38.

1.2.5 Research approaches

Four research approaches can be distinguished to conduct comparative management accounting research.[144] These approaches face different methodological challenges and provide different ways how to draw conclusions about cross-national differences and how similarities and differences are addressed.

- **Parochial research** is originally designed and conducted in one country by researchers from that country.[145] Hence, it comprises only monocultural studies and a comparison is not the original aim. As empirical studies differ in the way they are conducted, it is difficult to draw conclusions about cross-national differences from a meta-analysis. *Amat et al.*, for instance, reviewed the collection of parochial research on management accounting edited by *Bhimani* and *Birkett*, *Macintosh*, and *Shields* discuss this collection from an Anglophone perspective.[146]
- Studies that follow **impressionistic research** base their conclusions about cross-national similarities and differences on impressions rather than on facts. Three different types of impressionistic research are distinguished. Within the first type, research is originally designed and conducted in one country – either in the researcher's home or a foreign country – and compared with the researcher's impressions of another country. Predominantly practice oriented studies represent this research approach.[147] The researchers' impressions about the foreign country are often mainly limited to the findings of the particular research project. In the second type of impressionistic research, an international research team is formed that consists of members from all analyzed countries. Misunderstandings that are originated from shortcomings in knowledge of the foreign country and from biases that might stem, e.g., from national pride can thereby be reduced.[148] Unlike replicative and comparative research in a narrower sense, empirical data from only one country is collected and analyzed within the first two types of impressionistic research. Within the third type, management consultants and employees of MNC who have gained comprehensive practical knowledge of their profession about all compared countries are interviewed or mail-surveyed. Their impressions about cross-national differences are also subjective. However, like the second type of impressionistic research, the knowledge of national differences is based on comprehensive experience about all countries. Only few studies have identified cross-national differences in management accounting by following the third type of impressionistic research.[149]
- In **replicative research**, studies initially designed and conducted in one country are replicated in another. Comparability has to be ascertained by imitating the ini-

144 Cf. *Kajüter/Moeschler* (2011a), p. 2f. In taking a cross-cultural view, *Adler* distinguishes six approaches that share some aspects of the distinctions followed in this study. Cf. *Adler* (1983b).

145 Cf. *Adler* (1984), p. 33.

146 See *Amat et al.* (1999a), (1999b); *Bhimani* (1996); *Birkett* (1998); *Macintosh* (1998); *Shields* (1998) respectively.

147 See, e.g., *Winston* (1968); *Hiromoto* (1988); *Bennett* (1993); *Krumwiede* (2005).

148 Studies like *Tani et al.* represent this research approach. Cf. *Tani et al.* (1996).

149 See, e.g., *Weber* (1993), p. 270-272; *Boucoiran et al.* (2009).

tial study as far as the foreign setting admits, e.g., regarding the sample, sampling procedure, and research methods.[150] Studies can thereby test existing management methods or theories for their applicability to other countries.[151]

- In **comparative research in a narrower sense**, studies are initially planned to be carried through in at least two countries. Such studies face demanding challenges: The equivalence of the research process across countries must be assured to conduct comparative research (see section 1.2.6). When equivalence is not assured in all countries examined, the research would be rather replicative than comparative in a narrower sense. In contrast to the other types of research, comparative research in a narrower sense expends more time and costs. The researchers have to engage with at least two countries and they also have to collect data from these countries. The benefit of this approach is that more meaningful comparisons can be conducted than with the other research approaches, because the comparability of the findings can be ensured more comprehensively.

The present study is characterized as comparative research in a narrower sense. Issues in equivalence that this approach has to address as well as their solutions are discussed in the following section.

1.2.6 Issues in equivalence

Besides the general aspects of empirical research, comparative research in a narrower sense faces **further methodological difficulties**. Shortcomings in methodology have been identified as one significant reason why this research area has yielded only little significant insights so far.[152] Equivalence in comparative management accounting research, which constitutes an important and at the same time unique methodological issue in comparative research, is outlined in the following. These insights are valuable to evaluate the state of research on comparative management accounting (section 1.4) and to increase cross-national equivalence of this study (section 1.5.5). It further serves to set up the research design (section 1.5) as well as for statistical analysis and the interpretations of the results (chapter 3 and 4).

> *"The search for equivalence and comparability across nations and cultures appears as a natural understanding in cross-cultural research ... If researchers want to compare across cultural contexts, they need to use concepts and research instruments that are understood in similar ways in all the cultures studied. Moreover, they need to check that the same data collection procedures do not result in biased findings in one of the contexts under investigation. The search of equivalence is therefore the most important methodological aspect of cross-cultural management research."*[153]

To conduct comparative research, equivalence of the research process must be assured across countries. If equivalence is not ensured, the reasons for cross-national variation may

150 Cf. *Adler* (1984), p. 39.

151 See, e.g., *Brewer* (1998).

152 Cf. *Bhimani* (2007), p. 344, with further references; section 1.4.3.3.

153 *Usunier* (1998), p. 102.

not only exist due to country-specifics like national culture, but also due to other influences like differences in sample distribution or differences in the meaning of the aspects under investigation. This would impair a fair comparison of management accounting. Absolute equivalence, however, cannot be assured, because

> *"at a sufficiently high level of abstraction, the research topics, concepts, and approaches must be identical. But, at lower levels of abstraction – generally at the level of operationalizing the concepts and approaches – the definitions and methodologies should be culturally equivalent. The researcher must determine a way to design the study so that the MEANING in the two or more cultures is most similar."* [154]

The issues and problems in equivalence as well as their solutions that have to be considered are summarized in Table 1-2 and outlined in the following.[155]

Issue	Problem	Solution
Ethnocentric bias	• Implicit or explicit cultural dominance in research design and research process	• International research collaboration; intercultural training
Conceptual and functional equivalence	• Apparently identical concepts have a different meaning • Conceptually similar concepts and constructs serve different functions	• Pre-testing and advice from local researchers; consider social embeddedness of concepts and its functions
Translation equivalence	• Differences in meaning	• Back translation and equivalent meanings
Measure equivalence	• Identical or country-specific measurement instruments • Differences in perception, metric, calibration, and time	• Combination of emic and etic perspectives • Equivalent scales
Sampling equivalence	• Representativeness of samples • Non-independence of sample	• Use of matched samples • Choosing less globalized samples and use of 'cultunit'
Data collection equivalence	• Non-equivalence of responses • Biases	• Uniform procedures; international research collaborations • Pre-testing and advice from local researchers; international research collaborations

Table 1-2: Issues in equivalence, their problems, and proposals for their solution
Source: following *Firkola/Lim* (2003), p. 47

Ethnocentric bias

Ethnocentrism is "the inherent tendency to view one's own culture as the standard against which others are judged."[156] Researchers have learned to think, feel, and behave differently

154 *Adler* (1984), p. 50.

155 A similar and more extensive overview is provided by *Brislin et al.* (1973), p. 68-72; *Holzmüller* (1995), p. 271-276. A multiplicity how to classify equivalence is described in literature. The following distinction is based on *Usunier* (1998), p. 105-124; *Firkola/Lim* (2003). Further categorizations are provided, e.g., by *Frijda/Jahoda* (1966); *Ronen* (1986), p. 49-55; *Bauer* (1989); *Peng et al.* (1991).

across countries. They therefore perceive foreign cultural conditions in a biased way.[157] Ethnocentric bias can thus have an effect on the whole research project, including the identification of the research problem, the research method, the variables investigated, and the interpretation of the results.[158] Researchers should try to mask their national bias in order to consider for differences in research abroad and to deny national superiority.[159]

Intercultural training is suggested to sensitize researchers.[160] Furthermore, it is recommended to form **international research collaborations** to mask the researchers' ethnocentric bias.[161] "True international research, which is still quite rare, should always be the product of collaboration between native researchers coming from diverse cultural and linguistic contexts."[162] In spite of the significant consequences of ethnocentric bias, most of the cross-cultural studies do not discuss this issue of equivalence and do not apply any solutions.[163]

Conceptual and functional equivalence

Conceptual and functional equivalence are closely related.[164] *Conceptual equivalence* prevails when the operationalization of a concept has the same meaning in the investigated countries.[165] It means that the influence of certain concepts on other variables holds true in all investigated countries. *Functional equivalence* means that the concepts have to perform the same function.[166] Functional equivalence does not prevail for, e.g., friendship

---

156 *Senior/Bhopal* (1994), p. 329. Similarly, *Triandis* describes ethnocentrism as "using our own culture as the standard for judging how good other cultures are" (*Triandis* (1994), p. 38f.).

157 Cf. *Douglas/Craig* (2006), p. 4.

158 Cf. *v. Keller* (1982), p. 571-575.

159 Cf. *Hesseling* (1973), p. 129; *Adler* (1984), 49f.

160 Cf. *Holzmüller* (1995), p. 145-148.

161 Cf. *v. Keller* (1982), p. 633-635; *Adler* (1984), p. 49f. International research collaborations further allow scholars to complement each other's research experience and can thereby provide an important source of creativity. Cf. *Stead/Harrington* (2000), p. 331. Geographical, cultural, ideological, linguistic, and knowledge distance between the researchers may complicate the team work. Cf. *Wallace/Gernon* (1991), p. 251.

162 *Usunier* (1998), p. 66. Cf. also *Ricks* (1993), p. 11.

163 Cf. *Holzmüller* (1995), p. 12f.; section 1.4.

164 Cf. *Hui/Triandis* (1985), p. 133f.

165 Cf. *Sears* (1961); *Frijda/Jahoda* (1966), p. 115f.; *Berry* (1969), p. 125; *Berry/Dasen* (1974), p. 18; *Harpaz* (2004), p. 25f. Basic concepts like trust must have the same meaning across countries to ensure a fair comparison. Whereas the English concept of trust is about confidence in and reliance on truth, worth, and reliability of a person or thing, the initial position of the German concept is distrust, only after a positive change can trust be established. Cf. *Usunier* (1998), p. 106. Hence, asking US and German people, e.g., about trust and its influence on cost accounting would probably lead to distorted results. See further *Holzmüller* (1995), p. 96-98.

166 Cf. *Frijda/Jahoda* (1966), p. 116; *Berry/Dasen* (1974), p. 15; *Peng et al.* (1991), p. 98; *Usunier* (1998). "Functional equivalence exists when the behavior in question has developed in response to a problem shared by two cultural groups, even though the behavior in one society does not appear to be related to its counterpart in another society. These functional equivalents must pre-exist as naturally occurring phenomena" (*Berry* (1969), p. 122).

between Chinese and Western nationalities. For Chinese the function of friendship is important for doing business and to material advantage, whereas Western nationalities esteem not to exploit friendships for business purposes.[167]

One way to assure conceptual and functional equivalence is to investigate the **meaning** of the concepts and their functions **for the people** involved as well as their **social embeddedness**. International **research collaborations** can furthermore help to address and solve challenges in conceptual and functional equivalence.[168]

Translation equivalence

> *"Language is primarily a cultural or social product and must be understood as such."*[169]

As language influences the way in which we construct our reality, observers have the same picture of the universe, only when "their linguistic backgrounds are similar, or can in some way be calibrated"[170]. Language has a strong influence on perception and categorization. The word 'deadline', e.g., is literally translated to German as 'Stichtag' or 'Frist'. However, both translations do not render the intensity of this word, because the notion of deadly urgency is not comprised. Hence, translating deadline with 'Stichtag' or 'Frist' would be inappropriate.

Researchers should therefore try to achieve equivalent translations in meaning instead of literal translations of words. This, however, demands that the translator is familiar with linguistic and cultural backgrounds of the countries investigated as well as with the research project.[171] To ensure a highly qualitative translation, it is furthermore recommended to **translate** the research material **back** into the original language.[172]

Measure equivalence

From a methodological perspective the researcher has to decide, whether identical measurement instruments or country-specific instruments are more appropriate to address the research question. Cultural research can be classified along the dichotomy of **emic and etic research**. "Emic researchers tend to assume that a culture is best understood as an interconnected whole or system, whereas etic researchers are more likely to isolate particular components of culture and state hypotheses about their distinct antecedents and consequences"[173]. As a consequence, emic studies primarily focus on causes of phenomena

---

167 Cf. *Pye* (1986), p. 78f.

168 Cf. *Peng et al.* (1991), p. 98.

169 *Sapir* (1929), p. 214.

170 *Whorf* (1956), p. 214. Language can have an influence on the research process in three different ways. First, words can signal a specific meaning. Second, words may have a specific meaning in a specific context. Third, language provides the researcher with a specific world view.

171 Cf. *Adler* (1984), p. 54.

172 Cf. *Brislin* (1970); *Adler* (1984), p. 54; *Firkola/Lim* (2003), p. 56. A comprehensive demarcation of different translation methods is provided by *Holzmüller* (1995), p. 228-235. To increase translation equivalence for the linguistic arrangement of questionnaires and instructions, the 12 rules proposed by *Brislin* should be followed. See *Brislin* (1980), p. 432.

173 *Morris et al.* (1999), p. 782.

that are internal to an organization, whereas etic studies follow a more functionalist perspective mainly emphasizing relationships between external variables and behavior.[174] Whereas emic ensures an accurate measurement of the country-specific features, the etic aims at universal valid features.

The etic approach allows for cross-country comparisons, but it captures country-specific features in a less accurate way. Comparative research should for this reason not only apply the etic approach, but should also **comprise emic aspects.**[175] Measurement instruments should thus be to some extent identical to ensure comparability, but should also consider country-specifics.

Furthermore, four different **types of measure equivalence** can be differentiated:[176]

- *Perceptual equivalence.* National specifics may have a deep influence on the perception of the interviewees regarding the research objective. Perceptual equivalence is when a state of affairs produces "'the same, or a very similar' perceptual experience."[177]
- *Metric equivalence.* In comparative studies, the validity of a rating scale depends upon the metric equivalence of the scales. Researchers have to ensure that the distances between scale points are equivalent in the languages affected, because languages differ in expressing gradation in evaluation.[178] To solve this problem, *Sood* suggests applying the wordings based on scales that are used by the native researchers instead of lexically translating the scale terms.[179] Besides differences in distances between scale points, the sensitivity of answering a rating scale may also differ across countries.[180] *Malhotra et al.* recommend asking the respondents "to indicate their own anchor point and position relative to a culture-specific stimulus set"[181].
- *Calibration equivalence.* Regarding secondary data, difficulties in comparing across countries may occur due to differences in categories (e.g., comparing price changes between high- and low-inflation countries) and base years (e.g., some countries may have no recent data). Calibrations are required to "mark the scale of a measuring instrument so that readings can be made in appropriate units."[182]
- *Temporal equivalence.* On the one hand, temporal equivalence, similar to calibration equivalence, deals with the problem of calibrating dates and time periods. In high inflation countries, for instance, the exact date of collecting data is of importance. On the other hand, temporal equivalence also deals with cross-national

174 Cf. *Morris et al.* (1999), p. 790. See also *Berry* (1969), p. 122-124; *Triandis* (1994), p. 67-72.

175 Cf. *Holzmüller* (1995), p. 55-57. For an example how to integrate emic and etic insights see *Morris et al.* (1999).

176 Cf. *Usunier* (1998), p. 111-114.

177 Cf. *Goldman* (1992), p. 94.

178 Cf. *Sood* (1990), p. 34-39.

179 Cf. *Bauer* (1989), p. 183f., 194-201; *Sood* (1990), p. 31.

180 Cf. *Barry* (1969).

181 *Malhotra et al.* (1996), p. 21.

182 *Usunier* (1998), p. 113.

differences in the stage of development. China as a developing country, for example, is 'equivalent' to the characteristics of developing countries 20 years ago. Considering for time lags may be useful for making analogies, like assessing the development of management accounting systems in China.

Sampling equivalence

In comparative research a dilemma between **comparability and representativeness of samples** exists. Representative samples reflect the total population of each country or culture on all key demographic variables. Representative samples might, however, not be comparable, because the samples are likely to differ in composition. If samples are not comparable, cross-national differences cannot be traced back to country-specifics anymore, because differences might also stem from a different composition of the samples. To ensure comparability, full representativeness of the single samples has to be subordinated.[183] One solution is to define matched samples. These are functionally equivalent (regarding industry, company size, etc.) but not identical across the countries studied.[184] A similar strategy to improve the representativeness of samples is to constrain the comparison to a narrow subcategory, like an industry, of the investigated countries.[185]

The dilemma of drawing inferences from cross-national data is referred to the term '**Galton's problem**'.[186] Due to international diffusion, organizations from different countries can converge.[187] For comparative research the samples should be independent. The interactions between the samples are considered to contaminate the data leading to biased results.[188] Comparing, e.g., Chinese studying in the USA with US students is a simplified and inaccurate way to identify differences between China and the USA. The non-independence of samples should be minimized, e.g., by choosing samples that are less globalized or by utilizing the 'cultunit' as a unit of analysis. A cultunit is defined "as people who are domestic speakers of a common distinct language and who belong either to the same state or the same contact group"[189]. However, because the industrialized world is interrelated, independent samples of comparative management accounting research are unfeasible and also undesirable.[190] The researcher must therefore be aware of biases when interpreting his results.[191] Statistical analyses of relations between entities that do not consider non-independence of samples can lead to imprecise results or unjustifiably reject or non-reject hypotheses.[192]

---

183 Cf. *Holzmüller* (1995), p. 109-113.

184 Cf. *Sekaran* (1983), p. 64; *Adler* (1984), p. 52.

185 Cf. *Hofstede/Spangenberg* (1989), c. 955.

186 Cf. *Naroll* (1964), p. 863. For a discussion see *Erickson* (1974); *Ross/Homer* (1976); *Naroll et al.* (1980), p. 489-492.

187 Cf. *Nasif et al.* (1991), p. 85.

188 Cf. *Adler* (1984), p. 53; *Firkola/Lim* (2003), p. 54.

189 *Malhotra et al.* (1996), p. 25.

190 Such a sample would not be representative anymore, but atypical for the countries investigated.

191 Cf. *Adler* (1984), p. 53.

192 Cf. *Ross/Homer* (1976), p. 16.

Data collection equivalence

Various types of data collection equivalence should be considered in comparative research. To increase **respondents' co-operation equivalence** a uniform data collection is recommended.[193] However, respondents might have a different motivation to cooperate and might feel differently about the researchers contacting them. The **advice from foreign research partners** is therefore necessary when an adaptation of the data collection process is required.

Besides respondents' co-operation equivalence, **response style equivalence** should be considered, which include the following four issues.

- Questions are often culture-bound and can thus have a different *meaning* across countries. Nationalities respond differently, for instance, to culturally sensitive topics (e.g., questions about sex are taboo in some countries).[194] Respondents may even be unwilling to answer the questions (item non-response). Culturally sensitive topics should therefore be asked indirectly.[195]
- '*Yea-saying*' *patterns* occur, when respondents try to please the researcher,[196] whereas '*nay-saying*' patterns arise, when respondents try to avoid a loss of face.[197]
- *Sucker bias* arises when respondents try to deceive foreign researchers, e.g., to protect their country.[198]
- The *response patterns* of respondents differ internationally. The Japanese are most likely to soften their position and suppress their opinions by choosing the median value on questionnaire scales (middle response style).[199] Western countries like the USA on the contrary tend to overreact to questions by responding with more enthusiasm that leads to a higher standard deviation (extreme response style).[200]

To ensure response style equivalence ex-ante, **pre-testing** and **advice from local researchers** are useful.[201] To minimize biases ex-post, the national data sets could also be standardized, which are then normally distributed with a zero mean and unit standard

193 Cf. *Kim et al.* (1994), p. 55; *Sekaran* (1983), p. 63.

194 Cf. *Sekaran* (1983), p. 63.

195 *Usunier* (1998), p. 122.

196 *Mitchell* calls this phenomenon 'courtesy' or 'hospitality bias'. Cf. *Mitchell* (1969), p. 248. Cf. also *Brislin et al.* (1973), p. 70.

197 Cf. *Usunier* (1998), p. 122f.

198 Cf. *Mitchell* (1969), p. 249; *Brislin et al.* (1973), p. 70.

199 Cf. *Stening/Everett* (1984).

200 Cf. *Hui/Triandis* (1989); *Usunier* (1998), p. 123. Empirical investigations are provided by *Zax et al.* (1967); *Chun et al.* (1974); *Stening/Everett* (1984); *Harzing et al.* (2009). *Stening/Everett* investigated that education and age have a significant influence upon the response styles across nations. Cf. *Stening/Everett* (1984). To avoid this bias it is recommended to apply a seven-point- instead of a five-point-scale and ranking instead of rating. Cf. *Harzing et al.* (2009).

201 Cf. *Sekaran* (1983), p. 63; *Firkola/Lim* (2003), p. 59, respectively.

deviation.[202] This procedure, however, has strong effects, because significant differences in mean across national samples are eliminated.[203]

1.3 Theoretical perspectives for comparative management accounting research

A general agreement on how to carry out explanatory research on management is still missing. There is no theory that capably explains associations between culture, human behavior, and outcomes of organizations,[204] but theories from domestic research can also be applied to investigate phenomena cross-nationally. Following *Bhimani*, this chapter describes and criticizes alternative **theoretical perspectives** that were not all specifically developed for comparative research, but are still suitable for this research area. These perspectives differ in the explanatory contents regarding the view of homogenizing forces, the view of management accounting, methodological emphasis, and the level of analysis.[205] The strengths and weaknesses of the research perspectives are described in the following to identify a suitable research perspective for this study in section 1.3.8.

1.3.1 Theory of industrialism

According to the theory of industrialism, countries undergo an industrialization process, which leads to the same end-point industrialism that is characterized by common social, structural, and basic economic features. The underlying force of this process is productive technology.[206]

> *"Industrialization, according to this argument, brings about certain changes in the fabric of organizations, particularly their size and complexity. These changes, in turn, are seen as necessitating certain developments in organizational structuring: greater specialization, reliance upon rules, and decentralization."*[207]

The contingencies of technological development are seen to impose a logic that all societies must follow, "if they hope to conduct a successful march to industrialism"[208]. This force leads to a convergence in organizational structure and management systems across countries, irrespective of economic or political system and culture.[209] Among countries

202 Cf. *Usunier* (1998), p. 125. The underlying assumption of standardization is that the mean scores for the different countries investigated are equal.

203 Cf. *Usunier* (1998), p. 126. For a discussion between standardizing and not standardizing coefficients in cross-national research, see *Singh* (1995), p. 598-620.

204 Cf. *Bhimani* (2007), p. 344. Cf. also *Child* (1981), p. 304-307.

205 The selection of the theoretical perspectives largely follows *Bhimani* (1999); *Bhimani* (2005); *Bhimani* (2007). Theoretical perspectives for comparative financial accounting are described by *Gernon/Wallace* (1995).

206 Cf. *Kerr* (1960), p. 33-46; *Child/Tayeb* (1982), p. 27.

207 *Child/Tayeb* (1982), p. 23.

208 *Harbison/Myers* (1959), p. 117.

209 Cf. *Harbison/Myers* (1959), p. 117-133; *Child* (1981), p. 308. Technology "speaks a universal language attractive to all, whatever the form of government or the culture of a people" (*Hickson/Pugh* (2001), p. 305).

with a comparable stage of industrialization, companies are limited to a small set of functional possibilities that enable their survival.[210] Hence, cross-national and even cross-organizational differences are solely explained by the extent of industrialization – effects of nation-specific factors are downplayed.[211] *Form* illustrates this logic of industrialism in a comparative study of four countries. He concludes that the development of modern societies follows a similar path of technological-organizational structures and attitudes.[212] Based on this logic, developing countries like China require different management accounting systems than developed countries like Germany and Japan. Furthermore, management accounting between developed countries should be very similar and systems like those applied today in Germany and Japan will become popular in Chinese companies while China undergoes the industrialization process.

The argument of industrialization can be transferred on a more micro-organizational level in terms of other contextual variables' interdependencies with organizational structuring.[213] This approach is described in the following section.

1.3.2 Contingency theory

The contingency theory[214] can be traced back to the late 1950s. It was established by the organizational theorists *Woodward* and by *Burns/Stalker*.[215] It adopts some central assumptions of the theory of industrialism. Both theories assume that

> *"countries at similar stages of development adopt the same approach to the design of their business (and other) organizations and it posits the existence of a rationality, transcending national or cultural peculiarities."*[216]

However, the contingency theory does not follow the universalistic logic of 'one best way'.[217] Thus, unlike the theory of industrialism, cross-organizational differences within

---

210 Cf. *Bhimani* (1999), p. 414f. Similar to industrialism, some scholars have argued that contradictions within capitalism generate largely similar trends in management across countries. Cf. *Bhimani* (1999), p. 414, with further references. According to Marxist capitalist theory, the elite classes are driven by the same goals to increase capital accumulation. Cross-national convergence in business organization is assumed at a macro-level, because science and technology that drive industrial societies were universal. Divergence across national borders is interpreted by national differences in the world capital system. Cf. *Kerr* (1960); *Lane* (1995), p. 8f.; *Tempel* (2001), p. 28. Contrary to that, the theory of industrialism and the contingency theory (section 1.3.2) rather focus on the structure of organizations than highlighting and explaining similarities across economies. Cf. *Tempel* (2001), p. 28.

211 Cf. *Bhimani* (1999), p. 414f.

212 Cf. *Form* (1969).

213 Cf. *Bhimani* (2007), p. 345f., with further references.

214 This chapter mainly focuses on the contingency theory of organizational structure, which is termed 'structural contingency theory'. For structural contingency theory see *Pfeffer* (1982), p. 147-162.

215 Cf. *Woodward* (1958); *Burns/Stalker* (1961). See also *Lawrence/Lorsch* (1969), p. 185-210.

216 *Lane* (1989), p. 22.

217 Cf. *Donaldson* (2001), p. 3.

one society can also be explained by the contingency theory. To be efficient, organizations have to adapt their structures to the specific circumstances they are facing.[218] Furthermore, according to the contingency theory, organizational structure is not only influenced by productive technology, but also by other contingency factors like company size. It is assumed that the context factors can objectively be differentiated from other elements of the environment and knowing about these factors enables management accountants to design their systems purposefully.[219] The main objective of this approach is to **explain differences between the structures of different organizations** by means of the different circumstances they are facing.[220] From these insights practical recommendations can be derived.[221]

Early accounting researchers like *Waterhouse/Thiessen*[222] and *Otley*[223] drew on the work of organizational theorists and paved the way for contingency theory in management accounting research. Since then many researchers have attempted to examine the importance of context factors like environment, technology, and company size to design management accounting systems.[224]

The contingency theory has been criticized by several scholars.[225] *Kieser/Ebers* differentiate between methodological shortcomings and criticism that addresses the fundamental assumptions of the original contingency theory.[226] **Methodological shortcomings** include

1. relevant environmental and structural elements are not considered for,
2. the applied dimensions are not valid, not approvable, and not comparable across studies,
3. the applied statistical techniques are not adequate,
4. samples are not representative and not comparable, and
5. the information content of the empirical-based findings is low.

---

218 Cf. *Kieser/Ebers* (2006), p. 215. The contingency theory explains organizational change in a functional way. Cf. *Donaldson* (2001), p. 161f.

219 Cf. *Bhimani* (1999), p. 415.

220 Consequently, organizations "of similar size and other contextual characteristics, should demonstrate no significant differences in structure or in the nature of their approach to management" (*Child/Kieser* (1975), p. 5).

221 Cf. *Schreyögg* (1995), p. 11.

222 See *Waterhouse/Tiessen* (1978).

223 See *Otley* (1980).

224 For a review of empirical, contingency-based research see *Chenhall* (2003).

225 A summary of the criticism is provided in *Türk* (1989), p. 1-10; *Frese* (1992), p. 190-197; *Schreyögg* (1995), p. 159-219; *Kieser/Ebers* (2006), p. 231-239. See further *Aldrich* (1972), p. 27-29.

226 Cf. *Kieser/Ebers* (2006), p. 231-239.

Criticism that addresses the **fundamental assumptions** of contingency theory include

1. the organizational context does not determine the organizational structure,
2. the approach does not explain how organizational structure adapts to new organizational environments,
3. the approach ignores domination in organizations,
4. the approach pleads for a conservative organizational design, and
5. organizational structures cannot be designed and grasped irrespectively from apperception, intention, and action of the organizational members.

Besides these criticisms two important shortcomings of contingency theory for conducting comparative management accounting research exist.

- **Negligence to address national distinctiveness:** Contingency theory (and also the theory of industrialism) deems relationships between context factors and company's characteristics as invariant across national or societal settings. Hence, the country context is not seen as a rationale for variations in the dependent phenomenon under study.[227] The 'culture-free' perspective is thus not suitable for cross-national studies that aim to explain differences and similarities across countries.
- **Negligence of the process how structures adapt to new environmental conditions:** The contingency theory (and the theory of industrialism in particular) has considered only broad features of organizational characteristics. It reveals only little how structures become operationalized,[228] because the behavior of organizational members is not accounted for.[229] Although contingency theory postulates that organizational structures have to be adapted to the organizational environment, this process is not analyzed.[230] As this mechanism is missing, contingency theory has been accused to lack theoretical grounding.[231]

In a more contextual way with different methodological emphases, the following four theoretical perspectives explain variance in management accounting across nations and societies.

227 Cf. *Cheng* (2007), p. 29f. *Hickson et al.* state from a cross-national study: "Whether the culture is Asian or European or North American, a large organization with many employees improves efficiency by specializing their activities but also by increasing controlling and coordinating specialities" (*Hickson et al.* (1974), p. 64). See also *Smith/Meiksins* (1995), p. 242. *Donaldson* supports this 'culture-free' view by conducting a meta-analysis. He demonstrates that positive correlations between company size and bureaucracy exist and that theses coherences do not vary across 13 countries. Cf. *Donaldson* (1990).

228 Cf. *Bhimani* (1999), p. 416.

229 Cf. *Maurice/Sellier* (1979), p. 322; *Horváth et al.* (1981).

230 Cf. *Donaldson* (2001), p. 161. See also *Kieser* (1988).

231 Cf. *Aldrich* (1972); *Tosi/Slocum* (1984), p. 9.

1.3.3 Cultural contingency approach

Empirical research shows that company size has cross-nationally a positive effect upon formalization, specialization, and centralization.[232] However, on a more micro-level, considerable cross-national differences exist how formalization, specialization, and centralization are conducted.[233] There is systematic evidence in comparative management accounting research that formally identical instruments and tasks are carried out differently from one national society to another.[234] **Culture is seen as one factor that explains variation across countries.**[235] Understanding the implications of national culture therefore offers potential solutions to culture-specific problems in management accounting. To clarify the association between culture and national differences, researchers called for 'unbundling' the cultural variable into its subcomponents, which could make theoretical explanations of relations between culture and other variables possible.[236]

Through different studies[237] cross-national comparative researchers have gained "a readily accessible set of universal dimensions from which measures of culture could be derived."[238] In spite of this variety of concepts, most intensively, almost exclusively, the typology by **Hofstede**[239] was applied by cross-cultural studies.[240] This typology has been complimented as the most elaborate and most extensive cross-national study of values ever attempted –[241] before it was extended by the GLOBE study[242]. Around 1967 and 1973, *Hofstede* has surveyed attitudes of 116.000 employees within IBM subsidiaries in 66 coun-

---

232 Cf. *Hickson et al.* (1979).

233 Cf. *Kieser/Kubicek* (1992), p. 253-266.

234 The argument for the culture-free-thesis is therefore not "convincing in its own terms or when examined in the light of evidence of national variations" (*Child* (1981), p. 323).

235 "The less an activity is technically defined, the more it is ruled by values, and thus influenced by cultural differences. Values in turn are expressed in rituals, heroes, and symbols. Accounting is a field in which the technical imperatives are weak: historically based conventions are more important to it than laws of nature. So, we can expect accounting systems to vary along national cultural lines" (*Hofstede* (1987), p. 8).

236 Cf. *Bhagat/McQuaid* (1982), p. 675; *Harrison/McKinnon* (1999), p. 484f., with further references.

237 See, e.g., *Kluckhohn/Strodtbeck* (1961); *Hofstede* (1980); *Trompenaars/Hampden-Turner* (2005); *Schwarz* (1994); *House et al.* (2004). For an overview how national culture has been modeled by various researchers see *Myers/Tan* (2002), p. 6.

238 *Boyacigiller et al.* (2004), p. 106.

239 Cf., e.g., *Hofstede* (1980).

240 Cf. *Chandy/Williams* (1994), p. 722-724; *Harrison/McKinnon* (1999); *Sivakumar/Nakata* (2001), p. 555; *Chenhall* (2003), p. 153; *Tung/Verbeke* (2010), p. 1259.

241 Cf. *Triandis* (1982b), p. 90; *Robinson* (1983), p. 111f.

242 The GLOBE (Global Leadership and Organizational Behavior Effectiveness) study has investigated cultural, societal, organizational, and leadership differences across 62 societies. Cf. *House et al.* (2004). Solely the study by *Hofstede* is addressed in the following for three reasons. First, the cultural dimensions by the GLOBE study have hardly been applied in comparative management accounting research so far. Second, the general opportunities and limitations of both studies are very similar. Third, for this study, the cultural dimensions by *Hofstede* are sufficient to contrast German and Japanese cost accounting.

tries.[243] The connotations of each dimension and the comparisons drawn are of immediate interest for establishing and implementing management structures and systems.[244] *Hofstede* distinguishes five cultural dimensions.[245] These dimensions "describe basic problems of humanity with which every society has to cope; and the variation of country scores along these dimensions shows that different societies do cope with these problems in different ways."[246]

- (Low vs. high) **power distance** – "the extent to which the less powerful members of organizations and institutions (like the family) expect and accept that power is distributed unequally."[247]
- **Individualism** (vs. collectivism) – the extent "to which individuals are integrated into groups."[248] The ties between individuals are loose in individual societies, whereas in collectivist ones people are integrated into strong and cohesive groups from birth onward.
- **Masculinity** (vs. femininity) – "assertiveness and competitiveness versus modesty and caring"[249]. This dimension refers to the distribution of roles between the sexes. Men's values from one country to another "contain a dimension from very assertive, competitive, and maximally different from women's values on the one side, to modest and nurturing and similar to women's values on the other."[250]
- **Uncertainty avoidance** – "intolerance for uncertainty and ambiguity."[251] This dimension indicates to what extent people from different cultures feel either comfortable or uncomfortable in uncertain events or unstructured situations.
- **Long-** (vs. short-) **term orientation** – "persistence and thrift to personal stability and respect for tradition."[252] The dimension long-term orientation describes the

---

243 *Hofstede* initially found four central, bi-polar dimensions of a national culture explaining 49% of the variance. The dimension of Confucian dynamism – which is designated as long vs. short-term orientation – was developed and added in 1987. He statistically analyzed only 40 countries due to small numbers of respondents in the remaining countries. Cf. *Hofstede* (1983), p. 77; *Hofstede* (1993), p. 296.

244 Cf. *Mead* (2005), p. 51.

245 For a description of the dimensions see, e.g., *Hofstede/Bond* (1988); *Hofstede* (2001). *Hofstede* has recently added a sixth dimension – indulgence versus restraint. Cf. *Hofstede et al.* (2010), p. 277-298. This dimension, however, is not described in the following, because it has not significantly been applied in research so far and it is not relevant for this study.

246 *Hofstede* (1980), p. 212.

247 *Hofstede* (1991), p. 28.

248 *Hofstede* (1991), p. 51.

249 *Hofstede* (1991), p. 82f.

250 *Hofstede/Bond* (1988), p. 11.

251 *Hofstede* (1991), p. 113.

252 Cf. *Hofstede* (2001), p. 351. The dimension long-term orientation versus short-term orientation reflects the geographic division of cultures. Asian countries are rather characterized as long-term oriented, because they have been influenced by the teachings of Confucius that emphasize a long-

people's acceptance of change, perseverance, thrift, and pursuit of peace of mind. Short-term orientation is the opposite with spending now being more important than saving for tomorrow.[253]

Figure 1-5 demonstrates according to *Hofstede* that Germany shares more similarities with the USA regarding national culture than with Japan. Thus, according to the cultural contingency approach, stronger differences in management accounting are expected between Germany and Japan than between Germany and the USA.

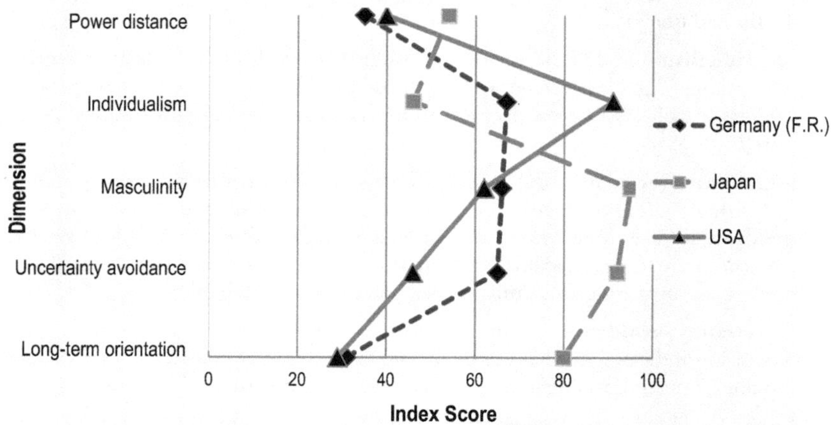

Figure 1-5: *Hofstede's* cultural scores for Germany, Japan, and the USA

Several **limitations** of *Hofstede's* work are discussed in literature.[254]

(1) Surveys as an inappropriate way to measure cultural differences. *Hofstede* concluded from questionnaire response differences to obtain cultural values. It is questioned, if "[t]he notions of culture as a force, and as a decipherable manifestation, are inappropriately conflated"[255]. In addition to that, further dimensions could have been 'found', if *Hofstede* had asked other questions.[256] Furthermore, his study ignores that response differences may have occurred due to other reasons but cul-

term orientation and an orientation towards future. Countries that have been influenced by Christianity are rather characterized as being short-term oriented. Cf. *Hofstede* (2001), p. 363.

253 Cf. *Hofstede* (2001), p. 354-368.

254 Cf. *Robinson* (1983); *Sorge* (1983); *Montagna* (1987); *Smith* (1992); *McSweeney* (2002); *Smith* (2002); *Baskerville* (2003); *Baskerville-Morley* (2005).

255 *McSweeney* (2002), p. 104, with a further reference.

256 *Smith* (1992), p. 41; *McSweeney* (2002), p. 105. It is questioned whether it is possible to identify cultural dimensions a priori to compare cultures and to explain variation across countries. Cf. *Child* (1981), p. 324f.; *Child/Tayeb* (1982), p. 44.

ture, like race, religion, or language. Finally, the questionnaire responses are likely to be biased.[257]

(2) **Lack of conceptual and functional equivalence.** Critics argue that *Hofstede's* study is heavily influenced by the Western culture. The dimension uncertainty avoidance has been identified as irrelevant, e.g., to the Chinese population.[258] The cultural dimensions are also not an exact point of comparison, because the dimensions carry different associations when describing different cultures.[259]

(3) **Nations should not be equated to cultures.** *Hofstede* assumes that national territory and culture corresponds and presumes national uniformity. This is problematic, because cultural borders rarely correspond to frontiers. Even within a country there is often more than one culture.[260]

(4) **Individuals working at IBM's subsidiaries cannot represent national cultures.** It is often criticized that *Hofstede* intended to measure national culture, but the results may be distorted by IBM's organizational culture.[261]

(5) ***Hofstede's* conceptualization of culture is superficial.** First, *Hofstede's* survey has measured *beliefs and not behavior.*[262] *Hofstede's* variables describe likely behavior in social context, but they neither specifically refer to decision making nor to management accounting.[263] Second, anthropologists view culture as *an integrated pattern of symbols and meanings.* Culture should therefore not be divided into dimensions.[264] Third, it is criticized that *Hofstede* only superficially compares cultures by *quantifying dimensions.* Culture, however, is much more complex in nature.[265]

---

257 See *McSweeney* (2002), p. 103.

258 In following studies, however, this drawback was partly reduced by adding a fifth cultural dimension. See *Hofstede/Bond* (1988); *Hofstede* (1999), p. 40. *Schwarz* concludes that "comparisons are virtually meaningless if there is no equivalence of meaning...Because *Hofstede* did not address this issue, the extent to which his items were conceptually equivalent across cultures is unknown" (*Schwarz* (1994), p. 94).

259 "Because individualism is expressed slightly differently in the United States and China, a statement such as 'the culture of the United States is more individualist than the culture of China' gives only a rough and ready guide to the two cultures" (*Mead* (2005), p. 28).

260 Cf. *Huo/Randell*, for instance, empirically demonstrate significant differences between the Chinese sub-populations Beijing, Wuhan, and Hong Kong regarding *Hofstede's* four initial dimensions. Cf. *Huo/Randall* (1991). There are also cultural differences between East and West Germany. Cf. *Brodbeck/Frese* (2007). Furthermore, *Hofstede* does not pay enough heed on non-national cultures or non-cultural forces that operate within nations, leading to the heterogeneity of values that tends to be common for many modern industrialized societies. Cf. *Bhimani* (1999), p. 420; *McSweeney* (2002), p. 109.

261 It is thus argued that the values of IBM employees are only representative to a small group that is educated, middle class, and city swelling. Cf. *Mead* (2005), p. 48.

262 Beliefs and behavior are not the same and individuals can show broad divergences between the two. Cf. *Lane* (1989), p. 29f.

263 Cf. *Sorge* (1983), p. 628; *McSweeney* (2002), p. 107; *Kirkman et al.* (2006), p. 297.

264 Cf. *Baskerville* (2003), p. 2.

265 Cf. *Sorge* (1983), p. 628; *Baskerville* (2003), p. 2, 8. Instead of describing cultures in numerate indices, an intensive analysis of cultures is required to discover the background of their characteris-

(6) ***Hofstede's* work is outdated.** *Hofstede's* scores were derived about four decades ago. Although cultures are relatively stable systems, Chinese managers, for instance, turned more individualistic and more short-term oriented over time.[266]

In spite of these shortcomings and the criticism from literature that "[t]he use of *Hofstede's* dimensions by accounting scholars raises more problems than it solves"[267], most of the research on comparative management accounting has chosen the cultural contingency approach to explain variance for two reasons. First, even though nations are not the best units to study culture, usually they are the only kind of units available and differences between nations – and only in very few cases differences between cultures – are of interest in accounting research.[268] Second, comparative studies follow different objectives than ethnocentric studies. Critics of *Hofstede* often argue from an anthropological point of view. They accept the subjectivity of the observer and focus on meaning. In business studies, however, researchers mainly focus on comparison and objectivity. As comparative researchers already face higher request compared to domestic studies, limitations in time and costs often force them not to comprehensively engage with cultures within the scope of ethnocentric studies, but to simplify.

Studies that applied *Hofstede's* concept lack further weaknesses that are beyond *Hofstede's* work. These studies usually explain cross-national differences only by national culture. Companies operating in different national settings might, however, also be subject to different laws, regulations, and local competitive factors. The impact of national culture can thus not be separated from other influences.[269] Furthermore, *Harrison/McKinnon* have identified three further weaknesses:[270]

(1) In many comparative studies, only some cultural dimensions are chosen to explain variance across countries and others are ignored. These studies fail to consider the totality of cultural domain.
(2) Studies tend to ignore that differences in the levels of cultural impact also depend on the centrality and importance of cultural characteristics.
(3) Culture is often treated simplistically. Studies assume that the cultural dimensions are uniform and unidimensional in nature. As a consequence, they claim that empirical results of one country are applicable to another country, when their cultural characteristics associated to the results are similar.

The challenges to conduct comparative research and the shortcoming in addressing culture as a main influence factor have caused **dissatisfying results** in comparative management accounting. Many *Hofstede*-inspired studies provide some empirical 'surprises'[271]

---

tics and their relationships to the environment. As a consequence, *Hofstede*'s work is criticized to be "useless for explaining the characteristics and dynamics of specific groups, organizations, and subsystems in concrete social settings" (*Alexander/Smith* (1993), p. 155).

266 Cf. *Ralston et al.* (1999), p. 422f.

267 *Baskerville* (2003), p. 10.

268 Cf. *Hofstede* (2003), p. 812.

269 Cf. *Chow et al.* (1999b), p. 442.

270 Cf. *Harrison/McKinnon* (1999).

271 Cf. *Harrison/McKinnon* (1998).

being either nonsignificant or contradictory to prediction.[272] *Bhimani* concludes that "[c]ulturalist explanations for international variety in management controls remain largely speculative and atheoretical"[273]. Furthermore, little overlap between studies exists and, where overlap exists, the research design of the studies significantly varies, which complicates generalizing empirical findings. Overall, only few new insights are gained and little variance is explained.[274]

For future research, it is recommended to explain the impact of culture with a greater explanatory content than simply applying *Hofstede's* concept. *Harrison/McKinnon* suggest "interpretational perspectives and methodologies of anthropology, sociology, and history"[275]. Furthermore, researchers should determine whether and how non-cultural variables interact with culture and they should examine the relative importance of cultural and non-cultural variables in explaining management accounting phenomena, either independently and/or in interaction.[276] *Kirkman et al.* recommend a contingency view to determine *when*, instead of *if*, culture matters most.[277] *Baskerville* proposes a cultural holism approach for accounting research by following "a diverse range of differing methodologies which, while being informed by anthropology, may have a variety of objectives and foci."[278] In addition to that, *Bhimani* criticizes that the cultural contingency perspective neglects the process how social phenomena become embedded in management accounting.[279] Suggestions for a greater explanatory content are provided by the following three theoretical perspectives.

1.3.4 Societal effects approach

Instead of the cultural contingency approach that looks upon culture as "sets of ideas, values, shared symbols, and meanings"[280], the societal effects approach[281] focuses on the expression of culture in institutions (including the educational system, the system of social stratification, the vocational education and training, and the division of labor), which shape actions.[282] Thus, unlike the cultural contingency approach, the societal effects approach expects culture to have an indirect impact through institutions upon managerial systems. Studies that follow this approach investigate the characteristics of organizations

272 Cf. *Chow et al.* (1999b), p. 442.

273 *Bhimani* (1999), p. 420f.

274 Cf. *Harrison/McKinnon* (1999), p. 502. See also *Kirkman et al.* (2006), p. 286, 313.

275 *Harrison/McKinnon* (1999), p. 501. Similarly *Chenhall* calls to conceive culture "in richer terms than the value systems of *Hofstede*" (*Chenhall* (2003), p. 155).

276 Cf. *Harrison/McKinnon* (1999), p. 503; *Chenhall* (2003), p. 154.

277 Cf. *Kirkman et al.* (2006), p. 313. See also *Briley/Aaker* (2006).

278 *Baskerville* (2003), p. 10.

279 Cf. *Bhimani* (2005), p. 253. *Montagna* explains that the "lack of emphasis on the social dynamics of culture limits the utility of their analysis of the relationships between culture and accounting" (*Montagna* (1987), p. 27).

280 *Child/Tayeb* (1982), p. 41.

281 See *Maurice* (1979); *Sorge/Warner* (1986); *Sorge/Maurice* (1993).

282 Cf. *Lane* (1989), p. 31-37; *Bhimani* (1999), p. 421. The state has been identified as the most important institution. Cf. *Whitley* (1992), p. 37.

that reflect the societies' institutional features in which they are located.[283] Thereby, differences between societies cannot be explained by one factor only, instead "there appears to be a close interaction between factors in different spheres of society which follows a logic upon which the identity of a particular society is built"[284].

Similar to contingency theory, the societal effects approach follows the isomorphism argument. Organizations are viewed as "social entities integrated into the institutional and value structures constituting the culture of a society. In this view organizations and society tend to reflect each other structurally."[285] Principles of the contingency theory are adopted to systematically analyze matched data across companies that are fairly identical regarding size, technology, location, and dependence.[286]

The societal effects approach **overcomes some drawbacks of the cultural contingency perspective.** First, "it taps culture relative to actions"[287] to avoid positing a priori, cultural value orientations to individuals. Second, it avoids treating culture as a separate causal factor that can be distinguished from economic factors.[288] Third, difficulties of the conceptual and functional equivalence are addressed. 'Comparison of the non-comparable' is no longer considered as a problem. Instead, the principle of comparability becomes the object of analysis. Analytical categories that acquire meaning in their very specificity through their location within a societal space are apprehended and analyzed across societies instead of comparing terms by terms only.[289] Fourth, the societal effects approach addresses interactions between institutions and organizational actors that can result in organizational change. Institutions influence the behavior of employees and the latter can also modify institutions in a non-deterministic relationship,[290] because institutions are seen as "patterns of habitualized reciprocal social action"[291]. The societal effects approach thereby opposes the determinism that is incorporated by the previous approaches.[292]

---

283 Cf. *Lane* (1989), p. 28, 31, 34.

284 *Sorge/Warner* (1986), p. 184.

285 *Inzerilli* (1980), p. 11.

286 Cf. *Maurice et al.* (1980), p. 61f.; *Bhimani* (1999), p. 422.

287 *Lane* (1989), p. 36.

288 Cf. *Lane* (1989), p. 36. In this approach, culture is seen to have a mediating influence. Cf. *Maurice* (1979), p. 46.

289 Cf. *Maurice* (2000), p. 16, 28f. However, studies that apply matched pairs for comparison often face limitations of the experimental research design that do not ensure that results can be comprehensively generalized. Cf. *Heidenreich* (1991), p. 184f.

290 Cf. *Maurice et al.* (1980), p. 61; *Lane* (1989), p. 35f.; *Mueller* (1994), p. 411; *Maurice/Sorge* (2000), p. 2; *Bhimani* (2007), p. 421.

291 *Lane* (1989), p. 35. Similarly, *Scapens* notes that "[i]nstitutions which influence actions are themselves the outcomes of those actions" (*Scapens* (1994), p. 309). The 'construction of the actors' has a historical dimension through which their identity (of professionalism) and their capacity for actions develop. Cf. *Maurice* (2000), p. 21.

292 Cf. *Hodgson* (1988), p. 10-12; *Liouville/Schmidt* (1996), p. 259f. Unlike the cultural contingency approach that explains national distinctiveness only in a static way, the societal effects approach can explain differences also in a dynamic way.

Although the societal effects approach overcomes some of the problems of the cultural contingency approach, it incorporates several **shortcomings**. First, "[i]t does not appeal to decontextualised structural relationships nor does it see human creativity as unbounded and organizational arrangement as unconstrained."[293] Second, by recognizing the historical nature of the interactions between actors and the institutions, the societal effects approach makes it possible to observe their relative stability and their dynamics of change.[294] The process how social phenomena become embedded in management accounting and the manner management accounting comes to exhibit specification and characteristics are, however, not addressed.[295] Third, like the cultural contingency approach, the societal effects approach does not examine organizational actors to explain national distinctiveness. Instead, organizational behavior is solely deduced from the environment. Autonomy and strategic freedom of the actors is not accounted for.[296] This, however, is necessary to understand how management accounting can be enacted rather than purposefully structured.[297] Fourth, *Lane* criticizes that the approach disregards that institutions are mostly designed by the powerful in society. Institutions do therefore rather reflect the values and interests of the powerful than of the powerless.[298] Fifth, the intensity of societal effects is questioned. As systems and practices effectively diffuse across borders, "organizational and globalization effects may complement or even counteract the societal effect."[299] The shortcomings of the societal effects approach are addressed by the new institutionalism approach.

1.3.5 New institutionalism

Institutionalism is an approach to study social, economic, and political phenomena.[300] It sees action rather as the output of institutions than autonomous decisions of individuals.[301] Institutionalization is the process by which actors reproduce what is socially defined as real and the meaning of an act is more or less taken for granted. Institutional acts must be perceived as rule-like and embedded in formal structures.[302] Thereby, the rationalism of actions is questioned. This approach investigates "the manner in which structures become institutionalized via interaction and how received opinions shape propriety as to the functioning of organizations."[303]

---

293 *Bhimani* (1999), p. 423.

294 Cf. *Maurice* (2000), p. 22.

295 Cf. *Bhimani* (1999), p. 424. Also *Lane* criticizes that the societal effects approach does not explain "how exactly institutions impact organizations" (*Lane* (1995), p. 13).

296 Cf. *Liouville/Schmidt* (1996), p. 260.

297 Cf. *Bhimani* (2005), p. 254.

298 Cf. *Lane* (1989), p. 37.

299 *Mueller* (1994), p. 407.

300 Cf. *DiMaggio/Powell* (1991a), p. 1.

301 Cf. *Zucker* (1987), p. 459; *Peters* (2005), p. 1.

302 Cf. *Zucker* (1977), p. 728.

303 *Bhimani* (2005), p. 254.

There is little agreement what 'institutions' are and how they are defined.[304] *Zucker* broadly distinguishes between two different **concepts of institutionalization.**[305] The '*environment as institution*' concept assumes that external, commonly state-linked institutional elements are reproduced or copied by organizations. The societal effects approach shares several aspects of this concept. The '*organization as institution*' concept, in contrast, emphasizes that institutional elements arise from within the organization itself or from similar organizations.[306] The *new institutionalism* is allocated to the second concept of institutionalization. This approach

> *"emphasises the ways in which action is structured and order made possible by shared systems of rules that condition the inclinations and capacities of individuals and influence the diffusion of organisational operation procedures. It seeks to explore how organizational ideals become embedded in language and symbols and how state of affairs are produced and constructed. It is thus partly concerned with the manner in which societal and symbolic order is maintained by means of rituals."*[307]

The **social dynamics** are more comprehensively explored by the new institutionalism approach than by the societal effects approach. "Past actions may have unanticipated consequences and the formation of rules may be the result of evolution, rather than rational choice. Furthermore, institutions do more than *inform* current actions, they create the concepts and cognitive frames through which certain behaviors become taken-for-granted."[308] As the actors' preference for familiar patterns creates resistance to change, patterns of actions persist even when they are perceived as inefficient.[309] **Three mechanisms of institutional change** are discussed by *DiMaggio/Powell*: coercive pressures, normative pressures, and mimetic processes (see section 1.2.3).[310] The authors choose isomorphism as the best way to comprehend the process of homogenization among organizations. They adopt *Hawley's*[311] description of isomorphism as "a constraining process that forces one unit in a population to resemble other units that face the same set of environmental conditions"[312].

Based on these mechanisms, specific practices "flow from organization to organization, sector to sector and even country to country ... Ultimately, they are taken for granted by

304 Cf. *DiMaggio/Powell* (1991a), p. 1.

305 Cf. *Zucker* (1987), p. 444-447. A comparison between traditional and new institutionalism is provided by *DiMaggio/Powell* (1991a), p. 11-15.

306 Cf. *Zucker* (1977), p. 727-730.

307 *Bhimani* (1999), p. 425.

308 *Scapens* (1994), p. 309.

309 Cf. *Lane* (1995), p. 11. This approach thereby shows similarities to the theory of structuration. For the theory of structuration see *Giddens* (2008) and for the structuration theory in management accounting in particular see *Macintosh/Scapens* (1990); *Macintosh/Scapens* (1991); *Coad/Herbert* (2009).

310 Cf. *DiMaggio/Powell* (1983), p. 150-154; *DiMaggio/Powell* (1991b), p. 67-74.

311 See *Hawley* (1968).

312 *DiMaggio/Powell* (1991b), p. 66.

individuals and organizations as the right way to do things"[313]. Hence, this approach stresses on the emergent nature of management accounting rather than on their technical purposefulness.[314] Furthermore, the approach of new institutionalism follows the **emic perspective** taking the insider's viewpoint in organizations. This is important especially for comparative management research to understand the thinking patterns of actors in organizations.[315] The previous theoretical perspectives on the contrary embody rather an etic perspective by focusing on universal aspects of organizational structuring revealing fewer insights of observed similarities and differences.[316]

Even though new institutionalism captures the social dynamics superior to the previous theoretical perspectives, *Bhimani* states that the existing work on new institutionalism has **limitations** in *explaining the historical rootedness* of the investigated phenomena.[317] Furthermore, the ability to explicate change with new institutionalism is less evident, because *revolutionary changes*, where established routines are significantly disrupted, *cannot be explained.*[318] Revolutionary changes are not considered, because this approach downplays conflicts within organizations by overlooking the actors' interests and their relative power.[319] Furthermore, new institutionalism does not sufficiently address how actors maintain their leading positions or respond to threats during instable periods.[320] Instead, changes are primarily attributed to extra-institutional changes.[321]

According to *Bhimani*, the interaction among actors and structural features of their organizations leading to changes in organizational structures can be clearer understood "by investigating the historical origins of institutional influences."[322]

---

313 *Meyer/Scott* (1992), p. 2. On the contrary, forces like law, professional ideologies, or custom institutionalize *standard* operation procedures.

314 Cf. *Bhimani* (1999), p. 427.

315 Cf. *Morey/Luthans* (1984). Emic research is carried through via open-ended and long-standing ethnographic observations. Its benefit is the 'thick description' (*Geertz* (1983) that enables the researcher to discover the depth of meaning that actors inscribe in their language and actions. Its disadvantage is the subjectivity of the results and the researcher's expenditure of time.

316 Cf. *Bhimani* (1999), p. 427.

317 Cf. *Bhimani* (1999), p. 428.

318 *Scapens* distinguishes between evolutionary and revolutionary changes. Only evolutionary change, where "current institutions will continue to play a significant role in the process of change" (*Scapens* (1994), p. 312) can be explained by the new institutionalism. The new institutionalists "attribute institutional persistence to the inability of individual actors to break out of, and transcend, established modes of cognition" (*Lane* (1995), p. 11). On the contrary, revolutionary change more likely leads to purposive action and conscious choice, because new routines have to be constructed.

319 The possibility that some organizational members benefit more than others from institutional changes is not considered for. Cf. *Lane* (1995), p. 11.

320 Cf. *DiMaggio/Powell* (1991a), p. 30. Cf. also *Tempel* (2001), p. 41f.

321 Cf. *DiMaggio/Powell* (1991a), p. 30, with further references.

322 *Bhimani* (1999), p. 428.

1.3.6 Historical analysis

When national distinctiveness is deemed to be originated from society's past,[323] *Bhimani* calls for showing **links between historical events and societal effects.**[324] The historical analysis is valuable to find a "'feel' of pattern, a process, or a series of accidents and contingencies"[325] that underlie enduring forces, which deepens the understanding of management accounting events and changes. Furthermore, by combining historical and institutional comprehensions,[326] deeper insights of their institutional origins can be provided.[327] This approach is also suitable for comparative management accounting research, because pattern of past action demonstrate contemporal cultural products[328] that can provide researchers a deeper understanding of practices' institutional origins of and sources of sustenance.[329] Researchers could apply this approach to investigate how cost accounting practices have changed over the course of history in different countries. It could be cross-nationally compared how networks of institutions and practices impose country-specific practices in cost accounting to assess the persistence of these country-specifics in the context of globalization and to draw conclusions about the future development of cost accounting in these respective countries.

Bhimani sees the approach by the **'new' historians** to be particularly suitable for determining the historical rootedness of management accounting change.[330] In this approach, the beliefs and value systems in specific historical situations are reconstructed by examining rituals and ceremony under an ethnological perspective.[331] "What is sought is to investigate the origins of modes of consciousness, the conditioning elements of human subjectivity, and the regularity of forms of thought in particular contexts."[332] This rich description of context allows exploring the rationalities that management practices underlie across different contexts. In this sense, management accounting is seen as emergent rather than intentionally designed a priori.[333]

---

323 "[T]he patterns of past action within a nation, particularly as reflected in its institutional development should draw attention to contemporary cultural products which are likely to be relatively persistent in nature" (*Child* (1981), p. 329). Furthermore, *Sahlins* states that "culture is precisely the organization of the current situation in the terms of the past" (*Sahlins* (1985), p. 155). Similarly, *Sheridan* describes "the present as a product of the past and as the seedbed of the new" (*Sheridan* (1980), p. 82).

324 Cf. *Bhimani* (1999), p. 428.

325 *Mann* (1986), p. 503.

326 Cf. *Child* (1981), p. 329.

327 Cf. *Bhimani* (1999), p. 429.

328 Cf. *Child* (1981).

329 Cf. *Bhimani* (2007), p. 355.

330 Cf. *Bhimani* (1999), p. 430-434.

331 See, e.g., *Foucault's* work on madness and criminality. In his writings he analyzes how networks of institutions and practices impose specific forms of subjectivity on individuals. See *Foucault* (1961); *Foucault* (1975).

332 *Bhimani* (1999), p. 430.

333 Cf. *Bhimani* (1999), p. 433f.

1.3.7 Discussion

The characteristics and distinguishing features of the six theoretical perspectives are summarized in Figure 1-6.

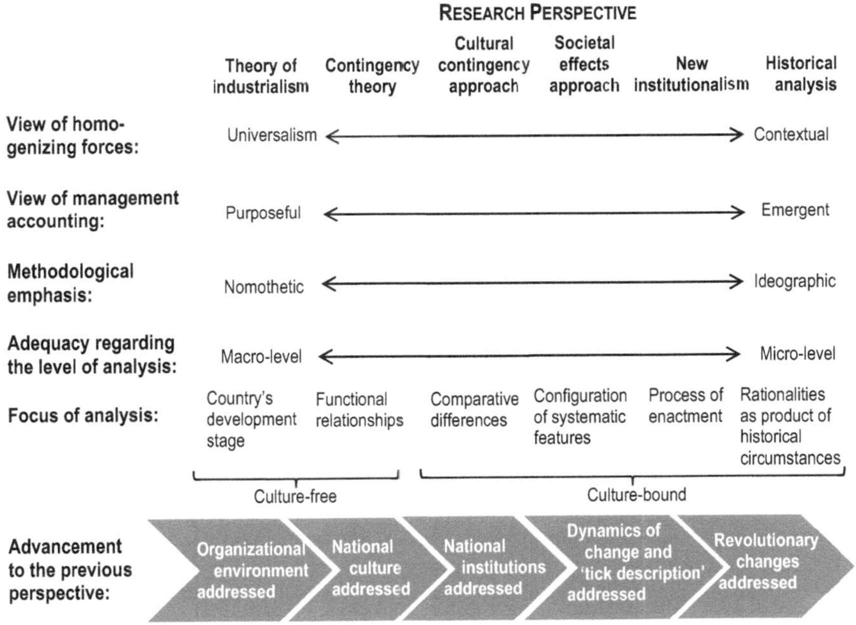

Figure 1-6: Differentiating features of alternative research perspectives
Source: extending *Bhimani* (1999), p. 416

The theory of industrialism and the contingency theory belong to the culture-free perspective. The theory of industrialism explains cross-national variance in management accounting in terms of the country's development stage in industrialization. This view is extended by the contingency theory in a more contextual way: Functional relationships between the organizational environment and management accounting are drawn to explain differences. The remaining perspectives belong to the culture-bound perspective.[334] Whereas the cultural contingency approach explains comparative differences exclusively by national culture, the expressions of national culture are addressed by the societal effects approach, new institutionalism, and historical analysis. The focus of analysis of these perspectives therefore differs from the cultural contingency approach: The societal effects

334 The culture-free-thesis assumes universality to organizational design and structures. On the contrary, the culture-bound-thesis expresses the thought that organizations match their structures to fit their cultural environment. Cf. *Oberg* (1963), p. 129; *Maurice* (1976), p. 5f.; *Tayeb* (1988), p. 21f. Thus, both theses are controversial – however, more on a methodological kind than on substance. Cf. *Tayeb* (1994), p. 438f.

approach addresses how national institutions configure management accounting features, new institutionalism analyses how management accounting practices become enacted, and the historical analysis addresses the rationalities of management accounting practices that stem from historical circumstances.

The sequence of the approaches reflects an increase in the **potential to explain national distinctiveness.** Whereas both culture-free approaches ignore national specifics as an independent variable, the other approaches address them – with the historical analysis being the most comprehensive one. The theory of industrialism in particular presupposes that homogenizing forces are *universal.* This view is *nomothetic*[335], as it has the tendency to establish generalizable relationships. Furthermore, according to this perspective, management accounting can *purposefully* be *constructed,* because instrumental rationality is assumed. These presuppositions are softened with increasing intensity by the other perspectives. The historical analysis reverses the presuppositions of the theory of industrialism: It views homogenizing forces as *contextual* and management accounting not as the product of rational choice but as *emergent.* Furthermore, as history deals with events which existed only once, not generalizable but unique, specific relationships are established (*idiographic*). As all theoretical perspectives comprise different methodological assumptions, they are suitable for different research purposes. The culture-free perspectives are most suitable for *macro-level* analyses, whereas the culture-bound perspectives are increasingly suitable to address research problems on a *micro-level* (in particular new institutionalism and historical analysis).[336]

The sequence of the approaches, however, also reflects an increase in the **required research resources.** As comparative research faces additional particularities, like issues in equivalence (see section 1.2.6), and requires sampling from at least two countries, limitations in time and cost often force researchers not to comprehensively engage with cultures within the scope of the societal effects approach, new institutionalism, or the historical analysis, but to simplify.[337] Most of the cross-cultural studies have therefore applied the "readily accessible set of universal dimensions"[338] by *Hofstede* to explain national distinctiveness.[339] Whether those simplifications are appropriate depends upon the specific research objective and the conditions of the research project.

---

335 For the antipode nomothetic-ideographic see *Thomae* (1999); *Cone* (1986). According to *Cone*, nomothetic is an approach, which "is concerned with (1) the discovery of general laws and (2) relating universally applicable variables in (3) research involving relatively large numbers of subjects" (*Cone* (1986), p. 112). Idiographic research on the contrary is "person-centered rather than variable-centered" and "emphasizes the discovery of relationships (laws) among variables uniquely patterned in each person" (*Cone* (1986), p. 112).

336 For potential research areas on a macro-, mezzo-, and micro-level in comparative management accounting see section 1.2.4.

337 Little comparative management accounting research has been guided by the new institutionalism and the historical analysis in any sustained manner to date. Cf. *Bhimani* (1999), p. 434; *Bhimani* (2007), p. 357.

338 *Boyacigiller et al.* (2004), p. 106.

339 See section 1.4.2.

The six presented perspectives are seen by some researchers as complementary and by others as alternatives.[340] Only few comparative studies have merged different theoretical perspectives,[341] although weaknesses of the single theoretical perspectives can thereby be compensated and a broader set of explanations for cross-national differences can be provided.[342]

1.3.8 Determination of the study's theoretical perspective

A theoretical perspective is required to investigate the five research questions of this study. It enables to observe the objective, to grasp the problem, and to phrase further research questions. This perspective embodies and demonstrates the researcher's preconception.[343]

The **contingency theory** is suitable to meet four out of the five research questions from section 1.1.1. By controlling for other external and internal context factors, a meaningful cross-national comparison can be conducted and it can be assessed whether stronger differences prevail across industries than across countries. Furthermore, the impact of context factors upon cost accounting and recommendations for practitioners how to purposefully design cost accounting systems can be provided. Nevertheless, the contingency theory does not explain national distinctiveness. Hence, the third research question – *why does cost accounting differ between Germany and Japan?* – cannot be answered by the contingency theory.

To explain national distinctiveness, a culture-bound perspective is required. The two perspectives **new institutionalism and historical analysis**, however, are not essential for this study, because behavioral aspects of cost accounting – that are assigned to the third level of analysis – are not addressed. Instead, the objective of this study is to compare cost accounting objectives and the conceptual design of cost accounting systems cross-nationally (see section 1.1.1). The biggest disadvantage of new institutionalism and historical analysis is the researcher's expenditure of time and costs. As this comparative research faces additional particularities, limitations in time and costs force the researcher not to comprehensively engage with countries, but to simplify. The **cultural contingency approach and the societal effects approach** are therefore more suitable for this research project. The drawback of all theoretical perspectives but the contingency theory and the theory of industrialism is that they are not engaged with other external and internal context factors. This, however, is necessary to address all five research questions comprehensively – either by determining their impact on cost accounting or by controlling for their influence.

As not all research questions can be met with one theoretical perspective, the **contingency theory is merged with the cultural contingency approach and the societal effects approach** to compensate for each other's weaknesses.[344] Thereby, this study can provide a broader set of explanations for cross-national differences than prior research on compara-

340 Cf. *Bhimani* (1999), p. 435.

341 For an exception see *Child* (1981).

342 Cf. *Kajüter/Moeschler* (2011a), p. 8.

343 Cf. *Kubicek* (1977), p. 17.

344 The perspectives presented in section 1.3 can either be seen as alternatives or as complementary. Cf. *Bhimani* (1999), p. 435.

tive cost accounting that has, if at all, adopted only one theoretical perspective.[345] As different theoretical perspectives might come to different conclusions, they can increase plausibility and explain why empirical outcomes are either nonsignificant or contradictory to prediction.[346] By merging the contingency theory with both culture-bound perspectives, two assumptions have to be accepted,[347] which are inconsistent with the original contingency theory. First, in reality structural designs are not rigidly determined by context factors and such factors are themselves affected by power-holders within organizations.[348] Second, culture and national institutions could theoretically be considered as further context factors.

Following *Child*, culture and national institutions are also regarded as **moderating variables** that have an effect on the magnitude of the contingency's functional relationships.[349] For example, following the contingency approach, company size is expected to positively affect the complexity of cost accounting systems. The direction of this influence is assumed to be universally valid, because this influence is rather technological than behavioral in nature. However, the magnitude of the change might vary across countries due to cultural and societal specifics (see Figure 1-7).[350]

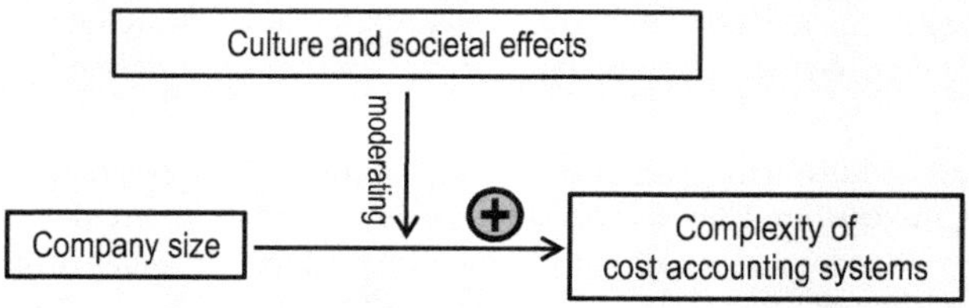

Figure 1-7: Culture and societal effects as moderating influences on functional relationships

1.4 Prior empirical research on comparative management accounting and implications for the study

Despite the increase in internationalization, the research reviews by *Adler* and *Shields* demonstrate that only **few articles examine international topics** in business studies and

345 Cf. *Kajüter/Moeschler* (2011a), p. 8.

346 *Hopper et al.*, e.g., suggest to emphasize further reasons besides national culture for conducting studies on cost accounting. Cf. *Hopper et al.* (1999), p. 83f.

347 Cf. *Child* (1981), p. 349.

348 Cf. *Child* (1972).

349 Cf. *Child* (1981). *Child* thereby agrees with *Donaldson*, who argues for a new synthesis of contingency theory as the core theory with selective propositions from other conceptual perspectives. Cf. *Donaldson* (1995), p. 5.

350 *Horovitz*, e.g., investigated that decentralization is on average higher in Great Britain than in France and Germany. As a consequence, keeping the size of organizations constant, British companies have a lower degree of detail in control than their French and German counterparts. Cf. *Horovitz* (1980), p. 171. The usefulness of integrating different methodological perspectives is demonstrated by *Child*. See *Child* (1981), p. 337-346.

management accounting. *Adler* analyzed the state on cross-cultural issues in business studies. She concludes that

> *"corporate activity has internationalized faster than has the publishing of articles in American management journals. The majority of the total articles and for the organizational behavior articles published in American management journals focus on the domestic US environment."* [351]

Also international topics in management accounting have suffered a lack of attention in the past. The review by *Shields* demonstrates that only 5 out of 152 articles published by North Americans during 1990 to 1996 in six leading journals have addressed cross-national differences in management accounting.[352] Due to the lack of research *Shields* concludes that comparative research on management accounting provides "modest evidence that national culture has a significant effect on the preference for and the design and use of management controls."[353]

Besides the lack of comparative research, *Harrison/McKinnon* demonstrate methodological shortcomings of prior research.[354] This review, however, is limited to "studies appearing in the main English-language research journals"[355] that have analyzed the relationships between cultural dimensions and management control systems.

A catalog of existing research on comparative management accounting is compiled in this section for three reasons. First, all three reviews mentioned above were published before 2000 and might thus be outdated. It is likely that with the increase in globalization over the past decade the number of publications in comparative management accounting research has grown and has caught up with the internationalization of corporate activity. Second, the reviews by *Shields* and *Harrison/McKinnon* are only limited to top-ranked academic journals. A comprehensive picture of comparative management accounting research has not been provided so far and it is possible that other journals have published more comparative articles. Third, this comprehensive review is required to demonstrate, whether comparative management accounting research has suffered a lack of attention in general, or whether this instance holds true for only specific topics in management accounting (e.g., cost accounting). When the number of cost accounting studies is compared with the number of studies of other topics, the relevance to conduct comparative research on cost accounting and the contribution of this study can better be assessed.

---

351 *Adler* (1983a), p. 231. *Werner/Brouthers*, however, demonstrate that many management journals increasingly publish more studies with international contents. Cf. *Werner/Brouthers* (2002).

352 Cf. *Shields* (1997).

353 *Shields* (1997), p. 7.

354 See *Harrison/McKinnon* (1999). Also *Hoffjan et al.* have reviewed studies on comparative management accounting, however, this review is not limited to empirical studies and the analyzed publications have not systematically been searched for. Therefore, only a minority of the comparative research on management accounting was identified and reviewed. See *Hoffjan et al.* (2009). Furthermore, *Riahi-Belkaoui* summarizes some empirical findings of comparative management accounting research. See *Riahi-Belkaoui* (2002), chapter 4.

355 *Harrison/McKinnon* (1999), p. 484.

In the following section the selection of the studies is outlined (section 1.4.1). Thereafter, an overview of all identified studies on comparative management accounting is provided (section 1.4.2). As the aim of this study is to compare cost accounting systems internationally, the studies on cost accounting are reviewed in depth (section 1.4.3). Methodological issues are thereby addressed and gaps for future research are identified. This review is based on the comprehensive descriptions of comparative management accounting from section 1.2 and theoretical perspectives for comparative research from section 1.3. Based on this review, implications for this study are drawn in section 1.4.4.

1.4.1 Selection of studies

A **qualifying article** is defined as one that is both comparative and empirical in nature. The studies, however, are limited to replicative and comparative research in a narrower sense (see section 1.2.5). As cross-national differences have been questioned in literature or criticized of being rather anecdotal than empirically proven,[356] research approaches that describe cross-national differences in a rather subjective way, like meta-analyses of parochial research as well as impressionistic research, are excluded from this review. In the following, the approaches 'replicative' and 'comparative in a narrower sense' are subsumed under the label 'comparative'. The studies of interest do not have to be limited to management accounting. They can also address management accounting among other management topics. However, they must contain instrumental, functional, or institutional aspects of management accounting or the use of management accounting information. Studies that compare management accounting only across continents are not included in this review,[357] because their findings are too aggregated to provide new insights about reasons for national distinctiveness. Also the comparison of textbooks is excluded,[358] because management accounting in organizations are to be investigated. As comparative research faces additional particularities compared to domestic research and requires sampling from at least two countries, limitations in time and cost often force researchers to simplify their research design. To investigate the consequences of simplifications in conducting a comparative study and to provide comprehensive recommendations for future research, the studies are not limited to any academic level. Unlike *Harrison/McKinnon*'s review on management control systems,[359] more methodological issues can thereby be discussed. Furthermore, a more comprehensive composition of empirical findings and of recommendations for future research is provided.

A comprehensive **sampling procedure** was designed to produce an exhaustive review on empirical and comparative research on management accounting. To find qualifying literature, the following procedure was followed:

356 Cf. *Shields et al.* (1991), p. 62; *Shields* (1998).

357 These studies include, e.g., *Rigby* (2001); *Rigby/Bilodeau* (2005); *Rigby/Bilodeau* (2007); *Stratton et al.* (2009).

358 These studies include *Pistoni/Zoni* (2000); *Roso et al.* (2003); *Hoffjan/Wömpener* (2005); *Roso et al.* (2005); *Hoffjan/Wömpener* (2006).

359 Cf. *Harrison/McKinnon* (1999).

(1) 17 English and two German (management) accounting journals as well as three journals that predominantly address international issues in management were searched over the years 1977 to 2009.[360] Prior articles have not been searched for, because the first study on comparative management accounting was published by *Horovitz* in 1978. The interest in this research area has awakened thereafter.

(2) A keyword search was performed using the EBSCOhost interface. Studies were identified that include at least one term of each following keyword groups in combination. Group 1: cross-national, cross-societal, cross-country, comparative, international, culture, *Hofstede*. Group 2: management accounting, cost accounting, costing, ABC, budgets, budgeting, transfer pricing, balanced scorecard, responsibility accounting, cost management, capital budgeting, controllership, management control systems.

(3) To identify comparative studies that were not found through both previous steps, snowballing was conducted with the above articles. Furthermore, articles quoted in reviews[361] on comparative and cross-national studies were searched.

1.4.2 Overview of comparative management accounting studies

112 research projects resulting in 148 publications have been identified by the sampling procedure in comparative management accounting research. It is thereby the largest collection of studies in comparative management accounting in literature.[362] The research projects are characterized in the following regarding the investigated countries, research method, topics, the application of *Hofstede's* cultural dimensions, and year of publication. The list of the research projects is provided in Appendix 1.

Investigated countries

Table 1-3 provides the frequencies of investigated countries. **Most frequently the USA is compared** with other countries (70 out of 114 research projects), followed by the UK (32), Japan (30), Germany (26), and Australia (22). Most frequently the USA has been

---

360 English speaking journals include *Abacus, Accounting Horizons, Accounting, Auditing and Accountability Journal, Accounting, Organizations and Society, Advances in Accounting Behavioral Research, Advances in Management Accounting, Behavioral Research in Accounting, Journal of Applied Management Accounting Research, Journal of Cost Management, Journal of International Accounting Research, Journal of International Financial Management and Accounting, Journal of Management Accounting Research, Management Accounting, Management Accounting Quarterly, Management Accounting Research, Strategic Finance* and *The International Journal of Accounting*. German-speaking journals include *Controlling* and *Zeitschrift für Controlling & Management*. Journals that address predominantly international issues in management include *Journal of Comparative International Management, Journal of International Business Studies* and *Management International Review*.

361 The reviews include *Harrison/McKinnon* (1999); *Riahi-Belkaoui* (2002), chapter 4; *Hoffjan et al.* (2009).

362 The literature review by *Harrison/McKinnon* (1999) addresses methodological issues of 19 empirical studies on management control. The literature review by *Hoffjan et al.* (2009) summarizes the findings of comparative studies on management accounting. Nine of the analyzed comparative studies are empirical.

compared with Japan (28 times) followed by the comparison with the UK (14) and the comparison with Germany (11). Most often the USA has been compared with other countries, because the majority of the studies were carried through by US researchers. Compared to their economic power, the Anglophone countries UK, Australia, Canada, and New Zealand are overrepresented, whereas the emerging countries Brazil, China, India, and Russia are underrepresented.

	Country	Frequency		Country	Frequency
1	USA	70	28	India	2
2	UK	32	29	Latin America	2
3	Japan	30	30	Malaysia	2
4	Germany	26	31	Thailand	2
5	Australia	22	32	Argentina	1
6	Canada	15	33	Caucasus	1
7	France	13	34	Central America (Costa Rica, Ecuador, El Salvador, Guatemala, Nicaragua, Panama)	1
8	China (including Hong Kong)	12			
9	Singapore	9	35	Colombia	1
10	New Zealand	8	36	Czech Republic	1
11	Italy	7	37	Europe (excl. UK)	1
12	Netherlands	7	38	Central and Eastern Europe	1
13	Spain	7	39	German-speaking countries	1
14	Sweden	7	40	Greece	1
15	Norway	5	41	Hungary	1
16	Belgium	4	42	Indonesia	1
17	Taiwan	4	43	Ireland	1
18	Korea	4	44	Israel	1
19	Mexico	4	45	Luxembourg	1
20	Taiwan	4	46	Philippines	1
21	Brazil	3	47	Poland	1
22	Switzerland	3	48	Portugal	1
23	Austria	2	49	Puerto Rico	1
24	Chile	2	50	Slovenia	1
25	Denmark	2	51	Ukraine	1
26	Europe	2	52	Venezuela	1
27	Finland	2			

Table 1-3: Investigated countries

Research method

The majority of the studies applied survey research followed by field research, and laboratory experiments (see Figure 1-8).[363] It is expected that the majority of the studies have applied survey research, because comparative research faces additional particularities, wherefore researchers are often forced to simplify by standardizing the data collection. The studies have almost exclusively applied mail surveys, the most standardized form of survey research. The researchers' language skills were a significant barrier for conducting valuable field research in comparative research when countries with a different national language are compared. Good skills in at least two languages are required to carry out valuable research, because the same researcher should conduct interviews and observations in

363 For the distinction between the three research methods see section 1.5.1.

all countries investigated.[364] When different researchers conduct a field study in each country, the results might be hard to compare, because the researchers might interpret the same issue differently. Survey research on the contrary can be conducted in each country by different researchers without losing comparability, because the data collection is standardized and there is thus little scope for subjective interpretations that might dilute the findings.[365]

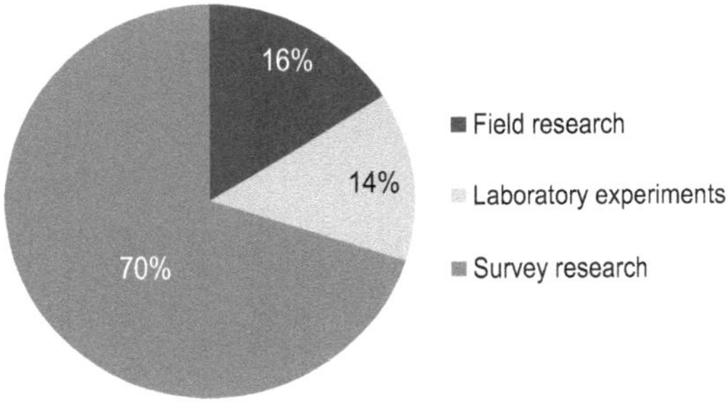

Figure 1-8: Distribution of research methods

Research topic

Table 1-4 provides the frequency distributions of the topics addressed by prior comparative research projects on management accounting. As comparative studies are usually less focused than domestic research, the majority of the research projects deal with multiple research topics. A wide variety of topics has been examined cross-nationally. The most frequently addressed topic is management control systems (74), followed by management accounting in general (57), cost accounting (17), and capital budgeting and investment decisions (6). Overall, comparative management accounting mainly focused on management control systems that are most relevant for governing MNC. Although cost accounting is an essential part of a company's information system, it has rather been neglected by prior research.

---

364 The research by *Ahrens* represents a valuable field study. See *Ahrens* (1996), (1997), (1999).

365 Besides language barriers, *Shields* enlists five further reasons explaining why only few field study articles are published in management accounting research. These include "lack of knowledge about how to do good studies; lack of colleagues with which to team; lack of incentives (annual performance reviews, short times for tenure and promotions); lack of access to good sites; and the journals' editorial styles and preferences" (*Shields* (1997), p. 10).

Topics	Frequency	
Management accounting		**57**
Management accounting overall	26	
Management accounting practices	16	
Decision making	14	
Controllership	2	
Information systems	10	
Education	2	
Learning style	2	
Career choice	2	
Management control systems		**74**
Management control systems overall	35	
Budgeting	24	
Transfer pricing	9	
International control (control exercised by MNC over their foreign subsidiaries)	7	
Performance measurement	31	
Value based management	2	
Balanced scorecard	3	
Incentives	5	
Cost accounting		**17**
Cost accounting overall	10	
ABC	6	
Product costing	2	
Use of cost information for decision making	3	
Capital budgeting and investment decisions		**6**

Table 1-4: Distribution of topics

Application of Hofstede's cultural dimensions

As comparative research faces additional particularities, many researchers did not comprehensively engage with culture but applied *Hofstede's* cultural dimensions for simplification. The majority of the research projects (53%) applied these dimensions to justify their research endeavor and to set up hypotheses about cross-national differences in management accounting. However, due to the shortcomings of the cultural contingency approach (see section 1.3.3) and the linear dependence of culture scores for all companies of a country,[366] none of the projects have applied the cultural scores by *Hofstede* in statistical ana-

366 A significant problem of *Hofstede's* dimensions is that all companies of the same country share the same scores for each dimension. All German companies, for example, are assigned with the score of 35 for power distance, 67 for individualism, 66 for masculinity, 65 for uncertainty avoidance, and 31 for long-term orientation. Cf. *Hofstede/Bond* (1988), p. 12. All country-specifics are linearly dependent, whereby only one cultural dimension can be applied to explain cross-national differences, when only two countries are compared. In multiple regression analysis variables that perfectly correlate with each other are removed from equations – when only two countries are compared, only one cultural dimension remains in the equation. Hence, whether cross-national differences either stem from, e.g., uncertainty avoidance or from long-term orientation cannot be determined. Instead of explaining differences in cost accounting with one cultural dimension, a dummy varia-

lyses. Ten studies have resampled two or more dimensions by *Hofstede* to verify that the samples of the investigated countries actually differ culturally.[367]

Year of publication

Figure 1-9 presents the development of publications in terms of three-year intervals from 1978 to 2010. The interest in comparative management accounting research (in terms of number of publications) has sharply increased at the end of the 1980s and has reached its peak at the end of the 1990s. The increase in comparative management accounting research is mainly explained by the rising awareness of management accounting after *Johnson/Kaplan* criticized the state of this discipline in 1987 and the rise of Japan's economic power that encouraged researchers to discover the reasons for Japan's success.

The interest in applying *Hofstede's* cultural dimensions, either as explanatory variables or to justify the research endeavor, has surprisingly not decreased over the years, in spite of its methodological shortcomings (see section 1.3.3) and the restriction that the findings could be outdated. The GLOBE study has extended *Hofstede's* survey in 2004, but it has stimulated little interest in comparative management accounting research so far.

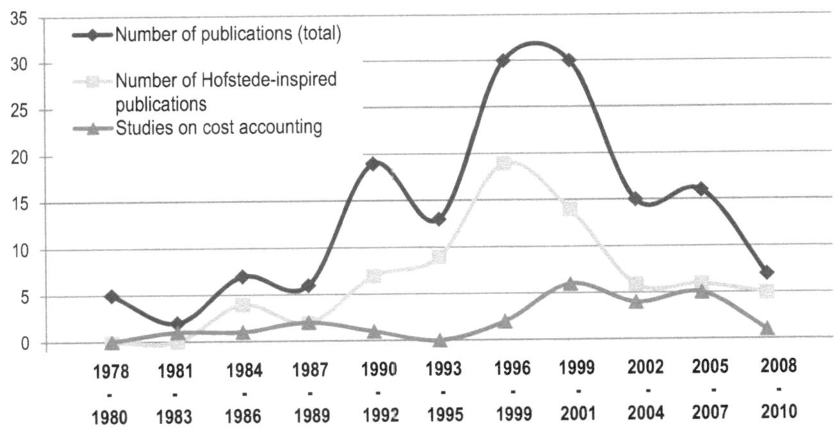

Figure 1-9: Development of comparative management accounting research over time

---

ble could just as well be included – the explanatory power would be the same. Studies comparing three countries could apply two cultural dimensions, comparing four countries allows to compare three cultural dimensions, and so forth. Hence, only those studies that compare many countries with each other could reasonably apply *Hofstede's* cultural scores in statistical analyses.

367 Only one of the ten studies applies the self-surveyed cultural values in statistical analyses. See *Chow et al.* (1991). Two studies have self-sampled cultural dimensions other than *Hofstede's*. See *Brownell/Hirst* (1986); *Douglas/Wier* (2005). Seven studies have applied dummy variables for countries in statistical analyses. See *Lau et al.* (1995); *Lau et al.* (1997); *Lau/Tan* (1998); *Chow et al.* (1999a); *Harrison et al.* (1999); *Salter/Sharp* (2001); *Choe/Langfield-Smith* (2004); *Salter/Schulz* (2005); *Feichter* (2008); *Salter et al.* (2008).

17 research projects have been identified that have compared cost accounting across countries. They resulted in 22 publications between 1983 and 2010, whereas only four of them have been published before 1998. Thus, comparative cost accounting research is a rather young field of research that has emerged in the past decade. Possible reasons for this are the growing dissatisfaction with cost accounting in the USA[368] and the raising interest in ABC.

Figure 1-9 shows that the number of publications in comparative management accounting has decreased after 2000. This research area has thus not caught up with the internationalization of corporate activity. Comparative management accounting research has suffered a lack of attention in general, but also for cost accounting in specific.

All in all, the overview of 148 studies on comparative management accounting shows that the USA has most frequently been compared with other countries and 70% of the studies have applied survey research. Topics in cost accounting have rather been neglected, although strong cross-national differences in cost accounting are expected[369] and in particular cost accounting systems have previously been transferred to other countries to improve domestic management accounting. The interest in cost accounting, however, has increased from 1996 onwards. The lack of comparative research in cost accounting demonstrates the relevance of this study.

1.4.3 Review on comparative research on cost accounting

To draw implications of prior research for this study in section 1.4.4, the comparative research on cost accounting is reviewed. First, some general characteristics of the existing studies are briefly described and their level of analysis is determined (section 1.4.3.1). The findings of prior research are summarized thereafter in section 1.4.3.2. To evaluate the explanatory power of prior research, general and specific methodological aspects of prior research are critically assessed (section 1.4.3.3).

1.4.3.1 Characteristics of the studies

In 12 out of 17 research projects only two countries are compared (see Figure 1-10, Table 1-5). Solely one project compares cost accounting across seven countries. Except for China, the seven countries with the highest gross domestic product are investigated. The absence of China is surprising, because comparative research on management accounting has considerably addressed this country. The studies also include countries with different societal backgrounds that enable to trace back cost accounting differences to national specifics. Although **16 different countries are compared**, an underlying systematic pattern with studies building upon earlier comparative studies is rare: the UK, the USA, and Japan are most often compared. Although eight countries are compared with each other in two different studies, New Zealand and the UK are compared three times, and Japan is compared with the USA four times, only two of these studies share about the same top-

368 See, e.g., *Garg et al.* (2003).
369 See section 1.1.1.

ic.[370] Thus, only the findings of these two studies have been affirmed by each other to some extent.

One study has already compared **cost accounting between Germany and Japan.**[371] This study, however, is limited to ABC and only few insights are reported. The Japanese respondents perceive ABC to be more useful and successful but they have installed this system to a lesser degree than their German counterparts. Insights about the conceptual design, factors that facilitate ABC adoption, and practical or theoretical contribution are not provided. Hence, only little empirical evidence about differences in cost accounting between Germany and Japan exists so far.

Country	Number of studies
UK	8
USA	8
Japan (JPN)	6
Canada (CAN)	3
Germany (GER)	3
New Zealand (NZL)	3
Australia (AUS)	2
Italy (ITA)	2
Finland (FIN)	1
France (Fra)	1
Ireland (IRL)	1
Korea (KOR)	1
Malaysia (MAS)	1
Netherlands (NED)	1
Sweden (SWE)	1
Singapore (SIN)	1

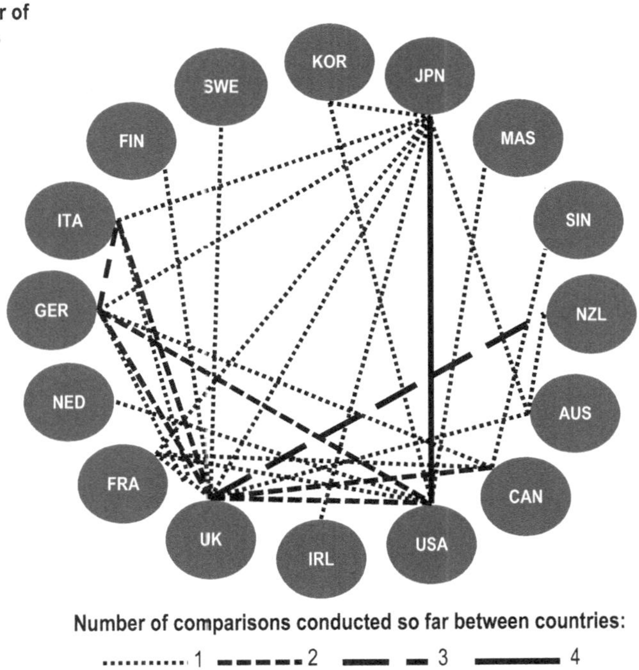

Figure 1-10: Distribution of comparative studies on cost accounting

370 See *Lamminmaki/Drury* (2001); *Cotton et al.* (2003).
371 See *Bhimani et al.* (2007).

Reference	Topic	Level of analysis		
		Level 1	Level 2	Level 3
Hawkins (1983)	Management accounting practices, budgeting, cost accounting overall	●	◐	◔
Yoshikawa (1989)	Management accounting overall, management accounting practices, cost accounting overall	●	◔	
Kim/Song (1990)	Management accounting overall, management control systems, cost accounting overall, product costing	●		
Groot (1997, 1999)	ABC	●	◐	
Brewer (1998)	ABC			◐
Guilding et al. (1998); *Lamminmaki/ Drury* (2001)	Cost accounting overall; budgeting, standard costing	●	◐	
Wijewardena/Zoysa (1999)	Management accounting overall, management accounting practices, cost accounting overall	●		
Ho/Kidwell (2000); *Kidwell et al.* (2002)	Management accounting practices, ABC, BSC, Benchmarking, Quality	●		
Aptel/Pourjalali (2001)	Cost accounting overall	●	◔	
Lapsley/Kurunmäki/Melia (2001); Kurunmäki/Lapsley/ Melia (2003)	Management accounting overall, management accounting practices, use of cost information for decision making			●
Williams/Seaman (2001)	Management accounting overall, management control systems, decision making, cost accounting overall, product costing		●	
Cotton et al. (2003)	ABC	●	◐	
Jacobs et al. (2004)	Use of cost information for decision making, information systems			●
Bhimani et al. (2005, 2007)	ABC	●		
Scarparo (2006)	Management accounting overall, management accounting practices, use of cost information for decision making			●
Krumwiede/ Suessmair (2007a, b)	Cost accounting overall		●	
Yazdifar/Askarany (2010)	ABC	●		

● = Focus of the study;

◐ = addresses several aspects of this level of analysis;

◔ = addresses some aspects of this level of analysis.

Table 1-5: Topics and level of analysis of comparative studies on cost accounting

Seven out of 17 studies are cross-sectional. The remaining ten studies focus on one **industry** only, whereas five of them investigate manufacturing companies, three investigate hospitals, one investigates food and beverage companies, and one investigates municipal governments. Six studies compare cost accounting across the **largest companies**. Comparing the largest companies in comparative research is criticized in literature,[372] because these companies are more likely to operate internationally than small and medium-sized companies. Thus, the samples from both countries might not be independent, which might lead to biased results.

Seven out of 17 comparative studies on cost accounting solely investigate the **topic** cost accounting. Seven of them focus on one cost accounting system only (six study ABC and one studies resource consumption accounting (RCA), which is similar to GPK) and three investigate the use of cost information for decision making. Only modern cost accounting systems are thus compared in detail cross-nationally, even though traditional cost accounting systems are more frequently applied in practice.[373] Nine studies compare further instruments of management accounting besides cost accounting, like budgeting and investment appraisal. One study also includes instruments that are in general not part of management accounting, such as total quality management and process reengineering.

Five out of 17 studies are **replicative**;[374] the majority is comparative in a narrower sense.

The predominant focus of the comparative studies on cost accounting is on the first **level of analysis** (see section 1.2.4; Table 1-5). 12 studies focus mainly on this level. In particular those studies that analyze also other topics than cost accounting merely shallowly investigate similarities and differences in cost accounting across countries. Only two studies analyze cost accounting primarily on the second[375] and four on the third level of analysis.[376] 13 studies address the *adoption rate* and eleven address the *assessment* of cost accounting. On the second level of analysis, *objectives* are investigated only by two studies. The *conceptual design* of cost accounting is solely analyzed by *Krumwiede/Suessmair* in detail.[377] The studies by *Yoshikawa et al.*, *Lamminmaki/Drury*, and *Cotton et al.* address only few aspects of the conceptual design of cost accounting.[378] Differences across countries in the *practice per se* of cost accounting are only analyzed by three studies yet.[379] Furthermore, *Brewer* investigates practice per se regarding actual ABC system usage – however, only the frequency that users queried the ABC system is analyzed.[380]

As most studies focus mainly on the first level of analysis, the research findings might be limited. To verify this assumption, the findings of prior research are summarized in the following section.

---

372 Cf. *Adler* (1984), p. 53; *Firkola/Lim* (2003), p. 54f.

373 Cf. *Garg et al.* (2003).

374 See *Kim/Song* (1990); *Groot* (1996); *Lamminmaki/Drury* (2001); *Williams/Seaman* (2001); *Cotton et al.* (2003).

375 See *Williams/Seaman* (2001); *Krumwiede/Suessmair* (2007a).

376 See *Brewer* (1998); *Kurunmäki et al.* (2003); *Jacobs et al.* (2004); *Scarparo* (2006).

377 See *Krumwiede/Suessmair* (2007a), (2007b).

378 See *Yoshikawa et al.* (1989); *Lamminmaki/Drury* (2001); *Cotton et al.* (2003).

379 See *Kurunmäki et al.* (2003); *Jacobs et al.* (2004); *Scarparo* (2006).

380 See *Brewer* (1998).

1.4.3.2 Summary of the research findings

Only three studies are explanatory in nature.[381] The remaining studies are descriptive, with seven of them providing conjectures and speculations of likely causes for cross-national differences.[382] The most relevant **findings of the descriptive studies** are outlined in the following.

The studies by *Lamminmaki/Drury* and *Askarany/Yazdifar* show that the **adoption rate of ABC** between New Zealand and the UK respectively Australia, New Zealand, and the UK are very similar.[383]

The findings regarding the **allocation of overhead costs** between Anglophone countries and Japan are controversial. Whereas *Wijewardena/Zoysa* found out that more Australian than Japanese companies choose direct labor hours/costs as their main overhead allocation bases (73% respectively 68%), *Yoshikawa et al.* find opposite results between the UK and Japan (34% respectively 50%).

Japanese companies probably provide cost information more often for **behavioral control** than for **cost control** compared to their Anglophone counterparts. In the study by *Wijewardena/Zoysa* Japanese companies rank the use of cost information for cost management significantly higher than their Australian counterparts.[384] However, Japanese companies also rank the purpose of standard costing for cost control much higher than Australian respondents. *Hawkins*' study supports this finding. He finds that US companies rank responsibility accounting higher and emphasized more to use accounting data for evaluating the performance of individual managers than their Japanese counterparts.[385] In the study by *Yoshikawa et al.*, Japanese respondents rank cost reduction as a reason for using variable costing higher than their Scottish counterparts.[386]

Japanese companies run cost accounting systems that provide more **current and future-oriented data** than their Anglophone counterparts. *Yoshikawa et al.* find that Japanese companies revise standard costs twice as frequently as their Scottish counterparts. *Wijewardena/Zoysa* found out that Japanese companies use more actual costing than their Australian counterparts.

Cross-national differences in institutions (in particular those that are related to health care reforms) lead to different behaviors of organizational members. In Finland and Sweden – unlike to the UK counterparts – the clinicians and managers carry out management accounting tasks themselves to determine and use cost information. The Finnish and Swedish employees accept their financial responsibilities and therefore use cost information for instrumental and conceptual use. UK clinicians and managers on the contrary occupy a dominant role and do not accept their financial responsibilities. Instead, they

381 See *Brewer* (1998); *Williams/Seaman* (2001); *Krumwiede/Suessmair* (2007a), (2007b).

382 See *Hawkins* (1983); *Yoshikawa et al.* (1989); *Groot* (1999); *Wijewardena/de Zoysa* (1999); *Kurunmäki et al.* (2003); *Jacobs et al.* (2004); *Scarparo* (2006).

383 Cf. *Lamminmaki/Drury* (2001); *Askarany/Yazdifar* (2010).

384 See *Wijewardena/de Zoysa* (1999).

385 See *Hawkins* (1983), p. 154f.

386 See *Yoshikawa et al.* (1989).

convince the management accountants to act in their interest. UK clinicians and managers "do not regard accounting information as an instrument for constraining their clinical activity, on the contrary they value the opportunity to it as a 'defensive shield'"[387] – to legitimize decisions and "to make sense of budgets after the event"[388]. Thus, instead of improving decision making or to improve their awareness, thinking, and comprehension about their situation, the British clinicians and managers mainly use information for symbolic purposes. Both studies see the health care reforms as the reason for cross-national differences. *Kurunmaki et al.* expand in their discussion further reasons that might have an impact including pressures from the external environment, the manner how health care reforms have been implemented by the state, and the presence or absence of professional or institutional barriers or constraints. These observed behavioral insights are strongly contextually dependent and can thus hardly be transferred to other countries or other industries.[389]

The most relevant **findings of the explanatory studies** are that the level of **ABC success and the complexity of cost accounting systems are culture-bound**. The survey by *Brewer* indicates that high-power-distance / collectivist cultures may generate a higher ABC success than low-power-distance / individualist cultures. The survey shows a higher level of ABC success in the Malaysian plant relative to the US plants, because ABC was implemented 'top-down' and more team-based work arrangements have been installed in the Malaysian plant before ABC implementation. More emphasis on cross-functional team-based work arrangements may have increased ABC success in Malaysia.[390] The study by *Krumwiede/Suessmair* indicates that German companies emerge to focus more on management accounting, have a higher long-term emphasis, and stress more importance to precision, whereas US companies stress their accounting emphasis on financial reporting. Therefore, German companies apply more principles of RCA than their US counterparts.[391]

The findings show that only little knowledge about cross-national differences in cost accounting exists so far and most of the knowledge is limited to differences between Anglophone and Japanese cost accounting. As 12 out of 17 studies focus on the first level of analysis, the little knowledge is mainly limited to the adoption of cost accounting systems. Even less is known about the reasons for cross-national differences.

As "methodological issues involved in conducting sophisticated comparative management research are numerous and complex"[392], it is necessary to assess the quality of the comparative studies besides summarizing their findings.[393] Thereby, the explanatory power of

387 *Scarparo* (2006), p. 152.

388 *Kurunmäki et al.* (2003), p. 136.

389 See *Kurunmäki et al.* (2003).

390 See *Brewer* (1998).

391 See *Krumwiede/Suessmair* (2007a), (2007b).

392 *Adler* (1984), p. 43.

393 Comparative management accounting research has been criticized before to be "largely speculative and atheoretical" (*Bhimani* (1999), p. 420f.).

these studies can be assessed in the following section, which is a basis to draw implications for this study.

1.4.3.3 Methodological issues

Research on comparative cost accounting encounters a number of methodological issues. These include issues in equivalence (see section 1.2.6), the theoretical perspectives of comparative management accounting research (see section 1.3), as well as more general issues including research methods, statistical methods for data analysis, and the application of control variables.

Looking at the particularities of comparative management accounting research reveals that only little attention has been awarded to ensuring equivalence. Furthermore, limitations in this respect are seldom discussed. Mainly translation **equivalence** was ensured by back translation and pre-tests. Only two studies discuss potential shortcomings in their studies that are related to equivalence.[394] Further aspects of equivalence (e.g., conceptual and functional equivalence, measure equivalence, aspects of sampling equivalence, and data collection equivalence) are not addressed in any study. It is therefore hardly possible for the reader to assess the validity of the results, which may even lead to false conclusions. Respondents in five studies,[395] for instance, have been required to place their own interpretations on the term ABC "with the potential consequences that their own interpretations might have been different from those of the researcher and from other respondents in the study"[396]. Comparisons regarding the adoption rate of ABC might therefore be diluted.

Looking specifically at *replicative studies*, four out of five studies have multiple shortcomings in imitating the initial studies. *Groot* has addressed different companies within the value added chain of the food and beverage industry.[397] Besides manufacturers and retailers, the US sample additionally includes distributors and brokers. Similarly, in *Cotton et al.* the distribution of companies across industries differs strongly between the sample in New Zealand and in the UK.[398] In the studies by *Kim/Song* and *Williams/Seaman* the research method even differs across the investigated countries.[399] In the study by *Kim/Song*, personal interviews were conducted by students in Korea, whereas the researchers in Japan and the USA have applied mail surveys.[400] Due to this distinctiveness, the proportion of

394 See *Williams/Seaman* (2001); *Jacobs et al.* (2004). *Jacobs et al.* struggled to find an equivalent word for 'accountability' in German and Italian. As this word is missing in German and Italian, the term 'responsibility' was chosen instead. This surrogate still proved difficult, because in Germany and Italy no accountability distinction between medical hierarchy and the management structure exists.

395 See *Askarany/Yazdifar* (2010); *Groot* (1999); *Wijewardena/de Zoysa* (1999); *Bhimani* (2007); *Krumwiede/Suessmair* (2007a).

396 *Baird et al.* (2004), p. 384.

397 See *Groot* (1999).

398 See *Cotton et al.* (2003).

399 See *Kim/Song* (1990); *Williams/Seaman* (2001).

400 See *NAA Tokyo Affiliate* (1988); *Howell et al.* (1987) respectively.

responders is different in Korea and only companies from few large cities were interviewed there. In the study by *Williams/Seaman* a mail survey was conducted, whereas the replicated study applied telephone interviews.[401] Furthermore, *Williams/Seaman* did not perfectly reproduce the independent variables. Consequently, the results of these studies may be distorted. Variations across countries may thus be existent not due to national factors like culture, but as a result of these shortcomings.

Another particularity in comparative management accounting is the **theoretical perspective**. Whereas the majority of the comparative studies on management control applies *Hofstede's* cultural dimensions,[402] only two out of 17 studies on cost accounting follow this methodological approach.[403] None of the studies have applied the societal effects approach, the new institutionalism approach, and the historical analysis. Instead of applying the cultural dimensions by *Hofstede*, cross-national differences in cost accounting are more often deduced from other country-specifics. One reason might be that the cultural dimensions by *Hofstede* are less appropriate to explain variations in cost accounting across countries: The cultural dimensions differ only little between Continental Europe and Anglophone countries and they are thus of inferior relevance to explain variation in cost accounting between Western countries. Although *Hofstede's* dimensions strongly vary between Western countries and Asia, different environmental conditions like institutions vary as well. Differences in systems and practices can therefore not be traced back solely to cultural differences.[404]

Krumwiede/Suessmair do not refer to *Hofstede's* cultural dimensions,[405] but rather operationalize culture in their own, more cost accounting specific way (including the focus on management accounting, long-term emphasis, and importance of precision). Thereby, stronger contrasts between Germany and the USA are highlighted than in Hofstede's work.[406]

Seven studies solely outline national specifics instead of applying *Hofstede's* cultural dimensions. Two of them describe national specifics by adopting the new institutionalism approach as a theoretical perspective to some extent.[407] Differences in the public sector and health care reforms across countries are outlined and associated to actors' behavior. However, the social dynamics and how they become embedded are only determined in a rather simplified way. The other five studies describe national specifics without operationalizing them and without a methodological grounding: *Hawkins* describes the development of management accounting in Japan and the USA and *Groot* briefly mentions aspects of the Dutch cost accounting environment.[408] *Jacobs et al.* describe institutional

401 See *Libby/Waterhouse* (1996).

402 Cf. *Harrison/McKinnon* (1999).

403 See *Brewer* (1998); *Williams/Seaman* (2001).

404 See *Chow et al.* (1999b).

405 See *Krumwiede/Suessmair* (2007a), (2007b).

406 In comparative management accounting research, ten studies have self-surveyed the cultural dimensions by *Hofstede* and two studies have self-sampled cultural dimensions other than *Hofstede's*.

407 Cf. *Kurunmäki et al.* (2003); *Scarparo* (2006).

408 See *Hawkins* (1983); *Groot* (1999).

differences across Germany, Italy, and the UK.[409] *Yoshikawa et al.* and *Wijewardena/Zoysa* highlight cultural and institutional specifics of Japan.[410] Whereas studies on management control systems are criticized to predominantly apply the simplistic cultural contingency approach,[411] most studies on cost accounting do not refer to any methodological perspective. Besides the studies that address the cultural contingency approach[412] and aspects of the new institutionalism approach,[413] only three studies apply the idea of the contingency theory by either controlling for company size[414] or by analyzing the impact of context factors upon cost accounting.[415]

Only three field studies[416] and one research triangulation[417] have been conducted to investigate similarities and differences in cost accounting cross-nationally. Experiments have not been carried out yet. Instead, 13 surveys have been conducted.[418] Therefore, the majority of the studies are rather limited in their potential to investigate behavioral aspects, because **research methods** like field studies and ethnocentric research are more suitable than surveys for this purpose. The richness of the natural content in survey research is often much more limited by only capturing the respondent's perceptions and the researcher's knowledge of the natural environment. Furthermore, the natural environment included in survey questions obtains only superficially relevant features of the 'natural world'.[419]

All 13 studies that have conducted survey research apply fairly simplistic **statistical methods** to determine cross-national differences. Two studies have conducted an analysis of variance and three studies have compared the rank for significance. All 13 survey-based studies have calculated comparisons of means; however, only four of them provide levels of significance.

Even if researchers comprehensively ensure equivalence in their studies, the sample might still differ across national borders, e.g., in company size or industry. Therefore, **control variables** should be applied to ensure that cross-national differences are not caused by these variables, but only by country-specifics.[420] Most comparative studies, however, lack control variables.[421] The results have to be treated with care, because it is expected that the

---

409 See *Jacobs et al.* (2004).

410 See *Yoshikawa et al.* (1989); *Wijewardena/de Zoysa* (1999).

411 Cf. *Harrison/McKinnon* (1999).

412 See *Brewer* (1998); *Williams/Seaman* (2001).

413 See *Kurunmäki et al.* (2003); *Scarparo* (2006).

414 See *Lamminmaki/Drury* (2001).

415 See *Hawkins* (1983); *Cotton et al.* (2003).

416 See *Kurunmäki et al.* (2003); *Jacobs et al.* (2004); *Scarparo* (2006).

417 See *Brewer* (1998).

418 The studies by *Kim/Song* and *Williams/Seaman* have applied different research methods than the initial studies they have replicated. Both studies are allocated to survey research though. See *Kim/Song* (1990); *Williams/Seaman* (2001).

419 Cf. *Birnberg et al.* (1990), p. 49-51.

420 Cf. *Schweikart* (1985), p. 95.

421 Particularly in the studies by *Groot* (1999), *Wijewardena/Zoysa* (1999), and *Cotton et al.* (2003) the average company size differs across countries.

adoption rates of cost accounting instruments as well as the characteristics of instruments are influenced by company size. The study by *Lamminmaki/Drury* supports this assumption and shows that many cross-country differences disappear when the country samples are matched by company size. They thus conclude that "inferences drawn from comparing cross-company data that fail to control for company size are overly simplistic and potentially highly misleading"[422]. Only the study by *Lamminmaki/Drury* controlled sophisticatedly for company size – all other studies might be biased. A similar occurrence applies for studies where the distribution of companies across industries differs strongly,[423] because *Frank/Reitmeyer* and *Brierley et al.* demonstrate that cost accounting instruments differ across industries.[424]

Overall, the quality of the reviewed studies is limited. Shortcomings in equivalence and the lack of control variables may have led to biased results. For this reason it is necessary that the reader critically scrutinizes the findings of the reviewed studies. The explanatory power of cross-national differences is furthermore limited, because fairly simplistic statistical methods have been applied. Finally, prior research provides only few insights about the reasons for cross-national differences in cost accounting, because only few studies are based on a theoretical perspective.

1.4.4 Implications of prior research

In the following the implications of prior research for this study are deduced. First, the *level of analysis* (see section 1.2.4) is chosen by referring to the foci and findings of prior research as well as their methodological shortcomings. To ensure that the research questions are purposefully addressed and to increase explanatory power of this study, *methodological issues* in comparative research are thereafter discussed. This discussion is based on the conclusions of the review.

1.4.4.1 Choice of the level of analysis

Comparative research should generally start off with the first level of analysis to obtain an overview about differences and similarities across countries. This overview drives further research by highlighting valuable research areas for the second level of analysis. On the second level of analysis, the results from the first level of analysis can be described in more detail. When sufficient knowledge about cross-national differences exists on the second level of analysis, the findings should be complemented by behavioral issues (third level of analysis). This order is reasonable, because the second and in particular the third level of analysis require more research resources. Hence, only those research areas should be addressed on the second and third level of analysis that justify time and effort. Furthermore, when studies on the first (second) level of analysis report contradictory findings, an investigation on the second (third) level of analysis can address further aspects to explain these outcomes.

422 *Lamminmaki/Drury* (2001), p. 344.

423 Cf., e.g., *Cotton et al.* (2003).

424 See *Frank/Reitmeyer* (1999); *Brierley et al.* (2006).

Most of the comparative studies on cost accounting are limited to the first level of analysis. Their findings provide a sufficient basis for this study to analyze cross-national differences in cost accounting between Germany and Japan on the **second level of analysis**. By *investigating the objectives and the conceptual design of cost accounting systems*, more recommendations for practitioners can be developed. Addressing the third level of analysis, on the contrary, would be inappropriate: Due to shortcomings in equivalence and the lack of studies addressing the second level of analysis, a sound and evidence-based picture of cross-national differences in objectives and conceptual design of cost accounting systems is still missing. Valuable insights about starting points for behavioral research do not exist for cost accounting, wherefore researchers would have to choose research areas without knowing whether they are worth the effort. It is therefore necessary to build on the findings of previous studies and to deepen them rather than to investigate behavioral aspects that lack reference to prior research.

1.4.4.2 Discussion of methodological issues to increase explanatory power

As a prerequisite to verify assumptions about cross-national differences and to provide recommendations for practitioners, cross-national **equivalence** has to be ensured. Prior comparative studies have addressed issues in equivalence only shallowly. This may have led to distorted results. As the shortcomings in equivalence and their impact upon the results are hardly discussed in prior studies, it is difficult for the reader to infer from these results. Researchers might even draw wrong conclusions, when variation across countries is due to shortcomings in equivalence and not due to country-specifics.

Prior research lacks in particular *conceptual equivalence*. Most studies focus on terminology, whereby respondents were required to place their own interpretations on the cost accounting terms like ABC that might differ from those of other (foreign) respondents and from that of the researcher. In contrast to that, solely *Krumwiede/Suessmair* investigated the conceptual design of cost accounting in detail.[425] The authors focused on one management accounting system, RCA, and surveyed themselves cultural differences between Germany and the USA. As the characteristics of the conceptual design fit to the country-specifics, this study provides solid evidence that German companies more intensively apply RCA than their US counterparts. A beneficial side effect of investigating the conceptual design is that the researcher instead of the respondents can determine the comprehensiveness of cost accounting systems and whether a company applies cost accounting systems like ABC and RCA or not.[426] Shortcomings in conceptual equivalence that stem from different meanings of terminology across nations can thereby be avoided. For both reasons this study breaks cost accounting objectives and systems down into their characteristics.

425 See *Krumwiede/Suessmair* (2007a), (2007b).

426 Prior studies "have rarely provided explicit definitions of the terms they have used such that it is difficult to compare results across studies and across time, and survey respondents have often been required to place their own interpretations on the terms with the potential consequences that their own interpretations might have been different from those of the researcher and from other respondents in the study" (*Baird et al.* (2004), p. 384).

Besides conceptual equivalence also *ethnocentric equivalence* is addressed. With the help of an international research cooperation an implicit cultural dominance in the research design and the research process is limited. The research design (section 1.5) and the conceptualization and operationalization of the conceptual framework (chapter 2) have been developed in cooperation with the Japanese research partner. To obtain a universally valid investigation, the research project and the questionnaire have furthermore been discussed with researchers from Australia, Italy, the UK, and the USA. The emic perspective has thereby been addressed to some extent to consider for country-specifics.[427]

Prior comparative studies on cost accounting lack **sophisticated statistical methods** for data analysis. The statistical methods applied by prior research are merely descriptive and limited to comparisons of means and comparisons of rank. Furthermore, only in four out of eleven surveys the level of significance has been provided. To comprehensively investigate the research questions developed in section 1.1.1, more sophisticated statistical methods like regression analysis and SEM are applied in this study.

The review demonstrates that comparability of the samples is a prerequisite to obtain meaningful results. The **control variables** company size and industry are applied to ensure comparability of the samples. The actions to ensure comparability of the German and Japanese sample are outlined in section 3.1.1.

1.5 Research design

Based on the implications of prior research for this study (section 1.4.4), the *research method* (section 1.5.1) is selected and the *conceptual framework* (section 1.5.2) is developed. The application and specification of the conceptual framework is outlined in sections 1.5.3 and 1.5.4 respectively. Furthermore, issues in cross-national equivalence are addressed (section 1.5.5).

1.5.1 Determination of the applied research method

Three different procedures to carry out empirical research are distinguished in business studies: field research, laboratory experiments, and survey research.[428]

- **Field research**. Three field research methods can be differentiated. A *case study* empirically investigates a contemporary phenomenon within the context of one organization only.[429] Unlike a case study, a *field study* examines two or more organizations. Apart from that, both methods typically describe a phenomenon by triangulating quantitative and qualitative information including archival data and interviews. *Field experiments* are carried through in any natural setting outside the laboratory that has been created for other purposes than research. "Typically, there is no experimental treatment, either natural or contrived."[430]

427 Other issues in equivalence, which are not relevant to determine the research method or to set up the conceptual research framework, are comprehensively addressed in section 1.5.5.

428 A detailed description of the three research methods is provided by *Birnberg et al.* (1990).

429 Cf. *Yin* (2009), p. 14, 22-26.

430 *Tunnell* (1977), p. 428.

- **Laboratory experiments**. Unlike field experiments, laboratory experiments occur in a setting that is intended primarily for research purposes. They allow the researcher to intervene into the research setting to investigate causal relationships among variables. By manipulating one independent variable and keeping all other influence factors constant, the effect on the dependent variables can be observed.
- **Survey research.** A survey employs a standardized approach to collect data on a large scale to describe practice and to test hypotheses. Unlike field research, which is allocated to qualitative research, survey research is a quantitative research method that generalizes the findings.[431]

A **case study** is **inappropriate** for this study, because at least two companies, one based in Germany and another one in Japan, would have to be compared to allow for a comparison. Regarding the study's research questions (section 1.1.1), neither are **field experiments nor** are **laboratory experiments** useful to determine the *conceptual design and the objectives of cost accounting* that are applied in practice across countries. Laboratory experiments are not suitable to describe how cost accounting systems are designed in practice and field experiments cannot be carried through, because it is assumed that no company agrees to experimentally change its cost accounting system.[432]

The remaining research methods (field study and survey research) are both **suitable to meet the research objectives.** They differ especially in *research application*, *observing and recording of behavior*, and *context*. The comparative advantages and disadvantages of both methods are analyzed following the criteria by *Birnberg et al.* to select the most beneficial method.[433] The criteria, their specification for both research methods, and the more appropriate method for the study are summarized in Table 1-6.

Research application

Both research methods are suitable to explore the cost accounting objectives and the conceptual design of cost accounting systems. The **purpose** of field studies is to investigate the phenomena in the natural occurring settings. Whereas the researcher observes and describes the setting, measures a variable of interest, or generates research ideas via a field study, survey research enables to test theories cross-sectionally and to generalize outcomes.[434] The objective of this study is to test theories and to generalize outcomes. Survey research is therefore preferred according to this criterion.

The construct **validity** depends upon the research design. As the measurement of variables is difficult and the control over extraneous variables is absent, statistical conclusion and internal validities are often low in field studies.[435] "Further, since availability limits the number of natural fields, the researcher may have difficulty determining causality due to

431 For the distinction between qualitative and quantitative research see, e.g., *Johnson/Christensen* (2011), p. 33-37.

432 Cf. *Kajüter* (2000), p. 63f.

433 See *Birnberg et al.* (1990).

434 Cf. *Birnberg et al.* (1990), p. 35, 38.

435 Cf. *Birnberg et al.* (1990), p. 40.

the lack of variation in the independent variables."[436] Therefore, a field study offers only few results from which to generalize (external validity). The survey method on the contrary has a medium level of statistical conclusion validity, because the researcher has some control over unintentional variables and can reliably measure the relevant ones.[437] Survey research is therefore more suitable for this study.[438]

	Field study	Survey research	Preferred method
Research application:			
Primary purpose	Exploration	Exploration	Survey research
Secondary purpose	Description	Test cross-sectional theories	Survey research
Validity:			
· Statistical conclusion	Low	Medium	Survey research
· Internal	Low	Low to medium	Survey research
· Construct	Low to high	Low to high	Survey research
· External	Low to medium	Medium	Survey research
Control	Low	Low to medium	Survey research
Observing and recording of behavior:			
Methods	Subjective self-report Trace Visible observer Hidden observer Archival record Public record	Subjective self-report	Field study
Context:			
Artificial vs. natural	Complete natural setting Incomplete natural setting Natural setting disturbed by researcher	Incomplete natural setting	Field study

Table 1-6: Advantages of field study and survey research for meeting the research questions
Source: following *Birnberg et al.* (1990), p. 36f.

Due to the complexity of the research site, field studies are very limited in **control** over independent and irrelevant variables while sampling. On the contrary, when a survey is

436 *Birnberg et al.* (1990), p. 40.

437 Cf. *Birnberg et al.* (1990), p. 41.

438 However, the researcher has difficulties in manipulating variables to establish causal relationships. Therefore the internal validity of a survey is often limited. The level of construct validity and external validity of a survey depends on the design of the questionnaire and the sampling strategy respectively. Cf. *Birnberg et al.* (1990), p. 38-42.

well-designed, unintentional variables can be controlled by excluding them in the questionnaire[439] or controlling for them while testing causal relationships.

Observing and recording of behavior

Studying behavior via survey research faces several shortcomings, because this method is only limited to subjective self-reports. This report is carried through by an actor "who is aware that his or her behavior is being observed and recorded"[440]. The validity of the study can be threatened by this method due to subjective bias and reactivity effects. Unlike survey research, field studies can apply further methods including participant observation, hidden observation, and examination of archival or public records to increase the validity of the study.[441]

Context

The richness of natural (field) context depends on the research design, in how far they address the three dimensions of naturalness:[442] The natural behavior "is part of the person's existing response repertoire"[443], the natural setting is a context to which the person is naturally exposed, and the natural treatment is an event that would have occurred in organizations without the researcher's presence. Field studies usually occur in a setting, which provides a richer source of data and information than most survey research. Whereas most field studies fail in at least the natural treatment,[444] the richness of the natural content in survey research is often much more limited by only capturing the respondents' perceptions and the researchers' knowledge of the environment. Furthermore, the environment included in survey questions obtains only superficially relevant features of the 'natural world'.[445]

Overall, the survey method is more suitable for this study, because it can meet all five research questions. Testing relationships between context factors, the objectives, and the conceptual design of cost accounting systems is limited for a *field study* and the results can hardly be generalized due to the small number of observations. A field study on the contrary is more suitable to observe and record behavior and to reflect the natural context of the organizations observed. These advantages, however, are only partially relevant for this study, because behavioral aspects are not investigated and because the findings are generalized, wherefore the companies' specific settings are only considered in a simplified way.[446]

439 Cf. *Birnberg et al.* (1990), p. 42.
440 *Birnberg et al.* (1990), p. 48.
441 Cf. *Birnberg et al.* (1990), p. 47f.
442 Cf. *Tunnell* (1977), p. 426-430.
443 *Tunnell* (1977), p. 426.
444 Cf. *Tunnell* (1977), p. 428.
445 Cf. *Birnberg et al.* (1990), p. 49-51.
446 Applying a field study would further offer a higher explorative potential in a more natural and mundane context, to develop a profound understanding of the research question, to specify supposed coherences between variables and to identify new research questions. Consequently, a field study would be valuable especially for understanding national differences and why they occur.

Different **data collection methods** can be chosen to carry out survey research. Content analysis is not suitable for this study, because the characteristics of cost accounting objectives and systems are usually not documented in medium-sized companies. Observations are not suitable for this study due to expenditure of time, because a large number of companies are investigated to meet the research objective. Hence, a more time-efficient data collection method is chosen – a *standardized questionnaire*. The questionnaire can either be self-completed by the respondents or can be filled out together with the researcher during structured interviews. The advantage of self-completed questionnaires over structured interviews is the saving of the researcher's time, which allows much larger samples, and that the questions are always phrased exactly the same for all respondents. The advantage of structured interviews over self-completion of questionnaires is that the researcher can more directly answer questions when the respondents have difficulties to understand the questionnaire. Hence, when the questionnaire is difficult to understand and the precision of the answers is highly relevant, structured interviews are more suitable than sending questionnaires to respondents for self-completion.[447] In the past, survey research has almost exclusively been sent to respondents for self-completion via mail.[448] In this study several actions were taken to ensure that the respondents properly understand the questionnaire. Pre-tests were carried out, some terms (e.g., actual costs, contribution margin accounting) were defined, and the respondents had the opportunity to contact the researcher to ask questions regarding the study.[449] Furthermore, to meet the objectives of this study, a large number of responses is required. For all reasons it is most suitable for this study to send out questionnaires to respondents for self-completion.

1.5.2 Development of the conceptual research framework and base hypotheses

According to *Kubicek*, the **starting point** of the conceptual framework is a theoretical problem. A theoretical problem comprises phenomena that are deemed by the researcher as being not sufficiently controlled or understood.[450] The five **research questions** in section 1.1.1 are the starting point in this study. To gradually specify the understanding of the research objective, a conceptual framework is developed. It guides the research process,[451] integrates single research results into a superior context, and visualizes the concept that is applied in the research process.[452]

The conceptual framework has to meet **three central requirements**. First, the conceptual framework has to *facilitate the research objective*. Considerable influence factors that have

447 For data collection methods see *Sapsford* (2007), p. 109f.

448 Cf. *Shields* (1997), p. 12.

449 For these measures see also section 1.5.5.

450 Cf. *Kubicek* (1977), p. 17. According to *Webb*, there are three fundamentals, which form the basis for good problems. *Knowledge* and *dissatisfaction* refer to the researcher himself and *generalizability* refers to the problem itself. Cf. *Webb* (1961), p. 225f.

451 Cf. *Grochla* (1978), p. 65.

452 Cf. *Al-Laham* (1997), p. 20. Hence, the research process can also be understood as a continuous advancement of the conceptual framework and its permanent empirical specification and modification. Cf. *Kubicek* (1975), p. 46.

already been identified in research should be controlled for to identify cross-national similarities and differences in cost accounting and country-specifics should be applied to explain variance. Second, the conceptual framework should address *issues in equivalence* (see sections 1.2.6 and 1.4.4.2). In particular the functional and conceptual equivalence should be assured. Third, the conceptual framework should fulfill the following three aspects to be preferably *objective, logical,* and *intersubjectively* verifiable:[453]

- The conceptual framework should have the ability to consider all relevant statements from literature (*function of integration*),
- it should be sufficiently specific to afford an *operationalization* of the construct for empirical research, and
- it should be *flexible* enough for further development and to fit different environmental conditions, like different countries and industries.

To answer all five research questions, the **conceptual framework is based upon the contingency theory**, which is merged with the **cultural contingency and the societal effects approach** (see section 1.3.8). The boxes in Figure 1-11 represent theoretical constructs[454] and the arrows demonstrate the relations between the constructs[455] that are hypothesized in chapter 2. Context factors, objectives, conceptual design of cost accounting systems, as well as the performance of the systems are components of the framework.

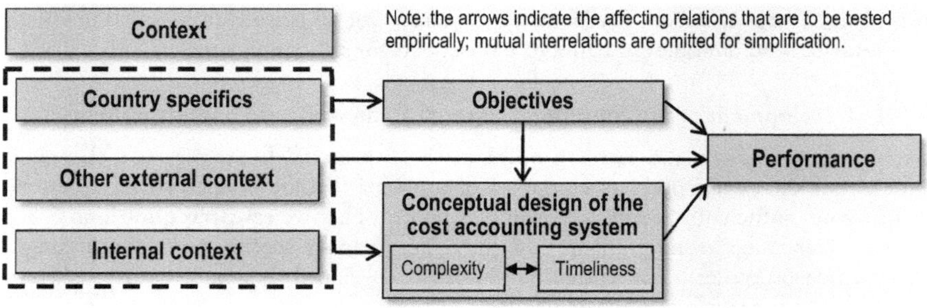

Figure 1-11: Conceptual framework

Context factors describe the organizational environment.[456] In this study three groups of context factors are distinguished: *country-specifics, other external context factors,* and *internal context factors.* All factors that can be influenced by the organization are assigned to internal context factors. Country-specifics and other external context factors are outside the

453 Cf. *Gabele* (1981), p. 99f.; *Kajüter* (2000), p. 56f.; *Horváth* (2009a), p. 84f.

454 Theoretical constructs are defined as "theoretical creations that are based on observations but that cannot be observed directly or indirectly" (*Babbie* (2010), p. 124).

455 Cf. *Kajüter* (2000), p. 60.

456 Cf. *Horváth* (2009a), p. 84f.

company's sphere of influence and can, if at all, be influenced only indirectly.[457] Country-specifics and other external context factors are distinguished in this study, because both are derived from different theoretical perspectives.[458]

This study follows the *cultural contingency and the societal effects approach* to derive *country-specifics* that explain why cost accounting differs between Germany and Japan (third research question). Hence, cross-national differences are explained by national culture and their expressions in national institutions. Country-specifics are applied in this study to contrast differences in country-specifics with differences in cost accounting systems.[459]

Following *contingency theory*, it is expected that also other factors than country-specifics determine the objectives and the conceptual design of cost accounting systems. To answer the fourth and fifth research question, the impact of *other external and internal context factors* upon cost accounting objectives, the conceptual design of cost accounting systems, and the performance of cost accounting systems is analyzed.[460]

The main research objective is to compare the objectives and the conceptual design of cost accounting systems between Germany and Japan. For this reason both elements are part of the conceptual framework. The **objectives** constitute aspired effects that shall be accomplished via a suitable cost accounting system under the given contextual conditions. Normative literature suggests that the conceptual design of cost accounting systems should differ depending on its intended objectives to be optimal.[461]

To meet cost accounting objectives, cost accounting systems have to be shaped accordingly. Two different dimensions regarding the **conceptual design of a cost accounting system** – *complexity*[462] and *timeliness* – are determined to further characterize German and Japanese cost accounting systems. Both dimensions are necessary to comprehensively describe cost accounting systems and the systems' potential to provide accurate, detailed,

457 Cf. *Becker* (1984), p. 42; *Krieger* (1995), p. 109, with further references; *Dobson et al.* (2004), p. 18f. A similar differentiation of context factors is applied by *Jaworski* (1988), p. 25; *Dobson et al.* (2004), p. 18f.

458 For the same reason many scholars distinguish between national culture and contingency factors as well. See, e.g., *Child* (1981); *Bhimani* (1999); *Bhimani* (2007).

459 Thereby, the call for "a better understanding of the factors that influence differences in the levels of adoption of recently-developed management accounting techniques between countries" (*Chenhall/Langfield-Smith* (1998), p. 15) is be addressed. This provides management accountants in MNC insights about the relevance of country-specifics for cost accounting.

460 The most relevant context factors and those that are suggested in literature (see, e.g., *Drury/Tayles* (2005), p. 78) are investigated in this study. Thereby, the call for further research is addressed. Cf. *Shields* (1998), p. 507. Also the motivation to install comprehensive cost accounting systems can thereby be answered. Calls from literature (see *Noreen* (1991), p. 165; *Drury/Tayles* (1995), p. 271f.; *Gerdin* (2005), p. 99; *Drury/Tayles* (2005), p. 77; *Tillema* (2005), p. 101f.; *Chenhall* (2007), p. 195) to enhance the understanding of factors that explain and lead to cost accounting sophistication are thereby empirically addressed. Understanding these factors is necessary, because "the appropriateness of using sophisticated techniques may depend on the circumstances in which these instruments are being used" (*Tillema* (2005), p. 101).

461 Cf. *Player/Keys* (1995); *Cokins* (2001).

462 See *Aust* (1999), p. 123f.; *Drury/Tayles* (2005); *Brierley et al.* (2006); *Abdel-Kader/Luther* (2008).

and timely cost information. Previous studies are thereby extended following the calls by *Drury/Tayles* and *Schoute* to improve the operationalization of cost accounting systems and its characteristics.[463] It is expected that German and Japanese companies differ in these dimensions due to country-specifics.

The construct **performance** is measured to investigate successful cost accounting systems. Thereby the fifth research question is answered. Following *contingency theory*, the cost accounting objectives as well as the conceptual design of cost accounting systems are expected to vary in their usefulness and under different contextual conditions. By highlighting these differences, recommendations for practitioners how to design cost accounting systems can be developed.[464] By comparing effective relationships cross-nationally recommendations for MNC can also be derived, which actions practitioners should choose to install and maintain cost accounting systems in a foreign country. This framework thereby seeks to consider the way in which multiple aspects of organizational context, cost accounting objectives, and cost accounting systems combine in a variety of ways to enhance performance. Optimal fit occurs when all characteristics of organizational context, cost accounting objectives, and cost accounting systems are congruent.[465]

Seven **basic research hypotheses** are distinguished, from which further hypotheses are specified in chapter 2. Hypotheses are understood as statements with objective truth content and subjective truth claim.[466] The hypotheses enable to test the validity of the conceptual framework.

The first purpose of the research framework serves to describe and explain cross-national differences in cost accounting (basic research hypothesis H_1). The cultural contingency and the societal effects approach is the theoretical basis for setting up and testing hypotheses on cross-national differences in cost accounting. The second purpose is to analyze the relationships between organizational context, cost accounting objectives, conceptual design of cost accounting systems, and performance of cost accounting systems (H_2, H_3, H_4, and H_5). This analysis, on the contrary, is based on the contingency theory. The respective basic hypotheses are listed below.

463 Cf. *Drury/Tayles* (2005), p. 77; *Schoute* (2009), p. 222.

464 This is necessary, because studies that are based on the contingency theory have been criticized to be "not specific enough to provide much useful guidance to practice" (*Malmi/Granlund* (2009), p. 603). Hence, this study applies the contingency theory in a more practical way. In order to provide recommendations how to design their cost accounting systems purposefully, it is necessary to have a choice between different alternatives to design cost accounting systems that are more efficient than others under given conditions. Cf. *Welge/Fessmann* (1980), c. 577; *Grabatin* (1981), p. 1.

465 "Variations in performance result from variations in this overall systemic fit" (*Selto et al.* (1995), p. 670).

466 Cf. *Chmielewicz* (1994), p. 119.

H_1:	*The context differs internationally and country-specifics have an influence upon the objectives, the conceptual design, and the performance of cost accounting systems.*
H_2:	*Other external context factors have an influence upon the objectives as well as on the conceptual design and the performance of cost accounting systems.*
H_3:	*Internal context factors have an influence upon the objectives as well as on the conceptual design and the performance of cost accounting systems.*
H_4:	*Cost accounting objectives have an influence upon the conceptual design and the performance of cost accounting systems.*
H_5:	*The conceptual design of cost accounting systems determines the performance of the systems.*

The conceptual framework is further suitable to test, whether cost accounting differs more strongly across industries than across countries (H_6). The conceptual framework is tested separately across industries and across countries to assess whether the cross-industry differences are stronger than the cross-national differences.

H_6:	*The objectives of cost accounting as well as the conceptual design and the performance of cost accounting systems differ more strongly across industries than across countries.*

The relationships between context factors, objectives, conceptual design of cost accounting systems, and the performance of cost accounting systems are compared across countries to test for the stability and the magnitude of relationships (H_7). This is necessary, because, following *Child*, country-specifics are also regarded as moderating variables that can have an effect on the magnitude of the contingency's functional relationships.[467] For analyzing moderating effects, the contingency theory is merged with the cultural contingency and societal effects approach. The moderating effects of country-specifics are not illustrated in Figure 1-11 for reasons of clarity. However, the principle of moderating influences is illustrated in Figure 1-7, p. 52.

H_7:	*The relationships between the elements are stable between Germany and Japan, but they differ in magnitude.*

1.5.3 Application of the conceptual framework

Mean comparisons of the theoretical constructs between countries and industries are conducted to answer the **first and second research question**: Cost accounting is distinguished between Germany and Japan and it is assessed whether cost accounting differs stronger between countries than across industries. To answer the third, fourth, and fifth research question, the relationships between theoretical constructs of the conceptual framework are analyzed. The relationships, however, are investigated differently for the third in comparison to the fourth and fifth research question (see Figure 1-12).

467 Cf. section 1.3.8. The call by *Schoute* to test for the influence of other context factors on cost accounting systems and on the effectiveness, as well as to test for the robustness of previous findings is thereby addressed. Cf. *Schoute* (2009), p. 222f.

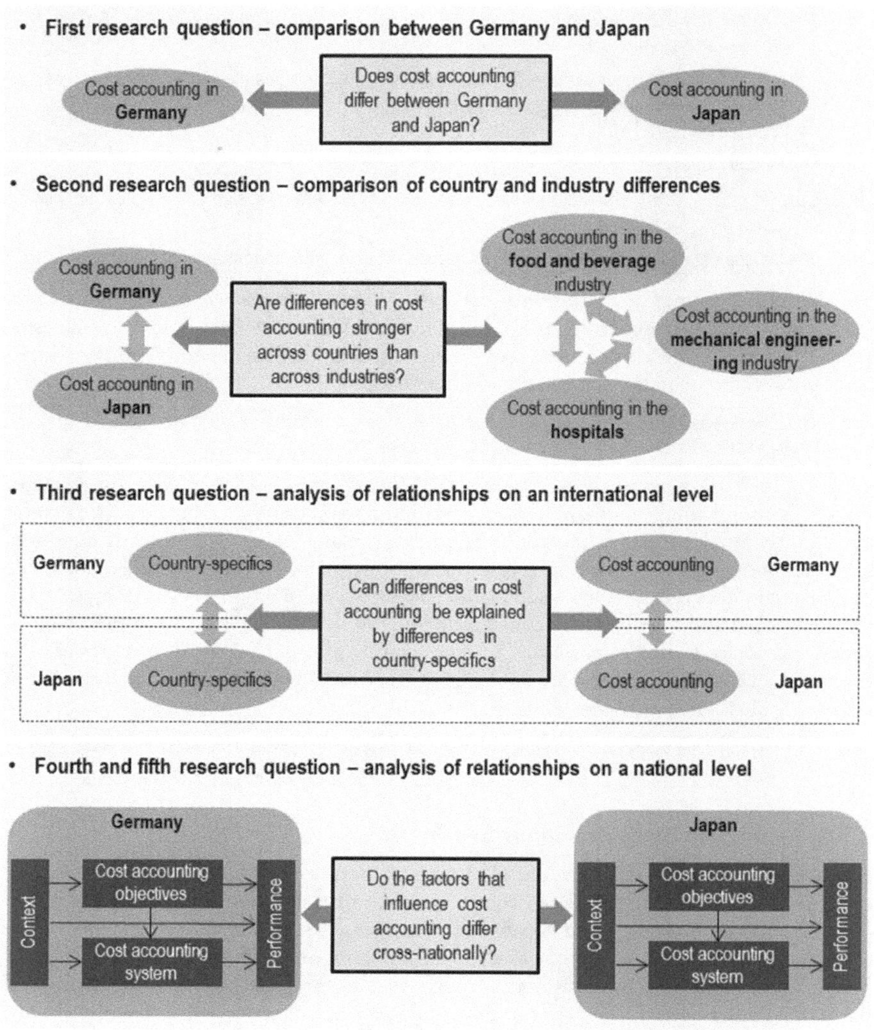

Figure 1-12: Application of the conceptual framework

For the **third research question**, an **analysis of relationships on an international level** is carried through. The impact of country-specifics upon cost accounting systems is analyzed by comparing cross-national differences in the country-specifics with cross-national differences in the objectives, the complexity and timeliness, and the performance of cost accounting systems. It is analyzed, whether differences in cost accounting between Germany and Japan fit with the differences in the institutional environment. Thereby, *indi-*

rect relationships based on plausibility are derived. A direct relationship between country-specifics and the characteristics of cost accounting on the contrary is not investigated, because of the linear dependence of country-specifics for all companies of a country.[468]

For the **fourth and fifth research question**, an **analysis of relationships on a national level** is carried through separately for Germany and Japan. For both research questions *direct relationships* between dependent and independent variables are investigated by applying correlations, regression analysis, and SEM. Thereafter, the impact of dependent variables upon cost accounting for the German and the Japanese data set is compared to test whether these relationships are universally valid or country-specific (see Figure 1-12). Not only the direction of the influence, but also the magnitude of the cause-and-effect relationships can be compared. Comparing cause-and-effect relationships between two countries can provide practitioners working in MNC with valuable recommendations. Given that, e.g., IT systems quality has a stronger impact upon the performance of cost accounting systems in Japan than in Germany, German management accountants should invest more resources in IT systems for their Japanese than for their German subsidiaries when they plan to improve their cost accounting systems.

Whereas for the analysis of relationships on an international level only country-specifics are applied to explain cross-national differences in cost accounting, all context factors – also country-specifics – can be applied to explain the complexity, timeliness, and performance of cost accounting systems on a national level as long as the country-specifics are self-surveyed.[469] Self-surveyed country-specifics can also be applied on a national level, because, e.g., the degree of specialization does not only differ internationally, but also across companies from the same country and thus also explains variance on a national level. The main purpose of country-specifics, however, is to explain cross-national differences. Therefore, only selected country-specifics are applied to answer the fourth and fifth research question on a national basis.

1.5.4 Specification of the conceptual framework

The conceptual framework of this study is developed to guide the research process and to visualize relationships that are expected between constructs. These abstract constructs have to be conceptualized and operationalized to convert the general research idea into effective and well-defined measurements in chapter 2. The process through which concepts like cost accounting systems are specified is called **conceptualization**. A definite meaning to a

---

468 When, e.g., the cultural dimensions by *Hofstede* are applied to explain cross-national variance, all German and all Japanese companies have the same score for power distance, individualism, masculinity, uncertainty avoidance, and long-term orientation. Due to multicollinearity, only one of the five dimensions can be inserted into a regression when two countries are compared. Hence, it cannot be investigated, whether power distance or individualism has a stronger impact upon cost accounting. See also footnote 366. For this reason, only indirect relationships between country-specifics and cost accounting can be set up.

469 Self-surveyed means that the researcher collects the attributes of country-specifics for each company separately. Then, all German and all Japanese companies do not have the same score for, e.g., the degree of specialization. Therefore, the variables that are self-surveyed are not linear dependent. Thus, these country-specifics can be inserted into the same regression.

concept is obtained by specifying one or more indicators that signal the presence or absence of the concept under investigation. The indicators or indicating variables are the empirical equivalents of the theoretical concepts that cannot be measured directly.[470] Besides the conceptualization, in chapter 2 "the development of specific research procedures (operations) that will result in empirical observations representing those concepts in the real world"[471] is set up. This is called **operationalization**. For each indicator the researcher has to measure the full range of variation unless otherwise requested. Furthermore, the required degree of precision should be considered for while operationalizing the indicators.[472] The researcher can choose between four different **scales** of measure that vary in permissible statistical calculations and methods:[473] nominal, ordinary, interval, and ratio measures.

Nominal measures are variables whose attributes are characterized solely by exhaustiveness and mutual exclusiveness. They assign numbers to labels or identify subjects or objects and have only the quantitative meaning to indicate presence or absence of the indicators being studied. Nominal measures therefore provide only the number of occurrences of the variable under investigation. One example is gender with male and female composing its attributes.

The next 'higher' level of measurement precision is *ordinary measures*. Variables allocated to this scale logically rank-order their attributes. They provide only the order of the values but not the amount of difference between them. Five-point-scales with the attributes 'very strong', 'strong', 'average', 'weak', and 'very weak' constitute one example for an ordinary measure. Equal distances between adjacent attributes are not provided for this example, because respondents may perceive unequal differences between, e.g., 'very strong' and 'strong' compared to 'strong' and 'average'.

In contrast to that, *interval measures* have equal distances between adjacent attributes. Celsius temperature scales are an example. However, many researchers demonstrate that ordinal scaled measures, like five-point-scales with the attributes 'very strong', 'strong', 'average', 'weak', and 'very weak', can be treated as interval measures.[474] It is assumed that when only the endpoints of a Likert scale are labeled and the remaining response options are only numerically anchored, it signals that the differences between adjacent attributes are equal and thereby interval-scaled.[475] It hence appears justified that Likert scales can be treated as interval-scaled data.[476] Attributing only the endpoints of a Likert scale is also

470 Cf. *Babbie* (2010), p. 121-128. For the proceedings of the conceptualization see *Kajüter* (2000), p. 61.

471 *Babbie* (2010), p. 135.

472 Cf. *Babbie* (2010), p. 135f. See also *Buch* (2007), p. 5f.

473 For an overview see, e.g., *Babbie* (2010), p. 138f.; *Hair et al.* (2010), p. 5-7.

474 Cf. *Borgatta/Bohrnstedt* (1980); *Kampen/Swyngedouw* (2000).

475 As the remaining scales are not verbally labeled, different perceptions of language by respondents are avoided. Cf. *Uterreitmeier* (2003), p. 68; *Porst* (2009), p. 73.

476 However, strictly speaking, it can only be assumed that the scales are ordinary-scaled, because it is not affirmed that the respondents actually treat adjoining categories equidistantly. Cf. *Backhaus et al.* (2011), p. 11.

necessary for comparative research to increase equivalence, because the perceived differences between, e.g., 'very strong' and 'strong' compared to 'strong' and 'average' may vary across different languages.

Ratio measures representing the highest form of measurement precision enhance all mathematical operations. The only difference between interval and ratio scales is that the former use an arbitrary zero point and the latter an absolute zero point. The turnover of a company in € is an example of a ratio measure.

In chapter 2 indicators are chosen and scales are developed for each variable. In order to apply SEM for data analysis (see section 3.1.3.2), interval scales are predominantly applied in the questionnaire. In this study interval measures are constructed by attributing only the endpoints of seven-point Likert scales (e.g., 1 = not at all, ..., 7 = completely).

1.5.5 Consideration of issues in equivalence

The relevance of equivalence in comparative cost accounting research is demonstrated in the literature review (see section 1.4.3). When issues in equivalence (see section 1.2.6) are not comprehensively addressed, the explanatory power of the studies suffers. For this reason issues in equivalence are addressed in this study with particular emphasis. Ethnocentric and conceptual equivalence are already considered for in section 1.4.4.2 to provide a basis for setting up the research design. After the theoretical perspective and the research method have been chosen and the conceptual framework has been developed, more specific issues in equivalence are addressed in the following to **ensure comparability of the whole research process**. This includes the selection of the companies, the development of the questionnaire, the data collection process, and the statistical analysis.

Sampling equivalence is ensured in this study by surveying companies from three industries (food and beverage, mechanical engineering, hospitals) that are of economic relevance for both countries. As it is necessary to define industries across countries in the same way, German and Japanese companies were selected following the same industry classification 'International Standard Industrial Classification of All Economic Activities by the United Nations (ISIC Rev.4)'. Medium-sized instead of large companies are selected to reduce the dependence between the samples in this study. It is expected that large companies are more globalized than smaller ones. The definition of the sample is outlined in section 3.1.1.

Besides general requirements that apply to domestic research,[477] several particularities to design a **questionnaire** for comparative research have to be considered for. In this study the questionnaire was originally developed in English to discuss it with foreign researchers. To ensure *translation equivalence*, the questionnaire was translated by the author and the Japanese research partner into their native languages and translated back by researchers who have not participated in the study. Differences between the original questionnaire

477 These include, e.g., comprehensible formulations, clear and specific questions, avoiding suggestive questions, well-arranged design of the questionnaire, 'correct' order of questions, variations of questioning techniques, and limiting the length of the questionnaire. After the questionnaire is designed, it should be pre-tested before launching.

and the one that has been translated back in English were investigated to signal the researchers potential for improvement. The equivalence between the German and the Japanese questionnaire was verified by the Japanese research partner, who speaks all three languages fluently and who is familiar with German and Japanese cost accounting. Furthermore, pre-tests were carried through in both countries. To ensure equivalence of scales (*metric equivalence*), the scales have thoroughly been discussed with the research partners. Instead of lexically translating the scale terms, the wording used by domestic research was applied while considering for cross-national equivalence in meaning. Metric equivalence was further addressed by labeling only the endpoints of the scales. To counteract *biases in response style*, mainly seven-point Likert scales were applied in the questionnaire. The use of seven-point-scales instead of five-point-scales has been identified as a solution to reduce differences in response style.[478]

Social norms to contact employees for research purposes differ between Germany and Japan. Advice from foreign researchers was therefore necessary to adapt the data collection process to the Japanese society (see section 3.1.2.1), to ensure **equivalence in the data collection process.**

Within **statistical analysis**, the equivalence of theoretical constructs (*construct equivalence*) is tested ex post (see section 3.1.3.2.3). Furthermore, *sampling equivalence* was ensured ex post. The composition of the German and Japanese data set was matched regarding industry and company size to avoid biases that stem from industry and size effects. Finally, all responses were checked for plausibility (see section 3.1.2.3).

As not only Germany and Japan, but also three industries are compared, **equivalence** has also to be ensured **across industries.** For this reason, the questionnaire for hospitals slightly differs from the questionnaire for both manufacturing industries.[479] Industry-specifics, like the fact that hospitals provide medical services to inpatients whereas food and beverage companies and companies operating in the mechanical engineering industry manufacture products, were considered for while formulating both versions of the questionnaire.

In Appendix 2 only the **written questionnaire** for the mechanical engineering and the food and beverage industry is provided. The **next chapter** specifies the conceptual framework and develops hypotheses.

478 Cf. *Harzing et al.* (2009), p. 424-429.

479 The questionnaire for both manufacturing industries (food and beverage as well as mechanical engineering) is completely identical, except for the heading.

2 Specification of the conceptual framework and hypotheses development

2.1 Context of cost accounting systems

Context factors are required for this study to answer all five research questions from section 1.1.1. Two internal context factors (company size and industry) are **applied as control variables** for the first two research questions. For the **analysis of relationships on an international level** (third research question), *country-specifics* are surveyed to explain why cost accounting differs internationally. For the **analysis of relationships on a national level** (fourth and fifth research question), not only *country-specifics*, but also *other external and internal context factors* are applied to explain the complexity, timeliness, and performance of cost accounting systems in Germany and Japan.

2.1.1 Country-specifics

In this section the history of cost accounting as well as three country-specifics are selected. These preliminary considerations provide a basis for describing how the selected country-specifics have influenced and still influence cost accounting systems in Germany and Japan (sections 2.1.1.2 and 2.1.1.3). Thereafter, the context of German and Japanese cost accounting are contrasted in section 2.1.1.4. The country-specifics are operationalized and hypotheses are developed in section 2.1.1.5.

2.1.1.1 Selection and preliminary considerations

To explain why cost accounting has developed differently between Germany and Japan, the cultural contingency and societal effects approach were chosen in section 1.3.8 as a theoretical basis. For reasons of simplification and because behavioral aspects are not addressed in this study, the new institutionalism and historical analysis are not applied. To still consider the development of cost accounting systems that are defined as real and are more or less taken for granted, the history of cost accounting in Germany and Japan is described.[480] Besides describing the history of cost accounting, country-specifics are selected that explain cross-national differences in cost accounting. The country-specifics are

480 Each country's history of cost accounting is unique and has considerably shaped today's practices. The necessity to investigate the history of financial and management accounting to conduct comparative research has already been highlighted in literature: "[I]t seems that more attention needs to be given to the social and historical development of accounting within different nations and at the global level. The fundamental limitation of the existing ICFAR [International Comparative Financial Accounting Research] literature is that it is narrowly or excessively accounting-centric. Insufficient attention is given to the historical and cultural conditions from which accounting practices emerge and by which they are transformed" (*Wallace/Gernon* (1991), p. 254). "[C]omparisons can be made within a culture in terms of the underlying logics of the social formations characterizing eras, and it should be possible to make similar comparisons across cultures in these terms without being swamped by differences of detail" (*Birkett* (1998), p. 493). See also *Hopwood* (1999), p. 378.

based on the cultural contingency and societal effects approach. Scholars have identified several country-specifics that explain cross-national differences in management accounting.[481] The most relevant ones for this study that belong to the cultural contingency and societal effects approach are national culture, the relationship of cost accounting towards financial and management accounting, and education. Preliminary considerations of the history of cost accounting and the country-specifics that explain the particularities of cost accounting in Germany and Japan are outlined in the following.

History of cost accounting

This study follows the taken for granted assumption that a demand for efficiency-increasing cost accounting systems exists. However, this demand does neither ensure if, when, and how this demand will be met.[482] If, when, and how cost accounting contributes to efficiency-increasing depends, besides coincidence and individual events, upon conditions like culture, the relevance of financial versus management accounting, and education. Caterpillar and General Electric, for instance, have implemented complex cost accounting systems similar to ABC far before *Kaplan* and *Cooper* have promoted this system.[483] The lower emphasis on management accounting compared to financial accounting in the USA might be one reason why ABC systems have not significantly diffused earlier across US companies.[484] By describing the history of cost accounting, the **underlying logic for cross-national differences and similarities in cost accounting** can be identified and traced back to their determinants.[485] This enables a more profound understanding of current practices and of national culture and institutions that shape them. Describing the history of cost accounting supports setting up hypotheses and interpreting the results, because links between the history of cost accounting and the country-specifics can be drawn. Furthermore, the stability of cost accounting differences and similarities as well as future developments can be deduced in a more reflective way.[486]

481 *Pistoni/Zoni* expects that national culture, the role of public sector in the economy, and the typical size of each nation's firms cause cross-national variance. Cf. *Pistoni/Zoni* (2000), p. 288f. *Shields* concludes from *Bhimani* (1996) that the following seven factors have shaped and currently influence management accounting in European countries: academics, education of students and employees, government intervention and regulation, professional associations, consultants, technology, and transfer of management accounting ideas and practices across countries. Cf. *Shields* (1998), p. 504. *Whitley* draws direct connections between (1) societal institutions including cultural conventions, state structure and policies, and (2) skill development and control, and control system characteristics. Cf. *Whitley* (1999), p. 515-520. *Shields et al.* suggest to attribute different practices across countries to different underlying goals (e.g., decision facilitating versus decision influencing) and to different roles and career paths of cost and management accountants. Cf. *Shields et al.* (1991), p. 69-72. See further *Farmer/Richman* (1964); *Schweikart* (1985); *Birkett* (1998), p. 493f.

482 Cf. *Luft* (2007), p. 272-277.

483 Cf. *Kellermanns/Islam* (2004), p. 33. See also *Jones* (1991).

484 Cf. *Johnson/Kaplan* (1987).

485 Cf. *Wallace/Gernon* (1991), p. 254; *Birkett* (1998), p. 493. See also *Hopwood* (1999), p. 378.

486 Cf. *Luft* (2007), p. 281. For the usefulness of historical analysis in science in general see also *Kuhn* (1996), p. 1-9, in economics see *Bellinger* (1967), p. 9f.; *Schneider* (2001), p. 1-9, and for the de-

Cost accounting as we know it today has emerged since the beginning of the 19th century. However, neither a uniform conceptualization of cost accounting nor a theoretical approach to determine profit on a periodical basis were existent.[487] For both reasons, the history of German and Japanese cost accounting is described from the end of the 19th century onwards.

National culture

Empirical[488] and conceptual studies[489] that explain cross-national differences in management accounting as well as literature that addresses German and Japanese management accounting on its own[490] assume that differences in **national culture** lead to variations in systems, because "[c]ultural factors are a part of the cost-benefit considerations that should underlie all management accounting choices."[491] Furthermore, several reviews demonstrate the impact of culture on cost and management accounting.[492]

To provide a stronger focus on cost accounting and to account for the criticism of *Hofstede's* work, the portrayal of Germany and Japan is not limited to the cultural dimensions by *Hofstede*.[493] It is supplemented by a wider description of cultural-specifics that are identified in literature to explain particularities in cost accounting. A **greater explanatory content** is provided by describing how cultural dimensions jointly manifest in the institutional environment of cost accounting.[494]

Relationship of cost accounting towards financial and management accounting

Culture indirectly affects cost accounting through financial accounting standards.[495] The requirements of financial accounting standards determine the relationship of cost accounting towards financial and management accounting. Compared to culture, this relationship has hardly been investigated before. *Johnson/Kaplan* claim that financial accounting dominates management accounting in the USA.[496] Prior US research indicates that most companies use a single data base to meet management and financial accounting purpos-

---

velopment of accounting see *Dorn* (1961), p. 13-19; *Edwards* (1989), p. 3-6; *Schneider* (1992), p. 3; *Bungenstock* (1995), p. 5; *Pleitgen* (2005).

487 Cf. *Dorn* (1993), c. 722f.; *Schweitzer/Wagener* (1998), p. 442.

488 See section 1.4.

489 Cf., e.g., *Brewer* (1997); *Lere* (2009).

490 Cf., e.g., *Nishimura* (2003); *MacArthur* (2006); *Portz/Lere* (2010).

491 *MacArthur* (2006), p. 10.

492 Cf. *Harrison/McKinnon* (1999); *Riahi-Belkaoui* (2002), p. 96-101; *Hoffjan et al.* (2009); *Kajüter/Moeschler* (2011).

493 See section 1.3.3. It is furthermore likely that the cultural dimensions vary in centrality between Germany and Japan. Cf. *Harrison/McKinnon* (1999), p. 490-492.

494 Investigating the interplay of cultural dimensions is expected to lead to more significant results and avoids a rather simple treatment of culture *Lere*, e.g., connects *Hofstede's* dimensions to draw conclusions about the design of cost accounting systems. Cf. *Lere* (2009), p. 12.

495 See *Nobes/Parker* (2008).

496 Cf. *Johnson/Kaplan* (1987). This claim was not empirically rejected by *Drury/Tales*. Cf. *Drury/Tayles* (2000), p. 60f.

es.[497] It is expected in this study that the stronger the emphasis on financial accounting, the less cost accounting systems serve managerial decision making. When cost accounting is primarily conducted for financial accounting, rather simple and annual calculations are sufficient.[498] For decision making purposes, however, more accurate, detailed, and timely cost information is required, e.g., to distinguish between profitable and unprofitable products.[499] Hence, companies in countries that put more emphasis on cost accounting for management accounting purposes than for financial accounting purposes are expected to have more comprehensive cost accounting systems. These companies are further expected to more often install separate data bases for financial accounting and management accounting to more specifically address these different objectives. On the contrary, the weaker the emphasis on management accounting, the more often an integrated data base for management and financial accounting is implemented.[500] The roots of cross-national differences in the relevance of financial and management accounting lie in national culture and primary source of finance.[501] The emphasis on financial versus management accounting is also expected to be reflected in the education of accountants.

Education

Education reflects national culture and ideology by creating and affecting prevalent values of a society. *Shields* assumes that textbooks and teaching influence the development and the spread of management accounting.[502] It is furthermore expected that the mix of qualifications, skills, and training of cost and management accountants determine cost accounting systems and their shape.[503] As institutions like universities, professional bodies, in-house training, and training on the job provide cost accountants with knowledge and skills, they have an indirect impact upon cost accounting systems. The relevance of institutions where cost accountants acquire their knowledge from is expected to be country-specific. The more practice-oriented the education, the more pragmatic and less theoretically sound is cost accounting expected to be applied. Furthermore, the stronger the emphasis on financial accounting versus management accounting within a country, the better cost accountants are skilled for financial than for management accounting purposes.

The history of cost accounting and the selected country-specifics that explain variance in cost accounting are comprehensively described for Germany and Japan in sections 2.1.1.2 and 2.1.1.3.

497 For an overview see *Johnson/Kaplan* (1987), p. 22.

498 Cf. *Brierley et al.* (2006), p. 316; *Drury* (2008), p. 51f.; *Kinney/Raiborn* (2008), p. 71f.

499 Cf. *Drury* (2005), p. 113f.

500 Specific calculations for managerial purposes that are beyond the scope of financial accounting requirements have then, however, to be carried out through more time consuming auxiliary calculations. This is one reason why ABC has failed in many US companies. Cf. *Sharman* (2003b), p. 46.

501 See in particular sections 2.1.1.2.1 and 2.1.1.2.2.1.

502 Cf. *Shields* (1998), p. 504.

503 Cf. *Rose* (1985), p. 69; *MacArthur* (2006), p. 15.

2.1.1.2 Specifics of German cost accounting

2.1.1.2.1 History

Little is known internationally about German traditions in cost accounting, because German scholars have published almost exclusively in their own language.

> *"This is particularly regrettable because German cost accounting looks back to a hundred-year-old tradition. And there appear to exist instances of early ideas that are re-invented decades later in other countries."* [504]

To address this gap and to provide an underlying logic why German cost accounting is different from other countries, its historical development is described in the following.

At the end of the 19th century, the first scientific and systematic examinations of cost accounting have been conducted.[505] The root of marginal costing can be traced back to the year 1899. The German scholar *Schmalenbach* suggested to apply direct costs for cost calculations, whereas overhead costs should be covered by the gross profit. Furthermore, he significantly contributed to the development of financial, management, and cost accounting.[506] Of great importance are his definition of the matching principle and his conclusion that the main purpose of management accounting is to support decisions.[507] *Schmalenbach* has additionally argued that financial accounting is improper for decision making, because of the connection between commercial and tax accounts ('Maßgeblichkeit') as well as because 'protection of creditors' ('Gläubigerschutz') and verifiability and reliability have been central principals in financial accounting.[508]

During the time of the National Socialism, cost accounting has been influenced through numerous orders, legal ordinances, and directives. Their purpose was to standardize cost accounting to improve production[509] and to stipulate price determination for controlling the quality and the quantity of production.[510] This regulation has dictated a uniform calculation of cost prices and has demanded a distinction between cost type, cost center, and product cost accounting leading to a more detailed and systematic cost ac-

---

504 *Christensen/Wagenhofer* (1997), p. 255.

505 Cf. *Mussnig* (1996), p. 23; *Schweitzer/Wagener* (1998), p. 442.

506 Due to his strong influence between 1919 and 1933, *Schäfer* calls these years the 'Schmalenbach-period'. Cf. *Schäfer* (1953), p. 207f. *Schmalenbach* had a strong influence upon cost accounting before the First and after the first years of the Second World War. Cf. *Schildbach* (1997), p. 264.

507 Cf. *Schildbach* (1997), p. 262; *Schweitzer/Wagener* (1998), p. 443.

508 Cf. *Lawrence* (1997), p. 23f.; *Schildbach* (1997), p. 263; *Nobes/Parker* (2008), p. 260. A 'true and fair' view on the contrary has been more important in the USA. Unlike in the USA where the major amount of capital is financed by investors, in Germany the banks finance most capital and are important owners of companies. Cf. *Nobes/Parker* (2008), p. 30f. Providing relevant information for investors has therefore been of minor relevance in Germany. Instead, a relevant feature of German financial accounting is to protect the providers of credits.

509 Cf. *Matz* (1940), p. 371f.

510 Cf. *Dorn* (1993). c. 728; *Messner* (2003), p. 58-60.

counting.[511] Furthermore, approaches to allocate overhead costs have been regulated. A blanket allocation of the overhead costs was not accepted. Instead, the companies were forced to use different allocation bases.[512] The regulation has also permitted companies to allocate imputed costs to the sales prices, which ensured the companies to make profit.[513] Imputed costs thereby became very popular in Germany and their diffusion can thus be traced back to the regulation during this period.[514] The current guidelines for determining the cost price for public contracts still share many similarities with those from the time of the National Socialism.[515]

After the Second World War, German companies grew bigger and decision making had to be decentralized. Cost accounting has therefore systematically been developed to support short-term decision making.[516] It is likely that the strong uncertainty avoidance in Germany has fostered this development. Three sophisticated, theoretically sound concepts like GPK by *Kilger*, Relative Einzelkosten- und Deckungsbeitragsrechnung by *Riebel*, and Plant Models by *Laßmann* have been developed in Germany. *GPK* [517] is based on the production theory of *Gutenberg*[518]. According to this theory, two different input-output relations exist in a firm – "direct relations between output and input of direct materials and direct labour, and indirect relations."[519] GPK is a direct costing technique that focuses on the control of efficiency in cost centers. The underlying idea is that product units are only assigned with direct costs that vary in relation to the output volume in a time horizon of one year. This follows the logic of decision theory with decision makers using marginal analysis to identify optimal choices of alternative actions.[520] GPK is widespread in Germany.[521] The main objective of the *Relative Einzelkosten- und Deckungsbeitragsrechnung* [522] is to offer a flexible and reliable decision support for a wide range of potential decision problems. It helps managers to understand complex cause-and-effect relations in cost accounting and provides different classifications of costs that are relevant for a specific decision. The author of this concept criticizes every sort of cost allocation. To him, only the principle of cause-and-effect (he calls it identity principle) is accurate enough to pro-

511 Cf. *Dorn* (1961), p. 156-205; *Schlegelberger* (1973), p. 300-309. The distinction between cost type, cost center, and product cost accounting is described in more depth in section 2.3.1.1.

512 Cf. *Dorn* (1961), p. 162-170.

513 Cf. *Dorn* (1961), p. 170-179; *Schneider* (2001), p. 233f.

514 Cf. *Seicht* (2001), p. 613; *Messner* (2003), p. 59.

515 A strict distinction between cost type, cost center, and product cost accounting, high detail in the allocation bases for overhead allocation, as well as a high adoption rate of imputed costs still exist today in German companies. Cf. *Franz* (1991); *Franz* (1992); *Zur* (1992); *Budäus* (2002); *Coenenberg et al.* (2003), p. 113-183.

516 Cf. *Weber/Weißenberger* (1997), p. 279.

517 See, e.g., *Kilger* (1961); *Sharman* (2003a); *Krumwiede* (2005); *Ewert/Wagenhofer* (2007), p. 1047-1050; See *Krumwiede/Suessmair* (2007a), (2007b); *Portz/Lere* (2010).

518 See *Gutenberg* (1983).

519 *Schildbach* (1997), p. 265.

520 Cf. *Weber/Weißenberger* (1997), p. 280.

521 Cf. See *Krumwiede/Suessmair* (2007a), (2007b). Its acceptance has been facilitated by ERP software like SAP R/3.

522 See *Riebel* (1959); *Weber/Weißenberger* (1997).

vide reliable and relevant cost information. Although virtually no company has fully implemented this concept, mainly because of its complexity, it has found significant consideration by German researchers and it is taught to business students.[523] *Plant Models*[524] mainly describe quantity relations to model the consumption of economic resources as well as the factors that cause their consumption. This concept controls the production process by input-output models and engineering production functions or process models. It demonstrates the short-term consequences in terms of costs of alternative actions that are related to the consumption of variable resources and the stress of limited fixed resources. It has found practical acceptance and was used especially in the steel industry.

From **1970 to 2000** researchers became increasingly interested in questions of detail (e.g., the inclusion of uncertainty), specific application areas of cost accounting (e.g., cost accounting for logistics, consolidated cost accounting), and decision influencing as a cost accounting objective.[525] During this period of time, the importance of variable costs in relation to fixed costs diminished over time due to an increase in fixed cost intensive production plants.[526] The cost accounting approaches developed after the Second World War are suitable only for short-term decision making. Therefore, other cost accounting instruments for rather long-term decision making were required,[527] like ABC that was imported from the USA and adapted to the German environment due to cultural and institutional differences.[528]

Since 2000 German researchers became less interested in cost accounting. Instead of developing new systems or improving them, German practitioners and researchers started criticizing cost and management accounting being too complex.[529] In particular for international companies it became more and more difficult to explain differences between expenses and costs[530] to their foreign employees. Furthermore, although cost accounting systems provide accurate and detailed information for decision making, the disadvantage of complex systems is that cost accountants often spend too much time on running and developing their systems and not enough time is left to discuss the provided information with their managers.[531]

One way to decrease complexity in accounting is to provide less detailed and accurate cost information. An alternative way, which is related to the former but has gained more atten-

---

523 Cf. *Luther et al.* (2010), p. 18f.

524 See *Laßmann* (1973); *Laßmann* (1993); *Schildbach* (1997), p. 270f.

525 Cf. *Kajüter* (2011), p. 92, with further references.

526 The increase in fixed and overhead costs has been confirmed by a series of studies. See *Miller/Vollmann* (1985); *Backhaus/Funke* (1994); *Schumann/Beinhauer* (1994); *Backhaus/Funke* (1996).

527 Cf. *Schildbach* (1997), p. 271f.

528 Cf. *Kellermanns/Islam* (2004), p. 38.

529 See, e.g., *Weber* (2004). About 30% of German executives assess cost accounting systems to be too complex. Cf. *Weber et al.* (2000), p. 94.

530 For the distinction between expenses and costs see section 2.1.1.2.2.2.

531 Cf. *Ahrens/Chapman* (1999), p. 43; *Weber* (2004), p. 9. The discussion of management accounting information with managers has been identified in many empirical studies as one important success factor. Cf. *Weber et al.* (2010a).

tion by practitioners and researchers, is to harmonize financial and management accounting and thereby to abolish the distinction between expenses and costs. The strict distinction between financial and management accounting has been questioned in Germany since German capital market oriented companies apply IFRS.[532] Unlike German GAAP (the German Commercial Code is called HGB), IFRS provides less biased information for managerial decision making, because the main objective of IFRS is decision-usefulness. Therefore, the purposes of financial accounting under IFRS better fit the purposes of management accounting. The change from German GAAP to IFRS consequently simplifies companies to harmonize financial and management accounting and the benefits to separate financial and management accounting decline.[533] Although there is a tendency in Germany to converge financial and management accounting, a complete integration is not possible due to the different functions and information needs of the users.[534] Furthermore, small and medium-sized companies have only little interest to apply IFRS, because the German Commercial Code was revised and became effective in summer 2009 to create particularly for small and medium-sized companies a less expensive and simpler alternative to the IFRS.[535] As a complete integration of financial and management accounting is not possible and as the German Commercial Code was revised, only a marginal convergence towards 'Anglophone' or 'international' management accounting is likely to occur. Object of the convergence is mainly the income statement, whereby only simplifications in terms of abandoning imputed cost may result.[536] The historical development of cost accounting in Germany is summarized in Figure 2-1.

532 The liberation of the capital markets and the increase in demand for capital has forced German companies to prepare their financial statements in accordance to international accounting standards. Cf. *Ernst et al.* (1998), p. 6. In the mid-1990s some of the large capital market oriented companies in Germany started to prepare their financial statements not only under German GAAP, but also under international accounting standards (IFRS and US-GAAP). Cf. *Christensen/Wagenhofer* (1997), p. 258; *Wagenhofer* (2006), p. 15. The German legislator addressed the wish for more international financial reporting by introducing a law that facilitates the raising of capital abroad (Kapitalaufnahmeerleichterungsgesetz, § 292a HGB). Since 2005 all capital market oriented companies are required by the IAS regulation (106/2002/EC) to prepare their consolidated accounts according to IFRS. Non-capital market oriented companies can apply IFRS optionally in their group accounts. Firms that were using US-GAAP outside the EU or debt only issuers had a two-year transition period until 2007 to apply IFRS.

533 Cf. *Wagenhofer* (2006), p. 15f. The definition of costs and how they should relate to financial accounting as well as the purposes of management accounting in general were questioned by scholars and practitioners. See, e.g., *Schweitzer/Ziolkowski* (1999).

534 Cf. *Klein* (1999), p. 68f.

535 Cf. *DRSC* (2010a), (2010b). However, through the revision of the German Commercial Code, the tax option rights have ceased to exist in the balance sheet. Hence, the benefit to separate financial and management accounting has declined because of the revision of the German Commercial Code. Cf. *Böge* (2009).

536 Cf. *Jones/Luther* (2005), p. 185; *Kajüter* (2008), p. 358.

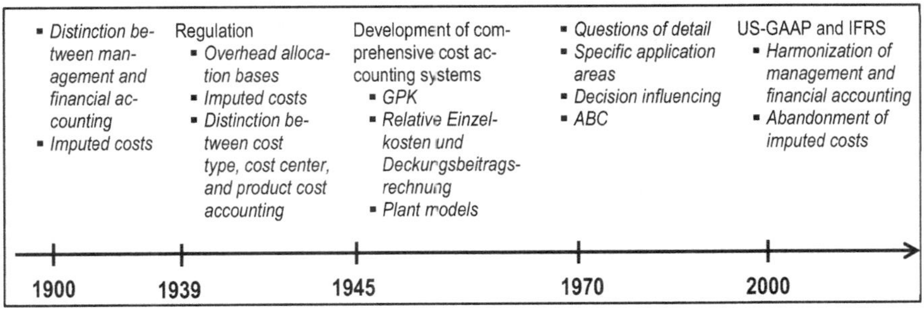

Figure 2-1: Historical development of cost accounting in Germany

2.1.1.2.2 Country-specifics

2.1.1.2.2.1 National culture

Two cultural dimensions – *individualism* and *uncertainty avoidance* – are associated in literature directly with German cost accounting and also indirectly through typical German organizational and managerial patterns as well as the education of cost accountants that constitute the institutional environment of cost accounting. Germany is classified as individualistic along with other Western countries. Compared to other Western countries, however, Germany is not that individualistic according to *Hofstede's* index.[537] Besides individualism, Germany is characterized to have a low tolerance for uncertainty.[538] According to *Hofstede*, however, Germany scores only average: 28 out of 53 countries including Japan are characterized to be more uncertainty avoiding.[539] In spite of this average score, uncertainty avoidance has in combination with other country-specifics a strong impact on cost accounting in Germany.

In the mid-ages the European culture was collective. The guild ensured that sufficient food was available and nobody should seek for individual benefits or profits. Competition was strictly forbidden. The European attitudes towards **individualism** changed over time and profit seeking became a virtue. This change has started off with merchants that adopted competitive attitudes from profit-oriented oriental competitors. Thereafter, the Renaissance and the Age of Enlightenment led to an increase in rationality of engineering and in the behavior of business people. Both cultural movements (spanning from 14th to the 17th century respectively centered upon the 18th century) legitimized individualistic exploratory urge. Finally, the success of the liberal economic policy in England leveraged

537 Germany is the 15th most individualistic country out of 53. Cf. *Hofstede/Bond* (1988), p. 12f.

538 See, e.g., *MacArthur* (2006); *Portz/Lere* (2010), p. 49.

539 Cf. *Hofstede/Bond* (1988), p. 12f. Furthermore, the Globe study indicates a decline in uncertainty avoidance in Germany. German managers want to reduce the amount of rules, regulations, and constraints. Cf. *Brodbeck/Frese* (2007), p. 163.

the success of liberalism – the belief in the importance of individual freedom.[540] Thereby, individualism has virtually been institutionalized.[541]

Employees in an individualistic society are expected to behave according to their interests. Work should therefore be organized in a way to align this self-interest with the employer's objectives.[542] One solution is to control and reward for the employees' performance.

> *"Management in an individualist society is management of individuals. Subordinates can usually be moved around individually; if incentives or bonuses are given, these should be linked to an individual's performance."* [543]

Controlling and rewarding is an important element of Western management control systems that is called **responsibility accounting**. Its objective is "to accumulate costs and revenues for each individual responsibility center so that the deviations from a performance target (typically the budget) can be attributed to the individual who is accountable for the responsibility centre."[544] One instrument to determine the performance of individuals is cost accounting. The costs incurred are compared with the budgeted costs.

Responsibility accounting has a **motivating effect** upon the responsible persons to operate efficiently. They are, e.g., encouraged to avoid unnecessary use of support cost centers when they are charged for each service they consume.[545] This motivating effect is less required in a more collective society, because employees are there already culturally encouraged to act in the company's interests. To ensure that responsibility accounting is accepted by the employees, an objective, easy comprehensible, and reliable cost control is required and it is necessary to charge the responsible persons only those costs they can influence.[546] For this reason variance analysis is frequently applied to distinguish between controllable and uncontrollable cost items so that cost variances can be traced back to the persons that are responsible.[547]

The dimension **uncertainty avoidance** by *Hofstede* addresses, amongst others, clichés about Germans that are world-wide prevalent. The prototype of a German is punctuality and accuracy in every detail; he loves orders and rules of every description and monitors

---

540 *Adam Smith* (1723-1790) has pinpointed the economic side of liberalism. "It is not from the benevolence of the butcher, the brewer, or the baker that we expect our dinner, but from their regard to their own self-interest. We address ourselves, not to their humanity but to their self-love, and never talk to them of our own necessities but of their advantages" (*Smith* (1776), p. I.ii.2, quoted after *Peil* (2000), p. 88).

541 Cf. *Kieser/Walgenbach* (2007), p. 281f.

542 "Employed persons in an individualist culture are expected to act according to their own interest, and work should be organized in such a way that this self-interest and the employer's interest coincide." *Hofstede* (1991), p. 63. Cf. also *Brodbeck/Frese* (2007), p. 164.

543 *Hofstede* (1991), p. 65.

544 *Kinney/Raiborn* (2008), p. 346.

545 Cf. *Kinney/Raiborn* (2008), p. 470.

546 Cf. *Schweitzer/Küpper* (2011), p. 614, 637.

547 German firms are more likely to report variances for each cost center than their US counterparts (83% versus 53% respectively). Cf. *Krumwiede/Suessmair* (2007b), p. 53-55; *Krumwiede/Suessmair* (2007a), p. 6f.

for compliance.[548] Finally, there is a historical connection between several countries with high uncertainty avoidance (in terms of the *Hofstede*-study) that have a fascist past and fought in the Second World War. Much evidence exists that *Hofstede's* concept of uncertainty avoidance is based on this relationship.[549] Before the Second World War Germany has already been torn apart several times, which has likely increased uncertainty avoidance.[550]

Employees in countries with a low tolerance for uncertainty tend to characterize the environment to be more uncertain than employees in societies with a high tolerance for uncertainty. The provision of more accurate, detailed, and timely information as well as organizational arrangements to reduce uncertainty are therefore popular in these countries.[551] The **provision of accurate and detailed cost information** in Germany has been associated in literature with uncertainty avoidance.[552] More accurate and detailed information facilitates decision making. Variance analysis, for instance, can be conducted to more comprehensively distinguish between controllable and uncontrollable cost variances. Organizational arrangements to reduce uncertainty include detailed, precise, and formal rules and instructions.[553] Strict **rules that govern workplace behavior** support to obtain high levels of operational efficiency that German companies typically target.[554] To ensure that employees behave in the company's interest, a high number of cost centers with much repetitive and predictable output are installed in Germany. Managers can thereby be controlled for operational efficiency. This operational emphasis requires more comprehensive cost accounting systems like GPK and detailed variance analyses. Both support German managers to learn how to conduct their tasks efficiently and effectively.[555] Cost variances are furthermore analyzed in depth to encourage individuals under control to avoid variances.[556] Uncertainty can further be reduced, when each employee has only one supervisor

548 Cf. *Behrens* (2007), p. 106. An extension of the German cliché is the exclusively negative expression 'the German angst'. *Traverso* sees the origin for 'the German Angst' in the years between the First and the Second World War and in particular in the experiences of the First World War. Cf. *Traverso/Bayer* (2008), p. 191-221.

549 Many countries with high uncertainty avoidance may superficially be functionally different, but all of them had a mental predisposition for fascism. Cf. *Hofstede* (1991), p. 128, 137; *Behrens* (2007), p. 108.

550 Cf. *Brodbeck/Frese* (2007), p. 151-153.

551 Cf. *Hofstede* (1991), p. 122.

552 See *MacArthur* (2006); *Lere* (2009), p. 12.

553 "In uncertainty avoiding societies there are many formal laws and/or informal rules controlling the rights and duties of employers and employees. There are also many internal rules and regulations controlling the work process" (*Hofstede* (1991), p. 120).

554 Cf. *Limprecht/Hayes* (1982); *Portz/Lere* (2010), p. 49. German companies might have a stronger emphasis for operational than for strategic tasks, because the latter are by definition unstructured and demand a greater acceptance for ambiguity. Cf. *Hofstede* (1991), p. 122.

555 Cf. *Lere* (2009), p. 12. Although Germany has been associated with high performance orientation, according to the Globe study Germany ranks only average in performance orientation. Cf. *Brodbeck/Frese* (2007), p. 160, 164.

556 Cf. *Schildbach* (1997), p. 269.

and when only one manager is responsible for a cost center.[557] The relationship between cultural and organizational patterns shaping the specifics in German cost accounting is pictured in Figure 2-2.

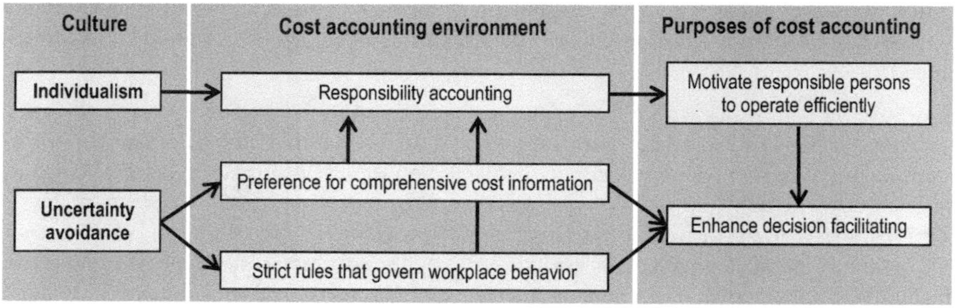

Figure 2-2: Relationship between cultural dimensions as well as organizational and managerial patterns shaping the specifics in German cost accounting

2.1.1.2.2.2 Relationship of cost accounting towards financial and management accounting

Cost accounting provides information for both financial and management accounting. Internationally, however, the focus of cost accounting differs. Due to the further developed capital markets in the USA, e.g., US companies put more emphasis upon financial accounting than on management accounting. For German companies, financial and management accounting are often equally relevant.[558] As financial accounting according to German common law provides distorted information that is less suitable for decision making and as Germany is an uncertainty avoiding society, German companies decided to run financial and management accounting systems independently at the beginning of the 20th century.[559] Cross-national differences in the relationship of cost accounting towards financial and management accounting have significant implications for cost accounting. As Germany has a stronger emphasis on management accounting than the USA, German

557 Cf. *MacArthur* (2006). When employees have to report to different supervisors, it may occur that the employees are uncertain to whom they have to report and how they should perform a task, if the supervisors issue different instructions. Similarly, a cost center with more than one responsible manager may lead to uncertain situations when the managers have different opinions who of them should conduct which task.

558 Cf. *Becker/Messner* (2005), p. 418. See also *Weber* (2011), p. 37.

559 Cf. *Kaplan/Atkinson* (1989), p. 9. The distinction between financial and management accounting can predominantly be traced back to the scholar *Schmalenbach*. Cf. *Schildbach* (1997), p. 262f.; *Schweitzer/Ziolkowski* (1999), p. 2; *Hebeler* (2003), p. 24; *Weißenberger* (2004), p. 72. Although he has suggested a distinction between financial and management accounting (cf. *Schmalenbach* (1919), p. 261, 265), he has confirmed that the financial and management accounting departments should cooperate to avoid duplication of work. Cf. *Schmalenbach* (1927), p. 4f.; *Schmalenbach* (1956), p. 30. Whereas in Germany two systems, one for inventory valuation and the other for decision making, are common, only 9% of the UK companies maintain this distinction. The remaining 91% run one cost accounting system for both inventory valuation and decision making. Cf. *Drury/Tayles* (2000), p. 45.

cost accounting systems better meet managerial needs for decision making. To meet managerial needs, cost accounting systems usually have to provide accurate, detailed, and timely information. Running two separate data bases for financial and management accounting and using imputed costs enhance the provision of relevant information for decision making, therefore both became widespread in Germany. Cost accounting had sufficient freedom and room for development in Germany leading to comprehensive cost accounting systems like GPK. Due to the harmonization of financial reporting standards, many German companies started to converge financial and management accounting. However, as outlined in section 2.1.1.2.1, a full convergence of financial and management accounting resulting in a one-circle system, which is prevalent in Anglophone countries, is unlikely. Hence, two separate data bases for financial and management accounting are expected to remain for Germany in future.

To correspond to the different purposes of financial and managerial accounting, *Schmalenbach* introduced the concept of imputed costs, which is unique for German-speaking countries. Whereas financial accounting deals with 'expenses', 'costs' are applied in management accounting. As little is known internationally about the distinction between expenses and costs, the differences between both terms are outlined in the following.

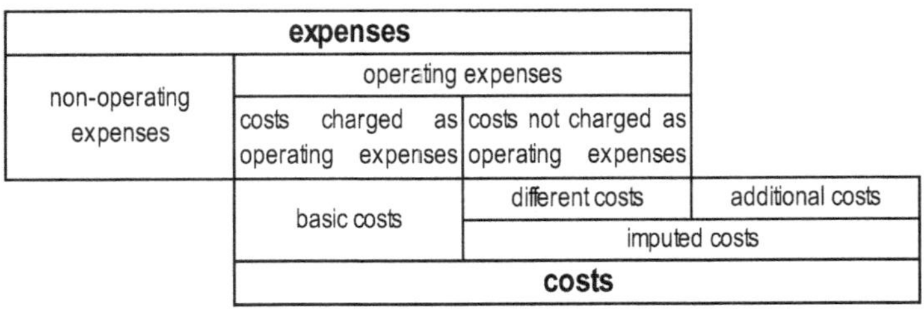

Figure 2-3: Differentiation between expenses and costs
Source: following *Schweitzer/Küpper* (2011), p. 20

To determine the 'operating expenses' (see Figure 2-3), German companies first subtract the 'non-operating expenses' from the expenses of a period. 'Non-operating expenses' include expenses that are not related to the main business activity (e.g., for charity), that do not regularly occur for providing operational services (e.g., fire, storm, and theft damages), as well as expenses that occurred in a former period (e.g., expenses have to be paid subsequently after a tax audit is carried through). The 'operating expenses' are further distinguished, whether they are charged as costs or not. The costs that are charged as operating expenses are called 'basic costs' on the cost level. Costs that are not charged as operating expenses, the so called 'different costs', result due to a valuation that differs from financial accounting. These include imputed interests, imputed depreciations, and imputed risks. The 'imputed costs' comprise besides 'different costs' also 'additional costs'. The 'additional costs' include cost types that are not expenses and therefore have to be considered additionally for cost accounting. They comprise imputed rent, imputed entrepreneurial profit, and imputed cost of equity capital.[560] The six different types of imputed costs are pictured in Figure 2-4 and explained in the following.[561]

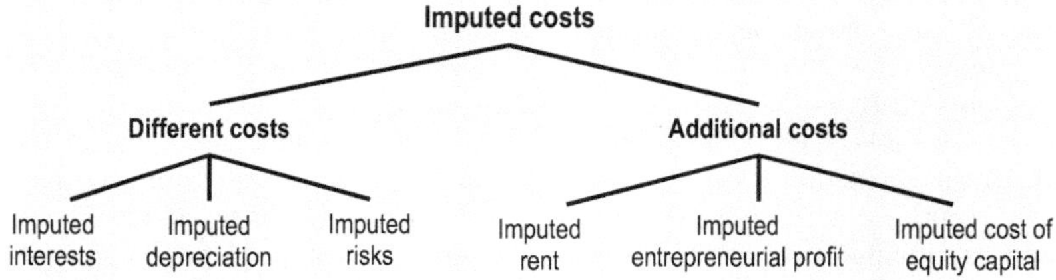

Figure 2-4: Types of imputed costs
Source: *Coenenberg et al.* (2009), p. 78

- *Imputed interests* differ to the interests paid, because only the interests for capital employed are costs. Assets that are capitalized for non-operational purposes are non-interest bearing on a calculative basis. Furthermore, to simplify and to improve comparability of periods, the interest payment is averaged.
- The measurement of *imputed depreciation* does not have to follow any regulations from financial or tax accounting systems. Instead, the internal requirements, i.e. the information needs of the management, are met. To ensure maintenance of assets, often replacement costs instead of acquisition and production costs are taken as a basis. The depreciation method should further reflect a fair consumption of assets.
- *Imputed risks* should take specific individual risks like fire, theft, and accidents into account in terms of a 'self-insurance premium'. Imputed costs further include only those risks that are not insured, because insurance premiums are basic costs (operating expenses that are charged as costs). Imputed risks are necessary, because expenses that do not regularly occur for providing operational services are not costs.[562] These events that can hardly be influenced by managers can have a strong impact upon the income statement. Paying a 'self-insurance premium' that equals the financial consequences of single events in the long-run therefore leads to smoother incomes. This facilitates to evaluate the performance of managers.
- *Imputed rent* is estimated for buildings and equipment that serve operational purposes and that are in private property of individual enterprises and private companies. No payments for these buildings and equipment occur due to the legal form of these companies. Payments occur, however, for other legal forms or when the buildings and equipment do not belong to the self-employed person. Imputed rent therefore ensures comparability across legal forms and of the assets contributed to the company by the self-employed. It further illustrates that the rent for buildings and equipment have to be gained by the company even when no payments occur.

560 Cf. *Schmalenbach* (1934), p. 115; *Schildbach* (1997), p. 263; *Fandel et al.* (2004), p. 11f., with further references.

561 For the description of imputed costs cf., e.g., *Coenenberg et al.* (2009), p. 77-93.

562 Cf. section 2.1.1.2.1.

- *Imputed entrepreneurial profit* is estimated for self-employed persons, if they cannot draw a salary. The imputed entrepreneurial profit is therefore a compensation for a manager who would otherwise be paid by individual enterprises and private companies. This type of imputed cost improves the comparability across companies with different legal structures and further illustrates that a company only makes an economic profit, when it gains the manager's salary.
- *Imputed costs of equity capital* illustrate the profit that investors would generate with an alternative investment. The internal income statement therefore represents a profit after an adequate return on equity.[563] Thereby, the costs of equity is already covered within the product costs. Comparisons between companies, within a company, and over time periods are more precise, because the impact of different financing structures is thereby compensated.

2.1.1.2.2.3 Education of cost accountants

It is believed in Western countries that efficiency rises when the division of work becomes finer and specialization is enhanced.[564] *Ahrens/Chapman* demonstrate for management accounting that this believe is more pronounced in Germany than in Britain. As cost accounting is an instrument that is applied by management accountants[565] and as specific education programs do not exist for cost accounting but for management accounting in Germany (including issues in cost accounting), the findings by *Ahrens/Chapman* are also relevant for this study.[566]

Unlike in Britain and the USA where accountancy is organized as a profession and management accountants are trained by professional institutes like CIMA and IMA, the **training of management accountants** in Germany is mainly part of university education.[567] Most of the German management accountants have completed a degree course of *Betriebswirtschaftslehre* (business economics/administration) with a specialization in management accounting.[568] The education of German management accountants is therefore

563 Therewith, the German scholar *Schmalenbach* has introduced the idea of economic profit already at the beginning of the 20th century.

564 Cf. *Nishimura* (2003), p. 60. This is contrary to Japan, where "the integrated and cooperative idea and the stratified relationship of cooperation between managers and workers lie at the heart of management." *Nishimura* (2003), p. 60f.

565 In Germany cost accounting is the instrument that is taught the most to business students at university. Cf. *Hirsch* (2003), p. 260f. Furthermore, knowledge of cost accounting belongs to the most relevant professional qualifications a management accountant in Germany should possess. Cf. *Hoffjan/Bebek* (2009), p. 619f.

566 See *Ahrens/Chapman* (1999a), (1999b), (2000).

567 A university degree is besides practical experience the most relevant professional requirement for management accountants in Germany. Cf. *Weber/Schäffer* (1998), p. 231. See also *Weber et al.* (2010b), p. 28f. German professional bodies like CIMA and IMA do not exist. Cf. *Ahrens/Chapman* (1999); *Horváth* (2009b), p. 18.

568 Students in *Betriebswirtschaftslehre* can therefore graduate in management accounting as a major in most business schools and universities. Cf. *Horváth* (2009b), p. 18. 72 out of 92 business admi-

very academically oriented. Bachelor and master degrees in *Betriebswirtschaftslehre* are provided. Most German students want to complete both, which takes between five and six years. As males used to do national service (it has recently been abolished) and many students of *Betriebswirtschaftslehre* have completed an apprenticeship before, which lasts for about two years, graduate job entrants are often older (between 25 and 29 years) than their counterparts from other countries. Few management accountants even obtain their BWL doctorate, which usually takes between three and five years. Besides university, it is also possible to study in a more vocational way by visiting *Fachhochschulen*, in evening courses at *Verwaltungs- und Wirtschaftsakademien*, and outside *Betriebswirtschaftslehre* the Chambers of Commerce as well as other public bodies offer courses for Certified Controllers. The latter have, however, gained only little importance so far. Practical outlook on management accounting is predominantly provided by workshops and seminars that only last up to a few weeks.

The **required qualifications of management accountants** differ internationally. German management accountants with non-relevant degrees are rare and have much fewer chances to enter the profession. To fulfill the management accounting tasks, entrants often require solid knowledge of management accounting instruments.[569] Due to an increase in complexity of management accounting tasks, an increasing number of German companies prefer to employ graduates.[570] In Britain on the contrary, management accountants with non-relevant degrees are common, because they have the opportunity to study management accounting in a more practical way while working.

German management accountants who are far more academically educated in comparison to their Anglophone counterparts view management accounting in highly theoretical terms. They see their **role** in understanding systematic economic relationships and providing their knowledge to operational managers without participating in operational tasks. This more theoretically oriented education of German management accountants with a strong emphasis on objective expertise results in a stronger emphasis on theoretically sound solutions in contrast to more ‘practical’ and ‘pragmatic’ solutions in Britain, Japan, and the USA.[571] It is common that German management scholars prefer descriptive models that express how organizations should work, than to express how they actually work.[572] German managers therefore spend a lot of time and effort on detailed theoretical problems allowing them to develop comprehensive decision-support systems. The career system in German companies furthermore enables managers to develop comprehensive func-

nistration faculties of German-language business schools and universities have a chair or institute that is specialized in management accounting. Cf. *Binder/Schäffer* (2005), p. 100f.

569 Cf. *Steinle/Daum* (2007), p. 53f.

570 Cf. *Görg* (1991), p. 98f. This trend towards academization has led to the creation of comprehensive cost accounting systems. Cf. *Rickards* (2005), p. 114f.

571 Cf. *Rickards* (2005), p. 115.

572 Cf. *Becker/Messner* (2005), p. 421. The emphasis of German scholars to describe how organizations should work instead of how they actually work might be due to the idealistic culture that stems from the philosophical traditions in Germany. Cf. *Palazzo* (2002), p. 206-208; *Becker/Messner* (2005), p. 421.

tional experience in a narrow defined area.[573] Due to the high degree in specialization of German management accountants, their role is formalized to rationalize and legitimize operational proposals that are generated by the functions.[574] A drawback of this specialization is that German management accountants collaborate less closely with managers and therefore might get stuck in complex management accounting systems that fail managers' requirements.

The reason why German cost and management accountants are more specialized than their Western counterparts is expected to stem from culture. By referring to the higher **uncertainty avoidance** in Germany compared to Anglophone countries, *MacArthur* deduces the need for specialized management accountants. As managers prefer precise answers, more career management accountants are employed.[575] High uncertainty can also foster a belief in experts leading to a professionalization of this function.[576] Specialization and relevant degrees of management accountants are preferred by the Germans, because they signal the skills that management accountants have and thus reduce uncertainty. The **separation between financial and management accounting** further enforces specialization. Accountants in Germany are more likely to specialize in financial or management accounting with both specializations having an own career-development path.[577] In the USA on the contrary, financial accounting dominates management accounting in education and practice.[578] Therefore, US cost and management accountants are likely to possess more knowledge of financial accounting and less knowledge of designing comprehensive cost and management accounting systems for managerial decision making than their German counterparts. The relationship between German culture and the specialization of cost accountants is depictured in Figure 2-5.[579]

573 Cf. *Goffee/Scase* (1992); *Walgenbach/Kieser* (1995), p. 281; *Lawrence/Edwards* (2000), p. 104f.

574 Cf. *Ahrens* (1997a), (1997b).

575 Cf. *MacArthur* (2006), p. 12.

576 Cf. *Hofstede* (2001), p. 168.

577 Cf. *Sharman* (2003a), p. 38. Separate courses for financial and management accounting are common in Germany. Cf. *Becker/Messner* (2005), p. 418; *Horváth* (2009b), p. 18.

578 This has been criticized by scholars. *Johnson/Kaplan* have triggered the discussion with their influential book 'Relevance Lost'. See *Johnson/Kaplan* (1987); *Clinton* (2007) respectively. *Clinton* supports their view. Professional accountants in business and accountancy professors "were (and still are) inappropriately reflecting an external financial accounting focus rather than internal decision support as the primary purpose of the accounting profession." *Clinton* (2007), p. 26. This shortcoming likely stems to a large degree from the limited number of cost and management accounting courses at university. The number of available senior-level cost/management accounting courses and the number of required senior-level cost/management accounting courses are significantly smaller than the number of other available and required senior-level accounting courses. The number of available senior-level cost/ management accounting courses is often only limited to one or two. Cf. *Tatikonda/Savchenko* (2010).

579 *Zimmermann* reports a positive relationship between functional specialization and performance of the management accounting system for German companies. Cf. *Zimmermann* (2001), p. 411f.

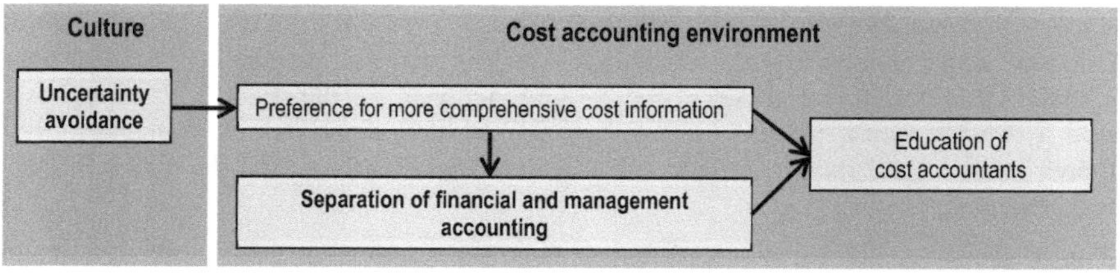

Figure 2-5: Reasons for highly specialized German cost accountants

2.1.1.3 Specifics of Japanese cost accounting

2.1.1.3.1 History

Before the Second World War, Germany and the UK and subsequently the USA had a significant influence on other countries. Japanese cost accounting owes much to Western countries. Therefore, many fundamental similarities in particular for traditional cost accounting exist between Japan and Western countries.[580] However, as Japan has adapted and modified the Western 'imports' and their use to fit its national culture,[581] considerable cross-national differences prevail. The development of Japanese cost accounting is outlined in the following to provide a better understanding why and how cross-national differences have emerged.

In the **middle of the 19th century**, Japan came under pressure to enter trade agreements and became interested in borrowing new industrial technology and economic institutions from Western countries.[582] Along with other Western 'imports', the double-entry bookkeeping by the Italian *Paciolo* was introduced in Japan in 1865 and was promoted through books and teachers from Western countries.[583]

During **1927 to 1937** Japan's main emphasis in accounting was like in the USA on financial accounting. Japanese businessmen and government officials have devoted little attention to management accounting until the economic depression in 1927. The necessity to rationalize and to apply accounting as a tool of management became more popular thereafter.[584] Management accounting – cost accounting and budgetary control being its most important instruments – started to become a recognized area of accounting and scholars started to demarcate management accounting from financial accounting. The Financial

580 Cf. *Winter* (2005), p. 32.

581 Cf. *Yoshikawa* (1994b), p. 279; *Yoshikawa* (2001), p. 269f.

582 Cf. *Someya* (1996), p. 12.

583 Two important publications have helped to stimulate adoption. The first important publication is a translation of an American bookkeeping textbook. The second book is a translation compiled from proposals by a Scotsman who was invited by the Ministry of Finance to teach bookkeeping methods. Cf. *Shimme* (1937), p. 292-294; *Someya* (1996), p. 13f.; *Okano/Suzuki* (2007), p. 1122f. To teach double-entry bookkeeping through the educational channels, the Japanese Government established commercial schools from 1875 onwards. Cf. *Shimme* (1937), p. 295.

584 Cf. *Matsumoto* (1953), p. 41.

Management Commission of the Ministry of Commerce and Industry started its work on a cost accounting guide in 1930 and published it in 1937 to diffuse and enlighten knowledge. Cost accounting was in an infant stage at this time. The Commission was convinced that this instrument had first of all to be improved before it can serve as a tool of control.[585] However, the industry community did not share the same interest in cost and management accounting during the 1930s, because industry lost the stimulus of rationalization when economic recovery started in 1932.[586]

During the Second World War, the army and navy formulated their own cost accounting rules in 1939 and 1940 respectively that were strongly influenced by European countries and the USA. As cost accounting was one of the most effective tools to tighten economic control, many norms and systems were developed. The plurality of rules has, however, hampered cost accounting for the munitions industry and has impeded national product price controls. As a consequence, the 'Rules on Cost Accounting in Manufacturing Factories' were introduced in 1942 to integrate the army's and navy's cost accounting rules.[587] As the war intensified in 1944, the 'Cost Accounting Guidelines for Manufacturing Companies' were adapted to reform and simplify cost accounting. Due to an increase in inflation and shortages of raw materials, the Japanese started to distrust monetary calculations. Instead of a production unit measured by a monetary term, a physical measure was therefore preferred by the new standard.[588]

After the Second World War, Japan started its rebuilding effort. Utmost efforts were necessary to rationalize organizations to attain economic stabilization. Cost and management accounting as a tool to improve decision making started to attract keen interest again.[589] The Japanese started to adapt American practices in scientific cost and management accounting to improve their competitiveness.[590] Although standard cost accounting has soon become widely accepted in Japanese academia, its implementation in the industry was hampered the first years after the Second World War for three reasons.[591] First,

---

585 Cf. *Matsumoto* (1953), p. 41; *Yoshikawa* (2001), p. 270.

586 Cf. *Matsumoto* (1953), p. 41-44.

587 The objective of this guideline was, besides to control prices, the increase in efficiency. Cf. *Yoshikawa* (2001), p. 270; *Okano/Suzuki* (2007), p. 1124.

588 Cf. *Okano/Suzuki* (2007), p. 1124f.

589 Cf. *Matsumoto* (1953), p. 45.

590 Research on scientific management methods began as early as 1911 when "The Principles of Scientific Management" by *Frederick Winslow Taylor* was translated into Japanese in an abridged form. The main emphasis of scientific management in Japan was the means of rationalizing production of Japan as a whole. It was introduced to eliminate useless efforts and a number of institutions and associations were founded to promote its notion, implementation, and practice. Cf. *Okano/Suzuki* (2007), p. 123f. Furthermore, the practices total quality control (TQC) and just-in-time (JIT) have their roots in the USA. See *Okano/Suzuki* (2007), p. 1125f.

591 Cf. *Matsumoto* (1953), p. 45f. Until the 1980s, standard cost accounting became widespread in Japanese companies. The adoption rate started to decline thereafter. Due to more competitive markets and increasing technological innovations, practices like TQC and JIT started to become widespread. Traditional management accounting techniques like standard costing are less useful under these conditions. Cf. *de Zoysa/Herath* (2007).

Japanese tax law was based on actual costs. Adopting a standard cost system required year-end adjustments. Second, Japan's industry was largely oriented towards export trade. This possessed a high degree of flexibility leading to a primarily job order-oriented production, which has complicated Japanese companies to define standardized production processes. Third, hardly any executives, superintendents, or workers understood this novel instrument at that time. In spite of these challenges, standard costing became the most effective management accounting instrument for improving operating efficiency.[592]

From **1962 to 1970**, the government started to improve national productivity by releasing a modern cost accounting standard in 1962.[593] It is based on the cost accounting standards that were developed during the Second World War. The new standard is a collection of best cost accounting systems around the world. The conception of this standard shares many similarities with the German standard 'Die allgemeinen Grundsätze der Kostenrechnung' (1939) and the US standard 'Report of the Committee on Cost Concepts and Standards by AAA' (1951).[594] Unlike the German and the US standard, only the Japanese standard is codified and therefore constitutes written and quasi compulsory methods of cost accounting. It was designed to have also a social binding for Japanese companies.[595] Consequently, the Japanese cost accounting standard became "the foundation for every company"[596] and has a significant influence upon practice.[597] In Germany and the USA on the contrary, solely companies in regulated industries or companies that submit an application for public contracts for products or services that have no market price have to follow their national cost accounting standards. As the Japanese cost accounting standard has not been updated, modern systems like ABC are not included, which may constitute a barrier for their diffusions.[598] The framework of the cost accounting standard indicates that cost accounting serves the following five purposes: price setting, preparing financial statements, cost management, budgeting and budgetary control, setting basic plans, and decision making.[599]

The guidelines of the Japanese cost accounting standard share many similarities with German cost accounting. The definition of costs is very similar to the German one.[600] Only operating expenses that are related to the main business activity are costs in Japan. Furthermore, costs constitute only the ordinary consumption of resources – not the consumption of resources due to extraordinary circumstances.[601] The Japanese standard reproduced the German three-tiered cost accounting system of cost type accounting, cost center accounting, and product cost accounting. Although the structure of Japanese cost

592 Cf. *Sakurai* (1997), p. 3.

593 Cf. *Yoshikawa* (2001), p. 270; *Winter* (2005), p. 7.

594 Cf. *Yoshikawa* (2001), p. 271; *Winter* (2005), p. 7.

595 However, companies that do not apply this standard cannot be punished by law. Cf. *Winter* (2005), p. 7, 28.

596 *Yoshikawa* (2001), p. 279.

597 Cf. *Winter* (2005), p. 28.

598 Cf. *Winter* (2005), p. 29, quoting *Yoshikawa* (2000), p. 37.

599 Cf. *Yoshikawa* (1994b), p. 279.

600 For the German definition of costs see section 2.1.1.2.1.

601 Cf. *Winter* (2005), p. 16f., 30f.

accounting is similar to the German one, the techniques and methods of cost accounting are expected to share more similarities with US cost accounting.[602]

From **1970 onwards**, cost management became very popular in Japan. After the oil crisis in 1973 cost pressure increased and companies were forced to become more proactive in managing their costs.[603] To survive competition, Japanese companies developed comprehensive cost management systems that build up pressure to reduce costs.[604] In the development stage of products between 70 and 80% of product costs are determined.[605] Japanese companies started to apply target costing to influence costs in this development stage.[606] After the product has been developed, costs can further be influenced during the production stage. According to the experience curve effect, costs of value added can potentially decline by approximately 20 to 30% each time accumulated output is doubled.[607] To exploit this potential, cost reduction systems like kaizen costing are employed to strive for small and continuous cost improvements of the production process.[608] Cost accounting has to support cost management by providing relevant information – with cost management being more comprehensive than cost accounting. "While cost accounting ... focuses on reporting costs, cost management takes a proactive role in planning, managing, and reducing costs."[609] A Japanese cost accounting instrument to support cost management are cost tables. They constitute a data base of costs. Japanese companies prepare cost tables throughout a product's life cycle. To help estimate the costs of future products, cost tables are prepared that include only a small number of key cost drivers to approximate future costs. More detailed cost tables with a comprehensive set of cost driver variables (e.g., kind of machine, type of material, and type of drilling) are set up to reduce the costs of existing products. Besides for negotiation purposes with suppliers and subcontractors, cost tables play an important role for cost management and cost reduction, because managers can efficiently conduct functional analyses. A cost table for a particular product provides managers with many sets of cost analyses, all of which dovetail together. This allows managers to quickly ascertain the implications of changes in production technology, type of material, etc. upon product costs. Cost accountants should have worked in other departments before to draw on their personal experience when they prepare cost tables.[610]

After 2000, performance evaluation became increasingly important for Japanese companies within heightened global competition and the erosion of the Japanese permanent employment and seniority principle.[611] Several companies have already started at the be-

602 Cf. *Winter* (2005), p. 31f.

603 Cf. *Sakurai* (1991), p. 40.

604 Cf. *Cooper/Slagmulder* (1997), p. 6-8.

605 Cf., e.g., *Schmidt* (1996), p. 54; *Franz/Kajüter* (2007), p. 279.

606 Cf. *Monden* (1995), p. 1-12.

607 Cf. *Henderson/Gälweiler* (1984), p. 19; *Henderson* (2003), p. 571.

608 Cf. *Monden* (1995), p. 7, 289f.; *Cooper/Slagmulder* (1997), p. 7f. This instrument is arranged on a long-term basis, and is part of the company's strategy. Besides kaizen costing, the instruments products costing and operational control can also be used to manage the costs of existing products.

609 *Berliner/Brimson* (1988), p. 3. See also *Kajüter* (2000), p. 12-14.

610 Cf. *Yoshikawa et al.* (1990).

611 For the erosion of Japanese permanent employment and seniority principle see section 2.1.1.3.2.1.

ginning of the 1990s generating more detailed cost information "to make segmental costs more visible and individuals more accountable"[612] and to adopt individualized payment systems.[613] This development has continued and performance evaluation and individual incentive systems have become more popular in Japanese companies over the years.[614] The evaluation of individuals and the implementation of individualized payment systems have been complemented in some companies by installing micro-profit centers.[615] Micro-profit centers make workers more conscious about profits and cost cutting. At the company Kyocera, the performance of the profit center is also announced or posted throughout the firm to increase the pressure to perform.[616] The historical development of cost accounting in Japan is summarized in Figure 2-6.

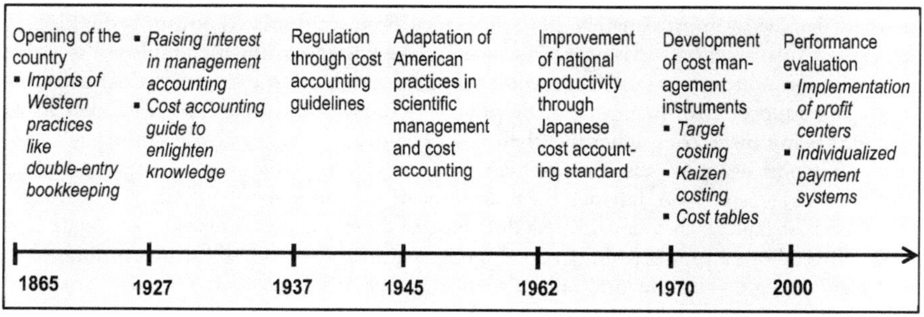

Figure 2-6: Historical development of cost accounting in Japan

2.1.1.3.2 Country-specifics

2.1.1.3.2.1 National culture

The impact of the Japanese culture upon management has been demonstrated in many comparisons with Western countries. Japan is characterized as a collective culture along with other Asian countries. Japan is according to *Hofstede's* index far more collective than Western countries like Germany, however, less collective than other Asian countries.[617] The concept of **Wa** is characteristic for Japan. It describes the harmony to attain for co-operation, fellowship, and mutual trust between workers, which is high in collective and low in individualistic societies.[618] Japan is further characterized as a long-term oriented

---

612 *Hopper et al.* (1999), p. 81.

613 *Takayanagi* states that progressive firms in Japan make deliberate efforts to increasingly install incentive systems that emphasize performance and ability. Cf. *Takayanagi* (1989), p. 425. See also *Yamada* (1991), quoted after *Hopper et al.* (1999), p. 81.

614 See *Pudelko* (2009), p. 448; *Haghirian* (2010), p. 29.

615 See, e.g., *Cooper* (1995), p. 304-316.

616 Cf. *Cooper* (1995), p. 315.

617 30 out of 53 countries are more collective than Japan. Cf. *Hofstede/Bond* (1988), p. 12f. One reason might be that Japan is wealthier than other Asian countries, with national wealth leading to more individualistic societies. Cf. *Hofstede* (1991), p. 75f.

618 Cf. *Huff/Kelley* (2003), p. 82f.

society. Japan scores the third highest out of 20 countries on this dimension.[619] Both cultural dimensions are perceived as relevant for Japanese cost accounting either directly or indirectly through organizational and managerial patterns.

The geographic conditions in Japan have facilitated the development of a **collective culture**. About 127 million Japanese live crowded together, because four-fifths of the country is undeveloped and uninhabited. Living in Japan therefore necessitates mutual respect, tolerance, and increased awareness of living in a society. Threats by natural catastrophes[620] as well as the focus on rice growing in Japan, which is highly complex and demands co-operation between farmers,[621] have facilitated the development of Japan's collective culture. Finally, the three major **spiritual systems** Shintoism, Buddhism, and Confucianism have shaped Japanese collective culture. Confucianism has been introduced in the fifth and Buddhism in the sixth century. Both were shaped by Shinto traditions and politics. All three spiritual systems share the idea that individuals are part of the greater whole and not the center of human endeavors.[622] To understand the Japanese culture it is suggested to go back to the Tokugawa era.[623]

The **Tokugawa feudalism** established a military regime in the 17th century with a hierarchy of four classes. The samurai warrior class was at the top. Farmers and peasants, craftsmen, and merchants followed in that order.[624] The Tokugawa military government turned to Confucianism to legitimize their regime and as a set of principles to govern the nation. Four out of five relationships that are taught by Confucianism are hierarchic in nature.[625] Behavioral rules for all classes have also been set up in accordance to Bushidō, a Japanese code of conduct and way of samurai life. From the supervisor it is expected that he puts the group's interest before his own. He owns the subordinate protection and consideration. The subordinate in return owns the supervisor respect and obedience. Acquittal comes first – all personal feelings and emotions that impede acquittal have to be suppressed. During this period, a person has been perceived as a member of a society with social obligation that is enmeshed in a web of social relationships and that is motivated by duties towards others.

Economic, political, and ideological crises have led to the downfall of the Tokugawa feudal regime in 1868. During the **Meiji era** the emperor reversed and the Shintoism became the state religion again. This has enforced loyalty to the emperor with the primary aim to

619 Cf. *Hofstede/Bond* (1988), p. 12f.

620 Cf. *Gendo/Konschak* (1999), p. 21.

621 Cf. *Schlieper* (1997), p. 68-73.

622 Cf. *Cyr* (2002), p. 92.

623 The further description is based on *Whitehill* (1995), p. 5-23; *Ohtsu/Imanari* (2002), p. 31-41, with further references; *Kieser/Walgenbach* (2007), p. 282-287. Furthermore, *Pauer* describes the impact of the Edo era that has also influenced the Japanese society to become collectivistic. Cf. *Pauer* (1985), p. 123.

624 *Lippert* assumes that the disesteem of merchants still prevails to some extent in the Japanese society and thereby hampers the development of management accounting in Japan. Cf. *Lippert* (2011), p. 32.

625 Cf. *Hofstede/Bond* (1988), p. 8.

modernize the country.[626] The role of businessmen became crucial to develop the economy with profit-making being subordinated to the industrialization of Japan. The focus was the duty to the nation and to behave in the interest of the public. The collectivistic orientations, that mainly stem from the Tokugawa feudalism, have been enforced and transferred to industrial companies during the Meiji era.[627]

Besides collectivism, Japan also became a **long-term oriented culture because of Confucianism.** Confucius' teachings are lessons in practical ethics that have been related to long-term orientation. "[T]he values on the one pole are more oriented towards the future (especially perseverance and thrift); they are more dynamic. The values on the opposite pole are more oriented towards the past and present; they are more static"[628] (see Table 2-1). Unlike Japan, Western countries have not been influenced by Confucius' teachings and therefore score lower on this dimension.

Pole labeled 'long-term orientation'	Opposite pole labeled 'short-term orientation'
·Persistence (perseverance)	·Personal steadiness and stability
·Ordering relationships by status and observing this order	·Protecting your 'face'
·Thrift	·Respect for tradition
·Having a sense of shame	·Reciprocation of greetings, favors, and gifts

Table 2-1: The poles long-term and short-term orientation
Source: following *Hofstede* (1991), p. 165f.

Whereas in Western countries cost control is important to motivate the employees, it is less necessary in collectivistic countries like Japan. The employees are far more loyal and motivated to work in the interest of the supervisor and the company compared to their Western counterparts. Instead of control, cost information is expected to be mainly applied for **implementing strategy** and for **directing employees' attention** to problems they have to solve collectively.[629] Due to the long-term orientation of Japanese companies, the Japanese approach to cost and management accounting combines control information more with planning to adopt a **proactive instead of a reactive emphasis**. Therefore, Japanese companies apply feedforward control more comprehensively than their Western counterparts. Whereas feedforward control is preventive in nature, the opposite, feedback control, is remedial.[630]

Permanent employment, which is also called long-term employment, remains one cultural-specific element of the Japanese business system.[631] It refers to "the practice whereby

626 The latter was an essential national concern to ensure political and economic independence against the threat of Western powers. For the historical development of loyalty in Japan see *Gendo/Konschak* (1999), p. 20f.

627 Cf. *Pauer* (1985), p. 123-125.

628 Cf. *Hofstede* (1991), p. 166.

629 Cf. *Hiromoto* (1988); *Yoshikawa* (1994b).

630 The performance of feedback control systems heavily depends on the performance and the rapidity of the error-detection process. Cf. *Riahi-Belkaoui* (2002), p. 59. For feedforward control see also *Collier/Agyei-Ampomah* (2008), p. 15.

631 For the historical development of permanent employment in Japan see *Pauer* (1985), p. 128-130.

an employee enters a company after school graduation, receives in-company training, and remains an employee of the same company until the retirement age"[632]. According to Confucianism, a son cannot be excluded from a family. Similarly, due to the collectivistic perspective in Japan, the relationship between employer and employee is not anonymous and it does not follow an economically rational relationship.[633] Instead, Japanese companies only dismiss workers with reluctance to avoid a disruption of harmony and togetherness within the group.[634] The obligation to loyalty applies not only to the company. The employees are expected as well to be loyal towards the company. Hence, investments into human capital are more worth spending, because they remain to the company.[635] Japanese companies hardly face the risk of heavily investing in employees and then losing the well-educated work force to their competitors.[636] When Western companies need new qualifications, they employ new staff from the labor market. Due to the low flexibility of the Japanese labor market, this way is only partly suitable in Japan.[637] To ensure the flexibility of the workforce, a more **general qualification** of the work force is required.

Not all employees benefit from permanent employment. Employees working at small companies, at the service industry, and at subcontractors,[638] as well as temporary workers and women are often excluded.[639] *Ernst* estimates that only 34% of the employees are permanently employed.[640] Furthermore, in the 1990s, a decline in permanent employment seemed to start off with Japanese managers striving for more flexibility in recruiting, dismissal of personnel, and change of employer.[641] As recruitment becomes more flexible, the need for a more generally skilled workforce diminishes. Consequently, managers started to increase the formation of specialists.[642] *Ahmadjian/Robinson* trace the **erosion of permanent employment** back to the diffusion of the concept downsizing.[643] *Witt* sees the development in the attitude of younger employees who show a different work ethic and

632 *Cole* (1979), p. 11.

633 Cf. *Kieser/Walgenbach* (2007), p. 284.

634 Judicial precedents in Japan make it also difficult to fire an employee. The company must be under economic pressures, the labor union has to agree, the employee has to be dismissed in a fair manner, and other methods of reducing labor cost must have already been exhausted. Cf. *Sugeno* (1992), p. 408-410, and further *Kono/Falkus* (1984), p. 319. This is consistent with the argument from *Hofstede* that higher uncertainty avoidance is related to a stronger loyalty to the employer and to a longer average duration of employment. Cf. *Hofstede* (2001), p. 165, 169.

635 Cf. *Kono/Falkus* (1984), p. 320.

636 Cf. *Vondran* (1985), p. 45.

637 Cf. *Kieser/Walgenbach* (2007), p. 285.

638 In these companies mobility is much higher than in larger manufacturing companies. Cf. *Kono/Falkus* (1984), p. 319.

639 Cf. *Stiles* (2009), p. 430. *Gendo/Koschak* even claim that the principle of permanent employment was made up by US researchers and has never been practiced in Japan. See *Gendo/Konschak* (1999), p. 97-107.

640 Cf. *Ernst/Herold* (1986), p. 22.

641 Cf. *Pudelko* (2009), p. 448.

642 Cf. *Pudelko* (2009), p. 448. Contrary to the decline of the seniority orientation and the permanent employment, far fewer managers mentioned to increase the formation of specialists.

643 Cf. *Ahmadjian/Robinson* (2001).

who may have recognized that prosperity through permanent employment has not led to job satisfaction.[644]

Another cultural-specific element of the Japanese business systems is the **seniority system.** Pay and promotion is chiefly based on the employee's education level and her or his years of membership.[645] Every working place requires a minimum seniority and also very talented employees are only then promoted when they reach this age.[646] Promotion according to the seniority system instead of the performance principle is more suitable for the Japanese culture. Individual career paths would contrast permanent employment as well as the collective and long-term oriented culture.[647] **Performance evaluation** is therefore less necessary for promotion or payment purposes.[648] The potential disadvantages of the seniority principle are the discouragement of new employees as well as potential complacency of the elder.[649] Due to changes in the demographics of the Japanese workforce, companies have to attract and retain more of the younger employees, e.g., by more performance-based payments and by promotions that are more based on merit than on seniority. Thus, companies that hold on the seniority principle might scare off younger employees.[650] A decline of the seniority orientation and a higher emphasis on performance orientation for promotion and compensation purposes has been observed in Japan in the last years.[651] Implications of Japan's collectivism and long-term orientation are depictured in Figure 2-7.

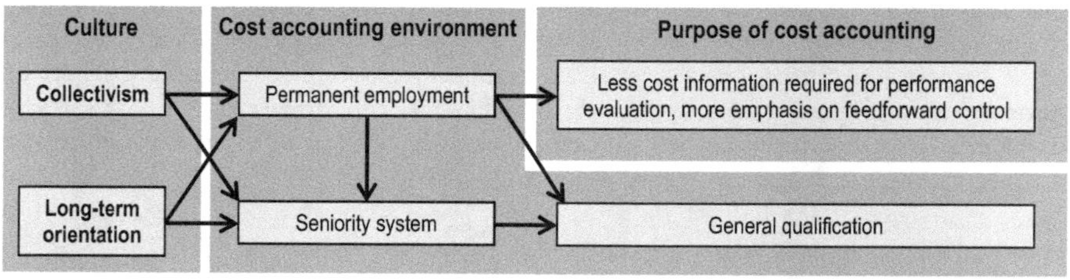

Figure 2-7: Relationships between cultural dimensions as well as organizational and managerial patterns shaping the specifics in Japanese cost accounting

644 Cf. *Witt* (2006).

645 Cf. *Stiles* (2009), p. 285. Japanese companies reward employees significantly less often according to their performance than their UK und US counterparts. Cf. *Kono/Falkus* (1984), p. 273f.

646 Cf. *Gendo/Konschak* (1999), p. 107-113.

647 Cf. *Kieser/Walgenbach* (2007), p. 285. Permanent employment only makes sense when with the principle of seniority career opportunities and potential for salary increase exist. Cf. *Hußmann* (1976), p. 57; *Gendo/Konschak* (1999), p. 30. Individual career paths provide less long-term security to the employees and do not reinforce high commitment and trust.

648 Even if bonuses and incentives prevail in companies, they should rather be given to the group and not to the individuals, if the work group should function as an emotional in-group. Cf. *Hofstede* (1991), p. 63-65.

649 Cf. *Stiles* (2009), p. 285.

650 Cf. *Ernst/Herold* (1986), p. 32; *Stiles* (2009), p. 285. Further economic reasons that reduce the usefulness of the seniority principle are described by *Hußmann* (1976).

651 See section 2.1.1.3.1.

2.1.1.3.2.2 Relationship of cost accounting towards financial and management accounting

Unlike in Germany, financial and management accounting have not been separated in Japan, although an important purpose of financial accounting is the protection of creditors.[652] *Otto* concludes from a comprehensive literature review that Japan has adapted the US concept of controllership – the scope of duties of management accountants – to their institutional environment. The orientation of the US concept towards financial accounting remained for Japan.[653] One further reason why cost accounting in Japan is closely linked to financial accounting is that the Japanese cost accounting standard is codified and a close relation towards financial accounting – particularly for inventory valuation – is thereby explicitly demanded. In Germany and in the USA, on the contrary, a regulation to link cost accounting to financial accounting does not exist.[654] The Japanese controllership concept therefore shares more similarities with the US financial accounting-oriented concept than with the German one. The duties of management accountants in Japan, similar to their US counterparts, include both the provision of information for internal and external users. Controllership in Japan is therefore defined much broader than in Germany, where management accountants provide information mainly for internal purposes. Management accountants in Japan are even more often responsible for treasury management than their US and German counterparts.[655] Due to the strong organizational link between financial and management accounting in Japan, cost accounting is stronger influenced by the requirements of financial accounting. This makes it more complicated to provide managers with relevant information for decision making.

2.1.1.3.2.3 Education of cost accountants

It is the "most striking feature of accounting education in Japan"[656] that many companies train and educate their employees extensively in-house. Expenditures on education within the company sum up to 3% of total sales in Japan. For Germany it is 2% and in Britain only 0.15%.[657] The high expenses for training can be explained with the specifics of the Japanese culture – in particular long-term orientation, seniority principle, and the consequential need for generally educated staff. As cost accounting is one of the most important instruments of management accounting in Japan,[658] the following descriptions in which

---

652 Due to changes in the funding of companies, the protection of creditors, however, became less important and modifications of the Japanese GAAP towards IFRS have occurred. Cf. *Mizuno* (2004).

653 Cf. *Otto* (2000), p. 282. The German concept on the contrary has developed over time and was subject to hardly any influence from the USA. Cf. *Stoffel* (1995), p. 254.

654 Cf. *Winter* (2005), p. 29.

655 Cf. *Otto* (2000), p. 278-281.

656 *Wijewardena/Cooray* (1995), p. 368.

657 Cf. *Porter* (1990), p. 498. In contrast to these findings and most literature on Japanese management education, *Hiramatsu* examines for corporate accountants that the majority is trained outside the company and only 11.7% of the companies provide education and training programs. Cf. *Hiramatsu* (1992), p. 60.

658 In the 1930s, cost accounting has already been the most important instrument of management accounting besides budgeting. Cf. *Matsumoto* (1953), p. 41-44. This topic also dominates Japa-

manner management accountants are educated and trained also apply to cost accounting. The education of managers and management accountants has hardly changed the last decades.[659]

The education of management accountants starts first off **at university** with more general lectures and by exposing fundamental theory with little respect to practice.[660] About the first third of the studies on accounting is devoted to general education and in the remaining time accounting is taught together with other subjects. The lack of specific and practical knowledge in management accounting is not seen as a disadvantage in Japan, because Japanese companies prefer hiring generally educated employees with promising qualities to provide them with practical training.[661] Japanese companies select students for employment first according to the name of the school, second according to extracurricular activities, and finally according to the student himself. Rarely do they consider for the field of study or the vocational attitude.[662] Accounting education is provided to students also on a postgraduate level. However, due to its highly theoretical and non-practical nature, these students often strive for a teaching career at the university level instead of becoming professional accountants or employees in large companies.[663] Similar to the Anglophone accounting system, graduates from university are with an age of about 22 years on average far younger than their German counterparts. In Japan, education starts off with six years of elementary and three years of junior high schooling. This is followed typically by further three years of high school and four years at university.[664] Besides universities, also professional bodies provide practical and theoretical education in Japan. Compared to similar institutions in the USA, the UK, and Australia, their size in terms of the number of professional accountants is quite small.[665]

After the graduates have obtained a theoretically oriented and rather general education at university, they are further educated **within the company**. This provides them with operational and technical knowledge to be able to cope with daily tasks that are specific to that company. This knowledge facilitates accountants to adapt accounting systems to the competitive environment.[666] In Japan, most employees in an organization are provided with a basic knowledge of accounting through a unique system of in-house education and

---

nese literature in terms of volume. About one third of all papers on management accounting addresses cost accounting and cost management. Cf. *Yoshikawa* (1994a), p. 19.

659 Cf. *Lippert* (2011), p. 32.

660 Cf. *Dubois/Someya* (1977), p. 502.

661 Cf. *Dubois/Someya* (1977), p. 502.

662 Cf. *Takemura/Takamatsu* (1987), p. 207. In Japan a person's future professional position and advancement depends upon her or his educational background. Everyone is therefore anxious to obtain education at a big, prestigious university. Cf. *Takemura/Takamatsu* (1987), p. 203. In a study by *Hiramatsu*, 69.4% of the companies have responded that there is no relationship between accountants and their accounting majors. Hence, 'non-relevant' degrees are very common for accountants in Japan. Cf. *Hiramatsu* (1992), p. 59.

663 Cf. *Wijewardena/Cooray* (1995), p. 368.

664 Cf. *Takemura/Takamatsu* (1987), p. 196.

665 Cf. *Wijewardena/Cooray* (1995), p. 371f.

666 Cf. *Wijewardena/Cooray* (1995), p. 369.

training, whereas the management accounting staff receives a much more comprehensive and advanced program of training in accounting.[667] The objective of this systematic training program is to increase the employees' general awareness of the accounting process, their concern for operations, and their consciousness about costs. In particular for small and medium companies, this training additionally enables management accountants to fulfill their tasks.[668]

Several forms of accounting education exist within Japanese companies. *In-house education and training* usually consists of lectures in cost accounting that last for about one month for new employees irrespective of type of work they perform.[669] For accountants, in-house education and training includes besides lectures also coursework and examinations.[670] *On-the-job training* starts when a new employee joins the accounting department after he has completed the initial training which is provided for all employees. This form of education is the best way for employees to acquire company-specific knowledge and skills on accounting on a case by case basis.[671] *Job rotation* is a system of planned rotation of personal. At the lowest level, accountants are rotated from department to department every five to ten years. Accountants are trained by reshuffling employees to the accounting department. On a higher level they are sent to subsidiaries and associated companies to learn accounting-specific methods of those organizations.[672] These companies thereby follow a rather generalist-oriented policy of accounting with a long range viewpoint instead of employing accounting specialists.[673] On-the-job training and job rotation further enable employees to build up a network of social relationships and thereby facilitate trust and cooperation at work.[674] Finally, employees are widely encouraged in *self-improvement and self-learning*. Some Japanese companies provide text material and correspondence courses, facilitate their employees to participate in classes and seminars outside the company, or to visit university.[675]

The education of cost accountants is far more general than in Western countries. As many Japanese management accountants have worked in other departments before, they can collaborate closer with managers from other functions than their Western counterparts to combine their accounting know-how with operational knowledge. Thereby, the employees can participate in a more cooperative form by assuming responsibility for plural sec-

667 Cf. *Wijewardena/Cooray* (1995), p. 368. However, the empirical study by *Hiramatsu* states that only about half of the Japanese companies provide accounting education for non-accountants. Cf. *Hiramatsu* (1992), p. 62.

668 Cf. *Takemura/Takamatsu* (1987), p. 211.

669 Cf. *Kono/Falkus* (1984), p. 320. Japanese companies regard cost management as crucial for their success and as a responsibility of all employees. Cf. *Howell* (1989).

670 Cf. *Wijewardena/Cooray* (1995), p. 370.

671 Cf. *Takemura/Takamatsu* (1987), p. 213.

672 Cf. *Wijewardena/Cooray* (1995), p. 371, quoting *Yagi* (1990).

673 Cf. *Hiramatsu* (1992), p. 68.

674 Cf. *Vondran* (1985), p. 44; *Esser/Kobayashi* (1994), p. 167. Employees thereby rather feel belonging to the company than to a certain occupational group. Cf. *Petzold et al.* (2005), p. 85.

675 Cf. *Kono/Falkus* (1984), p. 321; *Takemura/Takamatsu* (1987), p. 212f.; *Wijewardena/Cooray* (1995), p. 371.

tions of a production line.[676] The more general education of Japanese cost accountants can be explained by the principles **permanent employment** and **seniority system** as well as by the **Japanese collective culture.**[677]

The Japanese collective culture facilitates cost accountants to design systems that motivate and enable employees to improve operations and products as well as to better align the systems with the company's strategy and managerial needs. Japan is also characterized as a long-term oriented society. In combination with the principles permanent employment and seniority system "the expenditure incurred in training employees is seen as a long-term investment for the company"[678]. Therefore, Japanese companies spent more money on training its employees and it contains forms of education that are more suitable to provide employees with more company-specific knowledge. Besides cultural aspects, also the theory-oriented education at university motivates Japanese companies to train and educate their employees extensively in-house.[679]

German and Japanese specifics in cost accounting are contrasted in the following section to demonstrate that strong differences prevail between both countries.

2.1.1.4 Comparison between Germany and Japan

The history of cost accounting differs between Germany and Japan due to differences in the country-specifics national culture, relationship of cost accounting towards financial and management accounting, and education of cost accountants. The descriptions of the previous two sections are summarized and contrasted between Germany and Japan in the following.

The specifics of German cost accounting **history** are the strong emphasis on accurate and detailed cost information. This emphasis started off with running two separate data bases for financial and management accounting. During National Socialism, cost accounting standards forced German companies to employ comprehensive cost accounting systems. Comprehensive cost accounting systems were developed for short-term decision making in Germany after the Second World War. These systems were adapted, among others, to specific application areas and decision influencing has attracted attention from 1970 onwards. The last decade was characterized by international influences that are likely to reduce the application of imputed costs. Japan has adapted cost accounting instruments from Western countries to its environment and therefore many traditional instruments are very similar to the German ones. The government has strongly promoted Japanese companies to employ more comprehensive cost accounting systems. Over the years, cost ac-

676 Cf. *Nishimura* (2003), p. 61.

677 "In Japan the integrated and cooperative idea and the stratified relationship of cooperation between managers and workers lie at the heart of management. According to this idea, the specialization of management function and division of work develop and change their shapes. Therefore, multi-skilling, personal responsibility for plural sections for a production line, the redeployment, and continuous training play an important part in this cooperative management" (*Nishimura* (2003), p. 60f.).

678 *Wijewardena/Cooray* (1995), p. 368.

679 Cf. *Wijewardena/Cooray* (1995), p. 372f.

counting became more important. Japanese cost accounting systems are installed mainly to support cost management instruments like target costing and kaizen costing with timelier and future-oriented information. During the last decade, performance evaluation, individualized payment systems, and profit centers have increasingly become popular in Japanese companies.

Germany is characterized as an individualistic and uncertainty avoiding **culture**. Due to individualism, e.g., many cost centers are installed in German companies, where managers are responsible for their decisions. With detailed cost information their performance is evaluated in detail to increase the company's operational performance. Due to uncertainty avoidance, much accurate, detailed, and timely information should be provided so that the managers feel comfortable enough to make decisions. However, Japan is also a very uncertainty avoiding society, scoring higher on this dimension than Germany according to *Hofstede*.[680] Therefore, it is assumed that Japan has also a strong emphasis to reduce uncertainty with the help of cost information. Collectivism and long-term orientation have both led to a wide diffusion of permanent employment, seniority principle, and in-house education in Japan. Due to collectivism, cost variances are traced to a lesser degree back to individuals. Instead, Japanese companies try to avoid problems before they occur, e.g., with more future-oriented costs and continuous cost improvements. For this reason, Japanese companies are expected to require less accurate and detailed cost information, but they are also expected to require cost accountants with more operational knowledge of other business functions than accounting. Due to the concept of permanent employment and the seniority principle, cost accountants are educated more generally.

The **relationship of cost accounting towards financial and management accounting** differs between Germany and Japan (see Figure 2-8). In Germany, financial and management accounting have been separated at the beginning of the 20th century. Since then, cost accounting started to serve both managerial and financial accounting purposes. In Japan, cost accounting is linked more strongly to financial accounting than in Germany, because the Japanese cost accounting standard is codified and a close relation towards financial accounting is explicitly demanded. Furthermore, the Japanese have adapted the US concept of controllership that includes many financial accounting tasks.

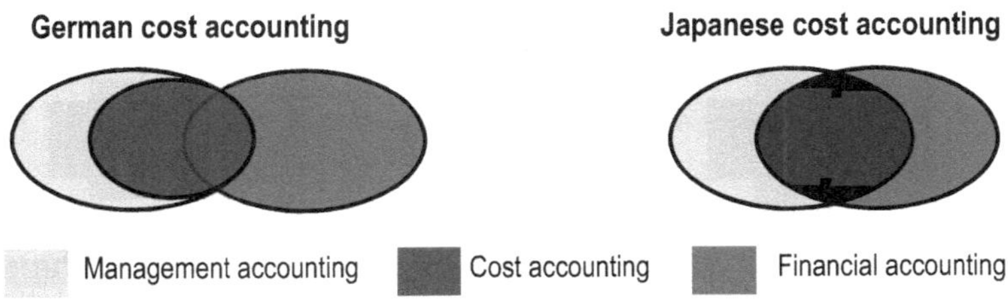

Figure 2-8: Relationships of financial and management accounting towards cost accounting

680 Cf. *Hofstede/Bond* (1988), p. 12.

A strong emphasis on cost and management accounting exists in Germany and Japan, but the way how cost and management accountants are educated differs strongly between both countries. German cost accountants are more theoretically educated and more specialized than their Japanese counterparts. The former mainly study *Betriebswirtschaftslehre* at university with a specialization in management accounting before working. This theoretical **education** provides them with a strong understanding of economic relationships to focus on theoretically sound solutions. In Japan on the contrary, cost accountants are mainly trained within companies through systematic training programs. They learn cost accounting among other functional areas at work to focus on 'practical' solutions and to enable cross-functional collaboration.[681] Education in both countries is also very distinctive from Anglophone countries (see Table 2-2). This demonstrates that Germany should not simply be allocated to Western countries in this respect and it also shows that the results of this study regarding the education of cost accounting can hardly be transferred to Anglophone countries.

	Anglophone countries	Germany	Japan
Course structure and teaching	· Emphasis on financial accounting	· Emphasis on management accounting	· Emphasis on management accounting
Nature of education	· Dominated by professional institutes	· Dominated by universities	· Dominated by companies
Relevance of field of study	· 'Non-relevant' degrees common	· Betriebswirtschaftslehre (business economics/ administration) degree expected	· 'Non-relevant' degrees common
Age of entrants	· Younger management accounting trainees	· Older Betriebswirtschaftslehre graduates	· Younger management accounting trainees
Main point of time of education	· Study management accounting whilst working	· Work after studying management accounting	· Study management accounting among other functional areas whilst working
Understanding of management and cost accounting	· Pick up 'bits of experience'; practice as a personal mobility project	· Understand systematic economic relationships	· Learn management accounting as part of a systematic training program
Attitude towards problem solving	· Focus on 'practical' solutions	· Focus on theoretically sound solutions	· Focus on 'practical' solutions
Characteristics of management and cost accountants	· Emphasis on personal attributes and motivation	· Emphasis on objective expertise	· Emphasis on collaboration

Table 2-2: Education of cost and management accountants in Anglophone countries, Germany, and Japan
Source: extending *Ahrens/Chapman* (1999), p. 43

2.1.1.5 Operationalization and hypotheses development

Cross-national differences in cost accounting can be explained by adopting country-specifics from prior research like the cultural dimensions by *Hofstede* or by **sampling country-specifics in one's own right**. The first problem of applying country-specifics identified by prior research is that they were determined for other purposes than cost ac-

681 For the advantages and disadvantages of general education of management accountants cf. *Lippert* (2011), p. 32.

counting. The centrality of these variables and their impact can vary across countries and across research objectives. The second problem is that the identified country-specifics might be outdated, because societies can converge over time due to internationalization.[682] The third problem is the linear dependence of culture scores for all companies of a country. Therefore, cultural dimensions cannot be included in statistical analysis when only two countries are compared.[683] For all three reasons several country-specifics are self-surveyed in this study:[684] *cultural preferences for cost information, relationship of cost accounting towards financial and management accounting*, and *education of cost accountants.* The cultural dimensions by Hofstede are not applied in statistical analysis, but it is referred to these dimensions in chapter 2 and 3 when hypotheses are set up and empirical findings are discussed. The operationalization of the country-specifics is outlined in the following.

Cultural preferences for cost information

Due to the shortcomings of *Hofstede's* cultural dimensions, preferences for different cost characteristics are surveyed to operationalize culture in a more cost accounting specific way. These country-specifics can be applied in regression analysis, because for each company the preferences for cost characteristics are surveyed. The respondents were asked to assess the extent to which managers require accurate, detailed, timely, and easily comprehensible cost information on a seven-point Likert scale (question A.12, Appendix 2).

Relationship of cost accounting towards financial and management accounting

The relationship of cost accounting towards financial and management accounting is surveyed by asking the respondents which body is responsible for cost accounting (question A.6, Appendix 2). The emphasis on financial and management accounting is surveyed by determining the workload of cost accountants for financial and managerial accounting (question A.9), by asking the respondents to assess on a seven-point Likert scale, whether cost accountants are rather qualified for financial accounting requirements than for management accounting requirements (question A.13, item 4), and by asking the respondents to which extent cost accounting systems are designed for managerial instead for financial accounting purposes (question A.10, item 3). For the workload of cost accountants the relative importance of management accounting compared to financial accounting is determined by dividing the percentage time of management accounting tasks by the percentage time of financial accounting tasks. It is expected that a higher quotient has a positive impact upon the potential to install and run comprehensive cost accounting systems –

682 See section 1.3.1; *Granlund/Lukka* (1998).

683 See footnote 366.

684 Most prior survey research has simply applied the cultural dimensions by *Hofstede* and solely *Krumwiede/Suessmair* have rudimentary surveyed cultural preferences in their survey. Cf. See *Krumwiede/Suessmair* (2007a), (2007b). Hence, the procedure of this study is special and enables to more comprehensively explain differences across countries than prior survey research did.

but at a declining rate. To consider for this non-linearity, all quotients are taken to the binary logarithm.[685]

1) $$x_i = \left(\frac{\text{\% time of management accounting tasks}}{\text{\% time of financial accounting tasks}}\right)$$

Education of cost accountants

The education of cost accounting is compared between Germany and Japan by asking the respondents where cost accountants acquire most of their knowledge from to fulfill their tasks (question A.13). The degree of specialization and the skills of cost accountants are determined by asking the respondents to assess on a seven-point Likert scale whether cost accountants are highly specialized in cost accounting only, whether they are experienced in other business functions other than cost accounting, and whether they are qualified to enhance and run sophisticated cost accounting systems (question A.13, item 1 to 3). The call for further research by *Drury/Tales* to explain the conceptual design of cost accounting systems by surveying the skills of cost accountants is thereby addressed.[686]

Hypotheses development

The operationalization of the country-specifics is necessary to explain cross-national differences in cost accounting. To answer the third research question, an analysis of relationships on an international level is conducted.[687] Cross-national differences in country specifics are contrasted with cross-national differences in cost accounting. The hypotheses to be tested are derived in the following.

Germany and Japan are both uncertainty avoiding societies with Japan scoring higher on this dimension. It is therefore concluded that both countries have a strong emphasis to reduce uncertainty with the help of cost information. The nature of cost information to reduce uncertainty, however, is expected to differ across both countries. German companies are characterized to prefer accurate and detailed in comparison to timely cost information, whereas Japanese companies are expected to favor timely in comparison to accurate and detailed cost information for continuous improvements and to solve problems before they occur. Although there is no empirical prove for these assumptions, previous comparisons with Anglophone countries support Germany's emphasis on detail and precision and Japan's emphasis on timeliness.[688] Consequently, the following hypotheses are

685 The highest and lowest number to be calculated is 6.63 and -6.63 respectively. 6.63 results when cost accountants spend 99% of their time for management accounting and 1% for financial accounting. When cost accountants spend 1% on management accounting and 99% on financial accounting, the number is -6.63. When cost accountants do not spend any time for financial or management accounting, the numbers 7 and -7 are assigned respectively to solve the problem of missing values that occur when dividing by zero.

686 Cf. *Drury/Tayles* (2005), p. 78.

687 See section 1.5.3.

688 In the study by *Krumwiede/Suessmair*, German companies emerged to focus more on management accounting and therefore stress more importance to accuracy and precision, which leads to more complex cost accounting systems compared to their US counterparts. Cf. See *Krumwiede/Suessmair*

derived. This hypothesis is tested by the operationalization of the country-specific 'cultural preferences for cost information'.

H_{1a}:	*German companies have a stronger emphasis on accurate and detailed than on timely cost information.*
H_{1b}:	*Japanese companies have a stronger emphasis on timely than on accurate and detailed cost information.*

The specialization of cost and management accountants varies internationally due to differences in **culture** and **education**. German cost accountants are characterized to be very specialized, to have more theoretical knowledge, and to be more distant from managers. Specialized cost accountants are preferred in Germany to reduce uncertainty. Japanese cost accountants on the contrary are likely more generally educated and they obtain more operational knowledge through, e.g., job rotation. Japanese cost and management accountants are furthermore expected to be more intensively trained in-house. The general education of Japanese employees meets the Japanese collective and long-term oriented culture as well as the practice of permanent employment. Consequently, the following two hypotheses are set up. This hypothesis is verified by the operationalization of the country-specifics 'Relationship of cost accounting towards financial and management accounting' and 'education of cost accountants'.

H_{1c}:	*German cost accountants are more specialized than their Japanese counterparts.*
H_{1d}:	*German cost accountants have more theoretical knowledge than their Japanese counterparts.*

Table 2-3 summarizes the contents of section 2.1.1.5. The country-specifics, their operationalization, and the hypotheses to be tested are compiled.

Country-specifics	**Operationalization**	**Hypotheses**
Cultural preferences for cost information	• Required characteristics of cost information	H_{1a}, H_{1b}
Relationship of cost accounting towards financial and management accounting	• Responsible body for cost accounting • Cost accountants' workload for management and financial accounting tasks • Focus on management accounting • Focus on management accounting education	H_{1c}, H_{1d}
Education of cost accountants	• Cost accountants' sources of knowledge • Degree of functional specialization	

Table 2-3: Overview of country-specifics, their operationalization, and the hypotheses to be tested

(2007a), (2007b). *Yoshikawa et al.* find that Japanese companies revise standard costs twice as frequently as their Scottish counterparts. Cf. *Yoshikawa et al.* (1989), p. 21. *Wijewardena/Zoysa* investigate that Japanese companies use more actual costing than their Australian counterparts. Cf. *Wijewardena/de Zoysa* (1999), p. 65.

2.1.2 Other external context factors

External context factors reflect the company's environment[689] and are outside the company's sphere.[690] Country-specifics also reflect one company's environment, but they are distinguished from other external context factors, because both are derived from different theoretical perspectives.[691] In prior research, several theoretical constructs of external context factors other than country-specifics have been developed.[692]

Many studies point out the importance of **environmental uncertainty.**[693] This theoretical construct is of relevance for information systems for two reasons. First, the demanded information depends upon the decider's perceived uncertainty of the environment. Second, information systems are characterized as mechanisms to overcome a too high degree of uncertainty in decision making.[694] Prior research has determined significant relationships between the perceived environmental uncertainty and **organizational information systems** in general and **management accounting systems** in specific.[695] Respondents have been more satisfied with systems that are broader in scope and provide timelier information in an uncertain environment.[696]

The competitive environment represents a further facet of environmental uncertainty.[697] Wrong decisions, which can result from distorted cost information from inappropriate **cost accounting systems**, are more readily exploited by competitors in a competitive environment. Therefore, more accurate and detailed cost information is then required to

689 The definition of the term 'environment' varies across studies due to differences in research areas and research objectives. An overview is provided by *Dess/Beard* (1984).

690 Cf. footnote 457.

691 See section 1.5.2.

692 An overview is provided by, e.g., *Aust* (1999), p. 102-104; *Frank* (2000), p. 136f.; *Chenhall* (2003), p. 137-141.

693 An overview of the studies is provided by *Chapman* (1997); *Aust* (1999), p. 136f.; *Frank* (2000), p. 103; *Chenhall* (2003), p. 137-139. *Chapman* further stresses the importance of uncertainty upon management accounting systems, "suggesting that accounting might perform a variety of different roles depending on the level of uncertainty" (*Chapman* (1997), p. 201).

694 Cf. *Aust* (1999), p. 136f.

695 Cf. *Gordon/Narayanan* (1984); *Mia/Clarke* (1999), p. 152. *Godron/Miller* further examine that a dynamic environment leads to forecasting difficulties and therefore frequent feedback is required; a hostile environment leads to sophisticated accounting control systems with a high frequency of feedback; and a complex environment leads to multiple focusing by the information system including multiple segment reporting. Cf. *Gordon/Miller* (1976).

696 Cf. *Chenhall/Morris* (1986), p. 27f.; *Gul/Chia* (1994). The usefulness of broad scope information and timely information is related to uncertainty. Cf. *Chenhall* (2003), p. 137, with further references. A positive relationship between environmental uncertainty and the implementation of comprehensive management accounting systems is also supported by literature. Cf. *Drury/Tayles* (2005), p. 79; *Abdel-Kader/Luther* (2008), p. 17.

697 *Khandwalla* also examines in his study a positive association between competition and the use of sophisticated management controls. The more competitive the environment, the more cost information is used. The type of competition the companies face (e.g., price, marketing, and product competition) influences the use of accounting controls. Cf. *Khandwalla* (1972), p. 282.

minimize the level of error.[698] *Rocheleau* states that competition encourages organizations to use IT systems to survive, wherefore organizations are more willing to invest in these resources.[699] A positive relationship between the intensity of a competitive environment and the adoption of complex cost accounting systems respectively ABC is supported by prior research.[700] *Schoute* furthermore shows a positive relationship between perceived uncertainty and the intensity to use cost information.[701]

To select suitable dimensions of environmental uncertainty, the idea of systems theory[702] as a theoretical basis is followed. A system can completely be described with the dimensions **complexity and dynamics**, because systems theory does not allow any further dimension. A system can be characterized with respect to number, dissimilitude, and state's variety of its elements and relationships. The number and dissimilitude of elements as well as their relationships constitute the system's complexity.[703] The variety of system elements and relationships represent a dynamic system.[704] The two environmental dimensions by *Duncan* are distinguished in the following: the simple-complex dimension (*external complexity*) and the static-dynamic dimension (*external dynamics*).[705] Both environmental dimensions are determined by the characteristics of their subsystems.[706] The subsystems 'suppliers' as well as the sales related subsystems 'customers' and 'competitors' are ac-

698 Cf. *Mia/Clarke* (1999), p. 137f.

699 Cf. *Rocheleau* (2006), p. 5.

700 For complex systems see *Al-Omiri/Drury* (2007), p. 415-419. This relationship is not supported by *Drury/Tayles* (2005), p. 72-75. The findings by *Guilding/McManus* suggest that competition intensity is positively associated with a greater incidence of customer accounting practices. Cf. *Guilding/McManus* (2002), p. 56. For ABC see *Anderson* (1995), p. 42; *Bjornenak* (1997), p. 12; *Nguyen/Brooks* (1997), p. 15; *Malmi* (1999), p. 659; *Anderson et al.* (2002), p. 206-209; *Sartorius et al.* (2007), p. 10-12. *Pizzini*, however, does not find significant associations between competition and the characteristics of cost accounting systems' level of detail, classification of cost according to behavior, frequency of cost reporting, and variance analysis. Cf. *Pizzini* (2006), p. 200.

701 Cf. *Schoute* (2009), p. 219f.

702 See *v. Bertalanffy* (1950); *Ulrich* (1970).

703 Cf. *Reiß* (1993), p. 58f.; *Ulrich/Probst* (1995), p. 36-50; *Hamprecht* (1996), p. 59f.; *Aust* (1999), 128f.

704 Cf. *Reiß* (1993), p. 57-59; *Hamprecht* (1996), p. 59f.; *Schreyögg* (2008), p. 260. Both dimensions are differentiated to facilitate their conceptualization and operationalization. Cf. *Frank* (2000), p. 105, with further references.

705 Cf. *Duncan* (1972) and further *Waterhouse/Tiessen* (1978); *Robbins* (1990), p. 218-220. Besides *Duncan's* approach, *Khandwalla* provides a taxonomy of environmental variables including turbulence, hostility, diversity, technical complexity, and restrictiveness and *Ewusi-Mensah* further distinguishes between controllable, partially controllable, and uncontrollable environments. Cf. *Khandwalla* (1977), p. 333-341; *Ewusi-Mensah* (1981) respectively. Environmental uncertainty is mostly operationalized by the respondent's subjective perception. However, few studies have operationalized this construct via objective measurements. For an overview see *Frank* (2000), p. 103.

706 Cf. *Lawrence/Lorsch* (1969), p. 8-10.

counted as relevant for this study.[707] Both dimensions have an impact upon the perceived uncertainty with individuals in dynamic-complex environments facing the highest uncertainty in decision making.[708] The more uncertain the environment is, the more accurate, detailed, and timely information is required for decision making.

External complexity

The simple part of the simple-complex dimension deals with the degree to which elements of the organizational environment are small in number, similar to one another, or not intensive in nature. The complex part indicates that the factors in the organizational environment are large in number or distinctive or intensive in nature.[709] The more complex the environment, the more complex are the company's operations. As cost accounting reproduces the company's reality, the external complexity has an indirect impact upon cost accounting systems. Companies that are collaborating with many suppliers have a more complex procurement and the benefits of many suppliers have to be evaluated. The more divers the customer needs are, the more important it becomes to address a higher number of customer segments individually. The more customer segments are individually addressed, the more time-consuming the analysis of these segments becomes.[710] When a company wants to determine the product costs for each variant that addresses a specific customer segment, the number of cost objects increases as well. Finally, the relevance of information systems increases in a competitive environment with a high number of competitors.[711] Both studies that have investigated the impact of external complexity upon the perceived complexity of cost accounting systems do not support this relationship.[712]

To determine external complexity, the respondents were asked to assess on a seven-point Likert scale the number of suppliers, the number of individually addressed customer segments, and the number of competitors (question A. 11, Appendix 2).

External dynamics

The static-dynamic dimension indicates the degree to which the factors of the organizational environment remain constant over time or are continually under change.[713] Companies operate in a dynamic environment when, e.g., the relationships with suppliers, customer needs, and competitors' actions change frequently.

In a static environment, cost information is valid for a long period, because only few environmental changes lead to modifications in organizational structures, resource consump-

707 Cf. *Flacke* (2006), p. 16. Following *Pugh et al.* (1969), *Amshoff* and *Flacke* determine the company's dependence upon other external organizations, which is one element of uncertainty, by the number of suppliers and customers. Cf. *Amshoff* (1993), p. 401; *Flacke* (2006), p. 159f.

708 Cf. *Duncan* (1972).

709 Cf. *Duncan* (1972), p. 314-316.

710 Cf. *Frank* (2000), p. 118f.

711 Cf. *Mia/Clarke* (1999), p. 137f.; *Frank* (2000), p. 103.

712 Cf. *Aust* (1999), p. 178; *Frank* (2000), p. 131. Instead, the external complexity has an impact upon the internal context of the company and thereby an indirect impact upon cost accounting systems.

713 Cf. *Duncan* (1972), p. 316f.

tion, and the valuation of costs. In a dynamic environment, however, cost information has to be updated frequently, to reproduce the current company's situation. Otherwise, the information is not valid anymore, which could lead to wrong decisions. When cost information has to be updated frequently, cost accounting can become very expensive.[714] As a consequence, more frequent cost updates have to be compensated by a decrease in complexity of cost accounting systems – **a highly dynamic environment and a complex cost accounting system misfit.**[715] The updating of cost information in a dynamic environment should be reduced to a smaller and more aggregated number of, e.g., cost types, cost centers, and products. In a dynamic environment, cost functions can hardly be determined, because processes are not stable over time. It is therefore less adequate to build up knowledge with the help of cost information that has become obsolete.[716] Detailed cost analyses, e.g., at the end of the year, are not necessary, because the reasons for differences between plan and actual incurred can hardly be traced back to inefficiencies, when the assumptions of the budgets are outdated. It might then be too late for managers to revise their actions after having analyzed results from plan and actual.[717] Cost accounting systems should instead update cost information frequently, but focus only on key variables to direct attention to changes in the environment and support the workforce to identify and learn critical factors for success.[718] The major consequences for the operations in a dynamic environment have to be highlighted promptly before the information loses validity. This enables employees to quickly react and to learn, which actions have to be accomplished for ensuring efficient operations. Similarly, companies that are characterized with short life cycles may be more interested in influencing the costs of future products rather than to know current product costs. Cost accounting systems should then be based on principles of learning and motivation and the systems should provide only the most relevant information for cost reduction.[719]

The respondents were asked to assess the stability of their relationships with suppliers, customer needs, and competitor's actions for determining the external dynamics of their companies on a seven-point Likert scale (question A.9, Appendix 2).

2.1.3 Internal context factors

Many different internal context factors have been investigated in prior cost and management accounting research including company size, cost structure, production type, internal complexity, competitive strategy, top management support, type of organization, industry, management and organizational structure, existence of external advisors, and IT

714 Cf. *Weber* (1996), p. 931.

715 Cf. *Aust* (1999), p. 151; *Weber* (2005), p. 35.

716 Empirical evidence shows that decision makers who perceive greater environmental uncertainty "tend to seek external, non-financial and ex ante information in addition to other types of information and increasingly move toward an organic form of organization" (*Gordon/Narayanan* (1984), p. 42). Similar results are provided by *Chenhall/Morris* (1986), p. 27f.

717 Cf. *Koontz/Bradspies* (1972).

718 Cf. *Merchant/Shields* (1993), p. 81. Cf. also *Weber* (2005), p. 33-35.

719 Cf. *Merchant/Shields* (1993), p. 81.

systems. In this study, the factors company size, potential for cost distortion, IT systems, and overall interest in cost accounting are chosen, because these factors have turned out to be of particular relevance in similarly designed studies.[720] The factor industry is also included. It enables to address the fifth research question by investigating whether cost accounting differs more strongly across industries than across countries (see section 1.1.1). The factor 'type of organization' is included to further assess the relative importance of the factors 'nation' and 'industry'.

2.1.3.1 Company size

Company size is one of the most important context factors in management accounting research.[721] Size, however, is not a context factor per se, because several factors are associated with size. Three derivative effects of size that possess a strong correlation to size exert a dominant influence on the design of cost accounting systems.[722] Employees in large companies have for these reasons also higher expectations on cost accounting systems than those in smaller companies.[723]

First, cost accounting systems **reflect the company's reality**.[724] The more products, customers, and organizational units the company has, the more cost objects and cost centers exist.[725] Due to specialization, the complexity of the production program and the production processes furthermore increases with company size. This creates the need to employ more complex cost accounting systems to comprise interrelations between cost centers and the large number of cost objects.

---

720 See, e.g., *Drury/Tayles* (2005); *Drury/Tayles* (2006); *Al-Omiri/Drury* (2007); *Krumwiede et al.* (2007); *Schoute* (2009). Other variables like competitive strategy are inconsistent in their effect on the conceptual design of cost accounting systems and have often not yielded significant results.

721 The importance of size upon organizational structure has early been emphasized by *Blau/Schoenherr* ("size is the most important condition affecting the structure of organizations" (*Blau/Schoenherr* (1971), p. 57)) and *Meyer* ("one cannot underestimate the impact of size on other characteristics of organizations" *Meyer* (1972), p. 440)).

722 Cf. *Frank* (2000), p. 108f.

723 Cf. *Lange/Schauer* (1996), p. 208.

724 Cf. *Krieger* (1995), p. 129; *Frank* (2000), p. 109. When organizations hire more operative employees, they attempt to give them more specialized tasks to increase their productivity. This leads to horizontal differentiation. To coordinate the horizontally differentiated employees, the management has to increase vertical differentiation. It is also likely that an increase in size results in spatial differentiation. Cf. *Robbins* (1990), p. 150; *Kieser/Walgenbach* (2007), p. 318f., 324f. The horizontal and vertical differentiation increases the complexity to manage the organization. The management is soon overburdened, if it has to make all decisions and supervises all employees. Therefore, other instruments to coordinate and to control are required to release the management, like delegation of decision making. Cf. *Robbins* (1990), p. 150; *Bluedorn* (1993), p. 174-178; *Kieser/Walgenbach* (2007), p. 328-330.

725 The constitution of cost centers often follows the area of responsibility, which directly depends on the number of employees. Cf. *Weber/Weißenberger* (2006), p. 364f.; *Schweitzer/Küpper* (2011), p. 125. For empirical evidence see, e.g., *Friedl et al.* (2009a), p. 112f.; *Friedl et al.* (2009b), p. 44.

Second, **larger companies can provide more resources** for cost accounting,[726] which is expected to increase the quality of cost accounting systems. Not before a company exceeds a certain size, institutionalized cost accountants are warrantable.[727] The more cost accountants a company employs, the more comprehensive can the systems be designed. Furthermore, more resources can also be provided to invest in IT-systems, to train the providers and the users of cost information,[728] or to experiment with the introduction of new instruments.[729]

Third, an increase in the number of organizational members leads inevitably to an **increase in communications complexity**, because more communication and more coordination are required for planning and control purposes.[730] Information systems are an integration mechanism to coordinate larger companies, which increase in complexity the more information is required.[731] Transfer prices, e.g., can be based on cost information to coordinate divisional units.[732]

Many studies have investigated the impact of size upon management accounting systems.[733] This relationship was also addressed for cost accounting. The intensity of using cost accounting instruments has been investigated by *Flacke*, *Kosmider*, *Schiller et al.*, and *Legenhausen*. All of them have identified a positive relationship between the intensity of usage and company size.[734] The impact of company size upon the complexity of cost ac-

---

726 Cf. *Krieger* (1995), p. 129; *Frank* (2000), p. 109. Furthermore, *Holmes et al.* conclude from their findings that larger companies having more resources can prepare or acquire more detailed accounting information than smaller ones. Cf. *Holmes et al.* (1991), p. 44f.

727 Whereas in German companies with less than 50 employees 5% employ more than four management accountants, 95% of the companies with more than 5,000 workers employ more than four management accountants. Cf. *Weber et al.* (2006), p. 22. Furthermore, the degree of specialization increases with company size. Cf. *Weber et al.* (2010b), p. 46.

728 Cf. *Krieger* (1995), p. 129; *Frank* (2000), p. 109.

729 Cf. *Chenhall/Langfield-Smith* (1998), p. 13f.; *Frank* (2000), p. 109. In small companies, improvements in cost accounting systems have often to be restricted due to economic reasons; it could even be advantageous to not establish cost accounting in a systematic way. Cf. *Gremillion* (1984), p. 6; *Krieger* (1995), p. 129. Many resources that are provided to improve cost accounting systems lead to an increase in fixed costs in the short-term. As in larger companies the fixed costs can be allocated to a higher number of employees who use cost information, the cost-benefit ratio for investing in cost accounting systems is more advantageous for larger than for smaller companies.

730 Cf. *Lange/Schauer* (1996), p. 208.

731 Cf. *Gremillion* (1984), p. 5f.; *Krieger* (1995), p. 129.

732 Cf. *Anthony/Govindarajan* (2007), p. 230f.

733 *Chenhall* concludes from his review that large companies are associated with "an emphasis on and participation in budgets and sophisticated controls" (*Chenhall* (2003), p. 149). See also *Abdel-Kader/Luther* (2008), p. 19.

734 Cf. *Kosmider* (1994), p. 110-117; *Legenhausen* (1998), p. 68; *Flacke* (2006), p. 259f. *Schiller et al.* have examined 539 companies from Switzerland and show that larger companies more often calculate product costs both at full and at marginal costs. Cf. *Schiller et al.* (2007), p. 304.

counting systems has been investigated in Germany and in the UK.[735] Most studies affirm that company size has a positive effect upon cost accounting complexity.[736] Finally, several studies demonstrate that larger companies tend to adopt ABC more frequently[737] and that small and medium-sized enterprises have difficulties in implementing them.[738]

Large companies have more resources to install more comprehensive cost accounting systems and thereby have a higher potential to satisfy the providers and users of cost information. However, employees in large companies might have higher expectations,[739] because cost accounting systems have to reflect more aspects of the companies' realities and because more coordination and communication is required. It is therefore expected that **company size** has no impact upon the performance of cost accounting systems.[740]

Company size can be defined by the number of employees, sales, total assets, or market capitalization. Prior studies report strong inter-correlations between different indicators for company size.[741] As this study aims to investigate medium-sized companies, the indicator 'market capitalization' would be inappropriate because many of these companies are not listed on the stock exchange. As country-specifics including culture are of predominant interest to explain cross-national differences, more behavioral aspects should be associated to the size indicator. The **number of employees** (full-time equivalents) is expected to have a more culture-specific impact upon the structure of cost accounting systems than the indicators 'total assets' or 'sales': "[S]ince it is people and their interactions that are structured, their number should be more closely associated with structure than with any other size measure."[742] To control for the stability of the findings and for the correctness of the responses, however, also the indicator 'sales turnover' is chosen in this study. The number of employees and sales are taken to the logarithm because previous studies

735 Whereas the studies in the UK define the comprehensiveness of cost accounting by few characteristics, like the number of cost centers (see *Drury/Tayles* (2005); *Drury/Tayles* (2006); *Al-Omiri/Drury* (2007)), the German studies define comprehensiveness regarding the characteristics of cost type, cost center, and product cost accounting (see *Becker* (1984), p. 148-164; *Aust* (1999), p. 166; *Frank* (2000), p. 116f.).

736 Studies that support this relationship include *Becker* (1984), p. 155f.; *Lange/Schauer* (1996); *Aust* (1999), p. 149; *Frank* (2000), p. 122-124; *Hunold* (2003), p. 158; *Drury/Tayles* (2005), p. 74f.; *Kajüter* (2005), p. 88; *Drury/Tayles* (2006), p. 419; *Al-Omiri/Drury* (2007), p. 412-420. Studies that do not support this relationship are *Pizzini* (2006), p. 200; *Lamminmaki* (2008), p. 177.

737 Cf. *Innes/Mitchell* (1995); *Bjornenak* (1997), p. 14; *Nguyen/Brooks* (1997), p. 14f.; *Krumwiede* (1998), p. 253f.; *Innes et al.* (2000), p. 351f.; *Pierce/Brown* (2004). *Gosselin* does not support this relationship. Cf. *Gosselin* (1997), p. 114-116.

738 Cf. *Gunasekaran et al.* (1999); *Gunasekaran/Singh* (1999); *Needy et al.* (2003). For activity-based management see *Wiersema* (1996).

739 Cf. *Lange/Schauer* (1996), p. 208.

740 *Zimmermann*, for instance, does not report a significant relationship between company size of small and medium-sized companies and the performance of management accounting systems. Cf. *Zimmermann* (2001), p. 405-407.

741 Cf. *Child* (1973), p. 170.

742 *Robbins* (1990), p. 151. See also *Child* (1973), p. 170; *Kieser/Walgenbach* (2007), p. 316f. For arguments against this variable see *Robbins* (1990), p. 151.

demonstrate that both size classifications have an impact upon specialization, horizontal and vertical differentiation, and decentralization – but at a declining rate.[743] Thus, the logarithm is used to consider for non-linearity that is associated with large values of both variables.[744] Sales turnover of Japanese companies are converted into € using the conversion rate between Japanese Yen and Euro at 113.16 Yen per Euro, as of January 27th 2011.

2.1.3.2 Potential for cost distortion

Assigning organizational overhead costs as a whole to products (or services) without allocating them to cost centers simplifies cost accounting.[745] It is sufficient for preparing financial accounts or when the company faces very small potential for cost distortion.[746] In companies with a high potential for cost distortion, however, this simplification leads to highly biased cost information. As managers use product costs for decision making,[747] it is necessary to provide them with comprehensive cost information.[748] Potential for cost distortion can be caused by many reasons. The most relevant ones addressed in literature having an impact upon the design of cost accounting systems are *product diversity*, *production process*, and *cost structure*.[749]

Product diversity "relates to the number of different types of products made"[750]. It can lead to a higher potential for cost distortion when products differ in resource consumption. Greater product diversity therefore requires more complex cost accounting systems to capture the products variety in resource consumption.[751] Cost accounting systems more accurately capture the difference in resource consumption when they, e.g., incorporate many cost centers, with each cost center representing a separate activity.[752] Product diver-

---

743 Cf. *Robbins* (1990), p. 152f.

744 Taking the logarithm of company size is very common in research. See, e.g., *Libby/Waterhouse* (1996), p. 141; *Davila* (2005), p. 231f.

745 Cf. *Drury* (2008), p. 51f. Single plant-wide overhead rates are applied by 0 to 30% of the companies across the world. Cf. *Drury/Tayles* (2000), p. 22.

746 Cf. *Brierley et al.* (2006), p. 316; *Drury* (2008), p. 51f.; *Kinney/Raiborn* (2008), p. 71f.

747 In the study by *Brierley et al.*, e.g., 238 out of 243 respondents use product costs in decision making. Cf. *Brierley et al.* (2006), p. 318.

748 Cf. *Park/Kim* (1995); *Charles/Hansen* (2008).

749 *Kinney/Raiborn* similarly identify three significant cost drivers that are traditionally related to variety and complexity of cost accounting: product variety, product complexity, and process complexity. Cf. *Kinney/Raiborn* (2008), p. 112. *Hwang et al.* describe the extent of product cost bias "as a function of the degree of heterogeneity in production technology, the level of unit input costs, and the product mix" (*Hwang et al.* (1993), p. 214). According to *Kumwiede*, potential for cost distortion "relates to diversity in products, support, processes, volume and relative degree of overhead costs" (*Krumwiede* (1998), p. 250). For production related aspects see further *Krieger* (1995), p. 177-211; *Weber* (2005), p. 9-37.

750 *Kinney/Raiborn* (2008), p. 112.

751 Cf. *Drury* (2005), p. 147; *Kinney/Raiborn* (2008), p. 116f.

752 Cf. *Malmi* (1999), p. 659; *Drury/Tayles* (2005), p. 60.

sity includes support, process, and volume diversity.[753] *Support diversity* occurs when products receive different support by various support cost centers, whereas *process diversity* refers to variation in consumption of activities that are related to product design, manufacture, and distribution. *Volume diversity* exists when products are manufactured in different batch sizes. To consider for volume diversity, a comprehensive cost accounting system requires cost centers for batch-level activities and non-volume based cost drivers.[754] Six out of eleven empirical studies support the often presented argument from literature that product diversity is a dominant motivation for implementing comprehensive cost accounting systems.[755] *Schoute* also provides evidence that more cost information is required for decision making the more diverse products are.[756]

The more complex the **production process**, the more complex cost accounting systems should be to model the setting in a more accurate and detailed way.[757] Looking more closely at the *type of manufacturing*, *Reeve* distinguishes between (1) discrete-part and assembly manufacturing and (2) continuous manufacturing.[758] *Reeve* expects ABC to be more suitable in a discrete-part and assembly manufacturing environment and less suitable in a continuous manufacturing environment due to a larger proportion of overhead costs

753 Cf. *Cooper* (1988a); *Estrin et al.* (1994), p. 40f.

754 The resource consumption is thereby measured by batch size rather than by volume. Volume-related cost drivers would undercost low volume products and overcost high volume products. Cf. *Drury/Tayles* (2005), p. 60.

755 *Aust*, *Frank*, *Drury/Tales*, and *Krumwiede/Suessmair* support the impact of product diversity upon the complexity of cost accounting systems. Cf. *Aust* (1999), p. 178; *Frank* (2000), p. 123; *Drury/Tayles* (2005), p. 74-76; *Krumwiede et al.* (2007), p. 32. *Drury/Tales* further find evidence for the relationship between the degree of customization and comprehensiveness of cost accounting. Cf. *Drury/Tayles* (2005), p. 74-76. *Becker* and *Al-Omiri/Drury* do not support this supposed relationship. Cf. *Becker* (1984), p. 150; *Al-Omiri/Drury* (2007), p. 419f. *Krumwiede* and *Malmi* provide evidence that companies with higher product diversity more likely adopt and apply ABC. Cf. *Krumwiede* (1998), p. 252f.; *Malmi* (1999), p. 659. *Bjornenak*, *Nguyen/Brooks*, and *Clarke et al.* do not support this relationship for ABC. Cf. *Bjornenak* (1997), p. 11; *Nguyen/Brooks* (1997), p. 13f.; *Clarke et al.* (1999), p. 452-454.

756 Cf. *Schoute* (2009), p. 219f. Furthermore, product diversity is positively related to ABC adoption and ABC use. Cf. *Schoute* (2011), p. 128-132.

757 Cf. *Malmi* (1999), p. 659; *Weber* (2005), p. 23f. For the impact of the number of production stages upon cost accounting see in particular *Krieger* (1995), p. 208-211. *Schoute* examines a negative relationship between cost system intensity of use and homogeneous mass production processes. Cf. *Schoute* (2009), p. 219. Two empirical studies verify this relationship for the complexity of cost accounting systems. See *Aust* (1999), p. 178; *Frank* (2000), p. 123. Similar to *Aust* and *Frank*, *Nguyen/Brooks* examine that companies having a more complex production are more likely to adopt ABC than their counterparts that have a lower production complexity. Cf. *Nguyen/Brooks* (1997), p. 13.

758 Discrete-part and assembly manufacturing are characterized as convergent manufacturing processes with parts being manufactured into sub-assemblies and then combined to form the finished product. Continuous manufacturing processes are characterized as divergent manufacturing processes with the input being divided into different products by the end of the production process. Hence, the complexity and diversity occurs further on in the manufacturing process.

in the former. Furthermore, in discrete-part and assembly manufacturing the product mainly determines activities and in continuous manufacturing engineering, continuous improvement and maintenance activities are caused by the production process instead.[759] Contrary to his assumptions, three studies identify more companies using ABC in continuous production process manufacturing.[760] The reason for ABC being less likely adopted in discrete-part and assembly manufacturing can be associated with the uncertainties of make-to-order production that hampers handling an ABC system.[761] The production process can further be distinguished regarding its *degree of repetition*.[762] Its frequency and duration significantly influence the efficiency of cost accounting.[763] Whereas in job production in the worst case each product has to be calculated separately, in continuous production in the best case the product costs have to be calculated only once for all products produced. Hence, the higher the degree of repetition, the more economic it is to conduct comprehensive cost accounting analyses.[764] However, more potential for cost distortion prevails for job production due to a higher potential of product diversity. The need for more comprehensive cost accounting systems is therefore stronger for production processes with a lower degree of repetition. Consequently, the relationship between production process and the characteristics of cost accounting systems are controversial. Former studies do not provide evidence for relationships regarding the degree of repetition.[765]

Another important argument for implementing more comprehensive cost accounting systems like ABC is the claimed change in **cost structure** over the last decades.[766] A major concern of these systems is to allocate overhead costs more accurately to cost objects to avoid cost distortion.[767] If overhead costs, however, constitute only a relative small proportion of total costs, it may not be desirable to invest in comprehensive cost accounting systems to allocate overhead costs in a more accurate way.[768] Only one out of five studies finds empirical support for cost structure leading to more comprehensive cost accounting

759 Cf. *Reeve* (1991).

760 Cf. *Krumwiede* (1998), p. 253f.; *Ittner et al.* (2002), p. 723; *Brierley et al.* (2006), p. 318-320. The results by *Brierley et al.* are not significant and "do not support the idea of differences in product costing practice between these two environments" (*Brierley et al.* (2006), p. 320).

761 Cf. *Krumwiede* (1998), p. 250f.; *Ittner et al.* (2002), p. 721.

762 For the degree of repetition of the production process and its impact upon the design of cost accounting systems see *Krieger* (1995), p. 178-183; *Weber* (2005), p. 16.

763 Particularly in Anglophone textbooks, cost accounting systems are often differentiated according to the repetition of the production process. Job costing is recommended for job production and process costing is recommended for continuous production. Cf., e.g., *Drury* (2008); *Kinney/Raiborn* (2008).

764 Cf. *Krieger* (1995), p. 183; *Weber* (2005), p. 16.

765 Cf. *Becker* (1984), p. 150; *Malmi* (1999), p. 659.

766 See *Miller/Vollmann* (1985); *Backhaus/Funke* (1994); *Schumann/Beinhauer* (1994); *Backhaus/Funke* (1996).

767 Cf. *Miller/Vollmann* (1985). As capital-intensive production techniques, e.g., are expected to lead to higher overhead costs (cf. *Sartorius et al.* (2007), p. 3), cost structure is also related to the production type.

768 Cf. *Kaplan/Cooper* (1998); *Brierley* (2008), p. 223.

systems.[769] The poor evidence from previous studies is surprising and contrasts conceptual considerations from literature. *Drury/Tales* conclude that one reason for this might be inappropriate measures for cost structure that previous studies have applied.[770]

Variables for production process and cost structure have resulted in poor empirical verification due to inconsistent relationships towards cost accounting systems and difficulties to measure the construct respectively. Therefore, potential for **cost distortion is defined in terms of product diversity**. This study investigates two manufacturing industries and one service industry. Due to the nature of services, product diversity is not characterized in terms of volume diversity because services are provided individually and not in batches. Therefore, product diversity is only indicated by support and process diversity on a seven-point Likert scale (question A.6, Appendix 2).

2.1.3.3 IT systems quality

Comprehensive cost accounting without an adequate IT system is barely imaginable[771] and IT systems are an important determinant of cost accounting systems.[772] They can influence cost accounting in three different ways.

First, advanced IT systems can run cost accounting systems at **lower costs** compared to less advanced or manual systems.[773] Integrated IT systems facilitate to implement and run cost accounting systems[774] and to track and measure costs by its type and in aggregation.[775] Furthermore, when data from subsystems can be accessed, information has to be updated only in one system whereby duplication of work is avoided. Advanced IT systems also provide data on a real-time basis.[776] The rationalization of data processing therefore enables the companies to implement and run more comprehensive cost accounting sys-

---

769 Only *Bjornenak* supports the relationship. Cf. *Bjornenak* (1997), p. 9f., 13. The following studies do not support this relationship. *Nguyen/Brooks* (1997), p. 12f.; *Clarke et al.* (1999), p. 453f.; *Malmi* (1999), p. 658; *Drury/Tayles* (2005), p. 74-76. Furthermore, *Stoi* reports that cost structure and its consequences constitute motives for implementing ABC. Cf. *Stoi* (1999), p. 152f.

770 Cf. *Drury/Tayles* (2005), p. 76.

771 Cf., e.g., *Dechow et al.* (2007), p. 633. Research further identifies a tendency towards using standard software solutions. Cf. *Friedl et al.* (2009a), (2009b).

772 Cf. *Friedl et al.* (2009b), p. 45. In the recent study by *Friedl et al.*, 58% of the German companies either 'fully' or 'largely' agree "that software was the main determinant in the adoption of their present cost accounting system" (*Friedl et al.* (2009b), p. 45). For the relations between IT systems and management accounting see *Granlund/Mouritsen* (2003); *Chapman* (2005); *Dechow et al.* (2007).

773 A comprehensive description of the development status of data processing systems and their impact upon cost accounting is provided by *Krieger* (1995), p. 124-126. See also *Ambos* (1974), p. 454-460.

774 Cf. *Lackes* (1989), p. 73.

775 Cf. *Krumwiede* (2005), p. 29f.

776 Cf. *Adam/Sammon* (2004), p. 100. 96% of international company managers adopt enterprise resource planning (ERP) due to an increased demand for real-time information. Cf. *Charalambos/Constantinides* (2004), p. 239f.

tems[777] and more complex cost accounting systems.[778] Second, IT systems can also have an impact upon the **structure of cost accounting**[779] and the **roles of cost accountants**[780] as they predetermine data collection and reporting patterns to produce accounting information. Third, *Krumwiede* concludes that **managers might feel reluctant to invest** the necessary resources **in advanced systems** like ABC when they are generally satisfied with the cost information provided by existing IT systems.[781]

The quality of IT systems is surveyed in this study on a seven-point Likert scale. The respondents were asked to assess the following characteristics of their IT systems: cross-functional integration, query capabilities, cost and performance information, and the nature of updates of the information (question A.5, Appendix 2). The call for further research by *Drury/Tales* is addressed by surveying the quality of IT systems to explain the conceptual design of cost accounting systems.[782]

Companies that face high potential for cost distortion might emphasize more advanced IT systems to obtain more comprehensive cost information.[783] The expected relationship between potential for cost distortion and IT systems quality are not supported by prior research.[784] Companies operating in a more complex and dynamic environment might also apply more advanced IT systems to reduce uncertainty, because IT systems quality facilitates to provide accurate, detailed, and timely cost information for decision making.

---

777 Cf. *Lackes* (1990), p. 328. The rationalization is achieved particularly by a better computing power, simpler updating of cost information, and improvements in the work flow. Cf. *Becker* (1984), p. 101; *Schweitzer/Küpper* (1991), p. 457f The form and the quality of data processing influence predominantly the efficiency in determining, presenting, and administrating information. Cf. *Mertens* (1992), p. 1210-1213; *Krieger* (1995), p. 125. *Krumwiede et al.'s* findings indicate that the choice of GPK practices is related to the capability of IT systems. Cf. *Krumwiede et al.* (2007), p. 32.

778 Companies with ERP information systems like SAP more likely use GPK cost accounting systems. Cf. *Krumwiede/Suessmair* (2008), p. 42. Furthermore, *Krumwiede* states that "[m]anagers with higher quality IT may feel better able to implement ABC than companies with less sophisticated IT systems because the costs of measurement are lower" (p. 251) and that "IT may be a critical factor to reach the highest level of ABC implementation. Strong existing information systems facilitate the integration with ABC and provide the needed operational data" (*Krumwiede* (1998), p. 264). Further, *Krumwiede et al.* report a significant relationship between (a) the quality of IT systems and the emphasis of the companies to provide precise information and (b) the number of GPK practices applied. Cf. *Krumwiede et al.* (2007), p. 31f., 43.

779 Increased use of PCs and local-area networks have led to a decentralization of information and data processing. Cf. *Kinney/Raiborn* (2008), p. 722. This can have an impact upon the structural and process organization and thereby indirectly alters cost accounting tasks. Cf. *Krieger* (1995), p. 126, with further references; *Drury* (2005), p. 17.

780 The automatization of routine tasks have facilitated a change in the roles of cost accountants, e.g., from 'bean-counters' to 'business analysts'. Cf. *Granlund/Malmi* (2002); *Drury* (2005), p. 17; *Dechow et al.* (2007), p. 633f., with further references. See also *Picot* (1986).

781 ABC might then not be worth the resource costs. Cf. *Krumwiede* (1998), p. 264.

782 Cf. *Drury/Tayles* (2005), p. 78.

783 Cf. *Krumwiede et al.* (2007), p. 9.

784 Cf. *Krumwiede et al.* (2007), p. 31.

The degree of long-term orientation can have an indirect impact upon cost accounting through IT systems quality. Short-term oriented cultures that emphasize the present might neglect investments in IT systems. Long-term oriented societies on the contrary primarily emphasize to take actions that improve the future of the organization.[785] Furthermore, companies in high uncertainty avoiding countries, e.g., are expected to install more comprehensive IT systems to provide their managers with more relevant information to reduce their inconvenience of decision making. As Japan is characterized as more long-term oriented and as more uncertainty avoiding than Germany, it is expected in the following hypothesis that Japanese companies have more comprehensive IT systems. Besides cultural aspects, however, further influences may explain cross-national differences in IT systems quality.[786]

H_{1e}: *Japanese companies have more comprehensive IT systems than their German counterparts.*

2.1.3.4 Overall interest in cost accounting

In prior research top management support has been identified as an essential prerequisite to implement ABC[787] and GPK[788]. The reason for this is that top management support determines what employees accept and work with. Top management allocates resources to systems that it believes are worthwhile and provides political help to motivate or push individuals and coalitions away who resist changes in cost accounting.[789] It furthermore encourages non-accounting managers to apply cost information.[790] By including top management support as a variable to explain the design of cost accounting systems, the call for further research by *Drury/Tales* is addressed.[791]

Top management support for cost accounting and the number of cost accountants per 100 employees and per € 10 mill. sales turnover are determined to measure the overall interest in cost accounting. Top management support is operationalized by asking the respondents on a seven-point Likert scale to assess to which extent cost accounting receives (1) strong, active support and (2) sufficient resources by top management (question A.10, item 1 and 2). The number of cost accountants is operationalized by asking the respondents how many employees were responsible for cost accounting (full-time equivalents) the last financial year (question A.14, item 2, Appendix 2). Anecdotal evidence indicates that Japanese companies employ more cost accountants than their German coun-

785 Cf. *Hasan/Ditsa* (1999), p. 11-13.

786 Further influences may include cooperation between companies with software consultants. *Krumwiede*, e.g., argues that the stronger German emphasis on comprehensive IT systems compared to US companies can be explained by the companies' closer contact with software consultants. Cf. *Krumwiede* (2005), p. 31.

787 Cf. *Shields* (1995), p. 161-164; *Krumwiede* (1998), p. 259-269; *Anderson/Young* (1999), p. 544-556.

788 Cf. *Krumwiede et al.* (2007), p. 30-32.

789 Cf. *Shields* (1995), p. 150. Top management support is further characterized as critical to implement activity-based management. Cf. *Player/Keys* (1995), p. 5-7.

790 Cf. *Krumwiede et al.* (2007), p. 11.

791 Cf. *Drury/Tayles* (2005), p. 78.

terparts, due to the broader range of responsibilities in Japan.[792] The measures regarding the number of cost accountants might therefore lack functional equivalence.

National culture, the relationship of cost accounting towards financial and management accounting, and education of cost accountants are expected to have a significant impact upon the relevance that is attached to cost accounting. As Germany and Japan are both uncertainty avoiding societies, decision makers in both countries perceive the environment to be highly uncertain. To overcome a too high degree of uncertainty in decision making, comprehensive cost information is required. Hence, top management is expected to be very interested in both countries to provide sufficient resources and political support for cost accounting as well as to employ sufficient cost accountants. Consequently, the following hypothesis is deduced.

H_{1f}: The overall interest in cost accounting is about the same in Germany and in Japan.

2.1.3.5 Industry

Industry is not a context factor per se; it is rather a conglomerate of context factors that is related to industries. When industries are narrowly circumscribed, the effects of many context factors can be analyzed in an aggregated way. However, the individual effects of the industry-related context factors upon cost accounting cannot be investigated, when they are not collected separately. It is suggested that recommendations for practitioners are superior when they are derived for industries separately, because recommendations that are valid for a specific environment might be less suitable in another.[793] Furthermore, the context factor industry is relevant to address the fifth research question (see section 1.1.1): The importance of nation and industry upon cost accounting can be compared and their relative importance can thereby be assessed.

Shields argues that cost information and cost accounting systems are contingent on industry characteristics.[794] This assumption is supported by the majority of prior research that has compared cost accounting across industries.[795] Modern cost accounting systems like GPK and ABC were initially introduced in manufacturing organizations. Thus, mimetic behavior of organizations suggests that manufacturers may have employed more of these

792 Cf. *Otto* (2000), p. 280f.

793 The increase in internal validity, however, is accompanied with a decrease in external validity. Cf., e.g., *Inkpen/Birkenshaw* (1994), p. 205.

794 Cf. *Shields* (1997), p. 6.

795 *Drury/Tales* and *Al-Omiri/Drury* show that the finance sector employs more complex cost accounting systems compared to other industries. Cf. *Drury/Tayles* (2005), p. 74f.; *Al-Omiri/Drury* (2007), p. 413-420. Without providing levels of significance, the study by *Legenhausen* demonstrates that companies that are allocated to the industries trading and manufacturing adopt the most comprehensive cost accounting instruments and companies of the building industry adopt the least comprehensive ones. Cf. *Legenhausen* (1998), p. 87. Other studies report cross-industry differences without further specifying. Cf. *Kosmider* (1994), p. 143-155; *Frank/Reitmeyer* (1999). *Becker* on the contrary does not demonstrate differences across a broader set of industries. Cf. *Becker* (1984), p. 149f.

systems.[796] Industry as an internal context factor is relevant for this study to answer the second research question, whether cost accounting differs more strongly across countries than across industries. Thereby the importance of nation as an influence factor can be assessed.[797]

2.1.3.6 Type of organization

The argument by *Shields*[798] that cost information and cost accounting systems are contingent on industry characteristics is transferred in this study to the type of organization. It is expected that cost accounting objectives and systems differ between private, public, and charitable organizations. Besides comparing cross-national with cross-industry differences in cost accounting, the relative importance of nation as an influence factor can further be assessed by contrasting differences between countries with differences across types of organizations.

The 'public-private difference' research stream started with the analysis of organizational differences found in the USA and their roles in the US society. These studies often conclude that different demand placed on public, private, and third sector organizations influences systems in these organizations.[799] For this reason the public-private distinction has obtained "a significant area of organizational research that needs further analysis"[800] and it may cause a stronger influence on cost accounting than country-specifics, like national culture. For this reason, three different types of organizations – **private, public, and charitable** – are compared. This distinction is limited to hospitals only, because, unlike in the other investigated industries, sufficient organizations of the three different types prevail.

It is expected that the type of an organization influences the organization's objectives and thereby the design of the systems. These differences stem from different roles that private, public, and charitable organizations play in a society.[801] Organizations of the private sector sell products and services mainly to create shareholder value.[802] Public organizations on the contrary are run by (usually local) government to ensure that, e.g., the health care in the local area is conform to the council's guidelines. Charitable organizations are a type of non-profit organizations and usually serve a public interest. Due to these different backgrounds, managers underlie different expectations. They address these expectations by setting **different objectives** and by installing and applying **different systems**. Consequently, the cost accounting objectives followed, the systems applied, and decisions made may be influenced by these diverse roles.

---

796 Cf. *Al-Omiri/Drury* (2007), p. 408f. For mimetic behavior of organizations see section 1.3.5 (new institutionalism).

797 This is necessary, because the importance of nation as an influence factor has been questioned in literature. Cf. *Shields* (1998), p. 512.

798 Cf. *Shields* (1997), p. 6.

799 Cf. *Nutt* (2000), p. 78, with further references.

800 *Perry/Rainey* (1988), p. 198.

801 Cf. *Rainey et al.* (1976); *Ring/Perry* (1985).

802 The relevance to create shareholder value, however, varies internationally. Cf. *Yoshimori* (1995).

Private organizations, e.g., are expected to rate financial objectives (e.g., profit) higher than public and charitable organizations that rather follow factual objectives (e.g., good patient care). The **pressure to cut costs** might therefore be stronger in private organizations that lead to more comprehensive cost saving-instruments like cost accounting.[803] As for cost and management accounting in public and charitable organizations only very little empirical evidence exists,[804] this assumption requires empirical verification by this study. The results can further indicate, to which extent empirical evidence from prior research on private organizations can be transferred to public and charitable organizations.

This section demonstrates that cost accounting objectives are likely to differ across different types of organizations. Also across countries and industries strong differences in cost accounting objectives are expected. It is important to compare cost accounting objectives across countries, industries, and types of organizations, because cost accounting systems should purposefully be designed to meet their objectives. Hence, it is necessary to investigate cost accounting objectives, because differences in cost accounting objectives are expected to lead to differences in cost accounting systems.

2.2 Cost accounting objectives

Cost accounting objectives are subordinate to the business objectives. The former are deduced in this study from the overriding business objectives because functional relationships between both are presupposed.[805] They constitute aspired affects that should be accomplished. Hence, cost accounting systems should be shaped accordingly to meet the cost accounting objectives.

Hardly any research has empirically investigated the relationship between objectives and the characteristics of management or cost accounting systems. Only two studies have addressed this issue for the complexity of cost accounting systems. However, they have either narrowed their investigation to profitability analysis[806] or to the distinction between cost system usage for cost management purposes and product planning purposes only.[807] Little knowledge of the relationship between objectives and the conceptual design of cost accounting systems therefore exists. Furthermore, no study has addressed this issue on an international basis yet. This, however, is a valuable endeavor, because it is likely that not

803 Cf. *Rainey et al.* (1976), 235f.

804 Cf. *Hunold* (2003), p. 108. The three types of organizations are for the first time comprehensively compared in management accounting research by this study. For an overview of empirical studies comparing public and private organizations in management research see *Rainey/Bozeman* (2000).

805 Cf. *Welge* (1988), p. 45-47.

806 Cf. *Drury/Tayles* (2006). They investigate that „the separate reporting of cause-and-effect indirect costs within the profitability analysis was higher in larger organizations and those that have implemented more complex costing systems. Additionally, the profit measures which involved the assignment of indirect costs were ranked most important by those organizations with higher levels of cost system sophistication or complexity" (*Drury/Tayles* (2006), p. 422).

807 Cf. *Schoute* (2009). Both objectives are determined by factor analysis, which do not meet by far the quality criteria that are applied in this study. The author demonstrates significant relationships between the complexity of cost accounting systems and both objectives.

only the conceptual design of cost accounting systems, but also cost accounting objectives differ internationally: The emphases of the overriding business objectives vary between Germany and Japan. Japanese companies follow an employee-centered and stakeholder-oriented perspective. The German counterparts often follow a stakeholder-oriented perspective as well, but they are significantly more oriented towards shareholder value.[808] Due to these differences and due to the country-specifics described in section 2.1.1, it is likely that the relevance and characteristics of the cost accounting objectives likewise differ between Germany and Japan – although cost accounting generally serves the same objectives internationally. It provides individuals or entities external to the organization with information through financial accounting reports and provides internal users with information for decision making. Hence, the **same cost accounting objectives prevail in both countries** (and are thus conceptually equivalent to a large extent) – **but they are likely to differ in relevance.**

In section 2.2.1 the information that cost accounting provides for individuals or entities external to the organization is outlined and the information provided for internal users is deduced in section 2.2.2.

2.2.1 Providing information for compiling financial reports

Financial accounting is governed by both local as well as international **financial accounting standards.** A key piece of information that is provided by cost accounting for financial accounting is **inventory valuation.** To meet the requirements for compiling financial reports, it is not necessary to update cost information during the reporting period or to generate accurate and detailed cost information. For management accounting purposes, however, timelier, more accurate, and more detailed cost information can improve decision making. German GAAP, Japanese GAAP, IFRS, etc. might differ in their requirements for cost accounting, e.g., whether inventory has to be recognized on a variable or full cost basis. Therefore, and to measure global pressures stemming from the harmonization of financial reporting standards, respondents were asked under which financial reporting system they prepare their individual and consolidated financial statements (question A.3, Appendix 2). The extent to which cost accounting is pursued to support the indicator '**inventory valuation**' is measured on a seven-point Likert scale (question B.3, item 5) to investigate the relevance of cost accounting for financial accounting.

In Japan the **Japanese cost accounting standard** is treated as a principle of proper accounting with written and quasi compulsory methods of cost accounting. It demands a close relationship between cost accounting and financial accounting.[809] German companies on the other side are not forced to apply a cost accounting standard that demands a close relationship of cost accounting towards financial accounting. Furthermore, German companies have already decided in the beginning of the 20th century to run financial and

808 Cf. *Yoshimori* (1995), p. 33-35. Unlike Germany, Japan clearly puts the interests of employees before that of shareholders. Cf. *Yoshimori* (1995), p. 33. The stakeholder concept is specific to Japan due to the principles of permanent employment and long-term trading relations with other stakeholders. This is in contrast to the shareholder-orientation of Anglophone countries.

809 Cf. *Winter* (2005), p. 29.

cost accounting systems independently (see section 2.1.1.2.1). Due to the Japanese cost accounting standard and the long traditions in Germany to separate financial and cost accounting systems, it is expected that cost accounting is stronger linked to financial accounting in Japan than in Germany. Consequently the following hypothesis is set up.

H_{1g}: Japanese companies pursue cost accounting for inventory valuation more intensively than their German counterparts.

2.2.2 Providing information for managerial use

The **management process of decision making** is separated into five sub-processes to derive different cost accounting objectives for managerial use (see Figure 2-9).[810] The management process starts with a goal or a set of goals of an organization. *Goal setting* is of strategic relevance and it is usually carried through by top management. Each decision maker has to know his role so that he can act in the organization's interests.[811] Plans for managers and employees are therefore derived from the organizational goal(s) to show them, how they can contribute to the overall performance of the company. The tasks of each manager and employee are thereby assigned to the company's goals. By preparing organizational plans, the basis for control is established – the last step of the management process. *Planning* includes only which targets the individual manager and employee has to achieve – it does not include how they have to achieve their targets. In the next step (*governance*), guidelines are induced. Managers can use information for facilitating their own decisions (*decision facilitating*) or for influencing the decisions of their subordinates (*decision influencing*). At the end of the period, the *execution* of tasks and the performance of individuals or groups are controlled by comparing actual versus planned outcomes. *Control* is often combined with rewards in Western countries to motivate employees. Controlling can furthermore provide managers and employees with feedback how to improve. To implement the management process of decision making, cost information is required for each sub-process.

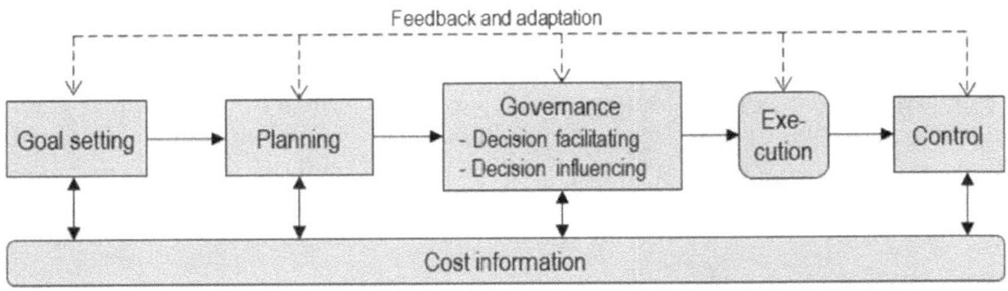

Figure 2-9: The management process
Source: following *Schweitzer/Küpper* (2011), p. 4

810 For the management process see *Fox* (1963), p. 3f.; *Schweitzer/Küpper* (2011), p. 2-7. This process extents the management process by *Fox*, who distinguishes between three sub-processes that are planning, organizing (the actual work of carrying out the planned activities), and controlling.

811 Cf. *Caplan* (1973), p. 23.

In this study it is furthermore distinguished between operational and strategic decision making, because both objectives require different cost information. Goal setting is thereby allocated to strategic decision making. Antipodes (planning versus control, facilitating versus influencing decisions, and supporting operational versus strategic decisions) are defined to better highlight the context dependence of cost accounting systems and expected cross-national differences. The objectives decision facilitating and decision influencing, for instance, require a different, oppositional conceptual design of cost accounting systems and they are expected to strongly differ in their relevance cross-nationally. The antipodes, their required conceptual designs of cost accounting systems, and their relevance in Germany and Japan are described in the following sections. A beneficial side effect of defining antipodes is that differences in response style between German and Japanese respondents are cancelled out, when the score for, e.g., decision facilitating is divided by decision influencing.[812]

2.2.2.1 Planning and control

The cost accounting objective **planning** encompasses the prediction of costs that occur for the production of goods in the future. It serves on the one hand as a basis for decision making, to demonstrate the consequences of alternative courses of action. On the other hand, it provides default values for cost control. **Control** should be designed to assist, guide, and motive managers and employees to act according to the overall organizational goal(s). As cost control might have a different psychological meaning or significance to the individuals involved (e.g., guidance, help, criticism) and is thereby charged emotionally,[813] significant cross-national differences in the relevance of cost control are expected.[814] Cost accounting for cost control provides information for measuring on-the-job performance, whether the planned costs have been exceeded or undercut. Furthermore, detailed cost variance analyses can show the reasons for differences between plan and actual. For instance, variances can occur due to external factors, like an increase in the market prices of pre-products, or due to inefficiencies in the execution of the tasks. Knowing whether costs are controllable is relevant for decision facilitating and decision influencing.[815]

As described in sections 2.1.1.2.2.1 and 2.1.1.3.2.1, particularly planning and controlling is expected to differ between **Germany and Japan**, with German companies putting more emphasis on cost control and Japanese companies focusing more on planning. In Germany controlling and rewarding is an important element to motivate employees to conduct their tasks efficiently. This motivating effect is necessary, because in individualistic countries like Germany the employees are less culturally encouraged to act in the company's

812 The respondents in Germany and Japan likely differ in response style. Whereas the Japanese are expected to choose the median value on questionnaire scales (middle response style), the German respondents are expected to answer the questions with more enthusiasm leading to a higher standard deviation (extreme response style). Cf. section 1.2.6. Differences in response style between countries are cancelled out, because respondents' specific response styles are present in both scores that are divided.

813 Cf. *Tannenbaum* (1962), p. 240.

814 Cf. *Riahi-Belkaoui* (2002), p. 48f.

815 Cf. *Schweitzer/Küpper* (2011), p. 34.

interests compared to collective societies like Japan. In Japan on the contrary feedforward control is often applied to avoid mistakes in advance.[816] Furthermore, less cost control is required in Japan, because performance evaluation of the staff is – with declining tendency though –[817] circumstantial due to the seniority system. Based on these assumptions, the following hypothesis is deduced.

H_{1h}: Whereas German companies place more emphasis on control, Japanese companies put more emphasis on planning.

2.2.2.2 Facilitating and influencing decisions

A comprehensive cost accounting system should provide relevant information. However, systems can fail when they are designed only from a technical point of view and not from a behavioral one: They can fail when they are not accepted by managers and employees or when they do not enable and encourage them to choose and implement organizationally desired courses of action. The governance of decision making is concerned with the influencing of behavior to a large extent. Consequently, it is suggested that the **two main principal purposes of cost accounting** are to provide managers and employees with the information they require to make decisions that are in the organization's interest (decision facilitating) and also to motivate subordinates to actually make the desired decisions (decision influencing).[818]

Cost accounting is according to **decision facilitating** an instrument that provides managers with information for decision making. Conflicts of aims within an organization are not accounted for. Accurate, detailed, and timely information provides a solid information basis and thus always leads to better decisions and are always superior – provided that information costs are disregarded. **Decision influencing** on the contrary considers for principal-agent relations within an organization, where decisions of subordinates (agents) are influenced by the supervisor (principal). This multiple person context can entail conflicts of aims. When information asymmetries between agents and principals additionally exist, more accurate, detailed, and timely information can lead to inferior decisions – even when information costs are disregarded. The subordinates can take advantage of their specific knowledge to act in their own instead of the company's interests. For decision influencing it is therefore very important that cost accounting systems align the aims of the supervisors and the subordinates. Goal congruence is ensured by control-

816 The study by *Hawkins* shows that US companies rank responsibility accounting higher and emphasize more to use accounting data for evaluating the performance of individual managers than their Japanese counterparts. Cf. *Hawkins* (1983), p. 154f.

817 For the increasing relevance of performance evaluation see sections 2.1.1.3.1 and 2.1.1.3.2.1.

818 Cf. *Caplan* (1973), p. 23. For the distinction between decision facilitating and decision influencing see *Demski/Feltham* (1976), p. 79-81, 84-86; *Wagenhofer* (1993); *Ewert/Wagenhofer* (2008), p. 6-10. Prior research has hardly investigated the impact of decision influencing on the design of cost accounting systems – although strong differences to decision facilitating are expected. For the expected impact of decision influencing on cost accounting see *Merchant/Shields* (1993). By investigating decision influencing the call for future research by *Schoute* is addressed. Cf. *Schoute* (2009), p. 222.

ling for the performance of individuals and by rewarding them,[819] when their actions are in the company's interests. Cost targets influence behavior because the employees have to direct their actions accordingly. Control information influences behavior as well because controls motivate employees to act according to the company's interests and to learn from mistakes to meet the cost targets in future. It is furthermore necessary to reduce information asymmetries, e.g., through IT systems that provide user-friendly query capabilities as well as comprehensive cost and performance data on a real-time basis. As decision making is contingent on the perception of information, goal congruence can further be ensured by providing the subordinates with selective cost information.[820] More accurate, detailed, and timely information can also harm decision facilitating, because a detailed cost accounting system might be "too complex to direct attention to the most important determinants of performance because it provides so many signals"[821]. For decision influencing, cost accounting systems have therefore to provide plain information.[822] To enhance the awareness, thinking, and comprehension of the operative company's situation, cost information should instead be updated more frequently. Timely information enables quick learning and the consequences of decisions can rather be identified, when the feedback information is provided promptly.

Compared to Western countries, a collective **culture** prevails in Asia.[823] Therefore, in particular Japanese companies focus more on behavioral control and motivating employees to reduce costs than on cost control to avoid tracing inefficiencies back to individuals.[824] Japanese companies comprehensively **educate** their employees to be aware about costs and benefits and to raise their concern for company operations. This enhances the awareness, thinking, and comprehension of the situation the employees are confronted with to facilitate cost and process improvements. To exploit this potential and to meet cultural-specifics, Japanese companies are expected to put more emphasis on decision influencing than their German counterparts. German companies on the contrary have likely a stronger emphasis on decision facilitating than their Japanese counterparts because a more individualistic culture prevails in Germany and the German employees are more specialized in a narrow area of responsibility. Empirical evidence for differences in the objectives of cost accounting between Germany and Japan does not exist. However, prior research indicates that Japanese companies put more emphasis on providing cost information for behavioral control than for cost control compared to their Anglophone counterparts.[825] The following hypotheses are consequently derived.

819 Incentives like bonuses enforce a target-oriented behavior. Cf. *Schweitzer/Küpper* (2011), p. 33.

820 Cf. *Ewert/Wagenhofer* (2008), p. 10.

821 *Merchant/Shields* (1993), p. 81.

822 Cf. *Weber* (2011), p. 36.

823 Cf. *Hofstede/Bond* (1988), p. 12f. Particularly the Japanese culture is characterized in literature by a horizontal relationship and mutual trust between managers and workers. Cf. *Nishimura* (2003), p. 59f.

824 Cf. *Hiromoto* (1988); *Yoshikawa* (1994b), p. 281.

825 See section 1.4.3.2.

> *H_{1i}: German companies place more emphasis on cost information for decision facilitating than their Japanese counterparts.*
>
> *H_{1j}: Japanese companies place more emphasis on cost information for decision influencing than their German counterparts.*

2.2.2.3 Supporting short-term and long-term decisions

The management process further varies between short-term (operational) and long-term (strategic) decision making. Whereas operational decision making has short-term implications upon the performance of the organization, strategic decision making has long-term implications upon the potential for future performance (see Table 2-4). Cost accounting has consequently to provide different information for short-term and for long-term decision making.[826]

Level of decision making	Operational	Strategic
Time-frame	Short-term implications	Long-term implications
Target variable of the company	Performance	Performance potential
Target variable for cost accounting	Accurate and detailed determination of costs	Influence costs proactively

Table 2-4: Characteristics of operational and strategic decision making
Source: following *Hoitsch/Lingnau* (2007), p. 236

Cost accounting for **short-term decisions** has to provide cost information for operational purposes. It requires short-term reporting periods to identify inefficiencies for expeditiously improving operating efficiency. The set of goals of an organization changes only in the long-run and it should not be based on short-term reporting periods, because "[d]ecisions regarding product design, introduction, abandonment, and pricing are strategic matters that should not be based on short-run fluctuations of manufacturing efficiencies."[827] The purpose of cost accounting for short-term decisions is therefore not to support goal setting. The purpose of short-term cost accounting is instead to support decision facilitating and influencing as well as planning and control. To support short-term decision facilitating and influencing, a strong emphasis on *operational planning* and control is required. For short-term decision facilitating, the capacities are given and therefore the main objective is to ensure high *capacity utilization*. For *pricing decisions*, whether an additional order should be accepted or rejected, only the variable costs are relevant because the fixed costs of capacity can only be influenced in the long-run. Fixed costs cannot be influenced in the short-term and are therefore irrelevant for operational decisions. For this reason, it is necessary to differentiate between variable and fixed costs. Short-term decision influencing includes motivating employees to *carry out operational tasks efficiently* and to *make cost savings* by proactively resolving problems before they occur. The last step of the management process for operational decision making comprises *cost control*, which often includes *trac-*

826 *Kaplan* even states that for operational control and for strategic profitability analysis two separate cost accounting systems are required. Cf. *Kaplan* (1988).

827 *Kaplan/Johnson* (1991), p. 398.

ing (in)efficiencies back to persons in charge to enable responsibility accounting (see Table 2-5).

Strategy is defined as "the determination of the basic long-term goals and objectives of an enterprise, and the adoption of courses of action and the allocation of resources necessary for carrying out these goals."[828] Hence, for **long-term decisions** cost accounting has to provide information for the whole management process.[829] Regarding goal setting, cost accounting can be applied to support *strategy development* and to define the organizational goal(s).[830] The company's future potential is based on advantages in differentiation and in costs. Cost information is relevant for both generic strategies. The more companies try to base their advantages on costs, the more important it becomes to *exploit the cost reduction potential* to improve the cost level (cost management).[831] Long-term plans (*strategic planning*) have to be derived from the organizational goal(s). Investments are often required to reach these long-term plans to build up advantages in differentiation or in costs. As decision facilitating for long-term decisions serves like goal setting to derive a competitive strategy, both include similar indicators. For reasons of simplification and to keep the questionnaire short, the same indicators are allocated to goal setting and to decision facilitating for long-term decisions. For influencing decisions that are strategic in nature, cost accounting provides information for implementing competitive strategies and to ensure that the employees *act according to the company's strategy*. Strategic control can be both reactive and pro-active in nature. Proactive controls include early indicators, e.g., cost drivers. Hence, rather cost management than cost accounting is suitable for pro-active strategic control. Value-based performance indicators like Economic Value Added (EVA) are frequently applied in practice to conduct reactive controls. Cost accounting is less

828 *Chandler* (1962), p. 13.

829 *Lord* similarly distinguishes different roles for strategic management accounting. According to these roles strategic management accounting systems should (1) provide a collection of competitor information, (2) support exploiting cost reduction opportunities, and (3) matching the company's accounting emphasis with its strategic position. Cf. *Lord* (1996), p. 354f. As cost accounting only provides cost information about the own company and not about its competitors, the first characteristic is not adequate for this investigation. The other two characteristics, however, are suitable for cost accounting as well and are thus adapted.

830 The application of cost information for the instruments target costing and kaizen costing demonstrates the strategic relevance that cost accounting can have. Cost benchmarks with competitors can further help to develop an organizational strategy and its goals. See, e.g., *Kreuz* (2002).

831 Companies that follow the cost leadership strategy shall more intensively manage their cost structure and cost behavior to obtain a cost advantage. Companies that follow the differentiation strategy also require cost information, because managers need to know how product features drive costs. When costs for a product feature are higher than its value to the customer, it should not be offered. To ensure the long-term competitiveness of the company, potential for cost improvements have to be identified and measures have to be planned accordingly – regardless of the company's competitive strategy. Some researchers argue that companies that follow a cost leadership strategy require a more comprehensive cost accounting system than those that follow a differentiation strategy. However, the arguments for and against this assumption, like the results of empirical investigations, are controversial. For an overview see *Aust* (1999), p. 152-154; *Frank* (2000), p. 198-214.

suitable for conducting periodical, reactive control, because, e.g., conducting cost benchmarking is far more complex than applying already existing information from the financial statements like value-based performance indicators.[832] Overall, cost accounting is of minor relevance for strategic control. For this reason no indicators for strategic cost control are investigated in this study.

The cost accounting objectives and its indicators investigated in this study are shown in Table 2-5. Respondents were asked to assess on a seven-point Likert scale to which extent they follow the indicators of the cost accounting objectives (question B.1 to B.3, Appendix 2).

	Short-term	**Long-term**
Goal setting		· Strategy development · Exploiting cost reduction potential
Planning	· Operational planning	· Strategic planning
Decision facilitating	· Short-term capacity planning · Pricing	· Strategy development · Exploiting cost reduction potential
Decision influencing	· Carry out operational tasks efficiently · Make cost savings	· Act according to the business strategy
Control	· Cost control · Trace (in)efficiencies back to persons in charge	

Table 2-5: Systematization of the indicators for cost accounting objectives

As described in section 2.1.1.2.2, in Germany cost accounting is mainly applied to improve operational efficiency. To motivate employees to increase operating efficiency, responsibility accounting is widespread in Germany. German companies therefore follow a rather short-term orientation on cost accounting and focus more on decision facilitating than on decision influencing. This is supported by prior empirical research.[833] On the other hand, in Japan as a long-term oriented society, cost improvements are often part of the company's strategy to influence the cost level and the cost structure to obtain competitive advantage.[834] Typical Japanese instruments like target costing and kaizen costing that apply cost information support this objective both in the product development and production stage. Consequently, the following hypotheses are derived.

H_{1k}: German companies apply cost accounting more intensively for short-term objectives than their Japanese counterparts.

H_{1l}: Japanese companies apply cost accounting more intensively for long-term objectives than their German counterparts.

---

832 For reactive and pro-active strategic control see *Finlay* (2000), p. 430-463.

833 Cf., e.g., *Weber* (1993), p. 259-262, 266f.; *Lange/Schauer* (1996), p. 204; *Friedl et al.* (2009b), p. 41.

834 See *Ferrara* (1990). Cf. also section 2.1.1.3.1.

Similarly to the assumptions by *Shields* that cost accounting systems differ more strongly across industries than across nations,[835] cost accounting objectives are expected to differ more strongly across industries than across nations. To identify the relative importance of nation and industry upon cost accounting objectives, the following two hypotheses are derived.

H_{3a}:	*Cost accounting objectives differ across industries.*
H_{6a}:	*Cost accounting objectives differ more strongly across industries than across countries.*

The business objectives differ between different types of organizations. Private organizations, e.g., are expected rate financial objectives higher than public and charitable organizations.[836] Private organizations might therefore pursue those cost accounting objectives more intensively that address **cutting costs.** It is consequently expected that private, public, and charitable organizations follow cost accounting objectives to different degrees.

To meet the cost accounting objectives, purposefully designed cost accounting systems are required. The conceptual design of cost accounting systems and its relationship towards cost accounting objectives is, among others, described in the following section.

2.3 Design of cost accounting systems

2.3.1 Preliminary considerations

2.3.1.1 Working definition of the cost accounting system

A system can be defined as a set of interacting elements.[837] This definition serves like in previous studies[838] to define relevant elements for this study. Cost accounting systems are characterized in this study by the **dimensions** *complexity* and *timeliness.*[839] The more complex the system is, the higher the potential to provide more accurate and detailed information[840] and timelier information can be prepared by timelier systems.[841] Both dimen-

835 Cf. *Shields* (1998), p. 512.

836 See section 2.1.3.6.

837 Cf. *v. Bertalanffy* (1950), p. 143; *Flechtner* (1966), p. 353; *Ulrich* (1970), p. 105.

838 See, e.g., *Kajüter* (2000), p. 57; *Kajüter* (2005), 81f.; *Blum* (2006), p. 47; *Esser* (2011), p. 75f.

839 This study does not follow the proceeding by *Aust* and *Frank* to characterize cost accounting systems by complexity and dynamics. Cf. *Aust* (1999), p. 128f.; *Frank* (2000), p. 113f. The system can thereby not be completely described in this study, because the dimension 'timeliness' does not include structural changes of the system over time. Cf. *Reiß* (1993), p. 58f.; *Ulrich/Probst* (1995), p. 36-50; *Hamprecht* (1996), p. 59f.; *Aust* (1999), p. 128f. In German literature, cost accounting systems are frequently systematized by two further dimensions. The first dimension differentiates between full and variable costing. The other dimension refers to the time reference of costs distinguishing between actual, normal, and planned costs. Cf. section 1.1.4.2. The alternative systematizations, however, are less suitable for the purpose of this study to draw relationships between context factors, cost accounting objectives, and cost accounting systems.

840 Cf. *Cooper* (1991), p. 147.

sions are thus relevant to determine the potential of cost accounting systems to provide comprehensive information in terms of accuracy, detail, and timeliness. Complex and timely cost accounting systems, however, lead to higher costs. The management is therefore forced to choose between cost accounting systems that provide accurate, detailed, and timely information and those providing less perfect information.[842] As cost-benefit considerations of cost accounting are expected to vary internationally,[843] cross-national differences on both dimensions are expected.

Subsystems are specified to characterize cost accounting systems in more depth to reduce the degree of abstraction. The **subsystems** cost type accounting, cost center accounting, and product cost accounting are chosen, which are geared to the flow of costs starting off with the procurement of resources, followed by the production, and the sales of products:

- With *cost type accounting* the question is answered, which type of costs has occurred in which amount. All costs are collected and structured in accordance to their specific type. They can be classified according to their consumption and their cost behavior.
- *Cost center accounting* answers the question, where costs have occurred in which amount. The purpose of cost center accounting is to provide information for determining the efficiency of operations. It further serves to allocate overhead costs as precisely as possible to cost objects.
- *Product cost accounting* answers the question, wherefore costs have occurred. Whereas product costing (also known as cost unit accounting) calculates the costs per product unit, the operating income statement determines the profit or loss of an organization on an annual basis or for a period of less than a year. Contribution margin accounting furthermore identifies the roots of financial success.

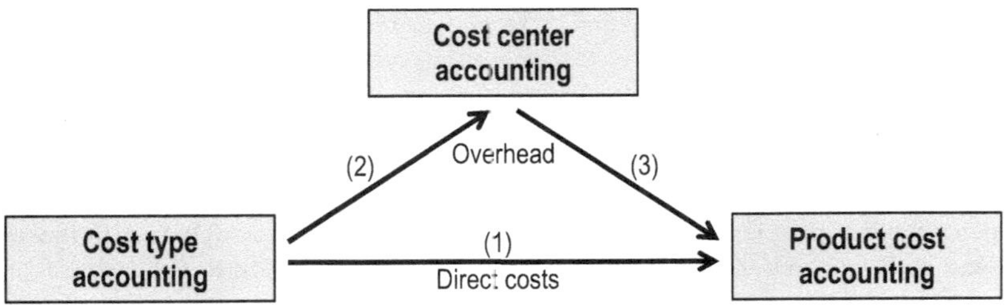

Figure 2-10: Elements and relationships of cost accounting systems

841 However, more complex and more timely cost accounting systems do not always lead to more accurate and detailed as well as timely cost information respectively. *Datar/Gypta*, for instance, show that more complex systems can also lead to less accurate cost information, when measurement errors increase. Cf. *Datar/Gupta* (1994).

842 Cf. *Cooper* (1991), p. 147.

843 Cf. *MacArthur* (2006).

Three *relations prevail between the tiers* cost type, cost center, and product cost accounting (see Figure 2-10). Direct costs of a cost unit can directly be assigned to it. Direct costs are therefore directly transferred from cost type accounting to product cost accounting (1). Overhead costs cannot be directly assigned to the cost unit. It is assumed that overhead costs do not directly occur for the production of a cost unit, but for the different services provided by cost centers. These services, however, are received by cost units. Therefore, overhead costs are first allocated to cost centers (2). Then, overhead costs are allocated to the cost units according to their consumption of the cost centers' services (3). Overhead rates are determined for this allocation to show how many costs have occurred on average for the provision of one service unit.[844]

The subsystems can further be broken down to elements. Although cost accounting is commonly distinguished into these tiers in Germany and Japan, their techniques and methods are expected to differ strongly between Germany and Japan.[845] Hence, this distinction offers a good basis to contrast cost accounting systems across both countries.

As cost accounting systems are expected to deliver a certain output in terms of relevant information, they are further characterized as **objective-oriented**. These systems are designed to fulfill cost accounting objectives. They are also characterized as **open systems** being related to the company's environment in terms of inputs (country-specifics, other external context factors, and internal context factors; see section 2.1) and outputs (provided cost information).[846]

2.3.1.2 Approach to describe the conceptual design of cost accounting systems

As the focus of this study is to compare the conceptual design of cost accounting systems between Germany and Japan, an objective characterization of cost accounting systems is required. If subjective characteristics were chosen, like asking the respondents how complex they perceive their cost accounting systems, systems could barely be compared cross-nationally. It is likely that the same cost accounting system is assessed differently in Germany and Japan. Perceptions what constitutes a complex cost accounting system already differs within a country.[847] It is very likely that the perceptions vary even more strongly internationally. Therefore, predominantly objective characteristics of cost accounting systems are surveyed, so that the researcher instead of the respondents can define the systems' complexity and timeliness. Aspects of **conceptual equivalence** as well as **differences in response style** (see sections 1.4.4.2 and 1.5.5) are thereby addressed to reduce biases.

---

844 For time reference of costs see, e.g., *Friedl* (2010), p. 44f.

845 The techniques and methods in Japan are expected to share more similarities with US than with German cost accounting. Cf. section 2.1.1.3.1; *Winter* (2005), p. 12f., 31. This distinction is very common in Germany. In nearly every German textbook on cost accounting this distinction is followed and at universities it is taught in more than 90% of all basic courses. Cf. *Laßmann et al.* (1995), p. 17. This tree-tired cost accounting system is, however, not common in the Anglophone literature. Cf. section 1.1.4.2.

846 Cf. *Ulrich* (1970), p. 112-115.

847 See *Brierley* (2008). It is further suggested that the expectations on the quality of cost accounting systems depend upon company size. Cf. *Lange/Schauer* (1996), p. 208.

Prior research often classifies cost accounting systems into two discrete alternatives: **traditional and ABC systems**, with ABC being more advanced.[848] In prior research it is usually not controlled for, whether a respondent who claims to apply cost accounting systems like ABC actually applies them or not.[849] Distinguishing solely between traditional and ABC systems does furthermore not "adequately capture the diversity of practices that exist"[850], because both traditional and ABC systems can vary from simple to complex.[851] As the perception what a complex or timely cost accounting system constitutes might differ internationally, it is necessary – as outlined in the previous section – to apply objective measures to determine the conceptual design of cost accounting systems.

Prior research applies different **approaches to determine the conceptual design of cost accounting systems**: In German literature, the conceptual design of cost accounting systems is often determined by the number of cost types, cost centers, and cost objects.[852] *Krumwiede et al.* investigate the number of RCA principles applied to determine the degree of RCA implementation.[853] *Aust* and *Frank* characterize cost accounting systems in a more subjective way by asking the respondents how they assess their cost accounting systems according to the number of and the changes in cost objects, valuation rates, allocation relations, and allocation bases.[854] *Drury/Tales* recently introduced four dimensions to determine the varying levels of cost system sophistication.[855] The authors assume that higher levels of sophistication are associated with "many first stage cost pools; assignments of costs to first stage cost pools based on using either direct charging or cause-and-effect resource cost drivers, many different types of second stage cost drivers, and an extensive reliance on second stage duration or intensity drivers."[856] The studies by *Drury/Tales* and *Al-Omiri/Tales* chose two out of the four elements – number of cost pools and number of cost allocation bases – to determine the degree of complexity. *Schoute* has extended this

848 The following studies have applied this approach: *Bjornenak* (1997); *Gosselin* (1997); *Krumwiede* (1998); *Clarke et al.* (1999); *Groot* (1999); *Malmi* (1999); *Joshi* (2001); *Al-Omiri/Drury* (2007); *Cinquini et al.* (2008). Traditional cost accounting systems are criticized due to changes in manufacturing technology, information costs, competition, and customer demands for greater product diversity. More comprehensive product costing systems like ABC are suggested to overcome those shortcomings. Cf. *Cooper* (1988b); *Kaplan* (1994); *Berens* (1997), p. 858.

849 Cf. footnote 426 and the comment by *Dugdale/Jones* (1997) on *Innes/Mitchell* (1997) questionnaire findings. For an exception see *Gosselin* (1997).

850 *Drury/Tayles* (2005), p. 54.

851 Cf. *Drury/Tayles* (2005), p. 54, 56f. The impact of a single element or instrument of a cost accounting system in isolation is often not the most informative issue. It is also suggested to investigate how management accounting instruments work as a package, because "why certain combinations work together and others do not, in various circumstances, needs more attention" (*Malmi/Granlund* (2009), p. 610). See also *Pizzini* (2006), p. 180f.; *Malmi/Brown* (2008).

852 Cf. *Aust* (1999), p. 124, with further references.

853 Cf. *Krumwiede et al.* (2007), p. 21. For an overview of the RCA principles see *Krumwiede/Suessmair* (2007a), p. 6.

854 Cf. *Aust* (1999), p. 166; *Frank* (2000), p. 116f.

855 See *Drury/Tayles* (2005). *Drury/Tayles* build upon the investigation by *Abernethy et al.* (2001) who has classified product costing systems according to their level of sophistication.

856 *Drury/Tayles* (2005), p. 57.

approach by taking both measures to the logarithm. In a second scale the author includes two further elements – nature of cost pools and nature of cost allocation bases. He then constructs a composite scale by standardizing the scores for each of the four elements and then takes the average of the resulting Z-scores.[857] *Pizzini* distinguishes in a more comprehensive way between four critical attributes. The system's ability to supply cost data on varying organizational levels is described with the factor 'level of detail'. To provide detailed cost information, it is further necessary to 'classify costs according to behavior'. 'Cost reporting frequency' supports managers for expedient decision making. With 'variance analysis', differences between expected and actual outcomes can be highlighted and reasons for such differences can be provided.[858] The studies outlined above either used factor analysis[859] or just equally weighted the specifications of cost accounting systems[860] to determine aggregated scores for cost accounting systems.

When a cost accounting system has to provide comprehensive information, companies can follow different solutions. They can, e.g., apply activity cost drivers to provide accurate and detailed cost information. Other elements of the cost accounting system that provide accurate and detailed cost information, however, might be more relevant in Germany and Japan.[861] Furthermore, the relevance of accurate, detailed, and timely cost information likely varies internationally. As outlined in section 1.1.1, researchers and practitioners in Western countries emphasize precision. Western researchers tend to define comprehensive cost accounting systems in terms of its *complexity*,[862] the potential to provide accurate and detailed cost information. In other countries like Japan, however, the complexity of systems might be less relevant and the timeliness of cost information could be more important. As previous studies have investigated only an extract of the characteristics that cost accounting systems can have, their approaches would be inappropriate to ensure cross-national comparability. Timeliness, the potential to provide timely information, is also relevant to ensure a fair comparison.[863] As the relevance of cost accounting elements and the accuracy, detail, and timeliness of cost information likely differs internationally, **this study investigates cost accounting systems on a broader basis and distin-**

857 Cf. *Schoute* (2009), p. 214.

858 Cf. *Pizzini* (2006).

859 See *Aust* (1999), p. 166; *Frank* (2000), p. 116f.; *Pizzini* (2006), p. 189f.

860 See *Drury/Tayles* (2005), p. 68-70; *Drury/Tayles* (2006), p. 414; *Al-Omiri/Drury* (2007), p. 411; *Krumwiede et al.* (2007), p. 21; *Schoute* (2009), p. 214.

861 In Germany, e.g., a very important objective of cost information is to analyze the efficiency of operations. Installing many cost centers could therefore be more suitable in Germany to provide accurate and detailed cost information.

862 All above mentioned studies measure the sophistication of cost accounting systems in terms of complexity. Only the factor 'cost reporting frequency' by *Pizzini* refers to timeliness of cost accounting systems. See *Pizzini* (2006).

863 Without the dimension timeliness a comparison would be incomplete. Determining that in one country more complex systems are run than in another is of limited explanatory power, because in the other country more timely cost accounting systems could be installed. Thus, without investigating both dimensions, it cannot be determined in which country more comprehensive systems are employed.

guishes the dimensions complexity and timeliness of cost accounting systems. Besides reducing ethnocentric bias, this course of action is also beneficial to provide more differentiated recommendations how practitioners should design their systems purposefully.

Based on the preliminary considerations, the following section 2.3.2 describes the relevant elements of cost accounting systems. Thereafter in section 2.3.3, the most relevant elements of the conceptual design are selected.

2.3.2 Conceptual design of cost accounting systems

Several **requirements** have to be considered **for** while **selecting the elements** that describe the conceptual design of cost accounting systems. First, all relevant elements should be recorded that describe the systems' complexity and timeliness. However, it is necessary to reduce the response time of the questionnaire to encourage practitioners participating in this study. Therefore, only the most relevant elements of cost accounting systems are investigated. The elements should furthermore have a different and independent effect upon the provision of cost information, should not record the same characteristics in a different way, should positively affect the complexity and timeliness of cost accounting systems, and should be measurable.

To facilitate the selection of all relevant system elements and to avoid sampling the same characteristics in a different way, a **hierarchical structure** is developed. It is first distinguished between the dimensions complexity and timeliness. The cost accounting system is further broken down into the subsystems cost type accounting, cost center accounting, and product cost accounting, where elements are allocated to. These subsystems provide different information about the costs incurred. The selection of the elements, however, remains subjective to some extent. To avoid shortcomings in equivalence that would impede to draw conclusions about cross-national differences, the selection of the elements has been discussed with foreign researchers.

2.3.2.1 Complexity

Complexity of cost accounting systems can most appropriately be defined by the processing effort of the elements (e.g., the nature of allocation bases) and by the number of elements taken into account (e.g., the number of cost centers). Characteristics of the relationships between the elements are of less relevance because the relationships in terms of arithmetic operations are largely standardized.[864] All relevant elements of the conceptual design of cost accounting systems identified in literature are outlined in the following.[865]

The complexity of **cost type accounting** can be described by (1) number of cost types, (2) distinction between fixed and variable costs, (3) existence of two separate data bases (one for financial accounting and one for management accounting), (4) existence of imputed costs, and (5) time reference of cost types.

864 See section 2.3.1.1. Only one relationship is relevant to characterize cost accounting systems: the transfer of costs from support cost centers to primary cost centers (first stage allocation).

865 Cf., e.g., *Weber* (1993); *Lompa* (1994), p. 48-79; *Drury/Tayles* (2005), p. 56f.; *Götze* (2007), p. 251.

- Ad (1): One important issue of cost type accounting is to allocate costs explicitly to the respective cost centers.[866] Within cost type accounting only primary costs (i.e. original costs that have to be booked in financial accounting) can be considered, because secondary costs (i.e. costs that have incurred for production factors a company has manufactured itself) are transferred from support cost centers to primary cost centers. As secondary costs belong to cost center accounting, only primary costs should be considered to describe cost type accounting. Secondary costs can indirectly be addressed by the first stage allocation. The more *cost types* are differentiated and allocated to determine product costs, the less costs are averaged leading to more accurate cost information.
- Ad (2): *Distinction between variable and fixed costs* provides additional information about cost characteristics that are relevant for planning and control purposes as well as for (in particular short-term) decision making.[867] Cost information is more accurate, the more intensively costs are separated into variable and fixed costs. When a manager is aware about fixed and variable costs, he can more accurately plan costs when the output volume changes. This is beneficial for budgeting purposes. Furthermore, planned costs can be compared with the actual costs to determine performance in the course of cost variance analysis. When an individual is only responsible for variable costs (e.g., because he is not responsible for the capacity utilization of a machine but only for its efficient operation), a separation of variable and fixed costs enhances the acceptance of cost control.
- Ad (3) and (4): As outlined in section 2.1.1.2.1, German companies have traditionally *two separate data bases*, one for financial accounting and one for management accounting. The content of the data bases differs when *imputed costs* are applied. These types of costs are necessary to more precisely capture the actual consumption of resources because then cost accounting can be designed for managerial needs without considering for external requirements. Running two separate data bases and applying imputed costs, however, increases the complexity of cost accounting systems in terms of a higher processing effort for three reasons. First, two data bases have to be installed and imputed costs have to be calculated additionally, which duplicates work. Second, reconciliations between financial and management accounting have to be carried through. Third, the differences of and the purpose for running two separate data bases have to be explained to the users of management accounting data.[868]
- Ad (5): For decision making and control purposes it is beneficial to differentiate cost information according to different *time references*. It can be distinguished between ac-

866 Cf. *Lompa* (1994), p. 49.

867 Cf. *Kloock/Schiller* (1997); *Drury* (2008), p. 237.

868 The necessity of imputed costs is difficult to comprehend in particular for managers from foreign countries that are not familiar with German cost accounting. For the difficulties to communicate two different income statements see *Lindner* (2009), p. 10f.

tual, normal, standard, and target cost information.[869] Cost information on different time references provides managers with better insights. When actual costs differ from expected costs (that can either be based on normal, standard, or target costs), the efficiency of operations for one period can be determined with a cost variance analysis.

Four elements determine the complexity of **cost center accounting**. They include (1) number and characteristics of cost centers, (2) cost variance analysis, (3) first stage allocation, and (4) average number and characteristics of second stage allocation bases.

- Ad (1): A higher *number of cost centers* and a higher number of allocation bases more comprehensively capture the variability of resource consumption by products or services.[870] The more cost centers are installed, the smaller they are on average. Smaller cost centers depend on fewer cost drivers in general and they lead to more homogeneous activities, whereby a more accurate resource consumption can be conducted. More precise cause-and-effect relations between cost driver(s) and cost level can thereby be determined reflecting the consumption of the activities by products and services in an accurate and detailed way.[871] This enables managers and cost accountants to gain greater insights into the monetary consequences of operations (e.g., for process optimization) and a more effective cost control.[872] Hence, the number of cost centers is expected to have a positive impact upon the complexity of cost accounting systems and the accuracy and detail of cost information. The *characteristics of cost centers* can also influence the choice of allocation bases. For instance, activity-based cost pools as opposed to responsibility-based cost pools support the implementation of activity-based cost drivers.[873]
- Ad (2): The *cost variance analysis* highlights differences between actual and expected costs (normal, standard, or target costs). It is an instrument to conduct cost control. By separating fixed and proportional costs, responsibility accounting can be enhanced.[874] Significant variances can be investigated in more depth to identify their causes. This information provides the responsible person with more insights how to avoid inefficiencies in future. The more intensively cost variances are analyzed, the

869 Actual costs are costs that have occurred during a reporting period. Normal costs are averaged costs – costs that have occurred on average over several reporting periods. Planned costs for a period are standard costs. Target costs are planned costs that are derived from market prices.

870 Cf. *Drury/Tayles* (2005), p. 56. *Datar/Gupta*, however, show that a higher number of cost centers not necessarily increases the accuracy of product cost accounting due to specification and aggregation errors. Cf. *Datar/Gupta* (1994).

871 Cf. *Drury* (2005), p. 118; *Friedl et al.* (2009b), p. 44.

872 Cf. *Götze* (2007), p. 73; *Portz/Lere* (2010), p. 48.

873 Cf. *Schoute* (2009), p. 210. Furthermore, qualitative characteristics of cost centers including the demarcation of areas of responsibility, transparency, clarity of cost center classification, and the adequacy to determine the factors that drive costs can drive complexity. Cf. *Lompa* (1994), p. 55f.

874 Cf. *Krumwiede* (2005), p. 30.

more accurate and detailed information is provided to increase the efficiency of operations.[875]

- Ad (3): The first stage of the traditional two stage cost allocation process (*first stage allocation*) contains (1) the estimation of costs incurred in each support and primary cost center and (2) the transfer of costs from support cost centers to primary cost centers.[876] In particular the second step of the first stage allocation is necessary to increase the accuracy of cost allocation and drives processing effort. The more support and primary cost centers are installed, the more interdependences can be considered for. Furthermore, the accuracy of cost information and the complexity of systems increase when not only unidirectional, but also interdependent interrelations between the cost centers are accounted for. Simple systems apply the direct method or the step method that do not consider all interdepartmental services. Complex systems on the contrary apply the reciprocal or the iterative method that gives full recognition to all interdepartmental services.[877] As this instrument serves full cost allocation, it is suitable for cost control in support cost centers to ensure their operating efficiency, and it ensures responsibility accounting of the respective persons in charge.[878]
- Ad (4): The second stage of the traditional two stage allocation process (*second stage allocation*) contains the allocation of costs from primary cost centers to cost objects.[879] The more allocation bases are used, the more visible the economics of production processes are. This leads to more accurate costs of cost objects.[880] Volume-based allocation bases often include direct materials respectively direct labor that is widespread in Germany and Japan.[881] As a direct relationship between overhead costs and the allocation base on a volume basis is missing, this form constitutes the least accurate allocation base.[882] Allocations on an hour rate basis, e.g., for labor or machinery use, are more accurate, because a direct relationship between overhead costs and the allocation base exists. To allocate overhead costs in a more accurate way, cost drivers have to be identified. Three different types of cost drivers can be distinguished. They differ in complexity, because the detail of the relationships between overhead costs and cost objects taken into account varies. Transaction drivers are the simplest ones, because it is assumed that for each time an activity is performed, the same quantity of resources is required. Duration drivers are more accurate, because the allocation of overhead costs is based on the duration to perform an activity. Intensity drivers are the most ac-

875 An overview of cost variance analysis applied in Germany is provided by *Scherrer* (1996), p. 106. Variance analysis is a powerful tool to motivate the responsible person to work efficiently, because variances he is responsible for are determined. Cf. *Ewert/Wagenhofer* (2008), p. 9.

876 See, e.g., *Atkinson et al.* (2004), p. 108-112. For the two stage allocation process see further *Cooper* (1991).

877 For the explanation of the different methods see *Kinney/Raiborn* (2008), p. 471-478.

878 Cf., e.g., *Kinney/Raiborn* (2008), p. 469f.; *Kalenberg* (2008), p. 84f. The need for support cost centers increases with the number of product lines or service types.

879 See, e.g., *Atkinson et al.* (2004), p. 108, 112-117.

880 Cf, e.g., *Kaplan/Cooper* (1998).

881 See *Schierenbeck* (2003), p. 691f.; *Hiromoto* (1988), p. 23, respectively.

882 Cf. *Drury* (2005), p. 112.

curate ones, because the resources used are directly charged each time an activity is performed.[883]

The complexity of **product cost accounting** can be described by (1) product costing, (2) number of cost objects, (3) operating income statement for managerial purposes, and (4) contribution margin accounting.

- Ad (1): *Product costing* provides more information when variable and full costs per product unit are reported. Variable costs constitute the lower price limit for short-term decisions and full costs constitute the lower price limit for long-term decisions. When only variable or full costs are reported, product costing should be categorized as simple.[884] Cost accounting systems are most comprehensive when they provide product costs both on a variable and a full cost basis.
- Ad (2): When product costs for each product variant are calculated, differences in resource consumption between product variants can be considered for. On the contrary, more simple systems reduce the number of calculations by subsuming products to product groups. The *number of cost objects* is hence an indicator for the degree of detail with which companies calculate their product costs.
- Ad (3): Cost accounting systems further increase in complexity, when besides the profit and loss statement also an *operating income statement for managerial purposes* is installed. Similar to running two separate data bases it duplicates work. Reconciliations between financial and management accounting have to be carried through and the differences and the purpose for distinguishing both have to be explained to the users of management accounting information.
- Ad (4): One further way to determine the income of a company and to investigate the roots for success is *contribution margin accounting*. The explanatory power and the complexity of it are mainly dependent upon how many different layers of fixed costs are differentiated. The simplest version of contribution margin accounting is direct costing. In direct costing the contribution margins of all cost objects are determined (sales less variable costs) and then fixed costs are subtracted as a lump sum. The most complex version differentiates fixed costs between a multitude of layers (e.g., department level, plant level, and product level) and allocates them to a multitude of cost objects (e.g., customers, products, sales regions).[885] Thereby, more information for decision making is provided.

---

883 For the characterization of the cost drivers see *Kaplan/Cooper* (1998), p. 95-100; *Drury/Tayles* (2000), p. 27f.; *Drury/Tayles* (2005); *Al-Omiri/Drury* (2007).

884 Whereas Anglophone practitioners assess full costing to be more sophisticated than variable costing (cf. *Brierley* (2008), p. 63, 69), in Germany variable costing is seen to be more comprehensive. The different German perception is explained by the long German traditions of variable costing and the sophisticated systems like GPK that have been developed after the Second World War. See section 2.1.1.2.1. Consequently, from an international point of view, neither full nor variable costing is assessed in this study to be more sophisticated or more complex than the other.

885 An empirical analysis for German companies is provided by *Friedl et al.* (2009b), p. 45.

Besides determining the complexity of cost type accounting, cost center accounting, and product cost accounting, the complexity of cost accounting systems can alternatively be described by the existence of **ABC**. In literature it is argued that ABC systems are often more complex and more sophisticated than traditional cost accounting systems.[886] However, traditional cost accounting systems can be more complex than ABC systems, e.g., when the first distinguish more cost centers than the latter.[887] Therefore, ABC might be a less precise indicator for the complexity of cost accounting systems. ABC is consequently applied in this study only as an alternative measure to test for the robustness of the results.

2.3.2.2 Timeliness

Timelier cost information enhances managers to expediently address problems and identify opportunities for improvement. It further provides feedback on prior decisions and information on recent events to purposefully guide future courses of action,[888] in particular when managers operate in highly uncertain environments.[889] To investigate the potential of cost accounting systems providing timely information, the timeliness of cost accounting systems in terms of the frequency of updating cost information or in terms of its internal processes of generating cost information can be determined.

The **frequency of updating cost information** should mainly be focused on standard costs, allocation bases, cost reports etc. Updating information about the relationships between the elements – which would rather characterize the dynamics of cost accounting systems in terms of the systems theory[890] – is of less relevance, because the relationships between the elements are largely standardized and only few are subject to change. Furthermore, structural changes of cost accounting systems are inappropriate for determining the potential of systems to provide timely cost information. For instance, changes in the number of products should not be included to define the timeliness of cost accounting systems, because the larger a company, the more frequently (among others) cost types, cost centers, and cost objects are rearranged. Hence, if structural changes were recognized, larger companies would appear to have timelier cost accounting systems. Other structural changes, like the number of fixed cost layers of the operating income statement and changes in the nature of allocation overhead bases, on the contrary, occur rather seldom.[891]

An alternative way to describe the timeliness of systems and thereby the potential to provide timely cost information is to investigate **internal processes** of cost accounting systems. Within a system the timeliness occurs in terms of 'activity' or 'behavior' of the elements and subsystems. A system is then not seen as a status anymore, which allows docu-

886 Cf., e.g., *Kaplan/Johnson* (1991); footnote 848.

887 Cf. *Drury/Tayles* (2005), p. 54, 56f.

888 Cf. *Pizzini* (2006), p. 184.

889 Cf. *Chenhall/Morris* (1986).

890 For systems theory see *v. Bertalanffy* (1950); *Ulrich* (1970).

891 In a study from 1993 only one out of 31 Germany's largest 48 companies has redesigned its cost accounting system within the last years. Cf. *Weber* (1993), p. 275.

menting the time-consuming consequences of activities.[892] The better the internal processes are designed, the less time is required to process the data, prepare reports, and distribute them to the users.[893] Like in previous studies, the process of generating cost information is not investigated in this study due to time restrictions of the questionnaire, the lack of prior research, and the research method. Hypotheses of cross-national differences in generating cost information can therefore hardly be set up. The survey method, which was chosen in section 1.5.1, is less suitable to describe the routine and the practically applied process of cost accounting in a natural context.[894] Therefore, solely the **frequency of updating of cost information** characterizes the timeliness of cost accounting systems in this study.

The timeliness of **cost type accounting** can be described by updating (1) the distinction between fixed and variable costs and (2) standard costs. When the nature of cost types differs strongly, e.g., due to changes in process sequence or due to restructuring of the company, fixed and variable costs have to be distinguished more frequently to provide decision makers with up-to-date information. As standard costs (e.g., for primary products, raw materials, and standard processes) can have a strong impact upon the profitability of services or products, companies frequently require updates of these costs in a dynamic environment.

Updating (1) cost variance analysis, (2) cost rates for support cost centers (first stage allocation), and (3) cost rates for overhead allocation bases (second stage allocation) can characterize the timeliness of **cost center accounting.** Cost variance analysis should be carried through more frequently, the more dynamic the environment is and the more changes in production sequence occur. When many changes occur, it is becoming more difficult to explain variances, because the causes and their significance for differences can hardly be distinguished. When variances are analyzed more frequently, fewer changes have occurred during the analyzed time period and it can thus more accurately be separated between controllable and uncontrollable cost variances. This enables a more accurate performance evaluation of individuals, countermeasures can earlier be carried through, and it enhances learning, because the reasons for variances become clearer.[895] The cost rates for support cost centers and overhead allocation bases should be updated more frequently, the more dynamic the environment is and the more changes in the production sequences or the structure of the cost centers occur.

Product cost accounting can be described by the frequency of updating (1) product costing, (2) the operating income statement for managerial purposes, and (3) contribution margin accounting. The more dynamic the environment and the more changes in the

892 Cf. *Ulrich* (1970), p. 113f.

893 Cf. *Riahi-Belkaoui* (2002), p. 7.

894 The survey method would be inappropriate to describe internal processes because this method can capture fewer features than field studies. Cf. *Birnberg et al.* (1990), p. 49-51. A field study like the one by *Weber et al.* would be more appropriate for this purpose. See *Weber et al.* (1997).

895 In particular Japanese companies are characterized in literature to provide their employees with easily understandable cost ratios within short intervals to visualize the impact of short-term improvements. Cf., e.g., *Reich* (1995), p. 113, 117.

production sequences, restructuring of the company, or changes in the product portfolio occur, the more frequently product costing, operating income statements, and contribution margin accounting should be updated. Providing managers with timelier product costs helps them to respond earlier to changes. It also shows managers timelier the cost implications of changes in the management of products. Cost savings, e.g., due to changes in the production process or the design of products can earlier be provided. This enhances learning, because the reasons for variances become clearer, and enables the managers to take further decisions to improve the costs per product. In addition to product costing, operating income statements and contribution margin accounting also show the financial consequences of managerial decisions for the whole company during a period of time.

2.3.3 Selection and operationalization of systems' elements

In only few studies the comprehensiveness of cost accounting systems has been analyzed before. Predominantly the complexity of cost accounting systems has been investigated (see Figure 2-11).

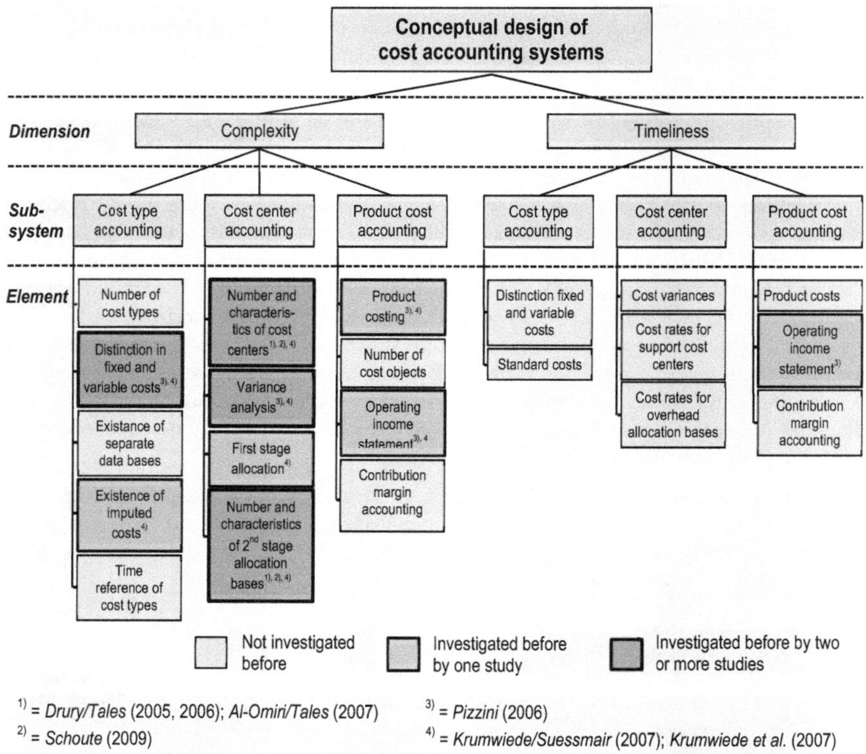

Figure 2-11: Prior research on the conceptual design of cost accounting systems

The distinction between fixed and variable costs, the number and characteristics of cost centers, cost variance analysis, as well as the number and characteristics of second stage allocation bases have been investigated by two or more studies before. The existence of imputed costs, first stage allocation, product costing, as well as operating income statements has only been addressed by one study. No study has investigated the number of cost types, the time reference of cost types, the existence of separate data bases, the number of cost objects, and contribution margin accounting. Furthermore, three out of four studies solely focused on the complexity of cost accounting systems and ignored the dimension 'timeliness', like the frequency of updating cost information or processing cost information. Only the study by *Pizzini* has investigated aspects of timeliness by addressing the element 'frequency of cost reports', which is similar to contribution margin accounting.[896]

This study extends prior research by addressing both system's dimensions (complexity and timeliness) and more elements of cost accounting systems.[897] In this study the following elements are chosen and operationalized to determine the **complexity of cost accounting systems:**

- *Number of cost types, cost centers,* and *average number of overhead allocation bases per cost center*: By question C.1 (Appendix 2) the respondents were asked to provide these figures for their companies.
- Existence of *imputed costs* and *operating income statement*: To determine the use of imputed costs, the respondents were asked to which extent they apply imputed depreciation and imputed interests (question C.3). As imputed costs are not very familiar outside of German-speaking countries, the English and Japanese questionnaires include a short explanation of this concept. Thereafter, the existence of operating income statements for managerial purposes is surveyed. When the respondents run this statement besides their profit and loss statement, they were further asked, to which extent both statements differ structurally from each other on a seven-point Likert scale (question C.4).
- *Contribution margin accounting*: The existence of contribution margin accounting was addressed by question C.5. When the respondents use this instrument, the number of distinguished contribution margins is surveyed. As this instrument is not well known in Japan, the English and Japanese questionnaires include a brief description of this instrument.

896 Cf. *Pizzini* (2006).

897 To cover most of the system's elements, only the most relevant characteristics of the elements are surveyed in this study. Some elements are therefore surveyed in a less detailed way than prior research did. Distinction between fixed and variable costs, the profit and loss account, as well as product costing have been investigated in more depth by *Pizzini* (2006). The characteristics of cost centers and second stage allocation bases have additionally been addressed by *Schoute* (2009). Furthermore, other aspects of the first stage allocation process are not investigated in this study. For those aspects see *Kinney/Raiborn* (2008), p. 470-472.

- *Distinction between fixed and variable costs, cost variance analysis*, and *first stage allocation*: For reasons of simplification, the complexity of the first stage allocation is only determined by the transfer of costs from support cost centers to primary cost centers. Respondents were asked to assess on a seven-point Likert scale the extent to which (1) fixed and variable costs are distinguished for each cost center, (2) cost variance analysis is carried through, and (3) output interdependencies are considered for while transferring costs from support cost centers to primary cost centers (question C.6).
- *Characteristics of second stage allocation bases*: By question C.7 the respondents were asked, on which bases overhead costs are allocated. Respondents had to choose between volume bases, hour rate bases, transaction drivers, and duration drivers. Intensity drivers were not included in the questionnaire, because many respondents have misunderstood this type of driver in the pre-tests of the questionnaire.
- *Product costing*: Question C.8 addresses the degree of cost allocation. The respondents were asked how product costs respectively medical treatments for the hospital industry are determined as part of regular cost accounting – either only on a full cost basis or only on a variable cost basis, or on both bases. In the following it is not further distinguished between product cost and medical treatment costs. The term 'product costing' represents both.
- *Time reference of costs*: The respondents had to assess on a seven-point Likert scale for how many products (respectively medical treatments for the hospital industry) actual costs, normal costs, standard costs, and target costs are determined (question C.9).
- *ABC*: To test for the robustness of the empirical findings, the complexity of cost accounting systems is further defined by the existence of ABC. To avoid shortcomings in equivalence, eight characteristics of ABC are distinguished. The respondents were asked to tick all the statements that apply to their cost accounting (question C.11). Five statements are based on *Gosselin's* distinction between 'activity analysis', 'activity cost analysis', and 'ABC':[898] 'Activity analysis' (characteristics 1 to 3) is a prerequisite to the process of installing an ABC system. It consists of identifying activities in cost centers, allocating cost center costs to activities, and determining cost driver volumes for each activity. When many activities are distinguished, activities should be aggregated to processes to reduce complexity (characteristic 4).[899] 'Activity cost analysis' is the next level of the ABC process, where activity cost driver rates are determined (characteristic 5). 'ABC' includes in addition to activity cost analysis that overhead allocation bases respectively service costs are calculated (characteristic 6). Activity cost driver rates can further be applied for process optimization and to analyze customer profitability (characteristics 7 and 8).

The number of cost objects and the characteristics of cost centers have not been surveyed, because the number of cost objects is expected to strongly differ across the three industries. Whereas in hospitals every inpatient is a cost objective, in the other industries the

898 For this distinction see *Gosselin* (1997), p. 106f.

899 Cf. *Gaiser* (1998), p. 72. It is expected that this is often the case for German-speaking countries. Cf. *Kellermanns/Islam* (2004), p. 42f.

products and not the customers are usually defined as cost objects. Thus, this element is not applied to determine systems' complexity. The characteristics of cost centers have also been excluded, because the number of cost centers is expected to have a stronger impact upon the accuracy and detail of cost accounting systems.

The **timeliness of cost accounting systems** is determined by question C.10. The respondents were asked how often they update (1) the distinction between fixed and variable costs, (2) standard costs, (3) cost variances, cost rates for (4) support cost centers and (5) overhead allocation bases, (6) product costs, and (7) the operating income statement for managerial purposes. Respondents had to choose between the following options: continuously, monthly, quarterly, semi-annually, annually, less often than annually, irregularly, and not applicable (N/A).[900]

The update of contribution margin accounting has not been surveyed. It is expected to be less relevant for determining the timeliness of cost accounting systems and it is expected to strongly correlate with the update of operating income statements for managerial purposes.

2.3.4 Aggregation rules for determining systems' degree of complexity and timeliness

After having selected the elements of cost accounting systems, **rules how to aggregate the elements' characteristics to determine the systems' degree of complexity and timeliness** are defined. The simplest way is to weight all elements equally.[901] An alternative way would be asking the respondents to assess the elements' relevance. This would be beneficial to consider for a different relevance of the elements across companies, countries, and industries. However, it would disproportionally extent the length of the questionnaire. Thus, like in prior research, all elements are weighted equally in this study. Then, however, the researcher instead of the cost accountants defines the relevance of systems' elements.

Two different **scores** for cost accounting complexity (systems' complexity score and ABC complexity score) and one score for cost accounting timeliness are developed in the following. For each element of the cost accounting system a single complexity respectively timeliness score is determined. Between zero and one point is awarded each. When respondents have not answered all questions on the elements' characteristics or have chosen the option 'no answer', no single complexity respectively timeliness score for the respective element is determined and the respective elements are not considered for calculating the

900 The intervals between the options are not equal to consider for the non-linearity of these figures. It is expected that timelier cost information has a positive impact upon decision making – but at a declining rate.

901 It is thereby expected that the elements of cost accounting systems are independent from each other. However, the number of cost centers, e.g., is probably associated with the number of second stage allocation bases.

aggregated complexity and timeliness scores.[902] The following equation shows that all calculated single complexity respectively timeliness scores (x_i) are added up and divided by the number of evaluable single scores to determine the aggregated complexity respectively timeliness scores (C_i): n represents the number of elements the respective overall score consists of. The maximum aggregated score is then 1.

2) $$C_i = \sum_{i=1}^{n} x_i$$

Systems' complexity score

Number of cost types, *cost centers*, and *average number of overhead allocation bases per cost center*: The studies by *Drury/Tales* and *Al-Omiri/Tales* define the complexity of cost accounting systems by the number of cost pools and the number of cost allocation bases. *Schoute* extends this approach by taking both measures to the logarithm. In a second scale, the author includes the nature of cost pools and the nature of cost allocation bases to determine systems' complexity.[903] *Brierley* concludes from field study interviews with British management accountants that the number of cost pools and the number of cost drivers (which is similar to overhead allocation bases) can both be used "as proxy measures of overhead assignment sophistication"[904]. However, he further states that both measures are highly related.[905] Thus, only one of both measures is chosen to indicate the complexity of cost accounting systems in this study. As the respondents had more difficulties to answer the question about the number of overhead allocation bases, the number of cost centers instead of the number of overhead allocation bases is chosen.

It is expected that large numbers of these elements have a positive impact upon the potential to provide accurate and detailed cost information – but at a declining rate. To consider for non-linearity of these elements, all values (labeled with x in the following formula) are taken to the logarithm. The company with the highest number for cost types and cost centers receives one point. The remaining companies obtain less, depending linearly upon their logarithmized values.

3) $$c_i = \frac{\log(x_i)-1}{\log(x_{max})-1}$$

Imputed costs and *operating income statement*: When imputed costs are not applied, no points are awarded. For imputed depreciation and imputed interests ¼ point is awarded each for 'in separate calculations only' and ½ point for 'as part of regular cost accounting'. Hence, the maximum score for imputed costs is 1. When no operating income statement

902 Thereby, those answers do not lead to a decrease in the overall complexity and timeliness scores. When less than 50% of the single complexity scores can be determined, no aggregated score is calculated for the respective company.

903 Cf. *Schoute* (2009), p. 214.

904 *Brierley* (2008), p. 75f.

905 Cf. *Brierley* (2008), p. 75f. Both elements are thus not independent.

is applied or when the operating income statement does not differ at all from the profit and loss statement, no points are awarded. The stronger the operating income statement differs from the profit and loss statement, the more points are awarded. A seven-point Likert scale is used for this question. For the first spot 0 points are given, for the second spot 1/6 point is given, for the third spot 2/6 points are given and so forth. When both statements differ very much (spot 7), 1 point is awarded.

Contribution margin accounting: ½ point is awarded, when contribution margin accounting is applied in a company. The remaining ½ point is distributed according to the number of contribution margins. Companies having 2 (3, 4, 5, 6 or more) contribution margins obtain further 0.1 (0.2, 0.3, 0.4, 0.5) points.

Distinction between fixed and variable costs, *cost variance analysis*, and *first stage allocation*: The higher respondents answered on a seven-point scale with 1 = not at all and 7 = completely that fixed and variable costs are distinguished, cost variances are analyzed, and that costs are transferred from support cost centers to primary cost centers, the more points are awarded. For each element 0 points are awarded for spot 1, 1/6 point is awarded for spot 2, 2/6 points are awarded for spot 3 and so forth. Hence, for each element the maximum score is 1 (which is the case, when respondents have marked spot 7).

Characteristics of second stage allocation bases: The more comprehensive the second stage allocation base, the more points are awarded. When a company allocates overhead costs on a volume basis, on an hour rate basis, on the number of times an activity is performed (transaction drivers), or on the amount of time taken to perform an activity (duration drivers), ¼, ½, ¾, or 1 points are awarded respectively. To ensure that the maximum score is 1, the companies obtain the points for the most comprehensive second stage allocation basis they apply. When a company, for example, allocates overhead costs both on a volume basis and on an hour rate basis, the company obtains ½ point. This means that no extra points are awarded for the variety of allocation bases applied.

Product costing: When product costs are determined only on a full cost basis or only on a variable cost basis, ½ point is awarded. Companies that determine product costs on both bases are awarded with 1 point.

Time reference of costs: The more actual, normal, standard, and target costs are provided for products respectively medical treatments, the more points are awarded. 1/24 point is awarded, when respondents have chosen spot 2, 2/24 points are awarded for spot 3 and so forth. The scores for actual, normal, standard, and target costs are then added up, so that the maximum score for time reference of costs is 1.

To ensure comparability across companies, the awarded points for each element are added up and divided by the number of single complexity scores. The maximum score of this measure is then 1.

ABC complexity score

Question C.11 (see Appendix 2) consists of eight items that characterize ABC complexity. 1 point is awarded for each item that applies to the respondents' cost accounting system. The maximum score of this measure is consequently 8. For comparability reasons across companies the score is then divided by the number of evaluable responses (see equation 2,

p. 161). The maximum score for ABC is then consequently 1. Furthermore, the adoption rate of ABC is determined by following the descriptions from section 2.3.3. It is distinguished between 'activity analysis', 'activity cost analysis', 'ABC', 'ABC for process optimization', and 'ABC for customer profitability analysis'.

Systems' timeliness score

For the **timeliness of cost accounting systems** a similar procedure is applied. The more frequently cost information is updated, the more points are awarded. No point is awarded when cost information is updated unregularly or less often than annually. 1/5 point is awarded when cost information is updated annually, 2/5 points when semi-annually, 3/5 points when quarterly, 4/5 points when monthly, and 1 point when continuously.[906] As timeliness distinguishes seven elements, the maximum score for timeliness would be 7. To ensure comparability across companies the awarded points for each of the seven elements are added up and divided by the number of evaluable responses (see equation 2, p. 161), so that the maximum score for timeliness of cost accounting systems is 1.

2.3.5 Hypotheses development

Context factors and cost accounting objectives are expected to have an impact upon the complexity and timeliness of cost accounting systems.

2.3.5.1 Influence of country-specifics upon cost accounting systems

Country-specifics are applied in this study within the *analysis of relationships on an international level* to explain cross-national differences in cost accounting (third research question) and to draw direct relationships between country-specifics and cost accounting within the *analysis of relationships on a national level* (fourth and fifth research question). The following hypotheses development is therefore distinguished between both types of analysis.

Hypotheses for the analysis of relationships on an international level

The complexity and timeliness of cost accounting systems are expected to vary internationally due to cross-national differences in culture, history of cost accounting, the relationship of cost accounting towards financial and management accounting, and education of cost accountants.

Germany is characterized by an uncertainty avoiding and individualistic and Japan by a collective and long-term oriented **culture**. German companies have therefore a strong emphasis on capturing the reality of costs as accurately and as detailed as possible to apply this information primarily for cost control and short-term decision support. This kind of cost information is also relevant for controlling the performance of individuals, which is very common in Germany to motivate employees to improve productivity. The German **history** of cost accounting has enforced and facilitated the implementation of complex cost accounting systems. Compared to Germany, the Japanese culture is characterized in

906 For the necessity of unequal intervals between the options see footnote 900 in section 2.3.4.

literature by a horizontal relationship and mutual trust between managers and workers.[907] Japanese companies therefore focus less on cost control and avoid tracing inefficiencies back to individuals.[908] To motivate employees to decrease costs proactively, Japanese companies frequently apply rather traditional cost accounting practices, like direct labor as an overhead allocation base, to reduce direct labor.[909] For decision influencing and for cost management rather timely instead of accurate and detailed cost information is required. According to national culture and history of cost accounting, German companies have more complex and less timely cost accounting systems than their Japanese counterparts.

To meet financial accounting requirements, less accurate, detailed, and timely cost information is sufficient compared to managerial requirements. In section 2.2.1 it was hypothesized that cost accounting in Japan is more influenced by the requirements of **financial accounting** than in Germany. According to this criterion, cost accounting systems in German companies should consequently be more comprehensive in terms of accuracy, detail, and timeliness.

A stronger **emphasis on cost and management accounting** is expected in Continental Europe[910] and Japan[911] than in Anglophone countries. Therefore, cost accountants in Germany and Japan are in general well educated and likely have enough resources to design and run comprehensive cost accounting systems.[912] Like Germany, Japan is also expected to have a strong emphasis on cost accounting for managerial purposes – however, it is assumed to be different in nature. Japanese companies are characterized to enable all employees a basic understanding of accounting for making them aware about costs and benefits and to raise their concern for the company's operations.[913] The roles and paths of cost and management accountants in Japan and their cultural specifics facilitate a cooperative and visible management.[914] This type of management enables and motivates employees to act proactively by discovering and resolving problems before they occur.[915] Instead of accurate and detailed cost information, more current, future-oriented, and plain information should be provided. As German management accountants are expected to be more specialized than their Japanese counterparts, it can be concluded that German companies have a higher potential to provide accurate, detailed, and timely cost information. Japanese cost accountants on the contrary are likely to provide more relevant cost information

907 Cf. *Nishimura* (2003), p. 59f.

908 Cf. *Hiromoto* (1988).

909 "[R]educing direct labor is essential for ongoing cost improvement. The company is committed to aggressive automation to promote long-term competitiveness. Allocating overhead based on direct labor creates the desired strong pro-automation incentives throughout the organization" (*Hiromoto* (1988), p. 23). Executives in Western countries might therefore dismiss the Japanese use of allocation bases as simple or even misguiding. Cf. section 1.1.1.

910 Cf. *Bhimani* (1996); *Krumwiede/Suessmair* (2007a), p. 2f.

911 Cf. *Wijewardena/Cooray* (1995), p. 368, 372-374.

912 For Germany cf. *Holzer/Norreklit* (1991); *MacArthur* (2006), p. 15; *Vikas* (2006), p. 33, 36.

913 Cf. *Hiramatsu* (1992); *Wijewardena/Cooray* (1995), p. 368, 372f.

914 Cf. *Nishimura* (2003), p. 59f.

915 Cf. *Cooper/Kaplan* (1991), p. 397f.; *Merchant/Shields* (1993), p. 80.

and are more capable of explaining cost information to managers due to their comprehensive operational knowledge.

As German companies have likely a higher potential to install complex and timely systems and as German companies are expected to have a stronger emphasis on accurate and detailed cost information, it is concluded that they run more complex and more timely cost accounting systems than their Japanese counterparts. Thus, the following two hypotheses are set up.

H_{1m}:	*German companies employ more complex cost accounting systems than their Japanese counterparts.*
H_{1n}:	*German companies employ timelier cost accounting systems than their Japanese counterparts.*

Hypotheses for the analysis of relationships on a national level

The more specialized cost accountants are, the more potential they have to install complex and timely cost accounting systems. Furthermore, the more theoretical knowledge they have, the more they emphasize theoretically sound systems and thus strive for more complexity and timeliness of cost accounting systems. Thus, the following hypotheses are set up.

H_{1o}:	*The more specialized cost accountants are, the more complex are cost accounting systems.*
H_{1p}:	*The more specialized cost accountants are, the timelier are cost accounting systems.*
H_{1q}:	*The more theoretical knowledge cost accountants have, the more complex are cost accounting systems.*
H_{1r}:	*The more theoretical knowledge cost accountants have, the timelier are cost accounting systems.*

2.3.5.2 Influence of other external and internal context factors upon cost accounting systems

To trace differences in cost accounting back to country-specifics and to identify factors that explain the conceptual design of cost accounting systems and their performance, other external and internal context factors are investigated in this study. In section 2.1.2 the **external context factors** 'external complexity' and 'external dynamics' have been outlined.

Hypotheses about the relationship between the context and cost accounting systems' complexity and timeliness are derived in the following. It is assumed that the direction of the influences between context factors and cost accounting systems' complexity and timeliness are universally valid, because they are rather technological than behavioral in nature. However, the magnitude of the changes is expected to be moderated by country-specifics to some extent, because, e.g., theoretical constructs differ in their relevance across countries (see section 1.3.8). As prior research provides hardly any insights in which country the magnitude might be stronger or weaker than in the other, the hypotheses are set up for both countries collectively without speculating about differences in magnitude. The robustness of the relationships is tested across nations in section 3.6, whereby differences in magnitude can be determined. Thus, the following hypothesis is deduced. This investigation is of practical relevance. For instance, the impact of top management support on cost accounting systems' complexity could be tested for the German and the Japanese sample. Then, in a second step, this impact can be compared for significant differences between both countries. If top management support has a significantly stronger impact on the systems' complexity in Japan than in Germany, a recommendation for German MNC could be to provide more resources and political support when the complexity of cost accounting systems should be increased in their Japanese subsidiaries.

H_{7a}: The impact of context factors upon the conceptual design of cost accounting systems has the same direction for both Germany and Japan, but it differs cross-nationally in magnitude.

Organizations that either face a more complex or a more dynamic environment require more complex respectively timelier cost accounting systems. In a **complex external environment** the company's operations are often complex. As cost accounting reproduces the company's reality, the external complexity has also an impact upon the complexity of cost accounting systems.[916] A **dynamic external environment** forces organizations to respond to changes promptly. Cost accounting can support decision making by frequently updating cost information to reflect the organizational reality. Thus the following hypotheses are set up.

H_{2a}: The more complex the environment is, the more complex are cost accounting systems.
H_{2b}: The more dynamic the environment is, the timelier are cost accounting systems.

In section 2.1.3 the **internal context factors** company size, potential for cost distortion, IT system quality, industry, and types of organizations have been described.

It is expected that **company size** has an impact upon the conceptual design of cost accounting systems. Cost accounting reflects the company's reality. Larger companies have more cost types, cost centers, and products on average. Due to a higher number of cost centers it is also more likely that, e.g., larger organizations transfer more intensively costs from support cost centers to primary cost centers. Larger companies can also provide more resources in terms of, e.g., stronger IT systems and better qualified cost accountants to run more comprehensive cost accounting systems. Whereas the impact of organizational size upon the complexity of cost accounting systems is apparent, its impact upon the timeliness of cost accounting systems is ambiguous. As size likely increases the complexity of cost accounting systems, it is on the one hand getting more costly to update all cost information.[917] On the other hand, larger companies have more resources to run these systems.[918] It is expected that both effects balance themselves out. Consequently, the following hypotheses are derived.

H_{3b}: The larger the company is, the more complex are cost accounting systems.
H_{3c}: Company size does not affect the timeliness of cost accounting systems.

Potential for cost distortion is defined in terms of product or service diversity. The more diverse products and services are, the more they usually differ in resource consumption, which leads to a higher potential for cost distortion. To better capture the products' varie-

916 Cf. *Khandwalla* (1977), p. 337f.

917 Cf. *Weber* (2004), p. 15f.

918 Cf. *Aust* (1999), p. 149; *Frank* (2000), p. 121f.

ty in resource consumption, more complex systems are required. In particular a higher number of cost centers and cost objects as well as more precise overhead allocation bases are relevant to provide managers with more accurate and detailed cost information.[919] Consequently, the following hypothesis is deduced.

H_{3d}:	*The higher the potential for cost distortion, the more complex are cost accounting systems.*

IT systems quality is expected to have an impact upon cost accounting systems. More comprehensive IT systems run cost accounting systems at lower costs and they facilitate implementing and running comprehensive systems. For both reasons it is expected that IT systems quality leads to more complex and timelier cost accounting systems.[920] These relationships are supported by prior research.[921] Thus, the following hypotheses are set up. The impact of IT systems quality is also tested for ABC application as an alternative measure for systems' complexity, to verify the argument by *Krumwiede* that IT systems quality has an impact upon implementing innovative systems like ABC.

H_{3e}:	*The higher IT systems quality, the more complex are cost accounting systems.*
H_{3f}:	*The higher IT systems quality, the timelier are cost accounting systems.*

It is further argued that the higher the overall interest in cost accounting is, the more resources and political support cost accountants have to install complex and timely cost accounting systems. Prior empirical research shows that resources and political support are a prerequisite to install sophisticated instruments like ABC and GPK.[922] Thus, the following two hypotheses are set up.

H_{3g}:	*The higher the overall interest in cost accounting is, the more complex are cost accounting systems.*
H_{3h}:	*The higher the overall interest in cost accounting is, the timelier are cost accounting systems.*

The environmental context of cost accounting systems differs across **industries.** By referring to the contingency theory it is concluded that the conceptual design of cost accounting systems differs across industries. Furthermore, the adoption rate of modern cost accounting instruments might vary because these instruments were mainly developed for the

919 It is expected that true product costs can be identified when all cause-and-effect relationships are considered for. Cf. *Charles/Hansen* (2008), p. 283.

920 As the focus of this study is on the complexity and timeliness of cost accounting systems and not on single instruments, the argument by *Krumwiede* that strong IT systems might serve as a disincentive to implement innovative instruments is of lower relevance. Cf. *Krumwiede* (1998), p. 264.

921 Cf. *Al-Omiri/Drury* (2007), p. 415-419. *Becker* shows significant differences in the design of cost accounting systems of small and medium-size companies, whether they have implemented IT-systems or not. Cf. *Becker* (1984), p. 162f. First stage allocation might be conducted in a more simple way when manual systems are employed. *Charalambos/Constantinides* further demonstrates that companies that adopt ERP-systems introduce more sophisticated cost accounting techniques like ABC. Cf. *Charalambos/Constantinides* (2004), p. 240.

922 Cf. section 2.1.3.3.

manufacturing sector. For both reasons, the following hypotheses are deduced in accordance with *Shields*.[923]

H_{3i}:	*The complexity of cost accounting systems differs across industries.*
H_{3j}:	*The timeliness of cost accounting systems differs across industries.*

Variations in management accounting are expected to diminish worldwide due to convergence factors. Against the background of globalization, the significance of country-specifics has been questioned while industry-specifics remain.[924] *Shields* therefore states that industry-specifics have a stronger impact than country-specifics upon the design of cost accounting systems.[925] So far, this assumption has not been tested before. To identify the relative importance of nation and industry upon the complexity and timeliness of cost accounting systems, the following two hypotheses are derived.

H_{6b}:	*The complexity of cost accounting systems differs more strongly across industries than across countries.*
H_{6c}:	*The timeliness of cost accounting systems differs more strongly across industries than across countries.*

It is expected that cost accounting objectives determine the conceptual design of cost accounting systems. As **private, public, and charitable organizations** likely follow the surveyed cost accounting objectives to a different extent, it is expected that the complexity and the timeliness of cost accounting systems differ across different types of organizations. By comparing the conceptual design of cost accounting systems across different types of organizations, the relevance of nation, industry, and type of organizations as an influence factor can be appraised.

H_{3k}:	*The complexity of cost accounting systems differs across private, public, and charitable organizations.*
H_{3l}:	*The timeliness of cost accounting systems differs across private, public, and charitable organizations.*

2.3.5.3 Influence of cost accounting objectives upon cost accounting systems

A strong **focus on financial accounting** is expected to have a negative impact upon the complexity and timeliness of cost accounting systems. The more intensively companies pursue cost accounting for financial objectives, the less cost accounting can serve managerial objectives to provide accurate, detailed, and timely cost information for decision making. Whereas for management accounting purposes timelier, more accurate, and more detailed cost information can improve decision making, financial accounting demands to update cost information only once during the reporting period and aggregated and less accurate cost information are sufficient. Thus the following hypotheses are derived.

923 Cf. *Shields* (1998), p. 512.

924 Cf. section 1.2.3.

925 Cf. *Shields* (1998), p. 512.

> *H_{4a}: The more intensively companies pursue cost accounting for inventory valuation, the less complex are cost accounting systems.*
>
> *H_{4b}: The more intensively companies pursue cost accounting for inventory valuation, the less timely are cost accounting systems.*

For **planning** more future-oriented cost information is required because realistic plans for the future have to be set up that anticipate prospective developments like prices for raw materials. As future-oriented cost information is uncertain and more difficult to obtain, only less accurate and detailed cost information can be provided. Thus, companies with a strong focus on planning require less complex cost accounting systems. *Schoute* supports this conclusion. He provides robust results indicating that for higher (lower) emphasis on product planning cost system complexity negatively (positively) affects cost system intensity of use.[926] Cost **control**, in particular in combination with responsibility accounting, requires accurate and detailed cost information. Otherwise, cost control is not accepted by the persons in charge.[927] Furthermore, accurate and detailed cost information is required to provide meaningful suggestions for improvement. Hence, the following hypotheses are deduced.

> *H_{4c}: The more important cost accounting is for planning, the less complex are cost accounting systems.*
>
> *H_{4d}: The more important cost accounting is for control, the more complex are cost accounting systems.*

For **decision facilitating**, accurate, detailed, and timely cost information is required because more comprehensive information leads to better decision making. More comprehensive cost information supports decision makers to determine the right decision because it enhances the comprehension of the situation.[928] Only the costs and benefits of complex and timely cost accounting systems have to be balanced. Thus, the following hypotheses are derived.

> *H_{4e}: The more important decision facilitating is, the more complex are cost accounting systems.*
>
> *H_{4f}: The more important decision facilitating is, the timelier are cost accounting systems.*

For **decision influencing** more complex cost accounting systems are not superior, because more comprehensive cost information can facilitate conflicts of aims when information asymmetries between agents and principals exist. Providing very accurate and detailed cost information might furthermore be "too complex to direct attention to the most important determinants of success because it provides so many signals"[929]. Cost accounting systems have therefore to provide plain information for decision influencing. Less detailed information directs managers' attention to the most important determinants of success, to help them learn and to motivate them: "Attention directing, learning, and motivation are most

926 Cf. *Schoute* (2009), p. 208.

927 By a more detailed cost variance analysis, e.g., the costs an employee is responsible for can more precisely be determined. Cf. section 2.3.2.1.

928 Timely information enables a quick learning and the consequences of decisions can rather be identified when feedback information is provided promptly. If cost information is outdated, it might be too late for decision makers to revise their actions after having analyzed differences between plan and actual. Cf. *Koontz/Bradspies* (1972).

929 *Merchant/Shields* (1993), p. 81.

effective and efficient when the employees' tasks are clarified and focused, when key variables are visible, and when few conflicts or trade-offs exist among the variables."[930] Companies striving for decision influencing are therefore expected to rather choose simple than complex systems that are easier to understand by product designers and process engineers.[931] The relationship between decision influencing and timeliness of cost accounting systems is not clear. Timelier information can constitute one source of information asymmetries between agents and principals, but could also facilitate to influence employees' behaviors in a more continuous manner. The following hypotheses are consequently set up.

H_{4g}:	*The more important decision influencing, the less complex are cost accounting systems.*
H_{4h}:	*The importance of decision influencing has no impact upon the timeliness of cost accounting systems.*

Cost accounting systems that are mainly applied for **operational objectives** have to provide more accurate, detailed, and timely cost information than for strategic objectives.[932] Cost information for operational objectives is often based on the past and can therefore be of higher accuracy and detail. As **strategic objectives** (e.g., reducing product costs by 20% within the next five years) reach farer into the future, they are more uncertain and more difficult to obtain than operational objectives (e.g., reducing product costs by 5% within one year). Consequently, less accurate and detailed cost information can only be provided for strategic objectives. Cost accounting for strategic objectives has further to direct managers' attention only to the most relevant information. A very complex cost accounting system that provides detailed cost information would be inappropriate for strategic objectives because it would generate too many signals to direct attention. Thereby, also learning and motivating employees to act in the company's interests are expected to be impeded. Furthermore, longer reporting periods for strategic objectives compared to operational objectives are required, because "[d]ecisions regarding product design, introduction, abandonment, and pricing are strategic matters that should not be based on short-run fluctuations of manufacturing efficiencies."[933] Hence, the following hypotheses are deduced.

H_{4i}:	*To meet short-term cost accounting objectives, more complex cost accounting systems are installed.*
H_{4j}:	*To meet short-term cost accounting objectives, timelier cost accounting systems are installed.*
H_{4k}:	*To meet long-term cost accounting objectives, less complex cost accounting systems are installed.*
H_{4l}:	*To meet long-term cost accounting objectives, less timely cost accounting systems are installed.*

Similar to H_{7a} it is expected that the impact of cost accounting objectives upon the conceptual design of cost accounting systems has the same direction cross-nationally, because these relationships are largely functional in nature. However, the **magnitude of the relationships** is expected to **differ cross-nationally**. Thus, the following hypothesis is set up.

---

930 *Merchant/Shields* (1993), p. 81.

931 See also *Kaplan/Johnson* (1991), p. 397.

932 Cf. *Schoute* (2009), p. 210f., with further references, p. 221f.

933 *Kaplan/Johnson* (1991), p. 398.

H_{7b}: The impact of cost accounting objectives upon the conceptual design of cost accounting systems has the same direction, but it differs cross-nationally in magnitude.

2.4 Performance of cost accounting systems

In order to **provide practitioners with recommendations** how to design their cost accounting systems purposefully, it is necessary to have a choice between different alternatives of cost accounting objectives and cost accounting systems that are more effective than others under given context factors.[934] It can thereby be demonstrated in how far designers can influence the performance of cost accounting systems – or whether the systems' performance mainly refers to factors that are beyond their sphere of influence. It is expected that the performance of the same conceptual design of a cost accounting system varies across different countries, under different other external and internal context factors, and when they are designed for different cost accounting objectives.

2.4.1 Selection of the approaches to measure performance

Several approaches are discussed in literature to measure organizational performance. The most relevant ones include the resource-based, internal process, goal, and system approach.[935] The first three approaches determine the performance on one of the three major cycle phases in the system model of organizational behavior: input, transformation, and output. The system approach combines all three major cycle phases (see Figure 2-12).[936] These approaches are described in the following.

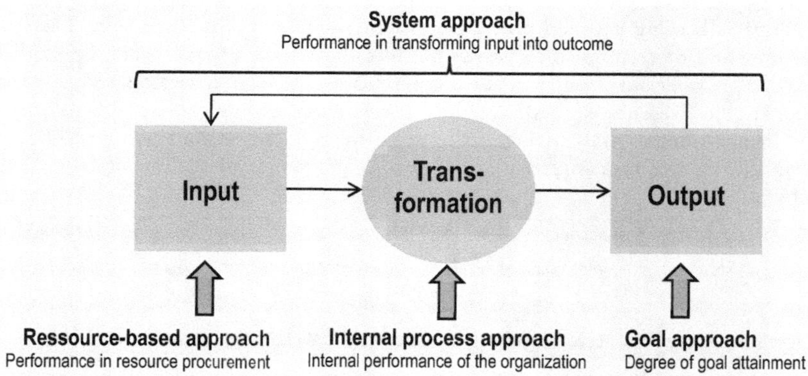

Figure 2-12: Traditional approaches to measuring organizational performance
Source: following *Daft* (2010), p. 76; *Daft* (2001), p. 27

The **resource-based approach** assesses the performance of organizations by observing the procurement activities and by determining, whether organizations are successful to acquire

934 Cf. *Welge/Fessmann* (1980), c. 577; *Grabatin* (1981), p. 1.

935 Cf., e.g., *Daft* (2001), p. 27-31; *Daft* (2010), p. 75-80.

936 Cf., e.g., *Daft* (2001), p. 27-31; *Vallabhaneni* (2008), p. 111; *Daft* (2010), p. 75-80.

scarce and valued resources for high performance from the environment. In other words, the negotiation power of organizations in respect to their suppliers is appraised. The resource-based approach is not suitable for this study, because it is not the task of cost accounting to procure resources like qualified cost accountants and IT systems.

The performance of transforming resources to generate output can be determined by the **internal process approach**. This approach investigates what organizations do with their resources. Thus, this approach focuses on the internal activities within organizations. "[A]n organization is effective if the internal processes of production, communication, cooperation and management develop promptly without conflicts."[937] This approach does not consider the external environment, wherefore it is unsuitable for this study. This approach is also not suitable because the process of generating cost information is not investigated in this study.[938]

The **goal approach** addresses the output side and assesses whether organizations attain their goals in terms of desired output. The performance of organizational instruments can thereby be investigated. As the usefulness of cost accounting systems strongly depends upon their applicability to meet their cost accounting objectives,[939] the performance of cost accounting systems is measured accordingly. Which resources are used and how efficient the internal processes operate is not considered for. Although the goal approach **fits best for this study**, there are two main assumptions that underlie this approach: (1) organizations have an ultimate goal and (2) this goal can be identified empirically.[940] The assumptions are often taken for granted, because orientation to a goal is often seen as the defining characteristic of organizations. However, the rationale and proceeding to identify the goals of organizations,[941] the fact that companies often follow several goals at the same time, and that goals may change over time is more problematic.[942] This study addresses the first two problems by deducing the cost accounting objectives from organizational goals. Prior research on cost accounting objectives is thereby considered for and the role of cost accounting within the management process is investigated to ensure that the most relevant cost accounting objectives are included (see section 2.2). The goal approach is a flexible instrument that can consider the relevance of cost accounting objectives to determine overall performance. This is useful, because the relevance of cost accounting objectives is expected to vary internationally.

Further approaches are discussed in literature, which are summarized to the **system approaches**, which include two or three phases of the model into a single framework.[943] As

---

937 *Hansen* (1995), p. 37.

938 Instead of describing the process of information generation, the system's dimension timeliness describes the frequency of updating cost information.

939 Cf. *Schweitzer/Küpper* (2011), p. 74.

940 Cf. *Yuchtman/Seashore* (1967), p. 892.

941 Cf. *Yuchtman/Seashore* (1967), p. 892, with further references.

942 Cf. *Grabatin* (1981), p. 25.

943 System approaches include, for instance, the system-resource approach (see *Yuchtman/Seashore* (1967)) and the competing values model (see *Quinn/Rohrbaugh* (1983)). See also *Paces et al.* (1999), p. 111f. The system resource and the goal approach are often considered in German litera-

measuring the resource-based and internal-process approach is inappropriate for this study, each system approach is also improper.

Performance of cost accounting systems can be defined both in terms of efficiency and effectiveness. Efficiency is commonly defined as 'doing the things right' and effectiveness as 'doing the right things'. Whereas efficiency describes the degree of productivity to achieve objectives, effectiveness refers to the degree of target achievement.[944] In this study effectiveness and satisfaction with cost accounting systems are addressed. The efficiency of cost accounting systems is not investigated because the internal process approach is not addressed and measuring the costs of running cost accounting systems to determine the systems' productivity is very difficult.[945] As in literature the terms 'efficiency' and 'effectiveness' are often used synonymously [946] and as the satisfaction with cost accounting systems is also determined, in the following the term '**performance**' and '**success**' instead of 'effectiveness' is used to avoid misunderstandings.

Economic indicators and subjective assessments can be applied to measure performance. **Economic indicators** like return on investment and return on sales measure the performance on an organizational and not on a functional level. These indicators are objective and are therefore less likely to be biased due to cultural differences in, e.g., response style. Although cost accounting has to contribute to the organizational goals, only few conclusions can be drawn from organizational performance to the performance of cost accounting systems and vice versa.[947] Furthermore, cost accounting is expected to have only a marginal effect on the company's overall performance. Other functions like marketing or research and development are expected to have a stronger impact. In spite of these shortcomings, the profitability of the companies is surveyed. The alternative to economic indicators, **subjective assessments**, is expected to have more significance for this study. *Drury/Tales*, e.g., call for subjective instead of economic performance measures to determine under which conditions companies adopt complex cost accounting systems.[948] Performance is subjectively assessed by the respondents on the functional level of cost accounting. Following the goal approach, this study determines the performance of cost accounting systems by investigating the attainment of cost accounting objectives. In addition to

ture to be the most relevant ones. Cf. *Fessmann* (1980), p. 213; *Grabatin* (1981), p. 19; *Kurrle* (1995), p. 56f.; *Grundei* (1999), p. 68.

944 Cf. *Grundei* (1999), p. 67f., with further references.

945 Two thirds of large German companies do not know how many resources their cost accounting systems consume. Cf. *Weber* (1993), p. 273.

946 Cf. *Fessmann* (1980), p. 26-31.

947 Cf. *Heigl* (1981), p. 429. The relevance of cost accounting for organizational performance is rather small compared to other functions. *Weber et al.* report that the costs of cost accounting are far below 1% of sales turnover. Cf. *Weber et al.* (1997), p. 32. The contribution of cost accounting to the overall performance of a company is therefore expected to be rather low. The performance of other functions thus likely distorts the impact of cost accounting upon organizational performance. Empirical research supports these conclusions. *Pizzini's* study indicates that the cost accounting system's characteristics are positively associated with the evaluation of relevance and usefulness of data but not with economic indicators. Cf. *Pizzini* (2006).

948 Cf. *Drury/Tayles* (2005), p. 77.

the goal approach, the managers' general satisfaction with cost accounting systems is surveyed. Both measures are expected to be interrelated. The better the cost accounting objectives are attained, the more satisfied managers are expected to be with the provided information.[949] Finally, the perceived characteristics of cost information including accuracy, detail, timeliness, and understandability for managers are assessed.

2.4.2 Operationalization of performance

The **attainment of cost accounting objectives** is operationalized by asking the respondents on a seven-point Likert scale to what extent they pursue eleven indicators of cost accounting objectives described in section 2.2 (question B.1 to B.3, Appendix 2) and to what extent these indicators are met (question D.4 to D.6). To consider that the relevance of cost accounting objectives may differ internationally, the **measure 'performance attainment'** is obtained individually for each company by weighting the performance of the indicators for cost accounting objectives by the extent to which they are pursued. Figure 2-13 shows that indicator B is more intensively pursued than indicator A (question 1). Therefore, the degree of performance for indicator B is weighted higher than the degree of performance for indicator A (question 2). The scale to calculate the performance of cost accounting systems is reduced by one from the scale of the questionnaire to obtain a range between 0 and 6. Without this transformation, the calculation would not correspond to the responses: When an indicator is not pursued at all, the indicator should not be relevant for the overall performance of cost accounting systems; when an indicator is not met at all, the performance should be zero. To determine the overall performance of cost accounting systems, the performance of the single indicators are each weighted by the extent to which the indicators are pursued. Thereafter, the obtained values for all single indicators are added up and divided by the sum of all evaluable scores for the first question. Finally, the outcome is added by 1 to obtain a range between 1 and 7. This is necessary to ensure comparability with the other performance measures that all lie between 1 and 7 except for profitability. To test for the stability of the results, the alternative performance **measure 'factor attainment'** is determined. This alternative measure aggregates the attainment of indicators with a factor analysis without weighting the attainment of these indicators according to their relevance.

949 This relationship is empirically supported by *Friedl et al.* (2009a), p. 116.

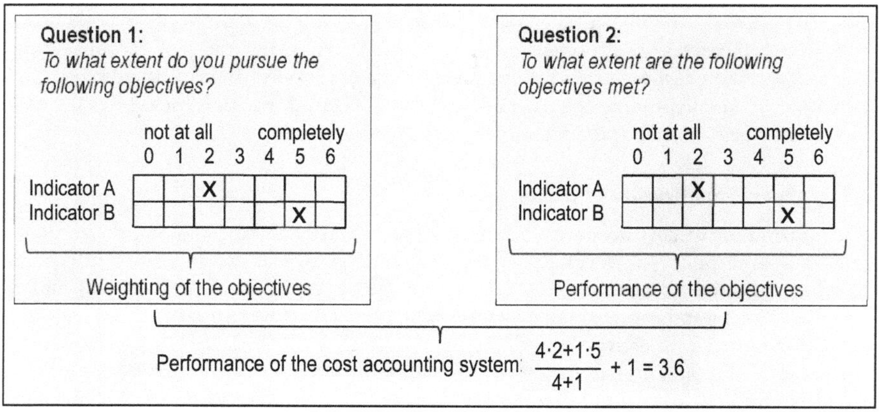

Figure 2-13: Operationalization of the attainment of objectives

The managers' **overall satisfaction** with cost accounting systems (question D.2, Appendix 2) does not require any transformation or calculation and thus directly represents the performance of cost accounting systems. The **characteristics of cost information** (accuracy, detail, timeliness, understandability for managers; cf. question D.1) are aggregated to one factor via factor analysis. Finally, the respondents are asked to appraise their companies' **profitability** relative to their competitors, being either less profitable, more profitable, or about the same (question A.16).

Solely *Pizzini* and *Schoute* have investigated the relationship between complexity of cost accounting systems and performance. *Pizzini* operationalized relevance in a comprehensive way by determining user needs and the actual information supplied with a set of questions. Thereafter, he subtracts the responses to user needs from the responses to actual information supplied. Usefulness, on the contrary, was solely measured with one question. *Schoute* operationalized performance by 'cost system intensity of use' and by 'cost system satisfaction'. The first measure rates the extent to which cost accounting systems are used for decision making. The second one rates the extent to which users are satisfied with the provided information. Both indicators of performance were measured by a single question on a five-point Likert scale.[950] Overall, the operationalization of performance in this study is more comprehensive compared to prior research. A comprehensive measurement for performance is required to reduce bias that might stem from cross-national differences in response style (see section 1.2.6) and in the perception of system quality.

2.4.3 Hypotheses development

In sections 2.1.1.5 and 2.3.5.1 it is concluded that German companies have a higher potential to install complex and timely cost accounting systems. Although more complex and timelier systems can provide more comprehensive cost information, it does not imply that comprehensive cost information leads to a higher satisfaction with cost accounting

950 Cf. *Schoute* (2009), p. 215.

systems. German cost accountants might spend too much time to install complex and timely systems instead of discussing the provided information with their managers.[951] In Japan on the contrary, a closer collaboration with managers to combine their accounting know-how with operational knowledge is assumed. Hence, although German cost accounting systems are likely to provide more comprehensive cost information, Japanese systems might provide more suitable cost information for decision makers. For this reason, the following hypothesis is set up without specifying in which **country** cost accounting is more successful.

H_{1s}: *The performance of cost accounting systems differs across countries.*

Schoute's study indicates that **context factors** are not significantly related to the cost accounting users' satisfaction with the system.[952] As in this study performance is operationalized in a more comprehensive way, assumptions about the impact of other external and internal context factors upon the performance of cost accounting systems are still drawn.

Advanced **IT systems** facilitate installing and running complex and timely cost accounting systems due to the rationalization of data processing.[953] Cost accountants may even have more time to discuss cost information with managers, when comprehensive IT systems avoid duplication of work, e.g., when the IT systems are cross-functionally integrated. Finally, comprehensive IT systems facilitate querying cost information. For all three reasons it is expected that IT systems quality leads to more successful cost accounting systems. Consequently, the following hypothesis is deduced.

H_{3m}: *The more comprehensive IT systems, the more successful are cost accounting systems.*

Industries represent a conglomerate of internal and external context factors. As these context factors differ across industries, the challenges to run cost accounting systems might also vary across industries leading to different expectations of the providers and users of cost information. As it is expected that the conceptual design of cost accounting systems differs more strongly across industries than across countries,[954] it is also concluded that the performance of cost accounting systems differs more strongly across industries than across countries. Consequently, the following hypotheses are derived.

H_{3n}:	*The performance of cost accounting systems differs across industries.*
H_{6d}:	*The performance of cost accounting objectives differs more strongly across industries than across countries.*

The cost accounting objectives likely differ across different types of organizations. As cost accounting systems differ in their potential to meet various cost accounting objectives, the

951 Cf. *Ahrens/Chapman* (1999), p. 43; *Weber* (2004), p. 9.

952 Cf. *Schoute* (2009), p. 222. In his analysis he has included competition, perceived environmental uncertainty, competitive strategy, vertical differentiation, formalization, centralization, organizational size, product diversity, advanced manufacturing technology, production lines, and production process.

953 This relationship has already been affirmed by *Krumwiede et al.* (2007), p. 26, 31f., 40.

954 Cf. *Shields* (1998), p. 512.

performance of cost accounting systems might differ as well between private, public, and charitable organizations. Consequently, the following hypothesis is set up.

H_{3o}: *The performance of cost accounting systems differs across private, public, and charitable organizations.*

Following the argument from hypothesis H_{3o}, it is expected that cost accounting **objectives** have an impact upon the performance of cost accounting systems. It is concluded that the more cost accounting serves for the financial accounting objective '**inventory valuation**', the less these systems are designed to support managerial objectives. Consequently, the providers and users of cost information are expected to be less satisfied with the provided information. On the contrary, the expectations of cost accounting systems that serve mainly financial accounting objectives might be lower. In spite of this counter-argument, the following hypothesis is deduced.

H_{4m}: *The more important cost accounting is for financial accounting purposes, the less successful are cost accounting systems.*

The **complexity and timeliness of cost accounting systems** as potentials to provide accurate, detailed, and timely information are expected to influence the performance of cost accounting systems. It is assumed that a more complex and timelier cost accounting system is perceived by the managers to be more successful.[955] Cost accounting systems are designed under cost-benefit considerations. Only when the providers and users of cost information are satisfied, they are willing to spend more money for further developing this instrument. This assumption is supported by discussion with practitioners *Timian's* findings. He concludes that

> *"when managers are interested in utilizing the accounting data, the system is usually expanded to provide the necessary information. On the other hand, if managers rely on alternative sources of information or models, which are not dependent upon accounting data, the accounting system is downscaled accordingly."*[956]

It is furthermore expected that the relationship between cost accounting systems' complexity and timeliness is non-linear, because – following *Kajüter*[957] – a diminishing marginal utility of complexity and timeliness is expected. With increasing accuracy, detail, and timeliness of cost information, the decision makers cannot exploit its full potential due to limitations in time and cognition. More accurate, detailed, and timely cost information can even lead to poorer results, if users are unable to cope with the amount of information and/or when the cost accountants spent too much time for installing and running the systems than discussing the information with the decision makers. Consequently, the following hypotheses are derived.

---

955 This assumption is supported by *Pizzini's* study. Cf. *Pizzini* (2006); section 2.4.2.

956 *Timian/Fleming* (2000), p. 44. This argument was also supported in discussions with practitioners. Cost accountants from the hospital industry have confirmed that the development of cost accounting systems is only worthwhile when chief and senior physicians actually use the provided cost information.

957 Cf. *Kajüter* (2005), p. 96f.

H_{5a}:	*The more complex cost accounting systems are, the more successful they are.*
H_{5b}:	*The timelier cost accounting systems are, the more successful they are.*
H_{5c}:	*A diminishing marginal utility of cost accounting systems' complexity prevails.*
H_{5d}:	*A diminishing marginal utility of cost accounting systems' timeliness prevails.*

As pointed out above, however, simpler cost accounting systems can be more suitable than more complex systems under certain environmental conditions and for different cost accounting objectives. Therefore, further hypotheses are derived by combining the conceptual design of cost accounting systems with context factors and cost accounting objectives.

As in a **complex external environment** more elements of the company's reality should be reproduced, more complex cost accounting systems are expected to be more successful than simple systems under these circumstances. In a **dynamic external environment** a company's reality should be reproduced more frequently with a timely cost accounting system to provide information that is still relevant for decision facilitating and influencing. Consequently, the following two hypotheses are set up.

H_{5e}:	*Complex cost accounting systems are more successful for companies with a complex external environment.*
H_{5f}:	*Timely cost accounting systems are more successful for companies with a dynamic external environment.*

In section 2.2.2 it was concluded that for **short-term decisions** and for **decision facilitating** more accurate, detailed, and timely cost information are required than for **long-term decisions** and for **decision influencing**. Hence, complex and timely cost accounting systems are expected to be more successful for short-term compared to long-term decisions and for decision facilitating compared to for decision influencing. The following hypotheses are therefore deduced.

H_{5g}:	*Complex cost accounting systems are more successful for decision facilitating than for decision influencing.*
H_{5h}:	*Timely cost accounting systems are more successful for decision facilitating than for decision influencing.*
H_{5i}:	*Complex cost accounting systems are more successful for short-term decision making than for long-term decision making.*
H_{5j}:	*Timely cost accounting systems are more successful for short-term decision making than for long-term decision making.*

It is furthermore assumed that more complex and timelier cost accounting systems are required, the more cost accounting serves **management accounting** than **financial accounting objectives**. Whereas financial accounting demands to update cost information only once during the reporting period and aggregated cost information are sufficient, for management accounting purposes timelier, more accurate, and more detailed cost information can improve decision making. This relationship is expressed in the following hypotheses.

H_{5k}: Complex cost accounting systems are more successful when cost accounting serves more for management than for financial accounting objectives.

H_{5l}: Timely cost accounting systems are more successful when cost accounting serves more for management than for financial accounting objectives.

The more complex cost accounting systems are, the more expensive it becomes to update all cost information. It is consequently expected that **complex and timely cost accounting systems misfit**. As the time of cost accountants is limited, they should make a compromise between complex and timely cost accounting systems. In a very complex and dynamic environment the cost accounting systems should consequently not be too complex to allow frequent updates of cost information under the given resources provided for cost accounting.

H_{5m}: Cost accounting systems that are both high or low in complexity and timeliness are less successful.

Similar to H_{7a} and H_{7b} it is expected that context factors, cost accounting objectives, and the conceptual design of cost accounting systems have cross-nationally the same impact regarding direction upon the performance of cost accounting systems. However, the **magnitude of the relationships** is expected to **differ cross-nationally**. Thus, the following hypothesis is set up.

H_{7c}: The impact of context factors, cost accounting objectives, and the conceptual design of cost accounting systems upon the performance of cost accounting systems has the same direction but, differs cross-nationally in magnitude.

2.5 Conclusions

In section 2 the conceptual framework from section 1.5.2 was specified by conceptualizing and operationalizing theoretical constructs in this chapter. The specified conceptual framework is provided in Figure 2-14.

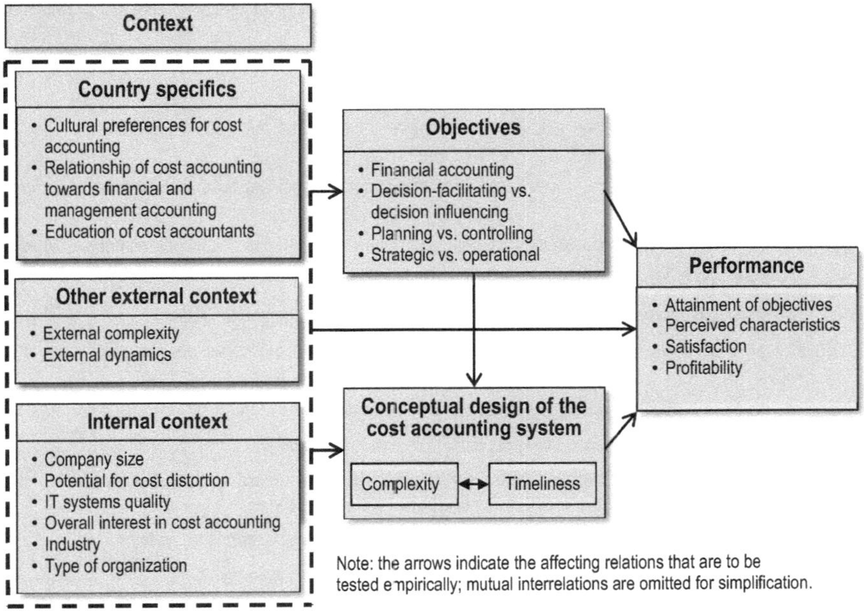

Figure 2-14: Specified conceptual framework

The basic research hypotheses from section 1.5.2 were furthermore specified. Table 2–1 summarizes the basic research hypotheses and the corresponding single hypotheses.

H_1: The context differs internationally and country-specifics have an influence upon the objectives, the conceptual design, and the performance of cost accounting systems.

H_{1a}: German companies have a stronger emphasis on accurate and detailed than on timely cost information.

H_{1b}: Japanese companies have a stronger emphasis on timely than on accurate and detailed cost information.

H_{1c}: German cost accountants are more specialized than their Japanese counterparts.

H_{1d}: German cost accountants have more theoretical knowledge than their Japanese counterparts.

H_{1e}: Japanese companies have more comprehensive IT systems than their German counterparts.

H_{1f}: The overall interest in cost accounting is about the same in Germany and in Japan.

H_{1g}: Japanese companies pursue cost accounting for inventory valuation more intensively than their German counterparts.

H_{1h}: Whereas German companies place more emphasis on control, Japanese companies put more emphasis on planning.

H_{1i}: German companies place more emphasis on cost information for decision facilitating than their Japanese counterparts.

H_{1j}: *Japanese companies place more emphasis on cost information for decision influencing than their German counterparts.*

H_{1k}: *German companies apply cost accounting more intensively for short-term objectives than their Japanese counterparts.*

H_{1l}: *Japanese companies apply cost accounting more intensively for long-term objectives than their German counterparts.*

H_{1m}: *German companies employ more complex cost accounting systems than their Japanese counterparts.*

H_{1n}: *German companies employ more timely cost accounting systems than their Japanese counterparts.*

H_{1o}: *The more specialized cost accountants are, the more complex are cost accounting systems.*

H_{1p}: *The more specialized cost accountants are, the timelier are cost accounting systems.*

H_{1q}: *The more theoretical knowledge cost accountants have, the more complex are cost accounting systems.*

H_{1r}: *The more theoretical knowledge cost accountants have, the timelier are cost accounting systems.*

H_{1s}: *The performance of cost accounting systems differs across countries.*

H_2: Other external context factors have an influence upon the objectives as well as on the conceptual design and the performance of cost accounting systems.

H_{2a}: *The more complex the environment is, the more complex are cost accounting systems.*

H_{2b}: *The more dynamic the environment is, the timelier are cost accounting systems.*

H_3: Internal context factors have an influence upon the objectives as well as on the conceptual design and the performance of cost accounting systems.

H_{3a}: *Cost accounting objectives differ across industries.*

H_{3b}: *The larger the company is, the more complex are cost accounting systems.*

H_{3c}: *Company size does not affect the timeliness of cost accounting systems.*

H_{3d}: *The higher the potential for cost distortion, the more complex are cost accounting systems.*

H_{3e}: *The higher IT systems quality, the more complex are cost accounting systems.*

H_{3f}: *The higher IT systems quality, the timelier are cost accounting systems.*

H_{3g}: *The higher the overall interest in cost accounting is, the more complex are cost accounting systems.*

H_{3h}: *The higher the overall interest in cost accounting is, the timelier are cost accounting systems.*

H_{3i}: *The complexity of cost accounting systems differs across industries.*

H_{3j}: *The timeliness of cost accounting systems differs across industries.*

H_{3k}: *The complexity of cost accounting systems differs across private, public, and charitable organizations.*

H_{3l}: *The timeliness of cost accounting systems differs across private, public, and charitable organizations.*

H_{3m}: *The more comprehensive IT systems, the more successful are cost accounting systems.*

H_{3n}: *The performance of cost accounting systems differs across industries.*

H_{3o}: *The performance of cost accounting systems differs across private, public, and charitable organizations.*

H_4: Cost accounting objectives have an influence upon the conceptual design and the performance of cost accounting systems.

H_{4a}: The more intensively companies pursue cost accounting for inventory valuation, the less complex are cost accounting systems.

H_{4b}: The more intensively companies pursue cost accounting for inventory valuation, the less timely are cost accounting systems.

H_{4c}: The more important cost accounting is for planning, the less complex are cost accounting systems.

H_{4d}: The more important cost accounting is for control, the more complex are cost accounting systems.

H_{4e}: The more important decision facilitating is, the more complex are cost accounting systems.

H_{4f}: The more important decision facilitating is, the timelier are cost accounting systems.

H_{4g}: The more important decision influencing, the less complex are cost accounting systems.

H_{4h}: The importance of decision influencing has no impact upon the timeliness of cost accounting systems.

H_{4i}: To meet short-term cost accounting objectives, more complex cost accounting systems are installed.

H_{4j}: To meet short-term cost accounting objectives, timelier cost accounting systems are installed.

H_{4k}: To meet long-term cost accounting objectives, less complex cost accounting systems are installed.

H_{4l}: To meet long-term cost accounting objectives, less timely cost accounting systems are installed.

H_{4m}: The more important cost accounting is for financial accounting purposes, the less successful are cost accounting systems.

H_5: The conceptual design of cost accounting systems determines the performance of the systems.

H_{5a}: The more complex cost accounting systems are, the more successful they are.

H_{5b}: The timelier cost accounting systems are, the more successful they are.

H_{5c}: A diminishing marginal utility of cost accounting systems' complexity prevails.

H_{5d}: A diminishing marginal utility of cost accounting systems' timeliness prevails.

H_{5e}: Complex cost accounting systems are more successful for companies with a complex external environment.

H_{5f}: Timely cost accounting systems are more successful for companies with a dynamic external environment.

H_{5g}: Complex cost accounting systems are more successful for decision facilitating than for decision influencing.

H_{5h}: Timely cost accounting systems are more successful for decision facilitating than for decision influencing.

H_{5i}: Complex cost accounting systems are more successful for short-term decision making than for long-term decision making.

H_{5j}: Timely cost accounting systems are more successful for short-term decision making than for long-term decision making.

H_{5k}: Complex cost accounting systems are more successful when cost accounting serves more for management than for financial accounting objectives.

H_{5l}:	*Timely cost accounting systems are more successful when cost accounting serves more for management than for financial accounting objectives.*
H_{5m}:	*Cost accounting systems that are both high or low in complexity and timeliness are less successful.*
H_{6}:	**The objectives of cost accounting as well as the conceptual design and the performance of cost accounting systems differ more strongly across industries than across countries.**
H_{6a}:	*Cost accounting objectives differ more strongly across industries than across countries.*
H_{6b}:	*The complexity of cost accounting systems differs more strongly across industries than across countries.*
H_{6c}:	*The timeliness of cost accounting systems differs more strongly across industries than across countries.*
H_{6d}:	*The performance of cost accounting objectives differs more strongly across industries than across countries.*
H_{7}:	**The relationships between the elements are stable between Germany and Japan, but they differ in magnitude.**
H_{7a}:	*The impact of context factors upon the conceptual design of cost accounting systems has the same direction for both Germany and Japan, but it differs cross-nationally in magnitude.*
H_{7b}:	*The impact of cost accounting objectives upon the conceptual design of cost accounting systems has the same direction, but it differs cross-nationally in magnitude.*
H_{7c}:	*The impact of context factors, cost accounting objectives, and the conceptual design of cost accounting systems upon the performance of cost accounting systems has the same direction but, differs cross-nationally in magnitude.*

Table 2-6: Research hypotheses of the study

The review on comparative research on cost accounting demonstrates that little theoretical and practical contribution has been provided, so that most arguments about cross-national differences remain rather anecdotal than empirically verified. This study addresses this research gap by conducting a theory-based and empirical comparison of German and Japanese cost accounting systems, whereby cost accounting is investigated in more depth, issues in equivalence are more comprehensively addressed, and cross-national differences are explained in a more comprehensive way. The empirical analysis is carried through in the following chapter to answer the five research questions from section 1.1.1.

3 Empirical analysis

3.1 Design of the empirical investigation

3.1.1 Definition of the sample

In this study **German and Japanese medium-sized companies** with between 250 and 2,000 employees were mail-surveyed. Small companies are not addressed in this study because they often lack resources and specialized employees to install comprehensive cost accounting systems. Recommendations on how to design comprehensive systems could thereby hardly be derived. Large companies are also excluded from the sample to avoid dependence between the German and Japanese samples.[958] It is expected that medium-sized companies are less exposed to globalization than larger ones and thus more likely represent 'domestic' cost accounting (section 1.2.6).[959]

Besides company size the sample is further limited to **three industries**. Previous studies on cost accounting have often narrowed their investigation to manufacturing industries.[960] However, the economic relevance of this group of industries has decreased over the years. For this reason and to test *Shields*' assumption that cost accounting differs more strongly across industries than across countries,[961] three industries are investigated. The explanatory power and the scope of application of this study significantly depend upon the chosen industries. A thoughtful selection of the three industries is therefore required. The industries have to be economically significant, sufficient companies must be available for contact, and they should be homogeneous. Furthermore, the industries should significantly differ in their requirements for cost accounting, because Germany and Japan constitute very distinctive countries in cost accounting as well. Hence, to test whether cost accounting differs more strongly across industries than across counties, it is necessary to contrast distinctive industries with distinctive countries. The industries mechanical engineering,

---

958 Interactions between the samples are thereby reduced to avoid contamination of the data, which could lead to biased results. Cf. *Adler* (1984), p. 53; *Firkola/Lim* (2003), p. 54.

959 Medium-sized companies are less frequently exposed to global pressures, like international reporting standards. IFRS for small and medium-sized companies, for example, is not frequently applied in Germany. Therefore, in Germany smaller companies apply more frequently national GAAP than IFRS in comparison to their larger counterparts. Cf. *Zwirner* (2010). See also *Kajüter et al.* (2007). Furthermore, it is not necessary to analyze large companies in this study, because only superficially relevant features of the 'natural world' (cf. *Birnberg et al.* (1990), p. 49-51) can be investigated via survey research. The particularities in which way large companies, e.g., allocate overhead cannot be described. A field study would be more appropriate for this kind of investigation to demonstrate sophisticated practices. Instead of observing particularities of cost accounting practices, broader characteristics of cost accounting systems are investigated in this study, like the frequency of updating cost information, and its impact on the performance of cost accounting systems. For this analysis large companies are not more beneficial than medium-sized companies, because these relationships are expected to stay constant irrespective of company size.

960 This study therefore mainly draws upon empirical studies on cost accounting that have investigated manufacturing industries. See chapter 2.

961 See *Shields* (1998), p. 512.

food and beverage, and hospitals meet all requirements. Whereas mechanical engineering companies and companies of the food and beverage industry are product-oriented, hospitals are service-oriented. The economic significance of the three industries and their different environmental contexts leading to varying requirements for cost accounting are described in the following.

The **food and beverage industry** belongs like the mechanical engineering industry to the manufacturing industries. Food companies process products of agriculture, forestry, and fishing into food for humans or animals. This also includes the production of intermediate products that are not directly food products. Beverage companies manufacture alcoholic and non-alcoholic beverages as well as mineral water. Companies creating a significant part of their value through wholesale and retail trade do not belong to the food and beverage industry.[962]

As this industry is more protected by national governments than other manufacturing industries and as the products of this industry are often perishable and costly to transport, the industry is largely domestic in production terms.[963] This makes it significant in all countries. In Germany and Japan 630,000 respectively 1,138,327 people are employed in the food and beverage industry generating a turnover of € 158 respectively 405 billion in 2008.[964] Small and medium-sized companies dominate the food and beverage industry in both countries. Only about 36% respectively about 10% of the companies have more than 49 employees in Germany and Japan.[965]

Unlike the mechanical engineering industry, the food and beverage industry is a relative low-tech, labor intensive industry with little research and development activities and patenting.[966] This industry is furthermore less subject to economic fluctuations.[967] Due to the relatively low technology a high proportion of low-skilled jobs prevails in this industry with often repetitive tasks.[968] Rivalry within the industry indicates that competition is very intensive. In addition to that, the increasingly dominant retail sectors exert pressures on the fragmented food and beverage industry. Product innovations, advertising, and product differentiation have therefore become a key success factor. Unlike the mechanical engineering industry, most of the innovations in production technologies and management

962 See *United Nations* (2011).

963 The export quota of German food and beverage companies is only 18.3 respectively 9.3%. See *Statistisches Bundesamt* (2010), p. 381.

964 For Germany see *Statistisches Bundesamt* (2010), p. 94, 375. For Japan see *Ministry of Internal Affairs and Communication* (2011), chapter 8-5, chapter 6-12. The Japanese values exclude the beverage industry.

965 For Germany the results were obtained for the year 2010 with the data base DAFNE. For Japan for 2006 including the tobacco and food industry see *Ministry of Internal Affairs and Communication* (2011), chapter 6-5.

966 Cf. *Connor* (1985); *Kubitzki* (2003); *Caroli et al.* (2010), p. 289f., with further references. See also *Avermaete et al.* (2004).

967 Cf. *Kubitzki* (2003), p. 22.

968 Cf. *Caroli et al.* (2010), p. 289f., with further references.

accounting were transferred from other industries.[969] More traditional and less modern cost accounting systems dominate this industry,[970] although stiff competition causes strong cost pressures.

The **mechanical engineering industry** belongs like the food and beverage industry to the manufacturing sector. It is a discipline of engineering that includes the design, production, and operation of machines and equipment. Around 999,000 respectively 1,730,340 employees in Germany and Japan generated a turnover of € 161 billion in 2009 respectively € 618 billion in 2008.[971] With its around 5,212 respectively 8,092 companies the mechanical engineering industry is the largest industry in Germany and Japan.[972] German and Japanese companies have a leading role in the mechanical engineering industry. German companies are in 18 out of 30 sub-industries world market leaders and three of these sub-industries are led by Japanese companies.[973] Germany is the largest exporting nation in this industry with a share of 19.2% of the world exports followed by the USA (11.7%) and Japan (10.7%) (see Figure 3-1).

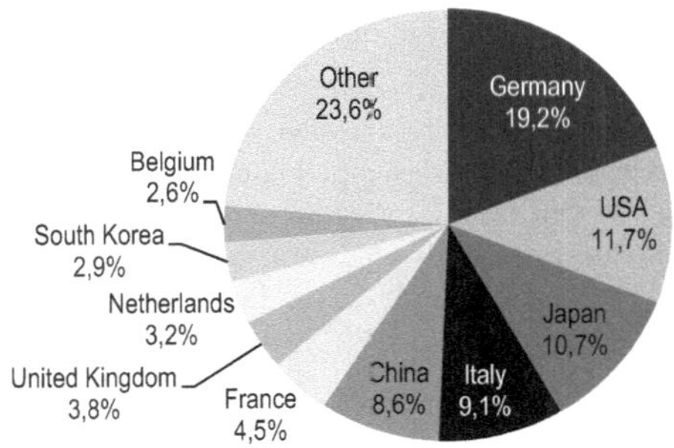

Figure 3-1: Share of world exports in the mechanical engineering industry
Source: own illustration, following *Poll* (2011)

Besides its economic significance, the mechanical engineering industry is very innovative and technical. It has a large proportion of innovating companies and employees working

969 This is one reason for few research and development activities and little patenting in this industry. Cf. *Kubitzki* (2003), p. 91.

970 *Asquer* concludes for Italian food manufacturers that most of them are far from adopting many of the state-of-the-art instruments like ABC. Cf. *Asquer* (2003). *Abdel-Kader/Luther* support this finding. They show that direct costing is widely practiced in comparison to ABC. Also *Groot* reports only low application rates of ABC in the Dutch and US food and beverage industry. See *Groot* (1999), p. 53-55.

971 See *Statistisches Bundesamt* (2010), p. 94, 375, 381; *Ministry of Internal Affairs and Communication* (2011), chapter 8-5, chapter 6-12, respectively.

972 For Germany see *Statistisches Bundesamt* (2010), p. 375; *VDMA* (2010), p. 4, 7. For Japan see *Ministry of Internal Affairs and Communication* (2011), chapter 6-12B.

973 See *VDMA* (2010), p. 33.

in research and development compared to other manufacturing industries.[974] The reasons for this are shortened product life cycles, increase in technological change and competition, as well as the customers' needs for comprehensive solutions. Manufacturing technology has been identified as a major factor of success for the efficiency of the manufacturing process. Over the last decades significant improvements have been achieved in factory automation and machine flexibility.[975] Innovations also include manufacturing management. Japanese companies have led the way to significantly increase productivity and overhead reductions through restructuring the way how products are produced. Significant improvements were realized through instruments like target costing and concepts like JIT.[976] The mechanical engineering industry has furthermore a long tradition of cost accounting and modern cost accounting systems like GPK and ABC. Thus, mimetic behavior of organizations suggests that manufacturers may have employed more comprehensive cost accounting systems than companies operating in other industries.[977]

The **hospital industry** is a branch of the health care industry. It includes hospital activities (i.e. medical, diagnostic, and treatment activities) that are chiefly directed to inpatients and are carried out under the supervision of medical doctors.[978]

The hospital industry is characterized by a large number of health care providers that are represented nationwide. The provision of the stationary services makes it a domestic industry that is of significant relevance in all developed countries. Another benefit of investigating hospitals in this study is that they are very homogeneous in service provision, because they often have to provide principally the same basic set of services by applying standard methods. The 2,083 German and 8,794 Japanese hospitals employ about 1,078,000 respectively 1,771,436 employees in 2008 (this includes about 139,000 respectively 187,948 medical doctors).[979]

Unlike in most industries, private, public, and charitable hospitals compete with each other and services are normally not charged to the customer (patient), but to the contribution-financed health insurance. Furthermore, as hospitals are service providers that underlie restricted legal requirements and witness strong structural changes, the hospital industry significantly differs from the mechanical engineering and the food and beverage industry. In former times hospitals have simply been reimbursed for the occurred costs to treat their inpatients. The pressure to install comprehensive cost and management accounting systems (e.g., for cost savings) was therefore rather low.[980] Structural changes in society, business, and medical progress have resulted in reorganizations and market-led reform strategies in the hospital sector in many countries around the world.[981] To modernize

974 See *Altmann* (2003), p. 11f., with further references.

975 Cf., e.g., *Kao et al.* (1995), p. 3207.

976 Cf. *Kao et al.* (1995), p. 3207.

977 Cf. *Al-Omiri/Drury* (2007), p. 408f.

978 See *United Nations* (2011).

979 For Germany see *Statistisches Bundesamt* (2010), p. 255f. For Japan see *Ministry of Internal Affairs and Communication* (2011), chapter 21-18 chapter 21-23.

980 See, e.g., *Langabeer II et al.* (2010).

981 See *McKee/Healy* (2002); *Preker/Harding* (2003).

public administration, concepts like 'New Public Management'[982] were introduced. The underlying assumption of this concept is to establish competition and markets in the public service industry to increase efficiency, effectiveness, and economy.[983] In this context a new payment systems for hospitals have been introduced in Germany and Japan.[984] These systems classify hospital cases that are expected to consume similar resources, the so called diagnosis-related group (DRG). Today hospitals are often paid a predetermined rate that is based on this system. Since then, the necessity to operate efficiently has increased. Hospitals have therefore raised their efforts to control whether the predetermined rate is sufficient for each DRG and in total to cover all of their costs.[985] One important tool to achieve this goal is to install a cost accounting system that allocates all costs occurred to patients in a case-related way and thereby determines patient respectively DRG profitability.[986] As the necessity to run comprehensive cost accounting systems in the hospital industry emerged only recently and as many traditional cost accounting instruments have originally been developed for the manufacturing sector, cost accounting is expected to be less developed in hospitals compared to manufacturing industries. As pressures to save costs emerged only few years ago, a lower acceptance of cost information in hospitals is furthermore expected. UK clinicians, for example, were characterized not to accept accounting information to constrain their clinical activities.[987]

Overall, the three industries are all of economic significance and strongly differ in their environmental context which is likely to lead to varying objectives and conceptual designs of cost accounting systems. This makes these three selected industries appropriate research sites for this investigation.

As for both countries different data bases are applied to identify the companies operating in the three industries, a universal standard has to be followed to ensure that the industries are circumscribed cross-nationally in the same way. Cost accounting differences in countries and industries may otherwise occur not only due to country and industry specifics, but also due to differences in circumscribing the sample. The **equivalence of industries** is ensured in this study by choosing data bases that follow the same statistical classification of economic activities – the 'International Standard Industrial Classification of all Economic Activities by the United Nations' (ISIC Rev.4). For all three industries and both

982 For 'New Public Management' see *Lane* (2001); *Schedler/Proeller* (2009).

983 For Germany see *Mosebach* (2009).

984 Since 2004 – or by option since 2003 – this new payment system is installed in Germany. Cf. *Brösel et al.* (2004), p. 247. See also *Doegel/Martini* (2009). In Japan a modified DRG, called the Diagnosis Procedure Combination (DPC) was introduced in 82 Japanese hospitals on a trial basis in 2003. Since 2004, this payment system has been introduced in many private hospitals. Cf. *Ishikawa et al.* (2005); *Yasunaga et al.* (2006), p. 577. The Japanese version slightly differs from the DRG system. See *Ishikawa et al.* (2005), p. 1618f.

985 Furthermore, weaknesses of service processes should be identified and recommendations for their solutions should be provided. Cf. *Tauch* (2003), p. 9.

986 Cf. *Brösel et al.* (2004).

987 Cf. *Scarparo* (2006), p. 152.

countries the population consists of companies with a size of between 250 and 2,000 employees that are assigned to the respective industry code.[988]

The identified companies belonging to the three industries were checked for duplicates and misspecifications. The distribution of the companies regarding industry and number of employees is provided in Table 3-1 for Germany and Japan.[989]

	Germany				Japan			
Number of employees **Industry**	250 - 499	500 - 999	1,000 - 2,000	**Sum**	250 - 499	500 - 999	1,000 - 2,000	**Sum**
Food and beverage	216	98	35	**349**	252	112	68	**432**
Mechanical engineering	448	168	80	**696**	210	116	82	**408**
Hospitals	258	261	117	**636**	339	294	98	**731**
Sum	**706**	**429**	**197**	**1,681**	**801**	**522**	**248**	**1,571**

Table 3-1: Distribution of companies in Germany and Japan regarding industry and number of employees

3.1.2 Data collection, quality of the sample, and preparation of the data

3.1.2.1 Procedure of data collection

In April 2010 the first version of the questionnaire was developed in English and translated into German and Japanese thereafter. Between April and September 2010 the questionnaire has been pre-tested in Germany and Japan to ensure that the questionnaire is understandable and to ensure conceptual and functional equivalence. Furthermore, issues in translation equivalence were addressed mainly by translating the German and Japanese research material back into English. Differences towards the original questionnaire were investigated for further improvements. The written version of the English questionnaire is printed in Appendix 2. The empirical data has been collected in Germany and Japan from October to December 2010.

The response rate of a study strongly depends upon three key factors. First, it is necessary to talk to the right person in charge. In **Germany**, the companies' headquarters were first called for transferring the calls to the employees who are responsible for cost accounting. Second, it was tried to convince the respective employees to participate in the study. Instead of writing a letter, the author decided to talk to the responsible cost accountants

988 See *United Nations* (2011). Companies operating in the mechanical engineering industry are assigned to code C.28 (manufacture of machinery and equipment n.e.c.), companies allocated to the food and beverage industry belong to code C.10 (manufacture of food products) and C.11 (manufacture of beverages), and hospitals are assigned to code Q.861 (hospital activities).

989 The German companies were identified via the database DAFNE. For the Japanese companies the databases Toyo Keizai, Inc., Kaisha-Shikiho 2010 (listed companies), Toyo Keizai, Inc., Mijyojyo-Kaisha 2010 (unlisted companies), Toyo Keizai, Inc., Yakuin-Shikiho 2011 (managers), Nikkei Telecom 21 Diamond, Inc., Kaisha-Shokuinroku Zenjyojyo-Kaisha 2010 (listed companies), Diamond, Inc., Kaisha-Shokuinroku Mijyojyo-Kaisha 2010 (unlisted companies), and Research and Development, Co., Ltd., Byoin Nenkan 2010 (Hospital Year Book) were used.

personally. The value of this research project was explained and a report of the results was promised for each participant. The insights of the report enable respondents to compare their cost accounting systems with those companies of the same industry and size and recommendations how to design a successful cost accounting system are provided. The respondents can thereby identify potential improvements for their cost accounting systems. The questionnaire was sent to the practitioners by e-mail. The respondents had the opportunity to choose between an online and a PDF version of the questionnaire.[990] Third, if the respondents have not answered the questionnaire within a time frame of two weeks, they were reminded twice via a follow-up call and email. With this procedure, sufficient responses were ensured so that the full spectrum of statistical methods for data analysis can be applied.

Industry	Food and beverage	Mechanical engineering	Hospitals	Total
Population	**349**	**696**	**636**	**1,681**
./. Exclusion criteria				
./. Insolvency	2	10	0	12
./. Wrong telephone number	1	10	1	12
./. No affiliation to industrial sector	25	187	33	245
./. Subsidiary	18	1	43	62
./. Other reasons	6	4	11	21
Adjusted sample	**297**	**484**	**548**	**1,329**
./. Reasons for refusal (before sending questionnaires)				
./. Lack of time	14	14	23	51
./. Generally no participation in surveys	87	139	32	258
./. No existing cost accounting	13	29	24	66
./. Other reasons	1	9	22	32
./. No reasons mentioned	48	40	77	165
Sent questionnaires	**134**	**253**	**370**	**757**
./. Reasons for refusal (after sending questionnaires)				
./. Lack of time	7	28	25	60
./. Generally no participation in surveys	5	6	12	23
./. No existing cost accounting	0	1	1	2
./. No affiliation to industry	1	2	0	3
./. Other	9	18	30	57
./. No reasons mentioned	12	34	96	142
Responses	**100**	**164**	**216**	**480**
Response rate (%)	**33.7%**	**33.9%**	**39.4%**	**36.1%**

Table 3-2: Response rates for Germany

The procedure to contact the employees who are responsible for cost accounting is different in **Japan** due to social norms. Whereas in Germany it is socially accepted that researchers call the respondents to convince them in participating, in Japan it is common to

990 For the written version of the questionnaire see Appendix 2.

send a letter to the accounting manager or the board of the company to ask for participation. In this study, the Japanese research partner sent letters to the head of the management of the Japanese companies and asked for participation and to forward the questionnaire to a cost accountant in charge. To increase the response rate, the aim of the project was explained, a report of the results was promised, and follow-up mails were conducted.

In total 3,252 companies were addressed in both countries. Several companies had to be removed from the statistical population, e.g., because they are listed twice or because they became insolvent. During the sampling process 1,329 respectively 1,571 companies were identified in Germany and Japan that meet the desired size and industry criteria, of whom 480 respectively 146 have responded. This is an overall response rate of 36.1% respectively 12.9%. An overview of the **addressed companies and the responses** for both countries and the three industries is given in Table 3-2 and Table 3-3. As the data collection processes differed in both countries, reasons why respondents refused to participate before and after sending the questionnaire were collected only in Germany. Furthermore, only for the German data set all responses were analyzable.[991] The response rate and the number of responses for Germany exceed those of comparable studies.[992] The value of the collected data depends besides a high response rate on further quality criteria that are outlined in the following.

Industry	Food and beverage	Mechanical engineering	Hospitals	Total
Sample	**432**	**408**	**731**	**1,571**
Sent questionnaires	**432**	**408**	**731**	**1,571**
Responses	**60**	**80**	**63**	**203**
Response rate (%)	13.9%	19.6%	8.6%	12.9%
Usable responses	**50**	**66**	**30**	**146**
Response rate (%)	11.6%	16.2%	4.1%	9.3%
Thereof early responder (%)	18.0%	12.1%	3.3%	12.3%

Table 3-3: Response rates for Japan

3.1.2.2 Quality of the sample

A relevant quality criterion for this study is the non-independence of samples (Galton's problem).[993] For this reason companies between 250 and 2,000 employees were selected that are large enough to run comprehensive cost accounting systems, but that are also less exposed to globalization.

991 All German responses were analyzable, because in case of non-analyzable responses the respective cost accountant was contacted to adjust his answers.

992 Cf. *Nazari et al.* (2006); Appendix 1.

993 Cf. section 1.2.6.

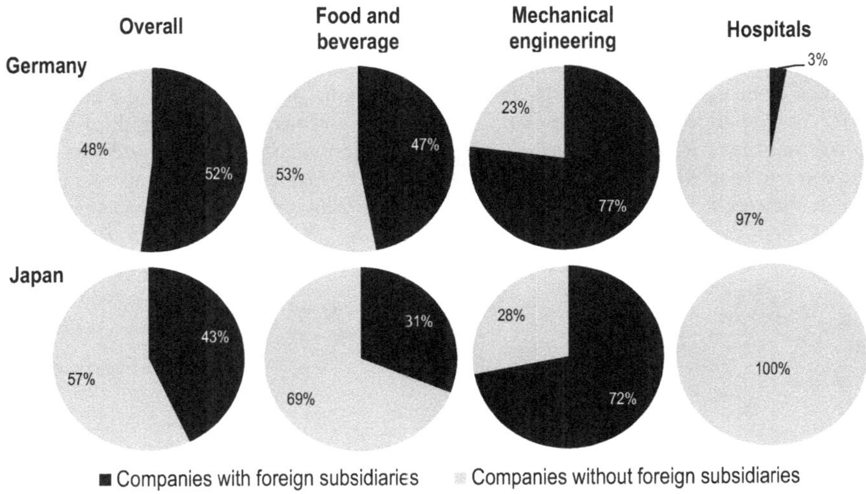

Figure 3-2: Percentage of companies owning foreign subsidiaries

Figure 3-2 indicates that the majority of the German and Japanese companies do not have foreign subsidiaries. Furthermore, 58% respectively 78% of the responding companies in Germany and Japan generate less than 15% of their sales turnover abroad (see Figure 3-3).

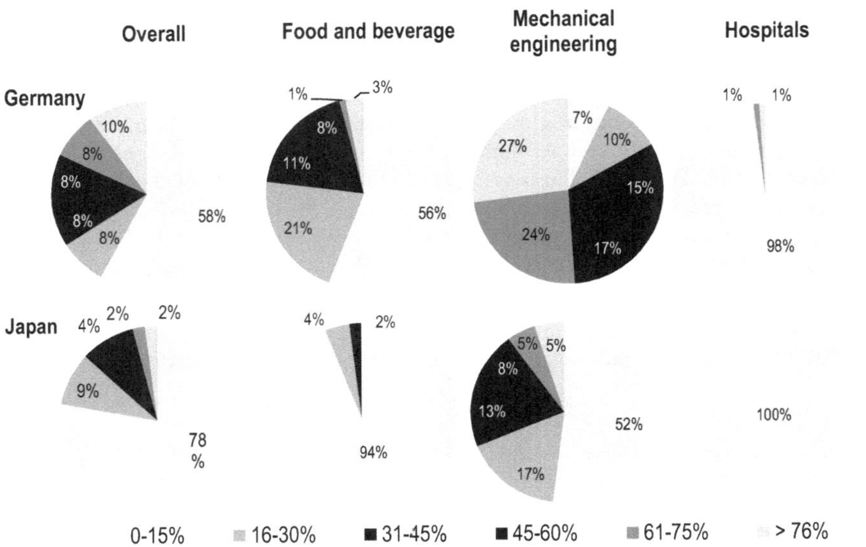

Figure 3-3: Percentage of sales turnover abroad

Finally, only the minority of the companies is exposed to international pressures that homogenize cost accounting systems internationally, because only 15% respectively 54% of the German and Japanese companies are capital market oriented and 27% respectively 6% of these companies apply IFRS or US-GAAP (see Figure 3-4).[994] Overall, the companies that have responded are little exposed to globalization. However, the strength of international pressures strongly differs across industries. Whereas hospitals (and food and beverage companies to a lesser extent) are fairly domestic, the majority of the companies operating in the mechanical engineering industry has a foreign subsidiary and generates more than 15% of their sales turnover abroad.

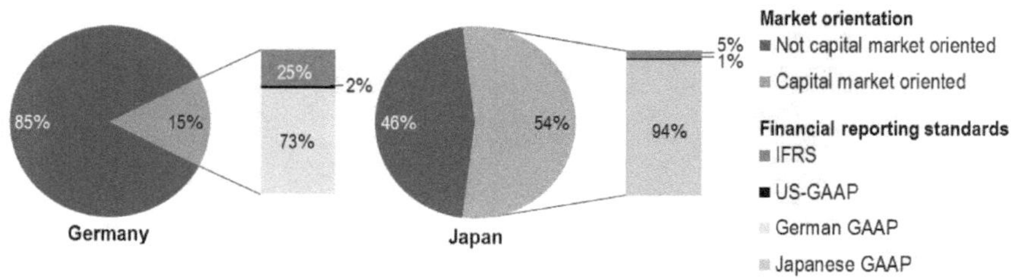

Figure 3-4: Capital market orientation and application of financial reporting standards

Another critical characteristic for this study is the group affiliation of a company. When a company is a subsidiary, it might be influenced by the parent company, which is in most cases larger than the subsidiary. It is thus likely that the parent company can provide more resources for designing the subsidiaries' cost accounting systems and that the parent company runs more complex operations.[995] As parent companies commonly require their subsidiaries to adopt similar cost and management accounting systems, this homogenizing impact might lead to more complex systems for the subsidiaries.[996] Furthermore, companies that are part of a group more intensively communicate with other members of the group. For these three reasons it is likely that subsidiaries are influenced by other members of a group regarding their cost accounting objectives and conceptual designs of cost accounting systems. Figure 3-5 illustrates that 41% respectively 33% of the German and Japanese companies are part of a group as a subsidiary, 17% respectively 25% as a subsidiary and as a parent company, equally 42% as a parent company, and 22% respectively 25% are not part of a group. Hence, in 58% of the German and Japanese companies the existence of a parent company might dilute the results of this study.

T-tests, however, show that systematic differences between parent companies and subsidiaries and between more and less globalized companies (in terms of sales turnover abroad

994 This finding supports prior research indicating small and medium-sized German companies have only little interest to apply IFRS. Cf. *Kajüter et al.* (2007).

995 Cf. section 2.1.3.1.

996 Cf. *Granlund/Lukka* (1998), p. 162f., with further references. This has also been noted for Japanese parent companies that introduced target costing and broadened this instrument to their subsidiaries. Cf. *Cooper/Slagmulder* (1997).

and IFRS adoption) do not prevail regarding complexity, timeliness, and performance of cost accounting systems.

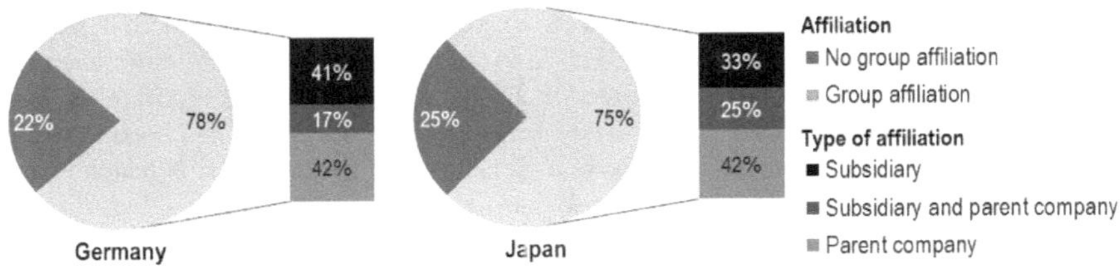

Figure 3-5: Group affiliation

Besides group affiliation and international pressures stemming from globalization, the **years of employment of the respondents** were surveyed. Years of employment within the company is an important criterion for the quality of the responses. It is expected that the years of employment of the respondents and their state of knowledge of cost accounting strongly correlate. The work experience varies between 3 months and 40 years for Germany and between 7 months and 45 years for Japan. The arithmetic mean is 10.49 respectively 18.36 years in Germany and Japan with a standard deviation of 8.14 respectively 14.49. The high average number of work experience in Germany and Japan suggests that the respondents have adequate knowledge to answer the questions and to reflect the context of their organizations and their cost accounting systems. The results of the survey are therefore very informative for the three industries under investigation. The informative value of the empirical investigation depends further on the representativeness of the sample.

A **test of representativeness** of the sample is implemented to verify whether the responding firms from both countries and the three industries represent the target population of the study. Representativeness is necessary to generalize statements for the whole population that are based on the sample.[997] In this study representativeness is tested for Germany by the *'known' values* 'number of employees' and 'sales turnover' that are both indicators for company size and for Japan for the 'number of employees' only.[998] For sales turnover five and for number of employees three size groups are distinguished and the response rate for each layer is analyzed. Appendix 3 to Appendix 7 show that the population is well represented by the sample, although some differences between the layers prevail. The chi-square test supports this descriptive finding, however, the sample is not representative for the population according to four out of nine criteria with a 5%-significance level or higher. Although the findings can generally be generalized to companies that have not participated, the statements developed in the course of this chapter should still be treated with care. This study's findings may not be entirely valid for the whole population.

997 Cf. *Armstrong/Overton* (1977), p. 397; *Stier* (1999), p. 157-160; *Bortz/Döring* (2009), p. 397f.

998 Sales turnover is not applied to test for the representativeness of the Japanese sample, because the distribution of sales turnover is incomplete.

"If persons who respond differ substantially from those who do not, the results do not directly allow one to say how the entire sample would have responded"[999]. To ensure that persons who have responded do not substantially differ from non-respondents, **nonresponse bias tests** are conducted. These tests are based on the assumption that subjects who respond less willingly – e.g., only after a follow-up e-mail or call – are more like non-respondents.[1000] The most common protection against nonresponse bias is a high response rate.[1001] The high response rate of this study with 36.1% in Germany thus counteracts a nonresponse bias. The Japanese response rate of 12.9%, on the contrary, is relatively low and is thus more vulnerable for nonresponse bias. In this study nonresponse bias is tested with the *extrapolation method*.[1002] The sample is divided into two groups. The first group consists of German and Japanese companies that have replied after the first contact (56.7% respectively 12.3%). The other group includes German and Japanese companies that have replied after they have been reminded via a follow-up e-mail and/or call. When the groups differ in relevant characteristics, it indicates that respondents vary from non-respondents. A t-test, however, shows that for the criteria company size as well as complexity, timeliness, and overall satisfaction with cost accounting systems no significant differences between both groups in Germany and Japan exist. Hence, according to the exploration method, the sample is also valid for companies that have refused participation (see Appendix 6).

Overall, the collected data can be assessed to be largely representative for the population and that respondents do not substantially differ from non-respondents. Therefore, the findings can generally be generalized.

3.1.2.3 Preparation of the data

To ensure the **correctness of the responses**, outliers were identified and plausibility checks were carried through. *Outliers* in number of cost types and number of cost centers were searched for. In Germany four respondents have indicated to distinguish more than 10,000 cost types and three indicated to have installed more than 2,000 cost centers, although the respective average number of cost types and cost centers are 425 respectively 221. In Japan two respondents have indicated to distinguish more than 1,200 cost types and one to have installed 2,000 cost centers, although the respective arithmetic means are 39 respectively 34. The number of cost centers for the four outliers from Germany and Japan are furthermore disproportional to the number of full-time equivalent employees – each employee was responsible for more than one cost center according to these figures. The respondents appear to have misinterpreted the respective questions. For these reasons all of the above mentioned outliers are treated as missing indicators. *Plausibility checks* were carried through regarding the number of distinguished contribution margins and the relation between number of employees and sales turnover. As the highest number of distinguished contribution margins is seven, which is very reasonable, no adjustment was

999 *Armstrong/Overton* (1977), p. 396.

1000 Cf. *Pace* (1939), p. 391f.

1001 Cf. *Armstrong/Overton* (1977), p. 396.

1002 For an overview of nonresponse bias tests see *Armstrong/Overton* (1977).

necessary for contribution margin accounting. In some companies, however, the sales turnover per employee was far above or below industry average. It is likely that some respondents have overlooked the provided measurement units. In 12 companies the responses for the number of employees and sales turnover are treated as missing indicators.

The responses to the **profitability indicator** strongly differ between Germany and Japan, with German respondents overestimating and Japanese respondents underestimating their companies' profitability. It is likely that this indicator is culturally biased, e.g., due to differences in response style between Germany and Japan. As the respondents were asked how profitable their companies are in comparison to their competitors, about the same proportion of the companies should be less and more profitable in both countries. This, however, is not the case. Furthermore, about half of the companies have indicated to be equally profitable, therefore only little potential for distinguishing between profitable and less profitable companies prevails (see Table 3-4). For both reasons it is concluded that the indicator for profitability is less suitable compared to other profitability indicators and it is thus excluded from the statistical analysis.

	Less profitable	Equally profitable	More profitable
Germany	13.9%	50.7%	35.4%
Japan	29.7%	50.0%	20.3%

Table 3-4: Responses to the profitability indicator

To **ensure cross-national comparability** of the German and Japanese sample, industry and size biases are eliminated by creating **data set 1**. The German and the Japanese sample differ regarding industry distribution and company size. Therefore, the German sample is adjusted to represent the same industry distribution like the Japanese sample (see Figure 3-6). The German companies are randomly selected for each industry, while controlling for preferably the same distribution within the size classes 250 to 499, 500 to 999, and 1,000 to 2,000 employees. The adjusted German sample contains 292 companies that have on average 716 full-time equivalent employees. The 146 companies of the Japanese sample are slightly larger with an arithmetic mean of 776 full-time equivalent employees. This difference, however, is not statistically significant (p = 0.500).

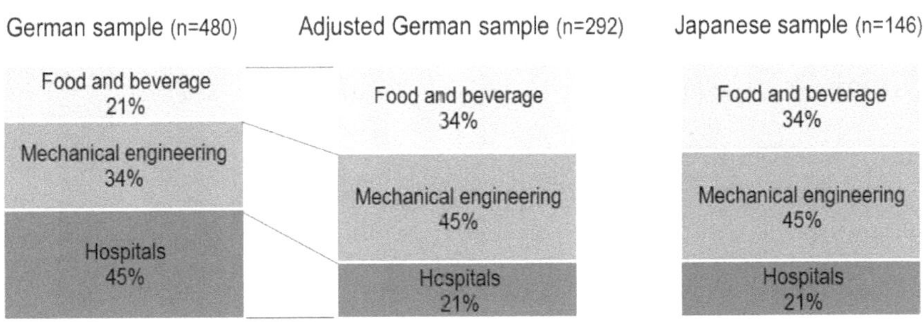

Figure 3-6: Elimination of industry and company size biases

Cross-national differences in cost accounting can vary across industries. Therefore, and to test for the stability of the findings the **data set 2** that contains only mechanical engineering industries from both countries is set up. As the data collection process has not delivered a sufficient high number of responses for the remaining two Japanese industries,[1003] the test for stability is mainly limited to the mechanical engineering industry. As the number of employees is very similar between Germany (with 552) and Japan (with 599) and no statistically significant differences prevail (p = 0.484), all 164 German and all 66 Japanese mechanical engineering companies are included in this data set.

Besides cross-national comparisons, also **cross-industry comparisons** are carried through to assess whether cost accounting differs more strongly between countries than across industries. Therefore, **data set 3** is created, which consists of all 480 responses from Germany. Japanese responses are not considered for this analysis, because their number is too small to conduct a meaningful comparison across industries. Furthermore, when companies from both countries were considered in data set 3, the cross-industry comparison could be distorted by national influences, e.g., when strong cross-national differences in the institutional environment of cost accounting prevail for the hospital sector. To measure solely cross-industry differences and to avoid distortions stemming from national influences, data set 3 is therefore limited to only one country. All 292 responses from Germany are applied for the cross-industry comparison. The average number of employees, however, slightly differs between two German industries: Companies of the food and beverage industry are statistically significantly larger at a 5%-significance level than their counterparts of the mechanical engineering industry.

	Purpose	Sample
Data set 1	Country comparison	292 German and 146 Japanese companies from three industries
Data set 2	Country comparison	164 German and 66 Japanese mechanical engineering companies
Data set 3	Industry comparison	292 German companies from three industries

Table 3-5: Data bases for cross-national and cross-industry comparisons

Overall, three different data bases are applied in this study to conduct cross-national and cross-industry comparisons. Table 3-5 summarizes the purpose and the composition of the three data sets.

3.1.3 Selection and fundamentals of the applied statistical methods

3.1.3.1 Overview of the applied statistical methods

Statistical tests are conducted by using the software SPSS 18 and SmartPLS 2.0. Three different types of statistical analyses are applied in this study: uni-, bi-, and multivariate analyses. An overview of the applied statistical methods is provided in Table 3-6.

1003 50 respectively 30 Japanese companies of the food and beverage and the hospital industry have responded. As not all indications are evaluable, both samples are too small to conduct meaningful comparisons.

Types of statistical analyses	Statistical methods
Univariate analyses	Arithmetic mean, standard deviation
Bivariate analyses	T-test, correlations
Multivariate analyses	Multiple regression analysis, logistic regression analysis, confirmatory factor analysis, partial least squares (PLS)

Table 3-6: Statistical methods applied

3.1.3.1.1 Univariate analyses

Univariate analyses investigate one single variable – they comprise in particular the distribution of attributes.[1004] This includes the two most relevant analyses, the **arithmetic mean** and the **standard deviation.**[1005] The arithmetic mean and the standard deviation are depicted by Ø and σ respectively. Univariate analyses are used to characterize the companies' context, the relevance of cost accounting objectives, the conceptual design of cost accounting systems, and their performance. Cross-national and cross-industry comparisons as well as relations between variables are carried through with bi- and multivariate analyses.

3.1.3.1.2 Bivariate analyses

Bivariate analyses are necessary to analyze two variables simultaneously.[1006] Stochastic tests of significance are applied to evaluate whether statistical results of the sample are valid and can be transferred to the population. Random differences between groups and random correlations between variables can thereby be excluded to a great extent. In this context two hypotheses, the null hypothesis and the alternative hypothesis, are compared in statistical **hypothesis testing.** Whereas the alternative hypothesis states that there is some kind of relation between the phenomena under investigation, the null hypothesis states the opposite. The researcher uses data from the sample to evaluate the reliability of the null hypothesis. When the data refutes the null hypothesis, it is rejected and the alternative hypothesis is accepted.[1007] This procedure corresponds with the methodological grounding of the critical rationalism that this study follows. Levels of significance are provided that indicate the probability of mistakenly rejecting the null hypothesis. The level of significance for bi- and multivariate analyzes is marked with the p-value. A level of significance of, e.g., $p < 0.10$ stands for a 90% probability that the null hypothesis is false. Levels of significance are depicted by asterisks (*). Coefficients on a 10%-, 5%-, and 1%-significance level are represented with one (*), two (**), and three (***) asterisks respec-

1004 Cf., e.g., *Babbie* (2010), p. 426.

1005 The arithmetic mean is the result when the sum of the values is divided by the total number of cases. The standard deviation is a measure of dispersion around the mean. Furthermore, the median (middle attribute in the ranked distribution of observed attributes) and the mode (most frequently occurring attribute) are also often applied to measure central tendencies. Cf. *Babbie* (2010), p. 422.

1006 Comparisons with univariate analyses are only descriptive. Levels of significance for group comparisons cannot be provided without bivariate and multivariate analyses. Cf. *Babbie* (2010), p. 429f.

1007 Cf., e.g., *Gravetter/Wallnau* (2009), p. 233-235.

tively. When three groups are compared, numbers labeled with asterisks printed in bold indicate that the value of the respective group is statistically significantly larger than those of the other two groups; non-bolded values labeled with asterisks indicate that the respective value is statistically significantly larger than the value with the lowest mean value. In this investigation, Student's t-tests and correlations are applied within the bivariate analyses. A hypothesis is not rejected, when the findings for data set 1 or 3 are statistically significant on a 10%-level or higher.

A **t-test** is a hypothesis test that evaluates whether mean differences between two samples exist and whether these differences are likely to be valid for the population. This test requires that the test statistic follows a normal distribution. When unequal variances are present, it can also be applied – given that the sample size exceeds 50 observations. When the sample size is smaller than 50, the assumption that the sample is normally distributed is tested in this study with the Shapiro-Wilk test. The t-test furthermore assumes that the data sets come from distributions with same variances, which is called homogeneity of variance or homoscedasticity.[1008] Homogeneity of variance is analyzed with the Levene-test.

Correlation is a numerical value that provides a concise description of the strength and the direction of relationships between two variables.[1009] It indicates the relationship with the help of a correlation coefficient ranging between -1 and +1. A zero correlation characterizes that the two variables are not linear dependent. The more linear dependent the variables are, the higher the absolute value. The sign shows whether the variables are either negatively (-) or positively (+) associated. A correlation of 1.0 constitutes a perfect correlation. In this study, the Spearman's rank correlation coefficient is applied to investigate the relationships between two variables, when they are either interval or ratio scaled. Correlations between nominal (dichotomous) and interval or ratio scaled variables are calculated with the point-biserial correlation coefficient. The results of this coefficient are abbreviated in the following by the letter *r*. This correlation solely describes statistical but not logical coherences between variables. The existence of correlations does not, by itself, imply cause-and-effect, because another variable than the two observed may cause a spurious relationship between the observed variables. To analyze more than two variables simultaneously, multivariate analyzes are applied.

3.1.3.1.3 Multivariate analyses

Multivariate analyses investigate more comprehensive relationships across a multitude of variables and constructs simultaneously.[1010] The multivariate statistical methods are preferably applied for hypothesis testing to verify the supposed relationships between variables. This study applies basic as well as complex multivariate statistical methods. The basic methods include regression analysis, logistic regression analysis, and factor analysis. Structural equation modeling (SEM) is chosen as a complex method. Hypotheses are accepted, when the findings of multiple regression analysis, logistic regression analysis, or SEM are

1008 Cf. *Backhaus et al.* (2011), p. 90-92.

1009 Cf., e.g., *Brosius* (2008), p. 503; *Gravetter/Wallnau* (2009), p. 520-525.

1010 Cf. *Babbie* (2010), p. 435; *Hair et al.* (2010), p. 4.

statistically significant on a 10%-level or higher. When alternative measures, e.g., for performance are applied, hypotheses are only accepted, if at least half of the respective findings are statistically significant on a 10%-level or higher. These multivariate methods applied in this study are outlined below.

A **multiple regression analysis** identifies relationships between a dependent variable and several independent variables.[1011] This method is mainly applied to analyze cause-and-effect relationships by proving correlations between the dependent and the independent variables. With the help of dummy variables it is possible to investigate, besides metric scales, also the impact of nominal-scaled variables upon the dependent variable.[1012] The quality of the regression models are assessed by its statistical significance as well as the coefficients of determination R^2 and the adjusted R^2. The latter adjusts for the number of independent variables. Furthermore, the statistical significance of single independent variables is determent. Three underlying assumptions of the multiple regression analysis are verified in this study.[1013] First, multicollinearity (high correlations between two or more independent variables in a multiple regression model) is detected by the variance inflation factor (VIF).[1014] The problem of multicollinearity is that it confounds the ability of statistical methods to measure the impact of any single variable, which makes interpretation less reliable.[1015] The VIF is calculated for each independent variable by the inverse of the tolerance value (VIF = $1/1\text{-}R^2$, with R^2 representing the coefficient of determination). R-square is calculated as follows:

4) $$R^2 = 1 - \frac{\sum_{n=1}^{N}(y_n - \hat{y}_n)^2}{\sum_{n=1}^{N}(y_n - \bar{y}_n)^2}$$

$(y_n - \hat{y}_n)^2$ represents the sum of squares of residuals (also called residual sum of squares) and $(y_n - \bar{y}_n)^2$ represents the regression sum of squares (also called explained sum of squares). A VIF-value of 1 indicates that the considered indicator is linearly independent from the remaining indicators of the same construct. Although a clear threshold value for multicollinerarity does not exist, it is suggested as a rule of thumb that the VIF should not be larger than 10.[1016] The second and third underlying assumptions are that the errors have to be uncorrelated (autocorrelation) and the variance of the errors should be constant across observations (homoscedasticity). Both assumptions are inspected visually. The visual inspections of the scatter diagram for all models analyzed in chapter 3 have not shown any evidence that both criteria are not satisfied. The test for autocorrelation of the errors is more serious for time series regression models than for cross-section analyses as carried through in this study. Nevertheless, the Durbin-Watson statistic was calculated to test for autocorrelation.

1011 Cf. *Hair et al.* (2010), p. 161.
1012 Cf. *Backhaus et al.* (2011), p. 14f.
1013 Cf. *Backhaus et al.* (2011), p. 84-97.
1014 It is the most used testing procedure for multicollinearity. Cf. *Meier* (2006), p. 96.
1015 Cf. *Hair et al.* (2010), p. 244.
1016 Cf. *Marquardt* (1970), p. 610; *Diamantopoulos/Winklhofer* (2001), p. 272.

In comparison to the multiple regression analysis, a **logistic regression analysis** (also called logit analysis) addresses complementary events, e.g., adoption or non-adoption of cost accounting instruments. With the maximum likelihood estimation the probabilities of occurrence of an event are predicted. It is recommended that the sample should consist of at least 50 cases and multicollinearity should not prevail to provide robust solutions. Different criteria are applied in this study to assess the appropriateness, adequacy, and usefulness of the model. The explanatory power of the model is assessed with likelihood ratio index, McFaddens-R^2, Cox and Snell-R^2, Nagelkerke-R^2, which are all similar to the coefficient of determination R^2, and the percentage of correct classifications. Furthermore, the VIF is determined to detect multicollinearity and the Hosmer-Lemeshow test is conducted to identify whether, e.g., companies adopting ABC are not statistically significantly different from those predicted by the logistic regression model. The significance of each explanatory variable is determined by the Wald statistic. To compare the effects and to show the influence of an impendent upon a dependent variable, odds ratios are determined. An odds ratio of 1 indicates that the variable has no influence; a ratio of 0.5 indicates that an increase of the independent variable by one unit leads to a decrease of occurrence of an event by a half (0.5:1); a ratio of 2 indicates that an increase of the independent variable by one unit leads to an increase of occurrence of an event by two (2:1).

For several elements of the conceptual framework different variables were set up within chapter 2. These variables have to be aggregated to a potentially lower number of unobserved variables that are highly interrelated, called factors.[1017] To reduce the set of variables for multiple regression analysis, the **confirmatory factor analysis** is applied.[1018] This type of factor analysis assumes mutual relationships between the various variables. These relationships can be quantified through correlations.[1019] To obtain reliable results, several quality criteria have to be met.[1020] Only metrically scaled variables can be aggregated to factors and the sample size should be three times the number of variables under investigation. Besides these general requirements, five further criteria have to be met (see Table 3-7). First, the Kaiser-Meyer-Olkin measure of sampling adequacy (KMO) is an index that examines the appropriateness of factor analysis. A KMO-value of between 0.5 and 1.0 indicates that the factor analysis is appropriate. Second, when only one factor is extracted, the threshold value of variance explained should be at least 50%. Third, the number of factors to be extracted often follows the Kaiser criterion. According to this criterion, each factor should have an eigenvalue (percentage of explained variance) of at least 1. Fourth, to assign variables to factors, the correlation coefficients between variables and factors (factor loadings) should be at least 0.5. Finally, the threshold values for Cronbach's Alpha, which is a coefficient of reliability used to measure the internal consistency of a factor, has to be met. Factors consisting of two or three variables should have a Cronbach's Alpha value of at least 0.5 and factors consisting of more than two variables should have a value of above 0.7.

1017 Cf. *Hair et al.* (2010), p. 94.

1018 Cf. *Singh* (2007), p. 203.

1019 Cf. *Liftin et al.* (2000), p. 283; *Bortz/Döring* (2009), p. 147f., 377f.

1020 Cf. *Backhaus et al.* (2011), p. 329-389; *Brosius* (2008), p. 771-801.

	Factor analysis				Reliability analysis
Criteria	KMO-value	% of variance explained	Kaiser	Factor loadings (max; min)	Cronbach's Alpha
Threshold value	≥ 0.5	≥ 50%	Eigenvalue ≥ 1	≥ 0.5	> 3 variables: ≥ 0.7 2-3 variables: ≥ 0.5

Table 3-7: Quality criteria for factor analysis
Source: following *Giering* (2000), p. 82; *Brast* (2006), p. 154

New factor loadings are derived separately for each subsample when a group comparison is conducted. As this study compares cost accounting across countries and industries, it is required to test for cross-country and cross-industry equivalence of the factors.[1021] The similarity of factor loadings is assessed by the measure **coefficient of congruence**[1022] – however, only for constructs that consist of more than two variables. The coefficient of congruence is calculated as follows:[1023]

5)
$$CC_A B = \frac{\sum p_v A \times p_v B}{\sqrt{(\sum p_v A^2) \times (\sum p_v B^2)}}$$

$CC_A B$ constitutes the coefficient of congruence between a factor in country A and a factor in country B. $p_v A$ and $p_v B$ are the factor loadings for the investigated factors in countries A and B respectively. According to *Teel/Verran* a factor of congruence value of 1.0 demonstrates a perfect agreement between the constructs and a value of 0.9 sufficiently indicates factor similarity.[1024] *Lorenzo-Seva/ten Berge* suggest that a value in the range 0.85 to 0.94 corresponds to a fair similarity and that a value higher than 0.95 implies that two factors can be considered as equal.[1025] In this study a threshold value of 0.9 is chosen.

More complex cause-and-effect relationships can be verified with the help of **SEM**. No comparative study on management accounting has applied this statistical method before,[1026] although this method extends multiple regression analysis. SEM is applied in this study to verify the findings of multiple regression analysis and to test for cross-national differences in the magnitude of relationships (hypotheses H_{7a} to H_{7c}). Unlike multiple

1021 This is supported by *Triandis'* call for ensuring functional equivalence – „[w]e must get empirical evidence that the construct operates the same way in the other culture...before we use it to compare the cultures" (*Triandis* (1994), p. 69). See also *Carte/Russell* (2003), p. 493f.; *Sin et al.* (2003), p. 921-925.

1022 Cf. *Gorsuch* (1983), p. 285. It is also called coefficient of concordance.

1023 See *Harman* (1976), p. 344; *Teel/Verran* (1991), p. 70.

1024 Cf. *Teel/Verran* (1991), p. 70.

1025 Cf. *Lorenzo-Seva/ten Berge* (2006).

1026 SEM, however, have already been applied in cross-national studies on management information systems and marketing. Cf., e.g., *Keil et al.* (2000); *Brettel et al.* (2008); *Engelen* (2007); *Brettel et al.* (2009a); *Brettel et al.* (2009b). Furthermore, only few studies on management accounting have applied this statistical method so far. Between 1980 and 2001 only 20 publications across ten leading accounting journals have applied SEM. Cf. *Smith/Langfield-Smith* (2004). See also *Henri* (2007). However, over the years more studies on management accounting have applied SEM.

regression analysis, SEM provides the opportunity to (1) additionally capture latent (e.g., non-observable) variables[1027], (2) investigate the measurement errors of latent variables, and (3) examine a network of causal relationships that link multiple constructs with the measurement model combining each construct with a set of indicators measuring the construct.[1028] Furthermore, the assumption that independent variables have cross-nationally the same impact regarding strength and magnitude upon a dependent variable can be tested.

Partial least squares (PLS) as the most accepted variance-based SEM is chosen instead of covariance-based SEM like LISREL or AMOS for three reasons.[1029] First, this statistical method is subject to fewer requirements than the other two. It is not contingent upon data having multivariate normal distributions, it works with much smaller and much larger samples, and it is more robust with fewer identification problems than covariance-based models.[1030] Second, unlike LISREL or AMOS, PLS can incorporate, besides reflective constructs, also formative constructs.[1031] Covariance-based models have difficulties with formative model specifications.[1032] Third, PLS is appropriate for testing theories that are in the early stages of development.[1033] *Holzmüller* recommends applying PLS in comparative management research due to the little insights prior research has provided so far and due to their complex research designs.[1034] For comparative management accounting as well, a specifically developed theory does not exist and only anecdotal insights about the impact of country-specifics upon objectives and the conceptual design of cost accounting systems prevail. Covariance-based SEM are most appropriate to test theories, because they assume that the model investigated is well defined. PLS on the contrary can additionally examine, where relations between variables might or might not exist and to advise propositions for testing later.[1035] It aims to maximize the explanatory power of the model and to best possibly predict latent variables.[1036] The disadvantage of PLS compared to covariance-

1027 For latent variables see *Fassott/Eggert* (2005), p. 34; *Buch* (2007), p. 4. Latent variables cannot be measured directly.

1028 Cf. *Fornell/Larcker* (1981), p. 39; *Amoroso/Cheney* (1991), p. 77f.; *Chin* (1998), p. 296f.; *Chin/Newsted* (1999), p. 308; *Hulland* (1999), p. 195; *Haenlein/Kaplan* (2004), p. 284. For an extensive description about the advantages of SEM over multiple regression and path analysis see *Smith/Langfield-Smith* (2004), p. 50-60.

1029 For the criteria to assess the appropriateness of variance-based SEM see *Chin/Newsted* (1999), p. 337.

1030 Cf. *Jöreskog* (1978), p. 444f.; *Fornell/Bookstein* (1982), p. 443; *Fornell/Cha* (1994), p. 55; *Chin* (1998), p. 295; *Smith/Langfield-Smith* (2004), p. 75f.; *Hair et al.* (2010), p. 776.

1031 For reflective and formative constructs see section 3.1.3.2.1.

1032 Cf. *Fornell/Bookstein* (1982), p. 442; *Chin* (1998), p. 299; *Hair et al.* (2010), p. 776-778.

1033 Cf. *Lohmöller* (1989), p. 28; *Götz/Liehr-Gobbers* (2004a), p. 721.

1034 Cf. *Holzmüller* (1995), p. 266f.

1035 Cf. *Chin* (1998), p. 295. As a consequence, PLS is most suitable for forcasting and for theory development. Cf. *Wold* (1980); *Wold* (1982), p. 341-343; *Chin/Newsted* (1999), p. 328; *Gefen et al.* (2000), p. 27.

1036 Cf. *Chin/Newsted* (1999), p. 312f.; *Gefen et al.* (2000), p. 14f.; *Götz/Liehr-Gobbers* (2004a), p. 721.

based methods is, however, that the former focuses on prediction rather than on explanation, which makes it more difficult to understand the relationships between variables.[1037]

For this study it is a **challenge to apply PLS**, because predominantly objective measures and a comprehensive description of the conceptual design of cost accounting systems were surveyed. Both issues complicate the aggregation of indicators to latent variables. In the following PLS is described in more depth to provide a better understanding of this advanced method.

3.1.3.2 Description of the partial-least-squares (PLS) method

PLS is based on the work of *Herman Wold*. It was developed in the 1960s and 1970s to avoid the restrictions of other methods. This method is used in this study to verify the findings of multiple regression analysis and to test for cross-national differences in the magnitude of relationships. It investigates (1) the impact of companies' context and cost accounting objectives upon the conceptual design of cost accounting systems and (2) the impact of the conceptual design of cost accounting systems upon the performance of cost accounting under different companies' contexts and cost accounting objectives.

3.1.3.2.1 Structure

The indicators or indicating variables are the empirical equivalents of the construct investigated. These indicators represent variables on the **observable level** (χ_1, χ_2, and χ_3) that are relevant to proxy the developed construct on the **theoretical level** (η_1 and η_2) that are not directly measurable (see Figure 3-7). The indicators χ_1 and χ_2 (χ_3) represent the theoretical construct η_1 (η_2). Among two observable indicators a covariance prevails that is characterized by the letter r. The supposed relationship H (that stands for hypothesis) between the constructs η_1 and η_2 is tested by investigating the covariance between r_2 and r_3 on the observable level. The theoretical constructs and their indicators are joined with correspondence rules (labeled as y). Two different rules can be distinguished. In **reflective models** the theoretical construct causes the indicators. The opposite is the case for **formative models** (see Figure 3-8).

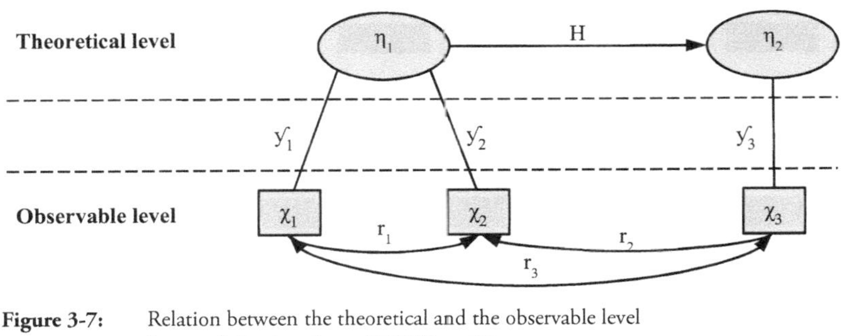

Figure 3-7: Relation between the theoretical and the observable level
Source: following *Bagozzi* (1998), p. 50

1037 Cf. *Hair et al.* (2010), p. 776.

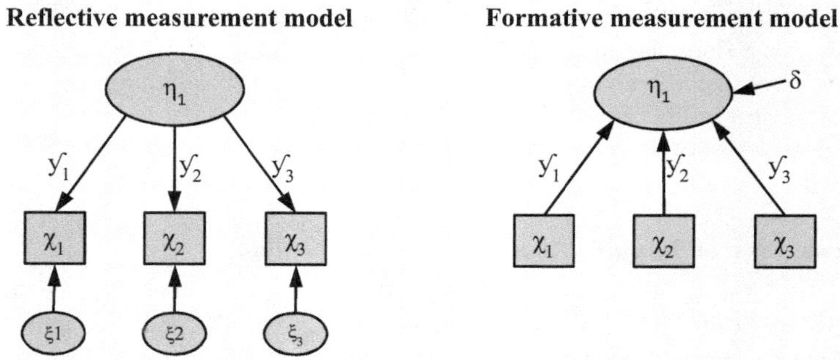

Figure 3-8: Reflective and formative measurement models
Source: following *Henseler* (2005), p. 72; *Götz/Liehr-Gobbers* (2004a), p. 717

PLS consists of two systems of equations. The **structural model** consists of the relations between the theoretical constructs on the theoretical level. The specification of the structural model is set up in this study with theoretical preliminary considerations that are theory based. The **measurement model** displays the relations between the constructs on the theoretical level and their respective indicators on the observable level (see Figure 3-9). The objective of the measurement models is to indicate the theoretical constructs as precisely as possible. They can either be reflective or formative in nature. To avoid biased results for PLS-based analyses, the sample size should be at least five times the largest number of independent constructs affecting a dependent construct.[1038] Some authors regard a multiplicator of ten as necessary.[1039] Smaller sample size than ten times the largest number of independent constructs affecting a dependent construct can be justified, when normal and elliptical theory is applied and when many indicators of latent variables are applied and the associated factor loadings are large.[1040]

1038 Cf. *Bentler/Chou* (1978), p. 90f.; *Gopal et al.* (1992), p. 57.

1039 Cf. *Barclay et al.* (1995), p. 292; *Chin* (1998), p. 311.

1040 Cf. *Bentler/Chou* (1978), p. 91.

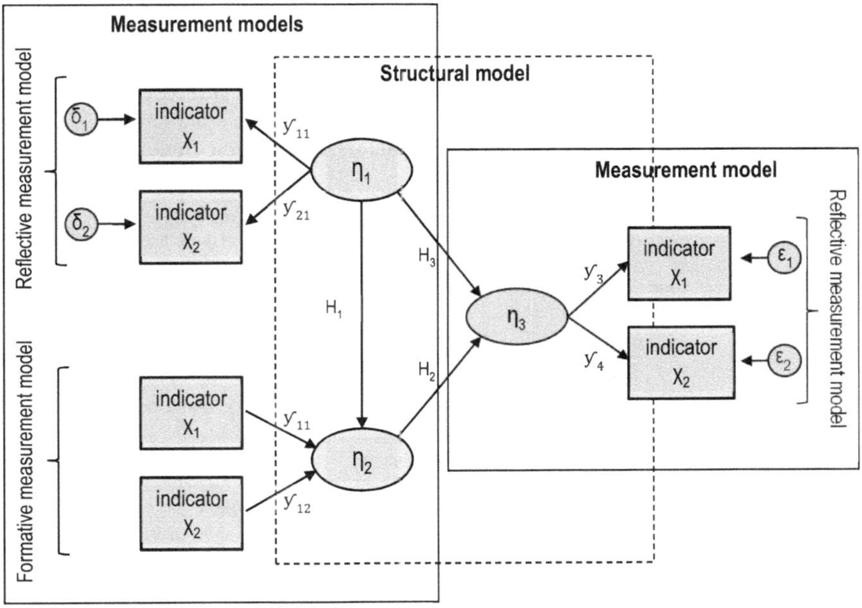

Figure 3-9: Relationship between the structural and measurement model
Source: following *Götz/Liehr-Gobbers* (2004a), p. 716

The **solution algorithm** consists of two parts. (1) Factor loadings are determined and factors are calculated for the measurement model. (2) Based on the factors a regression analysis is carried through that quantifies the relationships between the constructs of the structural model.[1041]

3.1.3.2.2 Specification of the constructs

Differentiating between formative and reflective constructs is necessary, because wrong specifications can lead to biased results and formative and reflective constructs require different quality criteria.[1042] *Jarvis et al.* provides a list of criteria to choose between formative and reflective measurement models (see Table 3-8).[1043]

The first criterion relates to the **direction of causality** between the theoretical construct and its indicators. Formative measures are characterized by a flow from the indicators to the constructs. For reflective measures the opposite is the case. The second criterion addresses the **interchangeability of the indicators**. The indicators should not be inter-

1041 Cf. *Fornell/Cha* (1994), p. 62-66; *Chin* (1998), p. 302f.; *Chin/Newsted* (1999), p. 320; *Hahn* (2002), p. 101-106; *Backhaus et al.* (2011), p. 520.

1042 Cf. *MacKenzie et al.* (2005), p. 711; *Eberl* (2006), p. 654f.

1043 Cf. *Jarvis et al.* (2003), p. 202f. An extensive discussion is also provided by *Fassott/Eggert* (2005).

changeable for formative instead of reflective measures. The third criterion relates to **co-variation among indicators.** Covariation among indicators does not necessary imply reflective measures, but it is a necessary condition for this type of construct. The last criterion addresses whether all indicators are required to have the same **antecedents and consequences** or not. Unlike formative measures, reflective measures should have the same antecedents and consequences, because all indicators reflect the same underlying construct and are expected to be interchangeable.

	Formative model	Reflective model
1. Direction of causality from construct to measure implied by the conceptual definition	Direction of causality is from items to construct. Indicators are defining characteristics of the construct. Changes in the indicators should cause changes in the construct. Changes in the construct do not cause changes in the indicators.	Direction of causality is from construct to items. Indicators are manifestations of the construct. Changes in the indicator should not cause changes in the construct. Changes in the construct do cause changes in the indicators.
2. Interchangeability of the indicators/items	Indicators need not be interchange-able. Indicators need not have the same or similar content/indicators need not share a common theme. Dropping an indicator may alter the conceptual domain of the construct.	Indicators should be interchangeable. Indicators should have the same or similar content/indicators should share a common theme. Dropping an indicator should not alter the conceptual domain of the construct.
3. Covariation among the indicators	Not necessary for indicators to covary with each other. Not necessarily.	Indicators are expected to covary with each other. Yes.
4. Nomological net of the construct indicators	Nomological net for the indicators may differ. Indicators are not required to have the same antecedents and consequences.	Nomological net for the indicators should not differ. Indicators are required to have the same antecedents and consequences.

Table 3-8: Decision rules for determining whether a construct is formative or reflective
Source: following *Jarvis et al.* (2003), p. 203

For the specification of the constructs *Albers/Hildebrandt* suggest that the researcher should also consider, whether he wants to derive **practical recommendations** from the constructs or not.[1044] This is more difficult for psychological constructs like customer satisfaction or the attainment of objectives. The constructs should be formative in nature, when the research objective is to identify which cause of action has resulted in satisfaction or attainment of objectives. Practical recommendations can thereby be obtained by investigating the consequences of individual causes of action. When the research objective on the contrary is to investigate how satisfaction or attainment of objectives manifests itself, reflective constructs should be chosen. Then, however, practical recommendations cannot be derived. The argument for defining the attainment of objectives as a reflective construct is that it can be seen as an integrated strategy with highly correlated indicators. Changes in the strategy consequently cause different characteristics of the associated indicators. The explanatory power of the model is then, however, limited, because the conse-

1044 Cf. *Albers/Hildebrandt* (2006).

quences of the integrated strategy are investigated and the researcher cannot ensure that the strategy is fully described.[1045] As in business studies most research serves to provide practical recommendations, most of the applied constructs are formative in nature.[1046]

3.1.3.2.3 Analysis of moderating effects

Investigating the relationship between, e.g., cost accounting objectives and the conceptual design of cost accounting systems could be extended by a more advanced model that includes a third aspect – country-specifics. This extension is appropriate for testing the impact of country-specifics upon the relationships between other constructs of the conceptual framework (hypotheses H_{7a}, H_{7b}, and H_{7c}). For this purpose, **moderating effects** stemming from country-specifics should be investigated. Moderators are variables that have an influence upon the magnitude of the relationship between two variables, e.g., between cost accounting objectives and the conceptual design of cost accounting systems.[1047] Moderating effects have not been considered for in most studies applying SEM, although its relevance has been pointed out in literature for investigating complex networks of causal relationships.[1048] The moderating effects of national specifics are examined by group comparisons.

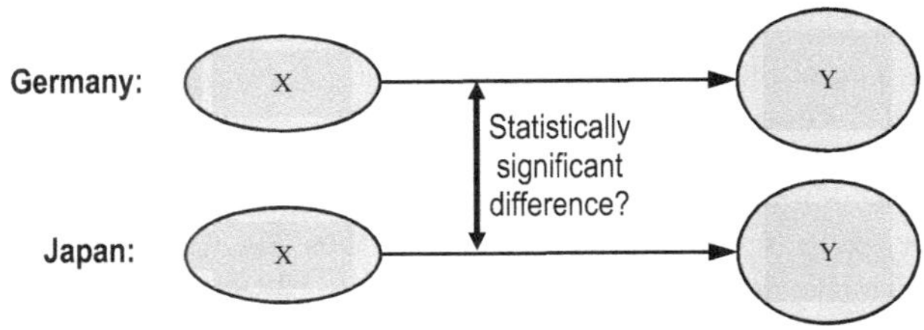

Figure 3-10: Principle of group comparisons

For **group comparisons** a SEM is estimated separately for Germany and Japan. Similar to the correlation analysis but in a more comprehensive way, corresponding path coefficients in SEM are compared across both countries. Differences in path coefficients between both models are then tested for significance (see Figure 3-10) with the following formula. m and n represent the sample sizes of the groups to be compared and SD stands for standard deviation.[1049]

1045 Cf. *Albers/Hildebrandt* (2006), p. 10-14.

1046 Cf. *Fassott* (2006).

1047 Cf. *James/Brett* (1984), p. 310; *Howell et al.* (1986), p. 89; *Venkatraman* (1989), p. 424.

1048 Cf. *Homburg/Giering* (2001), p. 47; *Chin et al.* (2003), p. 193; *Smith/Langfield-Smith* (2004), p. 76. Only few comparative studies have also investigated moderating effects. *Kirkman et al.*, e.g., mentions only one out of 54 studies that has applied *Hofstede's* cultural dimensions to apply culture as a moderator variable instead of a main effect. Cf. *Kirkman et al.* (2006), p. 309.

1049 Cf. *Keil et al.* (2000), p. 315.

6) $$t = \frac{\text{Path Coefficient}_{\text{Group 1}} - \text{Path Coefficient}_{\text{Group 2}}}{\left[\sqrt{\frac{(m-1)^2}{(m+n-2)} \times SD^2_{\text{Group 1}} + \frac{(n-1)^2}{(m+n-2)} \times SD^2_{\text{Group 2}}}\right] \times \left[\sqrt{\frac{1}{m} + \frac{1}{n}}\right]}$$

3.1.3.2.4 Quality criteria

One challenge of applying PLS is the evaluation of the model because no overall quality criterion exists. A comprehensive overview of quality criteria on a national level is reproduced from literature in this section.[1050] The quality criteria are distinguished in the following between formative and reflective constructs, for the structural model and for cross-national equivalence.

a) Formative constructs

By comparing the indicator's weights, the **relevance of indicators**, their relative contribution to their construct, can be assessed.[1051] Indicators with a small weight should, however, not be eliminated when their relative contribution is rather low, because this could lead to the omission of a substantial part of the construct.[1052]

The elimination of an indicator is only recommended for formative measurements, when substantial **multicollinearity** occurs. This is the case, when two or more indicators are highly correlated. This is tested by VIF, which should be below 10. A low VIF-value, however, does not mean that multicollinearity does not exist.[1053] Besides VIF it is therefore recommended to further determine the **condition indexes**, which measure the presence of collinear relations among indicators.[1054] It considers for near dependencies that describe pairwise correlations and their linear combinations: "High pairwise correlations between, say, X_1 and X_2 and between X_3 and X_4 could be due to a single near dependency involving all four variates, or to two separate near dependencies, one between X_1 and X_2 and one between X_3 and X_4."[1055] The condition index is determined by the square root of the ratio of the largest eigenvalue to each indicator's eigenvalue.

7) $$KI_i = \sqrt{\frac{\text{Eigenvalue}_{max}}{\text{Eigenvalue}_i}}$$

1050 See *Götz/Liehr-Gobbers* (2004a), p. 727-731; *Götz/Liehr-Gobbers* (2004b), p. 13-26; *Ringle* (2004); *Ringle/Spreen* (2007); *Götz et al.* (2010), p. 694-703.

1051 Cf. *Sambamurthy/Chin* (1994), p. 231.

1052 Cf. *Bollen/Lennox* (1991), p. 308; *Jarvis et al.* (2003), p. 202.

1053 Cf. *Belsley* (1991), p. 28; *Belsley et al.* (2004), p. 92.

1054 Cf. *Belsley* (1984), p. 184.

1055 *Belsley et al.* (2004), p. 93.

The highest condition index within a construct represents the condition index on the construct level. Condition indexes below 30 indicate an innocuous degree of multicollinearity.[1056] The quality criteria for formative constructs are summarized in Table 3-9.

Criterion	Requirement
• Relevance of indicators • Variance inflation factor (VIF) • Condition indexes	• No specified threshold • ≤ 10 • ≤ 30

Table 3-9: Quality criteria for formative measurement models
Source: following *Engelen* (2007), p. 205

b) Reflective constructs

The quality of reflective constructs can be assessed by reliability and validity. Both terms are relevant to determine the degree of measurement error of indicators. Validity is characterized as "the degree to which a measure accurately represents what it is supposed to"[1057] and reliability as "the degree to which the observed variable measures the 'true' value and is 'error free'"[1058]. A measurement is reliable, when the same result occurs every time the measurement is repeated. The measurement is then free of random errors. When the measurement is also free of systematic errors (errors that occur at each repetition and each time at the same level)[1059] that result from the design of the conceptual construct, the state is characterized as fully valid.[1060] Four different quality criteria are applied.[1061]

To measure the **individual item reliability** (also called indicator reliability), the squared correlation of the indicator with their respective constructs, the *factor loading*, is assessed. Items should be accepted with loadings of 0.707 or more.[1062] This implies that the shared variance between the construct and its indicator is larger than the variance of the measurement error.[1063] Indicators in an estimated model with a loading below the 0.707 threshold should consequently be eliminated. However, it is suggested that for new items or newly developed scales a threshold value of 0.4 or 0.5 is sufficiently reliable.[1064] As this study applies newly developed theoretical constructs, a threshold value of 0.4 is applied in this study.

The **reliability on a construct level** is assessed by the internal consistency for a given block of indicators. The indicators that are positively associated with the same construct have to be positively correlated with each other.[1065] Three criteria are applied. *Cronbach's*

1056 Cf. *Belsley et al.* (2004), p. 164.
1057 *Hair et al.* (2010), p. 7.
1058 *Hair et al.* (2010), p. 8.
1059 Cf. *Churchill/Lacobucci* (2005), p. 291, 680.
1060 Cf. *Peter* (1981), p. 134.
1061 These criteria are based on *Bagozzi* (1979); *Churchill* (1979); *Peter* (1981).
1062 Cf. *Hulland* (1999), p. 198; *Götz/Liehr-Gobbers* (2004a), p. 727.
1063 Cf. *Meier* (2006), p. 91. The required loading of 0.707 implies that more than 50% of the variance is explained, because correlations are the square of loadings.
1064 Cf. *Hulland* (1999), p. 198.
1065 Cf. *Bollen/Lennox* (1991), p. 307.

Alpha calculates the average of all correlations between the indicators with their construct. It quantifies how well a group of indicators measures its constructs. *K* stands for the number of indicators assigned to the construct and $\bar{r}$ for the average correlations of the indicators.[1066]

8) $$\alpha = \left(\frac{K\bar{r}}{1+\bar{r}(K-1)}\right)$$

A more accurate approximation of reliability is the *internal consistency measure.* Unlike Cronbach's Alpha, this measure does not assume that all indicators are equally weighted. Instead, it assumes that the parameters estimated by the PLS model are accurate. λ_i represents the component loading to an indicator and $var(\varepsilon_i)$ is the variance of the measurement error defined as $1 - \lambda_i^2$.[1067] j stands for the flow index across all reflective measurement models.

9) $$\rho_c = \frac{(\sum_i \lambda_{ij})^2}{(\sum_i \lambda_{ij})^2 + \sum_i var(\varepsilon_i)}$$

Values of 0.707 for Cronbach's Alpha and the internal consistency measure indicate a 'modest' reliability on the construct level.[1068] Some authors judge values larger than 0.6 as acceptable.[1069]

The third measure – that is very similar to the internal consistency measure, but more conservative – is the *average variance extracted.* It describes the amount of variance captured by the construct from its indicators relative to the variance of the measurement error. AVE should be greater than 0.5, which implies that 50% or more variance of the indicators is explained. Again, λ_i is the component loading to an indicator and $var(\varepsilon_i)$ is defined as $1 - \lambda_i^2$.[1070]

10) $$DEV = \frac{\sum_i \lambda_i^2}{\sum_i \lambda_i^2 + \sum_i var(\varepsilon_i)}$$

Content validity refers to the correct logical modeling of the constructs and cannot be tested quantitatively, but it can be ascertained qualitatively with the help of expert interviews and a comprehensive conceptualization of the study.

Discriminant validity, both on an indicator and construct level, represents the degree to which measures of different concepts vary. Measures of different concepts should have only little covariance, otherwise the uniqueness of the measure and/or the constructs are

1066 Cf. *Homburg/Giering* (1996), p. 22.
1067 Cf. *Hulland* (1999), p. 199. Cf. also *Chin* (1998), p. 320.
1068 Cf. *Nunnally* (1978), p. 245; *Götz/Liehr-Gobbers* (2004a), p. 727.
1069 See *Bagozzi/Yi* (1988), p. 82; *Hair et al.* (2010), p. 92.
1070 Cf. *Fornell/Cha* (1994), p. 69; *Chin* (1998), p. 321.

doubtful.[1071] *On the indicator level* each indicator should have the strongest correlation with its construct. When an indicator loads lower on the intended construct than on another one, the researcher should reconsider its appropriateness.[1072] *On the construct level* in a given model each construct should share more variance with its indicators than with other constructs.[1073] It is suggested that for each reflective construct the measure AVE should be greater than the squared correlation between two constructs.[1074]

The quality criteria for reflective constructs are summarized in Table 3-10. The quality of the measurement model is still acceptable, when not all quality criteria are met.[1075]

Criterion	Requirement
Reliability • Factor loading • Cronbach's Alpha • Internal consistency measure • Average variance extracted (AVE)	 • ≥ 0.4 respectively ≥ 0.707 • ≥ 0.6 • ≥ 0.6 • ≥ 0.5
Validity • Discriminant validity of indicators • Discriminant validity of concepts	 • Each indicator should have the strongest correlation with its construct. • The AVE for each reflective construct should be greater than the squared correlation between two constructs.

Table 3-10: Quality criteria for reflective measurement models
Source: following *Engelen* (2007), p. 203

c) Structural model

Three different criteria are applied to assess the quality of the structural model. The first criterion is the R-squares for each dependent latent variable.[1076] It measures how well the model approximates real data points. An R-squared of 1.0 indicates a perfect fit. The interpretation is the same to that of traditional regression models. Regarding the interpretation of the $\mathbf{R^2}$ values, there is no threshold value that can be considered as good or sufficient. Instead, the interpretation of this criterion depends on the particular situation and the nature of available data.[1077]

The change in R-squares can furthermore be measured to investigate the impact of a particular independent latent variable on a dependent latent variable. It is calculated as follows:[1078]

1071 *Bagozzi/Phillips* (1982), p. 469; *Hulland* (1999), p. 199.
1072 Cf. *Chin* (1998), p. 321.
1073 Cf. *Hulland* (1999), p. 199.
1074 Cf. *Fornell/Larcker* (1981), p. 46; *Hulland* (1999), p. 199f.
1075 Cf. *Homburg/Baumgartner* (1998), p. 363.
1076 Cf. *Chin* (1998), p. 316f.
1077 Cf. *Jain* (1994), p. 168.
1078 Cf. *Chin* (1998), p. 316.

11) $$f^2 = \frac{R^2_{included} - R^2_{excluded}}{1 - R^2_{included}}$$

$R^2_{included}$ and $R^2_{excluded}$ are the R-squares of the models with the predictor latent variable being used or omitted respectively. An **f^2** of 0.02, 0.15, and 0.35 indicates, whether a predictor latent variable has a small, medium, or large effect on the model.[1079]

Predictive power can also be assessed by applying the **Stone-Geisser Q^2**. It measures how well a model reproduces the indicators of an endogenous construct. The measure is estimated with the help of a blindfolding procedure, which omits during parameter estimation systematically data points for a particular block of indicators. The omitted part of data is predicted by drawing on the estimated parameters of the previous investigated blindfolded constructs. This procedure is carried through until every data point has been missed out and estimated. Positive Q^2-values imply that the model has predictive relevance.[1080] It is calculated as follows, with E_d representing the squares of prediction errors, O_d the squared errors using the mean of prediction, and D the omission distance:[1081]

12) $$Q^2 = 1 - \frac{\sum_{d=1}^{D} E_d}{\sum_{d=1}^{D} O_d}$$

Similar to f^2, the change in Q-squares can be measured to determine the relative impact of relations within the structural model upon the constructs. A **q^2** of 0.02, 0.15, and 0.35 indicates whether a construct is of small, medium, or large predictive relevance.[1082]

13) $$q^2 = \frac{Q^2_{included} - Q^2_{excluded}}{1 - Q^2_{included}}$$

Finally, the quality of the structural model can be assessed by the level of significance, the algebraic sign, and the value of the **path coefficients**. The value of the path coefficients should be larger than 0.1.[1083]

The quality criteria for the structural model are summarized in Table 3-11.

1079 Cf. *Chin* (1998), p. 317.

1080 Cf. *Fornell/Cha* (1994), p. 73; *Chin* (1998), p. 318.

1081 Cf. *Fornell/Cha* (1994), p. 72. The omission distance is used to estimate the omitted data points. Cf. *Chin* (1998), p. 317.

1082 Cf. *Ringle/Spreen* (2007), p. 215.

1083 Cf. *Götz/Liehr-Gobbers* (2004b), p. 23; *Huber et al.* (2007), p. 104.

Criterion	Requirement
• R^2 • f^2 • Stone-Geisser Q^2 • q^2 • Path coefficients	• No specific threshold value exists. • 0.02, 0.15, and 0.35 indicate small, medium, or large effects on the model. • Positive values imply predictive relevance of the model. • 0.02, 0.15, and 0.35 indicate small, medium, or large predictive relevance. • The value should be larger than 0.1.

Table 3-11: Quality criteria for the structural model

d) Quality criteria on a cross-national level

Besides the quality criteria on a national level, **quality criteria on a cross-national level** are required in this study. PLS derives new factor loadings and weights separately for each subsample when a group comparison is conducted. As the construct-level scores are estimated with different item weights for each subsample, the constructs may have a different meaning cross-nationally. Differences in the path coefficients may then occur due to the different meanings of the constructs or in fact due to the moderating effects. To ensure that cross-national differences exist due to the moderating effect, it is required to ensure that item weights of constructs are significantly similar across the groups.[1084] To test for equivalence, coefficients of congruence are determined as already outlined in section 3.1.3.1.3 for the factor analysis.

3.1.3.2.5 Application

Although PLS is recommended for comparative research to develop rather than to test theory,[1085] this method bears the risk for this study to provide results that lack cross-national comparability. PLS aims to maximize the explanatory power of the model and to best possibly predict latent variables,[1086] whereby the indicators are weighted accordingly. In comparison to confirmatory factor analysis, the weights of the indicators vary more strongly between PLS models. This can hamper cross-national comparability of the theoretical constructs, i.e. the theoretical constructs are more likely to differ in meaning. Furthermore, the outcomes can vary more strongly when a theoretical construct is included or excluded. Finally, the study faces further challenges to apply PLS, because the application of objective measures and a comprehensive description of the conceptual design of cost accounting systems complicate the aggregation of theoretical constructs that meet all quality criteria and that are cross-nationally comparable.

As the objective of this study is to provide solid knowledge of similarities and differences in cost accounting, PLS is applied in this study to **verify the findings of multiple regression analysis**. PLS is furthermore applied to increase the explanatory power of this study in three ways. Unlike multiple regression analysis, PLS can capture latent variables, inves-

1084 Cf. *Carte/Russell* (2003), p. 493f.

1085 Cf. *Holzmüller* (1995), p. 266f.

1086 Cf. *Chin/Newsted* (1999), p. 312f.; *Gefen et al.* (2000), p. 14f.; *Götz/Liehr-Gobbers* (2004a), p. 721.

tigate measurement errors of latent variables, and examine more complex relationships that consider for indirect effects that might distort the findings of multiple regression analysis. Furthermore, PLS is applied in this study to **test for statistically significant differences in the magnitude of path coefficients between theoretical constructs** by analyzing moderating effects.

The theoretical constructs conceptualized and operationalized in section 2 have to be characterized as either formative or reflective. This is necessary, because a wrong specification can lead to biased results and the applied quality criteria differ between both alternatives. As the research objective is to conduct a solid comparison, **equivalence** of theoretical constructs, however, **is of higher importance than an appropriate characterization of theoretical constructs**. Hence, the theoretical constructs are first characterized as either formative or reflective to meet issues in equivalence. Only when both characterizations ensure equivalence, the following considerations are followed to choose between formative or reflective constructs.

As the objective of this study is to provide practical recommendations for practitioners, the theoretical constructs that can be influenced by practitioners should be preferably **formative** in nature. These include the internal context factors, the *cost accounting objectives*, and the *conceptual design of cost accounting systems*. However, only for the internal context factor IT systems quality the direction of causality is from indicators to construct. Therefore IT systems quality is the only internal context factor that is formative in nature.

As already discussed in section 3.1.3.2.2, the performance of cost accounting systems can be both formative and reflective in nature. This construct should be formative, when the aim is to provide practical recommendations by identifying successful causes of action. It should be reflective on the other hand, when the objective of the study is to solely identify how well cost accounting systems manifest themselves. The construct performance is incorporated in the conceptual framework of this study to facilitate practical recommendations (see section 1.5.2). Hence, as far as possible, the construct should be **formative**. Performance is measured in four ways. To increase the quality of the model, however, the construct with the largest number of indicators, which is the measure '*factor attainment*', is applied to increase the explanatory power of the model.[1087]

The *country-specifics, other external context factors*, and the internal context factors *company size* and *potential for cost distortion* should be characterized as **reflective**, because of four main reasons. First, direction of causality is from construct to indicators. If, e.g., the country under investigation changes, the characteristics of the indications change as well. Second, the indicators have the same antecedents and consequences, because they all reflect the same underlying construct. Third, the indicators are thus expected to be interchangeable to some extent. Finally, country-specifics mainly serve to explain cross-national differences and the other external and both enlisted internal context factors cannot provide practical recommendations. Hence, solely the consequences of country-

1087 The weights of the indicators can be more adjusted to increase the explanatory power of the model, the more indicators a theoretical construct consists of.

specifics, other external context factors, and the internal context factors company size and potential for cost distortion should be described and explained.

3.2 Context of cost accounting systems

Country-specifics, other external context factors, and internal context factors are required as explanatory and control variables to meet the objectives of this study. The organizational context is expected to strongly influence cost accounting objectives as well as the conceptual design and the performance of cost accounting systems. The results of the context factors are presented in the following.

3.2.1 Country-specifics

3.2.1.1 Cultural preferences for cost information

Cultural preferences for cost information were operationalized by asking the respondents to what extent managers require accurate, detailed, up-to-date, and easily understandable cost information on a seven-point Likert scale (question A.12, Appendix 2).

Required cost information – comparisons of means	To what extent do managers at your company require the following cost information? (1=not at all; ... ; 7=very strongly)						
Type of comparison	**Country comparison**				**Industry comparison**		
Data set	**Data set 1**		**Data set 2**		**Data set 3**		
	Germany	Japan	Germany	Japan	Food and beverage	Mechanical engineering	Hospitals
Accurate cost information	5.27	5.22	5.28	5.61 *	5.44	5.28	5.22
Detailed cost information	4.77	4.88	4.87	5.09	4.98 **	4.87	4.57
Up-to-date cost information	5.43 ***	5.06	5.55	5.47	5.37	5.55 *	5.31
Easily understandable cost information	5.83 ***	5.12	5.88 ***	5.27	5.75	5.88 *	5.64

Table 3-12: Required characteristics of cost information

Table 3-12 provides comparisons of means between countries and industries of the three data sets. Coefficients on a 10%-, 5%-, and 1%-significance level are labeled with one (*), two (**), and three (***) asterisks respectively. For data set 3 numbers printed in bold (see, e.g., Table 3-13, page 218) indicate that the value of the respective group is statistically significantly larger than those of both other groups. Non-bolded values marked with asterisks indicate that the value of the respective industry is statistically significantly larger than the industry with the lowest respective mean value.

Table 3-12 illustrates for data set 1 (this data set compares all three industries cross-nationally; see section 3.1.2.3) that German companies have a stronger emphasis on up-to-date and easily understandable cost information. For mechanical engineering companies only (data set 2), however, German companies have only a stronger emphasis on easily understandable cost information and Japanese companies have a stronger emphasis on accurate cost information. Hence, the differences of required cost information between Germany and Japan vary across industries. Figure 3-11 pictures for data set 1 the extent to which accurate, detailed, up-to-date, and easily understandable cost information is required.

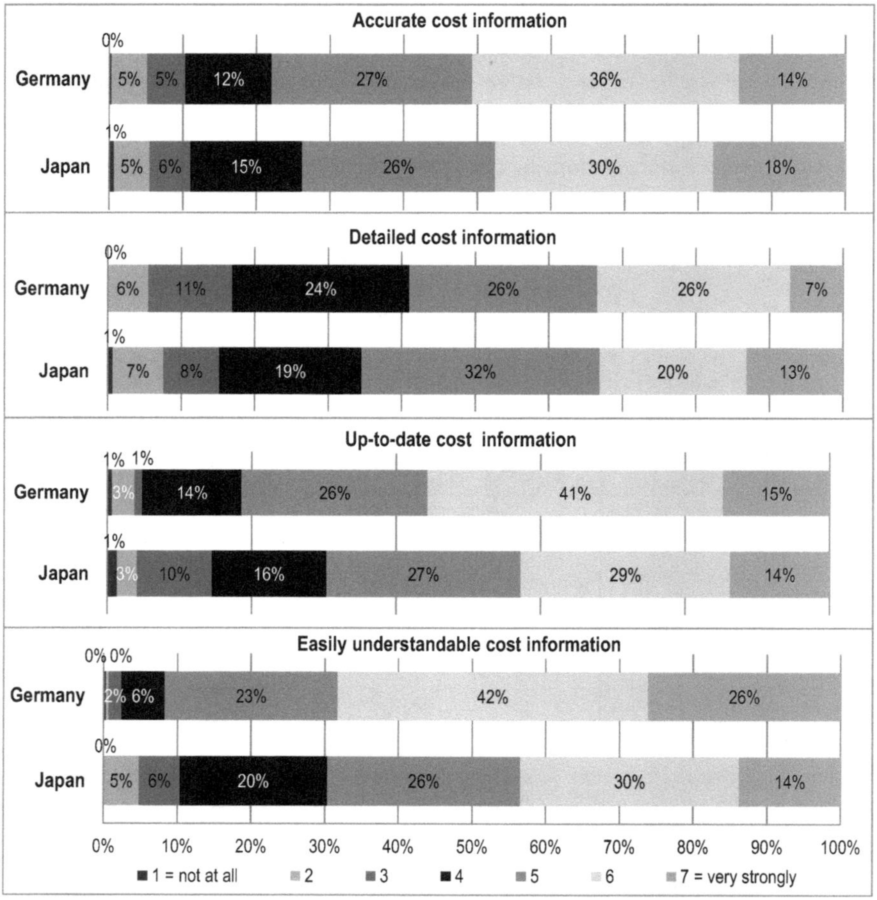

Figure 3-11: Required characteristics of cost information (data set 1)

The relevance of cost information also differs across industries (data set 3). Food and beverage companies prefer more detailed cost information and companies operating in the mechanical engineering industry have a stronger emphasis on up-to-date and easily understandable cost information than hospitals. As the relevance of cost information differs with about the same intensity across industries and across countries, the relevance of cost information seems to be both country and industry specific.

Hypotheses tests

In section 2.1.1.5 **hypotheses H_{1a} and H_{1b}** were set up. It is assumed that German companies have a stronger emphasis on accurate and detailed than on timely cost information respectively that Japanese companies have a stronger emphasis on timely than on accurate and detailed cost information. The results from Table 3-12 show that the preferences for cost information are in contrast to the conceptual considerations from section 2.1.1 and the conclusions drawn by *MacArthur* and *Krumwiede/Suessmair* that German companies have a strong focus on precise cost information.[1088] The surveyed German companies even put statistically significantly more emphasis on up-to-date and easily understandable cost information than on accurate and detailed cost information. These differences are significant on a 5%-significance level.[1089] Thus, both hypotheses are rejected. An explanation for these contradictory results is that German companies are used to accurate and detailed cost information and might therefore appraise the relevance of up-to-date and easily understandable cost information to be more relevant. For Japanese cost accountants the opposite might be the case for up-to-date and easily understandable cost information. Moreover, the question on required cost information is more susceptible to biased results than the other country-specifics, because it is up to the responder what he understands under accurate, detailed, up-to-date, and easily understandable cost information.

3.2.1.2 Relationship of cost accounting towards financial and management accounting

The relationship of cost accounting towards financial and management accounting was operationalized by the four measures (1) responsible body for cost accounting, (2) cost accountants' workload for management and financial accounting tasks, (3) focus on management accounting, and (4) focus on management accounting education. The first measure was operationalized by asking the respondents, which body is responsible for cost accounting (question A.7, Appendix 2). For the second measure the cost accountants' percentaged workload was surveyed for management accounting, financial accounting, and other tasks (question A.10). The relative importance of management accounting was determined by dividing the percentaged workload for managerial accounting tasks with the percentaged workload for financial accounting tasks. This measure is applied in section 3.4 and 3.5 to explain the conceptual design and the performance of cost accounting systems. For the third measure it was surveyed to what extent cost accounting systems are designed for managerial instead for financial accounting purposes (question A.11, item 3). Finally, to determine the relative importance of management accounting, the respondents were asked, whether cost accountants are rather qualified for management accounting or for financial accounting requirements (question A.14, item 4).

1088 Cf. *MacArthur* (2006); *Krumwiede/Suessmair* (2007a), (2007b).

1089 The results are stable for data set 2, where the differences are significant on a 99%-significance level. These levels for significance are not provided in Table 3-12. The comparisons are carried through with a paired sample t-test.

Responsible body for cost accounting

Table 3-13 illustrates the distribution of the responsible bodies for cost accounting in Germany and Japan for data set 1. The table shows that statistically significantly more management accounting departments and statistically significantly fewer financial accounting departments are responsible for cost accounting in Germany than in Japan. It is thus concluded that cost accounting is more aligned with management accounting purposes than with financial accounting purposes in Germany compared to Japan. Cost accounting in Japan is on the contrary more often assigned to specific cost accounting departments than in Germany. The cross-national differences are robust for the mechanical engineering industry (data set 2). Statistically significant variations also exist across industries; however, these differences are far smaller than those between both countries. Thus, the variable 'responsible body for cost accounting' is suitable to explain cross-national differences.

Responsible body for cost accounting – comparison of frequencies	Who is responsible for cost accounting in your company?						
Type of comparison	**Country comparison**				**Industry comparison**		
Data set	**Data set 1**		**Data set 2**		**Data set 3**		
	Germany	Japan	Germany	Japan	Food and beverage	Mechanical engineering	Hospitals
Specific department for cost accounting	10%	17% **	13%	25% **	8%	13% ***	3%
Management accounting department	80% ***	19%	78% ***	22%	82%	78%	85% *
Accounting/finance department	38%	65% ***	40%	77% ***	37%	40%	**49%** *
Operational departments	5%	31% ***	5%	28% ***	6% **	5%	2%
Other	2%	9%	1%	2%	3%	1%	2%

Table 3-13: Responsible body for cost accounting

Cost accountants' workload for management and financial accounting tasks

Figure 3-12 contrasts the cost accountants' percentaged time for management accounting, financial accounting, and other tasks between Germany and Japan (data set 1). It illustrates that German cost accountants spend more time for management accounting tasks and less time for financial accounting tasks than their Japanese counterparts.

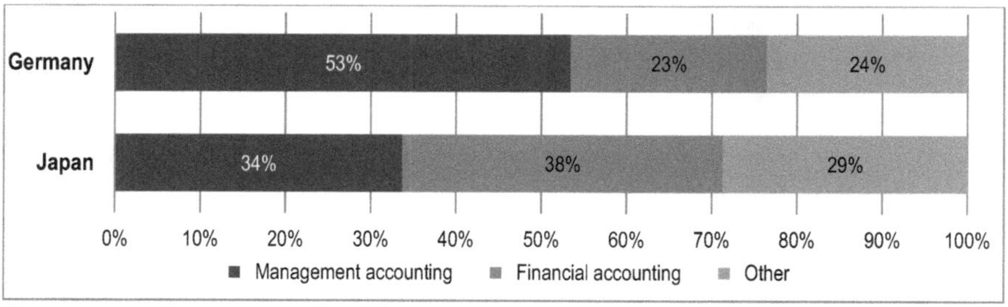

Figure 3-12: Cost accountants' workload (data set 1)

Table 3-14 shows that these cross-national differences are statistically significant and remain constant for data set 2. Far smaller differences of the cost accountants' workload prevails across industries. Cost accountants' workload is consequently a suitable variable to explain cross-national differences between Germany and Japan.

Cost accountants' workload – comparison of frequencies	How is the workload of the employees responsible for cost accounting divided?						
Type of comparison	**Country comparison**				**Industry comparison**		
Data set	**Data set 1**		**Data set 2**		**Data set 3**		
	Germany	Japan	Germany	Japan	Food and beverage	Mechanical engineering	Hospitals
Financial accounting	23%	38% ***	25%	46% ***	21%	25%	26% *
Management accounting	53% ***	34%	53% ***	35%	56% *	53%	45%
Other	24%	29% **	21%	18%	23%	21%	**28%** *

Table 3-14: Cost accountants' workload

Focus on management accounting

German companies design their cost accounting systems statistically significantly more for managerial instead for financial accounting purposes than their Japanese counterparts. The results are consistent for data set 1 and 2. Statistically significant, but weaker differences also prevail across industries. Food and beverage companies design their cost accounting systems significantly more for managerial instead for financial accounting purposes compared to hospitals (see Table 3-15). This variable is suitable as well to demonstrate cross-national differences between Germany and Japan.

Focus on management accounting – comparisons of means	To what extent do you agree with the following statements regarding your cost accounting? (1=not at all; ... ; 7=completely)						
Type of comparison	**Country comparison**				**Industry comparison**		
Data set	**Data set 1**		**Data set 2**		**Data set 3**		
	Germany	Japan	Germany	Japan	Food and beverage	Mechanical engineering	Hospitals
It is designed for managerial instead for financial accounting purposes.	4.99 ***	4.08	4.88 ***	3.77	5.11 ***	4.88	4.65

Table 3-15: Focus on management accounting

Focus on management accounting education

German cost accountants from data base 1 and 2 are compared to their Japanese counterparts statistically significantly more qualified for requirements in management than in financial accounting. The responses are reverse-scored. Only smaller differences prevail across industries. Cost accountants in the food and beverage industry are slightly more qualified for requirements in management than in financial accounting than their counterparts in hospitals. Hence, the qualification of cost accountants differs more strongly between Germany and Japan than across industries (see Table 3-16).

Focus on management accounting education – comparisons of means	To what extent do the following characteristics apply to your company's cost accountants? (1=not at all; ... ; 7=completely)						
Type of comparison	Country comparison				Industry comparison		
Data set	Data set 1		Data set 2		Data set 3		
	Germany	Japan	Germany	Japan	Food and beverage	Mechanical engineering	Hospitals
Rather qualified for requirements in financial than in managerial accounting. (R)	5.06 ***	3.81	4.99 ***	3.98	5.09 *	4.99	4.78

Table 3-16: Focus on management accounting education

Figure 3-13 summarizes for data set 1 to which extent cost accountants are qualified rather for management accounting than for financial accounting tasks.

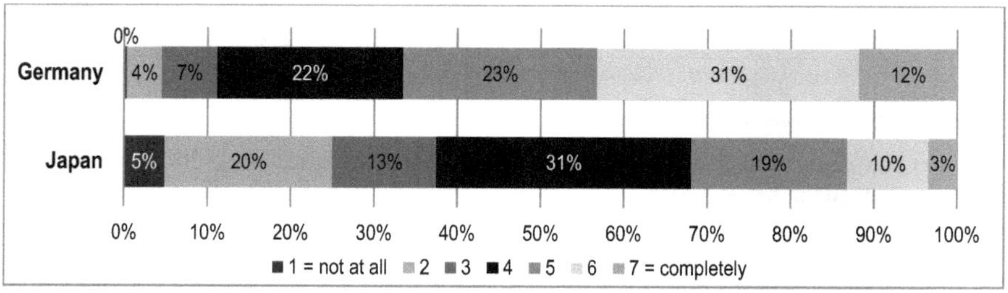

Figure 3-13: Focus on management accounting (data set 1)

Overall, all four indicators consistently show that German cost accounting is more aligned with management accounting than with financial accounting compared to Japanese cost accounting. Anecdotal evidence by *Otto*[1090] is thereby empirically verified. The indicators furthermore differ more strongly between Germany and Japan than across industries. They are therefore valuable to explain cross-national differences in cost accounting.

3.2.1.3 Education of cost accountants

The education of cost accountants was operationalized by the cost accountants' sources of knowledge and by the degree of functional specialization. The first measure characterizes the extent of theoretical knowledge and the second measure characterizes the degree of functional specialization of cost accountants. For the first measure respondents were asked, where the employees who are responsible for cost accounting have acquired most of their knowledge from (question A.13, Appendix 2). Multiple answers were possible. For the second measure it was surveyed, to which extent cost accountants are (1) highly specialized exclusively in cost accounting, (2) experienced in business functions other than accounting, and (3) qualified to enhance and run cost accounting systems (question A.14, item 1 to 3).

1090 See *Otto* (2000), p. 278-282.

Cost accountants' sources of knowledge

Figure 3-14 illustrates the distribution of the cost accountants' sources of knowledge in Germany and Japan for data set 1. German cost accountants have far more often acquired their knowledge from university and professional bodies than their Japanese counterparts (see also Table 3-17). For mechanical engineering companies (data set 2), only education at university remains statistically significantly different. Japanese cost accountants on the contrary obtain statistically significantly more knowledge at work than their German counterparts according to both data sets. Japanese cost accountants working for mechanical engineering companies furthermore obtain more in-house training than their German counterparts.

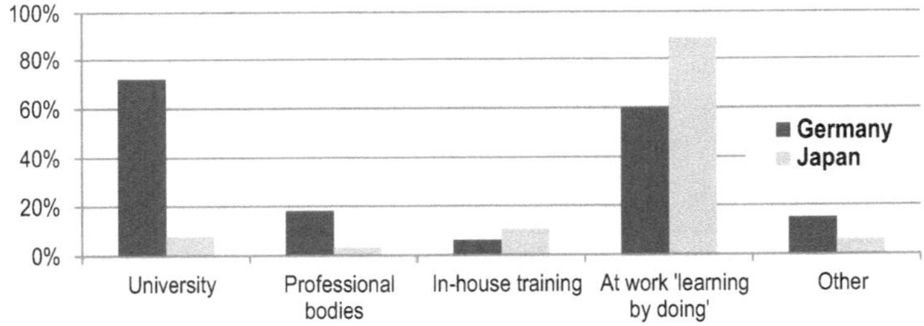

Figure 3-14: Cost accountants' sources of knowledge (data set 1)

The empirical data shows that in-house training is scarce for German companies operating in the mechanical engineering industry. Other German industries far more frequently apply this type of education. One reason for this industry-specific might be that German cost accounting was mainly developed for the mechanical engineering industry. Specifics for the food and beverage industry and for hospitals are far less often addressed at university and in textbooks. This gap might therefore more often be addressed by in-house training. Apart from in-house training, no significant differences prevail across industries. Overall, the cost accountants' sources of knowledge are suitable to explain cross-national differences in theoretical and practical knowledge between German and Japanese cost accountants.

Sources of knowledge – comparisons of frequencies	Where have employees responsible for cost accounting in your company acquired most of the knowledge required to fulfill their tasks?						
Type of comparison	**Country comparison**				**Industry comparison**		
Data set	**Data set 1**		**Data set 2**		**Data set 3**		
	Germany	Japan	Germany	Japan	Food and beverage	Mechanical engineering	Hospitals
University	72% ***	8%	79% ***	8%	54%	79%	81%
Professional bodies	18% ***	4%	15%	6%	33%	15%	13%
In-house training	6%	11%	2%	11% **	17% **	2%	13%
At work 'learning by doing'	60%	89% ***	65%	89% ***	67%	65%	59%
Other	15%	6%	11%	4%	21%	11%	10%

Table 3-17: Cost accountants' sources of knowledge

Degree of functional specialization

According to data set 1 German cost accountants are statistically significantly more specialized exclusively in cost accounting and more qualified to enhance and run cost accounting systems than their Japanese counterparts in a statistically significant way (see Table 3-18). For data set 2, however, only the qualification to enhance and run cost accounting systems is significantly different between both countries. Statistically significant differences also prevail across industries. Cost accountants of the mechanical engineering industry are significantly more functionally specialized than their counterparts working in hospitals. Cost accountants in the food and beverage industry have more experience in business functions other than accounting than their counterparts of the mechanical engineering industry (see Table 3-18). This empirical result can be explained by the impressions the author has obtained during the data collection process that more managers of the food and beverage industry than from the other two industries are responsible for cost accounting besides managerial tasks.

Functional specialization of cost accountants – comparisons of means	To what extent do the following characteristics apply to your company's cost accountants? (1=not at all; ... ; 7=completely)						
Type of comparison	**Country comparison**				**Industry comparison**		
Data set	**Data set 1**		**Data set 2**		**Data set 3**		
	Germany	Japan	Germany	Japan	Food and beverage	Mechanical engineering	Hospitals
Highly specialized exclusively in cost accounting	3.62 ***	3.17	3.81	3.54	3.65	3.81 ***	3.08
Experienced in business functions other than accounting	3.70	3.81	3.52	3.43	3.96 *	3.52	3.88
Qualified to enhance and run cost accounting systems	5.03 ***	4.08	5.11 ***	4.20	4.92	5.11	4.95

Table 3-18: Degree of functional specialization

Overall, the responses for both variables consistently show that German cost accountants have more theoretical knowledge and are more functionally specialized than their Japanese counterparts. As both indicators vary more strongly between countries than across industries, they are suited to explain differences in German and Japanese cost accounting.

Data set	**Analysis**	**Factor analysis**				**Reliability analysis**
	Criteria	**KMO-value**	**% of variance explained**	**Kaiser**	**Factor loadings (max; min)**	**Cronbach's Alpha**
1	Germany	0.498	40.9%	1.23	0.778; 0.406	0.241
	Japan	0.470	52.1%	1.56	0.869; 0.547	0.500

Table 3-19: Results of the factor analysis for degree of functional specialization

The three variables for the degree of functional specialization are not aggregated to one factor, because several quality criteria are not met (see Table 3-19). The KMO-value is below 0.5 for both countries, less than 50% of the variance is explained for Germany, the lowest factor loading is below 0.5 for Germany, and the Cronbach's Alpha is below 0.5 for Germany. Only the threshold value for the Kaiser criterion is fulfilled. Statements regarding the degree of specialization are therefore not drawn for this factor, but by its single indicators.[1091]

Hypotheses tests

In section 2.1.1.5 the **hypotheses H_{1c} and H_{1d}** were set up. It was expected that German cost accountants are more specialized and have more theoretical knowledge than their Japanese counterparts.

H_{1c} addressing the **specialization of cost accountants** is tested with the five indicators 'responsible body for cost accounting', 'cost accountants' workload for management and financial accounting tasks', 'focus on management accounting', 'focus on management accounting education', and 'degree of functional specialization'. The empirical results from section 3.2.1.2 consistently support that cost accounting and cost accountants are both more aligned with management accounting and are thus more specialized for management accounting purposes than for financial accounting purposes in Germany compared to Japan. The empirical results from section 3.2.1.3 support these findings: German cost accountants are educated in a more specialized way than their Japanese counterparts. As subjective and objective measures both lead to the same result, hypothesis H_{1c} is accepted.

H_{1d} addressing the **theoretical knowledge of cost accountants** is tested with the indicator 'cost accountants' sources of knowledge'. German cost accountants obtain more knowledge from university and professional bodies and less knowledge from in-house training and at work than their Japanese counterparts. German cost accountants therefore obtain more theoretical knowledge and the Japanese counterparts obtain more practical knowledge in cost accounting. Hypothesis H_{1d} is therefore accepted.

3.2.1.4 Conclusions on country-specifics

Country-specifics that are based on the cultural contingency and the societal effects approach were surveyed to explain cross-national differences in cost accounting. Seven indicators were surveyed to measure the cultural preferences for cost information as well as the degree of specialization and theoretical knowledge of cost accountants. The empirical results suggest that cultural preferences for cost information should not further be considered in this study to test hypotheses, because the results are contrary to prediction (H_{1a} and H_{1b}) and highly susceptible to biases. Nevertheless, cultural preferences for cost information and the cultural dimensions by *Hofstede* are still applied to interpret empirical findings. The remaining country-specifics that are based on the societal effects approach show that German cost accountants are more specialized and have more theoretical knowledge than their Japanese counterparts. The hypotheses H_{1c} and H_{1d} are therefore accepted (see Table 3-20). Based on the country-specifics, German companies have overall a higher potential to run complex and timely cost accounting systems than their Japanese counterparts. It is therefore likely that German companies also employ more complex and timelier cost accounting systems.

1091 To determine the factor for the degree of specialization the second indicator 'experienced in business functions other than accounting' was reverse-scored.

Hypothesis		Result
H_{1a}	German companies have a stronger emphasis on accurate and detailed than on timely cost information.	Rejected
H_{1b}	Japanese companies have a stronger emphasis on timely than on accurate and detailed cost information.	Rejected
H_{1c}	German cost accountants are more specialized than their Japanese counterparts.	Accepted
H_{1d}	German cost accountants have more theoretical knowledge than their Japanese counterparts.	Accepted

Table 3-20: Results of the hypotheses tests

For the analysis of relationships on an international level (third research question), cross-national differences in cost accounting systems are explained by the identified cross-national differences in country-specifics. Several country-specifics are also selected in section 3.2.4 as independent variables in regression analysis and PLS models to identify factors that explain the complexity, timeliness, and performance of cost accounting systems on a national level (fourth and fifth research question). The correlations between all country-specifics are summarized for data set 1 in Appendix 7 and Appendix 8. Both correlation matrices show that many indicators for the country-specifics are statistically significantly correlated, however, only two are highly correlated with each other. The specifications, e.g., accuracy and detail for the required cost information (r = 0.567 and r = 0.700 for Germany and Japan respectively) are significantly correlated. This, however, is reasonable, because they measure very similar aspects. Due to the overall low correlations between the country-specifics, all of them can be applied in the further analysis.

3.2.2 Other external context factors

3.2.2.1 External complexity

External complexity was operationalized by the companies' numbers of suppliers, customer (respectively patient) groups, and competitors (question A.8, Appendix 2).

External complexity – comparisons of means	How large is the number of the following aspects of your company? (1=very small; ... ; 7=very large)						
Type of comparison	Country comparison				Industry comparison		
Data set	Data set 1		Data set 2		Data set 3		
	Germany	Japan	Germany	Japan	Food and beverage	Mechanical engineering	Hospitals
Suppliers	4.60	4.84 *	4.76	4.75	4.57	4.76 ***	4.39
Customer/patient groups	4.27	4.50	4.08	4.20	4.20	4.08	**4.81** ***
Competitors	3.66	4.03 **	3.21	3.40	4.11 ***	3.21	3.98

Table 3-21: Companies' number of suppliers, customer respectively patient groups, and competitors

The Japanese respondents from all three industries (data set 1) assess their external complexity in terms of the number of suppliers and competitors to be more complex than their German counterparts. These differences, however, are not statistically significant for data set 2. External complexity varies more strongly across the three industries. Companies operating in the food and beverage industry suffer stronger competitive pressures than mechanical engineering companies. Mechanical engineering companies contrariwise operate in a more complex environment than hospitals regarding the number of suppliers. Finally, hospitals have more customer groups (i.e. patient groups) than the companies of both manufacturing industries (see Table 3-21). These findings are consistent with the descriptions of the industries in section 3.1.1.

Data set	Analysis	Factor analysis				Reliability analysis
	Criteria	KMO-value	% of variance explained	Kaiser	Factor loadings (max; min)	Cronbach's Alpha
1	Germany	0.541	45.3%	1.36	0.766; 0.509	0.393
	Japan	0.552	49.3%	1.48	0.793; 0.508	0.459

Table 3-22: Results of the factor analysis for external complexity

The **factor** of the three indicators does not meet all required criteria for data set 1. Less than 50% of the variance is explained and the threshold value of 0.5 for Cronbach's Alpha is not obtained (see Table 3-22). Factors consisting only of two out of the three indicators neither meet the threshold values. Statements regarding external complexity are therefore not drawn for this factor, but by its single indicators.

3.2.2.2 External dynamics

External dynamics was operationalized by the extent to which relationships with suppliers, customer respectively patient needs, and competitors' actions are stable (question A.9, Appendix 2). The answers are reversed to obtain the degree for external dynamics.

External dynamics – comparisons of means	How stable were the following aspects of your company over the last three years? (1=not stable at all; ... ; 7=very stable)						
Type of comparison	Country comparison				Industry comparison		
Data set	Data set 1		Data set 2		Data set 3		
	Germany	Japan	Germany	Japan	Food and beverage	Mechanical engineering	Hospitals
Relationships with suppliers (R)	2.58	2.61	2.55	2.72	2.53	2.55	2.74 *
Customer/patient needs (R)	2.84	3.56 ***	2.98	3.58 ***	2.75	**2.98** ***	2.66
Competitors' actions (R)	3.59	3.85 **	3.63	3.86	3.34	3.63	3.75 ***

Table 3-23: Stability of relationships with suppliers, of customer respectively patient needs, and of competitors' actions

The Japanese respondents from all three industries (data set 1) assess their external environment to be more dynamic in terms of customer respectively patient needs and competitors' actions than their German counterparts. The results are statistically significant. Only the results for customer respectively patient needs are stable for data set 2. Overall, Japanese respondents assess their environment on average to be more complex and more dynamic than their German counterparts. Respondents of the hospital industry assess their environment to be more dynamic in terms of relations with suppliers and in terms of competitors' actions than cost accountants working in the food and beverage industry. Cost accountants working in mechanical engineering companies furthermore assess customer needs to vary more frequently than the respondents from the other two industries (see Table 3-23).

The reason why Japanese companies perceive their environment to be more uncertain than their German counterparts might be due to the higher degree of uncertainty avoidance in Japan according to *Hofstede* and due to the Japanese practice to build up cost pressures within companies,[1092] whereas German companies rather emphasize quality than cost aspects while designing, producing, and selling products and services.

Data set	Analysis	Factor analysis				Reliability analysis
	Criteria	KMO-value	% of variance explained	Kaiser	Factor loadings (max; min)	Cronbach's Alpha
1	Germany	0.615	53.5%	1.61	0.780; 0.697	0.564
	Japan	0.637	63.3%	1.90	0.856; 0.743	0.710
2	Germany	0.565	51.6%	1.55	0.809; 0.641	0.525
	Japan	0.596	59.8%	1.79	0.842; 0.615	0.658

Table 3-24: Results of the factor analysis for external dynamics

All three indicators are aggregated to the **factor external dynamics** separately for each country for data set 1 and 2. This factor meets all required criteria for data set 1 and 2 (see Table 3-24). The mean of this factor is 0 and the standard deviation is 1 for each country for data set 1 and 2.

Coefficient of congruence for external dynamics		
Data set	Data set 1	Data set 2
	0.9995	0.9958

Table 3-25: Coefficients of congruence for external dynamics

For regression analyses of the subgroups (i.e. for Germany and Japan) the factor loadings are derived separately for each comparison group. For this reason it is necessary to test for equivalence of the factors, i.e. whether the factors have the same meaning in both countries.[1093] The **coefficients of congruence** are all above 0.9 and thus indicate that the factors for external dynamics are highly equivalent between Germany and Japan (see Table 3-25). Statements regarding external dynamics are therefore drawn for this factor only.

3.2.3 Internal context factors

3.2.3.1 Company size

Company size was operationalized by the number of employees (full-time equivalents) and sales turnover in mill. € and Yen (question A.15, items 1 and 2, Appendix 2).

For data set 1, the majority of the companies lie within the desired size range of 250 to 2,000 **employees.** Only 7% respectively 10% of the German and Japanese companies

1092 Cf., e.g., *Hiromoto* (1988); *Takatera/Yamamoto* (1989); *Cooper* (1996).

1093 Cf. section 3.1.3.1.

employ less than 250 workers and 2% respectively 5% employ more than 2,000 workers. The smallest company from both countries has 77 and the largest has 4,800 employees. About three quarters of the German and Japanese companies have between 250-999 employees. The arithmetic mean amounts to 716.24 (σ = 574.77) respectively 776.31 (σ = 994.23) for Germany and Japan (see Figure 3-15).

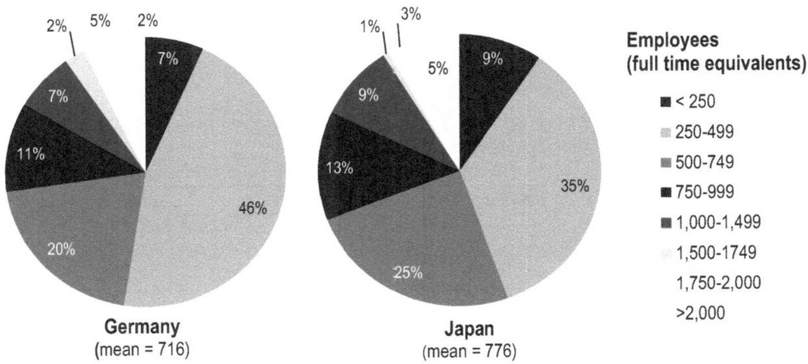

Figure 3-15: Size classification according to number of employees (full-time equivalents; data set 1)

Sales turnover varies between € 10 and 2,000 mill. (Ø = 165.72; σ = 242.57) for German companies and between € 3 and 5,625 mill. (Ø = 273.51; σ = 561.86) for Japanese companies. The distribution shows that 66% respectively 33% of the German and Japanese companies have yielded a sales turnover between € 20 and 100 mill. Only 4% respectively 12% reached less than € 20 mill. and 4% respectively 10% reached more than € 500 mill. sales turnover. The remaining companies (29% respectively 44%) realized a sales turnover of between € 100 to 500 mill. (see Figure 3-16).

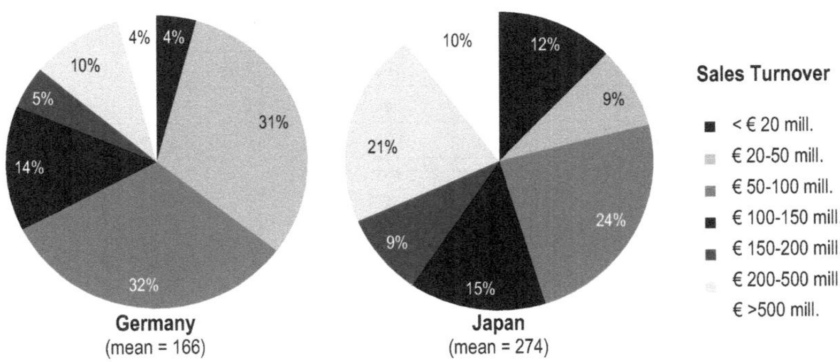

Figure 3-16: Size classification according to sales turnover (data set 1)

The arithmetic means of number of employees and sales turnover for all three data sets are summarized in Table 3-26. The number of employees is highly comparable across all data sets. Only food and beverage companies from data set 3 are statistically significantly larger than companies of the mechanical engineering industry. According to sales turnover, however, significant differences prevail. Japanese companies are statistically significantly larger than their German counterparts for data set 1 and 2. Furthermore, food and beverage companies are statistically significantly larger than firms from the other two industries (data set 3). This demonstrates that distortions due to company size are possible, however, previous studies indicate that cost accounting depends more on the number of employees than on sales turnover.[1094] Hence, minor distortions are expected to stem form cross-national and cross-industry differences in sales turnover.

Company size – comparisons of means	Please indicate the average number of employees (full-time equivalents) for the last financial year of your company.						
Type of comparison	**Country comparison**				**Industry comparison**		
Data set	**Data set 1**		**Data set 2**		**Data set 3**		
	Germany	Japan	Germany	Japan	Food and beverage	Mechanical engineering	Hospitals
Number of employees	716	776	552	599	697 **	552	677
Sales turnover in mill. €	166	274 **	124	205 ***	**251** ***	124	59

Table 3-26: Company size

The values for the number of employees and sales turnover are taken to the natural logarithm before aggregating them to the **factor company size.** For each data set and for each comparison group the factor company size is calculated separately. This factor meets all quality criteria for both data sets (see Table 3-27).[1095] Statements regarding company size are thus limited to this measure. As top management support consists only of two indicators, the coefficient of congruence cannot be calculated for this factor to test for cross-national equivalence.

Data set	**Analysis**	**Factor analysis**				**Reliability analysis**
	Criteria	**KMO-value**	**% of variance explained**	**Kaiser**	**Factor loadings (max; min)**	**Cronbach's Alpha**
1	Germany	0.500	81.2%	1.62	0.901; 0.901	0.729
	Japan	0.500	79.7%	1.60	0.893; 0.893	0.712
2	Germany	0.500	90.9%	1.82	0.953; 0.953	0.885
	Japan	0.500	87.5%	1.75	0.935; 0.935	0.817

Table 3-27: Results of the factor analysis for company size

3.2.3.2 Potential for cost distortion

Potential for cost distortion was operationalized by the extent to which products respectively medical treatments are similar regarding service processes and the utilization of support cost centers (question A.5, Appendix 2).

1094 Cf. section 2.1.3.1; *Weber/Weißenberger* (2006), p. 364f.; *Schweitzer/Küpper* (2011), p. 125. For empirical evidence see, e.g., *Friedl et al.* (2009a), p. 112f.; *Friedl et al.* (2009b), p. 44.

1095 As only two variables have been aggregated, the KMO criteria is 0.5 – as for all factors consisting of only two variables.

Potential for cost distortion – comparisons of means	To what extent are your company's product lines/medical treatments similar regarding the following characteristics? (1=very similar; ... ; 7=very heterogeneous)					
Type of comparison	Country comparison				Industry comparison		
Data set	Data set 1		Data set 2		Data set 3		
	Germany	Japan	Germany	Japan	Food and beverage	Mechanical engineering	Hospitals
Product/service processes	3.40 ***	2.66	3.42 ***	2.37	3.08	3.42	**4.00** ***
Utilization of support cost centers	3.00	5.00 ***	3.02	4.85 ***	2.94	3.02	3.14

Table 3-28: Potential for cost distortion

Table 3-28 compares the means of both items across Germany, Japan, and the three industries. German compared to Japanese companies have statistically significantly more heterogeneous product processes (respectively service processes for hospitals). This implies that German companies follow more intensively a differentiation strategy than their Japanese counterparts who are characterized in literature to intensively drive automation and standardization to promote long-term competitiveness.[1096] Product lines on the contrary utilize more heterogeneously support cost centers in Japan than in Germany. These variations remain constant for data set 2. For data set 3 it turns out that the service lines in hospitals are significantly more heterogeneous than the product lines in the food and beverage and the mechanical engineering industry. This result supports the common argument that services are usually less standardized than products.[1097]

Data set	Analysis	Factor analysis				Reliability analysis
	Criteria	KMO-value	% of variance explained	Kaiser	Factor loadings (max; min)	Cronbach's Alpha
1	Germany	0.500	79.4%	1.56	0.891; 0.891	0.735
	Japan	0.500	53.5%	1.07	0.732; 0.732	0.131

Table 3-29: Results of the factor analysis for potential for cost distortion

Both variables are not aggregated to the **factor potential for cost distortion**, because for the Japanese sample this factor *does not meet the threshold value of 0.5 for Cronbach's Alpha* (see Table 3-29). Statements regarding the potential for cost distortion are therefore not drawn by this factor, but by its single indicators.

3.2.3.3 IT systems quality

IT systems quality was operationalized by the extent to which IT systems are cross-functionally integrated, provide user-friendly query capabilities, provide comprehensive cost and performance information, and update most information in 'real time' instead of periodically (question A.6, Appendix 2).

1096 Cf., e.g., *Hiromoto* (1988), p. 23.

1097 This assumption is empirically verified by *Krumwiede/Suessmair* (2007a), p. 4; *Krumwiede/Suessmair* (2007b), p. 51. This study obtains similar responses for Germany in comparison to both references quoted before.

Hypothesis test

Japan is a more uncertainty-avoiding and more long-term oriented society than Germany according to *Hofstede's* cultural dimensions. It is thus expected that Japanese managers require more comprehensive IT systems to reduce their inconvenience of decision making and that Japanese managers are more interested to make investments for improving the future of the organization. In section 2.1.3.3 it was consequently hypothesized that IT systems are more comprehensive in **Japan** than in **Germany** (H_{1e}). Table 3-30 compares the means of the four indicators for IT systems quality across Germany, Japan, and the three industries.

IT systems quality – comparisons of means	To what extent do the following statements apply to your company's IT system? (1=not at all; ... ; 7=completely)						
Type of comparison	Country comparison				Industry comparison		
Data set	Data set 1		Data set 2		Data set 3		
	Germany	Japan	Germany	Japan	Food and beverage	Mechanical engineering	Hospitals
Cross-functionally integrated	5.01 ***	3.81	5.15 ***	4.04	4.86	5.15	5.04
Provides user-friendly query capabilities	4.41 ***	3.97	4.55 ***	4.11	4.38	4.55	4.37
Provides comprehensive cost and performance information	4.60 ***	3.82	4.71 ***	3.98	4.52	4.71	4.53
Most information is updated in 'real-time' and not periodically	4.64 ***	3.93	4.70 ***	3.66	4.51	4.70	4.77

Table 3-30: IT systems quality

In data set 1 and 2 it turns out that German companies employ superior IT systems than their Japanese counterparts, which means that German companies have thus a higher potential to install and run complex and timely cost accounting systems.[1098] Hypothesis H_{1e} is consequently rejected (see Table 3-31). Industry differences in IT systems quality on the contrary do not prevail.

Hypothesis		Result
H_{1e}	Japanese companies have more comprehensive IT systems than their German counterparts.	Rejected

Table 3-31: Results of the hypothesis test

From a cultural point of view, this result is surprising. It demonstrates that besides national culture other factors are relevant to explain cross-national differences in IT systems quality. *Krumwiede* argues that German companies employ more comprehensive IT systems and ERP software[1099] because they more closely cooperate with IT providers than their US counterparts.[1100] Furthermore, German companies have a long tradition to install complex cost accounting systems.[1101] It is likely that – although Japan scores higher

1098 Cf. section 2.1.3.3.

1099 This assumption is empirically verified by *Krumwiede/Suessmair* (2007a), p. 4; *Krumwiede/Suessmair* (2007b), p. 51. This study obtains similar responses for Germany in comparison to both references quoted before.

1100 Cf. *Krumwiede* (2005), p. 31.

1101 See section 2.1.1.2.1.

on uncertainty avoidance and long-term orientation – German companies have therefore a higher emphasis than their Japanese counterparts on investing in comprehensive IT systems.

All four variables are aggregated to the **factor IT systems quality**. This factor meets all required criteria for each data set (see Table 3-32).

Data set	Analysis	Factor analysis				Reliability analysis
	Criteria	KMO-value	% of variance explained	Kaiser	Factor loadings (max; min)	Cronbach's Alpha
1	Germany	0.818	72.8%	2.91	0.875; 0.781	0.870
	Japan	0.783	67.0%	2.68	0.896; 0.719	0.831
2	Germany	0.821	77.0%	3.08	0.897; 0.833	0.897
	Japan	0.743	62.5%	2.50	0.897; 0.667	0.788

Table 3-32: Results of the factor analysis for IT systems quality

The **coefficients of congruence** between the subsamples all lie above 0.9 and thus indicate that the factor IT systems quality is highly equivalent between Germany and Japan (see Table 3-33). Statements regarding IT systems quality are thus exclusively drawn for this factor.

Coefficient of congruence for IT systems quality		
Data set	Data set 1	Data set 2
	0.9990	0.9962

Table 3-33: Coefficients of congruence for the factor IT systems quality

3.2.3.4 Overall interest in cost accounting

The overall interest in cost accounting is measured by the construct 'top management support' as well as by the number of full-time cost accountants. The first measure was operationalized by the extent to which top management provides (1) strong and active support and (2) sufficient resources for cost accounting (question A.11, item 1 and 2, Appendix 2). For the second measure the respondents had to indicate the average number of full-time cost accountants responsible for cost accounting for the last financial year (question A.15, item 2). To measure the overall interest in cost accounting, the number of full-time cost accountants per 100 employees and per € 10 mill. sales turnover are determined.

Top management support

Figure 3-17 compares cross-nationally for data set 1 the extent to which top management provides political support and sufficient resources for cost accounting.

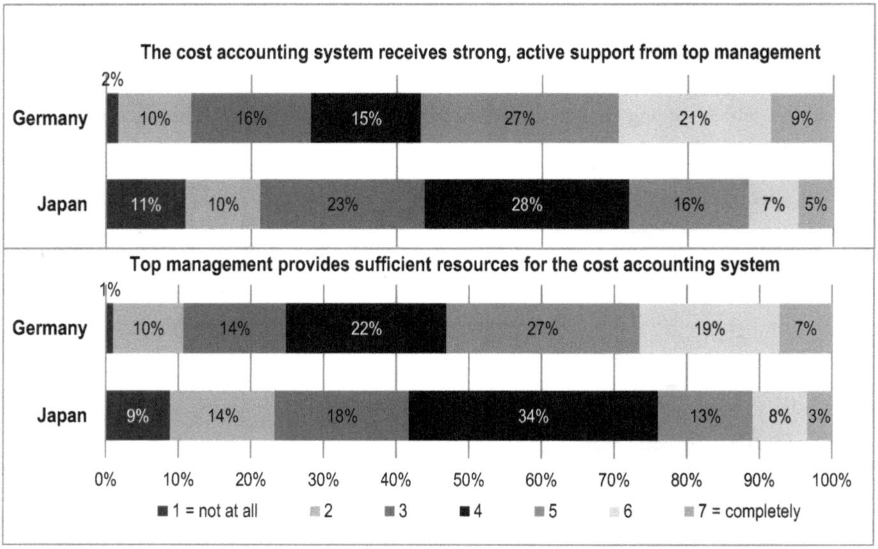

Figure 3-17: Top management support (data set 1)

Table 3-34 shows that cost accounting in Germany receives stronger, more active support and more resources from top management than their Japanese counterparts. The results are stable across both data sets. Differences between the three industries prevail to a lesser degree. Cost accounting obtains statistically significantly less top management support in hospitals than in the other two industries.

Top management support – comparisons of means	To what extent do you agree with the following statements regarding your cost accounting? (1=not at all; ... ; 7=completely)						
Type of comparison	**Country comparison**				**Industry comparison**		
Data set	**Data set 1**		**Data set 2**		**Data set 3**		
	Germany	Japan	Germany	Japan	Food and beverage	Mechanical engineering	Hospitals
It receives strong, active support from top management.	4.53 ***	3.69	4.63 ***	3.82	4.57	4.63	4.42
Top management provides sufficient resources.	4.50 ***	3.64	4.60 ***	3.74	4.61 ***	4.60 ***	4.06

Table 3-34: Top management support

Both indicators for top management support are aggregated to one factor separately for each country for data set 1 and 2. This factor meets all required criteria (see Table 3-35). Statements regarding top management support are thus limited to this measure. As top management support consists only of two indicators, the coefficient of congruence cannot be calculated for this factor to test for cross-national equivalence.

Data set	Analysis	Factor analysis				Reliability analysis
	Criteria	KMO-value	% of variance explained	Kaiser	Factor loadings (max; min)	Cronbach's Alpha
1	Germany	0.500	75.3%	1.51	0.868; 0.868	0.672
	Japan	0.500	92.3%	1.85	0.961; 0.961	0.916
2	Germany	0.500	74.5%	1.49	0.863; 0.863	0.656
	Japan	0.500	94.5%	1.89	0.972; 0.972	0.941

Table 3-35: Results of the factor analysis for top management support

Number of full-time cost accountants

Table 3-36 compares the number of full-time cost accountants per 100 employees and per € 10 mill. sales turnover. Japanese companies have more employees that are responsible for cost accounting. The results for the number of cost accountants per 100 employees remain constant for data set 2. These results are contrary to the variable top management support. Thus, the overall interest in cost accounting is expressed in different ways cross-nationally. Whereas German companies perceive more top management support, in Japanese companies more employees are responsible for cost accounting tasks. The higher number of cost accountants in Japan can partly be explained by the broader range of tasks that management accountants carry out in Japan.[1102] The results for the number of cost accountants might therefore lack functional equivalence, because German and Japanese cost accountants may have a different understanding which tasks cost accountants should fulfill. For this reason, 'top management support' is probably a better indicator for the overall interest in cost accounting. Furthermore, across industries strong differences prevail as well, especially for the measure 'number of cost accountants per 100 employees'.

Number of cost accountants – comparisons of means	Please indicate the average number of employees responsible for cost accounting (full-time equivalents) for the last financial year of your company.					
Type of comparison	Country comparison				Industry comparison		
Data set	Data set 1		Data set 2		Data set 3		
	Germany	Japan	Germany	Japan	Food and beverage	Mechanical engineering	Hospitals
Per 100 employees	0.53	0.89 ***	0.72	0.90 **	0.57	**0.72** **	0.32
Per € 10 mill. sales turnover	0.33	0.42 *	0.41	0.46	0.33	0.41 *	0.36

Table 3-36: Number of cost accountants

Hypothesis test

In section 2.1.1.5 **hypothesis** $\mathbf{H_{1f}}$ was set up stating that the overall interest in cost accounting is similar between Germany and Japan. Empirical evidence from this section shows that cost accounting receives more top management support in Germany than in Japan. On the contrary, more employees are responsible for cost accounting in Japan than in Germany. Hence, the overall interest in cost accounting is probably similar between both countries, but it is expressed in different ways. Hypothesis H_{1f} is therefore accepted with caution (see Table 3-37).

1102 See *Otto* (2000), p. 280f. *Otto's* anecdotal evidence is thereby empirically verified.

Hypothesis		Result
H_{1f}	The overall interest in cost accounting is about the same in Germany and in Japan.	Accepted

Table 3-37: Results of the hypothesis test

3.2.3.5 Type of organization

The type of organization was operationalized by asking the respondents of the hospital industry to characterize their organization as either private, public, or charitable.[1103] This measure is surveyed for hospitals only, because only in this industry all three types of the organization compete with each other.[1104]

Figure 3-18 provides the distribution of the three different types of organizations in Germany and Japan for data set 1. The three characteristics prevail with different frequencies in both countries. Whereas 58% of the German hospitals are charitable in nature,[1105] half of the Japanese hospitals are private. These contrasting results might lead to minor distortions, because the differences in the characteristics of the organizations are not controlled for while setting up data set 1.[1106] Industry effects and effects stemming from the types of organizations might thus interfere with each other to some extent. As hospitals represent only 21% of the German and Japanese companies in this study, a potential distorting effect in data set 1 is expected to be negligible.

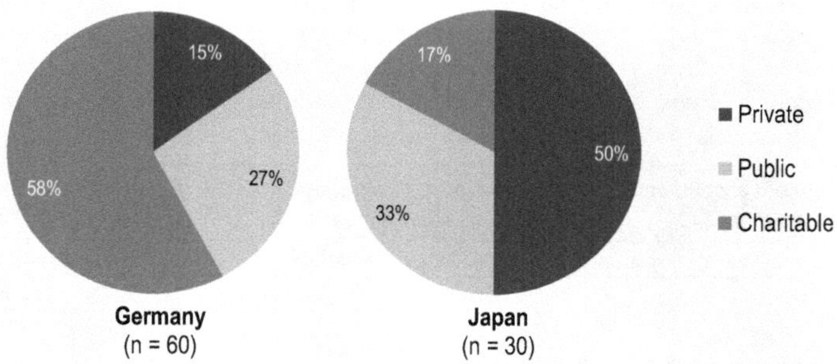

Figure 3-18: Distribution of the type of hospital organization (data set 1)

1103 This question is not included in Appendix 2, because only the questionnaire for the manufacturing sector is provided.

1104 Cf. section 3.1.1.

1105 The results for the complete German data set that consists of 216 hospitals are similar. 17% of the hospitals are characterized as private, 25% as public, and 58% as charitable.

1106 Type of organization was not controlled for, because company size and industry is expected to be of higher relevance.

3.2.4 Selection of context factors for regression analysis

14 variables for country-specifics,[1107] four variables for the other external context,[1108] and seven variables for the internal context[1109] are reported in previous sections. They can be applied to explain the complexity, timeliness, and performance of cost accounting systems. However, not all of the 25 context factors are applied for regression analysis in the following, because independent variables should explain different aspects. For this reason the number of context factors is reduced in the following, either because they strongly and statistically significantly correlate or because these variables are similar with regard to contents. Furthermore, stability of the results and the accuracy of the measure 'adjusted R^2' decreases,[1110] the more independent variables are applied in multiple regression analysis.

The variables for **required cost information** are excluded from further analysis, because the results are contrary to prediction and highly susceptible to biases.[1111]

The variable '**responsible bodies for cost accounting**' indicates the degree of specialization of cost accounting. It is excluded because sufficient other measures for both aspects are applied in regression analyzes that have a higher level of measurement – the measurements for 'responsible bodies for cost accounting' are only nominally scaled.

The factor '**potential for cost distortion**' of the Japanese responses has failed the quality criterion for Cronbach's Alpha. This demonstrates that both indicators are not internally consistent for the Japanese sample. Whereas both indicators strongly correlate for the German responses of data set 1 (r = 0.588***), both indicators are uncorrelated for the respective Japanese responses. This indicates that the two indicators for potential for cost distortion might also have a different meaning across both countries – it is probably not possible to compare the effect of both variables between Germany and Japan. Thus, both variables are excluded from regression analysis.

1107 These include four dummy-variables for responsible bodies for cost accounting, the relation between cost accountants' workload for management accounting and financial accounting, focus on management accounting, focus on management accounting education, four sources of cost accountants' knowledge, and three variables for the specialization of cost accountants.

1108 The external context factors include three variables for external complexity and the factor for external dynamics.

1109 These include the factor for company size, two variables for potential for cost distortion (the factor has not met the quality criteria and thus only the single variables can be applied), the factor for IT systems quality, the factor for top management support, and two variables for the relative number of cost accountants.

1110 This study uses the enter and the stepwise method of linear regression analysis. The larger the number of independent variables, the more the results vary between the stepwise method and the other methods like remove, backward, and forward. The adjusted R^2 penalizes the statistic according to the number of variables in the model. This procedure, however, is only a rule of thumb and can thus only more or less exactly compare models with different numbers of independent variables. The higher the number of independent variables, the higher the correction term and thus the lower the precision for how well the model explains variance.

1111 Cf. section 3.2.1.1.

External complexity is excluded from regression analysis for two reasons. First, the factor for external complexity does not meet all quality criteria. Its indicators are not internally consistent enough and do not strongly correlate with each other. Thus, applying the three indicators separately would insufficiently reflect external complexity. Second, instead of external complexity, the factor for external dynamics is applied in the following, which describes one facet of environmental uncertainty. Hence, environmental uncertainty is partly considered by external dynamics.

The **relative number of cost accountants** as an indicator for overall interest in cost accounting is not applied in regression analysis, because this measure might lack functional equivalence cross-nationally. Anecdotal evidence indicates that Japanese cost accountants might be in charge for a broader range of tasks in Japan than their counterparts in Germany.[1112]

By excluding the five groups of variables, the **number of context variables** to explain the complexity, timeliness, and performance of cost accounting systems via regression analysis **is reduced from 25 to 14.**[1113] Thereby, the most relevant influences are still analyzed and this study applies a slightly smaller number of independent variables like in previous studies.[1114] The correlations between the selected context factors for regression analysis of data set 1 are in most cases only weak (see Appendix 9 and Appendix 10). The highest correlation for Germany is between 'workload management over financial accounting' and 'focus on management accounting' ($r = 0.415$) and for Japan it is between 'factor top management support' and 'specification by high qualification' ($r = 0.454$). However, both correlations are reasonable because the first pair of variables measures similar aspects and because top management support might positively affect a high qualification of cost accountants to enhance and run cost accounting systems. The remaining correlations are weak or not statistically significant. Thus all selected variables are retained to ensure robust research findings.

3.3 Cost accounting objectives

12 variables were operationalized to measure seven cost accounting objectives by the degrees to which companies pursue them on a seven-point Likert scale (questions B.1 to B.3, Appendix 2). It is expected that cost accounting systems are purposefully designed and thus cost accounting objectives should have a significant impact upon the conceptual design of the systems.

1112 Cf. *Otto* (2000), p. 280f.

1113 The context variables include 'workload management over financial accounting', 'focus on management accounting', 'focus on management accounting education', 'education university', 'education professional institutes', 'education in-house training', 'education learning by doing', 'specialization in cost accounting only', 'specialization in other business functions', 'specialization by high qualification', 'factor external dynamics', 'factor company size', 'factor IT systems quality', and 'factor top management support'.

1114 *Pizzini* and *Schoute*, e.g., have applied 24 respectively 18 independent variables to explain the relevance, use, and satisfaction with cost accounting systems. Cf. *Pizzini* (2006), p. 196; *Schoute* (2009), p. 218f.

Cross-national and cross-industry differences prevail for **cost accounting objectives**. For data set 1 (see Figure 3-19), German companies pursue statistically significantly more intensively the four variables 'exploiting cost reduction potential', 'operational planning', 'cost control', and 'tracing (in)efficiencies back to persons in charge' than their Japanese counterparts. Japanese companies on the contrary significantly pursue more intensively 'short-term capacity planning', 'strategy development', and 'inventory valuation for financial accounting'. The results support earlier research findings that German companies put more emphasis on decision facilitating and control than on decision influencing.[1115]

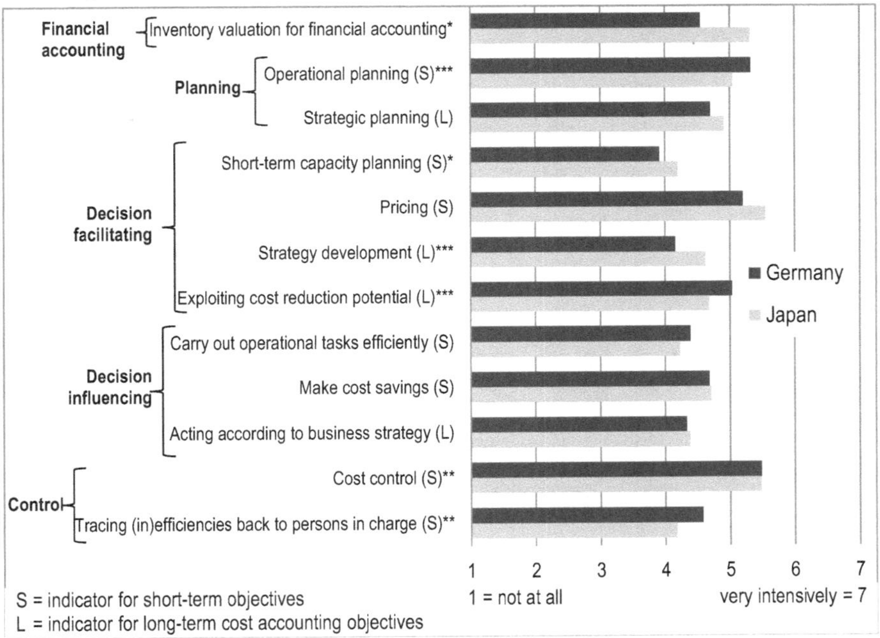

Figure 3-19: Intensity of pursuing cost accounting objectives (data set 1)

For data set 2, only two statistically significant differences remain for 'strategy development' and 'tracing (in)efficiencies back to persons in charge'. Significant differences prevail also across industries for seven variables (see Table 3-38). Three cross-industry differences can be explained by the nature of the industries: In most cases hospitals cannot set the prices for their services themselves and thus pricing is of less importance. Instead, they often get paid a predetermined rate that is based on DRGs. 'Pricing' is therefore of less relevance for hospitals. Second, mainly mechanical engineering companies use large machinery that demands a systematic capacity planning. 'Short-term capacity planning' is therefore highly relevant for this industry. Third, as services are usually immediately con-

1115 Cf. *Weber* (1993), p. 267f.; *Friedl et al.* (2009a), p. 111f.; *Friedl et al.* (2009b), p. 41.

sumed during the service processes, in most cases service providers like hospitals have no inventories that require valuation for financial accounting purposes.

Cost accounting objectives – comparisons of means	How intensively does your company pursue the following objectives? (1=not at all; ... ; 7=very intensively)						
Type of comparison	**Country comparison**				**Industry comparison**		
Data set	**Data set 1**		**Data set 2**		**Data set 3**		
	Germany	Japan	Germany	Japan	Food and beverage	Mechanical engineering	Hospitals
Financial accounting							
Inventory valuation for financial accounting	4.55	4.94 *	5.29	5.31	4.64 ***	**5.29** ***	3.33
Planning							
Operational planning (S)	5.32 ***	4.91	5.22	5.05	**5.59** **	5.22	4.98
Strategic planning (L)	4.70	4.76	4.65	4.91	4.90	4.65	4.76
Decision facilitating							
Short-term capacity planning (S)	3.92	4.21 *	4.28	4.20	3.75	**4.28** **	3.71
Pricing (S)	5.20	5.05	5.53	5.55	5.75 ***	5.53 ***	3.65
Strategy development (L)	4.16	4.66 ***	4.14	4.62 **	4.34	4.14	4.22
Exploiting cost reduction potential (L)	5.03 ***	4.59	4.94	4.68	5.25 *	4.95	5.18 *
Decision influencing							
Carry out operational tasks efficiently (S)	4.39	4.20	4.33	4.23	**4.65** *	4.33	4.28
Make cost savings (S)	4.68	4.64	4.62	4.71	4.91 *	4.62	4.71
Act in accordance with the business strategy (L)	4.33	4.44	4.37	4.38	4.46	4.37	4.45
Control							
Cost control (S)	5.48 **	5.22	5.46	5.48	5.57	5.46	5.44
Tracing (in)efficiencies back to persons in charge (S)	4.58 ***	4.10	4.60 *	4.18	4.56	4.60	4.50
S = indicator for short-term cost accounting objectives; L = indicator for long-term cost accounting objectives							

Table 3-38: Intensity of pursuing cost accounting objectives

The responses to the **intensity of pursuing cost accounting objectives** are susceptible to cross-national differences in response style[1116] and may thus provide biased results. To counteract this potential bias, first, **differences in rank** of the variables are compared cross-nationally. Figure 3-19 and Table 3-38 show that in both countries 'cost control', 'operational planning', 'pricing', and 'strategy development' belong to the five most important variables. The results are stable for both data sets. Among the four least important variables are in both countries 'short-term capacity planning' and 'motivating employees to act in accordance with the business strategy'. The results are also stable for data set 2. The strongest difference in rank between Germany and Japan is the variable 'tracing (in)efficiencies back to persons in charge'. Whereas for German companies this variable is the seventh most important one for data set 1 and the eighth most important for the mechanical engineering industry (data set 2), it is the least important one in Japan for data

1116 For this bias see section 1.2.6.

set 1 and 2. This outcome is reasonable, because (in)efficiencies have to be traced back to persons in charge when control is required for performance evaluation and to motivate employees working in the company's interests. In section 2.2.2.1 it was argued that both aspects are more relevant for German than for Japanese companies. According to the differences in rank it is concluded that only minor cross-national differences in cost accounting objectives prevail between Germany and Japan.

Second, to counteract cross-national differences in response style, the **relative importance** between management and financial accounting, decision facilitating and decision influencing, planning and control, and short-term and long-term objectives is determined. First, the means of the variables belonging to the same objective are averaged. E.g., the indicators 'cost control' and 'tracing (in)efficiencies back to persons in charge' belong to the objective control (see Table 2-5).[1117] The relative importance of the antipodes are thereafter determined by, e.g., dividing the index for planning by the index for control. Thereby, differences in response style between German and Japanese respondents are cancelled out. The results of this procedure are presented in Figure 3-20 for the German and Japanese responses of data set 1. They show that in both countries the objective management accounting dominates financial accounting, control dominates planning, and short-term dominates long-term objectives. Furthermore, German compared to Japanese companies pursue statistically significantly more intensively management accounting than financial accounting objectives, short-term than long-term objectives, and decision facilitating than decision influencing. Similar differences prevail also for data set 2, however, they are not statistically significant.

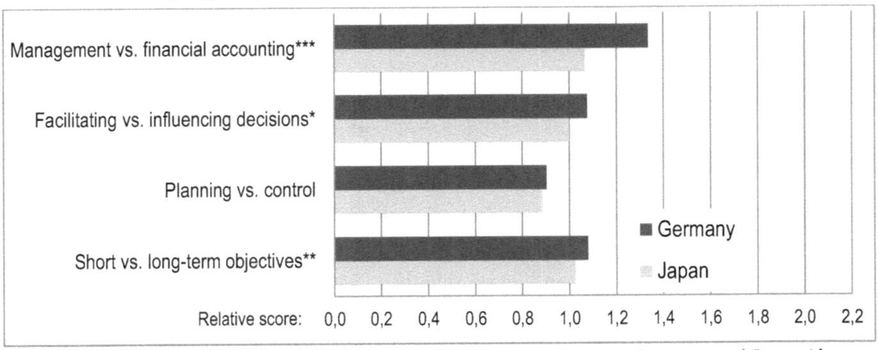

Figure 3-20: Relative importance of cost accounting objectives between Germany and Japan (data set 1)

Overall, the empirical results show statistically significant **variation in cost accounting objectives** between Germany and Japan. Regarding the popular assumption that Japanese

1117 Furthermore, all eleven cost accounting variables that serve managerial purposes are averaged and divided by the variable 'inventory valuation' that serves financial accounting purposes.

companies follow a different philosophy of cost accounting compared to their Western counterparts,[1118] stronger differences in cost accounting objectives were expected.

Hypotheses tests

In section 2.2.1 hypothesis H_{1g} was set up assuming that Japanese companies pursue **cost accounting for financial accounting** to a higher degree than their German counterparts. Based on the *intensity of pursuing cost accounting objectives* and according to the *relative importance* between management and financial accounting objectives this hypothesis is accepted. However, the relative importance between management and financial accounting objectives is not statistically significant for data set 2.

In section 2.2.2.1 it was concluded in hypothesis H_{1h} that German companies place more emphasis on **control** and Japanese companies place more emphasis on **planning**. The *intensity of pursuing cost accounting objectives* shows for data set 1 that German companies put more emphasis on cost control and on operational planning. For the mechanical engineering industry only the indicator for cost control 'tracing (in)efficiencies back to persons in charge' is statically significant. According to the *relative importance* between planning and control, German companies place more emphasis on control and the Japanese counterparts place more emphasis on planning (see Figure 3-20). This, however, is not statistically significant. As the relative importance of cost accounting objectives is expected to reduce response bias, more validity is attached to this measure than to the intensity of cost accounting objectives. Consequently, hypothesis H_{1h} is rejected.

In section 2.2.2.2 it was assumed that German companies place more emphasis on cost information for **decision facilitating** than their Japanese counterparts (hypothesis H_{1i}) and that Japanese companies place more emphasis on cost information for **decision influencing** than their German counterparts (hypothesis H_{1j}). The results for the *intensity of pursuing cost accounting objectives* are inconsistent or not statistically significant (see Figure 3-19 and Table 3-38). The *relative importance* of both objectives on the contrary is in accordance to both hypotheses (see Figure 3-20). The cross-national comparison based on the mechanical engineering industry does not show significant differences. Due to the contradictory results hypotheses H_{1i} and H_{1j} are rejected.

In section 2.2.2.3 hypotheses H_{1k} and H_{1l} stated that German companies put more emphasis on short-term objectives and less emphasis on long-term objectives than their Japanese counterparts. The relation between **short-term and long-term objectives** shows that German companies from data set 1 place statistically significantly more emphasis on short-term than on long-term objectives (see Table 3-38). Thus, hypothesis H_{1k} and H_{1l} are accepted. The results, however, are not statistically significant for data set 2.

In section 2.2.2.3 it was further assumed that cost accounting objectives differ **across industries** (hypothesis H_{3a}) and more strongly across industries than across countries (H_{6a}). For this analysis only the differences in the *relative importance* of cost accounting objectives between Germany and Japan (see Figure 3-20) are compared with the differences across industries (Figure 3-21) to avoid biases that stem from cross-national variation in

1118 See section 1.1.1.

response style. Across all industries more emphasis is put on management accounting than on financial accounting objectives with hospitals having the strongest focus on management accounting. Companies operating in the mechanical engineering industry put significantly more emphasis on short- versus long-term objectives than hospitals. In all three industries cost control dominates planning, however, statistically significant differences do not prevail. Finally, hospitals focus more on decision-facilitating than on decision-influencing compared to the food and beverage industry (see Figure 3-21). Comparing Figure 3-20 and Figure 3-21 and the arithmetic means from Table 3-38 it can be concluded that cost accounting objectives differ slightly more strongly between product and service industries than between Germany and Japan. Hypotheses H_{3a} and H_{6a} are thus both accepted.

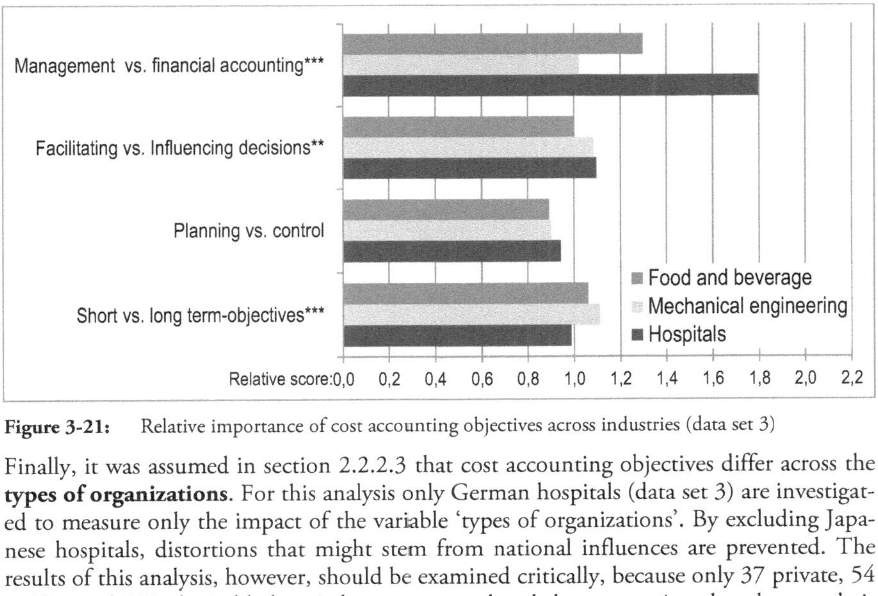

Figure 3-21: Relative importance of cost accounting objectives across industries (data set 3)

Finally, it was assumed in section 2.2.2.3 that cost accounting objectives differ across the **types of organizations**. For this analysis only German hospitals (data set 3) are investigated to measure only the impact of the variable 'types of organizations'. By excluding Japanese hospitals, distortions that might stem from national influences are prevented. The results of this analysis, however, should be examined critically, because only 37 private, 54 public, and 125 charitable hospitals are compared and the assumption that the sample is normally distributed does not hold for private hospitals.[1119] Statistically significant differences in the number of employees do not prevail on a 5%-significance level across the three types of organizations. Figure 3-22 shows that the relative importance of control over planning and facilitating over influencing decisions statistically significantly differs. However, these differences are smaller for the types of organizations than for the country and industry comparisons.

1119 Public and charitable hospitals are normally distributed and homoscedasticity prevails for all three types of organizations.

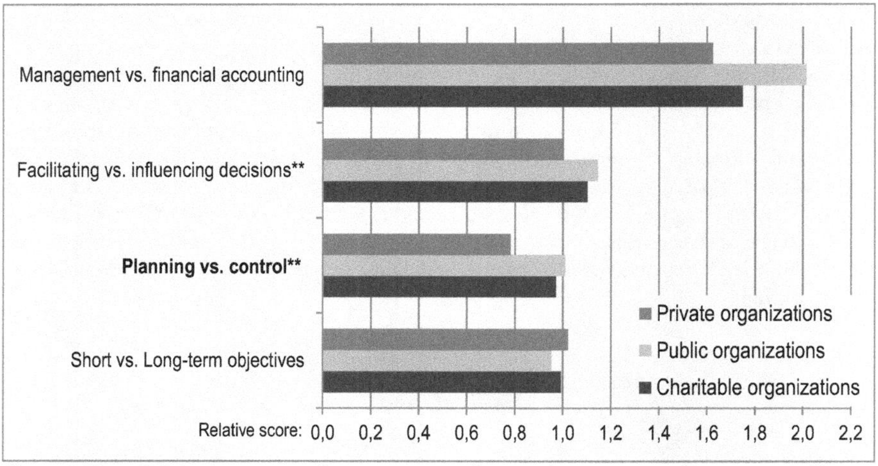

Figure 3-22: Relative importance of cost accounting objectives between types of organizations (data set 3)

The results of the hypotheses tests are summarized in Table 3-39.

Hypothesis		Result
H_{1g}	Japanese companies pursue cost accounting for inventory valuation more intensively than their German counterparts.	Accepted
H_{1h}	Whereas German companies place more emphasis on control, Japanese companies put more emphasis on planning.	Rejected
H_{1i}	German companies place more emphasis on cost information for decision facilitating than their Japanese counterparts.	Rejected
H_{1j}	Japanese companies place more emphasis on cost information for decision influencing than their German counterparts.	Rejected
H_{1k}	German companies apply cost accounting more intensively for short-term objectives than their Japanese counterparts.	Accepted
H_{1l}	Japanese companies apply cost accounting more intensively for long-term objectives than their German counterparts.	Accepted
H_{3a}	Cost accounting objectives differ across industries.	Accepted
H_{6a}	Cost accounting objectives differ more strongly across industries than across countries.	Accepted

Table 3-39: Results of the hypotheses tests

The eleven cost accounting variables that serve managerial purposes are reduced to the six **factors** planning, decision facilitating, decision influencing, cost control, short-term objectives, and long-term objectives. The factors short-term and long-term objectives do not meet the quality criteria of the factor analysis and the reliability analysis. Both factors are therefore not applied in multiple regression analysis. Furthermore, the indicators pricing and short-term capacity planning have a significant different relevance for hospitals compared to the food and beverage industry and for the mechanical engineering industry. Hospitals can seldom set the prices for their services themselves and capacity planning is of minor relevance, because most of the costs are personnel costs instead of costs for, e.g., operating rooms. Thus, both indicators have a different meaning across industries and should thus be excluded from the factor decision facilitating. The low values of indicator reliability[1120] for both indicators of 0.115 and 0.215 for the German sample and 0.251 and 0.363 for the Japanese sample of data set 1 support this argument.

Data set	Analysis	Factor analysis				Reliability analysis
	Criteria	KMO-value	% of variance explained	Kaiser	Factor loadings (max; min)	Cronbach's Alpha
Planning						
1	Germany	0.500	79.2%	1.58	0.890; 0.890	0.736
	Japan	0.500	88.9%	1.78	0.943; 0.943	0.875
2	Germany	0.500	76.8%	1.54	0.876; 0.876	0.695
	Japan	0.500	86.3%	1.73	0.929; 0.929	0.839
Decision facilitating						
1	Germany	0.500	75.7%	1.52	0.870; 0.870	0.676
	Japan	0.500	80.1%	1.60	0.895; 0.895	0.748
2	Germany	0.500	80.8%	1.62	0.899; 0.899	0.761
	Japan	0.500	88.2%	1.76	0.939; 0.939	0.860
Decision influencing						
1	Germany	0.734	77.4%	2.32	0.885; 0.875	0.854
	Japan	0.722	79.5%	2.39	0.920; 0.877	0.870
2	Germany	0.709	74.3%	2.23	0.889; 0.840	0.826
	Japan	0.693	77.1%	2.31	0.918; 0.831	0.848
Cost control						
1	Germany	0.500	80.5%	1.61	0.897; 0.897	0.746
	Japan	0.500	76.6%	1.53	0.875; 0.875	0.694
2	Germany	0.500	76.4%	1.53	0.874; 0.874	0.682
	Japan	0.500	76.6%	1.53	0.875; 0.875	0.689

Table 3-40: Results of the factor analysis for cost accounting objectives

Overall, the indicators 'operational planning' and 'strategic planning' are aggregated to the factor '*planning*', 'exploiting cost reduction potential' and 'strategy development' are aggregated to the factor '*decision facilitating*', 'carry out operational tasks efficiently', 'make cost savings', and 'act in accordance with the business strategy' are aggregated to the factor '*decision influencing*', and 'cost control' and 'tracing (in)efficiencies back to persons in charge' are aggregated to the factor '*cost control*'. All four factors meet each quality criterion (see Table 3-40).

1120 Indicator reliability is defined as the square of the correlation between a latent factor and that indicator. See section 3.1.3.2.4.

For decision facilitating (the only factor that consists of more than two variables) the **coefficients of congruence** between the subsamples all lie above 0.9 and thus indicate that this factor is highly equivalent between Germany and Japan (see Table 3-41).

Coefficient of congruence for decision influencing		
Data set	Data set 1	Data set 2
	0.9997	0.9979

Table 3-41: Coefficients of congruence for decision influencing

After having described the context factors in section 3.2 and the cost accounting objectives in section 3.3, the empirical results concerning the design of cost accounting systems are presented in section 3.4. The influence of the context factors and cost accounting objectives are examined in the following section.

3.4 Design of cost accounting systems

In this section the complexity (section 3.4.1) and the timeliness (section 3.4.2) of cost accounting systems are compared across countries, industries, and types of organizations. To better interpret the scope of cross-country differences, it is assessed in section 3.4.3 to which extent cost accounting systems are subject to convergence between Germany and Japan. A more comprehensive discussion and summary of the findings follows later in section 3.7.

3.4.1 Complexity

The complexity of cost accounting systems is defined by the processing effort of the systems' elements and by the number of elements taken into account. First, bivariate analyses are carried through in section 3.4.1.1. This includes the comparison of single systems' elements, correlations between the individual complexity scores, and the comparison of aggregated complexity scores of the cost accounting systems. Thereafter, multivariate analyses are carried though in section 3.4.1.2 to explain the complexity of cost accounting systems. The bi- and multivariate results are verified by the ABC complexity score as an alternative complexity measure in section 3.4.1.3.

3.4.1.1 Bivariate analysis

3.4.1.1.1 Single elements of the cost accounting system

3.4.1.1.1.1 Number of cost types

By question C.1 (item 1, Appendix 2) the respondents were asked to indicate their companies' numbers of cost types. Distinguishing many cost types drives processing effort and thereby complexity. A higher number of cost types, however, also leads to more accurate and detailed cost information, because less costs are averaged. The **score for cost types** is determined by taking the number of cost types to the natural logarithm for each company. Thereafter, this number is divided by the highest number of all companies from the respective data set.

German companies distinguish significantly more cost types than their Japanese counterparts. The results are stable for data set 1 and 2. Consequently, German companies have in both data sets on average a higher score for this element than their Japanese counterparts (see Table 3-42). 90% of the German and Japanese companies from data set 1 distinguish 694 or less respectively 100 or less cost types. The average number of cost types in Germany and Japan is 290 and 94 respectively.[1121] Strong differences also prevail across industries.[1122] Hospitals distinguish about three times more cost types (Ø = 765) than their counterparts of the food and beverage and the mechanical engineering industry (Ø = 294 respectively Ø = 227). Hospitals therefore score higher than the other two industries on this element. Companies of the mechanical engineering industry have statistically significantly the lowest number of cost types.

Average number of cost types – comparisons of means	Please indicate the number of cost types for your company.						
Type of comparison	**Country comparison**				**Industry comparison**		
Data set	**Data set 1**		**Data set 2**		**Data set 3**		
	Germany	Japan	Germany	Japan	Food and beverage	Mechanical engineering	Hospitals
Means	290.2 ***	94.4	227.2 ***	42.1	294.3 *	227.2	**765.3** **
Complexity score	0.566 ***	0.324	0.546 ***	0.328	0.539	0.546	**0.639** ***

Table 3-42: Number of cost types

The high number of cost types for Germany demonstrates the strong German emphasis on precision. As precision has already been identified as one particularity of German cost accounting,[1123] the very strong difference in the number of cost types between Germany and Japan is not unexpected..

3.4.1.1.1.2 Distinction between fixed and variable costs

Respondents were asked to indicate on a seven-point Likert scale to which extent fixed and variable costs are distinguished for each cost center (question C.6, item 1, Appendix 2). The more intensively companies distinguish fixed and variable costs, the higher the score for this element. Distinguishing between variable and fixed costs provides information that is relevant for planning and control purposes.

1121 In a recent survey on the 250 largest German companies in terms of sales turnover, the average number of cost types is 786 and three quarters of the companies use less than 1,080 cost types. Cf. *Friedl et al.* (2009a), p. 112; *Friedl et al.* (2009b), p. 43. Cf. also *Weber* (1993), p. 260.

1122 Cross-industry differences in the number of cost types have already been identified for German companies. Cf. *Friedl et al.* (2009a), p. 112; *Friedl et al.* (2009b), p. 43.

1123 See *MacArthur* (2006); *Krumwiede/Suessmair* (2007a), (2007b).

Distinction fixed and variable costs – comparisons of means	To what extent are fixed and variable costs distinguished for each cost center? (1=not at all; ... ; 7=completely)						
Type of comparison	Country comparison				Industry comparison		
Data set	Data set 1		Data set 2		Data set 3		
	Germany	Japan	Germany	Japan	Food and beverage	Mechanical engineering	Hospitals
Means	4.031	4.117	4.466	4.537	4.040 ***	**4.466** ***	3.067
Complexity score	0.513	0.517	0.578	0.589	0.507 ***	**0.578** ***	0.344

Table 3-43: Distinction between fixed and variable costs

No statistically significant differences regarding the distinction between fixed and variable costs prevail for both data sets between Germany (Ø = 4.031 and Ø = 4.466 respectively) and Japan (Ø = 4.117 and Ø = 4.537 respectively). 38% of all German companies and 47% of all Japanese companies of data set 1 have answered 5 or higher on a seven-point Likert scale (see Figure 3-23). Prior research that has compared German and US cost accounting has obtained similar results for Germany.[1124]

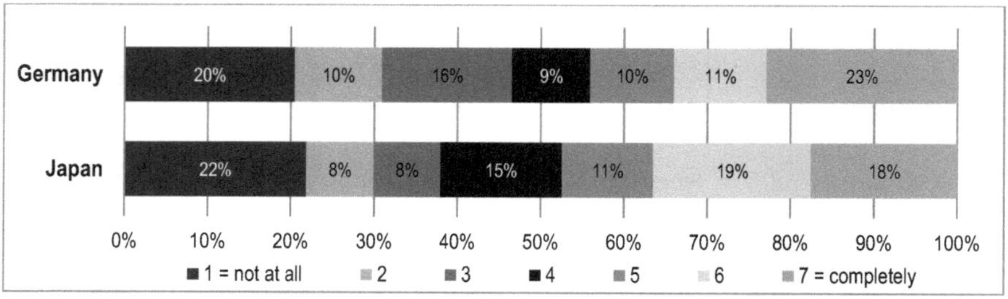

Figure 3-23: Distinction between fixed and variable costs (data set 1)

Across industries, on the contrary, fixed and variable costs are distinguished for each center to different extents (see Table 3-43). Fixed and variable costs are separated statistically significantly most intensively in the mechanical engineering industry (Ø = 4.466). Companies operating in the food and beverage industry (Ø = 4.040) distinguish significantly more intensively between fixed and variable costs than hospitals (Ø = 3.067).

The strong differences between the industries are explained by the low proportion of variable costs in hospitals.[1125] Hence, separating between fixed and variable costs is of less relevance for hospitals than for manufacturing companies.

1124 In the study by *Krumwiede/Suessmair* 40% of the German medium-sized manufacturing companies and 32% of the non-manufacturing companies have answered with 5 or higher on a seven-point Likert scale how intensively they distinguish fixed and variable costs for each resource cost center. 50% respectively 48% of the US companies have answered with 5 or higher on the same question. Cf. *Krumwiede/Suessmair* (2007a), p. 6. Cf. also *Krumwiede/Suessmair* (2007b), p. 53.

1125 Between 70 and 80% are labor costs and thereby overhead costs in hospitals. Cf. *Schlüchtermann* (1992), p. 434; *Rathje* (1993), p. 166; *Tscheulin/Helmig* (1994), p. 507.

3.4.1.1.1.3 Imputed costs

The existence of imputed depreciation and imputed interests were surveyed by question C.3 (Appendix 2). Imputed costs are statistically significantly more frequently applied in German than in Japanese companies. Whereas 72% respectively 66% of the German companies use imputed depreciation and imputed interests either in separate calculations or as part of regular cost accounting,[1126] only 46% respectively 19% of the Japanese companies apply both types of imputed costs (see Figure 3-24). Consequently, German companies score higher on this element than their Japanese counterparts. The cross-national results are stable for data set 1 (see Table 3-44). It is concluded in literature that many large German companies started to simplify management accounting by abandoning imputed costs due to the harmonization of management and financial accounting.[1127] The high application rate of imputed costs in Germany could be explained with the sample of this study. Medium-sized companies were selected from data set 1 that are less exposed to globalization. In this study only 15% of the German companies are capital market oriented, 25% apply IFRS for individual statements (see section 3.1.2.2), and 24.7% apply IFRS for consolidated statements. However, significant differences in applying imputed costs do not exist in Germany between capital market and non-capital market oriented companies as well as between IFRS adopters and non-adopters. It is hence concluded that the application of imputed costs remains in spite of global pressures a specific characteristic of German cost accounting.

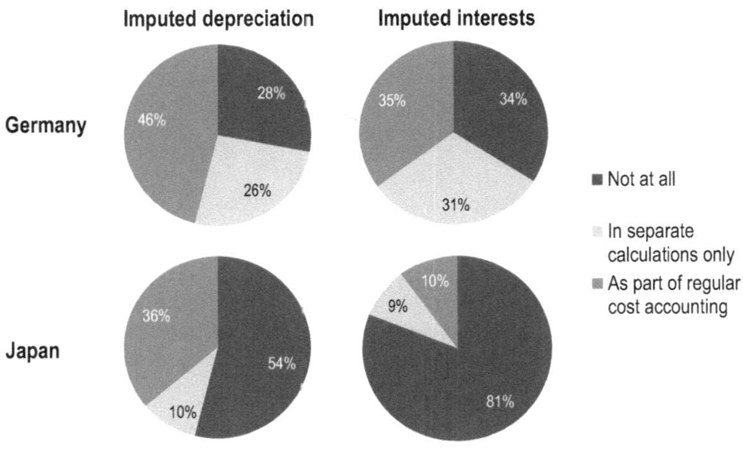

Figure 3-24: Distribution of imputed costs (data set 1)

1126 *Währisch* found out that 54.4% of the German companies apply the same depreciation rate for management and financial accounting and that 12.2% of the companies do not apply imputed interests at all. Cf. *Währisch* (1998), p. 101-111; *Währisch* (2000), p. 681-685.

1127 Cf. *Jones/Luther* (2005), p. 185; *Kajüter* (2008), p. 356. *Friedl et al.* show in their study a positive correlation between company size and efforts to converge financial and management accounting. Cf. *Friedl et al.* (2009b), p. 47.

When companies apply imputed depreciation and imputed interests in separate calculations only, ¼ points are awarded in each case to determine the complexity score for imputed costs. When both types of imputed costs are part of regular cost accounting, ½ point are awarded each. Imputed costs are beneficial to correspond to the different purposes that financial and management accounting pursue. These types of costs can provide more accurate and more relevant information for management accounting purposes.

Imputed costs	To what extent do you apply the following imputed costs?						
Type of comparison	**Country comparison**				**Industry comparison**		
Data set	**Data set 1**		**Data set 2**		**Data set 3**		
	Germany	Japan	Germany	Japan	Food and beverage	Mechanical engineering	Hospitals
Imputed depreciation							
Not at all	28%	54% ***	29%	58% ***	21%	29%	**40%** **
In separate calculations only	26% ***	10%	19% *	9%	25%	19%	38% **
As part of regular cost accounting	46% **	36%	52% ***	33%	54% ***	52% ***	21%
Imputed interests							
Not at all	34%	81% ***	32%	84% ***	34%	32%	**45%** *
In separate calculations only	31% ***	9%	29% ***	8%	26%	29%	38% *
As part of regular cost accounting	35% ***	10%	39% ***	8%	40% ***	39% ***	17%
Complexity score	0.550 ***	0.290	0.575 ***	0.266	0.598 ***	0.575 ***	0.383

Table 3-44: Imputed costs

Significant differences also prevail across industries. Hospitals apply imputed depreciation and imputed interests significantly less intensively than their counterparts from the remaining two industries. The application of imputed costs in both manufacturing industries is very similar.

3.4.1.1.1.4 Time reference of costs

Respondents were asked by question C.9 (Appendix 2) on a seven-point Likert scale for how many products (respectively medical treatments for the hospital industry) actual costs, normal costs, standard costs, and target costs are determined. The more of these costs are provided, the higher the complexity score. Cost information on different time references provides more information and it is a prerequisite for cost variance analysis that compares actual costs with expected costs.

Table 3-45 shows that German companies provide normal and standard costs (Ø = 4.090 respectively Ø = 4.978) statistically significantly for more products (respectively medical treatments for hospitals) than their Japanese counterparts (Ø = 3.430 respectively Ø = 4.397). These results are stable for both data sets. Although Japan is known for target costing, Japanese (Ø = 2.719) and German companies (Ø = 2.741) provide target costs with about the same frequency. The overall score for time reference of costs does not statistically significantly differ between Germany and Japan, because actual costs and target costs are provided with about the same frequency in both countries. Across industries strong differences prevail for actual costs and standard costs. Mechanical engineering companies provide both types of cost information more often than companies of the other two industries, and hospitals provide both types of information statistically significantly less often than its counterparts from both manufacturing industries. The frequency of normal and targets costs does not differ significantly across industries. The overall score for the time reference of costs is statistically significantly the highest for the mechanical engineering industry followed by the food and beverage industry.

Time reference of costs – comparisons of means	To what extent are costs for products respectively costs for medical treatments calculated on the following bases? (1=for non; ... ; 7= for all)						
Type of comparison	**Country comparison**				**Industry comparison**		
Data set	**Data set 1**		**Data set 2**		**Data set 3**		
	Germany	Japan	Germany	Japan	Food and beverage	Mechanical engineering	Hospitals
Actual costs	5.373	5.406	6.019	5.694	5.094 ***	**6.019** ***	4.222
Normal costs	4.090 ***	3.430	4.015 *	3.278	4.297	4.015	3.642
Standard costs	4.978 ***	4.397	5.641 **	4.689	5.253 ***	5.641 ***	2.557
Target costs	2.741	2.719	2.830	3.093	2.647	2.830	2.529
Complexity score	0.555	0.513	0.625	0.537	0.568 ***	**0.625** **	0.381

Table 3-45: Time reference of costs

The higher values for normal and standard costs in German companies can be explained by the stronger emphasis of German companies on cost variance analysis in comparison to their Japanese counterparts[1128] and the higher German emphasis on operating efficiency in combination with responsibility accounting. As identified before, German companies pursue the objective control more intensively than their Japanese counterparts.[1129] When actual and expected costs (normal, standard, or target costs) are compared, the cost variance analysis provides insights about the operating efficiency of the responsible persons. Furthermore, causes of inefficiencies and more insights how to increase operating efficiencies are provided.[1130]

Cross-industry differences are explained by the higher processing effort of hospitals to determine their medical treatment costs compared to product costs in manufacturing companies. Medical treatments are usually more specific than products of the food and beverage and the mechanical engineering industry. Therefore, the four types of cost information are provided for less medical treatments.

3.4.1.1.1.5 Number of cost centers

By question C.1 (item 2, Appendix 2) the number of cost centers was queried. A higher number of cost centers enables to more comprehensively capture the products' or services' variability in resource consumption. The score for cost centers is determined by taking the number of cost centers to the natural logarithm for each company. Thereafter, this number is divided by the highest number of all companies from the respective data set.

1128 Cf. section 3.4.1.1.1.6.

1129 Cf. section 3.3.

1130 Cf. section 2.3.2.1.

Statistically significantly more cost centers are installed in German compared to Japanese companies (see Table 3-46). This result is stable for both cross-national data sets. The scores for the number of cost centers likewise differ statistically significantly. 90% of the German and Japanese companies of data set 1 have 500 or less respectively 75 or less cost centers. The average number of cost centers in Germany and Japan is 217 respectively 35. Prior research that has compared German and US cost accounting has obtained similar results for Germany.[1131] Hence, a high number of cost centers is a specific of German companies. Statistically significant differences prevail across industries as well. These differences, however, are smaller than those between Germany and Japan. Hospitals have installed statistically significantly the most cost centers (Ø = 271) followed by the food and beverage industry (Ø = 267). The scores for this cost accounting element vary likewise.

Average number of cost centers – comparisons of means	Please indicate the number of cost centers for your company.						
Type of comparison	**Country comparison**				**Industry comparison**		
Data set	**Data set 1**		**Data set 2**		**Data set 3**		
	Germany	Japan	Germany	Japan	Food and beverage	Mechanical engineering	Hospitals
Means	216.9 ***	35.2	129.3 ***	28.3	266.8 ***	129.3	**270.7** ***
Complexity score	0.646 ***	0.294	0.593 ***	0.283	0.655 ***	0.593	**0.704** ***

Table 3-46: Number of cost centers

The higher number of cost centers in Germany is explained by the stronger German emphasis on cost control to improve operating efficiency and to enhance responsibility accounting.[1132] The higher emphasis on cost control and responsibility accounting in Germany compared to Japan is supported by the findings in section 3.3. The strongest difference in rank between Germany and Japan was, e.g., the variable 'tracing (in)efficiencies back to persons in charge'. This finding was supported by the relative importance of cost control compared to planning.

3.4.1.1.1.6 Cost variance analysis

Respondents were asked to assess on a seven-point Likert scale the extent to which cost variance analysis is carried through (question C.6, item 2, Appendix 2). The score for this element is determined by the degree of intensity with which companies conduct cost variance analysis. Cost variance analysis is an instrument to conduct cost control for responsibility accounting and to identify causes of variances.

1131 *Krumwiede/Suessmair* report an average number of resource cost centers of 176 respectively 207 for manufacturing and non-manufacturing medium-sized firms. The US figures are 17 and 44 respectively. Cf. *Krumwiede/Suessmair* (2007a), p. 6. Cf. also *Krumwiede/Suessmair* (2007b), p. 53. In the study by *Friedl et al.* on the 250 largest German companies, 90% of the companies have installed 3,000 cost centers or less and the arithmetic mean is 4,062. Cf. *Friedl et al.* (2009a), p. 112; *Friedl et al.* (2009b), p. 43f.

1132 Cf. section 2.3.2.1.

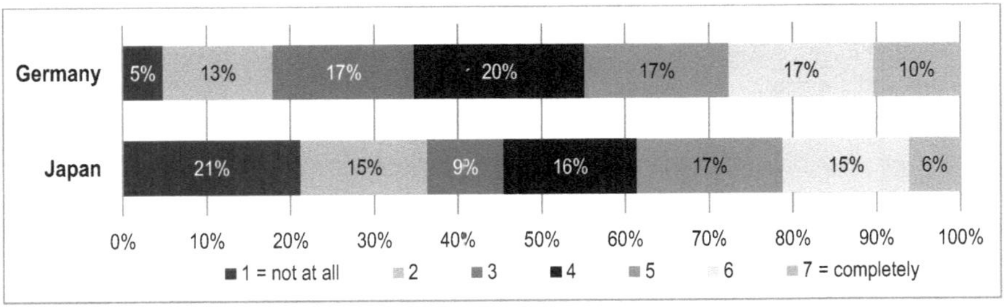

Figure 3-25: Cost variance analysis (data set 1)

German companies analyze cost variances statistically significantly more intensively in-depth for each cost center (Ø = 4.244) than their Japanese counterparts (Ø = 3.629). 45% of all German companies and 39% of all Japanese companies have answered 5 or higher on a seven-point Likert scale (see Figure 3-25).[1133] Similar cross-national results prevail for the mechanical engineering industry (data set 2). In both data sets German companies statistically significantly score higher on this element. Strong differences prevail also across industries. Companies from both manufacturing industries more intensively analyze cost variances than hospitals (see Table 3-47).

Cost variance analysis – comparisons of means	To what extent are cost variances analyzed in-depth for each cost center? (1=not at all; ... ; 7=completely)					
Type of comparison	**Country comparison**				**Industry comparison**		
Data set	**Data set 1**		**Data set 2**		**Data set 3**		
	Germany	Japan	Germany	Japan	Food and beverage	Mechanical engineering	Hospitals
Means	4.244 ***	3.629	4.422 *	3.983	4.360 ***	4.422 ***	3.687
Complexity score	0.548 ***	0.441	0.570 *	0.503	0.560 ***	0.570 ***	0.448

Table 3-47: Cost variance analysis

The higher intensity of cost variance analysis in Germany can be explained by the higher German emphasis on operating efficiency in combination with cost control and responsibility accounting. The higher emphasis on cost control and responsibility accounting in Germany compared to Japan is supported by the findings in section 3.3.[1134] The low intensity of cost variance analysis in hospitals is explained by the low acceptance of cost information and cost control by clinicians.[1135] UK clinicians, e.g., are characterized to regard

1133 83% respectively 71% of the German respondents from manufacturing and non-manufacturing medium-sized firms have answered 5 or higher on the seven-point Likert scale that variances are reported by resource cost centers. 53% respectively 64% of the US respondents have answered with 5 or higher on this question. Cf. *Krumwiede/Suessmair* (2007a), p. 6. Cf. also *Krumwiede/Suessmair* (2007b), p. 53.

1134 The variable 'tracing (in)efficiencies back to persons in charge', e.g., is the strongest difference in rank between Germany and Japan.

1135 See, e.g., *Lapsley et al.* (2001); *Kurunmäki et al.* (2003); *Kurunmäki* (2004); *Scarparo* (2006).

accounting information as an instrument to constrain their clinical activity.[1136] Similar structural changes, reorganizations, and market-led reform strategies have occurred in the German and Japanese hospital sector.[1137] Clinicians in Germany and Japan might therefore have also a low acceptance of cost information and cost control.

3.4.1.1.1.7 First stage allocation

The extent of first stage allocation was queried on a seven-point Likert scale (question C.6, item 3, Appendix 2). The more intensively companies transfer costs from support cost centers to primary cost centers, the higher the score. This element serves the purposes of full cost allocation, managerial motivation, and decision making.

First stage allocation – comparisons of means	To what extent are all service flows considered for while transferring costs from support cost centers to primary cost centers? (1=not at all; ... ; 7=completely)									
Type of comparison	**Country comparison**						**Industry comparison**			
Data set	**Data set 1**			**Data set 2**			**Data set 3**			
	Germany		Japan	Germany		Japan	Food and beverage	Mechanical engineering		Hospitals
Means	4.619	***	3.469	4.850	***	3.509	4.333	**4.850**	**	4.250
Complexity score	0.600	***	0.412	0.642	***	0.418	0.556	**0.642**	**	0.542

Table 3-48: First stage allocation

Table 3-48 shows that German companies more intensively transfer costs from support cost centers to primary cost centers (Ø = 4.619) than their Japanese counterparts (Ø = 3.469). 54% of all German companies and 30% of all Japanese companies have answered 5 or higher on a seven-point Likert scale for data set 1 (see Figure 3-26).[1138] This cross-national difference is consistent for both data sets. Consequently, the scores for this element also differ statistically significantly between both countries for both data sets. Smaller, but also statistically significant differences for this cost accounting element prevail across industries. Mechanical engineering companies (Ø = 4.850) more intensively transfer costs from support cost centers to primary cost centers and consequently have the highest score for this element compared to the companies from the other two industries.

It is likely that first stage allocation is more intensively applied in Germany than in Japan due to the strong German emphasis on operating efficiency and responsibility accounting.[1139] First stage allocation enables cost control in support cost centers for improving operating efficiency and to ensure responsibility accounting.[1140] Moreover, German com-

1136 Cf. *Scarparo* (2006), p. 152.

1137 See *McKee/Healy* (2002); *Preker/Harding* (2003). See also section 3.1.1.

1138 On a similar question 47% respectively 29% of German manufacturing and non-manufacturing firms have answered with 5 or higher on a seven-point Likert scale that they transfer costs from support cost centers to primary cost centers while maintaining the distinction between fixed and variable costs. 43% respectively 37% of the US respondents have answered this question with 5 or higher. Cf. *Krumwiede/Suessmair* (2007a), p. 6. Cf. also *Krumwiede/Suessmair* (2007b), p. 53.

1139 Cf. section 2.3.2.1. This is also supported by the findings in section 3.3.

1140 Cf. section 2.3.2.1.

panies score higher on this element although Japanese cost accountants assess that their product lines respectively medical treatments utilize more heterogeneously the resources of support cost centers than their German counterparts.[1141] Hence, the need to transfer costs from support cost centers to primary cost centers from a resource consumption point of view is lower for German than for Japanese companies. The low complexity score for hospitals is explained by the short traditions in cost accounting in this industry. As pressures to save costs emerged only few years ago, many hospitals have started only recently to implement to transfer costs from support cost centers to primary cost centers.[1142]

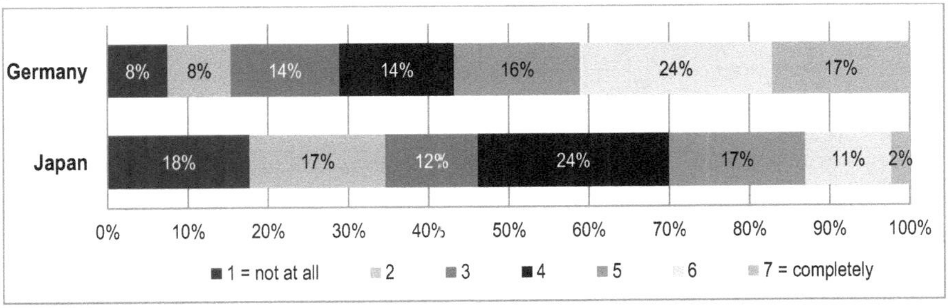

Figure 3-26: First stage allocation (data set 1)

3.4.1.1.1.8 Characteristics of second stage allocation bases

By question C.7 (Appendix 2) the bases to allocate costs from primary cost centers to cost objects were queried. Respondents had to choose between volume bases, hour rate bases, transaction drivers, and duration drivers. The sequence of the second stage allocation bases reflects an increase in processing effort and in accuracy of allocating overhead costs. The score for this element is therefore determined by the most comprehensive allocation base applied.

German companies use volume bases (Ø = 77%) and hour rate bases (Ø = 87%) statistically significantly more often to allocate overhead costs to products (respectively medical treatments for hospitals) than their Japanese counterparts (Ø = 68% respectively Ø = 76%). These results are stable for data set 2, except that Japanese mechanical engineering companies apply duration drivers significantly more often than their German counterparts. The scores do not statistically significantly vary between both countries for both data sets. The results show that for both countries traditional overhead allocation bases are more common than activity cost driver rates. Stronger differences prevail across industries. The industry comparison shows that in manufacturing industries traditional overhead allocation bases are far more common than activity cost driver rates. For hospitals, however, activity cost driver rates are more frequently applied than traditional overhead allocation bases (see Table 3-49). As the most comprehensive allocation base determines the complexity score for this element, hospitals yield statistically significantly the highest score. Whereas the two least accurate allocation bases are significantly more common in

1141 Cf. section 3.2.3.2.

1142 For an example see, e.g., *Bunzemeier et al.* (2010).

the mechanical engineering industry, the transaction and duration drivers are significantly more frequently applied in the food and beverage industry. However, no significant difference for the complexity score prevails between both manufacturing industries.

Second stage allocation	On which bases are overhead costs allocated to products/medical treatments?						
Type of comparison	**Country comparison**				**Industry comparison**		
Data set	**Data set 1**		**Data set 2**		**Data set 3**		
	Germany	Japan	Germany	Japan	Food and beverage	Mechanical engineering	Hospitals
On a volume basis	77% **	68%	**95%** ***	59%	68% ***	**95%** ***	47%
On an hour rate basis	87% ***	76%	**95%** ***	79%	82% **	**95%** ***	69%
On the number of times an activity is performed	29%	25%	11%	8%	31% ***	11%	**60%** ***
On the amount of time taken to perform an activity	33%	30%	16%	26% *	27% **	16%	**74%** ***
Complexity score	0.610	0.600	0.564	0.558	0.588	0.564	**0.781** ***

Table 3-49: Characteristics of second stage allocation bases

The high application rates of volume and hour rate bases in Germany and the low application rates of activity cost drivers can be explained by cost accounting traditions. During National Socialism, German companies were forced to apply different allocation bases – a blanket allocation of overhead costs was not accepted.[1143] After the Second World War sophisticated cost accounting systems like GPK were implemented by many German companies. The need to install ABC and thereby apply activity cost drivers was limited. The low application rates of activity cost drivers in Japan can be explained by the Japanese cost accounting standard that does not include ABC and may thus constitute a barrier for the diffusion of activity cost drivers.[1144]

In hospitals many overhead costs cannot be allocated on a volume or hour rate basis, but it requires the allocation by the number of times an activity is performed or by the time to perform an activity, because most medical treatments are inpatient-specific.

3.4.1.1.1.9 Product costing

By question C.8 (Appendix 2) the respondents were asked whether they determine their product costs either only on a variable cost basis, only on a full cost basis, or on both bases. Cost accounting systems provide more information when product costs are determined on both bases, because then the lower price limit for short-term and long-term decisions is provided. The complexity score is consequently higher when product costs are provided on both bases.

1143 Cf. section 2.1.1.2.1.

1144 Cf. *Winter* (2005), p. 29, quoting *Yoshikawa* (2000), p. 37.

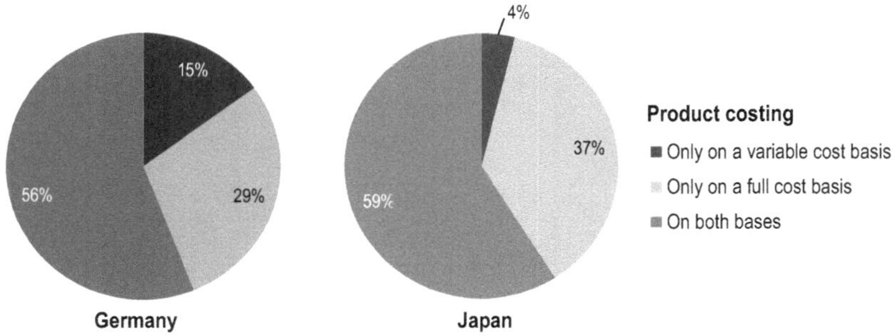

Figure 3-27: Product costing (data set 1)

For product costing stronger differences prevail across industries than between countries. Companies in both countries obtain about the same score. 56% of the German companies and 59% of the Japanese companies determine their product or service costs on both bases (see Figure 3-27). The only significant cross-national difference is that more German companies in both data sets (15% respectively 10%) determine product costs only on a variable cost basis than their Japanese counterparts (5% respectively 2%). Prior research has obtained similar results for German companies.[1145] This difference can be explained by the German traditions of marginal costing and that German GAAP used to allow determining product costs on a variable cost basis.[1146] The German food and beverage industry determines statistically significantly more frequently product costs only on a variable cost basis. This can be explained by a higher proportion of variable costs in this industry and the stronger competition that requires determining the price limit for short-term decisions. Contrariwise, companies of the food and beverage industry determine product costs only on a full cost basis significantly less frequently than their counterparts from the remaining two industries. Finally, food and beverage companies determine most frequently product costs on both bases, followed by the mechanical engineering industry. The food and beverage industry consequently scores the highest on this element followed by the mechanical engineering industry (see Table 3-50).

1145 According to a prior study, only 11% of the largest 250 German companies determine product costs only on a variable cost basis, 22% determine product costs only on a full cost basis, and 36% determine product costs on both bases. Cf. *Friedl et al.* (2009a), p. 113; *Friedl et al.* (2009b), p. 45. The proportion of variable cost bases has probably diminished the last years. About two decades ago 90% of the largest 100 German companies have calculated their product costs on a variable basis and 84% on a full cost basis. Cf. *Weber* (1993), p. 261. The study by *Währisch* shows that more than 90% of the companies determine product costs on a full cost basis and about 60% on a variable cost basis. Cf. *Währisch* (1998), p. 91.

1146 The German Commercial Code was revised in 2009. Since then product costs have to be determined on a full cost basis. See § 255 Abs. 2 HGB.

Product costing	How are product costs/costs for medical treatments determined as part of regular cost accounting?						
Type of comparison	**Country comparison**				**Industry comparison**		
Data set	**Data set 1**		**Data set 2**		**Data set 3**		
	Germany	Japan	Germany	Japan	Food and beverage	Mechanical engineering	Hospitals
Only on a variable cost basis	15% ***	5%	10% *	2%	20% **	10%	15%
Only on a full cost basis	30%	37%	34%	37%	17%	34% **	42% ***
On both bases	56%	59%	56%	61%	**63% ****	56% **	43%
Complexity score	0.778	0.791	0.780	0.800	**0.813 *****	0.780 **	0.717

Table 3-50: Product costing

The lower score for hospitals is explained by the difficulty to allocate overhead costs to medical treatments due to their specificity. Furthermore, knowing lower price limits for short-term decisions is seldom necessary because prices for hospital services are usually determined by government.[1147] Overall, hospitals put on average less emphasis on calculating medical treatment costs compared to manufacturing companies calculating product costs.

3.4.1.1.1.10 Operating income statement

The existence of an operating income statement was surveyed by question C.4 (Appendix 2). When respondents run this statement besides their profit and loss statement, they were further asked on a seven-point Likert scale to which extent both statements differ structurally from each other. No points are awarded to determine the complexity score when no operating income statement is applied. The stronger the difference between operating income statement and the profit and loss statement is, the higher the score. Operating income statements provide managers with information about their operating performance.

German companies of data set 1 run statistically significantly more often an operating income statement besides their profit and loss statements than their Japanese counterparts. Whereas 77% of the German companies apply operating income statements,[1148] only 46% of the Japanese companies have installed it. Furthermore, operating income statements differ statistically significantly more strongly from profit and loss statements in Germany (Ø = 3.950) than in Japan (Ø = 3.281) (see Figure 3-28). Consequently, German companies score higher on this element. The results are stable for data set 2. For the industry comparison no significant difference exists (see Table 3-51). Hence, the existence and the conceptual design of operating income statements are mainly country-specific.

1147 Cf. *Brösel et al.* (2004), p. 50.

1148 According to *Friedl et al.*, 84% of the 250 largest German companies apply this instrument. Cf. *Friedl et al.* (2009a), p. 113.

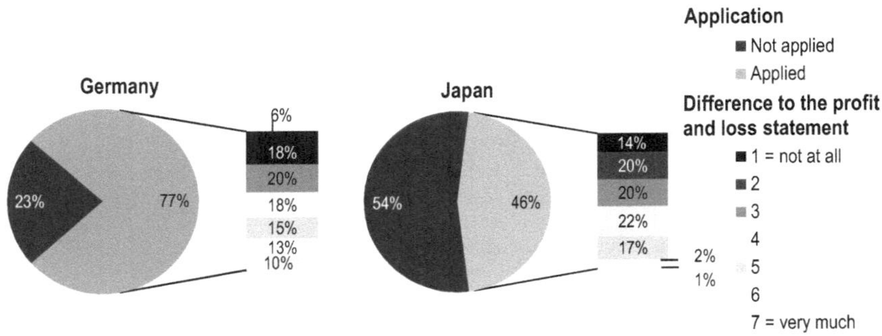

Figure 3-28: Operating income statement (data set 1)

Germany has a long tradition of separating financial and management accounting. It is argued in German literature that financial accounting is improper for decision making.[1149] For both reasons more German than Japanese companies run operating income statements to avoid distortions stemming from tax regulations or financial accounting standards.

Operating income statement							
Type of comparison	**Country comparison**				**Industry comparison**		
Data set	**Data set 1**		**Data set 2**		**Data set 3**		
	Germany	Japan	Germany	Japan	Food and beverage	Mechanical engineering	Hospitals
Existence	77% ***	46%	75% ***	49%	78%	75%	73%
Difference to P/L statement (1=not at all; … ; 7=very much)	3.950 ***	3.281	3.967 ***	3.031	3.838	3.967	3.630
Complexity score	0.372 ***	0.169	0.374 ***	0.155	0.367	0.374	0.320

Table 3-51: Operating income statement

3.4.1.1.1.11 Contribution margin accounting

The application of contribution margin accounting was surveyed by question C.5 (Appendix 2). When respondents apply this instrument, the number of contribution margins was requested. ½ complexity point is awarded when this instrument is applied and another ½ point is allocated according to the number of contribution margins. With this instrument the roots for success can be determined.

1149 Cf. section 2.1.1.2.1.

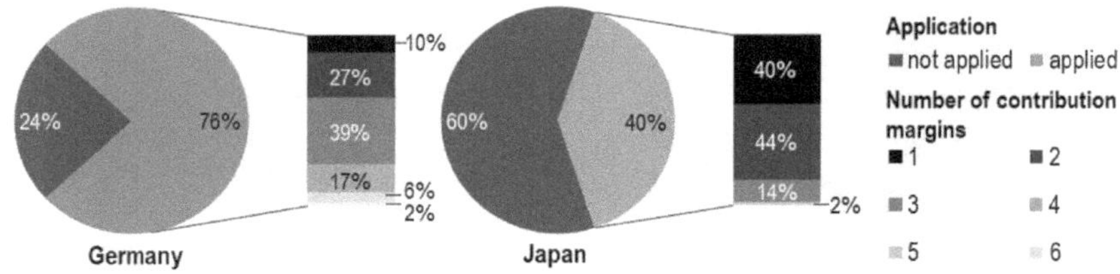

Figure 3-29: Contribution margin accounting (data set 1)

Figure 3-29 shows that more German than Japanese companies (76% and 40% respectively) apply contribution margin accounting. Prior research has obtained similar results for Germany.[1150] Furthermore, significantly more contribution margins are distinguished in German (Ø = 2.808) than in Japanese companies (Ø = 1.788) (see Table 3-52). Consequently, German companies score higher on this element than their Japanese counterparts. The results are stable for data set 2. The score for the food and beverage industry is the highest on this element, followed by the mechanical engineering industry. Both manufacturing industries use contribution margin accounting statistically significantly more often than hospitals, and food and beverage companies distinguish significantly more contribution margins than companies of the other two industries. For this element stronger differences prevail between countries than across industries (see Table 3-52).

Contribution margin accounting										
Type of comparison	**Country comparison**						**Industry comparison**			
Data set	**Data set 1**			**Data set 2**			**Data set 3**			
	Germany		Japan	Germany		Japan	Food and beverage		Mechanical engineering		Hospitals
Existence	76%	***	40%	79%	***	48%	84%	***	79%	***	49%
Average number of contribution margins	2.899	***	1.788	2.730	***	1.724	**3.210**	***	2.730		2.667
Complexity score	0.635	***	0.213	0.638	***	0.072	**0.680**	**	0.638	***	0.579

Table 3-52: Contribution margin accounting

Contribution margin accounting is more often applied in Germany than in Japan, because it is a traditional German instrument and it is intensively discussed in German textbooks. Following *Shields*[1151] it is assumed that textbooks significantly influence the spread of cost accounting instruments. Hospitals face more challenges than manufacturing companies to allocate overhead costs to cost objects, because medical treatments are more unique than products. Medical treatments are usually less standardized than products,

1150 *Krumwiede/Suessmair* report that 79% of manufacturing companies and 60% of non-manufacturing companies apply this instrument in Germany. Cf. *Krumwiede/Suessmair* (2007a), p. 6. Cf. also *Krumwiede/Suessmair* (2007b), p. 53. Furthermore, 69% of the 250 largest German companies apply contribution margin accounting. Cf. *Friedl et al.* (2009a), p. 113; *Friedl et al.* (2009b), p. 45.

1151 Cf. *Shields* (1998), p. 504.

because the inpatients are participating in service provision and thus demand a more individual execution. Consequently, fewer hospitals calculate medical treatment costs (see also section 3.4.1.1.1.9) and they can thus less frequently install contribution margin accounting to determine the financial contributions of medical treatments. Another reason for the lower adoption rates of contribution margin accounting in the hospital industry is that this instrument requires distinguishing between fixed and variable costs. The results from section 3.4.1.1.1.2, however, show that fixed and variables costs are less intensively distinguished in hospitals compared to the companies operating in the manufacturing sector.

3.4.1.1.2 Correlations between single complexity scores

In section 2.3.3 the most relevant elements of the cost accounting system were selected to measure the complexity and timeliness of cost accounting systems. During the selection process it was considered to select elements with a different and independent effect upon the provision of cost information and that the elements do not record the same characteristics in a different way.[1152] The complexity scores for single elements are – apart from few exceptions – only **weakly correlated with each other** and thus support the conceptual considerations from section 2.3.3 (see Table 3-53). The elements have a different and largely independent effect upon cost accounting systems' complexity. Although some elements are highly correlated, they still address different characteristics of the cost accounting system and thus do not record the same or similar characteristics in a different way for data set 1. Strong correlations and negative correlations are reproduced in the following.

For German companies of data set 1 cost types strongly correlate with cost centers (r = 0.533***), distinction between fixed and variable costs with first stage allocation (r = 0.377***), and cost variance analysis with first stage allocation (r = 0.348***). Furthermore, 23 elements correlate statistically significantly with each other with a coefficient below r = 0.3. Two correlations between elements even correlate negatively (cost centers with distinction between fixed and variable costs (r = -0.139**) and cost centers with time reference of costs (r = -0.232***)). The reason for both negative correlations might be that installing a large number of cost centers leads to more homogeneous activities within a cost center.[1153] This might simplify distinguishing between variable and fixed costs and enhancing cost control. For the Japanese sample 16 elements correlate positively with each other including five correlations that have a coefficient above r = 0.3: separation between fixed and variable costs with cost variance analysis (r = 0.472***) and with first stage allocation (r = 0.643***); cost variance analysis with first stage allocation (r = 0.606***) and with time reference of costs (r = 0.321***); first stage allocation with time reference of costs (r = 0.343***). Negative correlations between single complexity scores that are statistically significant do not exist for Japan.

1152 Cf. section 2.3.2, p. 148.

1153 Cf. *Drury* (2005), p. 118; *Friedl et al.* (2009b), p. 44.

	Distinction fixed and variable costs	Imputed costs	Time reference of costs	Number of cost centers	Cost variance analysis	First stage allocation	Second stage allocation	Product costing	Operating income statement	Contribution margin accounting	Aggregated complexity score
Germany											
Number of cost types	-0.047	-0.075	-0.098	0.533 ***	0.035	0.067	0.127 **	-0.012	0.058	0.022	0.079
Distinction fixed and variable costs		0.187 ***	0.251 ***	-0.139 **	0.234 ***	0.377 ***	-0.010	0.257 ***	0.089	0.213 ***	0.392 ***
Imputed costs			0.132 **	-0.058	0.104 *	0.165 ***	-0.024	0.057	0.141 **	0.189 ***	0.370 ***
Time reference of costs				-0.232 ***	0.177 ***	0.282 ***	0.102 *	0.164 ***	0.129 **	0.159 ***	0.458 ***
Number of cost centers					-0.053	-0.021	0.171 ***	-0.033	0.117 *	0.060	0.043
Cost variance analysis						0.348 ***	0.139 **	0.001	-0.057	0.136 **	0.260 ***
First stage allocation							0.149 **	0.027	0.099	0.116 *	0.373 ***
Second stage allocation								-0.024	-0.012	0.098	0.273 ***
Product costing									0.057	0.253 ***	0.186 ***
Operating income statement										0.167 ***	0.258 ***
Contribution margin accounting											0.262 ***
Japan											
Number of cost types	0.056	-0.090	-0.054	0.283 ***	0.169 *	0.069	-0.091	-0.091	0.111	-0.071	0.177 *
Distinction fixed and variable costs		0.146 *	0.239 ***	0.044	0.472 ***	0.643 ***	0.133	0.262	0.050	-0.173	0.678 ***
Imputed costs			-0.011	-0.142	0.071	0.198 **	0.248 ***	0.003	-0.090	0.109	0.412 ***
Time reference of costs				-0.113	0.321 ***	0.343 ***	0.076	0.176	0.143	-0.021	0.466 ***
Number of cost centers					-0.031	-0.048	0.047	0.141	0.222 **	-0.039	0.213 **
Cost cariance analysis						0.606 ***	0.141	0.026	0.093	0.028	0.655 ***
First stage allocation							0.278 ***	0.160	-0.016	0.056	0.752 ***
Second stage allocation								0.082	0.009	0.130	0.484 ***
Product costing									0.185 **	0.082	0.414 ***
Operating income statement										0.174	0.279 ***
Contribution margin accounting											0.173

Table 3-53: Spearman correlations of single complexity scores (data set 1)

Another criterion for selecting the elements of the cost accounting system was that they should positively affect the complexity and timeliness of cost accounting systems.[1154] As most of the single complexity scores are statistically significantly and **positively correlated with the aggregated complexity score** (see Table 3-53), the conceptual considerations from section 2.3.3 are supported. Only the single complexity scores for 'number of cost types' and 'number of cost centers' are not statistically significantly correlated with the aggregated complexity score for Germany. According to these results, both indicators are less appropriate to determine the complexity of cost accounting systems for German companies. The single complexity scores for both elements are furthermore correlated only with few other single complexity scores. Hence, a high number of cost types and cost centers is harly related to a high processing effort of other elements. For the Japanese responses from data set 1 only the single complexity score for 'contribution margin accounting' is not statistically significantly correlated with single complexity scores and the aggregated complexity score. These results indicate that contribution margin accounting is less adequate to determine the complexity of cost accounting systems for Japanese companies.

If the single complexity scores were strongly correlated with each other and with the aggregated complexity score, the single elements would be exchangeable to a large extent. The results, however, show that it is necessary to measure the complexity of cost accounting systems by a plurality of elements. As this study has measured the complexity of cost accounting systems is a more comprehensive way than prior research,[1155] **more meaningful results** are expected. The correlations of this study indicate that the number of cost centers is a less adequate indicator for determining the complexity of German cost accounting systems. *Brierley* indicates similar results for the UK.[1156] The studies by *Drury/Tales*[1157] and *Schoute*[1158] have determined the complexity of cost accounting systems for UK respectively Dutch companies mainly by the number of cost centers. Hence, the findings of prior research that explains the complexity of cost accounting systems might be limited.

3.4.1.1.3 Aggregated complexity scores

The aggregated score for the complexity of cost accounting systems is determined by the arithmetic mean of the single complexity scores. In eight out of eleven single elements and for the aggregated score, German companies have installed more complex cost accounting systems than their Japanese counterparts. These results remain constant for data set 2 except for cost variance analysis. Cross-national differences in cost accounting for both data sets are presented in Table 3-54, Figure 3-30, and Figure 3-31. Both figures show that the cross-national differences for both data sets are very similar. Only the cross-national difference for contribution margin accounting is larger for data set 2 compared to data set 1 and no significant difference prevails for cost variance analysis for data set 2.

1154 Cf. section 2.3.2, p. 150.
1155 See section 2.3.1.2.
1156 Cf. *Brierley* (2008).
1157 See *Drury/Tales* (2005, 2006).
1158 See *Schoute* (2009).

Complexity scores – comparisons of means							
Type of comparison	Country comparison				Industry comparison		
Data set	Data set 1		Data set 2		Data set 3		
	Germany	Japan	Germany	Japan	Food and beverage	Mechanical engineering	Hospitals
Number of cost types	0.566 ***	0.324	0.546 ***	0.328	0.539	0.546	**0.639** ***
Distinction fixed and variable costs	0.513	0.517	0.578	0.589	0.507 ***	0.578 ***	0.344
Imputed costs	0.551 ***	0.288	0.575 ***	0.266	0.598 ***	0.575 ***	0.383
Time reference of costs	0.555 *	0.513	0.625 ***	0.537	0.568 ***	**0.625** **	0.381
Number of cost centers	0.646 ***	0.294	0.593 ***	0.283	0.655 ***	0.593	**0.704** ***
Cost variance analysis	0.548 ***	0.441	0.570	0.503	0.560 ***	0.570 ***	0.448
First stage allocation	0.600 ***	0.412	0.642 ***	0.418	0.556	**0.642** **	0.542
Second stage allocation	0.610	0.600	0.564	0.558	0.588	0.564	**0.781** ***
Product costing	0.778	0.791	0.780	0.800	0.813 ***	0.780 **	0.717
Operating income statement	0.372 ***	0.169	0.374 ***	0.164	0.367	0.374	0.320
Contribution margin accounting	0.644 ***	0.213	0.638 ***	0.072	**0.680** ***	0.638 ***	0.579
Aggregated complexity score	0.576 ***	0.427	0.587 ***	0.427	0.586 ***	0.587 ***	0.517

Table 3-54: Single and aggregated complexity scores

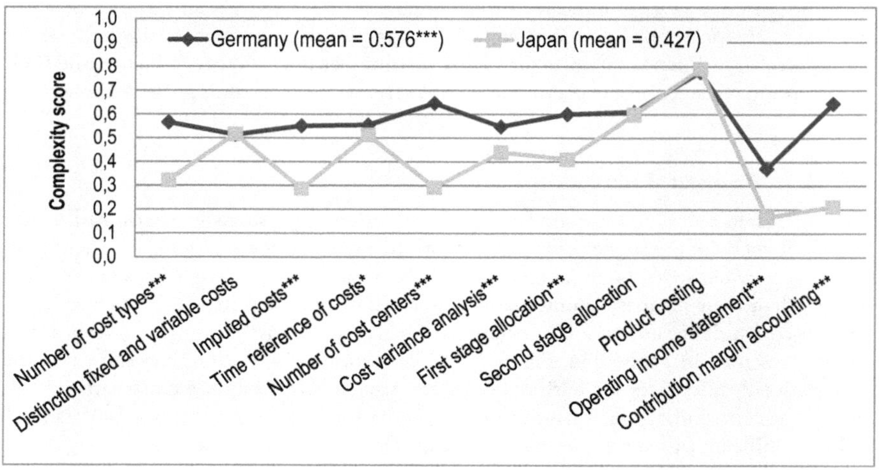

Figure 3-30: Cross-national comparison of single and aggregated complexity scores (data set 1)

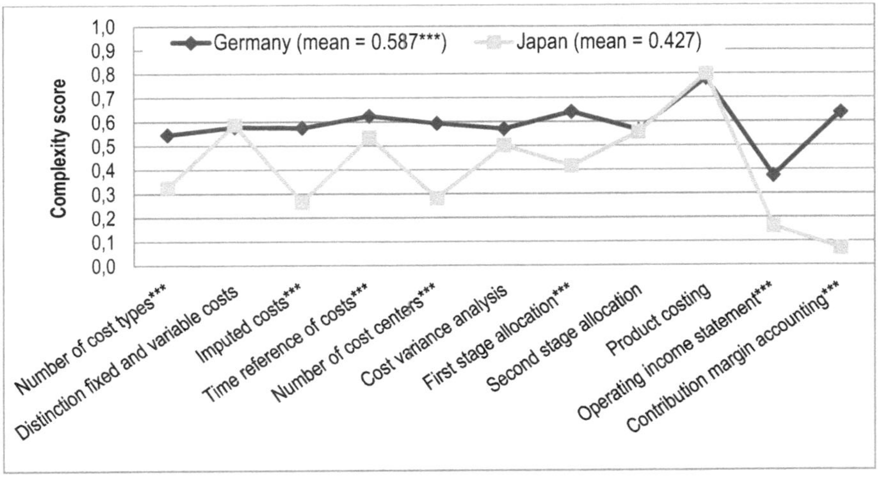

Figure 3-31: Cross-national comparison of single and aggregated complexity scores (data set 2)

In Table 3-55 country comparisons are also carried through on an industry basis for data set 1. The results show that **across all three industries German companies have installed more complex cost accounting systems** than their Japanese counterparts.[1159] The Japanese sample sizes for the food and beverage and the hospital industry are below 50 and should thus carefully be interpreted. The Levene and the Shapiro-Wilk test, however, show that the sample is normally distributed and homoscedasticity prevails for all three industries. The assumptions of the t-test are therefore fulfilled.

	Food and beverage	Mechanical engineering	Hospitals
Germany	0.586 ***	0.595 ***	0.517 ***
Japan	0.434	0.427	0.413

Table 3-55: Country comparison for systems' complexity on an industry basis (data set 1)

Hypotheses tests

Overall, German companies run more complex cost accounting systems than their Japanese counterparts. Hence, **hypothesis H_{1II}** stating that cost accounting systems are more complex in Germany than in Japan is accepted. This result is reasonable, because German companies have a higher potential to install complex cost accounting systems than their Japanese counterparts (see section 3.2.1.4).

Significant cross-industry differences for single element scores and for the aggregated score exist as well, but these differences are not as strong and unilateral than between Germany and Japan (see Figure 3-32). Food and beverage companies have two times a lower com-

1159 The values for the mechanical engineering industry from Table 3-55 slightly differ from Table 3-54, because data set 2 includes unlike data set 1 all German mechanical engineering industries. The implications for both data sets, however, are identical.

plexity score and two times a higher complexity score on single elements compared to their counterparts of the mechanical engineering industry. Overall, both industries have about the same aggregated complexity score. Hospitals have three times a higher complexity score for single elements than their counterparts from the other two industries. Food and beverage and mechanical engineering companies on the contrary have six respectively seven times a higher score for single elements than hospitals. Overall, both manufacturing industries have a statistically significantly higher aggregated score for the complexity of cost accounting systems than hospitals. This finding is reasonable, because modern cost accounting was initially introduced and developed in manufacturing organizations. Only since the introduction of DRG the necessity to operate efficiently and thereby to comprehensively apply cost accounting in hospitals increased. Furthermore, calculating medical treatment costs is usually more complicated than calculating product costs in manufacturing industries. Due to this higher processing effort, medical treatment costs are less frequently calculated and less emphasis is put on contribution margin accounting and on time reference of costs in hospitals than product costs in manufacturing companies. Overall, **hypothesis H_{3i}** stating that the complexity of cost accounting systems differs across industries is accepted and H_{6b} stating that the complexity of cost accounting systems differs more strongly across industries than across countries is rejected.

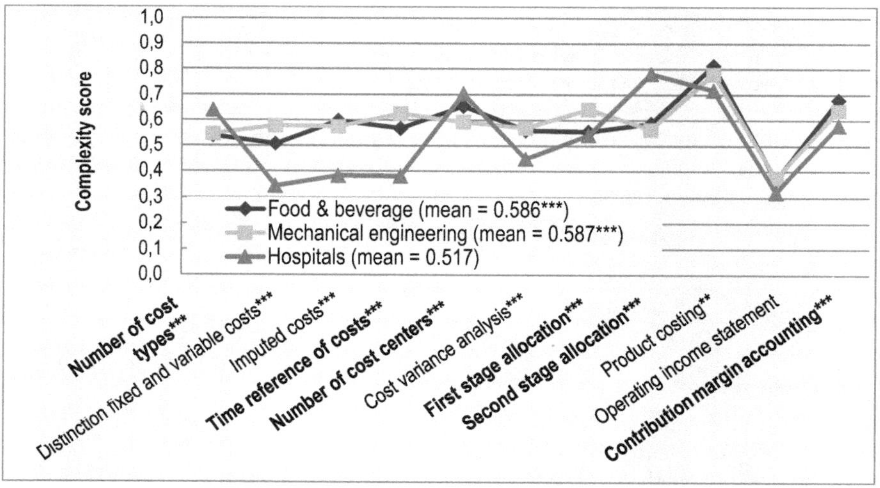

Figure 3-32: Cross-industry comparison for single and aggregated complexity scores (data set 3)

Smaller differences in the complexity scores prevail across private, public, and charitable hospitals than between Germany and Japan and across industries (see Figure 3-33). The following results, however, have to be critically examined. Data set 3 consists of only 37 private, 54 public, and 125 charitable hospitals from Germany and the assumption that the sample is normally distributed does not prevail for private hospitals.[1160] The strongest

1160 Public and charitable hospitals are normally distributed and homoscedasticity prevails for all three types of organizations.

statistically significant differences prevail for operating income statement, cost variance analysis, and first stage allocation. Private hospitals, surprisingly, obtain the lowest score and public hospitals the highest. This study supports the findings by *Wendel* and *Lachmann* that private companies run less complex cost accounting systems.[1161] These results of the hospital industry do not support the general assumption that private hospitals employ more comprehensive cost accounting systems.[1162] This surprising result is explained by the specific characteristics of private hospitals. Private hospitals are characterized in literature to be smaller and more specialized in Germany compared to public and charitable hospitals.[1163] Due to a lower potential of cost distortion, the need to install complex cost accounting systems is consequently lower. In addition to that, the empirical results show that cost accountants in private hospitals are statistically significantly less specialized (in terms of workload management over financial accounting) than their counterparts from private and charitable hospitals. Furthermore, cost accounting systems are statistically significantly less designed for managerial purposes and cost control is less intensively pursued in private compared to public hospitals. Overall, **hypothesis H_{3k}** stating that the complexity of cost accounting systems differs across private, public, and charitable organizations is accepted.

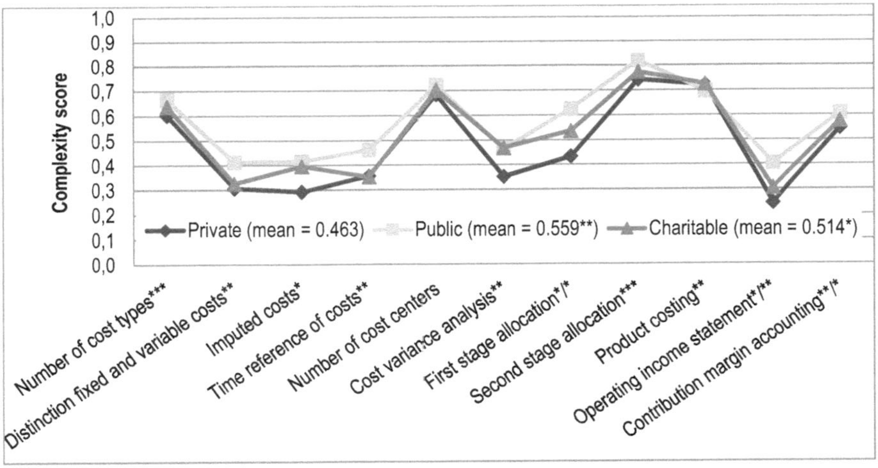

Figure 3-33: Comparison of the type of organization for single and aggregated complexity scores (hospitals of data set 3)

Besides group comparisons the study's objective is also to explain under which conditions companies install complex cost accounting systems. In section 2.3.5.2 it was hypothesized that **external complexity** (hypothesis H_{2a}) and **potential for cost distortion** (H_{3d}) have both a positive effect on the complexity of cost accounting systems. Both influences are not included in multiple regression analysis, because the factors for both theoretical con-

1161 See *Wendel* (2004), p. 166f.; *Lachmann* (2011), p. 190.

1162 For the general assumption see section 2.1.3.6.

1163 See *Henke/Göpffarth* (2010), p. 39.

structs do not meet all quality criteria (see sections 2.1.2 and 2.1.3.2). Therefore, Spearman correlations between the indicators for potential for cost distortion and external complexity and the aggregated complexity score for cost accounting are determined for data set 1. Table 3-56 shows that only for external complexity in terms of number of customers statistically significant correlations exist for both countries. Consequently, hypotheses H_{2a} and H_{3d} are rejected.

	Potential for cost distortion - processes	Potential for cost distortion - support cost centers	External complexity - suppliers	External complexity - customers	External complexity - competitors	Objective 'inventory valuation'
Germany Complexity of cost accounting systems	-0.044	-0.038	0.087	0.106 *	-0.033	0.232 ***
Japan Complexity of cost accounting systems	-0.129	-0.057	0.212	0.210 **	0.023	0.252 ***

Table 3-56: Spearman correlations among potential for cost distortion, external complexity, objective 'inventory valuation', and cost accounting systems' complexity

Furthermore, a negative impact of the financial accounting objective '**inventory valuation**' upon cost accounting systems' complexity was expected (**hypothesis H_{4a}**). This cost accounting objective is not included in the regression analysis, because it has a different meaning across industries (see section 3.3). For this reason the respective hypothesis H_{4a} is tested by correlation analysis. Surprisingly, Table 3-56 shows that the objective 'inventory valuation' is positively associated with cost accounting systems' complexity in Germany (r = 0.232***) and in Japan (r = 0.252***). Hence, hypothesis H_{4a} is rejected.

Finally, a positive impact of **short-term** cost accounting objectives (hypothesis H_{4i}) and negative impacts of **long-term cost accounting objectives** (H_{4k}) upon the complexity of cost accounting systems are expected. As the factor analysis failed (see section 3.3), the short-term and long-term objectives are aggregated to index scores for this analysis. No significant Spearman correlation between the index scores and the complexity of cost accounting systems prevail. Hence, **hypotheses H_{4i} and H_{4k}** are rejected.

The results of the hypotheses tests are summarized in Table 3-57. Bivariate analyses confirm that German companies have more complex cost accounting systems (H_{1m}) and that the complexity differs across industries (H_{3i}) and types of organizations (H_{3k}). In contrast to the expectations from hypothesis H_{6b} cost accounting differs more strongly between Germany and Japan than across industries. It can therefore be concluded that strong variance in the complexity of cost accounting systems still remains between both countries in spite of global pressures like IFRS. Unlike comparisons of means, all hypotheses tested by correlation analysis are rejected. The findings of the correlation analyses indicate that cost accounting systems are not aligned with the context factors external complexity and potential for cost distortion as well as with the addressed cost accounting objectives.

Hypothesis		Result
H_{1m}	German companies employ more complex cost accounting systems than their Japanese counterparts.	Accepted
H_{2a}	The more complex the environment is, the more complex are cost accounting systems.	Rejected
H_{3d}	The higher the potential for cost distortion, the more complex are cost accounting systems.	Rejected
H_{3i}	The complexity of cost accounting systems differs across industries.	Accepted
H_{3k}	The complexity of cost accounting systems differs across private, public, and charitable organizations.	Accepted
H_{4a}	The more intensively companies pursue cost accounting for inventory valuation, the less complex are cost accounting systems.	Rejected
H_{4i}	To meet short-term cost accounting objectives, more complex cost accounting systems are installed.	Rejected
H_{4k}	To meet long-term cost accounting objectives, less complex cost accounting systems are installed.	Rejected
H_{6b}	The complexity of cost accounting systems differs more strongly across industries than across countries.	Rejected

Table 3-57: Results of the hypotheses tests

3.4.1.2 Multivariate analysis of single and aggregated complexity scores

The effects of the 14 context factors that were selected in section 3.2.4 and the four cost accounting objectives upon the complexity of cost accounting systems are determined. **Multiple regression analyses** are carried through for data set 1 for each single complexity score and for the aggregated complexity score. All regressions are calculated separately for Germany and Japan by the enter method. The stepwise method is additionally calculated for the aggregated complexity score. The enter regression models for Germany and Japan yield both in ten out of eleven times higher adjusted R^2 for the aggregated score than for the single scores. For the German sample 31.9% and for the Japanese sample 15.6% of the variance for the aggregated complexity score is explained by the enter method and 25.4% respectively 23.5% of the variance for the aggregated complexity score is explained by the stepwise method (see Table 3-58). Thereby, more variance of cost accounting complexity is explained than in previous studies.[1164] Unlike most enter models for single elements, all quality criteria are met for the aggregated scores of both countries. 16 out of 22 regression analyses of the single elements with the enter method are not significant at the 95% confidence level. In none of the regression the VIF is above 5 and in only one regression the Durbin-Watson statistic is below 1. This demonstrates that a multifarious

1164 *Pizzini* explains 23.2%, 18.8%, and 11.3% of the variance for the dimensions detail, classify, and variance respectively. *Lamminmaki* explains 15%. See *Pizzini* (2006); *Lamminmaki* (2008), p. 17, respectively. *Drury/Tales* explain 38.3%, however, their complexity score consists only of the number of cost pools and the number of different types of second-stage cost drivers that are both highly correlated to company size. Other explanatory variables only marginally explain this complexity score. See *Drury/Tayles* (2005), p. 74.

measurement of cost accounting complexity increases the explanatory power of the models.

Dependent variable	Cost accounting complexity			
Country	Germany		Japan	
Linear regression method	Enter	Stepwise	Enter	Stepwise
R	0.676	0.536	0.562	0.509
R^2	0.457	0.288	0.316	0.259
adjusted R^2	0.319	0.254	0.156	0.235
F	3.319	8.578	1.979	10.738
Significance	0.000	0.000	0.021	0.000
VIF_{max}	2.690	1.118	3.089	1.037
Durbin-Watson statistic	2.163	1.944	1.870	1.912
Independent variables	**Standardized coefficients (Beta)**			
Workload management over financial accounting	-0.298 ***		0.026	
Focus on management accounting	0.241 *		0.077	
Focus on management accounting education	0.247 **		-0.023	
Education university	-0.117		0.112	
Education professional institutes	0.027		-0.039	
Education in-house training	0.178 *	0.215 **	0.096	
Education learning by doing	0.070		0.104	
Specialization in cost accounting only	0.040		-0.034	
Specialization in other business functions	0.070		0.113	0.214 **
Specialization by high qualification	-0.049		0.148	
Factor external dynamics	0.239 **		-0.071	
Factor company size	0.197 **	0.188 **	0.226 **	0.266 ***
Factor IT systems quality	-0.184 *		-0.067	
Factor top management support	0.160	0.234 **	0.210	0.324 ***
Factor decision facilitating objective	0.119		-0.071	
Factor decision influencing objective	0.023		0.060	
Factor planning objective	0.245 **	0.310 ***	-0.001	
Factor cost control objective	0.141		0.095	

Table 3-58: Regression analysis of cost accounting systems' complexity (data set 1)

For hypothesis testing, only the results of the enter method for single complexity scores and the aggregated complexity score are considered, because only this method controls for all other influences while analyzing the influences of single variables upon the complexity of cost accounting systems. Hence, this proceeding is more comprehensive than simply analyzing correlations that might be diluted by other influence factors. Table 3-59 provides an overview of the enter regression results. First, the table summarizes the statistically significant independent variables of the enter method for the single complexity scores. The numbers in the second and third column demonstrate for which single complexity score the respective independent variable is statistically significant. Positive and negative relationships are labeled with '+' and '-' respectively. To provide a better overview, the number of independent variables that have a statistically significant impact upon the single complexity scores are summarized in column four and five. The results of the aggregated complexity score from Table 3-58 are summarized in the last two columns.

Data set 1	Single elements' results				Aggregated results	
Independent variables	**Germany**	**Japan**	**Summary**		**Germany**	**Japan**
Workload management over financial accounting	6(-)	9(+)	-	+	-	
Focus on management accounting	2(+); 3(+); 6(-)		+++		+	
Focus on management accounting education	2(+); 8(+); 10(+); 11(+)		++++		+	
Education university	2(-); 9(+)		-/+			
Education professional institutes		9(-)		-		
Education in-house training	9(+)		+		+	
Education learning by doing	4(+); 7(+); 11(+)	6(+)	+++	+		
Specialization in cost accounting only	6(+); 7(+)	10(+)	++	+		
Specialization in other business functions	6(-); 11(-)	9(+)	- -	+		
Specialization by high qualification						
Factor external dynamics	3(+); 4(+)		++		+	
Factor company size	1(+); 5(+); 11(-)	5(+); 9(+)	++/-	++	+	+
Factor IT systems quality	3(-); 8(-)	8(+)	- -	+	-	
Factor top management support		1(+); 5(+); 7(+); 9(+)		++++		
Factor decision facilitating objective	8(+)		+			
Factor decision influencing objective		4(+)		+		
Factor planning objective	1(+); 2(+); 6(-)	9(-)	++/-	-	+	
Factor cost control objective	6(+)	1(-)	+	-		

1 = number of cost types; 2 = distinction fixed and variable costs; 3 = imputed costs; 4 = time reference of costs; 5 = number of cost centers; 6 = cost variance analysis; 7 = first stage allocation; 8 = second stage allocation; 9 = product costing; 10 = operating income statement; 11 = contribution margin accounting.

Table 3-59: Summary of regression analyses of cost accounting systems' complexity (data set 1)

Hypotheses tests

In section 2.3.5.1 it was hypothesized that the degree of specialization (hypothesis H_{1o}) and the theoretical knowledge of cost accountants (H_{1q}) positively affect the complexity of cost accounting systems. The **degree of specialization** is analyzed by six independent variables (see Table 3-59).[1165] For the German data set, the aggregated complexity score is positively associated with 'focus on management accounting' and 'focus on management accounting education' and negatively associated with 'workload management over finan-

1165 These include 'workload management over financial accounting', 'focus on management accounting', 'focus on management accounting education', 'specialization in cost accounting only', 'specialization in other business functions' (which indicates the opposite of specialization), and 'specialization by high qualification'.

cial accounting'. For 'focus on management accounting' and 'focus on management accounting education' the outcome is consistent with the results of three and four single complexity scores respectively. The results for 'workload management over financial accounting' are supported by one single element. For the Japanese data set one negative and two positive associations between degree of cost accounts' specialization and single complexity scores prevail. As the results for the German sample are controversial and only few significant and positive associations exist for the Japanese sample, the hypothesis H_{1o} is rejected for both countries.

Theoretical knowledge of cost accountants is analyzed by four different sources of knowledge: education in university, by professional bodies, in-house, and learning by doing (see Table 3-59). This sequence reflects an increase in practical knowledge. Theoretical knowledge of cost accountants is negatively associated with the complexity of cost accounting systems in Germany. Only education in-house is positively associated with the aggregated complexity score for the German data set 1. Whereas education in university (which is expected to provide cost accountants the most with theoretical knowledge) has one negative and one positive effect on single scores for systems' complexity, education in-house has one positive effect and education learning by doing has three positive effects on single complexity scores. The results for the Japanese data set are also controversial. Whereas education by processional institutes has a negative effect on the score for product costing, learning by doing is positively associated with the complexity score of cost variance analysis. Hence, hypothesis H_{1q} stating that theoretical knowledge of cost accountants has a positive effect on the complexity of cost accounting systems on a national level is rejected.

Systems' complexity	Germany		Japan	
Country specifics	Above average	Below average	Above average	Below average
Workload management over financial accounting	1.91 **	1.78	0.42	-0.33
Focus on management accounting	5.05	4.93	4.32 **	3.79
Focus on management accounting education	5.13	4.98	3.78	3.85
Education university	64%	80%	11%	4%
Education professional institutes	22%	14%	4%	4%
Education in-house	12% **	0%	14%	9%
Education learning by doing	66%	54%	89%	88%
Specialization in cost accounting only	3.89	3.33	3.45 **	2.84
Specialization in other business functions	3.77	3.63	4.08 *	3.49
Specialization by high qualification	5.35 **	4.69	4.39 ***	3.72

Table 3-60: Mean comparisons of country-specifics between companies having installed cost accounting systems that are above and below average complexity (data set 1)

The comparisons of means between companies scoring above and below average on the aggregated complexity score demonstrate that the country-specifics hardly vary on a national level between companies that have either installed systems above or below average complexity. The country-specifics vary even weaker between both groups than other external and internal context factors. This explains why the hypotheses H_{1o} and H_{1q} for specialization and theoretical knowledge are rejected. According to Table 3-60 German companies with an aggregated complexity score above average are more specialized in terms of 'workload management over financial accounting' and 'specialization by high qualification' than companies with systems' complexity below average. For Japan companies with systems' complexity above average are more specialized in terms of 'workload management over financial accounting', 'specialization in cost accounting only', and 'specialization by high qualification' than their counterparts with systems below average.

In section 2.3.5.2 it was hypothesized that company size (H_{3b}), IT systems quality (H_{3e}), as well as the overall interest in cost accounting (H_{3g}) have a positive effect on the complexity of cost accounting systems. The enter regression models for cost accounting systems' complexity (see Table 3-59) show that **company size** has a positive and significant impact upon the aggregated complexity score in both countries. This positive association is supported in Germany for the single scores 'number of cost types' and 'number of cost centers' and in Japan for the elements 'number of cost centers' and 'product costing'. Only for contribution margin accounting a negative effect for the German sample prevails. Overall, hypothesis H_{3b} stating that company size positively affects the complexity of cost accounting systems is accepted for both countries.

For the German sample **IT systems quality** has a negative effect on the aggregated score for complexity and on the single scores for imputed costs and second stage allocation. For the Japanese sample only one positive effect on the single score for second stage allocation prevails. Hence, hypothesis H_{3e} is rejected.[1166]

Overall interest in cost accounting in terms of **top management support** is not statistically significantly associated with complexity scores for the German data set. For Japan, this independent variable is associated positively with four single complexity scores ('number of cost types', 'number of cost centers', 'first stage allocation', and 'product costing'). Overall, hypothesis H_{3g} is rejected for Germany and accepted for Japan.

In section 2.3.5.3 it was hypothesized that the importance of decision facilitating (hypothesis H_{4g}) and cost control objectives (H_{4d}) have a positive effect on cost accounting systems' complexity. Only one significant association prevails between the factor '**decision facilitating**' and the single complexity score 'second stage allocation' for the German data set and no association prevails for the Japanese regressions. Thus, hypothesis H_{4g} is rejected. The factor for **cost control** has only a positive effect on the single score for cost variance analysis in Germany and a negative effect on the number of cost types in Japan. The hypothesis H_{4d} is therefore also rejected. It is further assumed that the importance of decision influencing objectives (H_{4e}) has a negative impact upon the complexity of cost accounting systems. The impact of decision influencing is contradictory for Japan. Whereas for Germany **decision influencing** objectives have no effect on any single or aggregated complexity scores, it has only a positive effect on the single score for time reference of costs in Japan. Hence, hypothesis H_{4e} is rejected as well. It is further expected that the

1166 One reason for this result might be that other influence factors are controlled for that might also be influenced by IT systems quality. Thus, IT systems quality might still positively affect complexity through other influence factors.

importance of **planning** objectives (H_{4c}) has a negative effect on the complexity of cost accounting systems. For the German responses a positive association between planning objectives and the aggregated score prevails. Planning has furthermore a positive effect on the German scores for 'number of cost types' and 'distinction fixed and variable costs'. In contrast to that it has a negative effect on 'cost variance analysis'. For the Japanese sample the factor for planning objectives has solely a negative effect on the single score for product costing. Due to these contradictory results in Germany and the little empirical evidence in Japan hypothesis H_{4c} is also rejected for both countries.

The results of the hypotheses tests are summarized in Table 3-61. Except for company size none of the expected independent variables that influence the complexity of cost accounting systems are accepted for both countries. Furthermore, top management support has only a statistically significant impact upon the complexity of cost accounting systems for Japan. Like in previous studies,[1167] most of the independent variables have turned out to be not statistically significant or to be in contrast to the expected direction. This outcome is surprising, given the arguments from literature that are summarized in sections 2.1 and 2.2. It is possible that this and prior studies have applied inappropriate measures for the context and the cost accounting objectives. Furthermore, a standardized data collection may be not accurate enough to identify influence factors of cost accounting systems. Finally, it is likely that companies follow different cost accounting objectives and that cost accountants have to design cost accounting systems that meet all these objectives. Consequently, the impact of single cost accounting objectives may be difficult to measure.

Hypothesis		**Result**
H_{1o}	The more specialized cost accountants are, the more complex are cost accounting systems.	Rejected
H_{1q}	The more theoretical knowledge cost accountants have, the more complex are cost accounting systems.	Rejected
H_{3b}	The larger the company is, the more complex are cost accounting systems.	Accepted
H_{3e}	The higher IT systems quality, the more complex are cost accounting systems.	Rejected
H_{3g}	The higher the overall interest in cost accounting is, the more complex are cost accounting systems.	Rejected for Germany, accepted for Japan
H_{4c}	The more important cost accounting is for planning, the less complex are cost accounting systems.	Rejected
H_{4d}	The more important cost accounting is for control, the more complex are cost accounting systems.	Rejected
H_{4e}	The more important decision facilitating is, the more complex are cost accounting systems.	Rejected
H_{4g}	The more important decision influencing, the less complex are cost accounting systems.	Rejected

Table 3-61: Results of the hypotheses tests

1167 Cf., e.g., *Drury/Tayles* (2005); *Drury/Tayles* (2006); *Pizzini* (2006).

3.4.1.3 Activity-based costing as an alternative measure for cost accounting systems' complexity

To test for the robustness of the findings, an alternative measure for cost accounting complexity – ABC – is examined in this section. To avoid shortcomings in conceptual equivalence, eight characteristics of ABC were surveyed so that the researcher instead of the practitioners could define whether ABC is applied or not. The indicators of ABC were operationalized by question C.11 (Appendix 2). The respondents were asked how many of the eight characteristics apply to their cost accounting systems. The characteristics are surveyed to determine the complexity score of ABC and to classify ABC according to *Gosselin's* typology.

3.4.1.3.1 Analysis of ABC complexity score

The more of the eight characteristics are applied, the more processing effort is required and the more accurate and relevant information can be provided.

Activity-based costing	Which of the following characteristics describe your cost accounting system? (Does apply; does not apply)						
Type of comparison	**Country comparison**				**Industry comparison**		
Data set	**Data set 1**		**Data set 2**		**Data set 3**		
	Germany	Japan	Germany	Japan	Food and beverage	Mechanical engineering	Hospitals
Activities in cost centers are identified.	66%	58%	63%	68%	66%	63%	73% *
Cost center costs are allocated to activities.	58%	57%	51%	70% **	61%	51%	59%
Activities are aggregated to processes.	37%	39%	29%	44% *	**45%** *	29%	32%
Cost driver volumes are determined for each activity.	44%	37%	33%	39%	54% ***	33%	44% *
Activity cost driver rates are determined.	34%	26%	22%	34%	**51%** ***	22%	27%
Activity cost driver rates are used for product/service costing.	31%	29%	23%	41% **	**50%** ***	23%	23%
Activity cost driver rates are used for process optimization.	25% **	14%	18%	21%	**40%** ***	18%	23%
Activity cost driver rates are used to analyze customer/patient profitability.	18%	12%	15%	18%	**27%** *	15%	17%
Complexity score	0.390	0.360	0.324	0.376 *	**0.366** ***	0.324	0.333

Table 3-62: Activity-based costing

For data set 1 only one statistically significant difference for the complexity score of ABC exists (see Table 3-62): German companies use activity cost driver rates more frequently for process optimization. More cross-national differences prevail for data set 2. Japanese mechanical engineering companies (1) allocate cost center costs to activities, (2) aggregate activities to processes, and (3) use activity cost driver rates for determining product costs statistically significantly more frequently than their German counterparts. The first two significant differences of the mechanical engineering industry are surprising. Ad (1): German companies were identified to more intensively transfer costs from support cost centers to primary cost centers than their Japanese counterparts.[1168] It is therefore feasible that also more German than Japanese companies allocate costs from cost centers to activities. Ad (2): Activities should be aggregated first to processes to reduce complexity of ABC calculations, when many cost centers and thus many activities are distinguished.[1169] Japanese companies install fewer cost centers than their German counterparts[1170] and the German version of ABC is characterized in literature to aggregate activities to processes before allocating costs to products or services. For both reasons it is surprising that more Japanese companies aggregate activities to processes. Ad (3): The result that Japanese mechanical engineering companies apply activity cost driver rates significantly more frequently for determining product and service costs is consistent with the finding that Japanese mechanical engineering companies apply more frequently duration drivers (see section 3.4.1.1.1.8). Whereas the complexity score for data set 1 is not statistically significantly different between German and Japanese companies, the Japanese mechanical engineering companies (data set 2) obtain a higher score for ABC than their German counterparts. **Hypothesis H_{1m}** stating that more complex cost accounting systems are installed in Germany cannot be supported for ABC complexity. One reason for this outcome could be the fact that the sophisticated German system GPK is widespread in German mechanical engineering companies.[1171] The need to install ABC is therefore lower for German compared to Japanese mechanical engineering companies.

Stronger differences than between Germany and Japan prevail across industries. Companies of the food and beverage industry apply six out of eight ABC characteristics statistically significantly more frequently than their mechanical engineering counterparts and five out of eight characteristics statistically significantly more frequently than hospitals. Hospitals only identify activities in cost centers more frequently than companies operating in the mechanical engineering industry. Overall, companies of the food and beverage industry obtain statistically significantly higher scores for ABC complexity than their counterparts from the other two industries. The results support **hypotheses H_{3i} and H_{6b}** for ABC that the complexity of cost accounting differs across industries and that the differences are stronger across industries than between Germany and Japan.

1168 See section 3.4.1.1.1.7.

1169 Cf. *Scheer/Berkau* (1993), p. 116; *Gaiser* (1998), p. 72f. Through the combination of subprocesses to processes, the German ABC version enables a more detailed allocation of costs. The German version assigns only the costs of indirect departments, whereas the US version on the contrary mainly allocates all overhead costs of the production cost centers. Cf. *Kellermanns/Islam* (2004), p. 38. Due to the conceptual differences, the type of use differs between both countries as well. See *Gaiser* (1998), p. 70; *Kellermanns/Islam* (2004), p. 37.

1170 Cf. section 3.4.1.1.1.5.

1171 Cf. See *Krumwiede/Suessmair* (2007a), (2007b).

Dependent variable	Activity-based costing			
Country	Germany		Japan	
Linear regression method	Enter	Stepwise	Enter	Stepwise
R	0.621	0.455	0.534	0.255
R^2	0.385	0.207	0.286	0.065
adjusted R^2	0.201	0.176	0.000	0.050
F	2.087	6.544	0.999	4.294
Significance	0.018	0.001	0.478	0.042
VIF_{max}	2.893	1.000	3.637	1.000
Durbin-Watson statistic	2.060	2.123	1.585	1.748
Independent variables	**Standardized coefficients (Beta)**			
Workload management over financial accounting	-0.338 **		0.016	
Focus on management accounting	0.484 ***	0.315 ***	0.005	
Focus on management accounting education	0.190		0.205	
Education university	-0.282 ***	-0.232 **	0.049	
Education professional institutes	-0.072		-0.013	
Education in-house training	0.203 *		-0.119	
Education learning by doing	0.108		0.168	
Specialization in cost accounting only	0.045		0.048	
Specialization in other business functions	0.126		0.127	
Specialization by high qualification	0.043		0.096	
Factor external dynamics	0.165		-0.088	
Factor company size	-0.158		0.194	
Factor IT systems quality	0.125		0.124	
Factor top management support	-0.162		0.006	
Factor decision facilitating objective	0.081	0.244 **	-0.023	
Factor decision influencing objective	0.108		-0.359 *	
Factor planning objective	0.068		0.128	
Factor cost control objective	0.068		0.300	0.255 **

Table 3-63: Regression analysis of ABC (data set 1)

Table 3-63 shows that the German enter and stepwise **multiple regression models** have a higher explanatory power (adjusted R^2 = 0.201 respectively 0.176) than the Japanese models (adjusted R^2 = 0.000 respectively 0.050). All quality criteria are met except for the Japanese enter model. For this reason only the German results of the regression analysis for cost accounting systems' complexity are verified by this alternative complexity measure. For the German responses (see Table 3-63) the independent variables focus on management accounting (r = 0.484***) and education in-house training (r = 0.203*) have a positive impact upon the ABC complexity score. Workload management over financial accounting (r = -0.338**) and education university (r = -0.282***) on the contrary have a negative effect. The results show that specialization has both a positive and a negative impact upon the ABC complexity score. Furthermore, theoretical education seems to have a negative impact upon the ABC complexity score. Hence, **hypotheses H_{1o} and H_{1q}** stating that specialization respectively theoretical knowledge have a positive impact upon cost accounting complexity are rejected for ABC. The other hypotheses assuming an impact of company size (H_{3b}), IT systems quality (H_{3e}), top management support (H_{3g}), and the cost accounting objectives planning, cost control, decision influencing, and decision facilitating (H_{4c}, H_{4d}, H_{4e}, H_{4g}) upon cost accounting system's complexity are not supported for the ABC complexity score. Finally, no significant correlations between ABC complexity score and the single indicators for external complexity and potential for cost distortion are prevalent. Hence, **hypotheses H_{2a} and H_{3d}** are rejected as well.

3.4.1.3.2 Analysis of ABC classification

Besides the complexity score of ABC, also *Gosselin's* typology[1172] of ABC is followed to investigate the application of ABC. This is necessary to determine the adoption rates of the different types of ABC and to investigate whether the motivation to adopt the different types of ABC differs internationally. *Gosselin* distinguishes between 'activity analysis', 'activity cost analysis', and 'ABC'. The application of ABC for process optimization and for customer profitability analysis is further analyzed in this study.

Following *Gosselin's* distinction, 35% respectively 32% of the German and Japanese companies apply 'activity analysis', 25% respectively 20% apply 'activity cost analysis', and 23% respectively 19% apply ABC. Only 18% respectively 10% of the German and Japanese companies use 'ABC for process optimization' and 14% respectively 9% apply 'ABC for customer profitability analysis'. German companies apply all five ABC classifications more frequently than their Japanese counterparts, however, only the difference for 'ABC for process optimization' is statistically significant (see Figure 3-34).

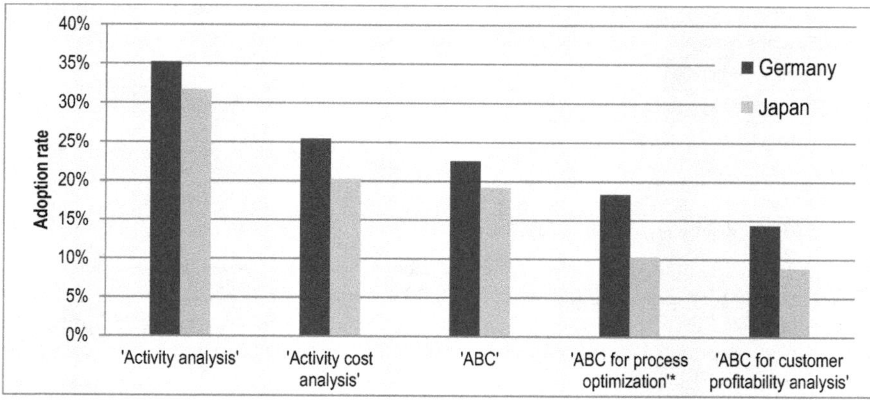

Figure 3-34: Adoption rates of ABC classifications for Germany and Japan (data set 1)

1172 See *Gosselin* (1997), p. 106f.

Overall, **hypothesis H_{1m}** stating that German companies have installed more complex cost accounting systems cannot be supported for *Gosselin's* ABC classification.[1173] In both countries only a small number of companies have installed ABC. The reason for few Japanese companies installing ABC systems can be explained by the Japanese cost accounting standard, which significantly influences the design of cost accounting systems. As modern systems like ABC are not included in the standard, the cost accounting standard may constitute a barrier for the ABC diffusion in Japan.[1174] In Germany on the contrary the higher degree of specialization may constitute a barrier to define activities across functions and to allocate costs to activities. Furthermore, the sophisticated system GPK is widespread in Germany,[1175] wherefore the necessity to install ABC for increasing the accuracy of product costing is lower than in other countries like the USA.[1176]

Stronger differences than between Germany and Japan prevail across industries. Food and beverage companies have implemented most frequently all five ABC classifications – the differences are statistically significant in five times in comparison with the mechanical engineering industry and three times in comparison with hospitals (see Figure 3-35). The **hypotheses H_{3i} and H_{6b}** stating that the complexity of cost accounting systems differs across industries respectively differs more strongly across industries than across countries can thus be accepted for the classification of ABC. The adoption rates of ABC determined in this study are comparable with earlier research[1177] and lower compared to *Gosselin's*[1178] and *Baird et al.'s*[1179] findings.

1173 The results are not verified by data set 2 due to the small number of responses.

1174 Cf. *Winter* (2005), p. 29, quoting *Yoshikawa* (2000), p. 37.

1175 See See *Krumwiede/Suessmair* (2007a), (2007b).

1176 Cf. *Gaiser* (1998), p. 69.

1177 For an overview see *Gosselin* (2007). Studies that have been published between 2001 and 2005 report adoption rates of between 20.3% and 40.9%. These studies, however, have not followed *Gosselin's* typology. Cf. *Gosselin* (2007), p. 654f.

1178 The adoption rate of 'ABC' (the third type according to Gosselin's typology) is 47.8%. Cf. *Gosselin* (1997), p. 112f.

1179 86.2% of the companies use 'activity analysis', 82.1% use 'activity cost analysis', and 78.1% use 'ABC'. Cf. *Baird et al.* (2004), p. 390f. Similar results are reported in *Baird et al.* (2007), p. 55f.

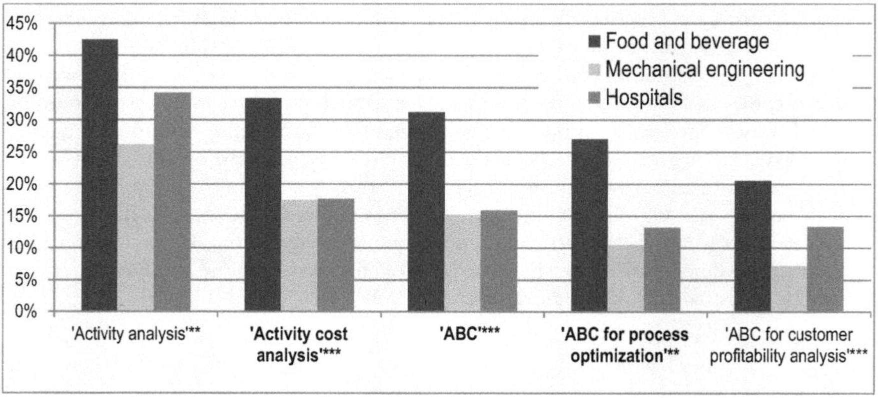

Figure 3-35: Adoption rates of ABC characteristics across industries (data set 3)

In the following the determinants for ABC adoption are analyzed via **logistic regression analysis.** Due to the small number of responses in Japan, where only 82 out of 146 responses are valid to analyze *Gosselin's* ABC classification, and due to the low application rates, determinants of ABC adoption can be compared between Germany and Japan only for 'activity analysis'. The other classifications of ABC can only be calculated for the German data set. Therefore, differences in the determinants of the five ABC classifications are compared only for the German data set. Furthermore, to increase stability of the findings, the four binary coded indicators for 'cost accountants' sources of knowledge' are excluded from the analysis. The stability of the findings can be increased, because a smaller number of independent variables requires a smaller number of observations per group.[1180] Furthermore, several observations were not analyzable, because of a too large number of missing indicators. By excluding the indicators for 'cost accountants' sources of knowledge' more observations were analyzable.

Quality of the models

The results of the logistic regression analysis of data set 1 show that only little variation can be explained (see Table 3-64 and Table 3-65). The McFaddens-R^2, Cox and Snell-R^2, and Nagelkerke-R^2, which are analog to the R^2 statistic applied in regression analysis indicators for the logit model's explanatory power, are between 0.111 and 0.266 for the German models and between 0.217 and 0.333 for the Japanese model. The percentage of correct classifications shows that the German models explain moderate variation. Hence, the logistic regression results have to be interpreted with care. All VIFs are far below 5 and thus multicollinearity is not problematic for all logit models.

1180 Cf. *Backhaus et al.* (2011), p. 295.

Dependent variable	**'Activity analysis'**			
Country	**Germany**		**Japan**	
McFaddens-R^2	0.111		0.217	
Cox and Snell-R^2	0.135		0.236	
Nagelkerke-R^2	0.185		0.333	
% correct classification non-adoption	88.1%		92.9%	
% correct classification adoption	48.0%		47.4%	
% correct classification overall	73.7%		78.7%	
Hosmer-Lemeshow-test	0.063		0.262	
VIF_{max}	2.401		3.489	
Independent variables	**Parameter estimate (B)**	**Odds ratio (exp (b))**	**Parameter estimate (B)**	**Odds ratio (exp (b))**
Workload management over financial accounting	-0.017	0.984	-0.128	0.880
Focus on management accounting	0.314 **	1.368	0.226	1.253
Focus on management accounting education	0.041	1.041	0.061	1.063
Specialization in cost accounting only	0.169	1.184	0.158	1.172
Specialization in other business functions	0.278 ***	1.320	-0.037	0.963
Specialization by high qualification	-0.210	0.811	0.292	1.339
Factor external dynamics	0.275	1.317	-0.199	0.820
Factor company size	-0.025	0.975	0.367	1.443
Factor IT systems quality	-0.027	0.974	0.191	1.210
Factor top management support	-0.195	0.823	-0.117	0.889
Factor decision facilitating objective	0.161	1.175	0.603	1.827
Factor decision influencing objective	-0.192	0.825	-0.097	0.907
Factor planning objective	0.514 **	1.671	-0.014	0.986
Factor cost control objective	0.190	1.209	0.427	1.533

Table 3-64: Logistic regression for 'activity analysis' (data set 1)

Comparison between Germany and Japan

Both logit models for 'activity analysis' show that the quality criteria strongly vary between Germany and Japan and that only three determinants explain the adoption of 'activity analysis' for the German data set (see Table 3-64). Whereas 'focus on management accounting', 'specialization in other business functions', and 'factor planning objective' statistically significantly and positively influence the adoption of 'activity analysis' in Germany, none of the determinants have a highly significant impact in Japan. The positive association between ABC and the variable 'specialization in other business functions' can be explained by the necessity that cost accountants require a basic understanding of operating departments to define activities and their costs.

Comparison of ABC classifications

Table 3-65 shows that the relevance of determinants varies across different ABC classifications for German companies.

Dependent variable	'Activity analysis'		'Activity cost analysis'		'ABC'		'ABC for process optimization'		'ABC for customer analyis'	
McFaddens-R²	0.111		0.169		0.180		0.171		0.166	
Cox and Snell-R²	0.135		0.174		0.177		0.147		0.118	
Nagelkerke-R²	0.185		0.256		0.266		0.238		0.208	
% correct classification non-adoption	88.1%		95.4%		97.4%		98.1%		98.8%	
% correct classification adoption	48.0%		32.7%		27.7%		18.9%		13.8%	
% correct classification overall	73.7%		79.3%		81.0%		83.2%		86.2%	
Hosmer-Lemeshow-test	0.063		0.084		0.082		0.134		0.665	
VIF_{max}	2.401		2.452		2.546		2.510		2.466	
Independent variables	**Parameter estimate (B)**	**Odds ratio (exp (b))**	**Parameter estimate (B)**	**Odds ratio (exp (b))**	**Parameter estimate (B)**	**Odds ratio (exp (b))**	**Parameter estimate (B)**	**Odds ratio (exp (b))**	**Parameter estimate (B)**	**Odds ratio (exp (b))**
Workload management over financial accounting	-0.017	0.984	-0.171 *	0.843	-0.179	0.836	-0.129	0.879	-0.015	0.985
Focus on management accounting	0.314 **	1.368	0.531 ***	1.701	0.475 **	1.608	0.359 *	1.432	0.124	1.132
Focus on management accounting education	0.041	1.041	-0.140	0.869	-0.146	0.864	-0.078	0.925	0.009	1.009
Specialization in cost accounting only	0.169	1.184	0.095	1.100	0.088	1.093	0.092	1.096	0.062	1.064
Specialization in other business functions	0.278 ***	1.320	0.390 ***	1.477	0.441 ***	1.554	0.353 **	1.424	0.408 **	1.504
Specialization by high qualification	-0.210	0.811	-0.329 **	0.720	-0.313 *	0.731	-0.302 *	0.739	-0.291	0.748
Factor external dynamics	0.275	1.317	0.194	1.214	0.241	1.273	0.212	1.236	0.024	1.024
Factor company size	-0.025	0.975	0.127	1.135	0.058	1.059	0.055	1.056	-0.092	0.912
Factor IT systems quality	-0.027	0.974	0.316	1.371	0.516 **	1.676	0.741 ***	2.098	0.793 **	2.209
Factor top management support	-0.195	0.823	-0.099	0.906	-0.089	0.915	-0.250	0.779	-0.189	0.827
Factor decision facilitating objective	0.161	1.175	0.510 **	1.666	0.491 *	1.634	0.462	1.588	0.549 *	1.731
Factor decision influencing objective	-0.192	0.825	0.129	1.137	-0.002	0.998	0.027	1.027	0.094	1.099
Factor planning objective	0.514 **	1.671	0.217	1.243	0.237	1.267	0.283	1.326	0.015	1.015
Factor cost control objective	0.190	1.209	-0.037	0.963	0.069	1.072	0.055	1.057	-0.074	0.928

Table 3-65: Logistic regressions for ABC classifications of German companies (data set 1)

IT systems quality is not a statistically significant influence factor for companies adopting 'activity analysis' or 'activity cost analysis', but it becomes significant for ABC and increases in significance and relevance[1181] when ABC is applied for process optimization and for customer profitability analysis. Hence, it can be concluded that IT systems quality is not a critical prerequisite to implement 'activity analysis' and 'activity cost analysis'. However, when the next higher classification of ABC is installed and in particular when ABC serves process optimization or assessing customer profitability, it becomes critical and increases in relevance. *Focus on management accounting* statistically significantly influences the implementation of the first four ABC classifications, whereby the relevance for the first classification ('activity analysis') is by far lower than for the types 'activity cost analysis' and 'ABC'. Like 'focus on management accounting', the *specialization in other business functions* statistically significantly influences the implementation of ABC, whereby for the ABC type 'activity analysis' the cost accountants' specialization in other business functions is by far the lowest. Unlike 'focus on management accounting', 'specialization in other business functions' remains statistically significantly relevant not only for 'ABC for process optimization', but also for 'ABC for customer profitability analysis'. A rather surprising result is that except for 'activity analysis' an increase in the *specialization by high qualification* statistically significantly reduces the probability to install the ABC types 'activity cost analysis', 'ABC' and 'ABC for process optimization'. According to these findings, the more cost accountants are qualified to enhance and run cost accounting systems, the less likely the respective companies install ABC systems. It can be concluded that highly qualified cost accountants have already installed more complex cost accounting systems and might therefore feel reluctant to invest further resources in advanced systems like ABC when they are already satisfied with their existing cost accounting systems. The results from section 3.4.1.2, however, do not support the assumption that more qualified cost accountants install more complex cost accounting systems. Finally, the *objective planning* has a strong impact upon adopting 'activity analysis', but no impact upon the remaining ABC classifications.

Overall, IT systems quality, focus on management accounting, and specialization in other business functions have a positive effect upon the adoption of ABC systems in Germany. Hence, the hypothesis H_{3e} stating that IT systems quality has an effect upon cost accounting systems' complexity is accepted. Furthermore, hypothesis H_{1o}, stating that the specialization of cost accountants has a positive effect on the complexity of cost accounting systems, is rejected for ABC for Germany and Japan due to inconsistent results. The hypothesis H_{4c} stating that planning leads to less complex cost accounting systems is also rejected. The remaining hypotheses (H_{1q}, H_{3g}, H_{3b}, H_{4d}, H_{4e}, and H_{4g})[1182] on cost accounting systems' complexity are rejected as well for both countries, because no significant influence was identified.

1181 The increase in parameter estimate (B) and in odds ratio (exp (b)) in Table 3-65 indicates the increase in relevance.

1182 The contents of these hypotheses are summarized in Table 3-67, p. 283.

3.4.1.3.3 Interpretation of the robustness test

In this study it is argued that measuring the complexity by simply distinguishing between the traditional and ABC systems might be not adequate enough to capture the diversity of practices that exist. For this reason, ABC was applied only as an alternative measure for the complexity of cost accounting systems. The results of ABC are summarized in Table 3-67. The analysis of the complexity score for ABC and the analysis of *Gosselin's* ABC classification have obtained similar results and according to both analyses only hypotheses H_{3i} and H_{6b} are accepted. According to ABC, German companies do not run more complex cost accounting systems than their Japanese counterparts. This outcome does not support the findings from section 3.4.1.1.3, where the aggregated complexity score for systems' complexity was compared cross-nationally. However, it is confirmed that the complexity of cost accounting systems in terms of ABC differs across industries. Unlike the result from section 3.4.1.1.3 the results show that differences in systems' complexity in terms of ABC are stronger across industries than across countries. From this result it can be concluded that specific systems like ABC that have extensively been discussed in literature are more subject to international convergence than more comprehensive systems comprising cost type, cost center, and product cost accounting. Whereas ABC rather incorporates a specific idea how to allocate overhead costs, the characterization of cost accounting systems that include cost type, cost center, and product cost accounting expresses a richer variety of elements, whereof only a few have attracted attention internationally.

The correlations between the complexity of cost accounting systems and ABC for data set 1 show that both measures are not very strongly correlated and that the correlations are much stronger for the Japanese data set (see Table 3-66). The complexity of cost accounting systems and ABC as an alternative measure therefore represent to some extent different aspects of the cost accounting system.

	ABC complexity score	'Activity analysis'	'Activity cost analysis'	'ABC'	'ABC for process optimization'	'ABC for customer profitability analysis'
Germany						
Complexity score	0.180***	0.126*	0.162**	0.179***	0.129*	0.142**
Japan						
Complexity score	0.633***	0.468***	0.401***	0.391***	0.332***	0.298***

Table 3-66: Correlations between the complexity score and alternative measures for systems' complexity

All hypotheses explaining the complexity of cost accounting systems are rejected. Unlike section 3.4.1.1.3 it is not confirmed by analyzing ABC as an alternative complexity measure that company size leads to more complex systems and that top management support leads to more complex systems in Japan.

Hypothesis		Result
H_{1m}	German companies employ more complex cost accounting systems than their Japanese counterparts.	Rejected
H_{3i}	The complexity of cost accounting systems differs across industries.	Accepted
H_{6b}	The complexity of cost accounting systems differs more strongly across industries than across countries.	Accepted
H_{1o}	The more specialized cost accountants are, the more complex are cost accounting systems.	Rejected
H_{1q}	The more theoretical knowledge cost accountants have, the more complex are cost accounting systems.	Rejected
H_{2a}	The more complex the environment is, the more complex are cost accounting systems.	Rejected
H_{3b}	The larger the company is, the more complex are cost accounting systems.	Rejected
H_{3d}	The higher the potential for cost distortion, the more complex are cost accounting systems.	Rejected
H_{3e}	The higher IT systems quality, the more complex are cost accounting systems.	Rejected
H_{3g}	The higher the overall interest in cost accounting is, the more complex are cost accounting systems.	Rejected
H_{4c}	The more important cost accounting is for planning, the less complex are cost accounting systems.	Rejected
H_{4d}	The more important cost accounting is for control, the more complex are cost accounting systems.	Rejected
H_{4e}	The more important decision facilitating is, the more complex are cost accounting systems.	Rejected
H_{4g}	The more important decision influencing, the less complex are cost accounting systems.	Rejected

Table 3-67: Results of the hypotheses tests

3.4.2 Timeliness

3.4.2.1 Bivariate analysis of single timeliness scores

The timeliness of cost accounting systems is surveyed by question C.10 (Appendix 2). The respondents had to indicate how often they update (1) distinction between fixed and variable costs, (2) standard costs, (3) cost variances, (4) cost rates for support cost centers (first stage allocation) and (5) cost rates for overhead allocation bases (second stage allocation), (6) product costs, and (7) operating income statement for managerial purposes. The following options were available: continuously, monthly, quarterly, semi-annually, annually, less often than annually, irregularly, and not applicable (N/A). Timely cost information is in general beneficial, because managers can earlier respond to changes and it facilitates learning. Consequently, the timelier the cost information, the higher the timeliness score. The aggregated score for the timeliness of cost accounting systems is determined by the arithmetic mean of the single timeliness scores.

More than half of the **German companies** update standard costs, cost rates for support cost centers, and cost rates for overhead allocation bases *annually* (see Table 3-68). About two-thirds of the German companies update cost variances, product costs, and operating income statements *monthly or continuously*. Similar results remain for **Japanese companies**: About every second company updates standard costs, cost rates for support cost centers, and cost rates for overhead allocation bases *annually*. Cost variances, product costs, and operating income statements[1183] are updated *monthly* by about every second company. The distinction between fixed and variable costs is handled differently in Germany and Japan. Whereas in Japan the largest group with 24% updates this cost information irregularly, the largest group in Germany with 38% updates this cost information annually (see Table 3-68).

How often is the following cost information updated?	Continuously	Monthly	Quarterly	Semi-annually	Annually	Less often than annually	Irregularly
Germany							
Distinction fixed and variable costs	11%	17%	9% *	4%	38% ***	5%	17%
Standard costs	6%	13%	17% ***	6%	52%	2%	5%
Cost variances	14% **	64% ***	13%	2%	3%	0%	4%
Cost rates for support cost centers	4%	11%	7%	6%	60% **	5%	8%
Cost rates for overhead allocation bases	4%	6%	8%	7%	60% **	6% *	9%
Product costs	28% ***	25%	9%	5%	23%	2%	9%
Operating income statement	7%	77% ***	9%	1%	5%	0%	1%
Japan							
Distinction fixed and variable costs	19% *	18%	3%	10% **	23%	3%	24%
Standard costs	8%	11%	3%	13% *	48%	3%	16% *
Cost variances	7%	40%	8%	13% ***	21% ***	2%	10% ***
Cost rates for support cost centers	2%	12%	5%	14% **	50%	3%	14% **
Cost rates for overhead allocation bases	2%	13% **	5%	15% ***	47%	2%	15% *
Product costs	10%	52% ***	7%	5%	18%	1%	8%
Operating income statement	5%	60%	7%	5% **	9%	1%	13% ***

Table 3-68: Frequency of cost updates (data set 1)

It is reasonable that in both countries cost variances, product costs, and operating income statements are updated more frequently than the other cost information: Updating cost variances is necessary to identify inefficiencies for expeditiously improving operating efficiency; updating product costs is required to know the price limit for short-term decisions; updating the operating income statement is necessary to promptly demonstrate financial consequences of decision making. These three types of cost information are overall necessary for short-term decision making and to enhance the awareness, thinking, and comprehension of the situation the employees are confronted with. Standard costs, dis-

1183 In the study by *Währisch* almost 90% of the German companies update the operating income statement monthly. Cf. *Währisch* (1998), p. 141.

tinction between fixed and variable costs, cost rates for support cost centers, and cost rates for overhead allocation bases on the contrary are usually less frequently updated to ensure comparability of the periods. These cross-national results are to a large extent stable for data set 2.

German companies update standard costs, cost variances, cost rates for overhead allocation bases, and operating income statements for managerial purposes on average statistically significantly more frequently than their Japanese counterparts. The strongest difference between Germany and Japan exists for the update of cost variances and for operating income statements. Whereas 78% respectively 84% of the German companies update cost variances and operating income statements monthly or annually, only 47% respectively 65% of the Japanese companies update both cost information with the same frequency (see Table 3-68). It is likely that German cost accountants update cost variances and operating income statements more frequently than their Japanese counterparts, because they have a stronger emphasis on cost control[1184] and because operating income statements are of higher relevance to German companies.[1185]

In section 2.3.3 the most relevant elements were selected to measure the timeliness of cost accounting systems. It was considered that the elements have a different and independent effect upon the provision of cost information, the elements should not measure the same characteristics in a different way, and they should be positively correlated with the aggregated timeliness score.[1186]

Many single timeliness scores correlate statistically significantly and strongly with each other (see Table 3-69). For German companies of data set 1 strong **correlations** prevail between the scores for standard costs with cost rates for overhead allocation bases (r = 0.333***), distinction between variable costs with cost rates for support cost centers (r = 0.303***) and with cost rates for overhead allocation bases (r = 0.311***), cost variances with operating income statement (r = 0.347***), cost rates for overhead allocation bases with cost rates for support cost centers (r = 0.555***), and cost rates for overhead allocation bases with product costs (r = 0.301***). Furthermore, 12 elements correlate statistically significantly but with a coefficient below r = 0.3. For the Japanese sample all elements correlate statistically significantly with each other. The strongest correlation prevails between cost rates for support cost centers and cost rates for overhead allocation bases (r = 0.897***). None of the correlations for both countries are negative. Overall, the single timeliness scores correlate more strongly with each other than the single complexity scores (see Table 3-53, p. 260). This indicates that the elements describing the timeliness of cost accounting systems are more exchangeable than the elements describing systems' complexity. Overall, the empirical results still confirm the conceptual considerations from section 2.3.3 that the selected elements that measure the timeliness of cost accounting systems have a different effect upon the provision of cost information.

The single timeliness scores are furthermore strongly correlated with the aggregated timeliness score (see Table 3-69). As all single timeliness scores are similarly strongly correlated

1184 Cf. section 3.3.

1185 Cf. section 3.4.1.1.1.10.

1186 Cf. section 2.3.2, p. 150.

with the aggregated score, **all elements** are considered as **relevant to determine the timeliness of cost accounting systems** and thus meaningful results can be expected.

	Standard costs	Cost variances	Cost rates for support cost centers	Cost rates for overhead allocation bases	Product costs	Operating income statement	Overall timeliness score
Germany							
Distinction fixed and variable costs	0.180 ***	0.289 ***	0.303 ***	0.311 ***	0.261 ***	0.171 **	0.680 ***
Standard costs		0.064	0.200 ***	0.333 ***	0.202 ***	0.153 **	0.565 ***
Cost variances			0.090	0.165 ***	0.176 ***	0.347 ***	0.433 ***
Cost rates for support cost centers				0.555 ***	0.089	0.149 **	0.615 ***
Cost rates for overhead allocation bases					0.301 ***	0.170 ***	0.715 ***
Product costs						0.224 ***	0.618 ***
Operating income statement							0.453 ***
Japan							
Distinction fixed and variable costs	0.316 ***	0.480 ***	0.371 ***	0.450 ***	0.490 ***	0.417 ***	0.723 ***
Standard costs		0.318 ***	0.442 ***	0.428 ***	0.293 ***	0.416 ***	0.580 ***
Cost variances			0.367 ***	0.415 ***	0.595 ***	0.455 ***	0.750 ***
Cost rates for support cost centers				0.897 ***	0.380 ***	0.338 ***	0.713 ***
Cost rates for overhead allocation bases					0.399 ***	0.405 ***	0.749 ***
Product costs						0.541 ***	0.762 ***
Operating income statement							0.710 ***

Table 3-69: Spearman correlations of single timeliness scores (data set 1)

3.4.2.2 Bivariate analysis of single and aggregated timeliness scores

German companies obtain a higher aggregated score for cost accounting systems' timeliness for both data sets (Ø = 0.501 and Ø = 0.483) than their Japanese counterparts (Ø = 0.411 and Ø = 0.454) (see Figure 3-36, Figure 3-37, and Table 3-70). Overall, it can be concluded that German companies run in general timelier cost accounting systems than their Japanese counterparts. This result is on the one hand reasonable, because German companies have a higher potential to install timely cost accounting systems than their Japanese counterparts: German cost accountants are more specialized and have more theoretical knowledge (see section 3.2.1.4). Furthermore, German companies have on average more comprehensive IT systems (see section 3.2.3.3) and obtain more top management support (see section 3.2.3.4). The higher scores for German companies are surprising though, because Japanese companies have been characterized in literature to frequently update cost information to motivate their employees acting proactively by discovering and resolving problems before they occur.[1187] Hence, **hypothesis H1n** stating that German companies employ timelier cost accounting systems is accepted.

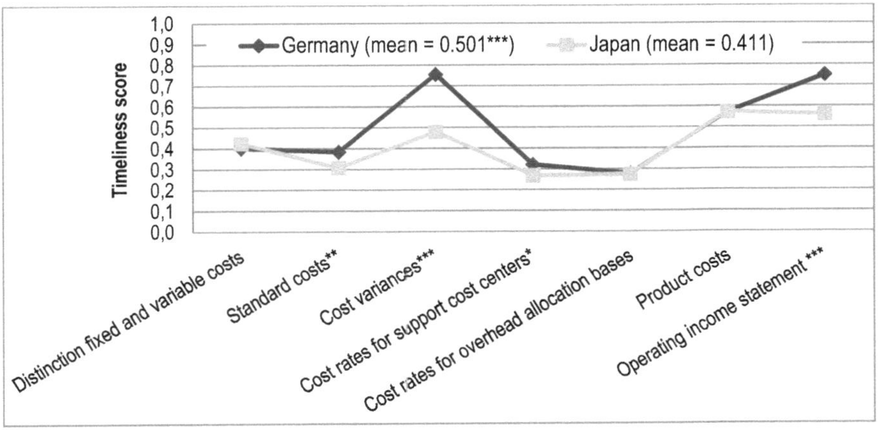

Figure 3-36: Cross-national comparison of single and aggregated timeliness scores (data set 1)

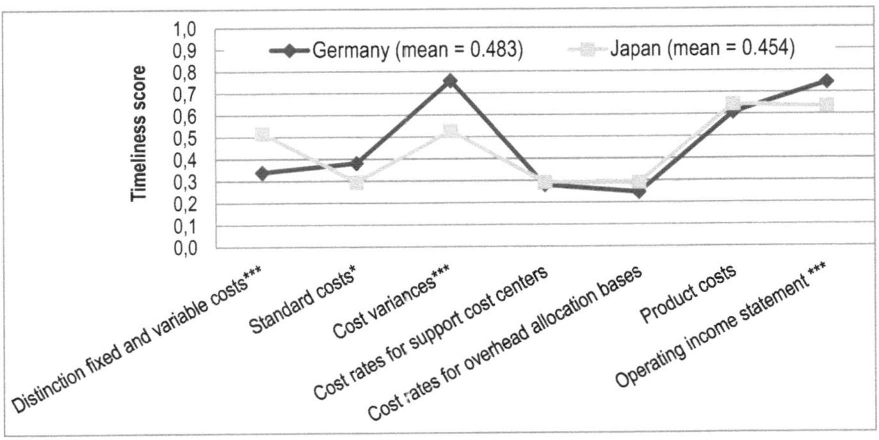

Figure 3-37: Cross-national comparison of single and aggregated timeliness scores (data set 2)

German companies from data set 1 have four out of seven times higher single timeliness scores than their Japanese counterparts. The higher scores in Germany for standard costs, cost variances, and cost rates for support cost centers can be explained by the stronger

1187 Cf. *Cooper/Kaplan* (1991), p. 397f.; *Merchant/Shields* (1993), p. 80. See also section 2.3.5.1. Japanese companies have been identified in prior research to revise standard costs twice as frequently as their Scottish counterparts (cf. *Yoshikawa et al.* (1989), p. 21) and to use more actual costing than their Australian counterparts. Cf. *Wijewardena/de Zoysa* (1999), p. 65.

German emphasis on operating efficiency in combination with cost control and responsibility accounting. The higher emphasis on cost control and responsibility accounting in Germany compared to Japan is supported by the findings in section 3.3 (see Figure 3-19 and Table 3-38). The more often cost variances are identified by comparing actual with expected costs, the earlier can cost variances and opportunities for improvement be identified.[1188] As operating income statements are of greater importance for German companies,[1189] the update of this information is also more relevant for German companies.

Timeliness scores – comparisons of means							
Type of comparison	Country comparison				Industry comparison		
Data set	Data set 1		Data set 2		Data set 3		
	Germany	Japan	Germany	Japan	Food and beverage	Mechanical engineering	Hospitals
Distinction fixed and variable costs	0.402	0.425	0.340	0.519 ***	**0.440** **	0.340	0.325
Standard costs	0.384 **	0.310	0.381 *	0.296	0.424 **	0.381	0.352
Cost variances	0.755 ***	0.480	0.757 ***	0.528	0.742	0.757 *	0.714
Cost rates for support cost centers	0.321 *	0.270	0.280	0.294	0.354 **	0.280	0.315
Cost rates for overhead allocation bases	0.279	0.275	0.246	0.292	**0.344** ***	0.246	0.228
Product costs	0.573	0.574	0.608	0.645	0.629 ***	0.608 ***	0.282
Operating income statement	0.750 ***	0.563	0.745 ***	0.636	**0.796** **	0.745 ***	0.679
Aggregated timeliness score	0.501 ***	0.411	0.483	0.454	**0.542** ***	0.483 **	0.439

Table 3-70: Single and aggregated timeliness scores

In Table 3-71 country comparisons are also carried through on an industry basis for data set 1. The results show that the German companies from the food and beverage and hospital industry have installed timelier cost accounting systems than their Japanese counterparts.[1190] The results, however, have to be interpreted critically, because the sample size for Japanese food and beverage companies and Japanese hospitals is below 50; the Shapiro-Wilk test indicates that the sample is not normally distributed for all three industries on a significance level; the Levene test indicates that homoscedasticity does not prevail for all three industries on a 10%-significance level. Nevertheless, the results still indicate that German companies have timelier cost accounting systems than their Japanese counterparts across all three industries. The strongest difference is between German and Japanese hospitals.

1188 Cf. section 2.3.2.2.

1189 Cf. section 3.4.1.1.1.9.

1190 The values for the mechanical engineering industry from Table 3-71 slightly differ from Table 3-70, because data set 2 includes unlike data set 1 all German mechanical engineering companies. The implications for both data sets, however, are identical.

	Food and beverage	Mechanical engineering	Hospitals
Germany	0.542 ***	0.489 ***	0.453 ***
Japan	0.432	0.454	0.259

Table 3-71: Country comparison for systems' timeliness on an industry basis (data set 1)

Strong differences prevail also across industries for data set 3 (see Table 3-70). Companies of the food and beverage industry update four out of seven pieces of cost information significantly more frequently than their counterparts of the mechanical engineering industry and five out of seven cost information significantly more frequently than hospitals. Companies of the mechanical engineering industry furthermore update three out of seven pieces of cost information more frequently than hospitals. Overall, cost information is updated most frequently in the food and beverage industry, followed by the mechanical engineering industry.

The more cost accounting serves operational than strategic objectives, the more accurate, detailed, and timely cost information has to be provided.[1191] The food and beverage industry is characterized by strong competition. The mechanical engineering industry on the contrary is more innovative.[1192] The difference in timeliness between both manufacturing industries can thus be explained by the stronger operational emphasis in the food and beverage industry and the stronger strategic emphasis in the mechanical engineering industry. The lower scores for the hospital industry may be explained by the lower acceptance of cost information and the late development of cost accounting in this industry.[1193] Only since the introduction of DRG the necessity to increase operating efficiency through comprehensive cost accounting systems increased. Furthermore, calculating medical treatment costs is usually more complicated than calculating product costs in manufacturing industries. Due to this high processing effort, medical treatment costs are less frequently updated in hospitals than product costs in manufacturing companies.

Figure 3-38 shows that the strongest difference between both manufacturing industries and hospitals is the update of product costs. Overall, the **hypothesis H_{3j}** assuming that the timeliness of cost accounting systems differs across industries is accepted. Cross-industry differences in cost accounting systems' timeliness are similar in strength to cross-national differences. **Hypothesis H_{6c}** stating that the timeliness of cost accounting systems differs more strongly across industries than across countries is consequently rejected.

1191 Cf. *Schoute* (2009), p. 210f., with further references, p. 221f.

1192 Cf. section 3.1.1.

1193 Cf. section 3.1.1.

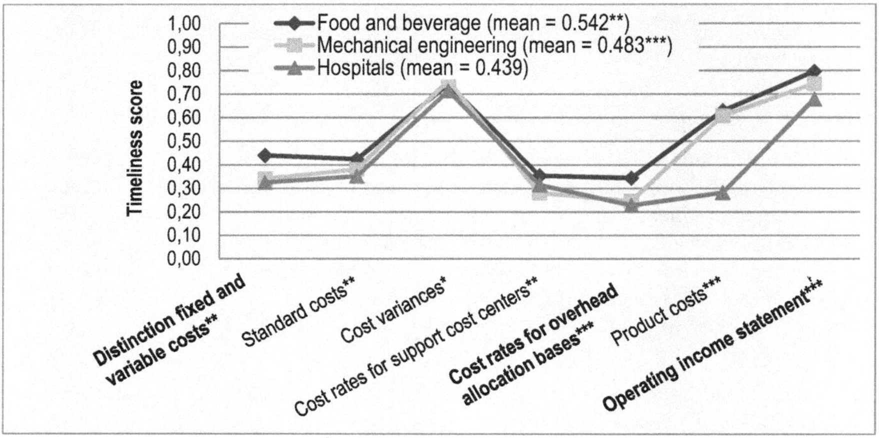

Figure 3-38: Cross-industry comparison for single and aggregated timeliness scores (data set 3)

Smaller differences in the timeliness scores prevail across private, public, and charitable hospitals (see Figure 3-39) than between Germany and Japan and across industries. The strongest difference exists for cost rates for overhead allocation bases. Like for complexity of cost accounting systems, private hospitals, surprisingly, obtain the lowest and public hospitals the highest aggregated score for the timeliness of cost accounting systems.[1194] Overall, **hypothesis H_{3I}** stating that differences in timeliness across organizational types prevail is accepted. These results, however, have to be carefully interpreted. The data set consists of only 37 private, 54 public, and 125 charitable organizations and the assumption that the sample is normally distributed is not fulfilled for public and charitable hospitals.[1195]

Besides group comparisons the study's objective is also to explain when companies install timely cost accounting systems. The impact of the **objective 'inventory valuation'** upon the timeliness of cost accounting systems is tested by correlation analysis. It is expected that companies having a strong emphasis on inventory valuation require less complex cost accounting systems (hypothesis H_{4b}). Surprisingly, like for systems' complexity, the Spearman correlations show that this objective is positively associated with cost accounting systems' timeliness in Germany (r = 0.120**) and in Japan (r = 0.340***). Hence, hypothesis H_{4b} is rejected. It is further expected that more (less) timely cost information is required for short-term (long-term) objectives. However, no significant correlations prevail between the index scores for **short-term and long-term cost accounting objectives** and the timeliness of cost accounting systems. Hence, hypotheses H_{4j} and H_{4l} are rejected. Both objectives are tested by Spearman correlations, because both objectives fail the quality criteria for factor analysis (see section 3.3).

1194 The number of employees does not statistically significant differ across the three types of organizations on a 95%-significance level.

1195 Private hospitals are normally distributed and homoscedasticity prevails for all three types of organizations.

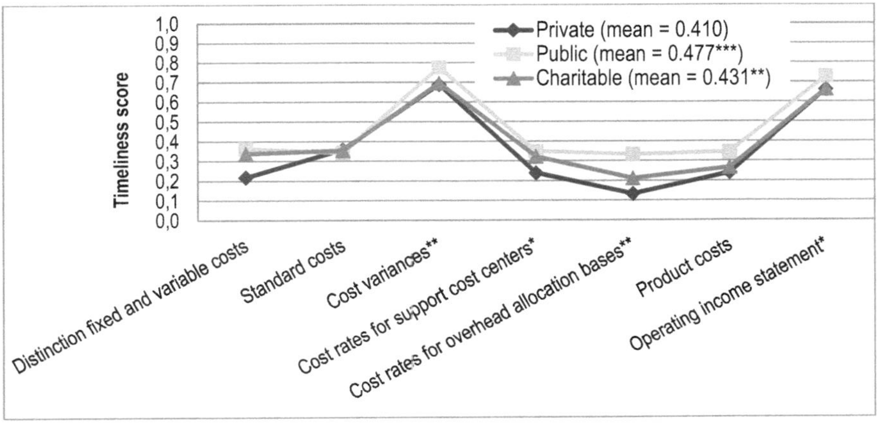

Figure 3-39: Comparison of the type of organization for single and aggregated timeliness scores (hospitals of data set 3)

The results for the timeliness of cost accounting systems are summarized in Table 3-72. The findings support the hypotheses that German companies have more timely cost accounting systems than their Japanese counterparts (H_{1n}) and that the timeliness of cost accounting systems differs across industries (H_{3j}) and across different types of organizations (H_{3l}). However, differences in timeliness of cost accounting systems are not stronger across industries than between Germany and Japan (H_{6c}). It can therefore be concluded that strong differences in the timeliness of cost accounting systems still remain between both countries in spite of global pressures. Three expected relationships between cost accounting objectives and the timeliness of cost accounting systems are not confirmed by correlation analyses. Hence, no empirical evidence is provided that cost accounting systems are purposefully designed.

Hypothesis		Result
H_{1n}	German companies employ more timely cost accounting systems than their Japanese counterparts.	Accepted
H_{3j}	The timeliness of cost accounting systems differs across industries.	Accepted
H_{3l}	The timeliness of cost accounting systems differs across private, public, and charitable organizations.	Accepted
H_{4b}	The more intensively companies pursue cost accounting for inventory valuation, the less timely are cost accounting systems.	Rejected
H_{4j}	To meet short-term cost accounting objectives, timelier cost accounting systems are installed.	Rejected
H_{4l}	To meet long-term cost accounting objectives, less timely cost accounting systems are installed.	Rejected
H_{6c}	The timeliness of cost accounting systems differs more strongly across industries than across countries.	Rejected

Table 3-72: Results of the hypotheses tests

3.4.2.3 Multivariate analysis of single and aggregated timeliness scores

Multiple regression analyses are carried through for each single and for the aggregated timeliness scores to determine the effect of 14 context factors and four cost accounting objectives. All regressions are calculated separately for Germany and Japan for data set 1 (see Table 3-73 and Table 3-74).

Dependent variable	Cost accounting timeliness			
Country	Germany		Japan	
Linear regression method	Enter	Stepwise	Enter	Stepwise
R	0.526	0.318	0.588	0.517
R^2	0.277	0.101	0.346	0.267
adjusted R^2	0.083	0.079	0.187	0.234
F	1.427	4.667	2.174	8.008
Significance	0.148	0.012	0.011	0.000
VIF_{max}	2.793	1.009	3.213	1.177
Durbin-Watson statistic	2.029	1.811	1.803	2.031
Independent variables	**Standardized coefficients (Beta)**			
Workload management over financial accounting	-0.280 **		0.000	
Focus on management accounting	0.170		-0.274 **	-0.201 **
Focus on management accounting education	0.035		-0.083	
Education university	0.060		-0.011	
Education professional institutes	-0.066		0.069	
Education in-house training	0.210 *		-0.066	
Education learning by doing	-0.025		-0.004	
Specialization in cost accounting only	-0.029		0.276 **	0.313 ***
Specialization in other business functions	-0.180	0.351 ***	0.104	
Specialization by high qualification	0.131	0.211 **	-0.200 *	
Factor external dynamics	-0.160		0.247 **	0.226 **
Factor company size	0.041		0.092	
Factor IT systems quality	0.166		0.273 **	0.283 ***
Factor top management support	-0.022		0.025	
Factor decision facilitating objective	0.006		-0.053	
Factor decision influencing objective	0.221		-0.068	
Factor planning objective	-0.084		0.042	
Factor cost control objective	-0.207		0.233	

Table 3-73: Regression analysis of cost accounting systems' timeliness (data set 1)

For the aggregated score the enter method explains 8.3% and 18.7% of the variance for the German and Japanese sample respectively. The step method explains 7.9% and 23.4% of the variance for Germany and Japan respectively. The German enter regression models provide in four out of seven times and the Japanese models in five out of seven times higher adjusted R^2 for the aggregated timeliness scores than for the single cost accounting elements. This demonstrates that in general a multifarious measurement of cost accounting systems' timeliness increases the explanatory power of the models. The German enter model and ten out of 14 enter model regressions of single elements are not significant at a 10%-significance level. The VIF is in no regression above 5 and the Durbin-Watson statistic is always between 1.5 and 2.5.

Table 3-74 summarizes the regression results of the single and the aggregated timeliness scores. Only the results of the enter method are considered for hypothesis testing. Column two and three provide the statistically significant independent variables for the respective single timeliness scores, which are summarized in column four and five. The last two columns summarize the results of the aggregated timeliness scores from Table 3-73. Positive and negative relationships between the independent variables and the timeliness scores are labeled with '+' and '-' respectively.

Data set 1	Single elements' results				Aggregated results	
Independent variables	**Germany**	**Japan**	**Summary**		**Germany**	**Japan**
Workload management over financial accounting	4(-); 6(-)		- -		-	
Focus on management accounting	4(+)	5(-)	+	-		-
Focus on management accounting education	3(+); 6(+)		++			
Education university	5(+)		+			
Education professional institutes						
Education in-house training	5(+)		+		+	
Education learning by doing		4(-)		-		
Specialization in cost accounting only	5(-)	6(+)	-	+		+
Specialization in other business functions	3(-); 6(-); 7(-)		- - -			
Specialization by high qualification		1(-)		-		-
Factor external dynamics	5(-)	1(+); 5(+); 6(+)	-	+++		+
Factor company size						
Factor IT systems quality	2(+); 5(+)	1(+); 2(+); 3(+); 6(+); 7(+)	++	+++++		+
Factor top management support		5(+)		+		
Factor decision facilitating objective		1(+)		+		
Factor decision influencing objective	1(+)	6(-)	+	-		
Factor planning objective	1(-)	6(+)	-	+		
Factor cost control objective	2(-)	3(+)	-	+		
1 = distinction fixed and variable costs; 2 = standard costs; 3 = cost variances; 4 = cost rates for support cost centers; 5 = cost rates for overhead allocation bases; 6 = product costs; 7 = operating income statement.						

Table 3-74: Summary of regression analyses of cost accounting systems' timeliness (data set 1)

Hypotheses tests

In section 2.3.5.1 it was hypothesized that the degree of specialization (hypothesis H_{1p}) and the theoretical knowledge of cost accountants (H_{1r}) positively affect the timeliness of cost accounting systems. The results for the **degree of specialization** are controversial in both countries (see Table 3-74). *For the German data set* the independent variables 'focus on management accounting' and 'focus on management accounting education' are positively associated with at least one single timeliness score. However, the aggregated timeliness score is negatively associated with the variable 'workload management over financial accounting' and the independent variables 'workload management over financial accounting' and 'specialization in cost accounting only' are further negatively associated with single timeliness scores. *For the Japanese data set* contradictory results prevail as well. The variables 'focus on management accounting' and 'specialization by high qualification' have both a negative impact upon the aggregated timeliness score. 'Specialization in cost accounting only', on the contrary, is conform to the supposed relationship by being positively associated to the aggregated timeliness score and to the single element 'product costs'. Due to the contradictory results for Germany and Japan the hypothesis H_{1p} is rejected for both countries. The specialization of cost accountants does not have a positive impact upon the timeliness of cost accounting systems on a national level.

For the German data set 'education in-house training' has a positive impact upon the aggregated timeliness score and 'education university' and 'education in-house training' have both a positive impact upon the single timeliness score for 'cost rates for overhead allocation bases'. For the Japanese data set only 'education learning by doing' is negatively associated with the single score for 'cost rates for support cost centers'. Due to little empirical evidence, hypothesis H_{1r} stating that **theoretical knowledge of cost accountants** has a positive impact upon the timeliness of cost accounting systems is rejected for both countries. It cannot be confirmed that the theoretical knowledge of cost accountants has a positive impact upon the timeliness of cost accounting systems on a national level.

Systems' timeliness	Germany		Japan	
Country specifics	Above average	Below average	Above average	Below average
Workload management over financial accounting	1.53	2.10 **	-0.15	0.31
Focus on management accounting	5.15 *	4.88	3.97	4.16
Focus on management accounting education	4.96	5.13	3.68	3.92
Education university	75%	68%	8%	8%
Education professional institutes	15%	21%	5%	4%
Education in-house	9%	2%	8%	14%
Education learning by doing	62%	57%	92%	86%
Specialization in cost accounting only	3.93 ***	3.38	3.56 ***	2.83
Specialization in other business functions	3.71	3.69	3.86	3.76
Specialization by high qualification	5.15	4.95	4.18	3.99

Table 3-75: Mean comparisons of country-specifics between companies having installed cost accounting systems that are above and below average timeliness (data set 1)

The comparisons of means between companies scoring above and below average on the aggregated timeliness score (see Table 3-75) support the regression results. 'Focus on management accounting' and 'specialization in cost accounting only' are statistically higher and 'workload management over financial accounting' is lower for German companies being above average timeliness. For Japan, solely 'specialization in cost accounting only' is statistically significantly higher for above average companies. The remaining country-specifics hardly vary on a national level between companies that have either installed systems above or below average timeliness. The country-specifics vary even less between both groups than other external and internal context factors.

In section 2.3.5.2 it was hypothesized that company size has no impact upon cost accounting systems' timeliness (hypothesis H_{3c}) and that external dynamics (H_{2b}), IT systems quality (H_{3f}), and overall interest in cost accounting (H_{3h}) positively affect systems' timeliness. The enter regression models (see Table 3-74) show for the German sample that no significant association prevails between **external dynamics** and the aggregated timeliness score. Only for the single element 'cost rates for overhead allocation bases' a negative association prevails. For the Japanese sample external dynamics has a positive effect on the aggregated score for timeliness and on the scores for the single elements 'distinction fixed and variable costs', 'cost rates for overhead allocation bases', and 'product costs'. Hence, hypothesis H_{2b} is only accepted for Japan and rejected for Germany.

Furthermore, Table 3-74 shows that **company size** has no impact upon the aggregated and the single scores for timeliness for both countries. Hypothesis H_{3c} is therefore accepted for both countries.

IT systems quality has a positive and significant impact upon the aggregated timeliness score for Japan. For the Japanese data set all the single element scores except 'cost rates for support cost centers' and 'cost rates for overhead allocation bases' are positively associated with IT systems quality. Positive relationships also exist for German companies for the single element 'standard costs' and 'cost rates for overhead allocation bases' (see Table 3-74). Overall, hypothesis H_{3f} stating that IT systems quality positively affects the timeliness of cost accounting systems is accepted for both countries.

Top management support as an indicator for the overall interest in cost accounting is solely positively associated with the score for 'cost rates for overhead allocation bases' for the Japanese data set (see Table 3-74). No significant associations prevail at all for the German data set. Overall, hypothesis H_{3h} is rejected for both countries.

In section 2.3.5.3 it was hypothesized by H_{4h} that the importance of **decision facilitating** has a positive effect on cost accounting systems' timeliness. No association prevails for the German data set and the Japanese data set is only positively associated with the single score for 'distinction fixed and variable costs' (see Table 3-74). Due to little empirical evidence hypothesis H_{4h} is rejected for both countries. It is further assumed that **decision influencing** has no impact upon the timeliness of cost accounting systems (H_{4f}). The regression results show that decision influencing has a positive effect for Germany on the distinction between variable and fixed costs and it has a negative impact upon the score for product costs in Japan. Like for the two previous objectives no effect prevails for the aggregated scores. Due to the small number of significant results only hypothesis H_{4f} is accepted.

The results for the timeliness of cost accounting systems are summarized in Table 3-76. The hypotheses stating that company size has no impact upon the timeliness of cost accounting systems (H_{3c}) and that IT systems quality (H_{3h}) and the objective decision facilitating (H_{4f}) has a positive impact upon timeliness are accepted. Furthermore, a positive association between external dynamics and the timeliness of cost accounting systems (H_{2b}) is confirmed for the Japanese data set. The remaining influence factors are rejected. Although the multiple regression models explain less variance of systems' timeliness compared to systems' complexity, more hypotheses are accepted for the former. However, like for the complexity of cost accounting systems, it can be concluded that only few independent variables explain the timeliness of cost accounting systems and there is hardly any evidence that cost accounting systems are purposefully designed. Like for the complexity of cost accounting systems it is possible that inappropriate measures were applied, the data collection might be not accurate enough, and that the impact of single cost accounting objectives is difficult to extract.[1196]

Hypothesis		Result
H_{1p}	The more specialized cost accountants are, the timelier are cost accounting systems.	Rejected
H_{1r}	The more theoretical knowledge cost accountants have, the timelier are cost accounting systems.	Rejected
H_{2b}	The more dynamic the environment is, the timelier are cost accounting systems.	Rejected for Germany, accepted for Japan
H_{3c}	Company size does not affect the timeliness of cost accounting systems.	Accepted
H_{3f}	The higher IT systems quality, the timelier are cost accounting systems.	Accepted
H_{3h}	The higher the overall interest in cost accounting is, the timelier are cost accounting systems.	Rejected
H_{4f}	The more important decision facilitating is, the timelier are cost accounting systems.	Accepted
H_{4h}	The importance of decision influencing has no impact upon the timeliness of cost accounting systems.	Rejected

Table 3-76: Results of the hypotheses tests

3.4.3 Future development

By question C.13 (Appendix 2) the extent to which changes of cost accounting systems have taken place over the last three years was queried on a seven-point Likert scale (1 = not at all; 7 = very much). Cost accounting systems have changed significantly more intensively in Germany than in Japan. The cross-national results are stable for both data sets. Nonsignificant differences prevail between the German industries (see Table 3-77). Hence, stronger differences in **cost accounting change** prevail between both countries than across the three industries. This strong cross-national difference is surprising, because strong differences between industries were expected as well, since the necessity to install comprehensive cost accounting systems have emerged after 2003 for German and Japanese hospitals.

1196 Cf. section 3.4.1.2.

Development of cost accounting systems – comparisons of means	To what extent have changes of your cost accounting system taken place over the last three years? (1 = not at all; 7 = very much)						
Type of comparison	Country comparison				Industry comparison		
Data set	Data set 1		Data set 2		Data set 3		
	Germany	Japar	Germany	Japan	Food and beverage	Mechanical engineering	Hospitals
Means	3.89 ***	2.91	3.78 ***	2.91	4.01	3.78	3.83

Table 3-77: Development of cost accounting systems (data set 1)

Only 25% of all German companies and 9% of all Japanese companies of data set 1 have answered 6 or higher on a seven-point Likert scale (see Figure 3-40). The results show that in both countries only few companies have strongly altered their cost accounting systems. In Japan even 28% of the companies have not changed their cost accounting systems at all over the last three years.

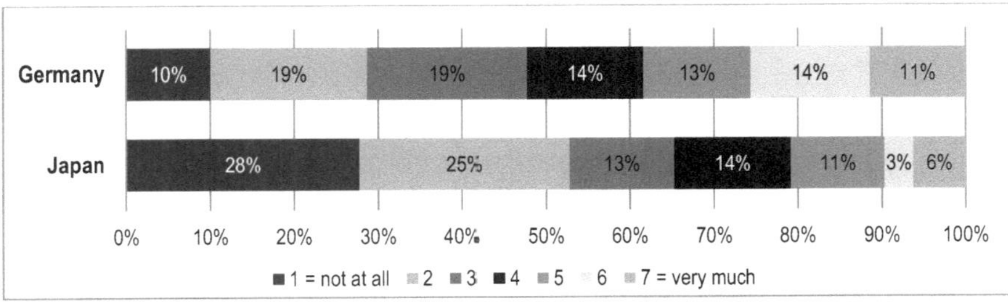

Figure 3-40: Development of cost accounting systems (data set 1)

The study by *Weber* has obtained similar results for large German companies. He found out that structural and strong changes in cost accounting occur rather seldom.[1197] This result is surprising, because prior research reports an increasing importance of cost accounting in Germany over time[1198] and that about 40% of German executives assess the quality of cost information as very poor.[1199] The results therefore suggest that cost accounting systems are insufficiently adapted to changes in the companies' environments.[1200]

By question C.14 it was surveyed whether cost accountants expect the accuracy, detail, timeliness, and understandability of cost information to decrease, remain the same, or to increase in the next three years. Between both countries and across the German industries only little variance prevails. In both countries and for all three industries less than 5% of the cost accountants believe that the **characteristics of cost information** will decrease. About 50% to 60% of the practitioners expect accuracy, detail, timeliness, and understandability to increase. The remaining respondents believe that the characteristics remain the same (see Table 3-78).

1197 Cf. *Weber* (1993), p. 275.
1198 Cf. *Weber* (1993), p. 268f.; *Friedl et al.* (2009a), p. 114; *Friedl et al.* (2009b), p. 47f.
1199 Cf. *Homburg et al.* (1998), p. 27-29.
1200 Similar conclusions are drawn for German companies by *Weber* (1993), p. 275.

Development of cost information – comparisons of frequencies	Please asses how the information provided by your cost accounting system will develop over the next three years.						
Type of comparison	Country comparison				Industry comparison		
Data set	Data set 1		Data set 2		Data set 3		
	Germany	Japan	Germany	Japan	Food and beverage	Mechanical engineering	Hospitals
Accuracy decreases	3%	4%	2%	3%	3%	2%	2%
Accuracy remains the same	44%	46%	47%	43%	39%	47%	38%
Accuracy increases	53%	50%	51%	54%	58%	51%	60%
Detail decreases	4%	3%	4%	2%	4%	4%	2%
Detail remains the same	38%	47%	43%	43%	35%	43%	31%
Detail increases	58%	50%	53%	56%	61%	53%	67%
Timeliness decreases	0%	1%	0%	2%	0%	0%	1%
Timeliness remains the same	47%	48%	47%	44%	48%	47%	45%
Timeliness increases	53%	51%	53%	54%	52%	53%	54%
Understandability decreases	0%	2%	0%	3%	0%	0%	1%
Understandability remains the same	44%	50%	43%	48%	44%	43%	44%
Understandability increases	56%	48%	57%	48%	56%	57%	55%

Table 3-78: Development of cost information

These results are similar to the findings by prior research: *Krumwiede/Suessmair* report that 58% of the German companies expect an increase in cost accounting systems' complexity, only 29% expect the complexity to stay the same, and only 6% expect a decrease.[1201] Also the studies by *Friedl et al.* and *Weber*, who have investigated large German companies, conclude that cost accounting systems will not become simpler in future.[1202] German companies have increased the number of cost centers over time[1203] and they plan to continue this in future.[1204] All cost accounting objectives investigated by *Friedl et al.* are expected to increase in importance, except precision for planning, which is expected to decline in importance.[1205] *Weber* shows for all cost accounting objectives he has investigated an increase in importance.[1206]

Empirical analyses do not indicate for data set 1 that those companies that have a more complex or timelier cost accounting system than expected[1207] have carried through more

1201 Cf. *Krumwiede/Suessmair* (2007a), p. 5; *Krumwiede/Suessmair* (2007b), p. 52.

1202 See *Weber* (1993), p. 268f.; *Friedl et al.* (2009a, 2009b).

1203 Cf. *Friedl et al.* (2009a), p. 112.

1204 Only very large German companies plan to decrease the number of cost centers. Cf. *Friedl et al.* (2009b), p. 47-49.

1205 Cf. *Friedl et al.* (2009a), p. 114-116; *Friedl et al.* (2009b), p. 47-49.

1206 Cf. *Weber* (1993), p. 268f.

1207 More or less complex cost accounting systems than expected, e.g., were identified by estimating the complexity score for each company separately by the enter regressions from section 3.4.1.2. Thereafter, the actual company's aggregated complexity score is subtracted by the estimated complexity score. Positive residuals indicate that companies have more complex cost accounting sys-

changes of their cost accounting system the last three years. Furthermore, those companies with a less complex and less timely cost accounting system than expected do not indicate to more likely increase the accuracy, detail, or timeliness of cost information than companies with a more complex and timelier cost accounting system than expected. These results indicate that companies from Germany and Japan that should increase the complexity or timeliness of their cost accounting systems do not plan to increase the accuracy, detail, and timeliness of their systems more intensively than other companies. Hence, the assumption of the contingency theory that companies adopt their cost accounting systems to their environments is not verified.

The responses to question C.13 and C.14 indicate that cost accounting systems have more intensively changed in German than in Japanese companies over the last three years. Furthermore, more German than Japanese cost accountants expect their cost accounting systems to provide more accurate, detailed, timely, and understandable cost information in future. It is thus expected that German companies remain to have more complex and timelier cost accounting systems than their Japanese counterparts – a **convergence** regarding the complexity and timeliness **is not expected**. The responses of Table 3-77 and Table 3-78 rather indicate a further divergence. Only a marginal convergence towards 'Anglophone' or 'international' management accounting is expected in literature, mainly in terms of abandoning imputed costs.[1208] The results from section 3.4.1.1.1.3 show, however, that many German medium-sized companies still apply imputed costs and that companies that are more exposed to globalization in terms of capital market orientation and IFRS adoption do not statistically significantly apply imputed costs to a lesser degree. These results support *Carr's* longitudinal study on strategic decision styles. He demonstrates that Japanese companies in general and German companies in particular exhibit deep-rooted differences from Anglo-Saxon practices implicating that cultural and institutional factors exert profound differences in management accounting.[1209] The only indication of convergence is that less German companies seem to determine their product costs only on a variable cost basis. This is reasonable, because in the context of globalization the German Commercial Code has been revised and since summer 2009 product costs have to be determined on a full cost basis.[1210]

Overall, the assumptions by *Granlund/Lukka* and *Shields* that management accounting systems converge internationally[1211] cannot be supported for German and Japanese medium-sized companies.

The performance of cost accounting systems is investigated in the following after the conceptual design of cost accounting systems has been analyzed. In particular the performance of cost accounting as well as recommendations for practitioners how to effectively

tems than expected. Negative residuals indicate the opposite. The same procedure was carried through for the timeliness of cost accounting systems.

1208 Cf. *Jones/Luther* (2005), p. 185; *Kajüter* (2008), p. 356.

1209 Cf. *Carr* (2005).

1210 See section 3.4.1.1.1.9.

1211 See *Granlund/Lukka* (1998); *Shields* (1998).

design cost accounting systems are compared between German and Japanese companies in the following section.

3.5 Performance of cost accounting systems

In section 3.5.1 the applied performance measures are determined. Thereafter, bivariate analyzes are conducted in section 3.5.2. This includes mean comparisons of the performance of cost accounting systems across countries, industries, and types of organizations. Furthermore, correlations among context factors, cost accounting objectives, the conceptual design of cost accounting systems, and the performance of cost accounting systems are determined. In section 3.5.3 multivariate analyses are conducted to investigate linear and non-linear relationships.

3.5.1 Determination of the applied performance measures

Performance was operationalized by the attainment of cost accounting objectives (questions D.3 to D.5, Appendix 2) and by the degree of satisfaction with the provided cost information (question D.1 and D.2).[1212] The attainment of cost accounting objectives and the degree of satisfaction with the provided cost information were determined on a seven-point Likert scale. Cost accountants were asked to assess to which extent the cost accounting objectives are met and to which extent they are satisfied with the cost information regarding accuracy, detail, timeliness, and understandability for managers. Furthermore, they were asked to assess how satisfied managers are overall with the provided cost information. A score of 1 indicates that a cost accounting system does not meet its objectives at all respectively that cost accountants and managers are not at all satisfied with the provided information. A score of 7 on the other side indicates that all cost accounting objectives are met respectively that cost accountants and managers are highly satisfied with the provided information.

Attainment of cost accounting objectives and the satisfaction indicators for accuracy, detail, timeliness, and understandability are each aggregated to factors. The **factor for attainment** of all 12 indicators for cost accounting objectives does not meet all quality criteria (see Table 3-79). As already argued in section 3.3, the variables 'pricing', 'short-term capacity planning', and 'inventory valuation' lack cross-industry comparability. The scores for indicator reliability for these three indicators are all below 0.5 for all three German data sets. The indicator 'inventory valuation' has only an indicator reliability of 0.322 and 0.222 for the German responses of data sets 1 and 2. A one-dimensional factor for all 12 indicators for cost accounting objectives does consequently not prevail.

1212 The profitability indicator, which was surveyed by question A.16 (cf. Appendix 2) is excluded from the statistical analysis. See section 3.1.2.3.

Data set	Analysis	Factor analysis				Reliability analysis
	Criteria	KMO-value	% of variance explained	Kaiser	Factor loadings (max; min)	Cronbach's Alpha
1	Germany	0.882	48.1%	5.77	0.790; 0.371	0.889
	Japan	0.929	73.7%	8.84	0.914; 0.737	0.966
2	Germany	0.896	50.0%	6.00	0.826; 0.280	0.898
	Japan	0.902	71.4%	8.57	0.810; 0.332	0.962

Table 3-79: Results of the factor analysis for performance attainment of objectives including all 12 indicators for cost accounting objectives

The factor for attainment of cost accounting objectives excluding the indicators 'pricing', 'short-term capacity planning', and 'inventory valuation' meets all quality criteria (see Table 3-80) and it is also highly comparable between Germany and Japan (see Table 3-81). This result supports the procedure from section 3.3 to exclude the three indicators 'pricing', 'short-term capacity planning', and 'inventory valuation' from the factor decision facilitating.

Data set	Analysis	Factor analysis				Reliability analysis
	Criteria	KMO-value	% of variance explained	Kaiser	Factor loadings (max; min)	Cronbach's Alpha
1	Germany	0.867	57.6%	5.19	0.811; 0.676	0.905
	Japan	0.903	77.3%	6.96	0.916; 0.837	0.963
2	Germany	0.878	58.1%	5.23	0.814; 0.625	0.906
	Japan	0.879	76.3%	6.87	0.896; 0.836	0.960

Table 3-80: Results of the factor analysis for performance attainment excluding the indicators pricing, capacity planning, and inventory valuation

Coefficient of congruence for factor attainment		
Data set	Data set 1	Data set 2
	0.9987	0.9979

Table 3-81: Coefficients of congruence for performance attainment of objectives

The **factor for satisfaction** meets all quality criteria for data set 1 and 2 (see Table 3-82) and it is highly comparable between both countries (see Table 3-83).

Data set	Analysis	Factor analysis				Reliability analysis
	Criteria	KMO-value	% of variance explained	Kaiser	Factor loadings (max; min)	Cronbach's Alpha
1	Germany	0.678	58.0%	2.32	0.819; 0.676	0.755
	Japan	0.813	76.4%	3.06	0.918; 0.821	0.895
2	Germany	0.722	60.5%	2.42	0.816; 0.702	0.780
	Japan	0.755	74.0%	2.96	0.889; 0.810	0.882

Table 3-82: Results of the factor analysis for satisfaction

Coefficient of congruence for satisfaction		
Data set	Data set 1	Data set 2
	0.9974	0.9996

Table 3-83: Coefficients of congruence for satisfaction

Besides 'factor attainment' and 'factor satisfaction', an alternative measure to 'factor attainment' is calculated: 'performance attainment'. This alternative is determined by weighting the performance of the indicators for cost accounting objectives by the extent to which they are met.[1213] Thereby, differences in the relevance of cost accounting objectives across companies and between countries can be considered for. A score of 7 for this measure indicates that all cost accounting objectives are met; 1 indicates that none of the objectives are met.[1214]

Performance measure	Application area
Performance attainment	Comparisons of means, correlations, multiple regressions
Factor attainment	Correlations, multiple regressions
Satisfaction – accuracy	Comparisons of means
Satisfaction – detail	Comparisons of means
Satisfaction – timeliness	Comparisons of means
Satisfaction – understandability for managers	Comparisons of means
Satisfaction overall	Comparisons of means, correlations, multiple regressions
Factor satisfaction	Correlations, multiple regressions

Table 3-84: Application areas of the performance measures

The analyses in sections 3.5.2 and 3.5.3 are not limited to factors, because both factors were determined separately for Germany and Japan and thus are normally distributed with a zero mean and unit standard deviation. Differences in mean across subgroups are thereby eliminated. Comparisons of means are therefore conducted by the measure 'performance attainment', by the four single indicators for satisfaction (accuracy, detail, timeliness, and understandability for managers), and by the managers overall satisfaction, which is labeled 'satisfaction overall'. For correlations and multiple regressions the measure 'performance attainment', the factors 'factor attainment' and 'factor satisfaction', and the single performance indicator 'satisfaction overall' are applied. The performance measures and their areas of application are summarized in Table 3-84.

3.5.2 Bivariate analysis

Hypotheses H_{1s}, H_{3n}, and H_{3o} respectively state that the **performance** of cost accounting systems **differs across countries, industries, and types of organizations.** Table 3-85 and Figure 3-41 show that all performance measures are higher for the German than for the Japanese data sets. This result, however, has to be treated with care. Unlike the relative cost accounting objectives (e.g., planning versus control) and the conceptual design of cost

1213 For an example see section 2.4.2.

1214 For the measure 'performance attainment' see section 2.4.2.

accounting systems, the performance measures are susceptible to biased results. Cost accountants were asked to assess the extent to which their systems meet cost accounting objectives and how satisfied they and managers are with the provided cost information. Furthermore, Japanese cost accountants might be more reserved than their German counterparts in assessing the performance of their cost accounting systems. The Japanese are known for their modesty instead of self-praise.[1215] As the results are stable for both data sets and for all measures, it is though overall concluded that German companies have more successful cost accounting systems than their Japanese counterparts.[1216] Hypothesis H_{1s} stating that the performance differs between Germany and Japan is therefore accepted.

Table 3-85 furthermore shows that the food and beverage and the mechanical engineering industry run more successful cost accounting systems than hospitals. Hence, cross-industry differences prevail between manufacturing and service industries. Hypothesis H_{3n} is consequently accepted. This result is reasonable, because the necessity to install comprehensive cost accounting systems has emerged after 2003 for German and Japanese hospitals. Furthermore, sophisticated instruments like GPK were originally developed for the manufacturing industry and may thus be less suitable for hospitals. For both reasons it is likely that cost accounting is less accepted and less purposefully designed in hospitals than in manufacturing industries.

Performance – comparisons of means							
Type of comparison	**Country comparison**				**Industry comparison**		
	Data set 1		**Data set 2**		**Data set 3**		
Data set	Germany	Japan	Germany	Japan	Food and beverage	Mechanical engineering	Hospitals
Performance attainment	4.81 ***	4.10	4.84 ***	4.32	4.88 **	4.84 **	4.60
Satisfaction – accuracy	5.34 ***	4.42	5.39 ***	4.71	5.31 **	5.39 **	4.98
Satisfaction – detail	5.23 ***	4.23	5.25 ***	4.53	5.34 ***	5.25 ***	4.70
Satisfaction – timeliness	5.32 ***	3.91	5.39 ***	4.08	5.33	5.39 *	4.90
Satisfaction – understandability for managers	4.93 ***	4.07	4.82 ***	4.14	5.01	4.82	4.77
Satisfaction overall	5.05 ***	3.83	5.07 ***	3.92	4.96	5.07 **	4.79

Table 3-85: Comparison of performance measures between countries and across industries

It is further assumed that the performance of cost accounting systems differs more strongly across industries than across countries (H_{6d}). Although the cross-national comparison of performance might lack equivalence due to differences in response style, it can be assessed that the performance of cost accounting systems varies more strongly across countries than across industries. Hence hypothesis H_{6d} is rejected. This result is not unexpected, because

1215 See *Lebra* (1998), p. 126-129. See also *Smith et al.* (2009), p. 121f.

1216 *Krumwiede/Suessmair* apply in their investigation different performance measures and conclude that German companies are more satisfied with their cost accounting systems than their US counterparts. Cf. *Krumwiede/Suessmair* (2007a), p. 4f.; *Krumwiede/Suessmair* (2007b), p. 51. The high satisfaction in cost accounting for German companies is supported by prior domestic research. See *Weber* (1993), p. 264f.; *Friedl et al.* (2009b), p. 47f.

the findings from sections 3.4.1.1.3 and 3.4.2.2 also show that the conceptual design of cost accounting does not differ more strongly across industries than between Germany and Japan as well.

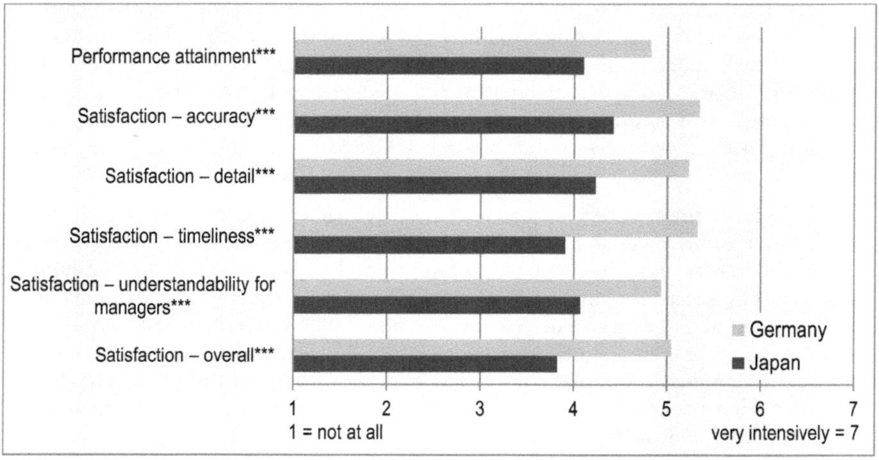

Figure 3-41: Comparison of performance measures between Germany and Japan (data set 1)

Accept for the cost characteristic 'timeliness' no significant differences prevail between the types of organizations (see Table 3-86). Due to this little empirical evidence, hypothesis H_{3o} is rejected. This outcome is reasonable, because similar cost accounting systems (cf. sections 3.4.1.1.3 and 3.4.2.3) are designed for similar cost accounting objectives (cf. section 3.3) across the three types of organizations. Hence, only few reasons exist why cost accounting systems should be more successful in one type of organization than in another.

	Satisfaction					Performance attainment
	Accuracy	Detail	Timeliness	Understandability for managers	Overall	
Private organizations	4.94	4.50	5.21 *	4.85	4.69	4.40
Public organizations	5.19	4.87	5.09 *	4.98	5.04	4.81
Charitable organizations	4.89	4.67	4.73	4.66	4.72	4.57

Table 3-86: Comparison of performance measures across types of organizations (hospitals of data set 3)

The **correlations** for the four performance measures 'performance attainment', 'factor attainment', 'factor satisfaction', and 'satisfaction overall' with the single scores for cost accounting systems' complexity and timeliness are provided in Table 3-87 and Table 3-88 respectively. The **complexity** scores for 'cost variance analysis', 'first stage allocation', and 'time reference of costs' have the strongest correlations with the four performance measures in both countries. This implies that the three elements are the most relevant ones in both countries for implementing successful cost accounting systems. The strong correlations can be explained by the German emphasis on operating performance and the prominence of continuous cost improvements in Japan. Cost variance analysis, which requires different cost types (e.g., actual and standard costs) for many products or services, support both objectives. Intensive transfers of costs from support cost centers to primary cost centers raise cost awareness as well. Table 3-87 furthermore shows that the complexity scores for 'operating income statement' and 'distinction fixed and variable costs' have stronger correlations with the performance measures in Japan than in Germany. Thus, both elements are expected to have a stronger impact upon the performance of cost accounting systems in Japan than in Germany. On the contrary, imputed costs and contribution margin accounting that are typical aspects of German cost accounting are stronger correlated with the performance measures in Germany and may thus lead to more successful cost accounting systems in Germany than in Japan. The score for imputed costs, however, is only very weakly correlated with performance in Germany and it is not correlated with performance in Japan. The low relevance of imputed costs may explain why it is suggested in German literature to abolish imputed costs.[1217] Surprisingly, operating income statements are more relevant in Japan compared to Germany, although this instrument is far more often applied in Germany.[1218]

The aggregated complexity score is statistically significantly correlated with the four performance measures in both countries. This indicates that the complexity of cost accounting leads to more successful systems. As in Japan stronger correlations prevail between the aggregated complexity score and the four performance measures, the correlations indicate that complexity has a stronger impact upon performance in Japan than in Germany.

Fewer statistically significant correlations prevail between the single **timeliness** scores and the four performance measures. For the German sample the most significant correlations exist for the scores 'distinction fixed and variable costs' and 'cost variances' (see Table 3-88). This can be explained by the German emphasis on operating efficiency, which requires timely cost information for facilitating and influencing decisions. In Japan the strongest correlations prevails for cost rates for overhead allocation bases. This can be explained by the Japanese practice to apply cost rates for overhead allocation bases for decision influencing.[1219] The aggregated timeliness score is four times statistically significantly correlated with the performance measures for Germany and two times for Japan. According to the correlations, the timeliness of cost accounting systems has a stronger impact upon performance for German than for Japanese companies.

1217 Cf. section 2.1.1.2.1.

1218 Cf. section 3.4.1.1.1.9.

1219 Cf. *Hiromoto* (1988), p. 22f.

	Number of cost types	Distinction fixed and variable costs	Imputed costs	Time reference of costs	Number of cost centers	Cost variance analysis	First stage allocation	Second stage allocation	Product costing	Operating income statement	Contribution margin accounting	Aggregated complexity score
Germany												
Performance attainment	0.095	0.187 ***	0.142 **	0.323 ***	-0.008	0.428 ***	0.324 ***	0.089	0.148 **	0.171 ***	0.236 ***	0.269 ***
Factor attainment	0.118 *	0.202 ***	0.149 **	0.377 ***	0.039	0.463 ***	0.319 ***	0.108	0.163 **	0.212 ***	0.274 ***	0.301 ***
Factor satisfaction	-0.025	0.135 **	0.113 *	0.308 ***	-0.068	0.313 ***	0.354 ***	0.054	-0.016	0.114 *	0.162 ***	0.201 ***
Satisfaction overall	-0.053	0.164 ***	0.081	0.240 ***	-0.009	0.240 ***	0.269 ***	0.050	-0.038	0.138 **	0.044	0.174 ***
Japan												
Performance attainment	-0.050	0.343 ***	0.033	0.419 ***	0.024	0.417 ***	0.400 ***	0.066	0.183 **	0.255 ***	0.153	0.424 ***
Factor attainment	-0.001	0.399 ***	0.056	0.452 ***	0.036	0.455 ***	0.409 ***	0.130	0.145	0.325 ***	0.072	0.505 ***
Factor satisfaction	0.059	0.289 ***	0.001	0.248 ***	0.024	0.426 ***	0.474 ***	0.058	0.147	0.230 ***	0.089	0.399 ***
Satisfaction overall	-0.016	0.183 **	-0.065	0.233 ***	-0.006	0.308 ***	0.393 ***	0.059	0.114	0.244 ***	0.192	0.295 ***

Table 3-87: Correlations between single elements of cost accounting systems' complexity and performance measures (data set 1)

	Distinction fixed and variable costs	Standard costs	Cost variances	Cost rates for support cost centers	Cost rates for overhead allocation bases	Product costs	Operating income statement	Aggregated timeliness score
Germany								
Performance attainment	0.141 **	0.008	0.201 ***	-0.020	0.075	0.052	0.052	0.132 **
Factor attainment	0.159 **	0.021	0.279 ***	0.016	0.074	0.093	0.093	0.165 **
Factor satisfaction	0.148 **	0.136 **	0.182 ***	0.080 ***	0.235 ***	0.166 ***	0.166 ***	0.297 ***
Satisfaction overall	0.030	0.130 **	0.130 **	0.054 ***	0.088	0.020	0.020	0.163 ***
Japan								
Performance attainment	0.124	-0.004	0.142	0.112	0.215 **	0.190 *	0.190 *	0.208 **
Factor attainment	0.141	0.000	0.128	0.090	0.232 **	0.162	0.162	0.219 **
Factor satisfaction	0.110	-0.001	0.064	0.112	0.092	0.117	0.117	0.134
Satisfaction overall	0.166 *	0.057	0.151	0.098	0.097	0.152	0.152	0.160

Table 3-88: Correlations between single elements of cost accounting systems' timeliness and performance measures (data set 1)

Besides group comparisons, it is also investigated when cost accounting systems are successful. Not all surveyed context factors were selected for multiple regression analysis (see section 3.2.4). The hypotheses that are based on the excluded context factors are therefore tested in the following by correlations. Hypothesis H_{4m} states that cost accounting systems are less successful, the more important the cost accounting objective '**financial accounting**' is. Table 3-89 shows for Germany that a strong emphasis on financial accounting has a negative impact upon the performance of cost accounting systems. For Japan no significant relations are identified.[1220] Hence, hypothesis H_{4m} is accepted for Germany and rejected for Japan. One reason for the negative effect of the financial accounting objective in Germany could be that German companies emphasize accurate and detailed cost information and try to avoid distortions stemming from financial accounting (see section 2.1.1.2.1). However, the more important cost accounting is for financial accounting, the less relevant are accurate and detailed cost information.

	Performance attainment	Factor attainment	Factor satisfaction	Satisfaction overall
Germany				
Financial over management accounting objectives	-0.257 ***	-0.252 ***	-0.050	-0.150 **
Japan				
Financial over management accounting objectives	0.014	0.050	-0.026	-0.059 ***

Table 3-89: Correlations between financial over management accounting objectives and performance indicators

1220 The relative measure 'financial over management accounting objectives' is chosen instead of the single financial accounting objective 'inventory valuation' to cancel out potential biases that stem from response style. Cf. section 3.3.

The results for the performance of cost accounting systems are summarized in Table 3-90. Germans have more successful cost accounting systems than their Japanese counterparts (H_{1s}). Furthermore, also cross-industry differences in cost accounting prevails (H_{3n}), however, the hypothesis that cross-industry differences are stronger than the differences in performance between Germany and Japan (H_{6d}) is rejected. The results of the bivariate analyses show that for German companies a stronger emphasis on financial accounting leads to less successful cost accounting systems (H_{4m}).

Hypothesis		Result
H_{1s}	The performance of cost accounting systems differs across countries.	Accepted
H_{3n}	The performance of cost accounting systems differs across industries.	Accepted
H_{3o}	The performance of cost accounting systems differs across private, public, and charitable organizations.	Accepted
H_{4m}	The more important cost accounting is for financial accounting purposes, the less successful are cost accounting systems.	Rejected
H_{6d}	The performance of cost accounting objectives differs more strongly across industries than across countries.	Rejected

Table 3-90: Results of the hypotheses tests

3.5.3 Multivariate analysis

3.5.3.1 Multiple regression analysis of linear relationships

Multiple regression analyses are carried through for the four performance measures to determine the effect of the 14 context factors, the complexity and timeliness of cost accounting systems, and the ABC complexity score. The ABC complexity score is included in the regressions, because it measures systems' complexity differently to the complexity score for cost accounting systems. Furthermore, both measures for complexity are, in particular for the German sample, only weakly correlated.[1221] The four cost accounting objectives that are applied to explain the complexity and timeliness of cost accounting systems are not considered, because two of the four performance measures ('performance attainment' and 'factor attainment') are based on the attainment of cost accounting objectives. All regressions are calculated separately for Germany and Japan. The German and Japanese enter regression models for data set 1 meet all quality criteria. The adjusted R^2 lie between 0.271 and 0.422 for Germany and between 0.373 and 0.561 for Japan (see Appendix 11 to Appendix 14). These models thereby explain more variance than prior research has obtained.[1222] The results are summarized in Table 3-91. The effects of the independent variables upon the four performance measures are summarized in the last two columns. The number of '+' and '-' indicates to how many performance measures the independent variable is positively respectively negatively associated.

1221 Cf. Table 3-66, p. 284.

1222 *Pizzini* obtains for relevance and use of cost information adjusted R^2 of 0.228 and 0.125 respectively. See *Pizzini* (2006), p. 196. *Schoute* attains adjusted R^2 of 0.286 and 0.093 for intensity of use of cost information and for satisfaction respectively. See *Schoute* (2009), p. 218f.

Nishimura argues that specialization has a different role in Western countries than in Japan. Whereas in the Western countries it is believed that specialization raises efficiency, cooperation through multi-skilling and personal responsibility for plural sections of a production line lie at the heart of management in Japan.[1223] The results of this study support *Nishimura's* argument for cost accounting. The results show that a higher **specialization** of cost accountants has a positive impact upon the performance of cost accounting systems in Germany, but not in Japan. 'Focus on management accounting' is positively associated with one performance measure, 'specialization in cost accounting only' is positively associated with three measures, 'specialization in other business functions' that measures the opposite of specialization is negatively associated with one measure, and 'specialization by high qualification' is positively associated with two performance measures for the German responses of data set 1.

The results from section 3.2.1.3 show that Japanese cost accountants are less theoretically educated and more educated at work than their German counterparts. The results from Table 3-91 indicate that **theoretical education** has a positive impact upon the performance of cost accounting systems for Japan but not for Germany. 'Education at university' is positively associated with two performance measures and 'education professional institutes' is positively associated with one measure for performance for the Japanese responses of data set 1. It is thus suspected that theoretical education has a positive impact upon the performance of cost accounting for countries where the theoretical education of cost accountants is rather low.

Large companies have more resources to install more comprehensive cost accounting systems and thereby have a higher potential to satisfy the providers and users of cost information. However, employees in large companies might have higher expectations,[1224] because cost accounting systems have to reflect more aspects of the companies' realities and because more coordination and communication is required. It can therefore be expected that **company size** has no impact upon the performance of cost accounting systems.[1225] Two of the four Japanese enter regression models, however, show a significant and positive relation between company size and performance. No significant relationships are identified for the German sample (see Table 3-91). This result may indicate that small Japanese companies have difficulties to install and run cost accounting systems, because of the Japanese education and employment system. As Japanese cost accountants are more intensively educated in-house than their German counterparts (see section 3.2.1.3) and as they are probably also more loyal to their companies, these particularities may hamper small Japanese companies to build up comprehensive knowledge in cost accounting. In Germany on the contrary, smaller companies can more easily acquire knowledge in cost accounting by employing staff that is either trained by university or by other companies.

1223 Cf. *Nishimura* (2003), p. 60f.

1224 Cf. *Lange/Schauer* (1996), p. 208.

1225 *Zimmermann*, for instance, does not report a significant relationship between company size of small and medium-sized companies and the performance of management accounting systems. Cf. *Zimmermann* (2001), p. 405-407.

Dependent variables / Data set 1	Performance attainment		Factor attainment		Factor satisfaction		Satisfaction overall		Summary	
Independent variables	Germany	Japan	Germany	Japan	Germany	Japan	Germany	Japan	Germany	Japan
Workload management over financial accounting										
Focus management accounting							0.348 **		+	
Focus education management accounting										
Education university		0.193 **		0.211 **						++
Education professional insitutes						0.203 *				+
Education in-house training										
Education learning by doing										
Specialization in cost accounting only	0.213 *		0.293 **				0.212 *		+++	
Specialization in other business functions	-0.187 *							-0.214 *	-	-
Qualified to run and enhance systems	0.216 *				0.248 **				++	
Factor top management support	0.246 **	0.376 ***		0.367 ***		0.352 **		0.543 ***	+	++++
Factor external dynamics										
Factor company size		0.222 ***		0.249 **						++
Factor IT systems quality		0.223 *		0.206 *		0.293 **	0.19 *		+	++
Complexity of cost accounting systems	0.437 ***		0.462 ***						++	
ABC Score		0.259 **								+
Timeliness of cost accounting systems		0.348 ***		0.282 **		0.231 *	-0.217 *	0.258 *	-	++++

Table 3-91: Summary of regression analyses of cost accounting systems' performance (data set 1)

A positive association between IT systems quality and performance (H_{3m}) is expected. Table 3-91 shows for one German and two Japanese regressions a positive impact of **IT systems quality** upon the performance of cost accounting systems. Consequently, hypothesis H_{3m} is accepted for both countries.

The findings further show that **top management support** has a stronger impact upon systems' performance in Japan than in Germany. One reason for this cross-national difference could be that a diminishing marginal utility of top management support for cost accounting systems prevails. The results from section 3.2.3.4 demonstrate that German cost accountants obtain more political support and more resources than their Japanese counterparts, wherefore the higher degree of top management support may lead to smaller increases in performance.

It was hypothesized that the **complexity** (H_{5a}) **and** the **timeliness of cost accounting systems** (H_{5b}) have both a positive effect upon the performance of cost accounting systems. The results from Table 3-91 show that systems' complexity is positively associated in two out of four regressions for German companies, the ABC complexity score is positively associated in one regression for Japanese companies, timeliness of cost accounting systems is negatively associated in one regression for the German sample and positively associated for all four regressions for the Japanese sample. Overall, the findings support that complexity of cost accounting systems has a positive impact upon performance in Germany and timeliness has a positive impact in Japan. Consequently, hypothesis H_{5a} is accepted for Germany and H_{5b} is accepted for Japan. The results demonstrate that complexity is more relevant in Germany and that timeliness is more relevant in Japan.[1226] The findings are consistent with the conclusions from section 2.1.1 that German companies rather prefer complex and Japanese companies rather prefer timely cost accounting systems.

The effect of complexity and timeliness upon the performance of cost accounting systems is more comprehensively analyzed in the following two sections by considering contextual conditions and cost accounting objectives to investigate non-linear relationships.

3.5.3.2 Analysis of interaction effects

In section 2.4.3 it was hypothesized that complex cost accounting systems are more successful for companies with a complex external environment (**H_{5e}**). As the factors for external complexity do not meet the quality criteria, the hypothesis is not tested. Hypothesis H_{5e} therefore remains unanswered.

Hypotheses H_{5f} states that timely cost accounting systems are more successful for companies in a dynamic external environment. **Hypothesis H_{5m}** states that cost accounting systems that are both high or low in complexity and timeliness are less successful. Both hypotheses are not concerned with a linear and additive effect of two independent variables

1226 These results are in contrast to the correlations provided in Table 3-87 and Table 3-88. The aggregated timeliness score is more strongly correlated to the performance measures for the German companies and the aggregated complexity score is more strongly correlated to the performance measure for the Japanese companies.

on the performance of cost accounting systems. Instead, they address non-linear relationships. The non-linear relationships can be investigated by integrating interaction terms into regressions.[1227] 14 context factors[1228] as well as systems' complexity and timeliness and the ABC complexity score are applied as control variables. To test interaction effects the interacting variables are standardized. Thereafter, interaction terms are determined by multiplying the interacting variables with each other. In hypothesis H_{5f} it is expected that when external dynamics is high (low), a more (less) timely cost accounting system is required. Hence, a positive product of the interaction term (timeliness x external dynamics) for a company states that both variables are either both positive or both negative and should thus have a positive impact on performance. When the product is negative, it shows that both variables are not properly aligned, which should have a negative impact on performance. Hypothesis H_{5m} states that when a cost accounting system's complexity is high (low), a less (more) timely cost accounting system is required. A positive product, which means that a cost accounting system is both above average complexity and timeliness, should consequently have a negative impact upon performance. A negative product means that either the system's complexity or timeliness is above average and the other dimension is below average. A negative product should have a positive impact on performance.

None of the interaction terms has a significant impact upon any performance measure for Germany. Also the results for Japan indicate that cost accounting systems are not adapted to the external environment. For Japan, however, both satisfaction measures show that high complexity and high timeliness misfit (see Table 3-92). This result indicates that successful Japanese companies do not run cost accounting systems that are both high or low in complexity and timeliness. Hypotheses H_{5f} and H_{5m} are consequently rejected for Germany and for Japan H_{5f} is rejected and H_{5m} is accepted. It was expected that complex and timely cost accounting systems misfit, because the more complex cost accounting systems are, the more expensive it becomes to update all cost information. As cost accountants in Japan have less comprehensive IT systems and receive less top management support than their Japanese counterparts,[1229] the results may show that Japanese cost accountants face stronger pressures to make a compromise between the complexity and timeliness of cost accounting systems.

1227 See *Aiken/West* (1991).

1228 The context factors include 'workload management over financial accounting', 'focus on management accounting', 'focus on management accounting education', 'education university', 'education professional institutes', 'education in-house training', 'education learning by doing', 'specialization in cost accounting only', 'specialization in other business functions', 'specialization by high qualification', factor external dynamics, factor company size, factor IT systems quality, and factor top management support.

1229 See sections 3.2.1.3 and 3.2.3.4.

Data set 1 / Dependent variables	Performance attainment		Factor attainment		Factor satisfaction		Satisfaction overall	
Country	Germany	Japan	Germany	Japan	Germany	Japan	Germany	Japan
Linear regression method	Enter	Enter	Enter	Enter	Enter	Enter	Enter	Enter
R	0.581	0.671	0.646	0.697	0.688	0.715	0.667	0.719
R^2	0.338	0.451	0.418	0.485	0.473	0.512	0.445	0.517
adjusted R^2	0.185	0.332	0.254	0.352	0.348	0.407	0.312	0.414
F	2.202	3.794	2.556	3.653	3.763	4.909	3.357	5.018
Significance	0.013	0.000	0.005	0.000	0.000	0.000	0.000	0.000
VIF_{max}	1.891	2.135	2.213	2.326	1.868	2.225	1.871	2.225
Durbin-Watson statistic	2.253	1.400	2.344	1.474	2.202	2.120	1.636	1.827
Independent variables	**Standardized coefficients (Beta)**							
Systems' timeliness * external dynamics	-0.170	0.134	-0.047	0.124	-0.090	0.070	0.059	0.005
Systems' complexity * systems' timeliness	0.127	-0.086	0.159	-0.097	-0.044	-0.190 **	-0.090	-0.158 *

Table 3-92: Interaction effects of timeliness with external dynamics and complexity (data set 1)

The hypotheses H_{5g}, H_{5i}, and H_{5k} state respectively that complex cost accounting systems are more successful, when cost accounting serves rather decision facilitating than decision influencing objectives, short-term than long-term objectives, and management than financial accounting objectives. It is further hypothesized that timely cost accounting systems are more successful, when cost accounting serves rather decision facilitating than decision influencing objectives, short-term than long-term objectives, and management than financial accounting objectives (hypotheses H_{5h}, H_{5j}, and H_{5l}). For this analysis, the relative importance of cost accounting objectives from section 3.3 is applied.[1230] The interaction terms are determined by multiplying the standardized score for **complexity respectively timeliness of cost accounting systems with** (standardized values for) **the relative importance of decision facilitating over decision influencing objectives, short-term over long-term objectives, and management over financial accounting objectives**. The interaction effects are simultaneously determined and regressed on all four performance measures for Germany and Japan. The same control variables like in section 3.4.1.2 are applied but not included in the table. Table 3-93 shows that many results are opposite to the hypotheses for data set 1 and that those results that support the hypotheses are not stable for data set 2. Overall, it cannot be supported that German and Japanese companies purposefully align the conceptual design of their cost accounting systems with cost accounting objectives. All six hypotheses are therefore rejected.

Normative literature strongly argues that the conceptual design of cost accounting systems should differ to meet the intended objectives.[1231] These results, however, do not confirm that cost accounting systems are purposefully designed. One reason for this unexpected result is that the large majority of companies has not only one cost accounting system, from which different types of cost information are provided for different objectives. Cost accountants have therefore to make a compromise between different cost accounting objectives.

Hence, those cost accounting objectives that are more relevant may have a stronger impact upon the design of cost accounting systems. Those objectives that require, e.g., more accurate and detailed cost information, might encourage cost accountants to install more complex cost accounting systems. However, other objectives that do not require detailed cost information would not necessarily encourage cost accountants to install less complex cost accounting systems, because less cost information could be extracted from the existing system to fulfill these objectives. Studies analyzing the impact of cost accounting objectives might therefore only identify, if at all, small effects on cost accounting systems.

1230 By applying relative objectives, cross-national equivalence is increased and the drawback that the measure 'factor attainment' and 'performance attainment' are related to cost accounting objectives is avoided.

1231 Cf. *Player/Keys* (1995); *Cokins* (2001).

Data set 1 — Dependent variables	Performance attainment		Factor attainment		Factor satisfaction		Satisfaction overall		Summary	
Independent variables	**Germany**	**Japan**	**Germany**	**Japan**	**Germany**	**Japan**	**Germany**	**Japan**	**Germany**	**Japan**
Systems' complexity * facilitating over influencing			0.292 ***						+	
Systems' complexity * short-term over long-term			0.182 *		-0.247 **				+/-	
Systems' complexity * management over financial accounting				-0.231 *				-0.296 **		--
Systems' timeliness * facilitating over influencing	-0.190 **		-0.274 ***						--	
Systems' timeliness * short-term over long-term			-0.199 *	0.328 **			-0.358 ***		--	+
Systems' timeliness * management over financial accounting		0.316 *		0.515 ***				0.378 **		+++
Data set 2										
Independent variables	**Germany**	**Japan**	**Germany**	**Japan**	**Germany**	**Japan**	**Germany**	**Japan**	**Germany**	**Japan**
Systems' complexity * facilitating over influencing			-0.402 *	0.290 *				0.354 *	-	++
Systems' complexity * short-term over long-term		-0.413 ***		-0.365 **				-0.364 **	-	--
Systems' complexity * management over financial accounting					-0.327 **				-	
Systems' timeliness * facilitating over influencing		-0.500 ***		-0.488 ***				-0.348 *		---
Systems' timeliness * short-term over long-term				0.314 *	0.313 **			0.331 *	+	++
Systems' timeliness * management over financial accounting	-0.455 ***		-0.389 **						--	

Table 3-93: Interaction effects of complexity and timeliness with cost accounting objectives (data set 1 and 2)

3.5.3.3 Analysis of diminishing marginal utility of systems' complexity and timeliness

The results from section 3.5.3.1 show that the complexity of cost accounting systems has a positive impact upon performance in Germany and that the timeliness of cost accounting systems has a positive impact upon performance in Japan. In this section the hypotheses H_{5c} and H_{5d} are analyzed. They state that a **diminishing marginal utility of complexity and timeliness of cost accounting systems** prevails. *Kajüter*[1232] shows that implementing a higher number of cost management instruments improves carrying through cost management. However, with a graphical analysis he indicates that with a higher number of instruments the exploitation of their potential and thereby the support for carrying through cost management decreases. In a more comprehensive way, non-linear relationships between complexity respectively timeliness of cost accounting systems and performance measures are investigated in this study. A diminishing marginal utility of cost accounting systems' complexity and timeliness cannot be investigated with a simple linear regression line. Hypotheses H_{5c} and H_{5d} are therefore tested with specific *mathematical* and *graphical analyses.*

For the **mathematical analysis** *Pizzini's* approach is followed.[1233] The aggregated complexity and timeliness scores for each company are estimated separately for Germany and Japan by applying multiple regression analysis following the proceedings from sections 3.4.1.2 and 3.4.2.3. Thereafter, the actual company's aggregated complexity and timeliness scores are subtracted by the estimated complexity and timeliness scores. Positive residuals indicate that the respective companies employ more complex respectively timelier cost accounting systems under the given operating environment and the cost accounting objectives than expected; they are denoted with the variables 'more complex' and 'timelier'. These variables are identical with the residual, when the residual is positive. Otherwise they are zero. Similarly, negative values indicate that the respective cost accounting systems are relatively less complex respectively less timely given the operating environment and cost accounting objectives; they are denoted with the variables 'less complex' and 'less timely'. Both variables equal the absolute value of the residual, when it is negative. Otherwise they are zero. The four variables 'more complex', 'less complex', 'timelier', and 'less timely' are included in the multiple regression analysis. *Pizzini's* approach has two advantages:

> *"First, it does not constrain the coefficients on the functionality measures to be the same regardless of whether a system has relatively 'too much' or 'too little' functional capability. Second, the approach provides a partial control for endogeneity by modeling cost-system functionally as a function of a number of exogenous variables."*[1234]

1232 Cf. *Kajüter* (2005), p. 96f.

1233 Cf. *Pizzini* (2006), p. 200. He has, however, not developed his approach to investigate non-linear relationships between the functionality of cost accounting systems and their performance.

1234 *Pizzini* (2006), p. 200.

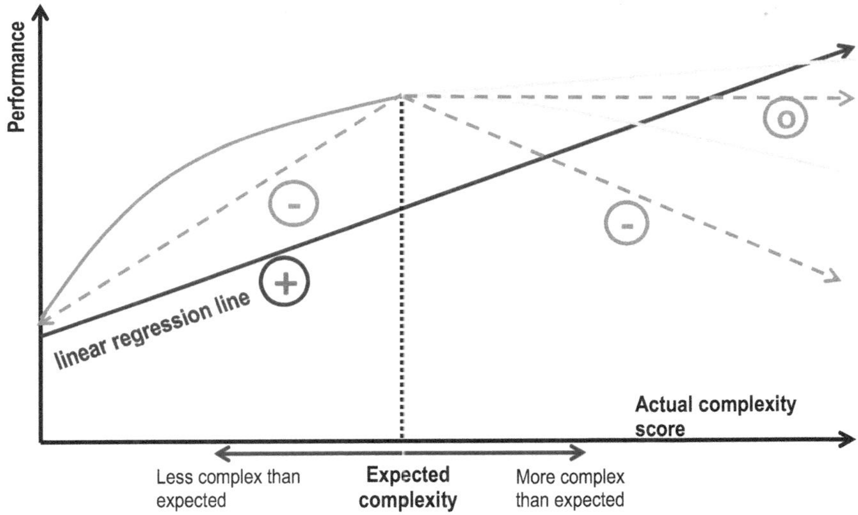

Figure 3-42: Rationale of the mathematical analysis for a diminishing marginal utility of complexity respectively timeliness of cost accounting systems

Figure 3-42 shows that a diminishing marginal utility of cost accounting systems' complexity and timeliness can be identified with this approach, when less complex respectively less timely cost accounting systems have a negative impact on the performance of cost accounting systems and more complex and timelier cost accounting systems have a nonsignificant influence on performance. When more complex and timelier cost accounting systems have a negative influence on performance, the analysis indicates that increasing the complexity and timeliness of cost accounting systems can even have a negative impact on performance. This can occur, when its users are overstrained by the amount of information and/or when cost accountants spend too much time to find theoretically sound solutions in cost accounting instead of discussing the provided information with their managers.[1235]

The **results** for data set 1 (see Table 3-94) illustrate that for Japan more complex and timelier systems lead to more successful cost accounting systems and less complex and less timely systems lead to less successful systems. For data set 2 only more complex cost accounting systems lead to more successful cost accounting systems for all four performance measures. For data set 2 this relationship is stronger than for data set 1. No significant results prevail for Germany. Hence, unlike for Germany, the mathematical analysis shows that a rather linear instead of a non-linear relationship between complexity respectively timeliness with cost accounting systems' performance prevails in Japan. Overall, a diminishing marginal utility of cost accounting systems' complexity and timeliness cannot be

1235 Literature indicates that this might be the case for German companies. See *Ahrens/Chapman* (1999), p. 43; *Weber* (2004), p. 9.

supported for both countries with the mathematical analysis. For this reason graphical analyses are carried through in the following, which investigate the non-linear relationship in a more detailed way.

Data set 1	Dependent variables: Performance attainment		Factor attainment		Factor satisfaction		Satisfaction overall		Summary	
Independent variables	Germany	Japan	Germany	Japan	Germany	Japan	Germany	Japan	Germany	Japan
More complex				0,205 *						+
Less complex						-0,187 *				-
More timely						0,231 **				+
Less timely		-0,184 *		-0,249 **						--
Data set 2										
Independent variables	Germany	Japan	Germany	Japan	Germany	Japan	Germany	Japan	Germany	Japan
More complex		0,211 *		0,304 **		0,441 ***		0,354 ***		++++
Less complex										
More timely										
Less timely										

Table 3-94: Mathematical analysis of non-linear relationships between systems' complexity respectively timeliness and performance measures (data set 1 and 2)

For the **graphical analysis** the actual scores for systems' complexity are compared with the estimated ones. For this analysis, however, the actual ($complexity_i^{actual}$) and estimated scores ($complexity_i^{estimated}$) are taken to the binary logarithm for each company before subtraction.

$$\Delta \text{ complexity} = \ln (complexity_i^{actual}) - \ln (complexity_i^{estimated})$$

This adjustment increases accuracy, because the relative variance between actual and estimated values can be determined.[1236] German and Japanese companies are split into two groups, those that have a positive score (i.e. those that have a more complex cost accounting system than expected) and those that have a negative score. Both groups are further split at the center to overall distinguish four groups: far less complex (--), less complex (-), more complex (+), and far more complex (++). Thereafter, the arithmetic mean scores for the standardized performance measures are determined for each group.

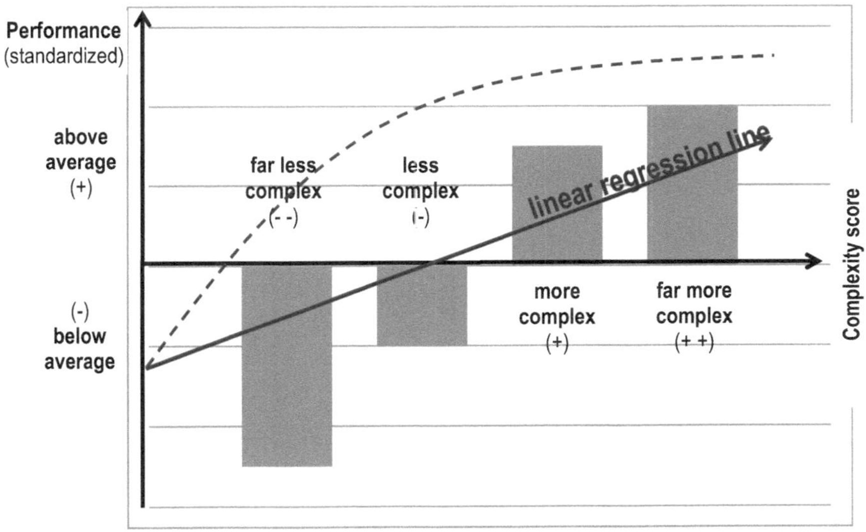

Figure 3-43: Rationale of the graphical analysis for a diminishing marginal utility of complexity respectively timeliness of cost accounting systems

When the arithmetic means for the standardized performance measures resemble those from Figure 3-43, a diminishing marginal utility of cost accounting systems' complexity prevails. The curved line visualizes the expected diminishing marginal utility of cost ac-

1236 The following example shall demonstrate the benefit to take the values to the binary logarithm. The estimated complexity score is 0.4 and the actual score is 0.1 for company A and 1 respectively 0.7 for company B. The absolute distance between estimated and actual scores are the same for both companies, however, company A is relatively farer away from the estimated score than company B. To account for the relative distance between estimated and actual scores, the scores are consequently taken to the binary logarithm first.

counting systems' complexity. The same procedure is carried through for the timeliness of cost accounting systems.

For reasons of clarity the diminishing marginal utility of systems' complexity and timeliness is limited to the measure 'performance attainment' and 'factor satisfaction'. Both measure performance differently and they are more comprehensive than the omitted measures 'factor attainment' and 'satisfaction overall': 'Factor attainment' does not consider that the relevance of cost accounting objectives might differ internationally and 'satisfaction overall' was only measured by a single question. As 'factor attainment' is highly correlated to 'performance attainment' (r = 0.986*** and 0.994*** for the German and Japanese responses from data set 1 respectively) and 'satisfaction overall' is highly correlated to 'factor satisfaction' (r = 0.594*** respectively 0.686***), similar results were obtained for the omitted performance measures.

The **results** for data set 1 and 2 are plotted in the following figures. The black curve in each diagram symbolizes the trend of all included bars between complexity respectively timeliness and performance. It is a trend line of a second degree polynomial.

Three out of four performance indicators demonstrate a diminishing marginal utility of cost accounting systems' complexity for the German data set 1 and 2 (see Figure 3-44). For data set 1, however, the performance measure 'factor satisfaction' shows that companies with far less complex systems are surprisingly the most satisfied ones.

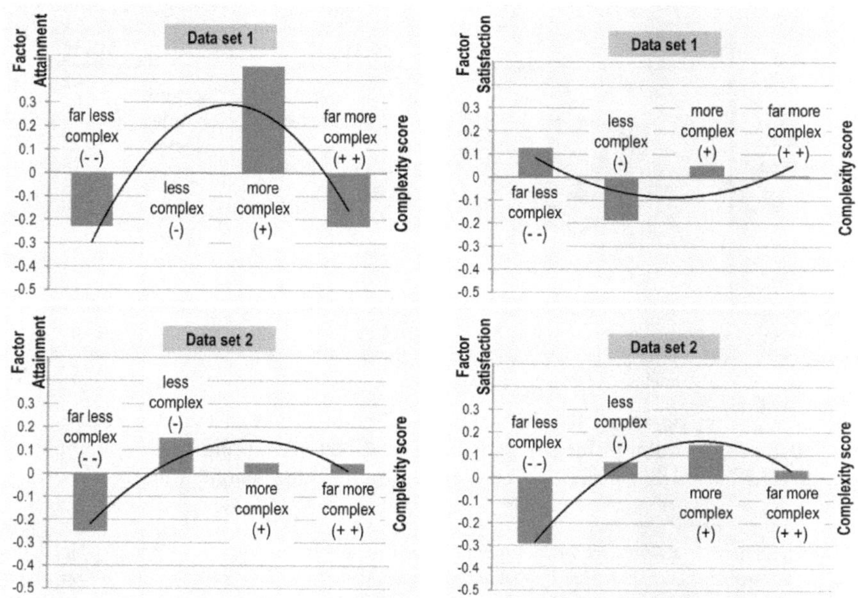

Figure 3-44: Graphical analysis for systems' complexity of German companies (data set 1 and 2)

Figure 3-45 shows that also for Japan three out of four performance measures indicate a diminishing marginal utility of cost accounting systems' complexity for data set 1 and 2.

The performance measure 'factor satisfaction', however, shows that for mechanical engineering companies (data set 2) the performance of cost accounting systems continuously increases with systems' complexity.

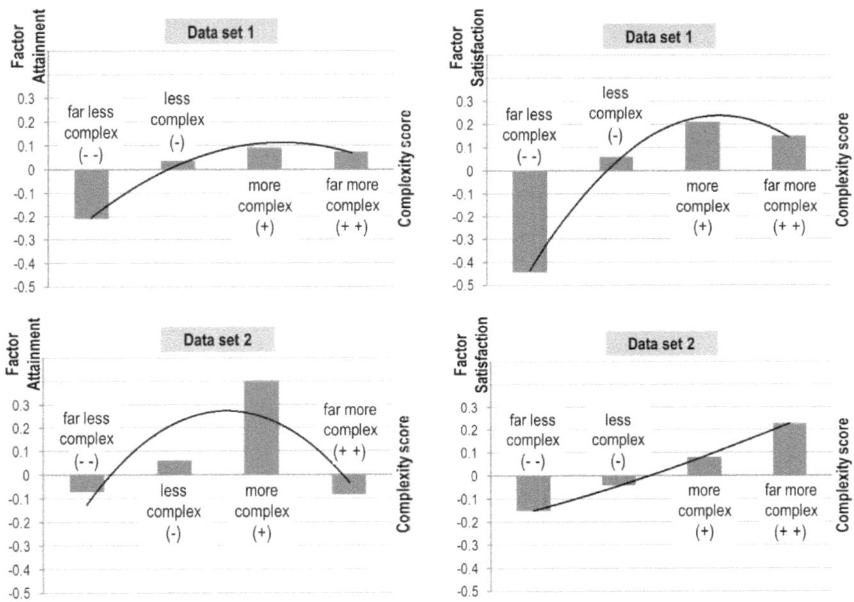

Figure 3-45: Graphical analysis for systems' complexity of Japanese companies (data set 1 and 2)

None of the performance measures indicate a diminishing marginal utility of cost accounting systems' timeliness for the German sample for data set 1 and 2 (see Figure 3-46). A consistent relationship between timeliness and performance does not prevail across both data sets and both types of performance indicators.

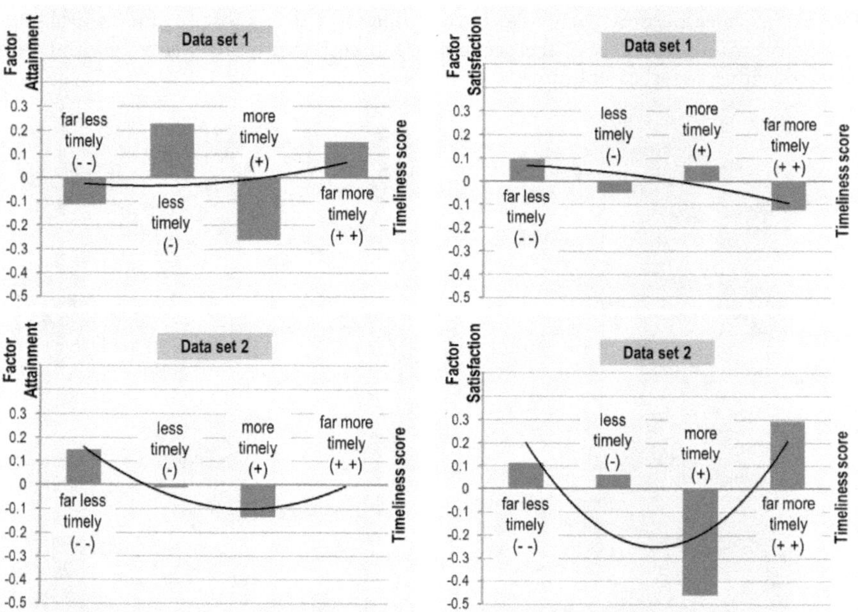

Figure 3-46: Graphical analysis for systems' timeliness of German companies (data set 1 and 2)

In contrast to the German sample, Figure 3-47 shows that three out of four performance measures indicate a diminishing marginal utility of cost accounting systems' complexity for the Japanese data set 1 and 2. The performance measure 'factor satisfaction' for data set 2, however, surprisingly show that Japanese companies having installed the least timely cost accounting systems are the second most satisfied with their cost accounting system. Apart from this group, the satisfaction increases the timelier the cost accounting system is.

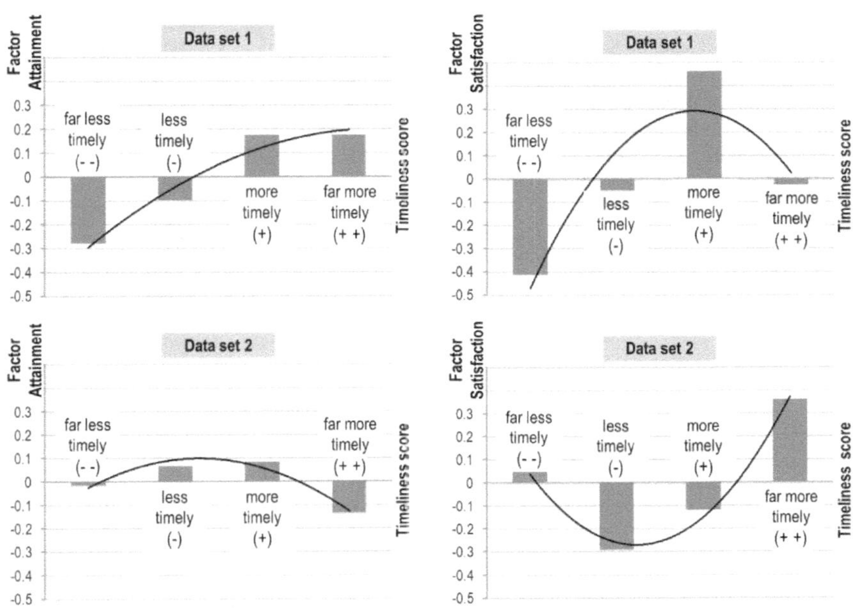

Figure 3-47: Graphical analysis for systems' timeliness of Japanese companies (data set 1 and 2)

Overall, Figure 3-44 and Figure 3-45 show a diminishing marginal utility of cost accounting systems' complexity for three out of four performance indicators of data set 1 and 2 for Germany and Japan. A diminishing marginal utility of timeliness prevails for none respectively three performance measures of data set 1 and 2 for Germany and Japan (see Figure 3-46 and Figure 3-47). These results indicate that German and Japanese companies having less (more) complex cost accounting systems than expected should (not) increase their complexity to improve performance. Furthermore, German and Japanese companies having less timely cost accounting systems than expected should increase timeliness of their systems to improve performance. However, German unlike Japanese companies having timelier cost accounting systems than expected should also increase timeliness of their systems to improve performance. Hence, whereas an increase in systems' complexity and timeliness of Japanese companies that are above average has no positive impact on performance, for the German counterparts only an increase in complexity has no positive impact on performance, but German companies having cost accounting systems above average timeliness should further improve timeliness.

Overall, the **mathematical analysis** indicates that for Japan a linear relationship between complexity respectively timeliness and performance prevails. The results for the German responses have not provided new insights for or against a diminishing marginal utility of cost accounting systems' complexity and timeliness. The results of the **graphical analysis** indicate for both countries that a diminishing marginal utility of cost accounting systems' complexity prevails. For Japan unlike for Germany, a diminishing marginal utility of cost accounting systems' timeliness prevails as well. Differences between the mathematical and graphical analysis can be explained by the fact that the graphical analysis investigates this non-linear relationship in a more detailed way. The graphical analysis, however, does not provide levels of significance, because the sample sizes for the four groups are below 50 responses. As a consequence, hypothesis H_{5c} (stating a diminishing marginal utility of systems' complexity) is accepted for Germany and Japan with caution and H_{5d} (stating a diminishing marginal utility of systems' timeliness) is rejected for Germany and accepted only for Japan with caution.

Hypothesis		Result
H_{3m}	The more comprehensive IT systems, the more successful are cost accounting systems.	Accepted
H_{5a}	The more complex cost accounting systems are, the more successful they are.	Accepted for Germany, rejected for Japan
H_{5b}	The timelier cost accounting systems are, the more successful they are.	Rejected for Germany, accepted for Japan
H_{5c}	A diminishing marginal utility of cost accounting systems' complexity prevails.	Accepted
H_{5d}	A diminishing marginal utility of cost accounting systems' timeliness prevails.	Rejected for Germany, accepted for Japan
H_{5e}	Complex cost accounting systems are more successful for companies with a complex external environment.	Not tested
H_{5f}	Timely cost accounting systems are more successful for companies with a dynamic external environment.	Rejected
H_{5g}	Complex cost accounting systems are more successful for decision facilitating than for decision influencing.	Rejected
H_{5h}	Timely cost accounting systems are more successful for decision facilitating than for decision influencing.	Rejected
H_{5i}	Complex cost accounting systems are more successful for short-term decision making than for long-term decision making.	Rejected
H_{5j}	Timely cost accounting systems are more successful for short-term decision making than for long-term decision making.	Rejected
H_{5k}	Complex cost accounting systems are more successful when cost accounting serves more for management than for financial accounting objectives.	Rejected
H_{5l}	Timely cost accounting systems are more successful when cost accounting serves more for management than for financial accounting objectives.	Rejected
H_{5m}	Cost accounting systems that are both high or low in complexity and timeliness are less successful.	Rejected for Germany, accepted for Japan

Table 3-95: Results of the hypotheses tests

The results for the performance of cost accounting systems are summarized in Table 3-95. The multivariate analysis show that comprehensive IT systems lead to more successful cost accounting systems in Germany and Japan. More complex systems are also more successful in Germany and more timely systems are more successful in Japan. Furthermore, a diminishing marginal utility of cost accounting systems' complexity is verified for Germany and Japan and a diminishing marginal utility of cost accounting systems' timeliness is demonstrated for the Japanese sample only. The remaining hypotheses postulate that the complexity and timeliness of cost accounting systems should be matched with cost accounting objectives to design successful cost accounting systems. The regression results, however, do not verify that cost accounting systems are purposefully designed. Only for the Japanese data set one out of nine assumptions how the conceptual design of cost accounting systems should be aligned with cost accounting objectives is accepted.

3.6 Partial-least-squares (PLS) analysis

3.6.1 Development of the PLS model

In this section two PLS models, one for the German and one for the Japanese responses of data set 1, are developed to verify the regression results from sections 3.4 and 3.5 and to test for cross-national differences in the magnitude of relationships by analyzing moderating effects. For this analysis, both models have to be comparable, i.e. the theoretical constructs must have the same meaning for the German and the Japanese model. The sample size of data set 1 for Germany and Japan is more than ten times the largest number of independent constructs affecting a dependent construct. To increase the explanatory power of the models, the performance measure 'factor attainment' was chosen in section 3.1.3.2.5.

At the beginning of the **model development**, all theoretical constructs (country-specifics, other external context factors, internal context factors, six groups of cost accounting objectives as well as complexity, timeliness, and performance of cost accounting systems) that are metric scaled are included. The theoretical constructs are first characterized as either formative or reflective to ensure comparability. When both characterizations of the theoretical constructs ensure comparability, the most suitable characterization is chosen following the conclusions from section 3.1.3.2.5. When neither a formative nor a reflective characterization of a theoretical construct is comparable across both countries or when in at least one country the quality criteria from section 3.1.3 are not met, the respective theoretical construct is excluded from the PLS model.[1237] This process has resulted in the PLS model that is presented in Figure 3-48.

All variables that describe country-specifics[1238] are excluded, either because they are not metric scaled (e.g., 'cost accountants' sources of knowledge') or because the theoretical constructs are not comparable between Germany and Japan (e.g., 'functional specialization of cost accountants'). Furthermore, potential for cost distortion, external complexity, and short-term and long-term objectives are excluded, because they do not meet all quality criteria. Unlike for timeliness, the reflective construct for cost accounting systems' complexity does not meet sufficient quality criteria. Complexity of cost accounting systems as a formative construct, on the other hand, consists of many negative loaded indicators, which are in contrast to the conceptual considerations that all elements should a have

1237 See section 3.1.3.1.3.

1238 For an overview of the variables that describe country-specifics see Table 2-3, p. 122.

a positive impact upon the complexity of cost accounting systems (see section 2.3). Hence, complexity of cost accounting systems as a formative construct would have a different meaning as intended. As systems' complexity does not meet the quality criteria for reflective and formative constructs, the complexity score determined in section 3.4.1.1.3 is applied as a single item indicator. The other theoretical constructs characterized as formative, in particular timeliness and 'factor attainment', face similar shortcomings like complexity of cost accounting systems in terms of negative loaded indicators. Therefore, all theoretical constructs are characterized as **reflective** to avoid biased outcomes and to ensure cross-national comparability. As it is concluded in section 3.1.3.2.5 that several of the theoretical constructs should rather be formative than reflective, this model has **limitations** in providing practical contributions.

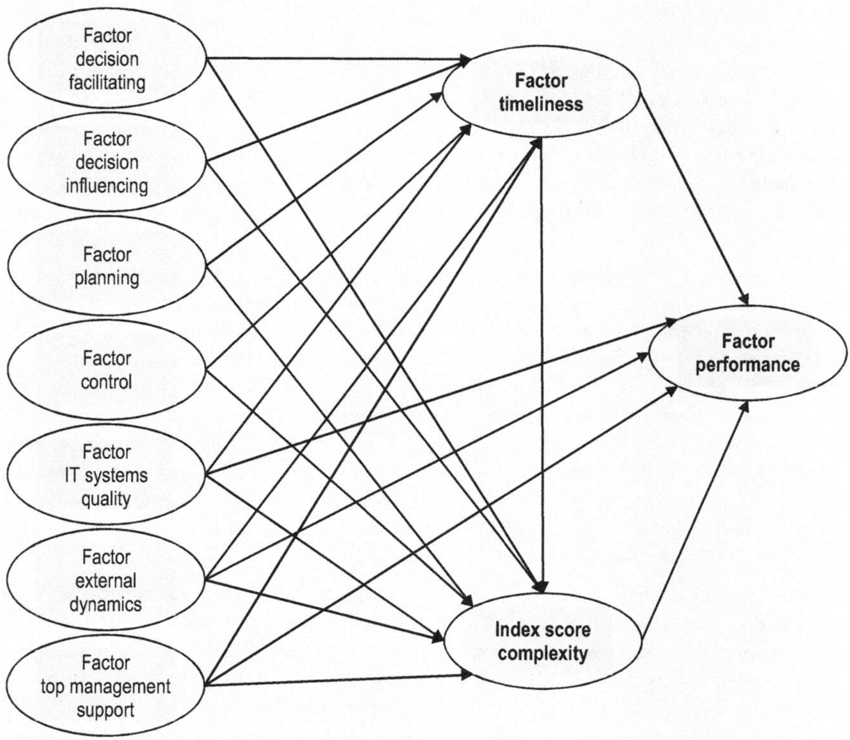

Figure 3-48: PLS model for the cross-national comparison

3.6.2 Quality criteria

The quality criteria for cross-national comparability of the theoretical constructs (*coefficient of congruence*), for the *reflective constructs*, and for the *structural model* are outlined in the following.[1239] Quality criteria for formative constructs are not included, because the PLS model comprises only reflective constructs.

The most relevant quality criterion for this study is the comparability of the theoretical constructs. As intended, the **coefficients of congruence** for all theoretical constructs with more than two indicators are all above 0.9 indicating that the constructs are cross-nationally equivalent (see Table 3-96).[1240]

	External dynamics	IT systems quality	Decision influencing	Timeliness of cost accounting systems	Performance attainment
Data set 1	0.9894	0.9977	0.9998	0.9784	0.9945

Table 3-96: Coefficients of congruence (data set 1)

The quality **criteria for reflective constructs** include

- *individual item reliability* (items should have a factor loading of at least 0.4),
- *reliability on a construct level* (Cronbach's Alpha and the internal consistency measure should be larger than 0.6; AVE should be larger than 0.5),
- *discriminant validity of indicators* (each indicator should have the strongest correlation with its construct), and
- *discriminant validity of concepts* (the AVE for each reflective construct should be greater than the squared correlation between two constructs).

Appendix 15 shows that all indicators have a factor loading of above 0.4 and that most of the factor loadings are above 0.707. All quality criteria for **individual item reliability** are thereby met.

Not all theoretical constructs meet all quality criteria for the **reliability on a construct level**. For the German model, the construct 'external dynamics' has a Cronbach's Alpha of 0.5642 and the construct 'timeliness' has an AVE of only 0.3152. For the Japanese model the construct 'timeliness' has an AVE of only 0.4539. The remaining quality criteria for the three theoretical constructs are all met. An elimination of the theoretical constructs only marginally improves the validity of the model and due to the theoretical considerations from section 2 the theoretical constructs are not eliminated.[1241]

1239 The quality criteria are described in section 3.1.3.2.4.

1240 The remaining theoretical constructs from Figure 3-48 consist only of two variables. Therefore, coefficients of congruence cannot be determined for them.

1241 Timeliness of cost accounting systems, e.g., was operationalized to measure the update of cost information and thus reflects a very important dimension of the cost accounting system. The main reason why less than 50% of the variance is explained is because of the objective measurement of this construct. The quality criteria for timeliness could have been improved by eliminating single indicators of the construct. Then, however, the cost accounting system would be less comprehensively described, which would impede cross-national comparability. See section 2.3.1.2.

		Cronbach's Alpha	Internal consistency measure	AVE
Germany	Factor decision facilitating	0.6784	0.8614	0.7566
	Factor decision influencing	0.8519	0.9092	0.7695
	Factor planning	0.7357	0.8817	0.7887
	Factor control	0.7570	0.8896	0.8014
	Factor IT systems quality	0.8271	0.8948	0.7401
	Factor external dynamics	0.5642	0.7489	0.5111
	Factor top management support	0.6685	0.8545	0.7466
	Factor timeliness	0.6327	0.7526	0.3152
	Factor attainment	0.8988	0.9179	0.5552
Japan	Factor decision facilitating	0.7513	0.8701	0.7220
	Factor decision influencing	0.8664	0.9182	0.7893
	Factor planning	0.8745	0.9409	0.8885
	Factor control	0.6938	0.8672	0.7656
	Factor IT systems quality	0.7139	0.8326	0.6278
	Factor external dynamics	0.7024	0.8335	0.6269
	Factor top management support	0.9162	0.9598	0.9226
	Factor timeliness	0.7980	0.8511	0.4539
	Factor attainment	0.9534	0.9603	0.7289

Table 3-97: Reliability on a construct level (data set 1)

The **discriminant validity** is met for all indicators and for all theoretical constructs (see Appendix 16, Appendix 17, Appendix 18).

The quality **criteria for the structural model** include

- *R-squares for each dependent latent variable* (no threshold value exists to assess the quality of the model),
- *f^2* – change in R-squares (investigates the relevance of independent latent variables),
- *Stone-Geisser Q^2* (Q^2 values should be positive),
- *q^2* – change in Q^2 (investigates the relevance of independent latent variables), and
- *significance and value of path coefficients* (path coefficients should be statistically significant to a 10%-significance level and should have a value of at least 0.1).

As only reflective constructs are applied, as several theoretical constructs are excluded from the study, and as complexity of cost accounting systems is only applied as a single item indicator, the explanatory power of the study in terms of R^2, Q^2, f^2, q^2, and path coefficients is low.

The largest **R^2** prevails for performance of the Japanese model with 35.6%. Timeliness of the German model has the lowest R^2 with 4.8%. Nevertheless, the **Stone-Geisser Q^2** implies that the German and Japanese models have predictive relevance (see Table 3-98).

Country	Quality criteria	Index score complexity	Factor timeliness	Factor attainment
Germany	R^2	0.170	0.048	0.276
	Q^2	0.121	0.014	0.147
Japan	R^2	0.179	0.108	0.356
	Q^2	0.077	0.046	0.250

Table 3-98: R-squares and Q-squares for complexity, timeliness, and performance of cost accounting systems (data set 1)

Germany	Index score complexity	Factor timeliness	Factor attainment
Factor decision facilitating	0.006	0.000	0.000
Factor decision influencing	-0.001	0.016	0.001
Factor planning	0.027	0.002	-0.001
Factor control	0.009	0.000	0.000
Factor IT systems quality	0.006	0.003	0.046
Factor external dynamics	0.001	0.001	0.002
Factor top management support	0.002	0.000	0.080
Factor timeliness	0.011		0.001
Index score complexity			0.031
Japan			
Factor decision facilitating	0.006	0.003	0.000
Factor decision influencing	0.020	0.004	0.000
Factor planning	0.009	0.004	0.000
Factor control	0.002	0.006	0.000
Factor IT systems quality	0.000	0.018	0.026
Factor external dynamics	0.008	0.029	0.007
Factor top management support	0.032	0.005	0.056
Factor timeliness	0.015		0.017
Index score complexity			0.081

Table 3-99: Change R-squares (data set 1)

The changes in R-squares (**f^2**) show that all constructs have only a small effect upon a dependent construct in Germany and Japan (see Table 3-99). For the German model the factor planning influences complexity of cost accounting systems and the factor attainment is influenced by factor IT systems quality, factor top management support, and complexity of cost accounting systems. For the Japanese model, the factor decision influencing and the factor top management support determine the complexity of cost accounting systems and the factor external dynamics influences the timeliness of cost accounting systems. The factor IT systems quality, factor top management support, and the complexity of cost accounting systems have furthermore an effect on the factor attainment for the Japanese model. The constructs that have a small effect on the complexity and timeliness of cost accounting systems differ cross-nationally. In contrast to that, the variables having a small effect on factor attainment are the same in both models, but their strengths differ.

Changes in Q^2 (**q^2**) indicate that the most relevant theoretical constructs in both countries are 'factor IT systems quality', 'factor top management support', and 'complexity of cost accounting systems' (see Appendix 19). These constructs, however, are only of little relevance, because they have an impact upon Q^2 below 0.15.

About half of the **path coefficients** are statistically significant and have a value above 0.1. These are marked gray in Table 3-100. However, only four out of 20 path coefficients have the expected sign and are statistically significant for Germany and Japan. Hence, only few similar patterns between context, objectives, conceptual design of cost accounting systems, and performance prevail in both countries.

Relationship	Coefficient		t-statistic	
	Germany	Japan	Germany	Japan
Factor decision facilitating → Index score complexity	0.093	-0.110	1.429	1.364
Factor decision facilitating → Factor timeliness	0.003	0.071	0.054	0.782
Factor decision influencing → Index score complexity	-0.040	0.210	0.081	2.331
Factor decision influencing → Factor timeliness	0.178	-0.109	2.083	1.024
Factor planning → Index score complexity	0.206	0.154	2.933	1.466
Factor planning → Factor timeliness	-0.066	0.106	0.898	0.964
Factor control → Index score complexity	0.136	-0.061	1.879	0.737
Factor control → Factor timeliness	0.027	0.159	0.423	1.262
Factor IT systems quality → Index score complexity	0.071	-0.013	1.561	0.214
Factor IT systems quality → Factor timeliness	0.088	0.142	1.431	1.782
Factor IT systems quality → Factor attainment	0.228	0.172	4.244	2.195
Factor external dynamics → Index score complexity	0.000	-0.103	0.009	1.397
Factor external dynamics → Factor timeliness	-0.049	0.181	0.824	1.877
Factor external dynamics → Factor attainment	-0.057	-0.090	1.185	1.402
Factor top management support → Index score complexity	0.001	0.215	0.019	2.215
Factor top management support → Factor timeliness	0.049	-0.084	1.093	1.205
Factor top management support → Factor attainment	0.300	0.273	5.793	3.948
Factor timeliness → Index score complexity	0.109	0.141	1.837	1.699
Index score complexity → Factor attainment	0.208	0.306	3.875	5.006
Factor timeliness → Factor attainment	0.044	0.139	0.681	2.018
Path coefficients marked grey are statistically significant at a 10%-significance level and have a value above 0.1.				

Table 3-100: Path coefficients (data set 1)

The structure of the German and the Japanese PLS models are depictured in Figure 3-49 and Figure 3-50. The scores on the arrows reproduce the path coefficients and their level of statistical significance.

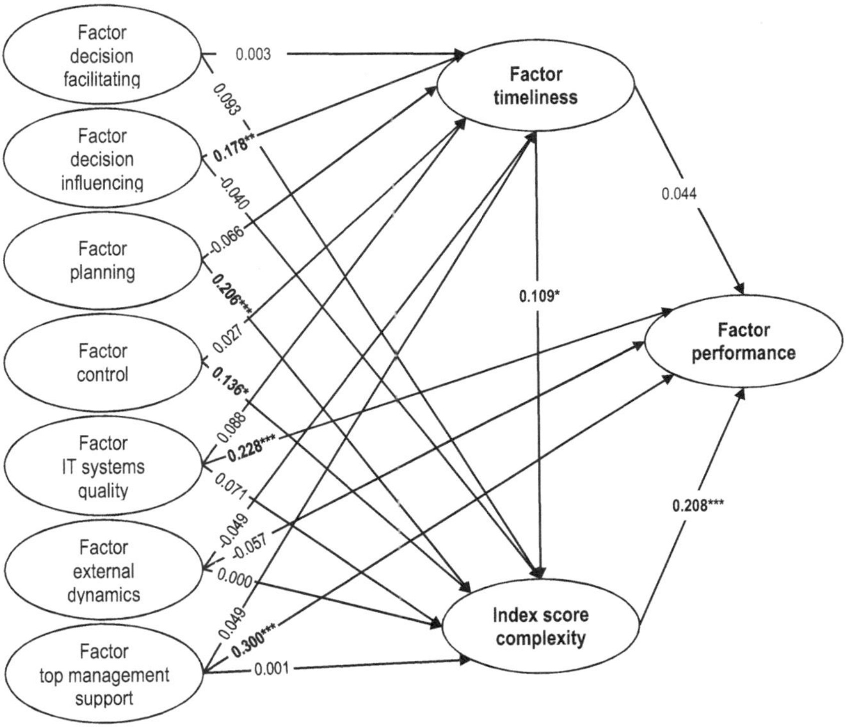

Figure 3-49: German PLS model (data set 1)

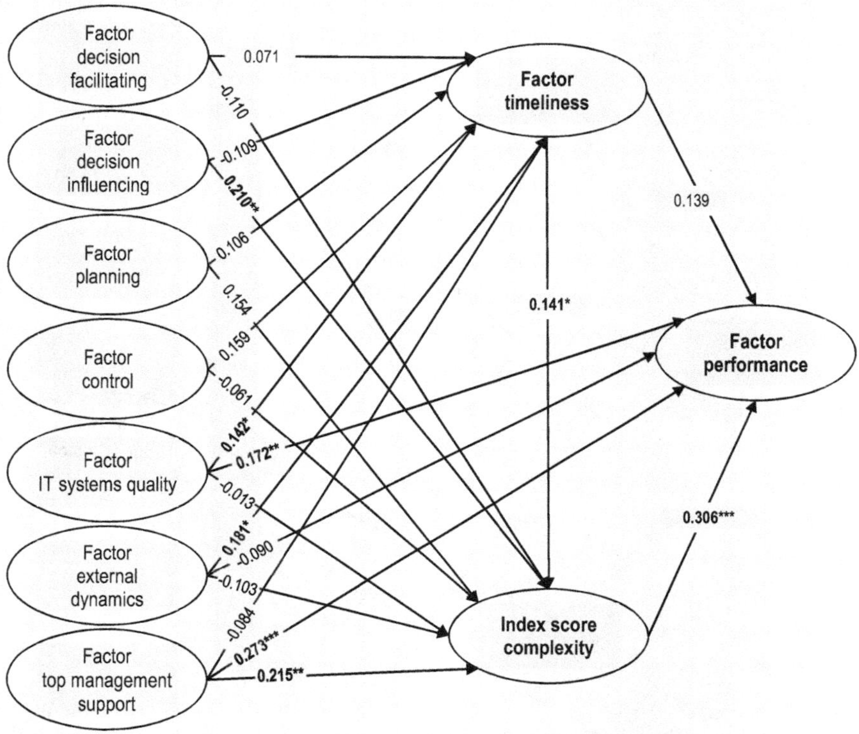

Figure 3-50: Japanese PLS model (data set 1)

3.6.3 Verification of the multiple regression results and hypothesis testing

The statistical method PLS supports most of the previous findings of the multiple regression analysis. In the following, the findings of PLS (see Table 3-100, Figure 3-49, and Figure 3-50) are contrasted with the findings for the complexity, timeliness, and performance of cost accounting systems outlined in sections 3.4 and 3.5.

Like for multiple regression analysis, PLS does not find any relationship between *IT systems quality* and the **complexity of cost accounting systems** (H_{3e}). PLS supports the results from regression analysis for Japan that *top management support* has a statistically significantly positive impact upon the complexity of cost accounting systems (H_{3g}). The results for *cost accounting objectives* (H_{4c}, H_{4d}, H_{4e}, H_{4g}) are, like for regression analysis, cross-nationally inconsistent and often in contrast to the hypotheses: Decision facilitating has a negative and decision influencing has a positive effect in Japan upon the complexity of cost accounting systems (both outcomes are in contrast to hypotheses H_{4e} and H_{4g} respectively), whereas for Germany no statistically significant relationships are determined with PLS. Planning has in both countries a positive impact upon systems' complexity, which is also in contrast to hypothesis H_{4c}. Cost control has as expected a positive impact in Germany (H_{4d}), but no significant relationship prevails for Japan.

The results from section 3.4.2.3 show that the **timeliness of cost accounting systems** is positively influenced by *IT systems quality* (H_{3f}) and the objective decision facilitating (H_{4f}) in both countries. The timeliness of cost accounting systems is furthermore positively associated with *external dynamics* (H_{2b}) in Japan. The positive impact of IT systems quality is only supported for Japan. The positive impact of *external dynamics* (H_{2b}) for Japan is also supported by PLS, whereas for Germany like in regression analysis no relationship is identified. Only few multiple regressions indicate that *cost accounting objectives* significantly influence the timeliness of cost accounting systems. Except for the factor 'decision influencing objectives' (H_{4h}) that has a positive impact upon the timeliness of cost accounting systems in Germany, no significant relationships are identified by the PLS model for Japan.

The regression analysis shows that the *complexity of cost accounting systems* (H_{5a}) has a positive effect upon the **performance of cost accounting systems** in Germany and *timeliness* (H_{5b}) has a positive effect in Japan. The results by the PLS model verify that systems' timeliness has only a positive effect in Japan, but complexity of cost accounting systems has a positive effect in both countries. PLS furthermore affirms the findings from section 3.4 that *IT systems quality* (H_{3m}) and *top management support* have a positive impact upon systems' performance for both countries. Overall, most of the findings for the complexity, timeliness, and performance of cost accounting systems outlined in sections 3.4 and 3.5 are verified by PLS.

The basic research hypothesis H_7 states that the relationships between the elements of the conceptual framework are stable between Germany and Japan, but they differ in magnitude. For this reason, an **analysis of moderating effects** is carried through with PLS, which cannot be calculated with multiple regression analysis. It is expected that the direction of relationships between two variables are universally valid, but the magnitude of the relationships is likely to be subject to country-specifics, because, e.g., theoretical constructs differ in their relevance between countries. Due to the small number of statistically significant path coefficients, only four path coefficients that have the expected sign and that are statistically significant in both countries are compared for cross-national differences in magnitude.[1242] These include factor IT systems quality → factor attainment, factor top management support → factor attainment, timeliness of cost accounting systems → complexity of cost accounting systems, and complexity of cost accounting systems → factor attainment. Although cross-national differences in the magnitude of relationships were expected due to cultural and institutional differences between Germany and Japan, the test for group comparisons from section 3.1.3.2.3 shows that the magnitude does not statistically significantly differ between both countries (see Table 3-101). Overall, only few context factors have the same impact upon the performance of cost accounting system, but they do not statistically significantly differ in relevance. Furthermore, although

1242 Furthermore, due to the small number of statistically significant path coefficients, mediating effects are not investigated in this study.

the regression results from section 3.5 indicate that systems' complexity is more relevant to German companies to attain cost accounting objectives and to provide comprehensive cost information, the results of the group comparison show that these differences are not statistically significant.

Path	German path value	Japanese path value	p-value
Factor IT systems quality → Factor attainment	0.228	0.174	0.6220
Factor top management support → Factor attainment	0.300	0.273	0.3133
Timeliness of cost accounting systems → Complexity of cost accounting systems	0.109	0.141	0.3166
Complexity of cost accounting systems → Factor attainment	0.208	0.306	1.1054

Table 3-101: Analysis of moderating effects – p-values (data set 1)

Due to the limitations of the applied PLS models, the hypotheses H_{7a}, H_{7b}, and H_{7c} are rejected and remain largely unverified in this study.

Hypothesis		Result
H_{7a}	The impact of context factors upon the conceptual design of cost accounting systems has the same direction for both Germany and Japan, but it differs cross-nationally in magnitude.	Rejected
H_{7b}	The impact of cost accounting objectives upon the conceptual design of cost accounting systems has the same direction, but it differs cross-nationally in magnitude.	Rejected
H_{7c}	The impact of context factors, cost accounting objectives, and the conceptual design of cost accounting systems upon the performance of cost accounting systems has the same direction but, differs cross-nationally in magnitude.	Rejected

Table 3-102: Results of the hypotheses tests

3.7 Summary and discussion of the empirical findings

3.7.1 Cross-national differences and similarities in cost accounting

The empirical results from section 3.2.1 consistently show that German cost accountants are more specialized and have more theoretical knowledge than their Japanese counterparts. The empirical findings support the theoretical assumptions about **country-specifics** from section 2.1.1. Country-specifics vary more strongly between countries than across industries. Hence, country-specifics are valuable variables to explain cross-national differences. Furthermore, German cost accountants have more comprehensive IT systems and receive more top management support. Based on these findings it is concluded that German companies have a higher potential to run complex and timely cost accounting systems than their Japanese counterparts.

Most of the theoretical assumptions about cross-national differences in cost accounting **objectives** are empirically verified as well. German compared to Japanese companies put statistically significantly more emphasis on management than on financial accounting, more on short-term than on long-term objectives, and more on decision facilitating than on decision influencing. The strongest difference prevails for the 'management versus financial accounting' antipode. Surprisingly little variation between Germany and Japan prevails for cost control, although the strongest differences are expected there, because control is charged emotionally and it is thereby subject to cultural differences.[1243] The variation in cost accounting objectives between Germany and Japan is overall far smaller than expected and the results are not statistically significant for mechanical engineering companies. This is surprising, because it is expected that Japanese companies follow a different philosophy of cost accounting compared to their Western counterparts.[1244]

Stronger cross-national differences exist for the conceptual design of cost accounting systems. German companies statistically significantly install more complex and timelier cost accounting systems than their Japanese counterparts. The results are stable for mechanical engineering companies. Cross-national variation in **complexity and timeliness of cost accounting systems supports** the conceptual considerations from section 2.3 and are consistent with the implications of cross-national differences in country-specifics. German companies, however, do not install ABC more frequently than their Japanese counterparts.

By comparing cross-national differences with differences across industries and types of organizations, the **relative importance of country as a variable** can be assessed. The cost accounting objectives vary more strongly between product and service industries than between Germany and Japan. Stronger cross-national differences exist for the conceptual design of cost accounting systems. Complexity of cost accounting systems differ more strongly between Germany and Japan than across industries and across types of organizations.[1245] Timeliness varies between Germany and Japan about as strong as across industries and more strongly than across types of organizations. Thus, German companies put relatively more emphasis on complexity than on timeliness of cost accounting systems in comparison to their Japanese counterparts. This is consistent with the conceptual considerations from section 2.1.1 that German companies put more emphasis on accurate and detailed than on timely cost information and that Japanese companies put more emphasis on timely than on accurate and detailed cost information.

It is expected that cost accounting only marginally converges internationally, when institutional differences like education of cost accountants remain country specific. Whereas the education and qualification of cost accountants has apparently not changed during the last decades in Japan,[1246] more **convergence** has probably occurred in terms of permanent

1243 Cf. *Tannenbaum* (1962), p. 240; *Riahi-Belkaoui* (2002), p. 48f.

1244 Cf. section 1.1.1.

1245 ABC as an alternative measure for systems' complexity, however, does not support this finding, probably, because ABC has been more exposed to globalization.

1246 Cf. *Lippert* (2011), p. 32. In the USA as well, little has changed in the education of cost accountants. Professional accountants in business and accountancy professors "were (and still are) inappropriately reflecting an external financial accounting focus rather than internal decision support as the primary purpose of the accounting profession" (*Clinton* (2007), p. 26). See also *Tatikonda/Savchenko* (2010).

employment and the seniority principle.[1247] The differences in convergence of country-specifics may affect the convergence of cost accounting in different ways. Whereas the conceptual design of cost accounting systems might be more affected by the education and qualification of cost accountants, cost accounting objectives might be more exposed to the principles of permanent employment and the seniority principle.[1248] The small differences in cost accounting objectives between Germany and Japan indicate that in Japan cost accounting objectives are already converging towards Western practices, probably because of the increasing importance of performance evaluation in Japan since the seniority principle becomes less important.[1249] Strong differences prevail in the conceptual design of cost accounting systems between Germany and Japan, probably, because the education and qualification of cost accountants remains distinctive. The findings from section 3.4.3 furthermore indicate that cost accounting systems' complexity and timeliness will probably not converge. Finally, the study shows that the German particularity to apply imputed costs is still widespread and companies being more exposed to globalization do not statistically significantly apply this instrument to a lesser degree.

3.7.2 Determinants of cost accounting systems' complexity, timeliness, and performance

To explain when cost accounting systems are complex, timely, and successful in Germany and Japan, a direct relationship is drawn between 14 independent variables and the complexity, timeliness, and performance of cost accounting systems. Multiple regression analyses and correlations were determined **on a national level** to investigate the determinants separately for Germany and Japan.[1250] It is thereby investigated whether, e.g., more specialized cost accountants lead to more complex, timely, and successful cost accounting systems in Germany and Japan. The results are discussed in the following.

Six variables[1251] are included in the regression analysis to investigate whether **specialization of cost accountants** leads to more complex, timely, and successful cost accounting systems in Germany and Japan. The regressions results for complexity (see Table 3-59, p. 269) and timeliness (see Table 3-74, p. 293) do not support the assumption for both countries that a higher specialization of cost accountants leads statistically significantly to more complex and timelier cost accounting systems. The regressions results for performance (Table 3-91, p. 310) on the contrary provide solid evidence that a higher specialization of cost accountants leads to more successful cost accounting systems for German

1247 Cf. *Takayanagi* (1989), p. 425; *Pudelko* (2009), p. 448; *Haghirian* (2010), p. 29.

1248 The less important, e.g., the seniority principle becomes, the more important cost control for performance evaluation is. Indirectly, through cost accounting objectives, it can also have an impact upon the conceptual design of cost accounting systems.

1249 Prior research supports this assumption that more Japanese companies start to increasingly use performance evaluation. See *Hopper et al.* (1999), p. 79, 81, with further references.

1250 See Figure 1-12, p. 80.

1251 They include 'workload management over financial accounting', 'focus on management accounting', 'focus on management accounting education', 'specialization in cost accounting only', 'specialization in other business functions', and 'specialization by high qualification'. The variable 'specialization in other business functions' measures the opposite of specialization.

companies. This result supports *Nishimura's* argument that specialization has a different role in Western countries than in Japan. Whereas in the Western countries it is expected that specialization improves efficiency, Japanese companies put more emphasis on cooperation through multi-skilling and personal responsibility for plural sections of a product line.[1252]

It is furthermore expected that a more **theoretical education of cost accountants** (by university and professional institutes) leads to more complex and timelier cost accounting systems compared to a practically oriented education (by in-house training and learning by doing). The results for the complexity of cost accounting systems do not support this assumption for both countries. The results rather indicate the opposite for Germany. A more practical oriented education leads to more complex cost accounting systems. For the timeliness of cost accounting systems a negative relationship prevails for Germany and no relationship is identified for Japan. However, a more theoretical education leads to more successful cost accounting systems in Japan. It is suspected that for countries where the theoretical education of cost accountants is rather low, more theoretically educated cost accountants have more valuable knowledge to install successful cost accounting systems.

It is argued that **external dynamics** has a negative impact upon the complexity and performance of cost accounting systems and a positive impact upon their timeliness. The results from the regression analysis for the Japanese responses show that external dynamics has no impact upon the complexity and a positive effect on timeliness cost accounting systems. The results for Germany are opposite to the Japanese results: External dynamics is positively associated with systems' complexity and not associated with systems' timeliness. The statistical method PLS shows that no significant relationship prevails between external dynamics and the conceptual design of cost accounting systems for Germany, but it confirms for Japan that external dynamics has a positive effect on the timeliness of cost accounting systems. These findings provide modest evidence that Japanese companies align their cost accounting systems better to the external environment. This result rudimentary supports prior anecdotal evidence that Japanese companies better direct their cost accounting systems to customers, external environment, and business strategy.[1253] Neither multiple regression analysis nor PLS identify any significant relationship between external dynamics and performance of cost accounting systems for Germany and Japan. No statistically significant relationship between **external complexity** and the complexity, timeliness, and performance of cost accounting systems prevails for Germany and Japan.[1254] Overall, unlike prior research,[1255] a direct relationship between the external environment and the conceptual design of cost accounting systems was verified for Japan. The results thereby confirm previous findings on organizational information systems and management accounting systems,[1256] but they do not support previous findings that have identi-

1252 Cf. *Nishimura* (2003), p. 61.

1253 Cf., e.g., *Hiromoto* (1988).

1254 These relationships are tested by correlations, because the quality criteria for factor analysis and for formative and reflective constructs are not met.

1255 See *Aust* (1999), p. 178; *Frank* (2000), p. 131.

1256 See *Gordon/Miller* (1976); *Gordon/Narayanan* (1984); *Mia/Clarke* (1999), p. 152.

fied respondents to be more satisfied with systems that are broader in scope and provide timelier information in an uncertain environment.[1257]

Company size is expected to have a positive effect on the complexity of cost accounting systems and no effect on the timeliness and the performance of cost accounting systems. The results from regression analysis support the hypotheses for complexity and timeliness for Germany and Japan. Unlike for Germany, a positive effect of company size upon the performance of cost accounting systems is determined for Japan, which is contrary to the expected hypothesis H_{3b}. This cross-national difference can be explained with the distinguishing features of the Japanese and German education and employment system: In Japan cost accountants are more intensively educated in-house and due to the Japanese collective culture, many employees are long-term employed. In Germany on the contrary, cost accountants acquire their knowledge mainly from university. Due to the more individualistic culture of Germany, employees change their employers more frequently. Both specifics likely hamper smaller Japanese companies to build up comprehensive knowledge in cost accounting to install well-performing systems. In Germany on the contrary, smaller companies can more easily acquire knowledge in cost accounting by employing staff that is either trained by university or by other companies.

In section 2.1.3.3 it was outlined that **IT systems quality** has a positive effect upon the complexity, timeliness, and performance of cost accounting systems. The regression results show that IT systems quality has a positive effect upon timeliness in Japan and a positive effect upon performance in both countries. A negative effect of IT systems quality upon the complexity of cost accounting systems is determined for Germany. This is surprising, because IT systems quality constitutes a critical factor to implement ABC in Germany. Hence, the effect of IT systems quality upon the complexity of cost accounting systems remains inconsistent for Germany, wherefore an in-depth analysis on this relationship is required. For Japan no statistically significant relationship between IT systems quality and complexity of cost accounting systems prevails. The Japanese results are supported by the PLS model. For the German PLS model only a positive association between IT systems quality and performance is identified. The strongest effect of IT systems quality is in both countries on performance of cost accounting systems. Furthermore, more statistically significant relationships prevail for Japan compared to Germany. As German companies have installed more comprehensive IT systems, this result may indicate a diminishing marginal utility of IT systems quality.

The overall interest in cost accounting in terms of **top management support** is expected to have a positive effect on the complexity and timeliness of cost accounting systems. The regression results show only a positive impact of top management support upon the complexity of Japanese cost accounting systems. These results are supported by the PLS model. This effect is significant in Japan unlike in Germany, probably because in Germany already a strong emphasis on precision and complex cost accounting systems prevails.[1258] According to the regression and PLS results, top management has a stronger positive im-

1257 See *Chenhall/Morris* (1986); *Gul/Chia* (1994).

1258 For the emphasis on precision and complex cost accounting systems in Germany see, e.g., See *Krumwiede/Suessmair* (2007a), (2007b).

pact on the performance than on the conceptual design of cost accounting systems in both countries. This indicates that top management support might be of less relevance to install complex and timely cost accounting systems. Other aspects that are not investigated in this study like the use of cost information might be more influenced by the top management through which top management support might exert a positive, indirect impact upon systems' performance.

Normative literature argues that cost accounting systems should be purposefully designed and **cost accounting objectives** should thus have a significant impact upon the conceptual design of the systems. The regression and PLS results are, however, cross-nationally inconsistent and often in contrast to the hypotheses. These results may indicate that cost accounting systems are not purposefully designed. However, it can also be argued that companies follow different cost accounting objectives. As cost accountants have then to make a compromise between different objectives, it might be difficult to identify an impact of individual objectives upon the conceptual design of cost accounting systems.

It is expected that the **complexity and timeliness of cost accounting systems** have a positive, but diminishing impact upon the performance of cost accounting systems. The regression analysis shows that complexity has a positive and timeliness has a negative effect on performance in Germany. In Japan only timeliness has a positive effect on performance. The PLS model, which also considers for indirect relationships, determines a positive effect of cost accounting system complexity upon performance for Germany and a positive effect of complexity and timeliness for Japan. The results of the group comparison show that the relevance of systems' complexity to install successful cost accounting systems does not statistically differ between both countries. To determine non-linear relationships, a specific mathematical and graphical analysis was carried through. No indication for linearity or non-linearity is determined for Germany by the mathematical analysis. For Japan, a linear and positive relationship between complexity and performance as well as between timeliness and performance is determined. The graphical analysis on the contrary indicates a diminishing effect of complexity on performance in Germany and Japan and for Japan also a diminishing effect of timeliness on performance. Although levels of significance are not provided for the graphical analysis it can be presumed that Japanese companies having installed cost accounting systems that are less complex and less timely (under the given operating environment and the cost accounting objectives) than expected should increase complexity and timeliness of their cost accounting systems. Japanese companies having installed more complex and timelier cost accounting systems than expected should, on the contrary, not further increase complexity and timeliness. For German companies the same conclusions can be drawn for the complexity of cost accounting systems. However, all German companies having either installed systems that are timelier or less timely than expected should further increase timeliness. This study thereby indicates that the predominant suggestions from literature[1259] to generally install more

1259 The studies investigating ABC often justify their endeavors by following the arguments by *Johnson/Kaplan* (1987) that more complex cost accounting systems such as ABC are required instead of traditional costing, because the latter systematically distort product costs, which can lead to wrong decision making.

complex cost accounting systems might not be suitable for all companies. These predominant suggestions are probably only appropriate for companies that have installed less complex cost accounting systems under their given operating environment and under the pursued cost accounting objectives than expected.

3.7.3 Implications for practitioners and researchers

Practical contributions are provided by identifying factors that statistically significantly influence the conceptual design and the performance of cost accounting systems. This provides practitioners with *recommendations how to purposefully design cost accounting systems* in Germany and Japan and where cross-national differences prevail. It is recommended, e.g., that German and Japanese companies having relatively less complex cost accounting systems should extend the complexity of their systems. German and Japanese companies having installed relatively more complex cost accounting systems should on the contrary not necessarily further extent complexity, because a diminishing marginal utility of cost accounting systems' complexity is likely to prevail. It would probably be more suitable to improve cost reporting[1260] or, in particular for Germany, that cost accountants spend more time for discussing the provided information with operative managers and to participate more in operational decision making. Unlike for Germany, Japanese companies having installed timelier cost accounting systems then expected should not necessarily further extend timeliness.

Cost variance analysis, first stage allocation, and time reference of costs are the most relevant cost accounting elements to install successful cost accounting systems in both countries. Furthermore, the update of the distinction between variable and fixed costs is most important in Germany and in Japan the update of cost rates for overhead allocation bases are most relevant. The score for imputed costs is only very weakly correlated with performance in Germany and it is not correlated with performance in Japan. This apparently low relevance of imputed costs supports recommendations from scholars[1261] to abandon imputed costs for simplifying German cost accounting. Finally, the typical German instrument contribution margin accounting is more relevant in Japan compared to Germany. It is concluded that this instrument could enhance Japanese cost accounting.

These insights are also relevant for *MNC* that adjust their cost accounting systems to their foreign subsidiaries. In German unlike in Japanese companies, consequently, the timeliness of cost accounting systems should still be increased, even when the timeliness is already high. This study furthermore shows that German companies install more complex and timelier cost accounting systems than their Japanese counterparts. These cross-national differences are explained by a higher specialization and a more theoretical education of cost accountants in Germany compared to Japan. Due to these country-specifics, German cost accountants are used to more complex and timelier cost accounting systems

1260 The author has obtained in discussions with practitioners the impression that cost accountants should rather improve cost reports and spend more time for discussing the provided information with managers than to further extend cost accounting systems, when the cost accounting systems are already above average in terms of complexity.

1261 Cf. section 2.1.1.2.1; *Jones/Luther* (2005), p. 185.

than their Japanese counterparts. Therefore, a standardization of cost accounting systems regarding complexity and timeliness might not be accepted by the German and Japanese employees. These cross-national differences might furthermore constitute barriers for transferring cost accounting systems between Germany and Japan. Unlike the conceptual design of cost accounting systems, only small differences in cost accounting objectives prevail between Germany and Japan. Hence, cost accounting objectives can be standardized in MNC to a large extent without losing acceptance, whereas the conceptual design of cost accounting systems should be differentiated to some extent. Only then local cost accounting systems can successfully be aligned with the global cost and management control systems to ensure homogenization of systems within MNC.[1262]

Besides highlighting cross-national differences in cost accounting and explaining their reasons, this study investigates the relevance of context factors and objectives to install and maintain cost accounting systems in Germany and Japan. This study shows that IT systems quality and top management support are more relevant in Japan than in Germany to install complex, timely, and successful cost accounting systems. This difference likely prevails, because German companies have already installed comprehensive IT systems and may more emphasize sophisticated cost accounting systems. Hence, some evidence is provided that the relevance of context factors to install and maintain cost accounting systems differs internationally.

Germany has a long tradition in cost accounting and German companies turned out in this study to have more complex and timelier cost accounting systems than their Japanese counterparts. Companies and professional or political institutions from Japan (but also from other countries, which want to increase complexity and timeliness of cost accounting systems) who want to promote comprehensive cost accounting systems might want to have a look at German companies. Comprehensive German systems include GPK and particularities of German cost accounting include the high number of cost types and cost centers. These systems and characteristics, however, have to be treated with care. Due to cross-national differences in national culture as well as in specialization and education of cost accountants, German systems have to be adapted to the foreign environment. Suggestions and examples how to adapt GPK to the US environment are already provided in literature.[1263]

Theoretical contributions are provided by highlighting *reasons for cross-national differences in cost accounting* and by assessing the extent of cross-national differences in cost accounting. This study has applied the cultural contingency and the societal effects approach to set up hypotheses about cross-national differences in cost accounting. Country-specifics were sampled in their own right to verify anecdotal evidence from literature and cross-national equivalence is ensured to obtain a solid knowledge base about cross-national differences and similarities in cost accounting. It turns out that the specialization and theoretical education of cost accountants are key determinants why German companies run more complex and timelier cost accounting systems than their Japanese counterparts. The propositions of the societal effects approach are thereby verified: Cost account-

1262 Cf. section 1.2.3 and footnote 139.

1263 See, e.g., *Clinton/Webber* (2004); *Webber/Clinton* (2004); *Friedl et al.* (2005); *Mackie* (2006).

ing differs internationally, because the expressions of national culture in the institutional environment of cost accounting vary cross-nationally. As the measure 'cultural preferences for cost information' was excluded from the analysis, because it has turned out to be more susceptible to biased results than the other country-specifics, the propositions from the cultural contingency approach have not been verified.

Cross-national differences in the institutional environment of cost accounting between Germany and Japan furthermore explain why strong differences in the conceptual design of cost accounting systems still remain between Germany and Japan in spite of global pressures (e.g., international financial reporting standards). Cost accounting objectives of Japanese companies on the contrary have possibly converged towards Western practices, because the prevalence of permanent employment and the seniority principle decreases in Japan.[1264]

Besides the reasons for cross-national differences, also the *relevance of cross-national research* is assessed by comparing cross-national with cross-industry differences in cost accounting. It turns out that cost accounting objectives differ more strongly across industries than between Germany and Japan, systems' timeliness differs with about the same strength, and systems' complexity differs more strongly between Germany and Japan than across industries. It is further shown that the conceptual design of cost accounting systems differs more strongly between Germany and Japan than across private, public, and charitable hospitals. These results demonstrate that strong differences in cost accounting still remain across borders in spite of globalization. Comparative research is therefore still relevant and merits further research.

Based on the sound findings of this study new valuable *research questions arise for future research*. These are outlined in section 4.3. Overall, this study contributes to the research area of comparative management accounting and to the stream of research that addressed the comprehensiveness of (cost) accounting systems. It has described and explained cross-national differences in cost accounting between Germany and Japan and provides practitioners with recommendations. Valuable insights were provided, because the conceptual design of cost accounting systems was measured in a more comprehensive way than in prior research, issues in equivalence were addressed, the samples were matched by company size and by industry, and sophisticated statistical methods were applied.

1264 These findings thereby support the endeavors of US researchers to adapt the German instrument GPK to the US environment. See *Clinton/Webber* (2004); *Webber/Clinton* (2004); *Thomson/Gurowka* (2005), p. 31; *White* (2009). For the necessity to adapt GPK to the US environment see also *Portz/Lere* (2010).

4 Summary and outlook

4.1 Main findings and contributions of the study

Knowledge of cross-national differences in cost accounting is of practical **relevance** for managing MNC and for enhancing national cost accounting systems by adapting foreign concepts. It is also of theoretical relevance, because it enlarges our knowledge base and offers much greater variance to test hypotheses.

Prior comparative research on cost accounting contributes only little practical and theoretical knowledge due to shortcomings in methodology and most of the prior findings are rather anecdotal than empirically verified. The **research objective** of this study was to conduct a theory-based and empirical comparison of cost accounting systems between Germany and Japan to provide knowledge of cross-national similarities and differences in cost accounting and their underlying rationale. To increase the explanatory power of this study, methodological shortcomings of prior research were carefully addressed. Furthermore, with Germany and Japan two of the three most influential countries in spreading management accounting systems around the world were surveyed that strongly differ in national culture and national institutions.

First, a **catalog of comparative management accounting research** was compiled to assess the state of research. An overview of 112 research projects resulting in 148 publications on comparative management accounting is provided and an in depth analysis of comparative research on cost accounting was carried through in section 1.4. This analysis demonstrates that comparative research should comprehensively address issues in equivalence, apply control variables, and use advanced statistical methods. Explanatory studies that explain cross-national differences should further apply at least one theoretical perspective and should preferably sample country-specifics in their own right. The conclusions drawn from this review and calls from literature were followed in this study to develop a **research design** that enables a theoretical and practical relevant survey. The results of this study are summarized following the order of the **five research questions** from section 1.1.1.

(1) Does cost accounting differ between Germany and Japan?

Although statistically significant differences in cost accounting **objectives** prevail between Germany and Japan, these differences are far smaller than expected. The strongest difference is that Japanese counterparts put more emphasis on financial accounting than their German counterparts. Stronger differences prevail for the **conceptual design** of cost accounting systems. German companies have installed more complex and timelier cost accounting systems than their Japanese counterparts. These findings suggest that for MNC little conflicts prevail for harmonizing cost accounting objectives, but stronger challenges possibly exist for harmonizing the conceptual design of cost accounting systems between German and Japanese affiliates.

(2) Are differences in cost accounting stronger across countries than across industries?

Complexity of cost accounting systems differs more strongly across countries, cost accounting objectives differ more strongly across industries, and timeliness of cost accounting systems differs with about the same strength between countries and industries. As strong differences in the conceptual design of cost accounting systems remain across national borders, comparative research is still relevant in the context of globalization and merits future research. For analyzing the relationship between cost accounting objectives and the conceptual design of cost accounting systems, however, cross-industry research is more promising, because cost accounting objectives differ more strongly across industries than across countries.

(3) Why does cost accounting differ between Germany and Japan?

National culture has led to different institutional environments of cost accounting in Germany and Japan. This study empirically confirms that German cost accountants are more specialized and have more theoretical knowledge. Furthermore, German cost accountants have more comprehensive IT systems and receive more top management support than their Japanese counterparts. German companies have therefore a higher potential to run complex and timely cost accounting systems than their Japanese counterparts, which is conform to the cross-national variations in the conceptual design of cost accounting systems. The institutional differences furthermore explain why variances in the conceptual design of cost accounting systems still remain in spite of global pressures like the harmonization of international financial reporting standards. Cost accounting objectives, on the contrary, differ to a lesser degree between both countries than often suspected in literature. It is likely that cost accounting objectives have converged in Japan towards Western practices due to global pressures that have encouraged Japanese companies to reduce permanent employment and to increase performance evaluation.

(4) Which factors influence cost accounting in Germany and Japan? Do these influences differ cross-nationally?

There is some empirical evidence for **Germany** that (1) external dynamics, (2) company size, and the cost accounting objective 'planning' lead to more complex and (3) IT systems quality leads to less complex cost accounting systems. For **Japan** the results indicate that (1) company size and (2) top management support have a positive effect on complexity of cost accounting systems. (1) External dynamics and (2) IT systems quality positively influence timeliness of cost accounting systems in Japan. **Overall**, different variables influence complexity and timeliness of cost accounting systems in Germany and Japan. It is expected that the factors influencing the conceptual design of cost accounting systems differ between both countries, because the cultural and institutional environment varies between both countries as well.

(5) Under which conditions is cost accounting successful in Germany and Japan? Are comprehensive cost accounting systems more successful than simple ones in Germany and in Japan?

Cost accounting systems are more successful in Germany, the more top management support it receives and the more complex the systems are. For Japan the results indicate that (1) a stronger orientation towards management compared to financial accounting, (2) a higher specialization of cost accountants, (3) company size, (4) IT systems quality, (5) top management support, and (6) the timeliness of cost accounting systems lead to more successful systems. As the performance of cost accounting systems dependents on different context factors between Germany and Japan, MNC should consider them, while installing and maintaining cost accounting systems in Germany and Japan. Hardly any successful relationships between cost accounting objectives and the conceptual design of cost accounting systems have been identified. This might indicate that cost accountants in both countries have difficulties to align the conceptual design of cost accounting systems with the objectives they have to fulfill.

Graphical analyses indicate that in Germany complexity of cost accounting systems has a positive but diminishing marginal effect upon performance. In Japan, this relationship is identified for complexity and timeliness of cost accounting systems. These results indicate that companies from both countries having installed less complex and less timely cost accounting systems should increase the complexity respectively timeliness of their systems. German companies having installed more complex and timelier systems should only increase the timeliness of their systems and Japanese companies having installed more complex and timelier systems should neither increase complexity nor timeliness to further augment performance of their systems.

Unlike for Germany, a positive effect of company size upon the performance of cost accounting systems is determined for Japan, which is contrary to the expected hypothesis H_{3b}. This cross-national difference is explained by the distinguishing features of the Japanese and German education and employment systems: In Japan cost accountants are more intensively educated in-house and due to the Japanese collective culture, many employees are long-term employed. In Germany on the contrary, cost accountants acquire their knowledge mainly from university. Due to the more individualistic culture of Germany, employees change their employers more frequently. Both specifics likely hamper smaller Japanese companies to build up comprehensive knowledge in cost accounting to install successful systems. In Germany on the contrary, smaller companies can more easily acquire knowledge in cost accounting by employing staff that is either trained by university or by other companies.

This study has answered all five research questions and provides thereby several theoretical and practical **contributions**. It has further addressed shortcomings of prior research to provide more meaningful results. The actions to increase the explanatory power of this study are summarized following the order of the five research questions.

This study provides insights about cross-national differences in cost accounting (first research question). To ensure *comparability of the responses from Germany and Japan*, issues in equivalence were comprehensively addressed. In particular the collaboration with the Japanese research partner, back translation of the questionnaire, and calculating the coefficient of congruence was important to ensure comparability. Furthermore, cost accounting systems were surveyed in a more comprehensive and in a more objective manner compared to previous studies and the distribution of the sample was matched by company size and industry to avoid distortions. Due to these measures a sound knowledge of cross-national differences in cost accounting between Germany and Japan is provided.

Unlike prior research this study has not only investigated whether cross-national differences prevail, but also how strong these differences are (second research question). To better assess the strength of cross-national differences, variations in cost accounting between Germany and Japan were compared with variations in cost accounting across industries. This study thereby provides indication about the extent of *cross-national differences in cost accounting* and thereby the *relevance of comparative management accounting research*. The finding that cost accounting differs with about the same strength between countries and industries may help researchers and practitioners to justify addressing cross-national differences in cost and management accounting. This is necessary, because several scholars have questioned the relevance of comparative management accounting research arguing that management accounting converges internationally and that management accounting differs more strongly across industries than across countries.[1265]

Besides investigating cross-national differences in cost accounting and assessing their strength, it is also valuable to explain cross-national differences (third research question). The cultural contingency and societal effects approach were merged to provide a *broader set of explanations for cross-national differences*. Anecdotal evidence that the institutional environment of cost accounting differs between Germany and Japan was furthermore empirically verified. None of the 148 comparative studies on management accounting have comprehensively compared the institutional environment across countries before. The strong differences in the institutional environment are expected to drive divergence and may suggest that cost accounting has only little converged between Germany and Japan over the last decades.

Prior research has almost exclusively explained cross-national differences in instruments and systems. Whether the motivation to install sophisticated management accounting systems and the factors that explain the success of cost accounting systems differ internationally (fourth and fifth research question) has been neglected. This study has addressed this research gap by applying *sophisticated statistical analyses* including multiple regression analysis and PLS. This study demonstrates that the *factors explaining the conceptual design and the performance of cost accounting systems* strongly differ between Germany and Japan – probably due to the different cultural and institutional environment in both countries. These findings show that the conclusions from prior research about the motivation to install sophisticated cost accounting systems may not apply to other countries with strong differences in national culture and the institutional environment of cost accounting.

1265 See *Granlund/Lukka* (1998); *Shields* (1998).

The most important actions that were applied in this study to increase the explanatory power are summarized in Table 4-1. These actions have contributed to provide a **sound knowledge of cross-national differences in cost accounting** between Germany and Japan. This study also extends prior domestic research on the complexity of cost accounting systems. By applying objective characteristics and a more comprehensive description of the cost accounting system, this study yields higher adjusted R^2 in the regressions than prior research.[1266]

Methodological issue	Actions to increase explanatory power of this study
Equivalence	• Comparative data sets • Back translations and pre-tests • Research collaboration • Objective characteristics • 7-point-Likert scale, labeling only the endpoints • Calculating coefficient of congruence
Control variables	• German and Japanese data sets matched by the control variables industry and company size
Methodological perspective	• Application of contingency theory merged with cultural contingency theory and societal effects approach
Statistical analysis	• Multiple regression analysis; PLS; test for equivalence • Test for stability of the findings

Table 4-1: Actions to increase the explanatory power of this study

4.2 Limitations

As in all research, the findings of this study are subject to conceptual and methodological limitations. These limitations should be considered while interpreting the results of this investigation. They further provide a basis to derive directions for future research.

Conceptual limitations

Conceptual limitations include the **selection of the sample**, the research topic, the selection and operationalization of theoretical constructs, and the explanation of cross-national differences. *Medium-sized companies* from *three industries* and *two countries* have been investigated in this study. Medium-sized companies were chosen to reduce the interrelations between the samples. Limiting this study to three industries is necessary to ensure sampling equivalence and to control for industry effects. Due to the complexity of comparative research, the study is limited to only two countries. Germany and Japan were chosen, because both belong to the three most influential countries in spreading management accounting systems around the world and because their cultural and institutional environments that shape cost accounting systems differ strongly. Section 3.1.2.2 shows that the data is representative to a large extent. Therefore, the findings are not only valid for the investigated companies, but they can generally be generalized to companies that have not participated in this study. Due to the selection of the sample, however, practical recommendations and theoretical conclusions can, strictly speaking, only be developed for medium-sized companies of these industries and countries. The transferability of the results to smaller and larger companies, to other industries, and to other countries than Germany

1266 See footnote 1164 and 1222.

and Japan is not directly possible. However, it is likely that the conclusions of the five research questions might also be valid to related industries (e.g., other manufacturing industries), and – to some extent – also to other countries like Austria and Switzerland that share a similar cultural and institutional environment with Germany. However, more valid conclusions can be developed when future research replicates this study by extending it to further industries and countries.[1267] Many statements might also be transferable to smaller and larger German and Japanese companies.[1268] Furthermore, as systems converge internationally,[1269] the differences in cost accounting may diminish over time. As the characteristics of the cost accounting objectives and systems have been surveyed only at one point of time, the results might be limited to only a certain period of time. The results of this study, however, do not indicate that harmonization in complexity and timeliness of cost accounting systems between Germany and Japan is imminent. To verify this assumption, however, longitudinal studies would be required.[1270]

Besides the sample, also the **research topic** has been narrowed. This study has investigated objectives, the conceptual design, and the performance of cost accounting systems. This limitation was necessary, due to shortcomings and the lack of prior research. Valuable insights about starting points for behavioral research did not exist before. Furthermore, the narrow focus of this study was necessary to ensure conceptual equivalence and to provide practitioners with more meaningful recommendations how to design cost accounting systems.[1271] Behavioral aspects in cost accounting were therefore not addressed in this study, although the strongest cross-national differences are expected there and the interplay between the conceptual design of cost accounting systems and type of use merits further research.[1272] Furthermore, this study has not investigate the relationship between cost accounting and other management accounting or cost management instruments, although their interplay is of theoretical and practical relevance.[1273] Cost accounting as an essential part of a company's information system should provide relevant information for other management accounting and cost management instruments as well.

Based on the conceptual framework, the **theoretical constructs** have been conceptualized and operationalized. The research design and the questionnaire have comprehensively

---

1267 To support credible international generalizations it would be required to extend this study to a minimum of further five to eight countries. Cf. *Franke/Richey* (2010).

1268 Although *Hopper et al.* concludes that small and medium sized Japanese companies have similar cost accounting systems to larger Japanese firms (cf. *Hopper et al.* (1999)), the transferability of the results to smaller or larger Japanese companies might still be limited. Unlike for German companies the results indicate that company size has a strong effect upon the complexity, timeliness, and performance of cost accounting systems in Japan. This might be linked to the Japanese education system that imposes barriers for smaller Japanese companies to acquire sufficient cost accounting knowledge to install comprehensive systems. See section 3.5.3.1.

1269 Cf., e.g., *Granlund/Lukka* (1998); *Shields* (1998).

1270 Longitudinal studies could further be applied to cross-nationally investigate the emergence of sophisticated cost accounting systems. Cf. *Drury/Tayles* (2005), p. 79.

1271 Cf. section 1.4.4.1.

1272 See section 4.3.

1273 Cf. *Malmi/Brown* (2008); *Malmi/Granlund* (2009), p. 610. See also section 4.3.

been discussed with researchers and practitioners. All relevant statements and empirical findings from literature were considered while specifying the conceptual framework. The conceptualization of the conceptual framework is theory-based. The results of this study show that the reality is well reflected by this conceptual framework. Nevertheless, it cannot be excluded that all relevant aspects have been considered and that all of them have been conceptualized and operationalized properly. It is possible that this and prior studies have applied inappropriate measures for the context as well as for the objectives, the conceptual design, and the performance of cost accounting systems. To keep the response time of the questionnaire below 30 minutes, only the most relevant *context factors* have been considered. Some of the omitted control variables, e.g., organizational structure, strategy, and other management (accounting) instruments, could also explain the conceptual design and the performance of cost accounting systems. Further research could also analyze more aspects of the *conceptual design of cost accounting systems.*[1274] Finally, the characteristics of cost accounting *elements were weighted equally* to obtain the overall score for the complexity and timeliness of the systems for reasons of simplification.

Cross-national variance in cost accounting between Germany and Japan were explained by contrasting cross-national differences in the institutional environment with cross-national differences in cost accounting. The **explanation of cross-national differences** is therefore based on indirect instead of statistical relationships. As cause-and-effect relationships can only be applied to determine the impact of country-specifics upon management accounting when sufficient countries are compared, none of the 148 prior studies on comparative management accounting have investigated statistical relationships before. Another limitation is that only of the expressions of national culture in the institutional environment and not national culture itself were contrasted to explain cross-national differences in cost accounting. Finally, it cannot be ensured that all variance between German and Japanese cost accounting objectives, systems, and performance are due to cross-national differences, because the German and Japanese sample were matched only by company size and industry.

Methodological limitations

Cross-national research is subject to specific and general methodological limitations. Specific limitations include **issues in equivalence**. It is likely that the research design and the findings are culturally formed by the researchers (ethnocentric bias) and that thus the supposed relationships and the interpretation of the empirical results are subject to a biased perception of the author.[1275] The questionnaire might not be equivalent in meaning, because in several questions instruments are named that might have a slightly different meaning across countries. Sampling equivalence is probably also not fully met, because

1274 E.g., not only the distinction between variable and fixed costs can be surveyed, but also their methods (like high-low method, statistical method, etc.) could be addressed to more accurately capture the complexity and timeliness of cost accounting systems. Furthermore, besides the frequency of updating cost information, the internal processes to generate cost information could be analyzed.

1275 Further steps to ensure measure equivalence could have been carried through. These, however, hamper comparability of the findings. See *Berry* (1980).

the selected industries might have a different economic relevance across countries. Furthermore, also medium-sized companies are operating internationally and might therefore be subject to international influences. They might thus not represent typical German and Japanese cost accounting. Unlike prior research, issues in equivalence have thoroughly been addressed in this study. This includes comparable data sets for Germany and Japan, back translations and pre-test of the questionnaire, selection of preferably objective characteristics to measure the conceptual design of the cost accounting systems, application of seven-point Likert scales, and collaboration with a Japanese research partner who is well familiar with German cost accounting and who fluently speaks German.[1276] In spite of these comprehensive efforts, limitations in equivalence can still lead to distorted results.

More general methodological limitations include the simplifications regarding survey research and statistical analyses. **Survey research** was the most appropriate research method to address the study's objective. Nevertheless, several limitations are associated with survey research. For example, it cannot be controlled, whether the addressed cost accountants have actually filled out the questionnaire by their own and under which conditions.[1277] This problem was considered for by personally contacting the responsible persons and sending them the questionnaire via e-mail in Germany. In Japan this problem was less comprehensively addressed, because the respondents were contacted only by mail. To avoid intended false declarations, the responders' anonymity was ensured in both countries.

Another related problem is the difference in response style, which is of particular relevance in cross-national studies. Seven-point Likert scales and prevalent objective measures for the conceptual design of cost accounting systems were applied as well as cost accounting objectives were contrasted with each other (e.g., planning versus control) to reduce such differences in response style and to ensure conceptual equivalence between Germany and Japan. A further advantage of this procedure is that this study, unlike most prior domestic research, avoids biases in the relationships between cost accounting objectives, cost accounting systems, and the performance of cost accounting systems that might solely stem from response style differences.[1278] Nevertheless, the responses are still based on perceptions of the addressed cost accountants. This is problematic in particular for evaluating the performance of cost accounting systems. Cost accountants were asked to assess the attainment of cost accounting objectives and the characteristics of the provided cost information (and thereby indirectly their own performance) themselves. It is likely that Japanese cost accountants are more reserved in assessing their own performance than their German counterparts.[1279] Further research may therefore survey the perception of the receivers of cost information to provide a more precise picture of cost accounting perfor-

1276 An overview of this effort is provided in sections 1.4.4.2 and 1.5.5.

1277 Cf. *Stier* (1999), p. 199.

1278 When respondents within a country systematically answer questions differently (e.g., some answer more positively and others less positively how intensively they pursue cost accounting objectives and how satisfied they are with the provided information), a positive coherence between objectives and performance prevails, which might only stem from differences in response style.

1279 This is likely, because the Japanese are known for their modesty. See *Lebra* (1998), p. 126-129. See also *Smith et al.* (2009), p. 121f.

mance for generating more comparable results. A dyadic or triadic sampling procedure was not carried through in this study, to obtain sufficient responses from practitioners, which was necessary to apply advanced statistical methods and to control for company size and industry effects. As described in section 1.5.1, a field study faces fewer of these disadvantages than survey research, because it better captures human behavior and the natural context of the observed organizations. A field study is more suitable to understand national differences and where they stem from. However, this method was not suitable for the research objective of this study, because it does not provide representative results and recommendations for practitioners cannot be developed.

The analysis of relationships between variables is mainly limited to linear regression analysis and PLS that do not allow to consider non-linear and recursive relationships. With both quantitative **statistical methods** it cannot be investigated, e.g., whether a diminishing marginal utility of cost accounting systems' complexity and timeliness prevails.[1280] To address this shortcoming for selective research questions, however, specific mathematical and graphical analyses were carried through to investigate non-linearity of relationships. For instance, interaction effects were integrated in regressions. More complex relationships, however, have to be analyzed qualitatively.

All these limitations may constrain the explanatory power of this investigation. However, many conceptual and methodological challenges have carefully been addressed in this study. It is therefore concluded that this study provides new insights that are relevant for theory and practice. Significant cross-national differences in cost accounting were reported and explained. Furthermore, recommendations how to design successful cost accounting systems in Germany and Japan were provided. This gives cost accountants in MNC a solid knowledge basis to solve their challenges that are associated to cross-national differences in cost accounting systems. It also provides researchers and practitioners with new insights why and how cost accounting systems differ between Germany and Japan. These findings provide a sound and evidence-based picture of cross-national differences in cost accounting objectives and the conceptual design of cost accounting systems that raise new research questions. The limitations outlined before provide additional suggestions for further research.

4.3 Further research

In this study several hypotheses are not verified – either because the theoretical conclusions were wrong or because the chosen research method is inadequate to fully address the respective hypotheses. Either way, these unsolved questions highlight valuable research areas. In particular the **interplay between objectives and the conceptual design of cost accounting systems** merits further research. It is, e.g., argued that "[a]ttention directing, learning, and motivation are most effective and efficient when the employees' tasks are clarified and focused, when key variables are visible, and when few conflicts or trade-offs exist among the variables."[1281] Instead of applying interaction terms in regression analysis,

1280 Cf. *Krumwiede* (1998), p. 264.

1281 *Merchant/Shields* (1993), p. 81.

a more detailed analysis via qualitative and behavioral research could be applied. The interplay between objectives and the conceptual design of cost accounting systems is of particular interest, because systems should be purposefully designed. Instead of aligning objectives with the conceptual design of cost accounting systems, solely the implementation of 'modern' systems like ABC and GPK are postulated in literature to improve cost accounting. However, whether more complex systems are in general better than simple ones requires empirical verification. The results of this study show that highly complex cost accounting systems can lead to inferior results. Hence, more research is required, e.g., about the **optimal degree of complexity and timeliness of cost accounting systems**. There is also a need for further research to examine why some companies do not align the conceptual design of their systems to their environments and to the objectives they are striving for.[1282]

This study investigated cost accounting systems without any reference to other instruments. Cost accounting systems, however, do not operate in isolation. They are instead connected to other management accounting and cost management systems that can either complement or substitute them.[1283] The complexity and timeliness of cost accounting systems thus depend on further instruments. Hence, further research should consider the **interplay between cost accounting systems and other instruments** to more comprehensively explain when cost accounting systems are complex or timely in nature, and whether or how cost accounting systems are complemented or substituted by other instruments in different contexts.

This study provides insights into cross-national differences in cost accounting objectives and the conceptual design of cost accounting systems. Thereby, valuable research questions for **behavioral research** (e.g., how cost information is actually used) arise. German companies employ more complex and timelier cost accounting systems than their Japanese counterparts, because German cost accountants are more specialized and have more theoretical knowledge than their Japanese counterparts. Furthermore, German companies have installed more comprehensive IT systems and German cost accountants receive more top management support for cost accounting. Although more complex and timelier systems have a higher potential to provide more accurate, detailed, and timely cost information, it does not imply that these systems lead to better decisions. First, because a diminishing marginal utility of both dimensions is likely to exist. Second, because German cost accountants might spend too much time to find theoretically sound solutions in allocating costs instead of discussing the provided information with their managers.[1284] In Japan on the contrary, cost accountants are less specialized and are more experienced in other business sections. This facilitates a closer collaboration with managers to combine their accounting know-how with operational knowledge. Hence, cost information is likely to be used differently in both countries and might have a different meaning. Furthermore,

1282 This call for further research extents the suggestions by *Drury/Tales*. Cf. *Drury/Tayles* (2005), p. 78.

1283 For suggestions how to investigate management control systems as a package see *Malmi/Brown* (2008).

1284 Cf. *Ahrens/Chapman* (1999), p. 43; *Weber* (2004), p. 9.

the role of cost accountants is likely to vary. Cross-national variation in the roles of management accountants that stem from differences in education is already described by *Ahrens* and *Ahrens/Chapman*.[1285] A new research area raised by this study is, which consequences the conceptual design of cost respectively management accounting systems have for the role of cost respectively management accountants and for the type of use of the provided information. Thereby, **effective relationships between the systems' characteristics, the role of cost respectively management accountants, and the type of use of cost information** could be compared cross-nationally. It is expected that German cost accountants can learn from Japanese companies how to effectively collaborate with managers. The discussion of management accounting information with managers has already been identified as one important success factor in many empirical studies for German companies.[1286] This interplay was neglected by prior empirical and conceptual research. Instead, merely better and 'sophisticated' systems were instead postulated in literature without any reference to the roles of cost accountants and the type of use of cost information.

The strong and significant cross-national differences indicate that caution is required while transferring cost accounting systems abroad. As German cost accountants are more specialized and have more theoretical knowledge than their Japanese counterparts, the expressions of national culture in the institutional environment of cost accounting (e.g., education, role of cost accountants) are likely to impose significant barriers for transferring German cost accounting systems to Japan. Further conceptual and empirical research can be based upon the findings of this study, to **enhance domestic cost accounting and to provide MNC with recommendations for integrating cost accounting systems** between Germany and Japan. The embeddedness of foreign systems, however, requires a more thorough understanding than provided in this study to successfully adapt these systems to other national settings: German companies, e.g., have failed to transfer GPK to the USA without adaptation.[1287] In the meantime, some US researchers started to adjust GPK to the US environment.[1288] One significant barrier to transfer German cost accounting to the USA that remains is the difference in cost accounting education between both countries. Adoption of German systems to foreign environments and solutions how to address this barrier also merits further research.

1285 Whereas the German management accountants' role is formalized to rationalize and legitimize operational proposals that are generated by the functions, the role in Britain is to early involve in emergent operational proposals. As a consequence, British management accountants are working more closely together with managers to combine their accounting know-how with operational knowledge than their German counterparts. In the British breweries observed, accounting is enacted to be immediately relevant for the daily ordering of organizational action. Cf. *Ahrens* (1997b). See also *Ahrens* (1996), (1997a), (1999), *Ahrens/Chapman* (2000). Similar cross-national differences in cost accountants' roles are expected between Germany and Japan.

1286 Cf. *Weber et al.* (2010a).

1287 See, e.g., *Krumwiede* (2005). The German company Stihl on the contrary has successfully implemented GPK in their US subsidiary.

1288 See *Clinton/Webber* (2004); *Webber/Clinton* (2004); *Thomson/Gurowka* (2005), p. 31; *White* (2009).

Finally, future research could **replicate this study by extending it to other industries and countries**. An extension to the USA would be of particular relevance, because then the three most influential countries in spreading management accounting systems around the world could be compared. Furthermore, the cultural and institutional environment differs significantly across the countries.[1289] Successful systems around the world could be identified, compared, and their embeddedness in different cultural and institutional environments could be explained.[1290] An extension to other industries would be of relevance, because the results of this study indicate that manufacturing industries run more complex and timelier cost accounting systems than hospitals. Whether in general manufacturing companies run more complex and timelier systems than companies from the service industry, however, demands further empirical evidence.[1291]

Overall, it can be concluded that this study has for the first time comprehensively considered issues in equivalence, theoretical perspectives, and advanced statistical methods to describe and explain cross-national differences in cost accounting objectives and the conceptual design of cost accounting systems. Particularities of German and Japanese cost accounting were empirically determined and their underlying rationale was identified. Furthermore, recommendations how to purposefully design cost accounting systems were provided. These findings provide a solid basis for further research: Valuable research areas for further research to cross-nationally compare behavioral aspects in cost accounting arose. Finally, the findings show that due to cross-national differences in national culture and institutions cost accounting should be adapted to the country-specific context when systems are transferred across countries or when MNC want to harmonize their cost accounting systems.

1289 See section 2.1.1.

1290 Addressing the specific challenges of small Japanese companies to acquire (cost) accounting knowledge would also merit further research.

1291 Further research indicates that some service industries run also highly comprehensive cost accounting systems. *Drury/Tales* and *Al-Omiri/Drury* demonstrate that the finance sector employs more complex cost accounting systems compared to other industries. Cf. *Drury/Tayles* (2005), p. 74f.; *Al-Omiri/Drury* (2007), p. 413-420. See also *Kosmider* (1994), p. 143-155; *Legenhausen* (1998), p. 87; *Frank/Reitmeyer* (1999).

Appendix

Appendix 1: List of research projects on comparative management accounting research

Reference	Countries/ nationalities	Setting (per country)	Database (response rate)	Research Method	Topic	Hofstede-inspired?
Ahrens (1996); Ahrens (1997a); Ahrens (1997b); Ahrens (1999)	Germany, UK	First group: Management accountants of large British and German manufacturing companies; Second group: Matched firms of the brewing industry	First observed group: 1 from the UK, 2 from Germany Second group: Observations in 2 firms and interviews in 7 firms from Germany, observations in 2 firms and interviews in 3 firms from the UK	Field study (interviews, observation)	Management accounting practices	No (1997a,b); Yes (1996; 1999)
Ahrens/ Chapman (1999); Ahrens/ Chapman (2000)	Germany, UK	64 management accountants in total	34 (30) individuals from 17 (12) German (British) firms	Field study (interviews)	Management accounting overall, career choice	No
Anyane-Ntow (1988)	Japanese, USA	Financial executives of manufacturing companies operating in the USA	45 Japanese companies (45%), 39 USA companies (39%)	Survey	Budgeting, management control systems, performance measurement	Yes
Appleyard/ Pallett (2003)	Germany, UK	2 acquisitions: one by a UK company of a German subsidiary and vice versa	1 from Germany, 1 from the UK	Field study	Management control systems, management accounting overall	No
Aptel/ Pourjalali (2001)	France, USA	Large hospitals	126 from France (6.3%), 75 from the USA (12.5%)	Survey	Management accounting practices, information systems, cost management, JIT, cost accounting overall	No
Au/Bemmels (2000)	Canada, Hong Kong	Undergraduate business students	98 from Canada (study 1), 120 from Hong Kong (study 3), 62 from Hong Kong (study 2)	Experiment (study 1 and 3), Survey (study 2)	Decision making	No
Auyeung/ Sands (1996); Auyeung/ Sands (1997)	Australia, China (Hong Kong), Taiwan	Accounting major students	303 Australian students (80.6%), 172 Chinese students, 157 Taiwanese students	Survey	Learning style, career choice	Yes
Awasthi/Chow/ Wu (1998); Awasthi/Chow/ Wu (2001)	Chinese (Taiwan) and USA nationals	Students from MBA and senior level undergraduate classes	75 USA nationals, 75 Chinese nationals	Experiment	Performance measurement	Yes
Bailes/Assada (1991)	Japan, USA	Large manufacturing companies	256 from Japan (39.6%), 80 from the USA (16%)	Survey	Budgeting, performance measurement, management control systems	No

Reference	Countries/ nationalities	Setting (per country)	Database (response rate)	Research Method	Topic	Hofstede-inspired?
Bailey/Chen/Dou (1997)	China, Japan, USA	Part-time MBA students, employees or trainees of medium-sized companies	82 from China, 57 from Japan, 77 from the USA	Survey	Performance measurement	Yes
Ballantine/ Brignall/Modell (1998)	Sweden, UK	Organizations in the public health sector	1 from Sweden, 1 from the UK	Field study	Performance measurement	Yes
Bhimani/ Gosselin/Ncube (2005); Bhimani et al. (2007)	Canada, France, Germany, Italy, Japan, UK, USA	Chief accountants or controllers of the 500 largest (450 in Italy) companies per country	35 from Canada (7%), 39 from France (8%), 73 from Germany (15%), 32 from Italy (7%), 95 from Japan (19%), 85 from the UK (17%), 57 from the USA (11%)	Survey	ABC	No
Bhimani/Ncube/ Soonawalla (2006)	Canada, France, Germany, Italy, Japan, UK, USA	Financial directors of the 500 largest (450 in Italy) companies per country	29 from Canada (5.8%), 34 from France (6.8%), 69 from Germany (13.8%), 29 from Italy (6.4%), 69 from Japan (13.8%), 63 from the UK (12.6%), 45 from the USA (9.0%)	Survey	Capital budgeting and investment decisions	No
Birnberg/ Hoffmann/Yuen (2008) replicating *Evan/Heiman-Hoffmann/Rau (1994)*(US study)	China, USA	MBA and doctoral students	34 from China, 56 from the USA	Experiment (question-naire includ-ed)	Management control systems	Yes
Birnberg/ Snodgrass (1988)	Japan, USA	Workers and managers of 11 large manufactur-ing and construction companies per country	550 from Japan, 501 from the USA	Survey (question-naire, inter-views)	Management control systems	No
Borkowski (1997)	Canada, USA	Transnational Corporations listed top 500 (or 1000) with Canadian-US cross-border subsidiaries	28 from Canada (22.2%), 62 from the USA (23.8%)	Survey	Transfer pricing	No
Borkowski (1999)	Canada, Germany, Japan, UK, USA	International vice presidents or controllers of transna-tional corporations (either parent or sub-sidiary from the USA)	71 from Canada (56.3%), 45 from Germany (39.8%), 105 from Japan (43.6%), 38 from the UK (31.4%), 292 from the USA (42.5%)	Survey	Performance measurement, transfer pricing	Yes

Reference	**Countries/ nationalities**	**Setting** (per country)	**Database** (response rate)	**Research Method**	**Topic**	**Hofstede-inspired?**
Borkowski (2010)	Australia, Canada, Japan, USA	Tax executives of the largest transnational corporations	7 from Australia (23%), 20 from Canada (25.7%), 22 from Japan (44%), 48 from the USA (27.4%)	Survey	Transfer pricing	No
Brewer (1998)	Malaysia, USA	Production managers and process engineers from Harris Semiconductor's plant locations (1 Malaysian and 3 US)	18 in Malaysia, 18 in the USA	Field study (survey, interviews, corporate database)	ABC	Yes
Brownell/Hirst (1986); replicating Brownell (1982a); Brownell (1982b) (US study)	Australia, USA	Line managers of a large manufacturing company headquartered in Sydney; managers of a large manufacturing company located in San Francisco	76 from Australia (82.6%), 48 from USA	Survey	Management control systems, budgeting, performance measurement	Yes
C&L Deutsche Revision (1997)	Austria, Belgium, Canada, France, Germany, Hungary, Italy, Netherlands, Spain, Sweden, Switzerland, UK, Ukraine	Chief financial officers and chief accountants or controllers of the largest companies	9 from Austria, 11 from Belgium, 17 from Canada, 23 from France, 45 from Germany, 10 from Hungary, 42 from Italy, 16 from the Netherlands, 17 from Spain, 8 from Sweden, 19 from Switzerland, 55 from the UK, 5 from Ukraine	Survey	Value based management, decision making	No
Cadez/Guilding (2007); Cadez (2006)	Australia, Slovenia	Australian top public companies and 500 largest Slovenian companies	111 from Australia (8.6%), 193 from Slovenia (49.7%)	Survey	Management accounting overall, management accounting practices	No
Calori/Lubatkin/Very (1994)	France, UK, USA	392 respectively 612 top managers of 29 French and 46 British acquired firms	70 from France (17.9%), 91 from the UK (14.9%)	Survey	International control	Yes
Carr (1998); Carr (2005); Carr/Tomkins (1996); Carr/Tomkins (1998); Carr/Tomkins/Bayliss (1991); Carr/Tomkins/Bayliss (1994); Carr/Harris (2004); Carr/Pudelko (2006)	Germany, Japan, UK, USA	90 vehicle component manufacturers	25 (+10 resp. 12 subsequent) from Germany, 11 (+2 subsequent and 1 re-interview) from Japan, 24 (+4 subsequent) from the UK, 11 (+3 subsequent and 1 re-interview) from the USA	Field study	Controllership, cost management	Yes (1998/2004/2006); No (1991/1994/1996/2005)

Reference	Countries/ nationalities	Setting (per country)	Database (response rate)	Research Method	Topic	Hofstede-inspired?
Chan (1998)	Australia, USA	Undergraduate and postgraduate business and accounting student volunteers	160 from Australia, 240 from the USA	Experiment (face-to-face negotiation)	Transfer pricing, performance measurement	Yes
Chan/DeGroote (2004)	Canada, USA	Chief administrative officers of municipal governments	52 from Canada (11.1%), 132 from the USA (29.3%)	Survey	Performance measurement, BSC	No
Choe/Langfield-Smith (2004)	Australia, Korea	Chief production managers or plant managers of automotive manufacturing firms	47 from Australia (25%), 74 from Korea (19%)	Survey	Management accounting overall, information systems	Yes
Choi/Czechowicz (1983)	Sweden, Switzerland, UK, USA, and others	Leading manufacturing US-based vs. non-US multinationals	Questionnaires: 64 from the USA (21.3%), 24 from non-US countries (8%); interviews of financial executives: 10 from the USA, 10 from non-US countries; telephone interviews: 10 further firms from the USA; roundtable discussions: 50 corporations from the USA	Field study	Performance measurement	No
Chow et al. (1997)	Chinese nationals from Taiwan, USA	192 undergraduate accounting students	83 Chinese students (69.2%), 109 US students (90.8%)	Experiment	Management accounting practices, decision making	Yes
Chow et al. (1998)	Chinese nationals from Taiwan, USA	144 upper-division undergraduate business students	72 from Taiwan, 72 from the USA	Experiment	Management control systems, performance measurement	Yes
Chow et al. (1999)	Australia, Taiwan	Middle-level managers of 14 Australian (13 Taiwanese) manufacturing companies	50 from Australia, 52 from Taiwan	Survey (and interviews)	Information systems	Yes
Chow/Deng/Ho (2000)	China, USA	142 managers (executive MBA students)	38 from China (100%), 104 from the USA (92%)	Survey	Information systems	Yes
Chow/Kato/ Merchant (1996); Merchant (1985,1990)	Japan, USA	Profit center managers from Toshiba and an American equivalent firm (out of the 50 largest industrial firms in the world)	28 from Japan (75.7%), 54 from the USA (87.1%)	Survey	Management control systems	Yes
Chow/Kato/ Shields (1994)	Japan, USA	93 MBA students	39 from Japan, 54 from the USA	Experiments (questionnaire included)	Management control systems	Yes

Reference	**Countries/ nationalities**	**Setting** (per country)	**Database** (response rate)	**Research Method**	**Topic**	**Hofstede-inspired?**
Chow/Lindquist/ Wu (2001)	Chinese nationals from Taiwan, USA	Students	13 Chinese nationals (58.1%), 13 USA nationals (72%)	Experiment	Management control systems	Yes
Chow/Shields/ Chan (1991)	Singapore, USA	192 undergraduate accounting students	93 from Singapore, 93 from the USA	Experiment	Management control systems, performance measurement	Yes
Chow/Shields/ Wu (1999)	Japan, Taiwan, USA	Top two levels of Taiwanese managers of foreign-owned computer/electronics companies (6 per country) in Taiwan	56 from Japanese-owned companies, 59 from Taiwan-owned companies, 44 from USA-owned companies; (40.7 % total response rate)	Survey	Management control systems, international control	Yes
Coates et al. (1992)	Germany, UK, USA	45 managers of 15 multinational companies (listed top 200) and 30 divisions or subsidiaries	5 MNCs from Germany, 5 MNCs from the UK, 5 MNCs from the USA	Field study (interviews with open-ended questions)	Performance measurement	No
Collins/ Holzmann/ Mendoza (2005)	Latin America, USA	Individuals working for corporations, mainly involved in primary industries (Latin America) or from the manufacturing sector (USA)	205 from Latin America (data collection at seminars), 159 from the USA (73%)	Survey	Budgeting	Yes
Collins/Almer/ Mendoza (1999)	Latin America, USA	Managers with budgetary responsibility	128 from Latin America (100%; data collection at seminars), 278 from the USA (23%)	Survey	Budgeting	Yes
Cotton/Jackman/ Brown (2003) replicating the UK survey Innes et al. (2000)	New Zealand, UK	Finance directors and accounting staff of the largest companies	299 from New Zealand (approximately 40%), 177 from the UK (22.9%)	Survey	ABC	No
Currie/Seddon (1992); Currie (1992a); Currie (1992b)	Japan, UK, USA	Senior and middle-level managers of manufacturing companies	8 from Japan, 1 from the UK 5 from the USA	Field study (interviews)	Information systems, performance measurement, management accounting overall, cost management, JIT	No
Daley et al. (1985)	Japan, USA	Controllers and line managers of the 500 largest industrial firms	Controllers: 207 from Japan (41%), 190 from the USA (38%) Managers: 173 from Japan (43%), 113 from the USA (30%)	Survey	Management control systems, budgeting	No

Reference	**Countries/ nationalities**	**Setting** (per country)	**Database** (response rate)	**Research Method**	**Topic**	**Hofstede-inspired?**
Daniel/Reitsperger (1991); Daniel/ Reitsperger (1992); Daniel/ Reitsperger (1994); Daniel/ Reitsperger/Gregson (1995)	Japan, USA	Manufacturing managers in 50 Japanese and 64 US electronics firms	698 from Japan (19%), 789 from the USA (6%)	Survey (plus interviews, observations)	Management control systems, quality, JIT, performance measurement	No (yes: 1991)
Douglas/Wier (2005)	China, USA	Chinese working graduate MBA students and American managers (members of The Institute of Certified Professional Managers)	142 from China, 220 from the USA (32%)	Survey	Budgeting, management control systems	Yes
Egelhoff (1984)	Europe, UK, USA	50 multinational corporations out of the 500 largest industrial corporations	20 from Europe, 6 from the UK, 24 from the USA	Survey (interview)	Management control systems, international control, performance measurement	Yes
Elliott (1998)	Australia/Japan, Europe (excluding UK), UK, USA	UK groups and foreign subsidiaries	3 from Australia/ Japan, 7 from Europe, 26 from the UK, 15 from the USA	Survey	Transfer pricing	No
Feichter (2008)	Central and Eastern European countries, German-speaking countries	Heads of investor relations or human resource departments of publicly listed companies	112 from Central and Eastern European countries (16.9%), 115 from German-speaking countries (23.1%)	Survey	Management control systems, performance measurement, incentives	Yes
Frucot/Shearon (1991) replicating the US study by *Brownell (1982)*	Mexico, USA	Managers of manufacturing companies	83 from Mexico, 48 from the USA	Survey	Management control systems, budgeting, performance measurement	Yes
Gentner (1994)	Germany, Japan, USA, Western Europe (France, Italy, Sweden, UK; excluding Germany)	Automobile companies	7 from Germany (100%), 3 from Japan (60%), 2 from the USA (67%), 3 from Western Europe (50%)	Survey	Performance measurement	No
Groot (1997); Groot (1999)	Netherlands, USA	Food and beverage producing companies	96 from the Netherlands (24.4%), 117 from the USA (17%)	Survey (plus additional interviews)	ABC	No
Guilding/ Cravens/Tayles (2000)	New Zealand, UK, USA	Senior accountants of the 230 [175; 937] largest New Zealand [British; US] companies	124 from New Zealand (51%), 63 from the UK (38%), 127 from the USA (13%)	Survey	Management accounting overall, management accounting practices	No

Reference	Countries/ nationalities	Setting (per country)	Database (response rate)	Research Method	Topic	Hofstede-inspired?
Guilding/ Lamminmaki/ Drury (1998)	New Zealand, UK	Accountants of 81 New Zealand and 260 British manufacturing companies	*Entire data set:* 85 from New Zealand (32%), 303 from the UK (24%) *Sub-sample:* 48 from New Zealand (17.5%), 47 from the UK (3.7%)	Survey	Budgeting, cost accounting overall, management accounting overall	Yes
Harrison (1992); Harrison (1993)	Australia, Singapore	Middle-level managers in the merchandising and buying functions of department and retail stores	96 from Australia (70.1%), 115 from Singapore (81%)	Survey	Budgeting, management accounting overall; performance measurement	Yes
Harrison et al. (1994)	Australia, Hong Kong, Singapore, USA	Senior accounting and finance executives	140 from Australia (70%), 55 from Hong Kong (27.5%), 65 from Singapore (32.5%), 104 from the USA (52%)	Survey	Budgeting, management control systems, decision making	Yes
Harrison et al. (1999)	Chinese and USA nationals	MBA students	119 Chinese subjects, 111 USA subjects	Experiment	Decision making	Yes
Hassall et al. (2005)	Spain, UK	Employers of management accountants	55 from Spain (20.4%), 214 from the UK (22.5%)	Survey	Management accounting overall, management accounting education	No
Hassel/ Cunningham (1996)	Belgium, Canada, Denmark, Finland, France, Germany, Netherlands, Norway, Spain, Sweden, UK	Domestic and foreign-unit managers of a multinational company headquartered in Finland	36 from domestic units (95%), 31 from foreign units (84%)	Survey	Budgeting	No
Hawkins (1983)	Japan, USA	Executives of large manufacturing companies	Pilot study: 9 from Japan(28.1%), 20 from the USA (57.1%); Full-scale study: 106 from Japan (33%), 147 from the USA (57%)	Survey	Management accounting practices, budgeting, cost accounting overall	No
Horovitz (1978); Horovitz (1980)	France, Germany, UK	High-ranking executives (4 per company) of 16 [18; 18] French [German; British] companies out of the top 500 companies per country	49 from France, 61 from Germany, 66 from the UK	Field study (interviews, document analysis)	Management control systems, management accounting practices	No

Reference	Countries/ nationalities	Setting (per country)	Database (response rate)	Research Method	Topic	Hofstede-inspired?
Horváth/ Minning (2001); Horváth et al. (2001); Horváth/Gehrke (2002); Gehrke/ Zarlowski (2002)	France, Germany, Italy, UK	The 125 top-selling companies, largest 50 companies of the new markets listed on the stock exchange, 25 companies shortly before admission to official listing	32 from France (10.4%), 49 from Germany (24.5%), 34 from Italy (17%), 30 from the UK (15%)	Survey	Management control systems, value based management, BSC, performance measurement	No
Ittner/Larcker (1997)	Canada, Germany, Japan, USA	Companies of the automotive and computer industries	53 from Canada, 50 from Germany, 54 from Japan, 92 from the USA; (85% total response rate)	Survey	Quality, management control systems, performance measurement, management accounting overall	Yes
Jacobs/Marcon/ Witt (2004)	Germany, Italy, UK	Clinicians of 2 hospitals	15 from Germany, 21 from Italy, 18 from the UK	Field study	Use of cost infor-mation for decision making, information systems	No
Jansen/ Merchant/Van der Stede (2007) replicating the US by study Gibbs et al. (2004)	Netherlands, USA	General, sales, service, and parts department managers of automobile companies	Survey: 206 from the Netherlands, 526 from the USA; interviews: in 2 Dutch companies, in 1 USA company	Survey, field study (interviews)	Incentives, perfor-mance measurement	Yes
Johnson/ Byington (1993)	Spain, USA	Mid- to upper-level managers	44 from Spain, 55 from the USA	Survey	Budgeting	Yes
Joshi (2001) replicating the Australian study *Chenhall/Smith (1998)*	*Australia*, India	Non-accounting man-agers or accounting and finance managers of large and medium size manufacturing companies (listed top 500)	78 from Australia (56%), 60 from India (24.4%)	Survey	Management accounting overall, management accounting practices	Yes
Kato (1989)	Japan, USA	Accounting executives of the largest compa-nies	168 from Japan (26.7%), 103 from the USA (20.6%)	Survey	Management accounting overall, management accounting practices	No
Kidwell et al. (2002); Ho/Kidwell (2000)	Canada, UK, USA	Chief administrative officers of municipal governments	157 from Canada (22.3%), 105 from the UK (22%), 140 from the USA (35.7%)	Survey	Management accounting practices, ABC, BSC, Bench-marking, Quality	No
Kim/Joo/Choi (1996)	Japan, Korea, USA	Manufacturing companies	Observations (1981-1986): 470 from Japan, 705 from Korea, 403 from the USA	Survey	Performance measurement	No
Kim/Song (1990) replicating *NAA Tokyo Affiliate (1988) and Howell (1987)*	Japan, Korea, USA	Manufacturing companies	375 from Korea (46.2%), other response rates unknown.	Survey (personal interviews in Korea)	Management accounting overall, management control systems, cost accounting overall, product costing	No
Kreder/Zeller (1988)	Germany, USA	Large companies	27 from Germany, 13 from the USA	Not mentioned	Management control systems	No

Reference	Countries/ nationalities	Setting (per country)	Database (response rate)	Research Method	Topic	Hofstede-inspired?
Krumwiede/ Suessmair (2007a); Krumwiede/ Suessmair (2007b)	Germany, USA	Manufacturing and non-manufacturing companies	148 from Germany (36%), 130 from the USA (27%)	Survey (plus additional site visits and inter-views)	Cost accounting overall	No
Kurunmäki/ Lapsley/Melia (2003); Lapsley/ Kurunmäki/ Melia (2001)	Finland, UK	Intensive care units from 2 hospitals	30 interviews with clinicians as well as finance and management staff in total	Field study	Management accounting overall, management accounting practices, Use of cost information for decision making	No
Lamminmaki/ Drury (2001)	New Zealand, UK	Senior accountants of large manufacturing companies	Sample: 85 from New Zealand (32%), 303 from the UK (24%) Subsample (matched by size): 43 from New Zealand, 47 from the UK	Survey	Product costing, management accounting overall, decision making, ABC	No
Lang (2001); Lang (2003)	Germany, Japan	Top 500 German companies and all listed Japanese companies	39 from Germany (26%), 59 from Japan (2.5%)	Survey	Management ac-counting overall	No
Lapsley/Pallot (2000)	New Zealand, UK (Scotland)	2 local governments	24 interviews per country	Field study	Management accounting overall	No
Lau/Buckland (2000) replicating Brownell/Dunk (1991) and Lau et al. (1995)	Australia, Norway, Singapore	Functional heads of mining companies	79 from Australia (66.9%), 71 from Norway (47.3%), 112 from Singa-pore (46.7%)	Survey	Budgeting	Yes
Lau/Low/ Eggleton (1995); Lau/Low/ Eggleton (1997)	Australia, Singapore	Functional heads of manufacturing companies	90 from Australia (52.9%), 107 from Singa-pore (44.6%)	Survey	Budgeting	Yes
Lau/Tan (1998)	Australia, Singapore	Middle-level managers from 20 [30] financial institutions in Australia [Singapore]	104 from Australia (65%), 85 from Singapore (53.1%)	Survey	Budgeting	Yes
Leach-López/ Stammerjohan/ McNair (2007)	Mexico, USA	American [Mexican] mid-level managers working for 15 US manufacturing companies [working for 49 US-controlled maquiladoras (re-exporting factories)]	98 from Mexico (55.6%), 45 from the USA (55.7%) [approximate values response rate in terms of number of companies/ maquiladoras]	Survey	Budgeting	Yes

Reference	Countries/ nationalities	Setting (per country)	Database (response rate)	Research Method	Topic	Hofstede-inspired?
Lee et al. (2001)	Asia-Pacific (Australia, Hong Kong, Japan, Korea, Singapore), UK, USA	Large multinational companies	53 from Asia-Pacific (26.5%) (including 14 (26%) [8 (15%), 17 (32%), 3 (7%), 11 (20%)] from Australia [Hong Kong, Japan, Korea, Singapore]), 79 from the UK (39.5%), 47 from the USA (23.8%)	Survey	Management accounting practices, management control systems	No
Li/Paisey (2005)	Australia, China, New Zealand	Financial officers of foreign subsidiaries of multinational companies and officials of four state tax authorities in China)	60 from Australia (27.8%), 47 from China (10.8%), 77 from New Zealand (28.1%)	Survey (including in-depth interviews)	Transfer pricing	Yes
McKee/Mock/ Ruud (1992)	Norway, USA	Accounting students	279 from Norway, 71 from the USA	Experiment (including questionnaire)	Learning style	No
Mendoza/Collins/ Holzmann (1997)	Central America (Costa Rica, Ecuador, El Salvador, Guatemala, Nicaragua, Panama), USA	Upper and mid-level managers with budgeting responsibilities	Central America (128 in total; data collection at seminars: 100%): 24 from Costa Rica, 50 from Ecuador, 20 from El Salvador, 7 from Guatemala, 19 from Nicaragua, 8 from Panama; USA: 276 from the USA (55%)	Survey	Budgeting	No
Merchant/Chow/ Wu (1995); Merchant (1989)	Taiwan, USA	Operating and profit center managers of 2 companies matched in terms of profit centers and industry (chemical, electronics)	23 from Taiwan, responses from the USA unknown	Field study	Incentives, performance measurement	Yes
Michalak (2002)	Germany, Poland	1 leading construction company	40 persons at different management levels in different departments	Field study (standardized interviews, analysis of documents and procedures, observation)	Management control systems	No
Patel (2003)	Australian, Indian, Chinese-Malaysian	Senior professional accountants from the Big Six multinational accounting firms	72 from Australia (60%), 84 from India (64.6%), 92 from Malaysia (68.1%)	Survey	Management control systems	Yes

Reference	Countries/ nationalities	Setting (per country)	Database (response rate)	Research Method	Topic	Hofstede-inspired?
Reitsperger/ Daniel (1991)	Japan, USA	Operating managers of 104 Japanese [110 US] manufacturing companies	1,582 from Japan (76.1%), 1,606 from the USA (73%)	Survey	Cost management, quality, JIT	No
Salter et al. (2008)	Australia, Chile	Undergraduate and MBA management accounting students	50 from Australia (86.2%), 108 from Chile (76.6%)	Experiment	Information systems, decision making	Yes
Salter/Schulz (2005)	Australian, Chinese	Management accounting students at an Australian university	60 Australian residents, 65 Chinese migrants	Experiment	Information systems, decision making	Yes
Salter/Sharp (2001)	Canada, USA	Managers participating in MBA, executive MBA and executive development programs in business schools	93 from Canada, 201 from the USA	Experiment	Management control systems, international control, decision making	Yes
Scapens/Sale (1985)	UK, USA	Corporate accounting personnel of large (mostly divisionalized) companies	300 from the UK (40.9%), 227 from the USA (46%)	Survey	Performance measurement, management control systems, decision making	No
Scarparo (2006)	Sweden, UK (Scotland)	2 Swedish [4 British] hospitals participating in the Hip Fracture Audit Programme	27 interviews with clinicians, nurses and hospital managers in total	Field study	Management accounting overall, management accounting practices, use of cost information for decision making	No
Scheytt/Soin/ Metz (2003)	Austria, France, Germany, UK	Business administration students	21 from Austria, 28 from France, 12 from Germany, 15 from the UK	Field study (narrative approach)	Management control systems, international control	Yes
Schuler/ Rogovsky (1998)	Argentina, Australia, Austria, Brazil, Canada, France, Germany, Ireland, Israel, Italy, Japan, Mexico, Netherlands, Norway, Spain, Sweden, UK, USA	Human resource specialists in companies	First data set: IBM-Towers Perrin; Second data set: International Social Survey Programme: over 1,000 respondents; Third data set: Price Waterhouse-Cranfield project: 4,684 respondents (14.2%)	Survey	Incentives, performance measurement	Yes
Schulz et al. (2009)	Chilean, Chinese	Chilean MBA students and Chinese visa students in Australia	105 Chilean subjects (91.3%), 44 Chinese subjects (69.8%)	Experiment	Information systems, decision making	Yes

Reference	Countries/ nationalities	Setting (per country)	Database (response rate)	Research Method	Topic	Hofstede-inspired?
Schweikart (1986)	Brazil, Colombia, Germany, Puerto Rico, Spain, USA, Venezuela	Large US multinational manufacturing company and its foreign plants	12 from Brazil (85.7%), 19 from Colombia (90.5%), 19 from Germany (90.5%), 7 from Puerto Rico (100%), 10 from Spain (71.4), 70 from the USA (97.2%), 15 from Venezuela (100%)	Survey	Management accounting overall, information systems, decision making, management control systems	Yes
Stoffel (1995,1997)	France, Germany, USA	Heads of controlling in industrial companies	49 from France (14%), 76 from Germany (21.7%), 36 from the USA (10.3%) (approximate values)	Survey	Controllership, management accounting overall	Yes
Tang/Chan (1979)	Japan, USA	Large industrial multinational companies	50 from Japan (13.6%), 76 from the USA (25.3%)	Survey	Transfer pricing	No
Tang/Walter/ Raymond (1979)	Japan, USA	Large industrial multinational companies	Pilot study: 13 from Japan (43%), 14 from the USA (47%); Full-scale study: 102 from Japan (27.6%), 145 from the USA (48.3%)	Survey	Transfer pricing	No
Tsui (2001)	Caucasian, Chinese	Subunit managers of manufacturing companies in China	38 Caucasian expatriates, 51 Chinese subjects; (71.8% in total)	Survey	Budgeting, management accounting overall	Yes
Ueno/Sekaran (1992); Ueno/Wu (1993); Ueno (2000)	Japan, USA	Controller or senior managers of manufacturing companies	149 from Japan (60.3%), 70 from the USA (34.1%)	Survey	Budgeting, management accounting practices, management control systems, performance measurement	Yes
Vallance/Fellow (1999)	Philippines, Singapore, Thailand	Not mentioned	Not mentioned	Not mentioned	Performance measurement	No
Van der Stede (2003)	Belgium, Europe (Czech Republic, Denmark, France, Germany, Greece, Luxembourg, Norway, Portugal, Netherlands, UK), Others (Canada)	153 business-unit managers of 37 large multinational companies headquartered in Belgium	*153 respondents (44.9%):* 115 from Belgium, 36 from Europe (excluding Belgium), 2 from other countries	Survey	Management control systems, incentives, budgeting, international control	Yes

Reference	Countries/ nationalities	Setting (per country)	Database (response rate)	Research Method	Topic	Hofstede-inspired?
Vance et al. (1992)	Indonesia, Malaysia, Thailand, USA	Managers representing diverse industries	177 from Indonesia, 192 from Malaysia, 182 from Thailand, 156 from the USA; (68% in total)	Survey	Performance measurement, management accounting practices	Yes
Welton/Davis (1990)	New Zealand, USA	College students	99 from New Zealand with (283 without) ethic exposure; 149 from the USA with (119 without) ethic exposure	Experiment (including questionnaire)	Ethical behavior, management accounting education	No
Whitt (1979)	Mexico, USA	Top managers in Mexican subsidiaries of USA multinational companies	Not mentioned	Survey	Management control systems, performance measurement, international control, budgeting	No
Wijewardena/De Zoysa (1999)	Australia, Japan	1000 largest manufacturing companies	231 from Australia (23.1%), 217 from Japan (21.7%)	Survey	Management accounting overall, management accounting practices, cost accounting overall	No
Williams/ Seaman (2001) replicating Libby/ Waterhouse (1996) [Canadian study]	Canada, Singapore	Assistant controllers (or above) of medium-sized manufacturing (industrial and service) companies	24 from Canada (34%), 121 from Singapore (58.7%)	Survey (telephone interviews)	Management accounting overall, management control systems, decision making, cost accounting overall, product costing	Yes
Wömpener (2010)	Brazil, Germany	Top-level management accountants	14 from Brazil, 14 from Germany	Field study	Management accounting overall, management accounting practices, decision making, information systems	Yes
Askarany/ Yazdifar (2010)	Australia, New Zealand, UK	CIMA members working in manufacturing and service companies	584 usable responses in total; Australia (28.5%), New Zealand (39.5%), UK (29%)	Survey (including interviews)	ABC	No
Yoshikawa/ Innes/Mitchell (1989)	Japan, UK (Scotland)	Top 500 manufacturing companies	137 from Japan (27.4%), 67 from the UK (33.5%)	Survey	Management accounting overall, management accounting practices, cost accounting overall	No

Appendix 2: Written version of the English questionnaire

WESTFÄLISCHE
WILHELMS-UNIVERSITÄT
MÜNSTER

IUR
Chair of International
Accounting
Prof. Dr. Peter Kajüter

Cost Accounting in the Mechanical Engineering Industry

This survey is part of an international research project being conducted by the Institute of Management Accountants, the University of Münster (Germany), Beppu University (Japan), and Osaka University of Commerce (Japan). The objective of the study is to identify worldwide best practices in cost accounting in the mechanical engineering industry. The insights provided by the results of this study will support companies to improve their cost accounting systems.

Contents:

A - **General questions about your company**

B - **Objectives of cost accounting**

C - **Design of the cost accounting system**

D - **Performance of the cost accounting system**

Please note:

This research is completely confidential and only aggregate (not individual) data will be published.

Please mark the appropriate response alternative(s) with an "x" or write in the designated boxes.

You can request a personal report summarizing the results of this project at the end of the questionnaire. This will enable you to benchmark your cost accounting system against those of other companies.

If you have any questions please contact Dipl.-Kfm. Matthias Moeschler at Matthias.Moeschler@wiwi.uni-muenster.de or by phone at +49 251 / 83-22858.

Section A – General questions about your company

A.1 Is your company part of a group?
☐ Yes, as a parent company ☐ Yes, as a parent company and as a subsidiary
☐ Yes, as a subsidiary ☐ No

A.2 Are shares of your company (or your parent company) listed on a stock exchange or are bonds issued?
☐ Yes ☐ No ☐ N/A (Not applicable)

A.3 Does your company own subsidiaries abroad? ☐ Yes ☐ No N/A

A.4 Under which financial reporting system do you prepare your... (Multiple answers possible)
individual financial statements? ☐ GAAP ☐ IFRS ☐ Other (please specify): ________________
consolidated financial statements? ☐ GAAP ☐ IFRS ☐ Other (please specify): ________________ ☐ Not applicable

A.5 To what extent are your company's product lines similar regarding the following characteristics?

	1 = very similar, ..., 7 = very heterogeneous							
	1	2	3	4	5	6	7	N/A
Production processes (e.g., setups, inspections)	☐	☐	☐	☐	☐	☐	☐	☐
Utilization of support cost centers (e.g., IT, internal power supply)	☐	☐	☐	☐	☐	☐	☐	☐

A.6 To what extent do the following statements apply to your company's IT system?

	1 = not at all, ..., 7 = completely							
	1	2	3	4	5	6	7	N/A
Cross-functionally integrated	☐	☐	☐	☐	☐	☐	☐	☐
Provides user-friendly query capabilities	☐	☐	☐	☐	☐	☐	☐	☐
Provides comprehensive cost and performance information	☐	☐	☐	☐	☐	☐	☐	☐
Most information is updated in "real-time" and not periodically	☐	☐	☐	☐	☐	☐	☐	☐

A.7 Who is responsible for cost accounting in your company? (Select all that apply)
☐ Specific department for cost accounting ☐ Management accounting department
☐ Accounting/finance department ☐ Operational departments (e.g., production, sales)
☐ Other (please specify): ________________________

A.8 How large is the number of the following aspects of your company (relative to your peers)?

	1 = very small, ..., 7 = very large						
	1	2	3	4	5	6	7
Suppliers	☐	☐	☐	☐	☐	☐	☐
Customer groups	☐	☐	☐	☐	☐	☐	☐
Competitors	☐	☐	☐	☐	☐	☐	☐

A.9 How stable were the following aspects of your company over the last three years?

	1 = not stable at all, .., 7 = very stable						
	1	2	3	4	5	6	7
Relationships with suppliers	☐	☐	☐	☐	☐	☐	☐
Customer needs	☐	☐	☐	☐	☐	☐	☐
Competitors' actions	☐	☐	☐	☐	☐	☐	☐

A.10 How is the workload of the employees responsible for cost accounting divided?
Tasks of financial accounting: ________%
Tasks of management accounting: ________%
Other tasks: ________%
Total 100%

A.11 To what extent do you agree with the following statements regarding your cost accounting?

	1 = not at all, ..., 7 = completely						
	1	2	3	4	5	6	7
It receives strong, active support from top management.	☐	☐	☐	☐	☐	☐	☐
Top management provides sufficient resources.	☐	☐	☐	☐	☐	☐	☐
It is designed for managerial instead for financial accounting purposes.	☐	☐	☐	☐	☐	☐	☐

A.12 To what extent do managers at your company require the following cost information?

	1 = not at all, ..., 7 = very strongly						
	1	2	3	4	5	6	7
Accurate cost information (in terms of: close to true value)	☐	☐	☐	☐	☐	☐	☐
Detailed cost information (in terms of: giving full particularities)	☐	☐	☐	☐	☐	☐	☐
Up-to-date cost information	☐	☐	☐	☐	☐	☐	☐
Easily understandable cost information	☐	☐	☐	☐	☐	☐	☐

A.13 Where have employees responsible for cost accounting in your company acquired most of the knowledge required to fulfill their tasks? ☐ College/University ☐ Professional associations (e.g., AICPA and IMA) ☐ In-house training ☐ At work "learning by doing" ☐ Other (please specify): ________________

A.14	To what extent do the following characteristics apply to your company's cost accountants?	1 = not at all, ..., 7 = completely						
		1	2	3	4	5	6	7
	Highly specialized exclusively in cost accounting	☐	☐	☐	☐	☐	☐	☐
	Experienced in business functions other than accounting (e.g., purchasing)	☐	☐	☐	☐	☐	☐	☐
	Qualified to enhance and run cost accounting systems	☐	☐	☐	☐	☐	☐	☐
	Rather qualified for requirements in financial than in managerial accounting	☐	☐	☐	☐	☐	☐	☐

A.15 **Please indicate the following figures for the latest financial year of your company:**
Average number of employees (full-time equivalents): ___________
Average number of employees responsible for cost accounting (full-time equivalents): ___________
Revenue ($ millions): ___________
Percentage of revenues from non-US sources: ☐ 0-15% ☐ 16-30% ☐ 31-45% ☐ 46-60% ☐ 61-75% ☐ more than 75%

A.16 **Over the last three years, how profitable was your company relative to its competitors ?**
☐ Less profitable ☐ Equally profitable ☐ More profitable

Section B – Objectives of cost accounting

B.1	How intensively does your company pursue the following objectives? • Providing cost information for decision making regarding...	1 = not at all,......, 7 = very intensively						
		1	2	3	4	5	6	7
	pricing	☐	☐	☐	☐	☐	☐	☐
	short-term capacity planning (e.g., for machines)	☐	☐	☐	☐	☐	☐	☐
	exploiting cost reduction potential	☐	☐	☐	☐	☐	☐	☐
	strategy development (e.g., cost leadership)	☐	☐	☐	☐	☐	☐	☐
B.2	• Providing cost information to motivate employees so that they...	1 = not at all,......, 7 = very intensively						
		1	2	3	4	5	6	7
	carry out operational tasks efficiently	☐	☐	☐	☐	☐	☐	☐
	make cost savings	☐	☐	☐	☐	☐	☐	☐
	act in accordance with the business strategy	☐	☐	☐	☐	☐	☐	☐
B.3	• Cost accounting to support...	1 = not at all,......, 7 = very intensively						
		1	2	3	4	5	6	7
	operational planning	☐	☐	☐	☐	☐	☐	☐
	strategic planning	☐	☐	☐	☐	☐	☐	☐
	cost control	☐	☐	☐	☐	☐	☐	☐
	tracing (in)efficiencies back to persons in charge	☐	☐	☐	☐	☐	☐	☐
	inventory valuation for financial accounting	☐	☐	☐	☐	☐	☐	☐

Section C – Conceptual design of the cost accounting system

C.1 **Please indicate the following for your company:**
Number of cost types: ___________ (each primary cost type that is distinguished in your company's cost accounting system)
Number of cost centers: ___________
Average number of overhead allocation bases per cost center: ___________

C.2 **Are separate databases maintained for financial and management accounting systems?**
☐ Yes ☐ No

C.3 **Imputed costs** are costs that are neither conform to actual cash flows nor to financial reporting requirements, but are recognized specifically for cost accounting purposes. They thereby more precisely capture the actual consumption of resources. Two main types of imputed costs exist:
- Imputed depreciation is calculated on replacement costs instead of historical costs in order to ensure maintenance of assets.
- Imputed interests comprise the cost of capital required by investors (opportunity cost).

To what extent do you apply the following imputed costs?

Imputed depreciation	☐ Not at all	☐ In separate calculations only	☐ As part of regular cost accounting
Imputed interests	☐ Not at all	☐ In separate calculations only	☐ As part of regular cost accounting

C.4 Besides your P/L statement do you also have an operating income statement for managerial purposes?

☐ Yes ☐ No ➔ **If no, please continue with C.5.**

If yes: To what extent does your P/L statement differ structurally from the operating income statement for managerial purposes?

1 = not at all, 7 = very much

1	2	3	4	5	6	7	N/A
☐	☐	☐	☐	☐	☐	☐	☐

C.5 Contribution margin accounting can be used to determine the profitability of cost objects (e.g., products, customers). In direct costing the contribution margins of all cost objects are determined (sales - variable costs) and then fixed costs are subtracted as a lump sum. Hence, only one contribution margin (**CM I**) is calculated (left example). If the fixed costs are further broken down, more contribution margins (**CM I, CM II, CM III**, ...) can be distinguished (right example).

• Example for direct costing - one CM distinguished

	Patient A	Patient B	Total
Sales	$ 120,000	$ 100,000	$ 220,000
- Variable costs	$ 80,000	$ 50,000	$ 130,000
= **CM I**	$ 40,000	$ 50,000	$ 90,000
- Fixed costs			$ 70,000
= Net operating income			$ 20,000

• Example for more than one CM (here: two CM distinguished)

	Patient A	Patient B	Total
Sales	$ 120,000	$ 100,000	$ 220,000
- Variable costs	$ 80,000	$ 50,000	$ 130,000
= **CM I**	$ 40,000	$ 50,000	$ 90,000
- Fixed costs (patient level)	$ 10,000	$ 20,000	$ 30,000
= **CM II**	$ 30,000	$ 30,000	$ 60,000
- Fixed costs (department level)			$ 40,000
= Net operating income			$ 20,000

Do you use contribution margin accounting? ☐ Yes ☐ No ➔ **If no, please continue with C.6.**

If yes: How many different contribution margins (CM) do you distinguish (CM I, CM II, CM III, etc.)? ______

C.6 To what extent do the following statements describe your cost accounting system?

1 = not at all, ..., 7 = completely

	1	2	3	4	5	6	7	N/A
Fixed and variable costs are distinguished for each cost center.	☐	☐	☐	☐	☐	☐	☐	☐
Cost variances are analyzed in-depth for each cost center.	☐	☐	☐	☐	☐	☐	☐	☐
All service flows are considered when allocating support cost centers to primary cost centers.	☐	☐	☐	☐	☐	☐	☐	☐

C.7 On which bases are overhead costs allocated to products?

	Yes	No	N/A
On a volume basis (e.g., direct materials, labor costs)	☐	☐	☐
On an hour rate basis (e.g., labor or machine hours)	☐	☐	☐
On the number of times an activity is performed (e.g., number of setups or inspections)	☐	☐	☐
On the amount of time taken to perform an activity (e.g., number of setups or inspection minutes)	☐	☐	☐

C.8 How are product costs determined as part of regular cost accounting?

☐ Only on a variable cost basis ☐ Only on a full cost basis ☐ On both bases

C.9 To what extent are costs for medical treatments calculated on the following bases?

1 = for no product, ..., 7 = for all products

	1	2	3	4	5	6	7	N/A
Actual costs (occurred costs)	☐	☐	☐	☐	☐	☐	☐	☐
Normal costs (averaged costs)	☐	☐	☐	☐	☐	☐	☐	☐
Standard costs (planned costs)	☐	☐	☐	☐	☐	☐	☐	☐
Target costs (costs derived from market prices)	☐	☐	☐	☐	☐	☐	☐	☐

C.10 How often is the following cost information updated? (Select only one response for each item.)

	continuously	monthly	quarterly	semi-annually	annually	less often than anually	irregulariarily	N/A
Standard costs	☐	☐	☐	☐	☐	☐	☐	☐
Distinction between fixed and variable costs	☐	☐	☐	☐	☐	☐	☐	☐
Cost variances	☐	☐	☐	☐	☐	☐	☐	☐
Charge rates for transferring costs from support cost centers to primary cost centers	☐	☐	☐	☐	☐	☐	☐	☐
Overhead allocation rates for product costing	☐	☐	☐	☐	☐	☐	☐	☐
Product costs	☐	☐	☐	☐	☐	☐	☐	☐
Operating income statement for managerial purposes	☐	☐	☐	☐	☐	☐	☐	☐

C.11	Which of the following characteristics describe your cost accounting system?	Does apply	Does not apply	N/A
	Activities in cost centers are identified.	☐	☐	☐
	Cost center costs are allocated to activities.	☐	☐	☐
	Activities are aggregated to processes.	☐	☐	☐
	Cost driver volumes are determined for each activity.	☐	☐	☐
	Activity cost driver rates are determined.	☐	☐	☐
	Activity cost driver rates are used for service costing.	☐	☐	☐
	Activity cost driver rates are used for process optimization.	☐	☐	☐
	Activity cost driver rates are used to analyze customer profitability.	☐	☐	☐

C.12 **Which ERP software do you use for cost accounting?**

☐ SAP ☐ Oracle ☐ Sage ☐ In-house software solutions
☐ Infor ERP ☐ Microsoft Dynamics ☐ Other (please specify): __________ ☐ None

C.13 **To what extent have changes of your cost accounting system taken place over the last three years?**

1 = not at all 7 = very much

1	2	3	4	5	6	7
☐	☐	☐	☐	☐	☐	☐

C.14 **Please assess how the information provided by your cost accounting system will change over the next three years.**

	decreases	remains the same	increases
Accuracy (close to true value)	☐	☐	☐
Detail (giving full particularities)	☐	☐	☐
Timeliness (being up to date)	☐	☐	☐
Understandability for managers	☐	☐	☐

Section D – Performance of the cost accounting system

D.1 **Please assess the following characteristics of the information provided by your cost accounting system.**

1 = very low, ..., 7 = very high

	1	2	3	4	5	6	7
Accuracy (close to true value)	☐	☐	☐	☐	☐	☐	☐
Detail (giving full particularities)	☐	☐	☐	☐	☐	☐	☐
Timeliness (being up to date)	☐	☐	☐	☐	☐	☐	☐
Understandability for managers	☐	☐	☐	☐	☐	☐	☐

D.2 **How satisfied are the managers overall with the information provided by your cost accounting system?**

1 = very unsatisfied 7 = very satisfied

1	2	3	4	5	6	7
☐	☐	☐	☐	☐	☐	☐

D.3 **To what extent has your company <u>met</u> the following <u>objectives</u> over the last three years in each of the following areas?**

1 = not at all, ..., 7 = completely

• **Providing cost information for decision making regarding...**	1	2	3	4	5	6	7	N/A
pricing	☐	☐	☐	☐	☐	☐	☐	☐
short-term capacity planning (e.g., for m)	☐	☐	☐	☐	☐	☐	☐	☐
exploiting cost reduction potential	☐	☐	☐	☐	☐	☐	☐	☐
strategy development (e.g., cost leadership)	☐	☐	☐	☐	☐	☐	☐	☐

D.4 1 = not at all, ..., 7 = completely

• **Providing cost information to motivate employees so that they...**	1	2	3	4	5	6	7	N/A
carry out operational tasks efficiently	☐	☐	☐	☐	☐	☐	☐	☐
make cost savings	☐	☐	☐	☐	☐	☐	☐	☐
act in accordance with the business strategy	☐	☐	☐	☐	☐	☐	☐	☐

D.5 1 = not at all, ..., 7 = completely

• **Cost accounting to support...**	1	2	3	4	5	6	7	N/A
operational planning	☐	☐	☐	☐	☐	☐	☐	☐
strategic planning	☐	☐	☐	☐	☐	☐	☐	☐
cost control	☐	☐	☐	☐	☐	☐	☐	☐
tracing (in)efficiencies back to responsible person	☐	☐	☐	☐	☐	☐	☐	☐
inventory valuation for financial accounting	☐	☐	☐	☐	☐	☐	☐	☐

Thank you for your help!

We would like to express our sincere thanks for spending some of your valuable time to participate in our survey. Your answers are of high importance to the success of this study. We will therefore gladly provide you with the results of our survey presumably in the fourth quarter of 2011 after having completed the investigation.

☐ If you are interested in the results of our study and would like to benchmark your company with others matched by industry and size, please tick this box.

Your name: ______________________________

Company: ______________________________

Address: ______________________________

____

Email-address: ______________________________

Telephone number: ______________________________

Further comments on this project:

If you have any questions or suggestions regarding this study, please contact Dipl.-Kfm. Matthias Moeschler at Matthias.Moeschler@wiwi.uni-muenster.de or by phone at +49 251 / 83-22858.

Appendix 3: Representativeness test of the German sample regarding sales turnover

Industry	Sales (mill. €)	Sample	Responses	Response rate (%)
Food and beverage industry	> 200	80 (35.7%)	38 (39.6%)	47.5%
	150 - 199.99	12 (5.4%)	5 (5.2%)	41.7%
	100 - 149.99	29 (12.9%)	12 (12.5%)	41.4%
	50 - 99.99	60 (26.9%)	18 (18.8%)	30.0%
	10 - 49.99	43 (19.2%)	23 (24.0%)	53.5%
	Total	224 (100.0%)	96 (100.0%)	**42.9%**
	Chi-square	Value	Degrees of freedom	P-value
		3.869	4	0.424

Industry	Sales (mill. €)	Sample	Responses	Response rate (%)
Mechanical engineering industry	> 200	87 (19.3%)	27 (16.7%)	31.0%
	150 - 199.99	32 (7.1%)	9 (5.6%)	28.1%
	100 - 149.99	72 (16.0%)	26 (16.0%)	36.1%
	50 - 99.99	189 (41.9%)	66 (40.7%)	34.9%
	10 - 49.99	71 (15.7%)	34 (21.0%)	47.9%
	Total	451 (100.0%)	162 (100.0%)	**35.9%**
	Chi-square	Value	Degrees of freedom	P-value
		4.004	4	0.406

Industry	Sales (mill. €)	Sample	Responses	Response rate (%)
Hospitals	> 200			
	150 - 499.99	10 (2.0%)	8 (3.9%)	80.0%
	100 - 149.99	31 (6.2%)	26 (12.6%)	83.9%
	50 - 99.99	146 (29.0%)	65 (31.4%)	44.5%
	10 - 49.99	317 (62.9%)	108 (52.2%)	34.1%
	Total	504 (100.0%)	207 (100.0%)	**41.1%**
	Chi-square	Value	Degrees of freedom	P-value
		21.723	3	0.000

Appendix 4: Representativeness test of the German sample regarding number of employees

Industry	Number of employees	Sample	Responses	Response rate (%)
Food and beverage industry	>2000		4 (4.1%)	
	2000-1000	28 (9.4%)	17 (17.3%)	60.7%
	999-500	81 (27.4%)	32 (32.7%)	39.5%
	499-250	188 (63.3%)	46 (46.9%)	24.5%
	<250		3 (3.1%)	
	Total	297 (100.0%)	98 (100.0%)	33.0%
	Chi-square	Value	Degrees of freedom	P-value
		11.704	2	0.003
Mechanical engineering industry	Number of employees	Sample	Responses	Response rate (%)
	>2000		5 (3.1%)	
	2000-1000	50 (10.3%)	16 (9.8%)	32.0%
	999-500	96 (19.8%)	41 (25.2%)	42.7%
	499-250	338 (69.8%)	94 (57.7%)	27.8%
	<250		10 (6.1%)	
	Total	484 (100.0%)	163 (100.0%)	33.7%
	Chi-square	Value	Degrees of freedom	P-value
		5.821	2	0.054
Hospitals	Number of employees	Sample	Responses	Response rate (%)
	>2000		2 (0.9%)	
	2000-1000	113 (20.6%)	34 (16.0%)	30.1%
	999-500	211 (38.5%)	74 (34.7%)	35.1%
	499-250	224 (40.9%)	77 (36.2%)	34.4%
	<250		19 (8.9%)	
	Total	548 (100.0%)	213 (100.0%)	38.9%
	Chi-square	Value	Degrees of freedom	P-value
		4.188	2	0.123

Appendix 5: Representativeness test of the Japanese sample regarding number of employees

Industry	Number of employees	Questionnaires mailed	Responses	Response rate (%)
Food and beverage industry	>2000		2 (4.0%)	
	2000-1000	68 (15.7%)	7 (14.0%)	10.3%
	999-500	112 (25.9%)	19 (38.0%)	17.0%
	499-250	252 (58.3%)	17 (34.0%)	6.7%
	<250		5 (10.0%)	
	Total	432 (100.0%)	50 (100.0%)	11.6%
	Chi-square	Value	Degrees of freedom	P-value
		48.020	2	0.000
Mechanical engineering industry	>2000		3 (4.5%)	
	2000-1000	82 (20.1%)	8 (12.1%)	9.8%
	999-500	116 (28.4%)	19 (28.8%)	16.4%
	499-250	210 (51.5%)	31 (47.0%)	14.8%
	<250		5 (7.6%)	
	Total	408 (100.0%)	66 (100.0%)	16.2%
	Chi-square	Value	Degrees of freedom	P-value
		2.352	2	0.308
Hospitals	>2000		4 (13.3%)	
	2000-1000	98 (13.4%)	4 (13.3%)	4.1%
	999-500	294 (40.2%)	17 (56.7%)	5.8%
	499-250	339 (46.4%)	3 (10.0%)	0.9%
	<250		2 (6.7%)	
	Total	731 (100.0%)	30 (100.0%)	4.1%
	Chi-square	Value	Degrees of freedom	P-value
		12.783	2	0.002

Appendix 6: Nonresponse bias test

Variables	Company size (employees)	Company size (sales turnover)	Complexity of cost accounting systems	Timeliness of cost accounting systems	Overall success of cost accounting systems
T-test (two tailed) for Germany	p = 0.788	p = 0.258	p = 0.318	p = 0.294	p = 0.481
T-test (two tailed) for Japan	p = 0.421	p = 0.306	p = 0.648	p = 0.152	p = 0.273

Appendix 7: Correlations between country-specifics for the German responses (data set 1)

	Required cost information - detail	Required cost information - timeliness	Required cost information - understandability	Specific department for cost accounting	Accounting/ finance department	Management accounting department	Operational departments	Workload management over financial accounting	Focus on management accounting
Required cost information - accuracy	0.567 ***	0.503 ***	0.311 ***	0.081	-0.128 **	0.012	0.004	0.115 *	0.243 ***
Required cost information - detail		0.360 ***	0.208 ***	0.101 *	-0.065	-0.004	-0.057	0.123 **	0.187 ***
Required cost information - timeliness			0.465 ***	-0.028	-0.037	0.043	0.029	0.116 **	0.195 ***
Required cost information – understandability				-0.031	-0.107 *	0.003	-0.011	0.096	0.165 ***
Specific department for cost accounting					-0.111 *	-0.184 ***	-0.023	0.027	0.040
Accounting/finance department						-0.379 ***	0.137 **	-0.245 ***	-0.186 ***
Management accounting department							-0.037	0.144 **	0.114 *
Operational departments								0.027	0.047
Workload management over financial accounting									0.415 ***

Correlations between country-specifics for the German responses (data set 1) (continued)

	Focus on management accounting education	Education university	Education professional institutes	Education in-house training	Education learning by doing	Specialization in cost accounting only	Specialization in other business functions	Specialization by qualification
Required cost information - accuracy	-0.090	0.020	0.006	0.152	0.086	0.221 ***	0.092	0.211 ***
Required cost information - detail	-0.103 *	-0.159	0.052	0.132	0.078	0.276 ***	0.100 *	0.218 ***
Required cost information - timeliness	-0.069	0.098	-0.114	0.071	0.005	0.138	0.069	0.219 ***
Required cost information - understandability	-0.068	0.037	-0.042	0.002	-0.090	0.087	0.131 **	0.158 ***
Specific department for cost accounting	-0.035	-0.037	0.034	0.215 **	0.185 *	0.185 ***	0.074	0.004
Accounting/finance department	0.256 ***	-0.186 *	-0.001	0.057	0.109	-0.119 **	0.041	-0.135 **
Management accounting department	-0.166 ***	0.266 ***	0.028	0.015	0.021	0.031	-0.052	0.031
Operational departments	0.082	0.064	-0.118	0.113	0.206 **	-0.040	0.009	-0.057
Workload management over financial accounting	-0.352 ***	-0.091	0.190 *	0.227 **	-0.026	0.116 **	0.014	0.080
Focus on management accounting	-0.245 ***	-0.011	0.028	0.144	0.124	0.022	-0.003	0.227 ***
Focus on management accounting education		-0.150	-0.181 *	-0.168 *	0.099	-0.097	0.052	-0.123 **
Education university			-0.230 **	-0.030	-0.055	-0.002	-0.092	0.071
Education professional institutes				0.210 **	-0.149	-0.009	0.161	0.077
Education in-house training					0.034	0.163	-0.027	-0.143
Education learning by doing						-0.032	-0.127	0.012
Specialization in cost accounting only							0.011	0.112 *
Specialization in other business functions								0.195 ***

Appendix 8: Correlations between country-specifics for the Japanese responses (data set 1)

	Required cost information - detail	Required cost information - timeliness	Required cost information - understandability	Specific department for cost accounting	Accounting/ finance department	Management accounting department	Operational departments	Workload management over financial accounting	Focus on management accounting
Required cost information - accuracy	0.700 ***	0.734 ***	0.544 ***	0.001	0.095	-0.072	0.098	0.078	0.015
Required cost information - detail		0.730 ***	0.578 ***	-0.106	0.010	-0.043	-0.002	0.023	0.021
Required cost information - timeliness			0.641 ***	-0.075	-0.036	-0.013	0.041	0.114	0.039
Required cost information – understandability				-0.065	-0.061	-0.019	0.047	0.122	0.100
Specific department for cost accounting					0.045	-0.170 **	-0.172 **	0.012	-0.159 *
Accounting/finance department						-0.285 ***	-0.093	-0.252 ***	-0.181 **
Management accounting department							-0.250 ***	0.076	0.030
Operational departments								0.127	0.125
Workload management over financial accounting									0.238 ***
Focus on management accounting									

Correlations between country-specifics for the Japanese responses (data set 1) (continued)

	Focus on management accounting education education	Education university	Education professional institutes	Education in-house training	Education learning by doing	Specialization in cost accounting only	Specialization in other business functions	Specialization by qualification
Required cost information - accuracy	-0.060	0.055	0.058	0.002	-0.045	0.308 ***	0.138 *	0.495 ***
Required cost information - detail	-0.009	-0.054	0.066	0.018	0.019	0.159 *	0.148 *	0.354 ***
Required cost information - timeliness	-0.051	-0.009	0.044	-0.034	0.025	0.148 *	0.244 ***	0.351 ***
Required cost information - understandability	-0.063	0.091	0.028	-0.036	-0.020	0.124	0.152 *	0.351 ***
Specific department for cost accounting	0.038	0.098	-0.098	0.028	0.035	0.111	-0.065	0.070
Accounting/finance department	-0.258 ***	0.155 *	0.088	-0.125	0.027	0.147 *	-0.101	0.077
Management accounting department	0.026	-0.071	-0.018	0.059	0.059	0.049	-0.073	-0.189 **
Operational departments	0.164 *	-0.007	0.010	0.017	0.085	0.112	0.164 *	0.117
Workload management over financial accounting	0.387 ***	0.009	-0.107	0.041	0.024	0.007	0.182 **	0.052
Focus on management accounting	0.212 **	0.033	-0.026	0.019	-0.054	0.079	0.331 ***	0.203 **
Focus on management accounting education		-0.094	-0.084	0.058	-0.009	-0.125	0.110	-0.152 *
Education university			-0.061	-0.020	-0.313 ***	0.076	0.030	0.065
Education professional institutes				-0.075	-0.036	-0.061	0.025	-0.059
Education in-house training					-0.437 ***	0.087	-0.010	0.090
Education learning by doing						0.020	0.116	-0.110
Specialization in cost accounting only							0.050	0.437 ***
Specialization in other business functions								0.340 ***

	Focus management accounting	Focus education management accounting	Education university	Education professional institutes	Education in-house training	Education learning by doing	Speciali-zation in cost accounting only	Speciali-zation in other business functions	Speciali-zation by quali-fication	Factor external dynamics	Factor company size	Factor IT systems quality	Factor top management support
Workload management over financial accounting	0.415 ***	0.352 ***	-0.091	0.190 *	0.227 **	-0.026	0.116 **	0.014	0.080	-0.032	0.075	0.122 **	0.147 **
Focus management accounting		0.245 ***	-0.011	0.028	0.144	0.124	0.022	-0.003	0.227 ***	-0.151 **	0.048	0.237 ***	0.235 ***
accounting			0.150	0.181 *	0.168 *	-0.099	0.097	-0.052	0.123 **	-0.028	0.095	0.086	0.166 ***
Education university				-0.230 **	-0.030	-0.055	-0.002	-0.092	0.071	-0.054	0.174 *	0.057	-0.055
Education professional institutes					0.210 **	-0.149	-0.009	0.162	0.077	0.037	-0.032	0.011	-0.032
Education in-house training						0.034	0.163	-0.027	-0.143	-0.024	-0.041	0.019	0.213 **
Education learning by doing							-0.032	-0.127	0.012	-0.116	0.003	0.038	0.166
Specialization in cost accounting only								0.011	0.112 *	-0.092	0.158 ***	0.263 ***	0.235 ***
Specialization in other business functions									0.195 ***	0.010	-0.126 **	-0.039	0.171 ***
Specialization by qualification										-0.140 **	-0.009	0.201 ***	0.223 ***
Factor external dynamics											-0.031	-0.092	-0.129 **
Factor company size												0.056	0.085
Factor IT systems quality													0.193 ***

Appendix 9: Correlations between the selected context factors for regression analysis for German responses (data set 1)

	Focus management accounting	Focus education management accounting	Education university	Education professional institutes	Education in-house training	Education learning by doing	Specialization in cost accounting only	Specialization in other business functions	Specialization by qualification	Factor external dynamics	Factor company size	Factor IT systems quality	Factor top management support
Workload management over financial accounting	0.238 ***	-0.387 ***	0.009	-0.107	0.041	0.024	0.007	0.182 **	0.052	0.078	0.127	0.024	0.077
Focus on management accounting		-0.212 **	0.033	-0.026	0.019	-0.054	0.079	0.331 ***	0.203 **	-0.196 **	0.118	0.188 **	0.423 ***
Focus on management accounting education			0.094	0.084	-0.058	0.009	0.125	-0.110	0.152 *	-0.049	0.097	-0.058	0.058
Education university				-0.061	-0.020	-0.313 ***	0.076	0.030	0.065	0.011	0.050	0.038	0.145 *
Education professional institutes					-0.075	-0.036	-0.061	0.025	-0.059	-0.053	-0.077	-0.093	0.012
Education in-house training						-0.437 ***	0.087	-0.010	0.090	0.077	-0.076	0.138	0.117
Education learning by doing							0.020	0.116	-0.110	0.021	0.097	-0.049	-0.136
Specialization in cost accounting only								0.050	0.437 ***	0.005	0.166 *	0.190 **	0.413 ***
Specialization in other business functions									0.340 ***	-0.189 **	0.065	-0.018	0.201 **
Specialization by qualification										-0.195 **	0.199 **	0.159 *	0.454 ***
Factor external dynamics											-0.096	-0.032	-0.286 ***
Factor company size												0.184 *	0.158 *
Factor IT systems quality													0.316 ***

Appendix 10: Correlations between the selected context factors for regression analysis for Japanese responses (data set 1)

Appendix 11: Regression analysis of performance attainment (data set 1)

Dependent variable	Performance attainment			
Country	**Germany**		**Japan**	
Linear regression method	Enter	Stepwise	Enter	Stepwise
R	0.708	0.658	0.810	0.758
R^2	0.502	0.433	0.657	0.574
adjusted R^2	0.360	0.402	0.530	0.545
F	3.552	13.950	5.173	19.875
Significance	0.000	0.000	0.000	0.000
VIF_{max}	2.347	1.220	2.168	1.256
Durbin-Watson statistic	1.928	1.938	1.972	1.754
Independent variables	**Standardized coefficients (Beta)**			
Workload management over financial accounting	0.011		-0.010	
Focus on management accounting	0.024		-0.084	
Focus on management accounting education	-0.012		-0.092	
Education university	-0.010		0.193 **	
Education professional institutes	0.067		0.015	
Education in-house training	-0.071		0.135	
Education learning by doing	-0.010		0.005	
Specialization in cost accounting only	0.213 *	0.216 **	0.006	
Specialization in other business functions	-0.187 *		0.035	
Specialization by high qualification	0.216 **	0.219 **	0.028	
Factor top management support	0.246 **	0.253 **	0.376 ***	0.358 ***
Factor external dynamics	-0.041		0.045	
Factor company size	-0.110		0.222 **	0.235 ***
Factor IT systems quality	0.067		0.223 *	0.234 **
Complexity of cost accounting systems	0.437 ***	0.369 ***	-0.092	
ABC complexity score	0.148		0.259 **	
Timeliness of cost accounting systems	-0.173		0.348 ***	0.408 ***

Appendix 12: Regression analysis of factor attainment (data set 1)

Dependent variable	Factor attainment			
Country	Germany		Japan	
Linear regression method	Enter	Stepwise	Enter	Stepwise
R	0.756	0.685	0.832	0.775
R^2	0.571	0.469	0.692	0.600
adjusted R^2	0.422	0.444	0.561	0.570
F	3.838	18.547	5.277	19.867
Significance	0.000	0.000	0.000	0.000
VIF_{max}	3.008	1.209	2.611	1.307
Durbin-Watson statistic	2.071	1.905	1.876	1.855
Independent variables	**Standardized coefficients (Beta)**			
Workload management over financial accounting	-0.105		0.040	
Focus on management accounting	0.021		-0.025	
Focus on management accounting education	0.046		-0.071	
Education university	-0.003		0.211 **	
Education professional institutes	0.057		0.030	
Education in-house training	-0.068		0.102	
Education learning by doing	0.014		0.101	
Specialization in cost accounting only	0.293 **	0.286 ***	0.024	
Specialization in other business functions	-0.122		0.037	
Specialization by high qualification	0.166		0.000	
Factor top management support	0.212	0.302 ***	0.367 ***	0.371 ***
Factor external dynamics	-0.109		0.105	
Factor company size	-0.152		0.249 **	0.255 ***
Factor IT systems quality	0.112		0.206 *	0.21 **
Complexity of cost accounting systems	0.462 ***	0.384 ***	0.061	
ABC complexity score	0.123		0.156	
Timeliness of cost accounting systems	-0.165		0.282 **	0.255 ***

Appendix 13: Regression analysis of factor satisfaction (data set 1)

Dependent variable	Factor satisfaction			
Country	**Germany**		**Japan**	
Linear regression method	Enter	Stepwise	Enter	Stepwise
R	0.661	0.533	0.792	0.735
R^2	0.437	0.284	0.627	0.541
adjusted R^2	0.271	0.254	0.490	0.510
F	2.643	9.524	4.556	17.371
Significance	0.003	0.000	0.000	0.000
VIF_{max}	2.312	1.111	2.272	1.391
Durbin-Watson statistic	2.201	1.893	1.950	2.070
Independent variables	**Standardized coefficients (Beta)**			
Workload management over financial accounting	0.219	0.02 **	0.096	
Focus on management accounting	-0.086		-0.135	
Focus on management accounting education	0.018		-0.046	
Education university	-0.149		0.047	
Education professional institutes	-0.021		0.203 *	
Education in-house training	0.027		0.114	
Education learning by doing	0.127		0.014	
Specialization in cost accounting only	0.192	0.295 ***	-0.022	
Specialization in other business functions	-0.162		-0.138	
Specialization by high qualification	0.248 **	0.257 **	0.084	
Factor top management support	0.120		0.352 **	0.295 ***
Factor external dynamics	-0.203		-0.236	-0.249 **
Factor company size	-0.136		0.045	
Factor IT systems quality	0.188		0.293 **	0.305 ***
Complexity of cost accounting systems	0.010		0.117	
ABC complexity score	0.050		-0.006	
Timeliness of cost accounting systems	-0.020		0.231 *	0.317 ***

Appendix 14: Regression analysis of satisfaction overall (data set 1)

Dependent variable	Satisfaction overall			
Country	Germany		Japan	
Linear regression method	Enter	Stepwise	Enter	Stepwise
R	0.666	0.576	0.736	0.695
R^2	0.443	0.332	0.542	0.482
adjusted R^2	0.280	0.304	0.373	0.457
F	2.717	11.904	3.201	18.640
Significance	0.002	0.000	0.001	0.000
VIF_{max}	2.254	1.151	2.272	1.017
Durbin-Watson statistic	1.730	2.068	1.795	1.898
Independent variables	**Standardized coefficients (Beta)**			
Workload management over financial accounting	-0.023		-0.001	
Focus on management accounting	0.348 **	0.423 ***	0.138	
Focus on management accounting education	0.063		0.091	
Education university	0.001		-0.001	
Education professional institutes	0.100		0.016	
Education in-house training	-0.141		0.176	
Education learning by doing	0.100		-0.004	
Specialization in cost accounting only	0.212 *	0.219 **	0.013	
Specialization in other business functions	-0.113		-0.214 *	-0.230 **
Specialization by high qualification	0.073		-0.040	
Factor top management support	0.134		0.543 ***	0.605 ***
Factor external dynamics	-0.067		-0.019	
Factor company size	-0.079		0.109	
Factor IT systems quality	0.190 *	0.21 **	0.02	
Complexity of cost accounting systems	0.091		-0.050	
ABC complexity score	0.149		0.019	
Timeliness of cost accounting systems	-0.217 *		0.258 *	0.237 **

Appendix 15: Individual item reliability (data set 1)

	Coefficient		t-statistic	
	Germany	Japan	Germany	Japan
Factor decision facilitating				
Strategy development	0.862	0.776	25.531	4.208
Exploiting cost reduction potential	0.877	0.971	23.754	6.337
Factor decision influencing				
Act according to the business strategy	0.845	0.869	26.936	26.251
Carry out operational tasks efficiently	0.894	0.918	50.266	57.620
Make cost savings	0.892	0.877	40.459	28.706
Factor planning				
Operational planning	0.917	0.941	48.016	64.384
Strategic planning	0.858	0.944	23.22	64.592
Factor control				
Cost control	0.863	0.873	26.637	13.373
Trace (in)efficiences back to individuals	0.926	0.877	37.439	17.807
Factor IT systems quality				
Integration	0.884	0.839	44.179	9.442
Cost information	0.909	0.876	62.993	21.561
Real-time	0.783	0.641	17.925	5.702
Factor external dynamics				
Suppliers	0.739	0.777	4.442	9.304
Customers	0.867	0.876	6.705	14.736
Competitors	0.435	0.713	2.238	7.085
Factor top management support				
Resources	0.911	0.963	42.729	109.343
Political support	0.815	0.958	22.359	90.128
Factor cost accounting systems' timeliness				
Update standards costs	0.428	0.484	2.878	4.269
Update distinction fixed and variable costs	0.697	0.672	4.814	9.424
Update cost variances	0.432	0.628	2.36	9.361
Update cost rates for support cost centers	0.671	0.706	5.832	8.951
Update cost rates for overhead allocation bases	0.730	0.785	7.117	13.295
Update operational income statement	0.387	0.658	2.749	7.209
Update product costs	0.448	0.741	2.589	12.548
Factor cost accounting systems' performance				
Strategy development	0.712	0.613	19.759	24.162
Exploiting cost reduction potential	0.809	0.835	30.944	28.329
Act according to the business strategy	0.787	0.864	29.417	34.923
Carry out operational tasks efficiently	0.785	0.869	27.232	33.492
Make cost savings	0.785	0.855	24.091	33.371
Operational planning	0.724	0.844	17.043	27.853
Strategic planning	0.640	0.853	14.552	28.577
Cost control	0.764	0.893	19.802	41.655
Trace (in)efficiencies back to individuals	0.682	0.855	14.521	32.811

	Index score complexity	Factor control	Factor external dynamics	Factor IT systems quality	Factor attainment	Factor planning	Factor top manage-ment support	Factor timeliness	Factor decision facilitating	Factor decision influencing
Act according to the business strategy	0.2178	0.4507	-0.1359	0.2045	0.7874	0.4559	0.3583	0.0538	0.4393	0.5315
Carry out operational tasks efficiently	0.2307	0.4927	-0.1057	0,2694	0.7849	0.4304	0.3108	0.2136	0.4216	0.5986
Cost control	0.2420	0.5795	-0.0795	0.2584	0.7640	0.3985	0.2583	0.0947	0.4066	0.4331
Exploiting cost reduction potential	0.2154	0.4969	-0.1294	0.3071	0.8094	0.3918	0.3098	0.1148	0.5536	0.4885
Make cost savings	0.1859	0.5662	-0.1185	0.2586	0.7853	0.3193	0.3104	0.1412	0.4884	0.5665
Operational planning	0.2943	0.4399	-0.0861	0.1910	0.7237	0.6226	0.2489	0.0975	0.3518	0.3882
Strategic planning	0.2744	0.2784	-0.0946	0.1940	0.6403	0.5552	0.2658	0.0464	0.3603	0,2915
Strategy development	0.2383	0.3454	-0.0125	0.2481	0.7119	0.4260	0.3321	0.0363	0.5464	0.3254
Trace (in)efficiences back to individuals	0.2822	0.6159	-0.1502	0.3005	0.6817	0.3069	0.2450	0.0676	0.3548	0.3957
Index score complexity	1.0000	0.3143	-0.0949	0.1928	0.3242	0.3405	0,1994	0.1574	0.2838	0.2509
Customers	-0.0789	-0.1578	0.8670	-0.0652	-0.1539	-0.1947	-0.1284	-0.0454	-0.0983	-0.1269
Suppliers	-0.0937	-0.2001	0.7387	-0.0805	-0.0695	-0.1454	-0.0899	-0.0711	-0.0583	-0.1428
Competitors	0.0170	-0.1395	0.4848	-0.0093	-0.0154	-0.0593	0.0090	-0.0871	0.0736	-0.0502
Cross-functional integration	0.1766	0.2313	-0.0460	0.8837	0.2589	0.1912	0.1639	0.0795	0.2222	0.1837
Cost and performance information	0.1914	0.2595	-0.0971	0.9089	0.3640	0.2411	0.2112	0.1288	0.2838	0.2382
Update of cost information in realtime	0.1167	0.1729	-0.0641	0.7831	0.2105	0.1593	0.0858	0.1064	0.1126	0.1121
Ressources	0.2262	0.2744	-0.1437	0.1998	0.3727	0.2895	0.9105	0.0904	0.2879	0.3231
Political support	0.0998	0.2536	-0.0634	0.1144	0.3041	0.3281	0.8147	0.0239	0.2564	0.2738

Appendix 16: Discriminant validity of indicators for the German model (data set 1)

	Index score complexity	Factor control	Factor external dynamics	Factor IT systems quality	Factor attainment	Factor planning	Factor top manage-ment support	Factor timeliness	Factor decision facilitating	Factor decision influencing
Act according to the business strategy	0.1862	0.5403	-0.1627	0.2302	0.5203	0.4686	0.3128	0.1134	0.4575	0.8454
Carry out operational tasks efficiently	0.2343	0.5324	-0.1224	0.2045	0.5200	0,4523	0.3057	0.1994	0.3897	0.8936
Make cost savings	0.2323	0.6280	-0.1446	0.1474	0.5516	0,4171	0.3010	0.1759	0.4701	0.8918
Exploiting cost reduction potential	0.2325	0.5494	-0.0470	0.1923	0.5648	0.4264	0.2411	0.1077	0.8625	0.5149
Strategy development	0.2605	0.3614	-0.0945	0.2472	0.4615	0.3798	0.3063	0.0701	0.8771	0.3521
Operational planning	0.3296	0.5501	-0.1849	0.2071	0.5583	0.9168	0.3245	0.1009	0,4252	0.5393
Strategic planning	0.2698	0.3461	-0.1845	0.2126	0.4603	0.8583	0.2977	0.0141	0.3957	0.3345
Cost control	0.2349	0.8630	-0.2159	0.2008	0.5869	0.5089	0.2370	0.1118	0.4803	0.5616
Trace (in)efficiencies back to individuals	0.3183	0.9263	-0.1868	0.2628	0.5656	0.4321	0.3024	0.1422	0.4592	0.5955
Update distinction fixed variable costs	0.0979	0.1384	-0.0199	0.0495	0.1352	0.0302	0.0447	0.6970	0.0766	0.1969
Update standards costs	0.0011	0.0122	-0.0521	0.0750	-0.0214	-0.0284	0.0234	0.4275	-0.0220	0.0609
Update cost variances	0.0133	0.1308	-0.0270	0.0493	0.1430	0.1471	-0.0298	0.4322	0.0843	0.1584
Update cost rates for support cost centers	0.1304	0.1125	-0.0403	0.0807	0.0760	0.0462	0.1206	0.6706	0.0857	0.1156
Update cost rates for overhead allocation bases	0.1247	0.0563	-0.1050	0.1047	0.0301	-0.0445	-0.0240	0.7297	0.0735	0.0621
Update operational income statement	0.0834	0.0374	-0.0373	0.0468	0.0337	0.0792	0.0374	0.3869	0.1055	0.0370
Update product costs	0.1341	-0.0252	-0.0458	0.1098	0.0189	0.0534	0.1175	0.4482	-0.0645	0.0226

Discriminant validity of indicators for the German model (data set 1) (continued)

	Index score complexity	Factor control	Factor external dynamics	Factor IT systems quality	Factor attainment	Factor planning	Factor top manage-ment support	Factor timeliness	Factor decision facilitating	Factor decision influencing
Act according to the business strategy	0.4298	0.3774	-0.1801	0.2783	0.8641	0.3537	0.3454	0.1436	0.3331	0.4837
Carry out operational tasks efficiently	0.3813	0.3874	-0.1742	0.2584	0.8686	0.3129	0.3811	0.1386	0.3542	0.5033
Cost control	0.3746	0.4872	-0.1361	0.2723	0.8930	0.4338	0.3693	0.1739	0.3197	0.4295
Exploiting cost reduction potential	0.3517	0.3622	-0.1772	0.2013	0.8354	0.2992	0.3735	0.1346	0.2543	0.3287
Make cost savings	0.3833	0.3719	-0.1849	0.2523	0.8550	0.2934	0.3310	0.1497	0.3209	0.4435
Operational planning	0.4022	0.4705	-0.2423	0.2580	0.8436	0.4725	0.3752	0.2061	0.3192	0.4099
Strategic planning	0.3729	0.4814	-0.1851	0.2953	0.8529	0.5245	0.4194	0.1706	0.3107	0.4055
Strategy development	0.3363	0.3709	-0.2007	0.2787	0.8134	0.4271	0.4258	0.1618	0.2623	0.3827
Trace (in)efficiences back to individuals	0.3710	0.4836	-0.1212	0.3053	0.8554	0.4115	0.3895	0.1640	0.2854	0.4190
Index score complexity	1.0000	0.2494	-0.1752	0.1137	0.4435	0.2964	0.3069	0.1333	0.1539	0.3072
Customers	-0.2015	-0.0539	0.8764	-0.0965	-0.1713	-0.0766	-0.3005	0.1800	-0.0902	-0.1198
Suppliers	-0.1080	-0.1273	0.7773	0.0499	-0.1987	-0.1706	-0.2412	0.0935	-0.0536	-0.1576
Competitors	-0.0856	-0.0890	0.7132	0.0109	-0.1273	-0.0139	-0.2009	0.1615	0.1076	0.0247
Cross-functional integration	0.1120	0.1710	0.0330	0.8394	0.2601	0.1250	0.2639	0.1259	0.2213	0.1661
Cost and performance information	0.1018	0.2295	-0.0611	0.8762	0.3055	0.1716	0.2549	0.1710	0.2014	0.1822
Update of cost information in realtime	0.0359	0.1847	-0.0382	0.6411	0.1366	0.2436	0.1740	0.0765	0.1654	0.2107
Ressources	0.3091	0.3454	-0.3159	0.2741	0.4377	0.3027	0.9632	-0.0131	0.3015	0.3254
Political support	0.2795	0.3948	-0.2940	0.2972	0.4158	0.3858	0.9578	-0.0113	0.3811	0.3405

Appendix 17: Discriminant validity of indicators for the Japanese model (data set 1)

	Index score complexity	Factor control	Factor external dynamics	Factor IT systems quality	Factor attainment	Factor planning	Factor top manage-ment support	Factor timeliness	Factor decision facilitating	Factor decision influencing
Act according to the business strategy	0.2656	0.5712	-0.1172	0.2214	0.4390	0.6329	0.3082	0.0361	0.4578	0.8691
Carry out operational tasks efficiently	0.2878	0.6396	-0.0662	0.2290	0.4783	0.6209	0.5080	0.1097	0.5370	0.9181
Make cost savings	0.2646	0.6090	-0.1232	0.1409	0.4029	0.5311	0.2612	0.0940	0.4553	0.8773
Exploiting cost reduction potential	0.1482	0.5831	-0.0070	0.2336	0.3409	0.5066	0.3062	0.2032	0.9707	0.5074
Strategy development	0.1226	0.4327	-0.0782	0.2077	0.3009	0.5380	0.3725	0.0158	0.7760	0.4824
Operational planning	0.2709	0.7215	-0.1115	0.1470	0.4482	0.9410	0.2884	0.1673	0.5058	0.6569
Strategic planning	0.2875	0.6865	-0.0955	0.2395	0.4241	0.9442	0.3831	0.1564	0.5528	0.6051
Cost control	0.2080	0.8727	-0.0903	0.1649	0.4059	0.7394	0.3594	0.1749	0.5400	0.5750
Trace (in)efficiencies back to individuals	0.2283	0.8772	-0.0984	0.2608	0.4603	0.5686	0.3137	0.1558	0.4940	0.6213
Update distinction fixed variable costs	0.0616	0.1317	0.1657	0.1877	0.1203	0.1518	-0.0141	0.6721	0.2749	0.1750
Update standards costs	-0.0511	0.0203	0.1650	0.0625	0.0010	0.0170	-0.0814	0.4841	0.0436	-0.0354
Update cost variances	0.1619	0.1290	0.1039	0.1052	0.1108	0.0851	-0.0314	0.6284	-0.0148	0.0724
Update first stage allocation	0.0801	0.1326	0.0929	0.0664	0.0712	0.0851	-0.0077	0.7057	0.0742	0.0551
Update second stage allocation	0.1385	0.1996	0.1268	0.1352	0.2077	0.1556	0.0394	0.7848	0.1453	0.1379
Update operational income statement	0.1056	0.0885	0.1557	0.0945	0.1696	0.0997	-0.0337	0.6580	0.0810	-0.0614
Update product costs	0.0529	0.1339	0.0683	0.0878	0.1073	0.1561	0.0236	0.7414	0.0982	0.0185

Discriminant validity of indicators for the Japanese model (data set 1) (continued)

Appendix 18: Discriminant validity of concepts (data set 1)

	Factor control	Factor external dynamics	Factor IT systems quality	Factor attainment	Factor planning	Factor top management support	Factor timeliness	Factor decision facilitating	Factor decision influencing
Germany									
Index score complexity	0.3143	-0.0949	0.1928	0.3242	0.3405	0.1994	0.1574	0.2838	0.2509
Factor control		-0.2216	0.2628	0.6391	0.5171	0.3052	0.1437	0.5207	0.6461
Factor external dynamics			-0.0833	-0.1370	-0.2073	-0.1267	-0.0773	-0.0820	-0.1602
Factor IT systems quality				0.3352	0.2351	0.1886	0.1236	0.2534	0.2169
Factor attainment					0.5784	0.3953	0.1306	0.5883	0.6038
Factor planning						0.3510	0.0706	0.4626	0.5046
Factor top management support							0.0720	0.3156	0.3476
Factor timeliness								0.1016	0.1910
Factor decision facilitating									0.4959
Japan									
Index score complexity	0.2494	-0.1752	0.1137	0.4435	0.2964	0.3069	0.1333	0.1539	0.3072
Factor control		-0.1078	0.2437	0.4952	0.7466	0.3844	0.1889	0.5906	0.6838
Factor external dynamics			-0.0267	-0.2091	-0.1097	-0.3178	0.1853	-0.0290	-0.1133
Factor IT systems quality				0.3134	0.2057	0.2969	0.1665	0.2470	0.2222
Factor attainment					0.4625	0.4446	0.1885	0.3597	0.4961
Factor planning						0.3569	0.1716	0.5619	0.6690
Factor top management support							-0.0127	0.3539	0.3464
Factor timeliness								0.1652	0.0918
Factor decision facilitating									0.5458

Appendix 19: Changes in Stone-Geisser Q^2 (data set 1)

Germany	Index score complexity	Factor timeliness	Factor attainment
Factor decision facilitating	-0.002	-0.003	0.000
Factor decision influencing	-0.004	0.005	0.000
Factor planning	0.021	-0.002	0.000
Factor control	0.005	-0.002	0.000
Factor IT systems quality	0.005	0.002	0.025
Factor external dynamics	-0.005	0.000	0.001
Factor top management support	-0.007	-0.002	0.045
Factor timeliness	-0.001		0.001
Index score complexity		0.000	0.016
Japan			
Factor decision facilitating	-0.010	-0.001	0.000
Factor decision influencing	0.011	0.003	0.000
Factor planning	-0.004	0.001	0.000
Factor control	-0.018	0.004	0.000
Factor IT systems quality	-0.020	0.008	0.018
Factor external dynamics	-0.007	0.013	0.003
Factor top management support	0.029	0.001	0.040
Factor timeliness	0.016		0.009
Index score complexity		-0.002	0.059

References

A

Abdallah, A. A.-N. (2008): Why Did ABC Fail at the Bank of China?, in: Management Accounting Quarterly, 9 (3), p. 7–17.

Abdel-Kader, M./Luther, R. (2008): The impact of firm characteristics on management accounting practices: A UK-based empirical analysis, in: British Accounting Review, 40 (1), p. 2–27.

Abernethy, M. A./Lillis, A. M./Brownell, P./Carter, P. (2001): Product diversity and costing system design choice: Field study evidence, in: Management Accounting Research, 12 (3), p. 261–279.

Adam, F./Sammon, D. (2004): The enterprise resource planning decade – Lessons learned and issues for the future, Hershey, PA (2004).

Adler, N. J. (1983a): Cross-Cultural Management Research: The Ostrich and the Trend, in: Academy of Management Review, 8 (2), p. 226–232.

Adler, N. J. (1983b): Cross-Cultural Management: Issues to be Faced, in: International Studies of Management & Organization, 13 (1/2), p. 7–45.

Adler, N. J. (1984): Understanding the Ways of Understanding: Cross-Cultural Management Methodology Reviewed, in: Advances in International Comparative Management, 1 (1), p. 31–67.

Ahmadjian, C. L./Robinson, P. (2001): Safety in Numbers: Downsizing and the Deinstitutionalization of Permanent Employment in Japan, in: Administrative Science Quarterly, 46 (4), p. 622–654.

Ahrens, T. (1996): Styles of Accountability, in: Accounting, Organizations & Society, 21 (2/3), p. 139–173.

Ahrens, T. (1997a): Strategic interventions of management accountants: everyday practice of British and German brewers, in: European Accounting Review, 6 (4), p. 557–588.

Ahrens, T. (1997b): Talking Accounting: An Ethnography of Management Knowledge in British and German Brewers, in: Accounting, Organizations & Society, 22 (7), p. 617–637.

Ahrens, T. (1999): Contrasting involvements – A study of management accounting practices in Britain and Germany, Amsterdam (1999).

Ahrens, T./Chapman, C. S. (1999): The Role of Management Accountants in Britain and Germany, in: Management Accounting, 77 (5), p. 42–43.

Ahrens, T./Chapman, C. S. (2000): Occupational identity of management accountants in Britain and Germany, in: European Accounting Review, 9 (4), p. 477–498.

Aiken, L. S./West, S. G. (1991): Multiple Regressions: Testing and Interpreting Interactions, Newbury Park et al. (1991).

Albers, S./Hildebrandt, L. (2006): Methodische Probleme bei der Erfolgsfaktorenforschung – Messfehler, formative versus reflektive Indikatoren und die Wahl des Strukturgleichungs-Modells, in: Zeitschrift für betriebswirtschaftliche Forschung, 58 (1), p. 2–33.

Albert, H. (1976): Wissenschaftstheorie, in: Grochla, E./Wittmann, W. (eds.): Handwörterbuch der Betriebswirtschaft, 4th edn., Stuttgart (1976), c. 4674–4692.

Aldrich, H. E. (1972): Technology and Organizational Structure: A Reexamination of the Findings of the Aston Group, in: Administrative Science Quarterly, 17 (1), p. 26–43.

Alexander, J. C./Smith, P. (1993): The discourse of American civil society: A new proposal for cultural studies, in: Theory and Society, 22 (2), p. 151–207.

Al-Laham, A. (1997): Strategieprozesse in deutschen Unternehmungen – Verlauf, Struktur und Effizienz, Wiesbaden (1997).

Al-Omiri, M./Drury, C. (2007): A survey of factors influencing the choice of product costing systems in UK organizations, in: Management Accounting Research, 18 (4), p. 399–424.

Altmann, G. (2003): Unternehmensführung und Innovationserfolg. Eine empirische Untersuchung im Maschinenbau, Wiesbaden (2003).

Amat, O./Blake, J./Oliveras, E. (1999a): Variations in National Management Accounting Approaches, Working Paper (1999).

Amat, O./Blake, J./Wraith, P. (1999b): Environmental Factors Giving Rise to Variations in National Management Accounting Practice, Working Paper (1999).

Ambos, M. (1974): Einsatz der elektronischen Datenverarbeitung in der Kostenrechnung, in: Bobsin, R. (ed.): Handbuch der Kostenrechnung, 2nd edn., München (1974), p. 419–546.

Amoroso, D. L./Cheney, P. H. (1991): Testing a Causal Model of End-User Application Effectiveness, in: Journal of Management Information Systems, 8 (1), p. 63–89.

Amshoff, B. (1993): Controlling in deutschen Unternehmungen. Realtypen, Kontext und Effizienz, Wiesbaden (1993).

Anderson, S. W. (1995): A framework for assessing cost management system changes: the case of activity-based costing implementation at General Motors 1986-1993, in: Journal of Management Accounting Research, 7, p. 1–51.

Anderson, S. W./Hesford, J. W./Young, S. M. (2002): Factors influencing the performance of activity based costing teams: a field study of ABC model development time in the automobile industry, in: Accounting, Organizations & Society, 27 (3), p. 195–211.

Anderson, S. W./Young, S. M. (1999): The impact of contextual and process factors on the evaluation of activity-based costing systems, in: Accounting, Organizations & Society, 24 (7), p. 525–559.

Anthony, R. N./Govindarajan, V. (2007): Management control systems, 12th. edn., Boston, Mass. (2007).

Anyane-Ntow, K. (1988): An Empirical Investigation of the Budgetary Process in American and Japanese Manufacturing Firms: A Comparative Analysis, in: Someya, K. (ed.): Accounting education and research to promote international understanding: the proceedings of the sixth International Conference on Accounting Education, October 7-10, 1987, Kyoto, Japan, New York et al. (1988), p. 491–505.

Appleyard, T./Pallett, S. (2003): Double trouble, in: Financial Management, 34 (1), p. 30–31.

Aptel, O./Pourjalali, H. (2001): Improving activities and decreasing costs of logistics in hospitals. A comparison of U.S. and French hospitals, in: The International Journal of Accounting, 36 (1), p. 65–90.

Armstrong, J. S./Overton, T. S. (1977): Estimating Nonresponse Bias in Mail Surveys, in: Journal of Marketing Research, 14 , p. 396–402.

Askarany, D./Yazdifar, H. (2010): A Comparative Investigation into the Diffusion of Management Accounting Innovations in the UK, Australia and New Zealand, in: Research Executives Summaries Series, 5 (9), p. 1–11.

Asquer, A. (2003): In for a penne…, in: Financial Management, 84 (3), p. 28–29.

Atkinson, A. A./Kaplan, R. S./Young, S. M. (2004): Management accounting, 4th. edn., Upper Saddle River NJ (2004).

Au, K./Bemmels, B. (2000): Determining the Effects of Exit, Voice, Loyalty, and Neglect on Changing a Dubious Decision in Canada and Hong Kong, in: Advances in International Comparative Management, 13, p. 205–225.

Aust, R. (1999): Kostenrechnung als unternehmensinterne Dienstleistung, Wiesbaden (1999).

Auyeung, P./Sands, J. (1996): A cross cultural study of the learning style of accounting students, in: Accounting & Finance, 36 (2), p. 261–274.

Auyeung, P./Sands, J. (1997): Factors influencing accounting students' career choice: a cross-cultural validation study, in: Accounting Education, 6 (1), p. 13–23.

Avermaete, T./Viaene, J./Morgan, E. J./Pitts, E./Crawford, N./Mahon, D. (2004): Determinants of product and process innovation in small food manufacturing firms, in: Trends in Food Science & Technology, 15 (10), p. 474–483.

Awasthi, V. N./Chow, C. W./Wu, A. (1998): Performance measure and resource expenditure choices in a teamwork environment: the effects of national culture, in: Management Accounting Research, 9 (2), p. 119–138.

Awasthi, V. N./Chow, C. W./Wu, A. (2001): Cross-cultural differences in the behavioral consequences of imposing performance evaluation and reward systems: An experimental investigation, in: International Journal of Accounting, 36 (3), p. 291–309.

B

Babbie, E. R. (2010): The practice of social research, 12th. edn., Belmont, Calif. (2010).

Backhaus, K./Erichson, B./Plinke, W./Weiber, R. (2011): Multivariate Analysemethoden – Eine anwendungsorientierte Einführung, 13th. edn., Berlin (2011).

Backhaus, K./Funke, S. (1994): Fixkostenintensität und Kostenstrukturmanagement: Ergebnisse einer empirischen Studie, in: Controlling, 6 (3), p. 124–129.

Backhaus, K./Funke, S. (1996): Auf dem Weg zur fixkostenintensiven Unternehmung?, in: Zeitschrift für betriebswirtschaftliche Forschung, 48 (2), p. 95–129.

Bagozzi, R. P. (1979): The role of measurement in theory construction and hypothesis testing: toward a holistic model, in: Ferrell, O. C./Brown, S. W./Lamb, C. W. (eds.): Conceptual and theoretical developments in marketing, Chicago, Ill. (1979), p. 15–32.

Bagozzi, R. P. (1998): A Prospectus for Theory Construction in Marketing: Revisited and Revised, in: Hildebrandt, L./Homburg, C. (eds.): Die Kausalanalyse: Ein Instrument der empirischen betriebswirtschaftlichen Forschung, Stuttgart (1998), p. 45–81.

Bagozzi, R. P./Phillips, L. W. (1982): Representing and Testing Organizational Theories: A Holistic Construal, in: Administrative Science Quarterly, 27 (3), p. 459–489.

Bagozzi, R. P./Yi, Y. (1988): On the Evaluation of Structural Equation Models, in: Journal of the Academy of Marketing Science, 16 (1), p. 74–94.

Bailes, J. C./Assada, T. (1991): Empirical Differences between Japanese and American Budget and Performance Evaluation Systems, in: International Journal of Accounting, 26 (2), p. 131–142.

Bailey, J. R./Chen, C. C./Dou, S.-G. (1997): Conceptions of Self and Performance-Related Feedback in the U.S., Japan and China, in: Journal of International Business Studies, 28 (3), p. 605–625.

Baird, K. M./Harrison, G. L./Reeve, R. C. (2004): Adoption of activity management practices: a note on the extent of adoption and the influence of organizational and cultural factors, in: Management Accounting Research, 15 (4), p. 383–399.

Baird, K. M./Harrison, G. L./Reeve, R. C. (2007): Success of activity management practices: the influence of organizational and cultural factors, in: Accounting & Finance, 47 (1), p. 47–67.

Ballantine, J./Brignall, S./Modell, S. (1998): Performance measurement and management in public health services: a comparison of U.K. and Swedish practice, in: Management Accounting Research, 9 (1), p. 71–94.

Barclay, D. W./Thompson, R./Higgins, C. A. (1995): The Partial Least Squares Approach to Causal Modeling: Personal Computer Adoption and Use as an Illustration, in: Technology Studies: Special Issue on Research Methodology, 2 (2), p. 285–309.

Barrett, G. V./Bass, B. M. (1976): Cross-Cultural Issues in Industrial and Organizational Psychology, in: Dunnette, M. D. (ed.): Handbook of industrial and organizational psychology, Chicago (1976), p. 1639–1686.

Barry, H. (1969): Cross-Cultural Research with Matched Pairs of Societies, in: The Journal of Social Psychology, 79 (2), p. 25–33.

Bartel, R. (1990): Charakteristik, Methodik und wissenschaftsmethodische Probleme der Wirtschaftswissenschaften, in: Wirtschaftswissenschaftliches Studium, 19 (2), p. 54–59.

Baskerville, R. F. (2003): Hofstede never studied culture, in: Accounting, Organizations & Society, 28 (1), p. 1–14.

Baskerville-Morley, R. F. (2005): A research note: the unfinished business of culture, in: Accounting, Organizations & Society, 30 (4), p. 389–391.

Bauer, E. (1989): Übersetzungsprobleme und Übersetzungsmethoden bei einer multinationalen Marketingforschung, in: Jahrbuch der Absatz- und Verbrauchsforschung, 35 (2), p. 174–205.

Beck, U. (2000): What is globalization?, Cambridge et al. (2000).

Becker, A. (2003): Controlling als reflexive Steuerung von Organisationen, Stuttgart (2003).

Becker, A./Messner, M. (2005): After the scandals. A German-speaking perspective on management accounting research and education, in: European Accounting Review, 14 (2), p. 417–427.

Becker, H. P. (1984): Verwendung und Gestaltung der Kosten- und Leistungsrechnung in mittelgroßen Industrieunternehmen, Darmstadt (1984).

Behrens, G. (1993): Wissenschaftstheorie und Betriebswirtschaftslehre, in: Wittmann, W./Kern, W./Köhler, R./Küpper, H.-U./Wysocki, K. von (eds.): Handwörterbuch der Betriebswirtschaftslehre, 5th edn., Stuttgart (1993), c. 4763–4772.

Behrens, L. (2007): Konservierung von Stereotypen mit Hilfe der Statistik. Geert Hofstede und sein kulturvergleichendes Modell, Working Paper (2007).

Bellinger, B. (1967): Geschichte der Betriebswirtschaftslehre, Stuttgart (1967).

Belsley, D. A. (1984): Collinearity and Forecasting, in: Journal of Forecasting, 3 (2), p. 183–196.

Belsley, D. A. (1991): Conditioning Diagnostics: Collinearity and Weak Data in Regressions, New York (1991).

Belsley, D. A./Kuh, E./Welsch, R. E. (2004): Regression diagnostics – Identifying influential data and sources of collinearity, New York (2004).

Bennett, S. (1993): Chinese and western accounting practices compared, in: Management Accounting, 71 (2), p. 26–27.

Bentler, P. M./Chou, C.-P. (1978): Practical Issues in Structural Modeling, in: Sociological Methods & Research, 16 (1), p. 78–117.

Berens, W. (1997a): Kosteneinflußgrößen, in: Bloech, J./Ihde, G. B. (eds.): Vahlens Großes Logistiklexikon, München (1997), p. 452–454.

Berens, W. (1997b): Prozeßkostenrechnung, in: Bloech, J./Ihde, G. B. (eds.): Vahlens Großes Logistiklexikon, München (1997), p. 858–859.

Berliner, C./Brimson, J. A. (1988): Cost management for today's advanced manufacturing – The CAM-I conceptual design, 2nd. edn., Boston, Mass. (1988).

Berry, J. W. (1969): On cross-cultural comparability, in: International Journal of Psychology, 4 (2), p. 119–128.

Berry, J. W. (1980): Introduction to Methodology, in: Triandis, H. C./Berry, J. W. (eds.): Handbook of cross-cultural psychology. Volume 2: Methodology, Boston (1980), p. 1–28.

Berry, J. W./Dasen, P. R. (1974): Introduction: History and method in the cross-cultural study of cognition, in: Berry, J. W./Dasen, P. R. (eds.): Culture and cognition. Readings in cross-cultural psychology, London (1974), p. 1–25.

Berstecher, D. (1970): Zur Theorie und Technik des internationalen Vergleichs, Stuttgart (1970).

Bertalanffy, L. v. (1950): An Outline of General System Theory, in: The British Journal for the Philosophy of Science, 1 (2), p. 134–165.

Bhagat, R. S./McQuaid, S. J. (1982): Role of Subjective Culture in Organizations: A Review and Directions for Future Research, in: Journal of Applied Psychology, 67 (5), p. 653–685.

Bhimani, A./Ncube, M./Soonawalla, K. (2006): Intuition and Real Options-Based Investment Appraisal: A Cross-National Study of Financial Executives, in: The Journal of Applied Management Accounting Research, 4 (2), p. 11–33.

Bhimani, A. (ed.) (1996): Management accounting – European perspectives, Oxford (1996).

Bhimani, A. (1999): Mapping methodological frontiers in cross-national management control research, in: Accounting, Organizations & Society, 24 (5/6), p. 413–440.

Bhimani, A. (2005): International comparative management accounting, in: Abdel-Khalik, A. R./Cooper, C. L./Argyris, C. (eds.): The Blackwell encyclopedic dictionary of accounting, Cambridge, Mass. (2005), p. 250–255.

Bhimani, A. (2007): Comparative management accounting research – Past forays and emerging frontiers, in: Chapman, C. S./Hopwood, A. G./Shields, M. D. (eds.): Handbook of Management Accounting Research, Amsterdam et al. (2007), p. 343–363.

Bhimani, A./Gosselin, M./Ncube, M. (2005): Strategy and activity based costing: a cross national study of process and outcome contingencies, in: International Journal of Accounting, Auditing and Performance Evaluation, 2 (3), p. 187–205.

Bhimani, A./Gosselin, M./Ncube, M./Okano, H. (2007): Activity-based costing: how far have we come internationally?, in: Journal of Cost Management, 21 (3), p. 12–17.

Binder, C./Schäffer, U. (2005): Deutschsprachige Controllinglehrstühle an der Schwelle zum Generationswechsel, in: Zeitschrift für Controlling & Management, 49 (2), p. 100–104.

Birkett, W. P. (1998): Management accounting in Europe: a view from down-under, in: Management Accounting Research, 9 (4), p. 485–494.

Birnberg, J. G./Hoffman, V. B./Yuen, S. (2008): The accountability demand for information in China and the US – A research note, in: Accounting, Organizations and Society, 33 (1), p. 20–32.

Birnberg, J. G./Shields, M. D./Young, S. M. (1990): The Case for Multiple Methods in Empirical Management Accounting Research (with an Illustration from Budget Setting), in: Journal of Management Accounting Research, 2, p. 33–66.

Birnberg, J. G./Snodgrass, C. (1988): Culture and Control: A field study, in: Accounting, Organizations and Society, 13 (5), p. 447–464.

Bjornenak, T. (1997): Diffusion and accounting: the case of ABC in Norway, in: Management Accounting Research, 8 (1), p. 3–17.

Blake, J./Amat, O./Wraith, P. (2000): Developing a new national management accounting framework – the Spanish case, in: European Business Review, 12 (3), p. 122–128.

Blake, J./Soldevila, P./Wraith, P. (2003): The dimensions of, and factors giving rise to, variations in national management accounting approaches, in: European Business Review, 15 (3), p. 181–188.

Blau, P. M./Schoenherr, R. A. (1971): The structure of organizations, New York et al. (1971).

Bluedorn, A. C. (1993): Pilgrim's Progress: Trends and Convergence in Research on Organizational Size and Environments, in: Journal of Management, 19 (2), p. 163–191.

Blum, H. S. (2006): Logistik-Controlling – Kontext, Ausgestaltung und Erfolgswirkungen, Wiesbaden (2006).

Boddewyn, J. J. (ed.) (1969): Comparative management and marketing – Text and readings, Glenview (1969).

Boesch, E. E./Eckensberger, L. H. (1969): Methodische Probleme des interkulturellen Vergleichs, in: Graumann, C. F. (ed.): Sozialpsychologie, Göttingen (1969), p. 515–566.

Böge, H. (2009): Konzernrechnungslegung: Das Zusammenspiel zwischen IFRS-Konzernabschluss und HGB-Einzelabschluss, in: Gleich, R./Klein, A. (eds.): BilMoG und Controlling. Alle neuen Anforderungen für das Controlling, Freiburg et al. (2009), p. 223–252.

Bollen, K./Lennox, R. (1991): Conventional Wisdom on Measurement: A Structural Equation Perspective, in: Psychological Bulletin, 110 (2), p. 305–314.

Borgatta, E. F./Bohrnstedt, G. W. (1980): Level of Measurement: Once Over Again, in: Sociological Methods & Research, 9 (2), p. 147–160.

Borkowski, S. C. (1997): Factors Affecting Transfer Pricing and Income Shifting (?) Between Canadian and U.S. Transnational Corporations, in: The International Journal of Accounting, 32 (4), p. 391-415.

Borkowski, S. C. (1999): International managerial performance evaluation – A five country comparison, in: Journal of International Business Studies, 30 (3), p. 533–555.

Borkowski, S. C. (2010): Transfer pricing practices of transnational corporations in PATA countries, in: Journal of International Accounting, Auditing & Taxation, 19 (1), p. 35–54.

Bortz, J./Döring, N. (2009): Forschungsmethoden und Evaluation – Für Human- und Sozialwissenschaftler, 4th. edn., Heidelberg (2009).

Boucoiran, T./Brandau, M./Hoffjan, A./Trapp, R. (2009): Influence of National Culture on Management Accounting. An Exploration of German and French Management Accounting Instruments from the Perspective of German Companies, Working Paper (2009).

Boyacigiller, N. A./Adler, N. J. (1991): The Parochial Dinosaur: Organizational Science in a Global Context, in: Academy of Management Review, 16 (2), p. 262–290.

Boyacigiller, N. A./Kleinberg, J./Phillips, M. E./Sackmann, S. A. (2004): Conceptualizing culture: Elucidating the streams of research in international cross-cultural management, in: Punnett, B. J./Shenkar, O. (eds.): Handbook for international management research, 2nd edn., Ann Arbor (2004), p. 99–167.

Brast, C. (2006): Post Merger Integration betrieblicher Forschung und Entwicklung (F&E), Wiesbaden (2006).

Brettel, M./Engelen, A./Heinemann, F. (2009a): Der Einfluss nationaler Kultur auf Stellhebel und Wirkung der Marktorientierung in deutschen und thailändischen jungen Unternehmen, in: Zeitschrift für Betriebswirtschaft, 79 (1), p. 59–92.

Brettel, M./Engelen, A./Heinemann, F. (2009b): New entrepreneurial ventures in a globalized world: The role of market orientation, in: Journal of International Entrepreneurship, 7 (2), p. 88–110.

Brettel, M./Engelen, A./Heinemann, F./Vadhanasindhu, P. (2008): Antecedents of Market Orientation: A Cross-Cultural Comparison, in: Journal of International Marketing, 16 (2), p. 84–119.

Brewer, P. C. (1997): Managing Transnational Cost Management Systems, in: Journal of Cost Management, 11 (6), p. 35–40.

Brewer, P. C. (1998): National culture and activity-based costing systems: a note, in: Management Accounting Research, 9 (2), p. 241–260.

Brierley, J. A. (2008): Toward an Understanding of the Sophistication of Product Costing Systems, in: Journal of Management Accounting Research, 20, p. 61–78.

Brierley, J. A./Cowton, C. J./Drury, C. (2006): A comparison of product costing practices in discrete-part and assembly manufacturing and continuous production process manufacturing, in: International Journal of Production Economics, 100 (2), p. 314–321.

Briley, D. A./Aaker, J. L. (2006): When Does Culture Matter? Effects of Personal Knowledge on the Correction of Culture-Based Judgments, in: Journal of Marketing Research, 43 (3), p. 395–408.

Brislin, R. W. (1970): Back-Translation for Cross-Cultural Research, in: Journal of Cross-Cultural Psychology, 1 (3), p. 185–216.

Brislin, R. W. (1980): Translation and Content Analysis of Oral and Written Material, in: Triandis, H. C./Berry, J. W. (eds.): Handbook of cross-cultural psychology. Volume 2: Methodology, Boston (1980), p. 389–444.

Brislin, R. W./Lonner, W. J./Thorndike, R. M. (1973): Cross-cultural research methods, New York (1973).

Brodbeck, F. C./Frese, M. (2007): Societal Culture and Leadership in Germany, in: Chhokar, J. S./Brodbeck, F. C./House, R. J. (eds.): Culture and leadership across the world. The GLOBE book of in-depth studies of 25 societies, Mahwah (2007), p. 147–214.

Brösel, G./Köditz, F./Schmitt, C. (2004): Kostenträgerrechnung im Krankenhaus – Anforderungen unter DRG-Bedingungen, in: Zeitschrift für Controlling & Management, 48 (4), p. 247–253.

Brosius, F. (2008): SPSS 16 – Das mitp-Standardwerk, Heidelberg (2008).

Brownell, P. (1982a): A Field Study Examination of Budgetary Participation and Locus of Control, in: The Accounting Review, 57 (4), p. 766–777.

Brownell, P. (1982b): The Role of Accounting Data in Performance Evaluation, Budgetary Participation, and Organizational Effectiveness, in: Journal of Accounting Research, 20 (1), p. 12–27.

Brownell, P./Hirst, M. (1986): Reliance on Accounting Information, Budgetary Participation, and Task Uncertainty: Tests of a Three-Way Interaction, in: Journal of Accounting Research, 24 (2), p. 241–249.

Bruhn, M. (2006): Qualitätsmanagement für Dienstleistungen, 6th. edn., Berlin et al. (2006).

Buch, S. (2007): Strukturgleichungsmodelle – Ein einführender Überblick, Working Paper, Berlin (2007).

Budäus, D. (2002): Öffentliches Vergabewesen und Kalkulation öffentlicher Aufträge, Hamburg (2002).

Bungenstock, C. (1995): Entscheidungsorientierte Kostenrechnungssysteme: eine entwicklungsgeschichtliche Analyse, Wiesbaden (1995).

Bunzemeier, H./Fiori, W./Sitterlee, C./Brüning, K./Helling, J./Zimmer, D./Hoppenheit, C./Roeder, N. (2010): Erlösverteilung unter DRG-Bedingungen am Universitätsklinikum Münster. Ein wichtiger Baustein für erfolgreiche Krankenhausführung, in: Das Krankenhaus, 102, p. 946-961.

Burns, T./Stalker, G. M. (1961): The management of innovation, London (1961).

Burrell, G./Morgan, G. (1979): Sociological paradigms and organisational analysis – Elements of the sociology of corporate life, London (1979).

Busco, C./Giovannoni, E./Riccaboni, A. (2007): Globalisation and the international convergence of management accounting, in: Hopper, T./Northcott, D./Scapens, R. (eds.): Issues in management accounting, 3rd edn., Harlow (2007), p. 65–92.

C

C&L Deutsche Revision (1997): Wertorientierte Unternehmensführung – Die Ergebnisse einer internationalen Studie von C&L bei 300 Unternehmen in 13 Ländern zum Thema Shareholder Value, Frankfurt am Main (1997).

Cadez, S. (2006): A Cross-Industry Comparison of Strategic Management Accounting Practices: An Exploratory Study, in: Economic and Business Review, 8 (3), p. 279–298.

Cadez, S./Guilding, C. (2007): Benchmarking the incidence of strategic management accounting in Slovenia, in: Journal of Accounting & Organizational Change, 3 (2), p. 126–146.

Calori, R./Lubatkin, M./Very, P. (1994): Control Mechanisms in Cross-Border Acquisitions: An International Comparison, in: Organization Studies, 15 (3), p. 361–379.

Caplan, E. H. (1973): The Behavioral Implications of Management Accounting, in: Management International Review, 13 (2/3), p. 21–31.

Caroli, E./Gautié, J./Lloyd, C./Lamanthe, A./James, S. (2010): Delivering Flexibility: Contrasting Patterns in the French and the UK Food Processing Industry, in: British Journal of Industrial Relations, 48 (2), p. 284–309.

Carr, C./Tomkins, C. (1996): Strategic investment decisions: the importance of SCM. A comparative analysis of 51 case studies in U.K., U.S. and German companies, in: Management Accounting Research, 7 (2), p. 199–217.

Carr, C. (1998): Strategic Investment Decisions and Short-Termism: Germany versus Britain, in: Papadakis, V./Barwise, P. (eds.): Strategic decisions, Dordrecht (1998), p. 107–125.

Carr, C. (2005): Are German, Japanese and Anglo-Saxon Strategic Decision Styles Still Divergent in the Context of Globalization?, in: Journal of Management Studies, 42 (6), p. 1155–1188.

Carr, C./Harris, S. (2004): The Impact of Diverse National Values on Strategic Investment Decisions in the Context of Globalization, in: International Journal of Cross Cultural Management, 4 (1), p. 77–99.

Carr, C./Pudelko, M. (2006): Convergence of Management Practices in Strategy, Finance and HRM between the USA, Japan and Germany, in: International Journal of Cross Cultural Management, 6 (1), p. 75–100.

Carr, C./Tomkins, C. (1998): Context, culture and the role of the finance function in strategic decisions. A comparative analysis of Britain, Germany, the U.S.A. and Japan, in: Management Accounting Research, 9 (2), p. 213–239.

Carr, C./Tomkins, C./Bayliss, B. (1991): Strategic controllership - a case study approach, in: Management Accounting Research, 2 (2), p. 89–107.

Carr, C./Tomkins, C./Bayliss, B. (1994): Financial or Strategic Controls? An Anglo-German Case Study, in: European Management Journal, 12 (1), p. 102–113.

Carte, T. A./Russell, C. J. (2003): In Pursuit of Moderation: Nine Common Errors and Their Solutions, in: Management Information Systems Quarterly, 27 (3), p. 479–501.

Chan, C. W. (1998): Transfer pricing negotiation outcomes and the impact of negotiator mixed-motives and culture empirical evidence from the U.S. and Australia, in: Management Accounting Research, 9 (2), p. 139–161.

Chan, Y.-C. L./DeGroote, M. G. (2004): Performance measurement and adoption of balanced scorecards. A survey of municipal governments in the USA and Canada, in: The International Journal of Public Sector Management, 17 (3), p. 204–221.

Chandler, A. D. (1962): Strategy and structure, 22nd. edn., Cambridge, Mass. (1962).

Chandy, P. R./Williams, T. G. E. (1994): The impact of journals and authors on international business research: A Citational Analysis of JIBS Articles, in: Journal of International Business Studies, 25 (4), p. 715–728.

Chapman, C. S. (1997): Reflections on a Contingent View of Accounting, in: Accounting, Organizations & Society, 22 (2), p. 189–205.

Chapman, C. S. (2005): Not because they are new: developing the contribution of enterprise resource planning systems to management control research, in: Accounting, Organizations & Society, 30 (7/8), p. 685–689.

Charalambos, S./Constantinides, S. (2004): Enterprise Resource Planning Systems' impact on Accounting Processes, in: Business Process Management Journal, 10 (2), p. 234–247.

Charles, S. L./Hansen, D. R. (2008): An evaluation of activity-based costing and functional-based costing: A game-theoretic approach, in: International Journal of Production Economics, 113 (1), p. 282–296.

Cheng, J. L. C. (1989): Toward a contextual approach to cross-national organization research: a macro perspective, in: Advances in International Comparative Management, 4 (1), p. 3–18.

Cheng, J. L. C. (2007): Critical issues in international management research: an agenda for future advancement, in: European Journal of International Management, 1 (1/2), p. 23–38.

Chenhall, R. H. (2003): Management control systems design within its organizational context: findings from contingency-based research and directions for the future, in: Accounting, Organizations & Society, 28 (2/3), p. 127–168.

Chenhall, R. H. (2007): Theorizing contingencies in management control systems research, in: Chapman, C. S./Hopwood, A. G./Shields, M. D. (eds.): Handbook of Management Accounting Research, Amsterdam et al. (2007), p. 163–205.

Chenhall, R. H./Langfield-Smith, K. (1998): Adoption and benefits of management accounting practices: an Australian study, in: Management Accounting Research, 9 (1), p. 1–19.

Chenhall, R. H./Morris, D. (1986): The Impact of Structure, Environment, and Interdependence on the perceived Usefulness of Management Accounting Systems, in: The Accounting Review, 61 (1), p. 16–35.

Child, J. (1972): Organizational Structure, Environment and Performance: The Role of Strategic Choice, in: Sociology, 6 (1), p. 1–22.

Child, J. (1973): Predicting and understanding organization structure, in: Administrative Science Quarterly, 18 (2), p. 168–185.

Child, J. (1981): Culture, contingency and capitalism in the cross-national study of organizations, in: Research in Organizational Behavior, 3 (1), p. 303–356.

Child, J./Kieser, A. (1975): Organization and managerial roles in British and West German companies: An examination of the culture-free thesis, Berlin (1975).

Child, J./Tayeb, M. (1982): Theoretical Perspectives in Cross-National Organizational Research, in: International Studies of Management & Organization, 12 (4), p. 23–70.

Chin, W./Marcolin, B. L./Newstead, P. R. (2003): A Partial Least Squares Latent Variable Modeling Approach for Measuring Interaction Effects: Results from a Monte Carlo Simulation Study and an Electronic-Mail Emotion/Adoption Study, in: Information Systems Research, 14 (2), p. 189–217.

Chin, W./Newsted, P. R. (1999): Structural Equation Modeling Analysis With Small Samples Using Partial Least Squares, in: Hoyle, R. H. (ed.): Statistical Strategies for Small Sample Research, Thousand Oaks Calif. et al. (1999), p. 307–341.

Chin, W. W. (1998): The partial least squares approach for structural equation modeling, in: Marcoulides, G. A. (ed.): Modern Methods for Business Research, Mahwah, NJ (1998), p. 295–358.

Chmielewicz, K. (1994): Forschungskonzeptionen der Wirtschaftswissenschaft, 3rd. edn., Stuttgart (1994).

Choe, J.-m./Langfield-Smith, K. (2004): The Effects of National Culture on the Design of Management Accounting Information Systems, in: Journal of Comparative International Management, 7 (1), p. 1–14.

Choi, F. D. S./Czechowicz, I. J. (1983): Assessing Foreign Subsidiary Performance: A Multinational Comparison, in: Management International Review, 23 (4), p. 14–25.

Choi, F. D. S./Mueller, G. G. (1978): An Introduction to Multinational Accounting, Englewood Cliffs (1978).

Chow, C. W./Deng, F. J./Ho, J. L. (2000): The Openness of Knowledge Sharing within Organizations. A Comparative Study of the United States and the People's Republic of China, in: Journal of Management Accounting Research, 12, p. 65–95.

Chow, C. W./Harrison, G. L./McKinnon, J. L./Wu, A. (1999a): Cultural influences on informal information sharing in Chinese: an exploratory study, in: Accounting, Organizations & Society, 24 (7), p. 561–582.

Chow, C. W./Harrison, P./Lindquist, T./Wu, A. (1997): Escalating commitment to unprofitable projects – replication and cross-cultural extension, in: Management Accounting Research, 8 (3), p. 347–361.

Chow, C. W./Hwang, R. N.-C./Liao, W./Wu, A. (1998): National Culture and Subordinates' Upward Communication of Private Information, in: The International Journal of Accounting, 33 (3), p. 293–311.

Chow, C. W./Kato, Y./Merchant, K. A. (1996): The use of organizational controls and their effects on data manipulation and management myopia: A Japan vs. U.S. comparison, in: Accounting, Organizations & Society, 21 (2/3), p. 175–192.

Chow, C. W./Kato, Y./Shields, M. D. (1994): National Culture and the Preference for Management Controls – an Exploratory Study of the Firm-Labor Market Inferface, in: Accounting, Organizations & Society, 19 (4/5), p. 381–400.

Chow, C. W./Lindquist, T. M./Wu, A. (2001): National Culture and the Implementation of High-Stretch Performance Standards: An Exploratory Study, in: Behavioral Research in Accounting, 13, p. 85–109.

Chow, C. W./Shields, M. D./Wu, A. (1999b): The importance of national culture in the design of and preference for management controls for multi-national operations, in: Accounting, Organizations & Society, 24 (5/6), p. 441–461.

Chow, C. W./Shields, M. D./Yoke, K. C. (1991): The Effects of Management Controls and National Culture on Manufacturing Performance: an Experimental Investigation, in: Accounting, Organizations & Society, 16 (3), p. 209–226.

Christensen, J./Wagenhofer, A. (1997): Editorial: Special Section: German cost accounting, in: Management Accounting Research, 8 (3), p. 255–259.

Chun, K.-T./Campbell, J. B./Yoo, J. H. (1974): Extreme Response Style in Cross-Cultural Research: A Reminder, in: Journal of Cross-Cultural Psychology, 5 (4), p. 465–480.

Churchill, G. A. (1979): A Paradigm for Developing Better Measures of Marketing Constructs, in: Journal of Marketing Research, 16 (2), p. 64–73.

Churchill, G. A./Lacobucci, D. (2005): Marketing research – Methodological foundations, 9th. edn., Mason Ohio (2005).

Cinquini, L./Collini, P./Marelli, A./Tenucci, A. (2008): An exploration of the factors affecting the diffusion of advanced costing techniques: a comparative analysis of two surveys (1996-2005), Working Paper (2008).

Clarke, P. J./Hill, N. T./Stevens, K. (1999): Activity-Based Costing in Ireland: barriers to, and opportunities for change, in: Critical Perspectives on Accounting, 10 (4), p. 443–468.

Clinton, B. D. (2007): Crisis!, in: Strategic Finance, 88 (7), p. 24–30.

Clinton, B. D./Webber, S. A. (2004): RCA at Clopay, in: Strategic Finance, 86 (4), p. 21–26.

Coad, A. F./Herbert, I. P. (2009): Back to the future: New potential for structuration theory in management accounting research?, in: Management Accounting Research, 20 (3), p. 177–192.

Coates, J. B./Davis, E. W./Emmanuel, C. R./Longden, S. G./Stacey, R. J. (1992): Multinational companies performance measurement systems: international perspectives, in: Management Accounting Research, 3 (2), p. 133–150.

Coenenberg, A. G./Cantner, J./Fink, C./Mattner, G. (2003): Kostenrechnung und Kostenanalyse, 5th. edn., Stuttgart (2003).

Coenenberg, A. G./Fischer, T. M./Günther, T. (2009): Kostenrechnung und Kostenanalyse, 7th. edn., Stuttgart (2009).

Cokins, G. (2001): Activity-based cost management – An executive's guide, New York (2001).

Cole, R. E. (1979): Work, Mobility and Participation. A Comparative Study of American and Japanese Industry, Berkeley Calif. (1979).

Collier, P. M./Agyei-Ampomah, S. (2008): Management accounting, Amsterdam (2008).

Collins, F./Almer, E. D. (1999): Budget Games and Effort Differences Between the United States and Latin America, in: Journal of International Accounting, Auditing & Taxation, 8 (2), p. 241.

Collins, F./Holzmann, O. J./Mendoza, R. (2005): The relationship between machistic tendencies and budgeting: A cross-cultural study, in: Journal of International Accounting, Auditing & Taxation, 14 (2), p. 139–156.

Cone, J. D. (1986): Idiographic, Nomothetic, and related Perspectives in Behavioral Assessment, in: Nelson, R. O./Hayes, S. C. (eds.): Conceptual foundations of behavioral assessment, New York (1986), p. 111–128.

Connor, J. M. (1985): The food manufacturing industries – Structure, strategies, performance and policies, Lexington, Mass. (1985).

Cooper, R. (1988a): The rise of activity-based costing – part two: when do I need an activity-based cost system?, in: Journal of Cost Management, 2 (3), p. 41–48.

Cooper, R. (1988b): The rise of activity-based costing – part three: how many cost drivers do you need, and how do you select them?, in: Journal of Cost Management, 2 (4), p. 34–46.

Cooper, R. (1991): The Two-Stage Procedure in Cost Accounting: Part One, in: Cooper, R./Kaplan, R. S. (eds.): The design of cost management systems. Text and cases, 1st edn., Upper Saddle River, NJ (1991), p. 147–156.

Cooper, R. (1995): When lean enterprises collide – Competing through confrontation, Boston, Mass. (1995).

Cooper, R. (1996): Costing techniques to support corporate strategy: evidence from Japan, in: Management Accounting Research, 7 (2), p. 219–246.

Cooper, R./Kaplan, R. S. (eds.) (1991): The design of cost management systems – Text, cases, and readings, Englewood Cliffs, NJ (1991).

Cooper, R./Slagmulder, R. (1997): Target costing and value engineering, Portland, Or. (1997).

Corsten, H./Gössinger, R. (2007): Dienstleistungsmanagement, 5th. edn., München (2007).

Cotton, W. D. J./Jackman, S. M./Brown, R. A. (2003): Note on a New Zealand replication of the Innes et al. UK activity-based costing survey, in: Management Accounting Research, 14 (1), p. 67.

Crowningshield, G. R./Gorman, K. A. (1979): Cost accounting – Principles and managerial applications, 4th. edn., Boston (1979).

Cruz, I./Major, M./Scapens, R. W. (2009): Institutionalization and practice variation in the management control of a global/local setting, in: Accounting, Auditing & Accountability Journal, 22 (1), p. 91–117.

Cruz, I./Scapens, R./Major, M. (2008): The Localisation of a Global Performance Measurement System, Working Paper (2008).

Currie, W. L. (1993a): The strategic management of AMT in Japan, the USA, the UK and West Germany – Part 2: Managing AMT in a UK automotive plant: the cost of machine downtime, in: Management Accounting, 70 (1), p. 38–39.

Currie, W. L. (1993b): The strategic management of AMT in Japan, the USA, the UK and West Germany – Part 1: Developing a performance measurement system for CAD in a US manufacturing company, in: Management Accounting, 70 (1), p. 32–33.

Currie, W. L./Seddon, J. J. M. (1992): Managing AMT in a Just-in-Time Environment in the UK and Japan, in: British Journal of Management, 3 (3), p. 23–31.

Cyert, R. M./March, J. G. (1963): A behavioral theory of the firm, Englewood Cliffs, NJ (1963).

Cyr, D. (2002): The art of global thinking – Integrating organizational philosophies of East and West, West Lafayette Ind. (2002).

Czycholl, R. (1971): Vergleichende Wirtschaftspädagogik. Möglichkeiten und Grenzen einer vergleichenden erziehungswissenschaftlichen Disziplin, Trier (1971).

D

Daft, R. L. (2001): Essentials of organization theory and design, 2nd. edn., Cincinnati, Ohio (2001).

Daft, R. L. (2010): Organization theory and design, 10th. edn., Mason, Ohio (2010).

Daley, L./Jiambalvo, J./Sundem, G. L./Kondo, Y. (1985): Attitudes Towards Financial Control Systems in the United States and Japan, in: Journal of International Business Studies, 16 (3), p. 91–110.

Daniel, S. J./Reitsperger, W. D. (1991): Management Control Systems for J.I.T.: An Empirical Comparison of Japan and the U.S, in: Journal of International Business Studies, 22 (4), p. 603–617.

Daniel, S. J./Reitsperger, W. D. (1992): Management Control Systems for Quality: An Empirical Comparison of the U.S. and Japanese Electronics Industries, in: Journal of Management Accounting Research, 4, p. 64–78.

Daniel, S. J./Reitsperger, W. D. (1994): Strategic Control Systems for Quality: An Empirical Comparison of the Japanese and U.S. Electronics Industry, in: Journal of International Business Studies, 25 (2), p. 275–294.

Daniel, S. J./Reitsperger, W. D./Gregson, T. (1995): Quality Consciousness in Japanese and U.S. electronics manufacturers: an examination of the impact of quality strategy and management control systems on perceptions of the importance of quality to expected management rewards, in: Management Accounting Research, 6 (4), p. 367–382.

Datar, S. M./Gupta, M. (1994): Aggregation, specification and measurement errors in product costing, in: Accounting Review, 69 (4), p. 567–591.

Davila, T. (2005): An exploratory study on the emergence of management control systems: formalizing human resources in small growing firms, in: Accounting, Organizations & Society, 30 (3), p. 223–248.

Dechow, N./Granlund, M./Mouritsen, J. (2007): Management Control of the Complex Organization: Relationships between Management Accounting and Information Technology, in: Chapman, C. S./Hopwood, A. G./Shields, M. D. (eds.): Handbook of Management Accounting Research, Amsterdam et al. (2007), p. 625–640.

Demski, J. S./Feltham, G. A. (1976): Cost determination, a conceptual approach, Ames Iowa (1976).

Dess, G. G./Beard, D. W. (1984): Dimensions of Organizational Task Environments, in: Administrative Science Quarterly, 29 (1), p. 52–73.

Deutsch, K. W. (1996): Prologue: Achievements and Challenges in 2000 Years of Comparative Research, in: Inkeles, A./Sasaki/Masamichi (eds.): Comparing nations and cultures. Readings in a cross-disciplinary perspective, Englewood Cliffs NJ (1996), p. 3–8.

Diamantopoulos, A./Winklhofer, H. M. (2001): Index Construction with Formative Indicators: An Alternative to Scale Development, in: Journal of Marketing Research, 38 (2), p. 269–277.

DiMaggio, P. J./Powell, W. W. (1983): The Iron Cage Revisited: Institutional Isomorphism and Collective Rationality in Organizational Fields, in: American Sociological Review, 48 (2), p. 147–160.

DiMaggio, P. J./Powell, W. W. (1991a): Introduction, in: Powell, W. W./DiMaggio, P. J. (eds.): The new institutionalism in organizational analysis, Chicago et al. (1991), p. 1–38.

DiMaggio, P. J./Powell, W. W. (1991b): The Iron Cage Revisited: Insitutional Isomorphism and Collective Rationality in Organizational Fields, in: Powell, W. W./DiMaggio, P. J. (eds.): The new institutionalism in organizational analysis, Chicago et al. (1991), p. 63–82.

Dobson, P./Starkey, K./Richards, J. (2004): Strategic management – Issues and cases, 2nd. edn., Malden, Mass. (2004).

Doege, V./Martini, S. (2009): Krankenhäuser auf dem Weg in den Wettbewerb – Der Implementierungsprozess der Diagnosis Related Groups, Wiesbaden (2009).

Donaldson, L. (1990): Size and bureaucracy in East and West: a preliminary meta analysis, in: Clegg, S. R./Dunphy, D./Redding, S. G. (eds.): The enterprise and management in East Asia, 2nd edn., Hong Kong (1990), p. 67–91.

Donaldson, L. (1995): American anti-management theories of organization – A critique of paradigm proliferation, Cambridge etc. (1995).

Donaldson, L. (2001): The contingency theory of organizations, Thousand Oaks Calif. et al. (2001).

Dorn, G. (1961): Die Entwicklung der industriellen Kostenrechnung in Deutschland, Berlin (1961).

Dorn, G. (1993): Geschichte der Kostenrechnung, in: Chmielewicz, K./Schweitzer, M. (eds.): Enzyklopädie der Betriebswirtschaftslehre: Band 3 – Handwörterbuch des Rechnungswesens, 3rd edn., Stuttgart (1993), c. 722–729.

Douglas, P. C./Wier, B. (2005): Cultural and Ethical Effects in Budgeting Systems: A Comparison of U.S. and Chinese Managers, in: Journal of Business Ethics, 60 (2), p. 159–174.

Douglas, S. P./Craig, C. S. (2006): On Improving the Conceptual Foundations of International Marketing Research, in: Journal of International Marketing, 14 (1), p. 1–22.

DRSC (2010a): Final Report of the Survey on the IFRS for SMEs among German SMEs, available at: http://www.standardsetter.de/drsc/dox.php?do=docs_index&type_id=9&cat _id=30, last revised 16.09.2011.

DRSC (2010b): IFRS for SMEs - Ergebnisse einer Befragung von nicht kapitalmarktorientierten Unternehmen in Deutschland, available at: http://www.standardsetter.de/drsc/dox.php?do=docs_index&type_id=9&cat_id=30, last revised 16.09.2011.

Drucker, P. F. (1971): Men, ideas and politics, essays, New York et al. (1971).

Drury, C. (2005): Management accounting for business, 3rd. edn., London (2005).

Drury, C. (2008): Management and cost accounting, 7th. edn., London (2008).

Drury, C./Tayles, M. (1995): Issues arising from surveys of management accounting practice, in: Management Accounting Research, 6 (3), p. 267–280.

Drury, C./Tayles, M. (2000): Cost System Design and Profitability Analysis in UK Companies, London (2000).

Drury, C./Tayles, M. (2005): Explicating the design of overhead absorption procedures in UK organizations, in: British Accounting Review, 37 (1), p. 47–84.

Drury, C./Tayles, M. (2006): Profitability analysis in UK organizations: An exploratory study, in: The British Accounting Review, 38 (4), p. 405–425.

Dubois, D. A./Someya, K. (1977): Accounting Development in Japan: The Convergence Theory, in: Accountant, 176 (May 5th), p. 500–502.

Dugdale, D./Jones, T. C. (1997): How many companies use ABC for stock valuation? A comment on Innes and Mitchell's questionnaire findings, in: Management Accounting Research, 8 (2), p. 233–240.

Duncan, R. B. (1972): Characteristics of Organizational Environments and Perceived Environmental Uncertainty, in: Administrative Science Quarterly, 17, p. 313–327.

Dyer, J. H. (2000): Examining interfirm trust and relationships in a cross-national setting, in: Earley, C. P./Singh, H. (eds.): Innovations in international and cross-cultural management, Thousand Oaks (2000), p. 215–244.

E

Eberl, M. (2006): Formative und reflektive Konstrukte und die Wahl des Strukturgleichungsverfahrens, in: Die Betriebswirtschaft, 66 (6), p. 651–668.

Edwards, J. R. (1989): A History of Financial Accounting, London, New York (1989).

Egelhoff, W. G. (1984): Patterns of Control in U.S., UK, and European Multinational Corporations, in: Journal of International Business Studies, 15 (2), p. 73–83.

Elger, T. (1994): Global Japanization? – The transnational transformation of the labour process, London et al. (1994).

Elliot, J. (1998): International Transfer Pricing. A survey of UK and non-UK groups (Part 2), in: Management Accounting, 76 (11), p. 48–51.

Engelen, A. (2007): Marktorientierung junger Unternehmen – Einflussgrößen und Wirkung im interkulturellen Vergleich zwischen Deutschland, Thailand und Indonesien, Wiesbaden (2007).

Erickson, E. E. (1974): Galton's Worst: A Note on Ember's Reflection, in: Schaefer, J. M. (ed.): Studies in cultural diffusion: Galton's problem, New Haven, Conn. (1974), p. 62–83.

Ernst, A./Herold, R. (1986): Japans langer Abschied von der Vollbeschäftigung – Arbeitsmarktstrukturen und Arbeitsmarktentwicklung, Hamburg (1986).

Ernst, C./Seibert, U./Stuckert, F. (1998): KonTraG, KapAEG, StückAG, EuroEG. Gesellschafts- und Bilanzrecht – Textausgabe mit Begründungen des Bundesrates mit Gegenäusserungen der Bundesregierung, Berichten des Rechtsausschusses des Deutschen Bundestages, Stichwortverzeichnis, Düsseldorf (1998).

Esser, M./Kobayashi, K. (1994): Kaishain: Personalmanagement in Japan – Sinn und Werte statt Systeme, Göttingen (1994).

Esser, S. (2011): Produktorientiertes Kostenmanagement in der chemischen Industrie – Eine empirische Analyse, Frankfurt am Main (2011).

Estrin, T. L./Kantor, J./Albers, D. (1994): Is ABC suitable for your company?, in: Management Accounting, 75 (4), p. 40–45.

Ewert, R./Wagenhofer, A. (2007): Management Accounting Theory and Practice in German-Speaking Countries, in: Chapman, C. S./Hopwood, A. G./Shields, M. D. (eds.): Handbook of Management Accounting Research, Amsterdam et al. (2007), p. 1035–1069.

Ewert, R./Wagenhofer, A. (2008): Interne Unternehmensrechnung, 7th. edn., Berlin Heidelberg (2008).

Ewusi-Mensah, K. (1981): The External Organizational Environment and its Impact on Managerial Information Systems, in: Accounting, Organizations & Society, 6 (4), p. 301–316.

F

Fandel, G./Fey, A./Heuft, B./Pitz, T. (2004): Kostenrechnung, 2nd. edn., Berlin, Heidelberg (2004).

Farmer, R. N./Richman, B. M. (1964): A Model for Research in Comparative Management, in: California Management Review, 7 (2), p. 55–68.

Fassott, G. (2006): Operationalisierung latenter Variablen in Strukturgleichungsmodellen: eine Standortbestimmung, in: Zeitschrift für betriebswirtschaftliche Forschung, 58 (2), p. 67–88.

Fassott, G./Eggert, A. (2005): Zur Verwendung formativer und reflektiver Indikatoren in Strukturgleichungsmodellen: Bestandsaufnahme und Anwendungsempfehlungen, in: Bliemel, F./Eggert, A./Fassott, G./Henseler, J. (eds.): Handbuch PLS-Pfadmodellierung, Stuttgart (2005), p. 31–47.

Feichter, A. (2008): National Culture and its Impact on Performance Evaluation Systems: An Exploratory Study of German Speaking and Central and Eastern European Countries, Working Paper (2008).

Ferrara, W. (1990): The new cost/management accounting – More questions than answers, in: Management Accounting, 68 (10), p. 48–52.

Fessmann, K.-D. (1980): Organisatorische Effizienz in Unternehmungen und Unternehmungsteilbereichen, Düsseldorf (1980).

Fickert, R. (1993): Management accounting – quo vadis?, in: Die Unternehmung, 47 (3), p. 203–224.

Finlay, P. N. (2000): Strategic management – An introduction to business and corporate level strategy, London (2000).

Firkola, P./Lim, L. (2003): Cross-Cultural Management Research Issues, in: Economic journal of Hokkaido University, 32, p. 45–68.

Flacke, K. (2006): Controlling in mittelständischen Unternehmen – Ausgestaltung, Einflussfaktoren der Instrumentennutzung und Einfluss auf die Bankkommunikation (2006).

Flechtner, H. J. (1966): Grundbegriffe der Kybernetik, Stuttgart (1966).

Form, W. H. (1969): Occupational and social integration of automobile workers in four countries: A comparative study, in: International Journal of Comparative Sociology, 10 (1/2), p. 95–116.

Fornell, C./Bookstein, F. L. (1982): Two Structural Equation Models: LISREL and PLS Applied to Consumer Exit-Voice Theory, in: Journal of Marketing Research, 19 (4), p. 440–452.

Fornell, C./Cha, J. (1994): Partial Least Squares, in: Bagozzi, R. P. (ed.): Advanced Methods of Marketing Research, Cambirdge Mass. (1994), p. 52–78.

Fornell, C./Larcker, D. F. (1981): Evaluating Structural Equation Models with Unobservable Variables and Measurement Error, in: Journal of Marketing Research, 18 (1), p. 39–50.

Foucault, M. (1961): Folie et déraison: Histoire de la folie à l'Age classique, Paris (1961).

Foucault, M. (1975): Surveiller et punir: Naissance de la prison, Paris (1975).

Fox, W. M. (1963): The Management Process. An Integrated Functional Approach, Homewood (1963).

Frank, S. (2000): Erfolgreiche Gestaltung der Kostenrechnung. Determinanten und Wirkungen am Beispiel mittelständischer Unternehmen, Wiesbaden (2000).

Frank, S./Reitmeyer, T. (1999): Gestaltung und Erfolgsfaktoren der Kostenrechnung im Mittelstand, in: Kostenrechnungspraxis (special edition no. 2), p. 15–25.

Franke, G. R./Richey, R. G. J. (2010): Improving generalizations from multi-country comparisons in international business research, in: Journal of International Business Studies, 41 (8), p. 1275–1293.

Franz, K.-P. (1991): Preisbildung bei öffentlichen Aufträgen, in: Wirtschaftswissenschaftliches Studium, 20 (11), p. 831–835.

Franz, K.-P. (1992): Kalkulation von Selbstkostenpreisen für öffentliche Aufträge, in: Wirtschaftswissenschaftliches Studium, 21 (1), p. 40–46.

Franz, K.-P./Kajüter, P. (2007): Kostenmanagement, in: Busse von Colbe, W./Coenenberg, A. G./Franz, K.-P./Kajüter, P./Linnhoff, U./Pellens, B. (eds.): Betriebswirtschaft für Führungskräfte. Eine Einführung in wirtschaftliches Denken und

Handeln für Ingenieure, Naturwissenschaftler, Juristen und Geisteswissenschaftler, 3rd edn., Stuttgart (2007), p. 275–306.

Frese, E. (1992): Organisationstheorie – Historische Entwicklung, Ansätze, Perspektiven, 2nd. edn., Wiesbaden (1992).

Frey, F. W. (1970): Cross-cultural survey research in political science, Cambridge, Mass. (1970).

Friedl, B. (2010): Kostenrechnung – Grundlagen, Teilrechnungen und Systeme der Kostenrechnung, 2nd. edn., München (2010).

Friedl, G./Frömberg, K./Hammer, C./Küpper, H.-U./Pedell, B. (2009a): Stand und Perspektiven der Kostenrechnung in deutschen Großunternehmen, in: Zeitschrift für Controlling & Management, 53 (2), p. 111–116.

Friedl, G./Hammer, C./Burkhard Pedell/Küpper, H.-U. (2009b): How Do German Companies Run Their Cost Accounting Systems?, in: Management Accounting Quarterly, 10 (2), p. 38–52.

Friedl, G./Küpper, H.-U./Pedell, B. (2005): Relevance Added Combining ABC with German Cost Accounting, in: Strategic Finance, 86 (12), p. 56–61.

Frijda, N./Jahoda, G. (1966): On the Scope and Methods of Cross-Cultural Research, in: International Journal of Psychology, 1 (2), p. 109–127.

Frucot, V./Shearon, W. T. (1991): Budgetary participation, locus of control, and Mexican managerial performance and job satisfaction, in: Accounting Review, 66 (1), p. 80–99.

G

Gabele, E. (1981): Die Einführung von Geschäftsbereichsorganisationen, Tübingen (1981).

Gaiser, B. (1998): Prozeßkostenrechnung und Activity Based Costing (ABC), in: Horváth & Partner (ed.): Prozeßkostenmanagement. Methodik und Anwendungsfelder, 2nd edn., München (1998), p. 65–77.

Garg, A./Ghosh, D./Hudick, J./Nowacki, C. (2003): Roles and Practices in Management Accounting Today, in: Strategic Finance, 85 (1), p. 30–35.

Geertz, C. (1983): Local knowledge – Further essays in interpretive anthropology, New York (1983).

Gefen, D./Straub, D. W./Boudreau, M.-C. (2000): Structural Equation Modeling and Regression: Guidelines for Research Practice, in: Communications of AIS, 4 (August), p. 1–77.

Gehrke, I./Zarlowski, P. (2002): Modelling cross-national variations in management control practices: the example of France and Germany (2002).

Gendo, F./Konschak, R. (1999): Mythos Lean Production – Die wahren Erfolgskonzepte japanischer Unternehmen, Essen (1999).

Gentner, A. (1994): Entwurf eines Kennzahlensystems zur Effektivitäts- und Effizienzsteigerung von Entwicklungsprojekten, München (1994).

Gerdin, J. (2005): Management accounting system design in manufacturing departments: an empirical investigation using a multiple contingencies approach, in: Accounting, Organizations & Society, 30 (2), p. 99–126.

Gernon, H./Wallace, O. R. S. (1995): International Accounting Research – A Review of its Ecology, Contending Theories and Methodologies, in: Journal of Accounting Literature, 14, p. 54–106.

Gernon, H. M./Meek, G. K. (2001): Accounting – An international perspective, 5th. edn., Boston (2001).

Giddens, A. (1991): Modernity and self-identity – Self and society in the late modern age, Cambridge (1991).

Giddens, A. (2008): The constitution of society – Outline of the theory of structuration, Cambridge (2008).

Giering, A. (2000): Der Zusammenhang zwischen Kundenzufriedenheit und Kundenloyalität – Eine Untersuchung moderierender Effekte, Wiesbaden (2000).

Glaser, B. G./Strauss, A. L. (1967): The discovery of grounded theory, Strategies for Qualitative Research, Chicago (1967).

Glaskiewicz, J./Wasserman, S. (1989): Mimetic Processes within an Interorganizational Field: An Empirical Test, in: Administrative Science Quarterly, 34 (3), p. 454–479.

Goffee, R./Scase, R. (1992): Organizational Change and the Corporate Career: The Restructuring of Managers' Job Aspirations, in: Human Relations, 45 (4), p. 363–385.

Goldman, A. I. (1992): Liaisons: Philosophy meets the cognitive and social sciences, Cambridge, Mass. (1992).

Goody, J. (1977): The domestication of the savage mind, Cambridge et al. (1977).

Gopal, A./Bostram, R. P./Chin, W. (1992): Applying Adaptive Structuring Theory to Investigate the Process of Group Support Systems Use, in: Journal of Management Information Systems, 9 (3), p. 45–69.

Gordon, L. A./Miller, D. (1976): A Contingency Framework for the Design of Accounting Information Systems, in: Accounting, Organizations & Society, 1 (1), p. 59–69.

Gordon, L. A./Narayanan, V. K. (1984): Management accounting systems, perceived environmental uncertainty and organizational structure: an empirical investigation, in: Accounting, Organizations & Society, 9 (1), p. 33–47.

Görg, B. (1991): Was erwarten Unternehmen von einem Controller? – Was erwarten Controller von einem Unternehmen?, in: Eschenbach, R. (ed.): Der Controller – Controlling als Serviceleistung. Was kann das Unternehmen vom Controller fordern? Tagungsbericht vom Österreichischen Controllertag 1990, Wien (1991), p. 95–104.

Gorsuch, R. L. (1983): Factor analysis, Hillsdale (1983).

Gosselin, M. (1997): The Effect of Strategy and Organizational Structure on Adoption and Implementation of Activity-Based Costing, in: Accounting, Organizations & Society, 22 (2), p. 105–122.

Gosselin, M. (2007): A Review of Activity-Based Costing: Technique, Implementation, and Consequences, in: Chapman, C. S./Hopwood, A. G./Shields, M. D. (eds.): Handbook of Management Accounting Research, Amsterdam et al. (2007), p. 641–671.

Götz, O./Liehr-Gobbers, K. (2004a): Analyse von Strukturgleichungsmodellen mit Hilfe der Partial-Least-Squares(PLS)-Methode, in: Die Betriebswirtschaft, 64 (6), p. 714–738.

Götz, O./Liehr-Gobbers, K. (2004b): Der Partial-Least-Squares (PLS)-Ansatz zur Analyse von Strukturgleichungsmodellen, Working Paper, Münster (2004).

Götz, O./Liehr-Gobbers, K./Krafft, M. (2010): Evaluation of Structural Equation Models Using the Partial Least Squares (PLS) Approach, in: Vinzi, V. E./Chin, W. W./Henseler, J./Wang, H. (eds.): Handbook of Partial Least Squares. Concepts, Methods and Applications, Berlin, Heidelberg (2010), p. 691–711.

Götze, U. (2007): Kostenrechnung und Kostenmanagement, 4th. edn., Berlin (2007).

Grabatin, G. (1981): Effizienz von Organisationen, Berlin (1981).

Granlund, M./Lukka, K. (1998): It's a Small World of Management Accounting Practices, in: Journal of Management Accounting Research, 10, p. 153–179.

Granlund, M./Malmi, T. (2002): Moderate impact of ERPS on management accounting: a lag or permanent outcome?, in: Management Accounting Research, 13 (3), p. 299–321.

Granlund, M./Mouritsen, J. (2003): Problematizing the relationship between management control and information technology, in: European Accounting Review, 12 (1), p. 77–83.

Graves, D. (1972): A Cross-Cultural Comparison of Managerial Behavior in England and France, in: International Studies of Management & Organization, 2 (1), p. 105–116.

Gravetter, F. J./Wallnau, L. B. (2009): Statistics for the behavioral sciences, 8th. edn., Belmont CA (2009).

Gray, S. J. (1983): International Accounting: A Review of Academic Research in the United Kingdom, in: International Journal of Accounting, 19 (1), p. 15–42.

Gremillion, L. L. (1984): Organization Size and Information System Use: An Empirical Study, in: Journal of Management Information Systems, 1 (2), p. 4–17.

Grochla, E. (1978): Einführung in die Organisationstheorie, Stuttgart (1978).

Groot, T. L. C. M. (1996): Managing Costs in the Netherlands: Past Theory and Current Practice, in: Bhimani, A. (ed.): Management accounting. European perspectives, Oxford (1996), p. 164–179.

Groot, T. L. C. M. (1997): Activity-Based Costing in the Food Industry, Working Paper (1997).

Groot, T. L. C. M. (1999): Activity based costing in US and Dutch food companies, in: Advances in Management Accounting, 7, p. 47–63.

Grundei, J. (1999): Effizienzbewertung von Organisationsstrukturen – Integration verhaltenswissenschaftlicher Erkenntnisse am Beispiel der Marktforschung, Wiesbaden (1999).

Guilding, C./Cravens, K. S./Tayles, M. (2000): An international comparison of strategic management accounting practices, in: Management Accounting Research, 11 (1), p. 113–135.

Guilding, C./Lamminmaki, D./Drury, C. (1998): Budgeting and Standard Costing Practices in New Zealand and the United Kingdom, in: International Journal of Accounting, 33 (4), p. 569–588.

Guilding, C./McManus, L. (2002): The incidence, perceived merit and antecedents of customer accounting: an exploratory note, in: Accounting, Organizations & Society, 27 (1/2), p. 45–59.

Gul, F. A./Chia, Y. M. (1994): The effects of management accounting systems, perceived environmental uncertainty and decentralization on managerial performance: A test of three-way interaction, in: Accounting, Organizations & Society, 19 (4/5), p. 413–426.

Gunasekaran, A./Marri, H. B./Grieve, R. J. (1999): Activity-based costing in small and medium enterprises, in: Computers & Industrial Engineering, 37 (1/2), p. 407–411.

Gunasekaran, A./Singh, D. (1999): Design of activity-based costing in a small company: a case study, in: Computers & Industrial Engineering, 37 (1/2), p. 413–416.

Gutenberg, E. (1983): Grundlagen der Betriebswirtschaftslehre. Band 1: Die Produktion, 24th. edn., Springer (1983).

H

Haenlein, M./Kaplan, A. M. (2004): A Beginner's Guide to Partial Least Squares Analysis, in: Understanding Statistics, 3 (4), p. 283–297.

Haghirian, P. (2010): Understanding Japanese Management Practices, New York (2010).

Haghirian, P. (2011): Japanese Management Revisited, in: Zeitschrift für Controlling & Management, 55 (1), p. 33–37.

Hahn, C. H. (2002): Segmentspezifische Kundenzufriedenheitsanalyse: Neue Ansätze zur Segmentierung von Märkten, Wiesbaden (2002).

Hair, J. F./Black, B./Babin, B. J./Anderson, R. E./Tatham, R. L. (2010): Multivariate data analysis – A global perspective, 7th. edn., Upper Saddle River, NJ (2010).

Hamprecht, M. (1996): Controlling von Konzernplanungssystemen – Theoretische Ableitung und betriebliche Realität führungsstrukturabhängiger Ausprägungsmuster, Wiesbaden (1996).

Hansen, H. F. (1995): Organizing for Quality – A Discussion of Different Evaluation Methods as Means for Improving Quality in Research, in: Science Studies, 8 (1), p. 36–53.

Harbison, F. H./Myers, C. A. (1959): Management in the industrial world – An international analysis, New York et al. (1959).

Harman, H. H. (1976): Modern factor analysis, 3rd. edn., Chicago (1976).

Harpaz, I. (2004): The essence of performing meaningful comparative international survey research, in: Punnett, B. J./Shenkar, O. (eds.): Handbook for international management research, 2nd edn., Ann Arbor (2004), p. 17–48.

Harrison, G. L. (1992): The cross-cultural generalizability of the relation between participation, budget emphasis and job related attitudes, in: Accounting, Organizations & Society, 17 (1), p. 1–15.

Harrison, G. L. (1993): Reliance on Accounting Performance Measures in Superior Evaluative Style – The Influence of National Culture and Personality, in: Accounting, Organizations and Society, 18 (4), p. 319–339.

Harrison, G. L./McKinnon, J. L. (1998): Editorial culture and management accounting, in: Management Accounting Research, 9 (2), p. 113–118.

Harrison, G. L./McKinnon, J. L. (1999): Cross-cultural research in management control systems design a review of the current state, in: Accounting, Organizations & Society, 24 (5/6), p. 483–506.

Harrison, G. L./McKinnon, J. L./Panchapakesan, S./Leung, M. (1994): The Influence of Culture on Organizational Design and Planning and Control in Australia and the United States Compared with Singapore and Hong Kong, in: Journal of International Financial Management & Accounting, 5 (3), p. 242–261.

Harrison, P. D./Chow, C. W./Wu, A. (1999a): A Cross-Cultural Investigation of Managers' Project Evaluation Decisions, in: Behavioral Research in Accounting, 11, p. 143–159.

Harzing, A.-W./Baldueza, J./Barner-Rasmussen, W./Barzantny, C./Canabal, A./Davila, A./Espejo, A./Ferreira, R./Giroud, A./Koester, K./Liang, Y.-K./Mockaitis, A./Morley, M. J./Myloni, B./Odusanya, J. O. T./O'Sullivan, S. L./Palaniappan, A. K./Prochno, P./Choudhury, S. R./Saka-Helmhout, A. (2009): Rating versus ranking: What is the best way to reduce response and language bias in cross-national research?, in: International Business Review, 18 (4), p. 417–432.

Hasan, H./Ditsa, G. (1999): The impact of culture on the adoption of IT: an interpretive study, in: Journal of Global Information Management, 7 (1), p. 5–15.

Hassall, T./Joyce, J./Montano, J. L. A./Anes, J. A. D. (2005): Priorities for the development of vocational skills in management accountants: A European perspective, in: Accounting Forum, 29 (4), p. 379–394.

Hassel, L. G./Cunningham, G. M. (1996): Budget Effectiveness in Multinational Corporations: An Empirical Test of the Use of Budget Controls Moderated by Two Dimensions of Budgetary Participation Under High and Low Environmental Dynamism, in: Management International Review, 36 (3), p. 245–266.

Hatfield, H. R. (1966): Some Variations in Accounting Practices in England, France, Germany and the United States, in: Journal of Accounting Research, 4 (2), p. 169–182.

Hawkins, C. E. (1983): A comparative study of the management accounting practices of industrial companies in the United States and Japan, Nebraska (1983).

Hawley, A. H. (1968): Human Ecology, in: Sills, D. L. (ed.): International Encyclopaedia of the Social Sciences, New York (1968), p. 328–337.

Hebeler, C. (2003): Harmonisierung des internen und externen Rechnunungswesens. US-amerikanische Accounting-Systeme als konzeptionelle Grundlage für deutsche Unternehmen?, Wiesbaden (2003).

Heidenreich, M. (1991): Problems of Generalisation in Cross-National Studies of Organisations, in: International Sociology, 6 (2), p. 181–200.

Heigl, A. (1981): Controlling im Mittelbetrieb, in: Zeitschrift für Organisation, 50 (8), p. 425–430.

Heiner, R. A. (1983): The Origin of Predictable Behavior, in: American Economic Review, 73 (4), p. 560–595.

Henderson, B. D. (2003): Noch einmal: Die Erfahrungskurve (1980), in: Oetinger, B. von (ed.): Das Boston Consulting Group Strategie-Buch. Die wichtigsten Managementkonzepte für den Praktiker, 8th edn., München (2003), p. 571–574.

Henderson, B. D./Gälweiler, A. (1984): Die Erfahrungskurve in der Unternehmensstrategie, 2nd. edn., Frankfurt/Main (1984).

Henke, K.-D./Göpffarth, D. (2010): Das Krankenhaus im System der Gesundheitsversorgung, in: Hentze, J./Kehres, E. (eds.): Krankenhaus-Controlling. Konzepte, Methoden und Erfahrungen aus der Krankenhauspraxis, 4.th edn., Stuttgart (2010), p. 35–52.

Henri, J.-F. (2007): A Quantitative Assessment of the Reporting of Structural Equation Modeling Information: The Case of Management Accounting Research, in: Journal of Accounting Literature, 26, p. 76–115.

Henseler, J. (2005): Einführung in die PLS-Pfadmodellierung, in: Wirtschaftswissenschaftliches Studium, 34 (2), p. 70–75.

Hesseling, P. (1973): Studies in Cross-Cultural Organization, in: Columbia Journal of World Business, 8 (4), p. 120–134.

Hickson, D. J./Hinings, C. R./McMillan, C. J./Schwitter, J. P. (1974): The Culture-Free Context of Organization Structure: A Tri-National Comparison, in: Sociology, 8 (1), p. 59–80.

Hickson, D. J./McMillan, C. J./Azumi, K./Horváth, D. (1979): Grounds for comparative organization theory: Quicksands or hard core?, in: Lammers, C. J./Hickson, D. J. (eds.): Organizations alike and unlike. International and interinstitutional studies in the sociology of organizations, London (1979), p. 25–41.

Hickson, D. J./Pugh, D. S. (2001): Management worldwide – Distinctive styles amid globalization, 2nd. edn., London (2001).

Hiramatsu, K. (1992): Accounting Education in Japanese Corporations, in: Asian Review of Accounting, 1 (1), p. 57–68.

Hiromoto, T. (1988): Another Hidden Edge – Japanese Management Accounting, in: Harvard Business Review, 66 (4), p. 22–26.

Hirsch, B. (2003): Zur Lehre im Fach Controlling – Eine empirische Bestandsaufnahme an deutschsprachigen Universitäten, in: Weber, J./Hirsch, B. (eds.): Zur Zukunft der Controllingforschung. Empirie, Schnittstellen und Umsetzung in der Lehre, Wiesbaden (2003), p. 249–266.

Ho, S.-J. K./Kidwell, L. A. (2000): A Survey of Management Techniques Implemented by Municipal Administrators, in: Government Accountants Journal, 49 (1), p. 46–52.

Hodgson, G. M. (1988): Economics and institutions – A manifesto for a modern institutional economics, Cambridge (1988).

Hoecklin, L. A. (1995): Managing cultural differences – Strategies for competitive advantage, Wokingham (1995).

Hoffjan, A./Bebek, M. (2009): Anforderungen an den Controller aus Sicht der Praxis. Eine Bestandsaufnahme, in: Controlling, 21 (11), p. 617–623.

Hoffjan, A./Nevries, P./Stienemann, R. (2009): Comparative Management Accounting: Literature Review on Similarities and Differences Between Management Accounting in Germanic and Anglophone Countries, in: Berens, W./Hoffjan, A./Burgartz, T. (eds.): Controlling in einem globalen Markt, Frankfurt am Main (2009), p. 115–146.

Hoffjan, A./Wömpener, A. (2005): Comparative management accounting – similarities and differences in German and English language management accounting textbooks, in: Weber, J./Meyer, M. (eds.): Internationalisierung des Controllings. Standortbestimmung und Option, Wiesbaden (2005), p. 49–65.

Hoffjan, A./Wömpener, A. (2006): Comparative Analysis of Strategic Management Accounting in German- and English-language General Management Accounting Textbooks, in: Schmalenbach Business Review, 58 (3), p. 234–258.

Hofstede, G. (1980): Culture's consequences, international differences in work-related values, 1st. edn., Beverly Hills (1980).

Hofstede, G. (1983): The Cultural Relativity of Organizational Practices and Theories, in: Journal of International Business Studies, 14 (2), p. 75–89.

Hofstede, G. (1987): The Cultural Context of Accounting, in: Cushing, B. E. (ed.): Accounting and culture, Sarasota, Fla. (1987), p. 1–11.

Hofstede, G. (1991): Cultures and organizations – Software of the mind, London (1991).

Hofstede, G. (1993): Interkulturelle Zusammenarbeit – Kulturen – Organisationen – Management, Wiesbaden (1993).

Hofstede, G. (1999): Problems Remain, But Theories Will Change – The Universal and the Specific in 21st-Century Global Management, in: Organizational Dynamics, 28 (1), p. 34–44.

Hofstede, G. (2001): Culture's consequences – Comparing values, behaviors, institutions and organizations across nations, 2nd. edn., Thousand Oaks, Calif. (2001).

Hofstede, G. (2003): What is culture? A reply to Baskerville, in: Accounting, Organizations & Society, 28 (7/8), p. 811–813.

Hofstede, G./Bond, M. H. (1988): The Confucius Connection: From Cultural Roots to Economic Growth, in: Organizational Dynamics, 16 (4), p. 5–21.

Hofstede, G./Hofstede, G. J./Minkov, M. (2010): Cultures and organizations – Software of the mind; intercultural cooperation and its importance for survival, 3rd. edn., New York, NY (2010).

Hofstede, G./Spangenberg, J. (1989): Internationale(n) Vergleiche, Technik der, in: Macharzina, K. (ed.): Handwörterbuch Export und Internationale Unternehmung, Stuttgart (1989), c. 948–963.

Hoitsch, H.-J./Lingnau, V. (2007): Kosten- und Erlösrechnung – Eine controllingorientierte Einführung, 6th. edn., Berlin et al. (2007).

Holmes, S./Kelly, G./Cunningham, R. (1991): The Small Firm Information Cycle: A Reappraisal, in: International Small Business Journal, 9 (1), p. 41–53.

Holzer, P. H./Norreklit, H. (1991): Some thoughts on cost accounting developments in the United States, in: Management Accounting Research, 2 (1), p. 3–13.

Holzmüller, H. H. (1995): Konzeptionelle und methodische Probleme in der interkulturellen Management- und Marketingforschung, Stuttgart (1995).

Homburg, C./Baumgartner, H. (1998): Beurteilung von Kausalmodellen: Bestandsaufnahme und Anwendungsempfehlungen, in: Hildebrandt, L./Homburg, C. (eds.): Die Kausalanalyse: Ein Instrument der empirischen betriebswirtschaftlichen Forschung, Stuttgart (1998), p. 343–369.

Homburg, C./Giering, A. (1996): Konzeptualisierung und Operationalisierung komplexer Konstrukte, in: Marketing – Zeitschrift für Forschung und Praxis, 18 (1), p. 5–24.

Homburg, C./Giering, A. (2001): Personal Characteristics as Moderators of the Relationship Between Customer Satisfaction and Loyalty: An Empirical Analysis, in: Psychology and Marketing, 18 (1), p. 43–66.

Homburg, C./Weber, J./Aust, R. (1998): Interne Kundenorientierung der Kostenrechnung – Ergebnisse der Koblenzer Studie, Vallendar (1998).

Hopper, T. (1999): Postcard from Japan: a management accounting view, in: Accounting, Auditing & Accountability Journal, 12 (1), p. 58–68.

Hopper, T./Koga, T./Goto, J. (1999): Cost accounting in small and medium sized Japanese companies: an exploratory study, in: Accounting & Business Research, 30 (1), p. 73–86.

Hopwood, A. G. (1999): Situating the practice of management accounting in its cultural context: an introduction, in: Accounting, Organizations & Society, 24 (5/6), p. 377–378.

Horngren, C. T./Datar, S. M./Foster, G. (2006): Cost accounting – A managerial emphasis, 12th. edn., Upper Saddle River, NJ (2006).

Horovitz, J. H. (1978): Management Control in France, Great Britain and Germany, in: Columbia Journal of World Business, 13 (2), p. 16–22.

Horovitz, J. H. (1980): Top management control in Europe, London (1980).

Horváth, D./Koya Azumi/Hickson, D. J./McMillan, C. (1981): Bureaucratic Structures in Cross-National Perspective: A Study of British, Japanese, and Swedish Firms, in: Dlugos, G./Weiermair, K. (eds.): Management Under Differing Value Systems, Berlin, New York (1981), p. 537–563.

Horváth, P. (2009a): Controlling, 11th. edn., München (2009).

Horváth, P. (2009b): What is German Controlling?, in: Journal of Cost Management, 23 (2), p. 16–19.

Horváth, P./Minning, F. (2001): Wertorientiertes Management in Deutschland, Großbritannien, Italien und Frankreich, in: Controlling, 13 (6), p. 273.

House, R. J./Hanges, P. J./Javidan, M./Dorfman, P. W./Gupta, V. (2004): Culture, leadership, and organizations – The GLOBE study of 62 societies, Thousand Oaks, Calif. (2004).

Howell, J. P./Dorfman, P. W./Kerr, S. (1986): Moderator Variables in Leadership Research, in: Academy of Management Review, 11 (1), p. 88–102.

Howell, R. A. (1989): Foreword, in: Monden, Y./Sakurai, M. (eds.): Japanese management accounting. A world class approach to profit management, Cambridge, Mass. (1989), p. xix.

Howell, R. A./Brown, J. D./Sourcy, S. R./Seed, A. H. (1987): Management accounting in the new manufacturing environment – Current cost management practice in automated (advanced) manufacturing environments, Montvale, NJ (1987).

Huber, F./Herrmann, A./Meyer, F./Vogel, J./Vollhardt, K. (2007): Kausalmodellierung mit Partial Least Squares – Eine anwendungsorientierte Einführung, Wiesbaden (2007).

Huff, L./Kelley, L. (2003): Levels of organizational trust in individualist versus collectivist societies: a seven nation study, in: Organisation Science, 14 (1), p. 81–90.

Hui, H. C./Triandis, H. C. (1985): Measurement in Cross-Cultural Psychology – A Review and Comparison of Strategies, in: Journal of Cross-Cultural Psychology, 16 (2), p. 131–152.

Hui, H. C./Triandis, H. C. (1989): Effects of culture and response format on extreme response styles, in: Journal of Cross-Cultural Psychology, 20 (3), p. 296–309.

Hulland, J. (1999): Use of Partial Least Squares (PLS) in Strategic Management Research: A Review of four Recent Studies, in: Strategic Management Journal, 20 (2), p. 195–204.

Hummel, S. (1998): Kostenrechnungssysteme, in: Busse von Colbe, Walther. (ed.): Lexikon des Rechnungswesens. Handbuch der Bilanzierung und Prüfung, der Erlös-, Finanz-, Investitions- und Kostenrechnung, 4th edn., München (1998), p. 453–457.

Hunold, C. (2003): Kommunale Kostenrechnung – Gestaltung Nutzung und Erfolgsfaktoren, Wiesbaden (2003).

Huo, Y. P./Randall, D. M. (1991): Exploiting Subcultural Differences in Hofstede's Value Survey: The Case of the Chinese, in: Asia Pacific Journal of Management, 8 (2), p. 159–173.

Hußmann, K. (1976): Der Wandel des japanischen Lohnsystems, Tübingen (1976).

Hutchinson, R./Liao, K. (2009): Zen Accounting: How Japanese Management Accounting Practice Supports Lean Management, in: Management Accounting Quarterly, 11 (1), p. 27–35.

Hwang, Y./Evans III, J. H./Hegde, V. G. (1993): Product Cost Bias and Selection of an Allocation Base, in: Journal of Management Accounting Research, 5, p. 213–242.

I

Inkpen, A. C./Birkenshaw, J. (1994): International Joint Ventures and Performance: an Interorganizational Perspective, in: International Business Review, 3 (3), p. 201–217.

Innes, J./Mitchell, F. (1995): A survey of activity based costing in the U.K.'s largest companies, in: Management Accounting Research, 6 (2), p. 137–153.

Innes, J./Mitchell, F. (1997): Survey research on activity-based costing: a reply to Dugdale and Jones, in: Management Accounting Research, 8 , p. 241–249.

Innes, J./Mitchell, F./Sinclair, D. (2000): Activity-based costing in the U.K.'s largest companies: a comparison of 1994 and 1999 survey results, in: Management Accounting Research, 11 (3), p. 349–362.

Inzerilli, G. (1980): Preface: Some conceptual issues in the study of the relationships between organizations and societies, in: International Studies of Management & Organization, 10 (4), p. 3–14.

Ishikawa, K./Yamamoto, M./Kishi, D. T./Nabeshima, T. (2005): New prospective payment system in Japan, in: American Journal of Health-System Pharmacy, 62 (15), p. 1617–1619.

Ittner, C. D./Lanen, W. N./Larcker, D. F. (2002): The Association Between Activity-Based Costing and Manufacturing Performance, in: Journal of Accounting Research, 40 (3), p. 711–726.

Ittner, C. D./Larcker, D. F. (1997): Quality Strategy, Strategic Control Systems, and Organizational Performance, in: Accounting, Organizations & Society, 22 (3/4), p. 293–314.

J

Jacobs, K./Marcon, G./Witt, D. (2004): Cost and performance information for doctors: an international comparison, in: Management Accounting Research, 15 (3), p. 337–354.

Jain, D. (1994): Regression Analysis for Marketing Decisions, in: Bagozzi, R. P. (ed.): Principles of marketing research, Cambridge (1994), p. 162–194.

James, L. R./Brett, J. M. (1984): Mediators, Moderators, and Tests for Mediation, in: Journal of Applied Psychology, 69 (2), p. 307–321.

Jamieson, I. (1982): The concept of culture and its relevance for an analysis of business enterprise in different societies, in: International Studies of Management & Organization, 12 (4), p. 71–105.

Jansen, E. P./Merchant, K. A./van der Stede, W. A. (2007): National Differences in Performance-Dependent Compensation Practices: The United States vs. the Netherlands, Working Paper (2007).

Jarvis, C. B./MacKenzie, S. B./Podsakoff, P. M. (2003): A Critical Review of Construct Indicators and Measurement Model Misspecification in Marketing and Consumer Research, in: Journal of Consumer Research, 30 (2), p. 199–218.

Jaworski, B. J. (1988): Toward a Theory of Marketing Control Environmental Context, Control Types, and Consequences, in: Journal of Marketing, 52 (3), p. 23–39.

Johnson, B./Christensen, L. B. (2011): Educational research – Quantitative, qualitative, and mixed approaches, 4th. edn., Thousand Oaks Calif. (2011).

Johnson, G. H./Byington, J. R. (1993): Accounting Competence, Machiavellianism, and Budget-Related Behavior: A Comparative Study of US and Spanish Managers, in: The International Journal of Accounting, 28 (4), p. 335–346.

Johnson, H. T./Kaplan, R. S. (1987): Relevance lost – The rise and fall of management accounting, Boston, Mass. (1987).

Jones, J. M./Munday, M./Brinn, T. (1998): Speculations on barriers to the transference of Japanese management accounting, in: Accounting, Auditing & Accountability Journal, 11 (2), p. 204–215.

Jones, L. F. (1991): Product Costing at Caterpillar, in: Management Accounting, 72 (2), p. 34–42.

Jones, T. C./Luther, R. (2005): Anticipating the Impact of IFRS on the Management of German Manufacturing Companies: Some Observations from a British Perspective, in: Accounting in Europe (1), p. 165–193.

Jöreskog, K. G. (1978): Structural Analysis of Covariance and Correlation Matrices, in: Psychometrika, 43 (4), p. 443–477.

Joshi, P. L. (2001): The international diffusion of new management accounting practices: the case of India, in: Journal of International Accounting, Auditing & Taxation, 10 (1), p. 85–109.

K

Kajüter, P. (2000): Proaktives Kostenmanagement – Konzeption und Realprofile, Wiesbaden (2000).

Kajüter, P. (2005): Kostenmanagement in der deutschen Unternehmenspraxis – Empirische Befunde einer branchenübergreifenden Feldstudie, in: Schmalenbachs Zeitschrift für betriebswirtschaftliche Forschung, 57 (1), p. 79–100.

Kajüter, P. (2008): Harmonisierung des Rechnungswesens: Ein Ansatz zur Vereinfachung des Controllings?, in: Vom Brocke, J./Becker, J. (eds.): Einfachheit in Wirtschaftsinformatik und Controlling. Festschrift für Heinz Lothar Grob, München (2008), p. 347–363.

Kajüter, P. (2011): Kostenrechnungssysteme im internationalen Vergleich, in: Kajüter, P./Mindermann, T./Winkler, C. (eds.): Controlling und Rechnungslegung. Bestandsaufnahme, Schnittstellen, Perspektiven, Stuttgart (2011), p. 89–118.

Kajüter, P./Barth, D./Dickmann, T. (2007): Rechnungslegung nach IFRS im deutschen Mittelstand? – Der Standardentwurf "IFRS für kleine und mittelgroße Unternehmen" im Licht empirischer Befunde, in: Der Betrieb, 60 (35), p. 1877–1884.

Kajüter, P./Moeschler, M. (2011a): Comparative Management Accounting: A review of research in international differences of cost accounting, Working Paper (2011).

Kajüter, P./Moeschler, M. (2011b): Management Accounting, in: Busse von Colbe, W./Crasselt, N./Pellens, B. (eds.): Lexikon des Rechnungswesens, 5th edn., München (2011), p. 545–549.

Kalenberg, F. (2008): Kostenrechnung – Grundlagen und Anwendungen, 2nd. edn., München (2008).

Kampen, J./Swyngedouw, M. (2000): The Ordinal Controversy Revisited, in: Quality & Quantity, 34 (1), p. 87–102.

Kao, C./Wang, T. Y./Kuo, S./Chen, L. H./Horng, S. D. (1995): Production pattern of machinery firms: viewpoints of technology and management, in: International Journal of Production Research, 33 (11), p. 3207–3215.

Kaplan, R. S. (1988): One Cost System isn't Enough, in: Harvard Business Review, 66 (1), p. 61–66.

Kaplan, R. S. (1994): Management Accounting (1984–1994): Development of New Practice & Theory, in: Management Accounting Research, 5 (3/4), p. 247–260.

Kaplan, R. S./Atkinson, A. A. (1989): Advanced management accounting, 2nd. edn., Englewood Cliffs, NJ (1989).

Kaplan, R. S./Cooper, R. (1998): Cost & Effect – Using integrated cost systems to drive profitability and performance, Boston Mass. (1998).

Kaplan, R. S./Johnson, H. T. (1991): Using Activity-Based Cost Systems to Influence Behavior, in: Cooper, R./Kaplan, R. S. (eds.): The design of cost management systems. Text and cases, 1st edn., Upper Saddle River, NJ (1991), p. 396–432.

Kato, Y. (1989): Applying Quantitative Methods to Cost and Management Accounting Practices: A U.S. - Japanese Comparison, in: Monden, Y./Sakurai, M. (eds.): Japanese management accounting. A world class approach to profit management, Cambridge, Mass. (1989), p. 449–473.

Keil, M./Tan, B. C./Wei, K.-K./Saarinen, T./Tuunainen, V./Wassenaar, A. (2000): A Cross-Cultural Study on Escalation of Commitment Behavior in Software Projects, in: Management Information Systems Quarterly, 24 (2), p. 299–325.

Keller, E. v. (1982): Management in fremden Kulturen – Ziele, Ergebnisse und methodische Probleme der kulturvergleichenden Managementforschung, Bern (1982).

Kellermanns, F. W./Islam, M. (2004): US and German activity-based costing: A critical comparison and system acceptability propositions, in: Benchmarking: An International Journal, 11 (1), p. 31–51.

Kern, M. (1979): Klassische Erkenntnistheorien und moderne Wissenschaftslehre, in: Raffée, H./Abel, B. (eds.): Wissenschaftstheoretische Grundfragen der Wirtschaftswissenschaften, München (1979), p. 11–27.

Kerr, C. (1960): Industrialism and industrial man – The problems of labor and management in economic growth, Cambridge Mass. (1960).

Khandwalla, P. N. (1972): The Effect of Different Types of Competition on the Use of Management Controls, in: Journal of Accounting Research, 10 (2), p. 275–285.

Khandwalla, P. N. (1977): The design of organizations, New York (1977).

Kidwell, L. A./Ho, S.-J. K./Blake, J./Wraith, P./Roubi, R./Richardson, A. W. (2002): New Management Techniques: An International Comparison, in: CPA Journal, 52 (2), p. 63–66.

Kieser, A. (1988): Adapting organizations to micro-electronics and micro-electronics to organizations: Experiences in the Federal Republic of Germany, in: Urabe, K./Child, J./Kagono, T. (eds.): Innovation and management. International comparisons, Berlin (1988), p. 319–336.

Kieser, A./Ebers, M. (2006): Organisationstheorien, 6th. edn., Stuttgart (2006).

Kieser, A./Kubicek, H. (1992): Organisation, 3rd. edn., Berlin (1992).

Kieser, A./Walgenbach, P. (2007): Organisation, Stuttgart (2007).

Kilger, W. (1961): Flexible Plankostenrechnung und Deckungsbeitragsrechnung, 1st. edn., Wiesbaden (1961).

Kim, I.-W./Ansari, S./Bell, J./Swenson, D. (2002): Target Costing Practices in the United States, in: Controlling, 14 (11), p. 607–614.

Kim, I.-W./Song, J. (1990): U.S., Korea, & Japan – Accounting Practices in Three Countries, in: Management Accounting, 72 (2), p. 26–30.

Kim, J. H./Joo, I. K./Choi, F. D. S. (1996): The Information Content of Productivity Measures: an International Comparison, in: Journal of International Financial Management & Accounting, 7 (3), p. 167–190.

Kim, U./Triandis, H. C./Kagitcibasi, C./Choi, S./Yoon, G. (eds.) (1994): Individualism and collectivism – Theory, method, and applications, Thousand Oaks, Calif (1994).

Kinney, M. R./Raiborn, C. A. (2008): Cost accounting, 6th. edn., Mason Ohio et al. (2008).

Kirkman, B. L./Lowe, K. B./Gibson, C. B. (2006): A quarter century of "Culture's Consequences" a review of empirical research incorporating Hofstede's cultural values framework, in: Journal of International Business Studies, 37 (3), p. 285–320.

Klein, G. A. (1999): Konvergenz von internem und externem Rechnungswesen auf Basis der International Accounting Standards (IAS), in: Kostenrechnungspraxis, 43 (3), p. 67–77.

Kloock, J./Schiller, U. (1997): Marginal costing, cost budgeting and cost variance analysis, in: Management Accounting Research, 8 (3), p. 299–323.

Kluckhohn, F. R./Strodtbeck, F. L. (1961): Variations in value orientations, Evanston Ill. (1961).

Kolbe, C. (1989): Investitionsrechnungen zur Beurteilung von Auslandsinvestitionen, Bergisch Gladbach (1989).

König, R. (1975): Beobachtung und Experiment in der Sozialforschung, in: König, R. (ed.): Beobachtung und Experiment in der Sozialforschung, 8th edn., Köln (1975), p. 17–49.

Kono, T./Falkus, M. (1984): Strategy and structure of Japanese enterprises, London (1984).

Koontz, H./Bradspies, R. W. (1972): A future-directed view, in: Business Horizon, 15 (3), p. 25–36.

Kornmeier, M. (2007): Wissenschaftstheorie und wissenschaftliches Arbeiten – Eine Einführung für Wirtschaftswissenschaftler, Heidelberg (2007).

Kosmider, A. (1994): Controlling im Mittelstand – Eine Untersuchung der Gestaltung und Anwendung des Controllings in mittelständischen Industrieunternehmen, 2nd. edn., Stuttgart (1994).

Kreder, M./Zeller, M. (1988): Control in German and U.S. Companies, in: Management International Review, 28 (3), p. 58–66.

Kreuz, W. (2002): Kosten-Benchmarking: Konzept und Praxisbeispiel, in: Franz, K.-P./Kajüter, P. (eds.): Kostenmanagement. Wertsteigerung durch systematische Kostensteuerung, 2nd edn., Stuttgart (2002), p. 91–106.

Krieger, R. (1995): Betriebsindividuelle Gestaltung der Kostenrechnung – Ein Beitrag zur Weiterentwicklung der situativen Kostenrechnungstheorie unter besonderer Berücksichtigung der Industriebetriebe, Berlin (1995).

Krumwiede, K. R. (1998): The Implementation Stages of Activity-Based Costing and the Impact of Contextual and Organizational Factors, in: Journal of Management Accounting Research, 10, p. 239–277.

Krumwiede, K. R. (2005): Rewards and Realities of German Cost Accounting, in: Strategic Finance, 86 (10), p. 27–34.

Krumwiede, K. R./Suessmair, A. (2007a): Comparing U.S. and German Cost Accounting Methods, in: Management Accounting Quarterly, 8 (3), p. 1–9.

Krumwiede, K. R./Suessmair, A. (2007b): Getting Down to Specifics on RCA, in: Strategic Finance, 88 (12), p. 50–55.

Krumwiede, K. R./Suessmair, A. (2008): A Closer Look at German Cost Accounting Methods, in: Management Accounting Quarterly, 10 (1), p. 37–50.

Krumwiede, K. R./Suessmair, A./MacDonald, J. (2007): An Exploratory Study of the Factors Affecting the Implementation Success of German Cost Accounting Methods, Working Paper (2007).

Kubicek, H. (1975): Empirische Organisationsforschung, Stuttgart (1975).

Kubicek, H. (1977): Heuristische Bezugsrahmen und heuristisch angelegte Forschungsdesigns als Element einer Konstruktionsstrategie empirischer Forschung, in: Köhler, R. (ed.): Empirische und handlungstheoretische Forschungskonzeptionen in der Betriebswirtschaftslehre. Bericht über die Tagung in Aachen März 1976, Stuttgart (1977), p. 3–36.

Kubitzki, S. (2003): Innovationsaktivitäten im Ernährungsgewerbe – Eine branchenspezifische Untershcung des Mannheimer Innovationspanels 1999, Gießen (2003).

Kuhn, T. S. (1996): The structure of scientific revolutions, 3rd. edn., Chicago (1996).

Küpper, H.-U. (2008): Controlling – Konzeption, Aufgaben, Instrumente, 5th. edn., Stuttgart (2008).

Kurrle, A. (1995): Controlling und Effizienz – Die Messung der Effizienz des Controlling in der Industrie auf der Grundlage einer empirischen Einzelanalyse, Bielefeld (1995).

Kurunmäki, L. (2004): A hybrid profession – the acquisition of management accounting expertise by medical professionals, in: Accounting, Organizations & Society, 29 (3/4), p. 327–347.

Kurunmäki, L./Lapsley, I./Melia, K. (2003): Accountingization vs. legitimation: a comparative study of the use of accounting information in intensive care, in: Management Accounting Research, 14 (2), p. 112–139.

L

Lachmann, M. (2011): Der Einsatz von Controllinginstrumenten in Krankenhäusern – Verbreitung, Kontextfaktoren und Erfolgspotenziale, Wiesbaden (2011).

Lackes, R. (1989): EDV-orientiertes Kosteninformationssystem – Flexible Plankostenrechnung und neue Technologien, Wiesbaden (1989).

Lackes, R. (1990): Herausforderungen an ein fortschrittliches Kosteninformationssystem, in: Kostenrechnungspraxis, 5 (6), p. 327–338.

Lamminmaki, D./Drury, C. (2001): A comparison of New Zealand and British product-costing practices, in: International Journal of Accounting, 36 (3), p. 329–347.

Lamminmaki, D. (2008): Accounting and the management of outsourcing: An empirical study in the hotel industry, in: Management Accounting Research, 19 (2), p. 163–181.

Lane, C. (1989): Management and labour in Europe – The industrial enterprise in Germany, Britain and France, Aldershot (1989).

Lane, C. (1995): Industry and society in Europe – Stability and change in Britain Germany and France, Aldershot (1995).

Lane, J.-E. (2001): New public management, London (2001).

Lang, H. A. (2001): Controlling in japanischen Unternehmen – Die Gestaltung des Controllings im westlichen Sinne und seine Ausprägung in der japanischen Controllingpraxis, Berlin (2001).

Lang, H. A. (2003): Controlling in japanischen Unternehmen, in: Controlling, 15 (1), p. 19–26.

Langabeer II/James R./DelliFraine, J. L./Helton, J. (2010): Mixing Finance and Medicine, in: Strategic Finance, 91 (12), p. 27–34.

Lange, J.-U./Schauer, B. D. (1996): Ausgestaltung und Rechenzwecke mittelständischer Kostenrechnung, in: Kostenrechnungspraxis, 40 (4), p. 202–208.

Lapsley, I./Kurunmäki, L./Melia, K. (2001): Sensitive operators, in: Financial Management (2), p. 15–16.

Lapsley, I./Pallot, J. (2000): Accounting, management and organizational change: A comparative study of local government, in: Management Accounting Research, 11 (2), p. 213–229.

Laßmann, G. (1973): Gestaltungsformen der Kosten- und Erlösrechnung im Hinblick auf Planungs- und Kontrollaufgaben, in: Die Wirtschaftsprüfung, 26 (1), p. 4–17.

Laßmann, G. (1993): Betriebsplankostenrechnung, in: Chmielewicz, K./Schweitzer, M. (eds.): Enzyklopädie der Betriebswirtschaftslehre: Band 3 – Handwörterbuch des Rechnungswesens, 3rd edn., Stuttgart (1993), p. 168–183.

Laßmann, G./Wischermann, B./Währisch, M. (1995): Die Grundausbildung im Bereich der Kosten- und Erlösrechnung an deutschen Universitäten, Working Paper (1995).

Lau, C. M./Buckland, C. (2000): Budget emphasis, participation, task difficulty and performance: the effect of diversity within culture, in: Accounting & Business Research, 31 (1), p. 37–55.

Lau, C. M./Low, L. C./Eggleton, I. R. C. (1995): The Impact of Reliance on Accounting Performance Measures on Job-Related Tension and Managerial Performance: Additional Evidence, in: Accounting, Organizations and Society, 20 (5), p. 359–381.

Lau, C. M./Low, L. C./Eggleton, I. R. C. (1997): The interactive effect of budget emphasis, participation and task difficulty on managerial performance: a cross-cultural study, in: Accounting, Auditing & Accountability Journal, 10 (2), p. 175–197.

Lau, C. M./Tan, J. J. (1998): The impact of budget emphasis, participation and task difficulty on managerial performance: a cross-cultural study of the financial services sector, in: Management Accounting Research, 9 (2), p. 163–183.

Law, K. S./Song, L. J./Wong, C.-S./Chen, D. (2009): The antecedents and consequences of successful localization, in: Journal of International Business Studies, 40 (8), p. 1359–1373.

Law, K. S./Wong, C.-S./Wang, K. D. (2004): An empirical test of the model on managing the localization of human resources in the People's Republic of China, in: The International Journal of Human Resource Management, 15 (4/5), p. 635–648.

Lawrence, P. R./Lorsch, J. W. (1969): Organization and environment. Managing differentiation and integration, Homewood (1969).

Lawrence, P. A./Edwards, V. (2000): Management in Western Europe, London (2000).

Lawrence, S. (1997): International accounting, London et al. (1997).

Leach-López, M. A./Stammerjohan, W. W./McNair, F. M. (2007): Differences in the Role of Job-Relevant Information in the Budget Participation – Performance Relationship among U.S. and Mexican Managers: A Question of Culture or Communication, in: Journal of Management Accounting Research, 19, p. 105–136.

Lebra, T. S. (1998): Japanese patterns of behavior, 6th. edn., Honolulu (1998).

Lee, F. M./Marshall, A./Szto, Y. K./Tang, J. (2001): The Practice of Financial Risk Management: An International Comparison, in: Thunderbird International Business Review, 43 (3), p. 365–378.

Legenhausen, C. (1998): Controllinginstrumente für den Mittelstand, Wiesbaden (1998).

Lere, J. C. (2009): Benchmarking Accounting Practices in a Global Economy, in: CPA Journal, 79 (11), p. 10–12.

Li, J./Paisey, A. (2005): International Transfer Pricing in Asia Pacific. Perspectives on Trade between Australia, New Zealand and China, New York (2005).

Libby, T./Waterhouse, J. H. (1996): Predicting change in management accounting systems, in: Journal of Management Accounting Research, 8, p. 137–150.

Liftin, T./Teichmann, M.-H./Clement, M. (2000): Beurteilung der Güte von explorativen Faktorenanalysen im Marketing, in: Wirtschaftswissenschaftliches Studium, 30 (5), p. 283–286.

Limprecht, J. A./Hayes, R. H. (1982): Germany's world-class manufacturers, in: Harvard Business Review, 60 (6), p. 137–145.

Lindner, T. (2009): Harmonisierung des internen und externen Rechnungswesens – Theoretische Grundlagen und Beispiele aus der Praxis, Norderstedt (2009).

Liouville, J./Schmidt, G. (1996): Gibt es eine ideale Methode für die international vergleichende Managementforschung? – Folgerungen aus einer empirischen Studie, in: Engelhard, J. (ed.): Strategische Führung internationaler Unternehmen. Paradoxien, Strategien und Erfahrungen, Wiesbaden (1996), p. 257–271.

Lippert, S. (2011): Controlling in Japan, in: Zeitschrift für Controlling & Management, 55 (1), p. 30–32.

Lohmöller, J.-B. (1989): Latent Variable Path Modelling with Partial Least Squares, Heidelberg (1989).

Lompa, B. (1994): Weiterentwicklung der Kostenrechnung zu einem CIM-gerechten Controlling-Instrument, Hannover (1994).

Lord, B. R. (1996): Strategic management accounting: the emperor's new clothes?, in: Management Accounting Research, 7 (3), p. 347–366.

Lorenzo-Seva, U./ten Berge, J. M. F. (2006): Tucker's Congruence Coefficient as a Meaningful Index of Factor Similarity, in: Methodology, 2 (2), p. 57–64.

Luft, J. L. (2007): Historical Theorizing in Management Accounting Research, in: Chapman, C. S./Hopwood, A. G./Shields, M. D. (eds.): Handbook of Management Accounting Research, Amsterdam et al. (2007), p. 269–284.

Luther, R./Jones, T. C./Saxl, A. (2010): Experiencing change in German controlling – Management accounting in a globalizing world, Amsterdam (2010).

M

MacArthur, J. B. (2006): Cultural Influences on German versus U.S. Management Accounting Practices, in: Management Accounting Quarterly, 7 (2), p. 10–16.

Macintosh, N. B. (1998): Management accounting in Europe: a view from Canada, in: Management Accounting Research, 9 (4), p. 495–500.

Macintosh, N. B./Scapens, R. W. (1990): Structuration Theory In Management Accounting, in: Accounting, Organizations & Society, 15 (5), p. 455–477.

Macintosh, N. B./Scapens, R. W. (1991): Management accounting and control systems: A structuration theory analysis, in: Journal of Management Accounting Research, 3, p. 131–158.

MacKenzie, S. B./Podsakoff, P. M./Jarvis, C. B. (2005): The Problem of Measurement Model Misspecification in Behavioral and Organizational Research and Some Recommended Solutions, in: Journal of Applied Psychology, 90 (4), p. 710–730.

Mackie, B. (2006): Merging GPK and ABC on the Road to RCA, in: Strategic Finance, 88 (5), p. 33–39.

Malhotra, N. K./Agarwal, J./Peterson, M. (1996): Methodological issues in cross-cultural marketing research – A state-of-the-art review, in: International Marketing Review, 13 (5), p. 7–43.

Malmi, T. (1999): Activity-based costing diffusion across organizations an exploratory empirical analysis of Finnish firms, in: Accounting, Organizations & Society, 24 (8), p. 649–672.

Malmi, T./Brown, D. A. (2008): Management control systems as a package – Opportunities, challenges and research directions, in: Management Accounting Research, 19 (4), p. 287–300.

Malmi, T./Granlund, M. (2009): In Search of Management Accounting Theory, in: European Accounting Review, 18 (3), p. 597–620.

Mann, M. (1986): The sources of social power, Cambridge (1986).

Marquardt, D. W. (1970): Generalized Inverses, Ridge Regression, Biased Linear Estimation, and Nonlinear Estimation, in: Technometrics, 12 (3), p. 591–612.

Marsh, R. M. (1967): Comparative Sociology: A Codification of Cross-Societal Analysis, New York et al. (1967).

Matsumoto, M. (1953): The development of managerial accounting in Japan, in: The Annals of the Hitotsubashi Academy, 4 (1), p. 40–54.

Matz, A. (1940): Cost Accounting in Germany, in: Accounting Review, 15 (3), p. 371–379.

Maurice, M. (1976): Introduction: Theoretical and Ideological Aspects of the Universalistic Approach to the Study of Organization, in: International Studies of Management & Organization, 6 (3), p. 3–10.

Maurice, M. (1979): For a study of the "societal effect": Universality and specificity in organization research, in: Lammers, C. J./Hickson, D. J. (eds.): Organizations alike and unlike. International and interinstitutional studies in the sociology of organizations, London (1979), p. 42–60.

Maurice, M. (2000): The paradoxes of societal analysis. A review of the past and prospects for the future, in: Maurice, M./Sorge, A. (eds.): Embedding organizations. Societal analysis of actors, organizations, and socio-economic context, Amsterdam (2000), p. 13–36.

Maurice, M./Sellier, F. (1979): Societal Analysis of Industrial Relations: A Comparison between France and West Germany, in: British Journal of Industrial Relations, 17 (3), p. 322–336.

Maurice, M./Sorge, A. (2000): General introduction, in: Maurice, M./Sorge, A. (eds.): Embedding organizations. Societal analysis of actors, organizations, and socio-economic context, Amsterdam (2000), p. 1–6.

Maurice, M./Sorge, A./Warner, M. (1980): Societal Differences in Organizing Manufacturing Units: A Comparison of France, West Germany, and Great Britain, in: Organization Studies, 1 (1), p. 59–86.

McKee, M./Healy, J. (2002): Hospitals in a changing Europe, Buckingham (2002).

McKee, T. E./Mock, T. J./Ruud, T. F. (1992): A comparison of Norwegian and United States accounting students' learning style preferences, in: Accounting Education, 1 (4), p. 321–341.

McSweeney, B. (2002): Hofstede's model of national cultural differences and their consequences – A triumph of faith – a failure of analysis, in: Human Relations, 55 (1), p. 89–118.

Mead, R. (2005): International management – Cross-cultural dimensions, 3rd. edn., Malden, Mass. (2005).

Meier, D. (2006): Post-investment value addition to buyouts – Analysis of European private equity firms, Wiesbaden (2006).

Mendoza, R./Collins, F./Holzmann, O. J. (1997): Central American budgeting scorecard: Cross cultural insights, in: Journal of International Accounting, Auditing & Taxation, 6 (2), p. 190.

Merchant, K. A. (1985): Organizational Controls and Discretionary Program Decision Making: A Field Study, in: Accounting, Organizations and Society, 10 (1), p. 67–85.

Merchant, K. A. (1989): Rewarding Results: Motivating Profit Center Managers, Boston, MA (1989).

Merchant, K. A. (1990): The Effects of Financial Controls on Data Manipulation and Management Myopia, in: Accounting, Organizations and Society, 15 (4), p. 297–313.

Merchant, K. A./Chow, C. W./Wu, A. (1995): Measurement, Evaluation and Reward of Profit Center Managers: A Cross-Cultural Field Study, in: Accounting, Organizations and Society, 20 (7/8), p. 619–638.

Merchant, K. A./Shields, M. D. (1993): When and Why to Measure Costs Less Accurately to Improve Decision Making, in: Accounting Horizons, 7 (2), p. 76–81.

Mertens, P. (1992): DV-Unterstützung der Kostenrechnung, in: Männel, W. (ed.): Handbuch der Kostenrechnung, Wiesbaden (1992), p. 1199–1214.

Messner, S. (2003): Die Kostenrechnung im Spannungsfeld internationaler Entwicklungen – Über die Amerikanisierung des Rechnungswesens und ihre Bedeutung für die interne Unternehmensrechnung in Österreich und Deutschland, Wien (2003).

Meyer, J. W./Scott, W. R. (1992): Organizational Environments: Ritual and Rationality, Newbury Park et al. (1992).

Meyer, M. W. (1972): Size and the Structure of Organizations: A Causal Analysis, in: American Sociological Review, 37 (4), p. 434–441.

Mia, L./Clarke, B. (1999): Market Competition, Management Accounting Systems and Business Unit Performance, in: Management Accounting Research, 10 (2), p. 137–158.

Michalak, J. : Comparison of controlling systems in Polish and German constructioncompanies, in: (no editor): Accounting and companies' performance management, Tartu (2002), p. 153–161.

Miller, E. L. (1984): Comparative Management Conceptualization: An Assessment, in: Advances in International Comparative Management, 1 (1), p. 69–82.

Miller, J. G./Vollmann, T. E. (1985): The Hidden Factory, in: Harvard Business Review, 63 (5), p. 142–150.

Ministry of Internal Affairs and Communication (2011): Japan Statistical Yearbook 2011, available at: http://www.stat.go.jp/english/data/nenkan/index.htm, last revised 16.09.2011.

Mitchell, R. E. (1969): Survey Materials Collected in the Developing Countries: Sampling, Measurement, and Interviewing Obstacles to Intra- and Inter-National Comparisons, in: Boddewyn, J. J. (ed.): Comparative management and marketing. Text and readings, Glenview (1969), p. 232–252.

Mizuno, M. (2004): The Impact of new Accounting Standards on Japanese Companies, in: Pacific Economic Review (4), p. 357–369.

Monden, Y. (1995): Cost reduction systems – Target costing and kaizen costing, Portland Or. (1995).

Montagna, P. D. (1987): Discussion Comments, in: Cushing, B. E. (ed.): Accounting and culture, Sarasota, Fla. (1987), p. 23–27.

Morey, N. C./Luthans, F. (1984): An Emic Perspective and Ethnoscience Methods for Organizational Research, in: Academy of Management Review, 9 (1), p. 27–36.

Morris, M. W./Kwok Leung/Ames, D./Lickel, B. (1999): Views From the Inside and Outside Integrating Emic and Etic Insights about Culture and Justice Judgment, in: Academy of Management Review, 24 (4), p. 781–796.

Mosebach, K. (2009): Commercializing German Hospital Care? Effects of New Public Management and Managed Care under Neoliberal Conditions, in: German Policy Studies, 5 (1), p. 65–98.

Mueller, F. (1994): Societal Effect, Organizational Effect and Globalization, in: Organization Studies, 15 (3), p. 407–428.

Mussnig, W. (1996): Von der Kostenrechnung zum Management Accounting, Wiesbaden (1996).

Myers, M. D./Tan, F. B. (2002): Beyond Models of National Culture in Information Systems Research, in: Szewczak, E./Snodgrass, C. (eds.): Human Factors in Information Systems (2002), p. 1–19.

N

NAA Tokyo Affiliate (1988): Management Accounting in the Advanced Manufacturing Surrounding: Comparative Study on Survey in Japan and U.S.A., Tokyo (1988).

Naroll, R. (1964): A Fifth Solution to Galton's Problem, in: American Anthropologist, 66 (4), p. 863–867.

Naroll, R./Michik, G. L./Naroll, F. (1980): Holocultural Research Methods, in: Triandis, H. C./Berry, J. W. (eds.): Handbook of cross-cultural psychology. Volume 2: Methodology, Boston (1980), p. 479–521.

Näsi, S./Rohde, C. (2007): Development of cost and management accounting ideas in the Nordic countries, in: Chapman, C. S./Hopwood, A. G./Shields, M. D. (eds.): Handbook of Management Accounting Research, Amsterdam et al. (2007), p. 1091–1118.

Nasif, E. G./Ai-Daeaj, H./Ebrahimi, B./Thibodeaux, M. S. (1991): Methodological Problems in Cross-Cultural Research. An Updated Review, in: Management International Review, 31 (1), p. 79–91.

Nath, R. (ed.) (1988): Comparative management – A regional view, Cambridge, Mass. (1988).

Nazari, J./Kline, T./Herremans, I. (2006): Conducting Survey Research in Management Accounting, in: Hoque, Z. (ed.): Methodological issues in accounting research. Theories, methods and issues, London (2006), p. 427–459.

Needy, K. L./Nachtmann, H./Roztocki, N./Warner, R. C./Bidanda, B. (2003): Implementing activity-based costing systems in small manufacturing firms: a field study, in: Engineering Management Journal, 15 (1), p. 3–10.

Nguyen, H. V./Brooks, A. N. (1997): An empirical investigation of adoption issues relating to activity-based costing, in: Asian Review of Accounting, 5 (1), p. 1–17.

Nishimura, A. (1995): Transplanting Japanese Management Accounting and Cultural Relevance, in: International Journal of Accounting, 30 (4), p. 318–330.

Nishimura, A. (2003): Management accounting – Feed forward and Asian perspectives, Basingstoke (2003).

Nobes, C./Parker, R. (eds.) (2008): Comparative international accounting, Harlow (2008).

Noreen, E. (1991): Conditions under which activity-based cost systems provide relevant costs, in: Journal of Management Accounting Research, 3, p. 159–168.

Nunnally, J. C. (1978): Psychometric theory, 2.th. edn., New York (1978).

Nutt, P. C. (2000): Decision-Making Success in Public, Private and Third Sector Organisations: Finding Sector Dependent Best Practice, in: Journal of Management Studies, 37 (1), p. 77–108.

O

Oberg, W. (1963): II. Cross-Cultural Perspectives on Management Principles, in: Academy of Management Journal, 6 (2), p. 129–143.

Ohtsu, M./Imanari, T. (2002): Inside Japanese business – A narrative history, 1960 – 2000, Armonk, NY (2002).

Okano, H./Suzuki, T. (2007): A history of Japanese management accounting, in: Chapman, C. S./Hopwood, A. G./Shields, M. D. (eds.): Handbook of Management Accounting Research, Amsterdam et al. (2007), p. 1119–1137.

Oliver, N./Wilkinson, B. (1992): The Japanization of British industry, 2nd. edn., Oxford et al. (1992).

O'Neill, H. M./Pouder, R. W./Buchholtz, A. K. (1998): Patterns in the Diffusion of Strategies across Organizations. Insights from the Innovation Diffusion Literature, in: Academy of Management Review, 23 (1), p. 98–114.

Otley, D. T. (1980): The contingency theory of management accounting: Achievement and prognosis, in: Accounting, Organizations & Society, 5 (4), p. 413–428.

Otto, S.-S. (2000): Controllership in Japan – Eine ländervergleichende Analyse von Controllership-Konzeptionen und Controllership-Praxis unter Einbeziehung Japans, Vallendar (2000).

Ouchi, W. G. (1981): Theory Z, how American business can meet the Japanese challenge, 5th. edn., Reading Mass. et al. (1981).

P

Pace, C. R. (1939): Factors influencing questionnaire returns from former university students, in: Journal of Applied Psychology, 23 (3), p. 388–397.

Paces, V./Pivec, L./Teich, A. H. (1999): Science evaluation and its management, Amsterdam (1999).

Palazzo, B. (2002): U.S.-American and German Business Ethics: An Intercultural Comparison, in: Journal of Business Ethics, 44 (3), p. 195–216.

Park, C. S./Kim, G.-T. (1995): An Economic Evaluation Model for Advanced Manufacturing Systems Using Activity-Based Costing, in: Journal of Manufacturing Systems, 14 (6), p. 439–451.

Pascale, R. T./Athos, A. G. (1981): The art of Japanese management – Applications for American executives, New York (1981).

Patel, C. (2003): Some Cross-Cultural Evidence on Whistle-Blowing as an Internal Control Mechanism, in: Journal of International Accounting Research, 2, p. 69–96.

Pauer, E. (1985): Arbeit und Unternehmen in historischer Sicht, in: Hanau, P./Kimoto Saburo/Markmann, H./Tezuka, K. (eds.): Die Arbeitswelt in Japan und in der Bundesrepublik Deutschland, Neuwied (1985), p. 117–133.

Peil, J. (2000): Deconstructing the canonical view on Adam Smith. A new look at the principles of economics, in: Psalidopoulos, M. (ed.): The canon in the history of economics. Critical essays, London (2000), p. 68–91.

Pelz, D. C. (1978): Some Expanded Perspectives on Use of Social Science in Public Policy, in: Yinger, M. J./Cutler, S. J. (eds.): Major social issues. A multidisciplinary view, New York (1978), p. 346–357.

Peng, T. K./Peterson, M./Shyi, Y.-P. (1991): Quantitative Methods in Cross-National Management Research: Trends and Equivalence Issues, in: Journal of Organizational Behavior, 12 (2), p. 87–107.

Perlitz, M. (2004): Internationales Management, 5th. edn., Stuttgart (2004).

Perry, J. L./Rainey, H. G. (1988): The Public-Private Distinction in Organization Theory: A Critique and Research Strategy, in: Academy of Management Review, 13 (2), p. 182–201.

Peter, P. J. (1981): Construct Validity: A Review of Basic Issues and Marketing Practices, in: Journal of Marketing Research, 18 (2), p. 133–145.

Peters, B. G. (2005): Institutional theory in political science – The 'new institutionalism', 2nd. edn., London (2005).

Petzold, I./Ringel, N./Thomas, A. (2005): Beruflich in Japan – Trainingsprogramm für Manager, Fach- und Führungskräfte, Göttingen (2005).

Pfeffer, J. (1982): Organizations and organization theory, Boston (1982).

Picot, A. (1986): Zehn Thesen zur Bedeutung der Informationstechnik für die Betriebswirtschaftslehre, in: Information Management (3), p. 52–54.

Pierce, B./Brown, R. (2004): An empirical study of activity-based systems in Ireland, in: The Irish Accounting Review, 11 (1), p. 33–55.

Pistoni, A./Zoni, L. (2000): Comparative management accounting in Europe: an undergraduate education perspective, in: European Accounting Review, 9 (2), p. 285–319.

Pizam, A./Pine, R./Mok, C./Shin, J. Y. (1997): Nationality vs industry cultures: which has a greater effect on managerial behavior?, in: International Journal of Hospitality Management, 16 (2), p. 127–145.

Pizzini, M. J. (2006): The relation between cost-system design, managers' evaluations of the relevance and usefulness of cost data and financial performance: an empirical study of US hospitals, in: Accounting, Organizations & Society, 31 (2), p. 179–210.

Player, S./Keys, D. E. (1995): Activity-based management – Arthur Andersen's lessons from the ABM battlefield, New York (1995).

Pleitgen, V. (2005): Die Entwicklung des betriebswirtschaftlichen Rechnungswesens von 1890 bis 1940 am Beispiel der Firmen Krupp, Scheidt und Farina, Köln (2005).

Poll, D. (2011): VDMA: Leichtes Wachstum im Jahr 2010, available at: http://www.produktion.de, last revised 16.09.2011.

Popper, K. R. (1965): Das Elend des Historizismus, Tübingen (1965).

Popper, K. R. (1966): Logik der Forschung, 2nd. edn., Tübingen (1966).

Popper, K. R. (2002): The logic of scientific discovery, London (2002).

Popper, K. R./Kiesewetter, H. (1992): Gegen den Zynismus in der Interpretation der Geschichte, Regensburg (1992).

Porst, R. (2009): Fragebogen – Ein Arbeitsbuch, 2nd. edn., Wiesbaden (2009).

Porter, M. E. (1990): The Competitive Advantage of Nations, London, Basingstoke (1990).

Portz, K./Lere, J. C. (2010): Cost Center Practices in Germany and the United States: Impact of Country Differences on Managerial Accounting Practices, in: American Journal of Business, 25 (1), p. 45–51.

Preker, A. S./Harding, A. (2003): Innovations in health service delivery – The corporatization of public hospitals, Washington, DC (2003).

Pudelko, M. (2009): The End of Japanese-Style Management?, in: Long Range Planning, 42 (4), p. 439–462.

Pugh, D. S./Hickson, D. J./Hinings, C. R./Turner, C. (1969): The Context of Organization Structures, in: Adminsitrative Science Quarterly, 14 (1), p. 91–114.

Pye, L. W. (1986): The China trade: making the deal, in: Harvard Business Review, 64 (4), p. 74–80.

Q

Quinn, R. E./Rohrbaugh, J. (1983): A Spatial Model of Effectiveness Criteria: Towards a Competing Values Approach to Organizational Analysis, in: Management Science, 29 (3), p. 363–377.

R

Raffée, H./Abel, B. (1979): Aufgaben und aktuelle Tendenzen der Wissenschaftstheorie in den Wirtschaftswissenschaften, in: Raffée, H./Abel, B. (eds.): Wissenschaftstheoretische Grundfragen der Wirtschaftswissenschaften, München (1979), p. 1–10.

Rainey, H. G./Backoff, R. W./Levine, C. H. (1976): Comparing Public and Private Organizations, in: Public Administration Review, 36 (2), p. 233–244.

Rainey, H. G./Bozeman, B. (2000): Comparing Public and Private Organizations: Empirical Research and the Power of the A Priori, in: Journal of Public Administration Research and Theory, 10 (2), p. 447–469.

Ralston, D. A./Egri, C. P./Stewart, S./Terpstra, R. H./Yu Kaicheng (1999): Doing Business in the 21st Century with the New Generation of Chinese Managers. A Study of Generational Shifts in Work Values in China, in: Journal of International Business Studies, 30 (2), p. 415–427.

Rathje, E. (1993): Änderungen von Kostenmanagement und Krankenhausorganisation bei Einführung von pauschalierten Sonderentgelten und Fallpauschalen, in: Das Krankenhaus, 85 (4), p. 165–169.

Reeve, J. M. (1991): Cost management in continuous-process environments, in: Journal of Cost Management, 5 (1), p. 22–34.

Reich, T. (1995): Prozeßverbesserung durch Kosteninformation – Japanisches, amerikanisches und europäisches Kostenmanagement im Vergleich, Wien (1995).

Reiß, M. (1993): Komplexitätsmanagement (I), in: Wirtschaftswissenschaftliches Studium, 22 (1), p. 54–60.

Reitsperger, W. D./Daniel, S. J. (1991): A Comparison of Quality Attitudes in the U.S. and Japan: Empirical Evidence, in: Journal of Management Studies, 28 (6), p. 585–599.

Riahi-Belkaoui, A. (2002): Behavioral management accounting, Westport, Conn. (2002).

Richman, B. M. (1965): Significance of Cultural Variables, in: Academy of Management Journal, 8 (4), p. 292–308.

Rickards, R. C. (2005): Management Perspectives on Problems in Controlling and Cost Accounting, in: Investment Management and Financial Innovations (3), p. 109–127.

Ricks, D. . A. (1993): International Management Research: Past, Present and Future, in: Wong-Rieger, D./Rieger, F. (eds.): International management research. Looking to the future, Berlin (1993), p. 9–12.

Riebel, P. (1959): Das Rechnen mit Einzelkosten und Deckungsbeiträgen, in: Zeitschrift für handelwissenschaftliche Forschung – Neue Folge, 11 (5), p. 213–238.

Rigby, D. (2001): Management Tools and Techniques. A Survey, in: California Management Review, 43 (2), p. 139–160.

Rigby, D./Bilodeau, B. (2005): The Bain 2005 management tool survey, in: Strategy & Leadership, 33 (4), p. 4–12.

Rigby, D./Bilodeau, B. (2007): Bain's global 2007 management tools and trends survey, in: Strategy & Leadership, 35 (5), p. 9–16.

Ring, P. S./Perry, J. L. (1985): Strategic Management in Public and Private Organizations: Implications of Distinctive Contexts and Constraints, in: Academy of Management Review, 10 (2), p. 276–286.

Ringle, C. M. (2004): Gütemaße für den Partial least Squares-Ansatz zur Bestimmung von Kausalmodellen. Industrielles Management, Arbeitspaper Nr. 16, Hamburg (2004).

Ringle, C. M./Spreen, F. (2007): Beurteilung der Ergebnisse von PLS-Pfadanalysen, in: Wirtschaftswissenschaftliches Studium, 36 (2), p. 211–216.

Robbins, S. P. (1990): Organization theory: structure, design, and applications, Englewood Cliffs, NY et al. (1990).

Roberts, K. H. (1970): On looking at an elephant: An evaluation of cross-cultural research related to organizations, in: Psychological Bulletin, 74 (5), p. 327–350.

Robinson, R. V. (1983): Book review: Geert Hofstede, in: Work and Occupations, 10 (1), p. 110–115.

Rocheleau, B. (2006): Public management information systems, Hershey, Pa. (2006).

Rokkan, S. (1960): The comparative study of political participation: notes towards a perspective on current research, Ann Arbor Mich. (1960).

Ronen, S. (1986): Comparative and multinational management, 3rd. edn., New York (1986).

Rose, M. (1985): Universalism, Culturalism and the Aix Group: Promise and Problems of a Societal Approach to Economic Institutions Universalism, Culturalism and the Aix Group: Promise and Problems of a Societal Approach to Economic Institutions, in: European Sociological Review, 1 (1), p. 65–83.

Roso, M./Vormweg, R./Wall, F. (2003): Controlling-nahe Begriffe in Deutschland und USA – Eine vergleichende Lehrbuchanalyse, in: Zeitschrift für Controlling & Management, 47 (1), p. 56–61.

Roso, M./Vormweg, R./Wall, F. (2005): Controlling im Spiegel deutscher und angloamerikanischer Literatur – Eine vergleichende Lehrbuchanalyse, in: Weber, J./Meyer, M. (eds.): Internationalisierung des Controllings. Standortbestimmung und Option, Wiesbaden (2005), p. 67–83.

Ross, M. H./Homer, E. (1976): Galton's Problem in Cross-National Research, in: World Politics, 29 (1), p. 1–28.

S

Sachs, S./Hauser, A. (2002): Das ABC der betriebswirtschaftlichen Forschung – Anleitung zum wissenschaftlichen Arbeiten, Zürich (2002).

Sahlins, M. D. (1985): Islands of history, Chicago (1985).

Sakurai, M. (1991): Target Costing and How to Use it, in: Journal of Cost Management, 3 (2), p. 39–50.

Sakurai, M. (1997): Integratives Kostenmanagement – Stand und Entwicklungstendenzen des Controlling in Japan, München (1997).

Salter, S. B./Schulz, A. K. D. (2005): Examining the Role of Culture and Acculturation in Information Sharing, in: Advances in Accounting Behavioral Research, 8, p. 189–212.

Salter, S. B./Schulz, A. K. D./Lewis, P. A./Lopez, V. J. C. (2008): Otra Empanada en la Parilla: Examining the Role of Culture and Information Sharing in Chile and Australia, in: Journal of International Financial Management & Accounting, 19 (1), p. 57–72.

Salter, S. B./Sharp, D. J. (2001): Agency effects and escalation of commitment – Do small national culture differences matter?, in: The International Journal of Accounting, 36 (1), p. 33–45.

Sambamurthy, V./Chin, W. (1994): The Effects of Group Attitudes Toward Alternative GDSS Designs on the Decision-making Performance of Computer-Supported Groups, in: Decision Sciences, 25 (2), p. 215–241.

Sapir, E. (1929): The Status of Linguistics as a Science, in: Language, 5 (4), p. 207–214.

Sapsford, R. (2007): Survey research, 2nd. edn., London (2007).

Sartorius, K./Eitzen, C./Kamala, P. (2007): The design and implementation of Activity Based Costing (ABC): a South African survey, in: Meditari Accounting Research, 15 (2), p. 1–21.

Saudagaran, S. M./Diga, J. G. (1999): Evaluation of the Contingency-Based Approach in Comparative International Accounting – A Case for Alternative Research Paradigms, in: Journal of Accounting Literature, 18, p. 57–95.

Scapens, R. W. (1994): Never mind the gap: towards an institutional perspective on management accounting practice, in: Management Accounting Research, 5 (3/4), p. 301–321.

Scapens, R. W./Sale, J. T. (1985): An International Study of Accounting Practices in Divisionalized Companies and Their Associations with Organizational Variables, in: The Accounting Review, 60 (2), p. 231–247.

Scarparo, S. (2006): The Integration of Clinical and Costing Information: A Comparative Study between Scotland and Sweden, in: Financial Accountability & Management, 22 (2), p. 133–155.

Schäfer, E. (1953): Von der statischen zur dynamischen Betriebswirtschaftslehre, in: Zeitschrift für handelswissenschaftliche Forschung, 48, p. 205–211.

Schanz, G. (1977): Jenseits von Empirismus[1]: Eine Perspektive für die betriebswirtschaftliche Forschung, in: Köhler, R. (ed.): Empirische und handlungstheoretische Forschungskonzeptionen in der Betriebswirtschaftslehre. Bericht über die Tagung in Aachen März 1976, Stuttgart (1977), p. 65–84.

Schedler, K./Proeller, I. (2009): New Public Management, 4th. edn., Stuttgart (2009).

Scheer, A./Berkau, C. (1993): Wissensbasierte Prozesskostenrechnung – Baustein für das Lean Controlling, in: Kostenrechnungspraxis, 6 (2), p. 111–119.

Scherrer, G. (1996): Management Accounting: A German Perspective, in: Bhimani, A. (ed.): Management accounting. European perspectives, Oxford (1996), p. 100–122.

Scheuch, E. K. (1967): Society as Context in Cross-Cultural Comparisons, in: Social Science Information, 6 (5), p. 7–23.

Scheytt, T./Soin, K./Metz, T. (2003): Exploring notions of control across cultures: a narrative approach, in: European Accounting Review, 12 (3), p. 515–547.

Schierenbeck, H. (2003): Grundzüge der Betriebswirtschaftslehre, 16th. edn., München (2003).

Schildbach, T. (1997): Cost accounting in Germany, in: Management Accounting Research, 8 (3), p. 261–276.

Schiller, U./Keimer, I./Egle, U./Keune, H. (2007): Kostenmanagement in der Schweiz: Eine empirische Studie, in: Controlling, 19 (6), p. 301–307.

Schlegelberger, F. (1973): Handelsgesetzbuch, Band 1: §§ 1-47a, 5th. edn., München (1973).

Schlieper, A. (1997): Die Nähe fremder Kulturen – Parallelen zwischen Japan und Deutschland, Frankfurt (1997).

Schlüchtermann, J. (1992): Prozeßkostenrechnung im Krankenhaus?, in: Führen und Wirtschaften im Krankenhaus, 9 (6), p. 434–437.

Schmalenbach, E. (1919): Selbstkostenrechnung I, in: Zeitschrift für handelswissenschaftliche Forschung, 13, p. 257-299; 321-356.

Schmalenbach, E. (1927): Der Kontenrahmen, 1st. edn., Leipzig (1927).

Schmalenbach, E. (1934): Selbstkostenrechnung und Preispolitik, 6th. edn., Leipzig (1934).

Schmalenbach, E. (1956): Kostenrechnung und Preispolitik, 7th. edn., Köln et al. (1956).

Schmidt, F. (1996): Gemeinkostensenkung durch kostengünstiges Konstruieren, Wiesbaden (1996).

Schneider, D. (1992): Theorien zur Entwicklung des Rechnungswesens, in: Zeitschrift für betriebswirtschaftliche Forschung, 44 (1), p. 3–31.

Schneider, D. (2001): Betriebswirtschaftslehre, Band 4: Geschichte und Methoden der Wirtschaftswissenschaft, München et al. (2001).

Schneider, S. C./Barsoux, J.-L. (2003): Managing across cultures, 2nd. edn., Harlow et al. (2003).

Schoenfeld, H.-M. W. (1992): Entwicklung des Management Accounting in den USA, in: Männel, W. (ed.): Handbuch Kostenrechnung, Wiesbaden (1992), p. 348–359.

Schoute, M. (2009): The relationship between cost system complexity, purpose of use, and cost system effectiveness, in: The British Accounting Review, 41 (4), p. 208–226.

Schoute, M. (2011): The relationship between product diversity, usage of advanced manufacturing technologies and activity-based costing adoption, in: The British Accounting Review, 43 (2), p. 120–134.

Schreyögg, G. (1995): Umwelt, Technologie und Organisationsstruktur – Eine Analyse des kontingenztheoretischen Ansatzes, 3rd. edn., Bern et al. (1995).

Schreyögg, G. (2008): Organisation, 5th. edn., Wiesbaden (2008).

Schuler, R. S./Rogovsky, N. (1998): Understanding Compensation Practice Variations Across Firms: The Impact of National Culture, in: Journal of International Business Studies, 29 (1), p. 159–177.

Schulz, A. K. D./Salter, S. B./Lopez, V. J. C./Lewis, P. A. (2009): Revaluating Face: A Note on Differences in Private Information Sharing Between Two Communitarian Societies, in: Journal of International Accounting Research, 8 (1), p. 57–65.

Schumann, M./Beinhauer, M. (1994): Empirische Analysen zur Kostenentwicklung des administrativen Bereichs, in: Kostenrechnungspraxis, 38 (5), p. 297–305.

Schwarz, S. H. (1994): Beyond Individualism / Collectivism. New Cultural Dimensions of Values, in: Kim, U./Triandis, H. C./Kagitcibasi, C./Choi, S./Yoon, G. (eds.): Individualism and collectivism. Theory, method, and applications, Thousand Oaks, Calif (1994), p. 85–119.

Schweikart, J. A. (1985): Contingency Theory as a Framework for Research in International Accounting, in: The International Journal of Accounting, 21 (1), p. 89–98.

Schweikart, J. A. (1986): The relevance of managerial accounting information: A multinational analysis, in: Accounting, Organizations & Society, 11 (6), p. 541–554.

Schweitzer, M./Küpper, H.-U. (1991): Systeme der Kosten- und Erlösrechnung, 5th. edn., München (1991).

Schweitzer, M./Küpper, H.-U. (2011): Systeme der Kosten- und Erlösrechnung, 10th. edn., München (2011).

Schweitzer, M./Wagener, K. (1998): Geschichte des Rechnungswesens, in: Wirtschaftswissenschaftliches Studium, 27 (9), p. 438–446.

Schweitzer, M./Ziolkowski, U. (1999): Interne Unternehmensrechnung: aufwandsorientiert oder kalkulatorisch?, in: Zeitschrift für betriebswirtschaftliche Forschung, 51 (special edition no. 42).

Searcy, d. W. L./Mentzer, J. T. (2003): A Framework for Conducting and Evaluating Research, in: Journal of Accounting Literature, 22, p. 130–167.

Sears, R. R. (1961): Transcultural Variables and Conceptual Equivalence, in: Kaplan, B. (ed.): Studying personality cross-culturally, New York (1961), p. 445–455.

Seicht, G. (2001): Moderne Kosten- und Leistungsrechnung – Grundlagen und praktische Gestaltung, 11th. edn., Wien (2001).

Sekaran, U. (1983): Methodological and Theoretical Issues and Advancements in Cross-Cultural Research, in: Journal of International Business Studies, 14 (2), p. 61–73.

Selmer, J. (2004): Motivating Western business expatriates in China to localize, in: Journal of Asian Business, 20 (1), p. 49–69.

Selto, F. H./Renner, C. J./Young, S. M. (1995): Assessing the organizational fit of a just-in-time manufacturing system: Testing selection, interaction and systems models of contingency theory, in: Accounting, Organizations & Society, 20 (7/8), p. 665–684.

Senior, P. A./Bhopal, R. (1994): Ethnicity as a variable in epidemiological research, in: British Medical Journal, 309, p. 327–330.

Sharman, P. A. (2003a): Bring on German Cost Accounting, in: Strategic Finance, 85 (6), p. 30–38.

Sharman, P. A. (2003b): The Case for Management Accounting, in: Strategic Finance, 85 (4), p. 43–47.

Shenkar, O. (2000): On the Integration of Comparative and International Management: Comments on Child's Essay, in: Advances in International Comparative Management, 13, p. 107–112.

Sheridan, A. (1980): Michel Foucault – The will to truth, London (1980).

Sheridan, T. T. (1995): Management accounting in global European corporations: Anglophone and continental viewpoints, in: Management Accounting Research, 6 (3), p. 287–294.

Shields, M. D. (1995): An empirical analysis of firms' implementation experiences with activity-based costing, in: Journal of Management Accounting Research, 7 (3), p. 148–166.

Shields, M. D. (1997): Research in Management Accounting by North Americans in the 1990s, in: Journal of Management Accounting Research, 9, p. 3–61.

Shields, M. D. (1998): Management accounting practices in Europe. A perspective from the States, in: Management Accounting Research, 9 (4), p. 501–513.

Shields, M. D./Chow, C. W./Kato, Y./Nakagawa, Y. (1991): Management Accounting Practices in the U.S. and Japan. Comparative Survey Findings and Research Implications, in: Journal of International Financial Management & Accounting, 3 (1), p. 61–77.

Shimme, S. (1937): Introduction of double-entry bookkeeping into Japan, in: Accounting Review, 12 (3), p. 290–295.

Siegel, G. (1996): The Practice Analysis of Management Accounting, Montvale, NJ (1996).

Sin, L. Y. M./Chow, R./Lee, J. S. Y. (2003): Market Orientation and Business Performance – A Comparative Study of Firms in Mainland China and Hong Kong, in: European Journal of Marketing, 37 (5/6), p. 910–936.

Singh, J. (1995): Measurement Issues in Cross-National Research, in: Journal of International Business Studies, 26 (3), p. 597–619.

Singh, K. (2007): Quantitative social research methods, Los Angeles (2007).

Sivakumar, K./Nakata, C. (2001): The Stampede Toward Hofstede's Framework: Avoiding the Sample Design Pit in Cross-Cultural Research, in: Journal of International Business Studies, 32 (3), p. 555–574.

Smith, A. (1776): An Inquiry into the Nature and Causes of the Wealth of Nations, London (1776).

Smith, C./Meiksins, P. (1995): System, Society and Dominance Effects in Cross-National Organisational Analysis, in: Work, Employment and Society, 9 (2), p. 241–267.

Smith, D./Langfield-Smith, K. (2004): Structural Equation Modeling in Management Accounting Research: Critical Analysis and Opportunities, in: Journal of Accounting Literature, 23, p. 49–86.

Smith, P. B. (1992): Organizational Behavior and National Cultures, in: British Journal of Management, 3 (1), p. 39–51.

Smith, P. B. (2002): Culture's consequences: Something old and something new, in: Human Relations, 55 (1), p. 119–135.

Smith, P. B./Bond, M. H./Kagitcibasi, C. (2009): Understanding social psychology across cultures – Living and working in a changing world, Los Angeles (2009).

Someya, K. (1996): Japanese Accounting – A Historical Approach, Oxford (1996).

Sood, J. (1990): Equivalent Measurement in International Market Research. Is It Really a Problem?, in: Journal of International Consumer Marketing, 2 (2), p. 25–41.

Sorge, A. (1983): Culture's Consequences. International Differences in Work-Related Values, in: Administrative Science Quarterly, 28 (4), p. 625–629.

Sorge, A./Maurice, M. (1993): The societal effect in the strategies of French and west German machine tool manufacturers, in: Kogut, B. (ed.): Country competitiveness. Technology and the organizing of work, New York (1993), p. 75–95.

Sorge, A./Warner, M. (1986): Comparative factory organisation – An Anglo-German comparison of manufacturing management and manpower, Aldershot Hants et al. (1986).

Stählin, W. (1973): Theoretische und technologische Forschung in der Betriebswirtschaftslehre, Stuttgart (1973).

Stanzel, F. K. (1997): Europäer – Ein imagologischer Essay, Heidelberg (1997).

Stanzel, F. K. (1999): Europäischer Völkerspiegel – Imagologisch-ethnographische Studien zu den Völkertafeln des frühen 18. Jahrhunderts, Heidelberg (1999).

Statistisches Bundesamt (2010): Statistisches Jahrbuch 2010, Wiesbaden (2010).

Stead, G. B./Harrington, T. F. (2000): A Process Perspective of International Research Collaboration, in: Career Development Quarterly, 48 (4), p. 323–331.

Steinle, C./Daum, A. (2007): Controlling – Kompendium für Ausbildung und Praxis, 4th. edn., Stuttgart (2007).

Stening, B. W./Everett, J. E. (1984): Response styles in a cross-cultural managerial study, in: Journal of Social Psychology, 122 (2), p. 151–156.

Stier, W. (1999): Empirische Forschungsmethoden, 2nd. edn., Berlin (1999).

Stiles, P. (2009): The Changing Nature of the Japanese Business System and its Impact on Asia, in: Long Range Planning, 42 (4), p. 427–438.

Stoffel, K. (1997): Controllership im internationalen Vergleich, in: Krystek, U./Zur, E. (eds.): Internationalisierung. Eine Herausforderung für die Unternehmensführung, Berlin et al. (1997), p. 333–352.

Stoffel, K. (1995): Controllership im internationalen Vergleich, Wiesbaden (1995).

Stoi, R. (1999): Prozeßorientiertes Kostenmanagement in der deutschen Unternehmenspraxis – Eine empirische Untersuchung, München (1999).

Stratton, W./Desroches, D./Lawson, R./Hatch, T. (2009): Activity-Based Costing: Is It Still Relevant?, in: Management Accounting Quarterly, 10 (3), p. 31–40.

Sugeno, K. (1992): Japanese Labor Law, Seattle, WA (1992).

Swanson, G. (1971): Frameworks for comparative research: Structural anthropology and the theory of action, in: Vallier, I. (ed.): Comparative methods in sociology, Berkeley Calif. (1971), p. 141–202.

Sweeney, R. B. (1983): MAP Committee Promulgates Definition of Management Accounting, in: Thomas, W. E. (ed.): Readings in cost accounting, budgeting and control, 6th edn., Cincinnati (1983), p. 466–469.

T

Takatera, S./Yamamoto, M. (1989): The Cultural Significance of Accounting in Japan, in: Scandinavian Journal of Management, 5 (4), p. 235–250.

Takayanagi, S. (1989): Personnel Evaluation and Incentive Systems in Japanese Corporations, in: Monden, Y./Sakurai, M. (eds.): Japanese management accounting. A world class approach to profit management, Cambridge, Mass. (1989), p. 424–432.

Takemura, N./Takamatsu, M. (1987): Accounting Education in Japan, in: Choi, F. D. S./Hiramatsu, K. (eds.): Accounting and financial reporting in Japan. Current issues and future prospects in a world economy, Wokingham, Berkshire (1987), p. 196–217.

Tang, Roger Y. W./Chan, K. H. (1979): Environmental Variables of International Transfer Pricing – A Japan-United States Comparison, in: Abacus, 15 (1), p. 3–12.

Tang, Roger Y. W./Walter, C. K./Raymond, R. H. (1979): Transfer Pricing – Japanese vs. American Style, in: Management Accounting, 60 (7), p. 12–16.

Tani, T./Horváth, P./Wangenheim, S. v. (1996): Genka Kikaku und marktorientiertes Zielkostenmanagement, in: Controlling, 8 (2), p. 80–89.

Tannenbaum, A. S. (1962): Control in Organizations: Individual Adjustment and Organizational Performance, in: Administrative Science Quarterly, 7 (2), p. 236–257.

Tatikonda, L. U./Savchenko, O. (2010): Crisis in Accounting: Are Accounting Curricula Following the Path of General Motors?, in: Management Accounting Quarterly, 11 (2), p. 33–45.

Tauch, J. G. (2003): Kostenrechnung und Controlling im Krankenhaus, Gütersloh (2003).

Tayeb, M. (1994): Organizations and National Culture: Methodology Considered, in: Organization Studies, 15 (3), p. 429–445.

Tayeb, M. H. (1988): Organizations and national culture – A comparative analysis, London (1988).

Teel, C./Verran, J. A. (1991): Factor comparison across studies, in: Research in Nursing & Health, 14 (1), p. 67–72.

Tempel, A. (2001): The cross-national transfer of human resource management practices in German and British multinational companies, München, Mering (2001).

Thomae, H. (1999): The Nomothetic-Ideographic Issue: Some Roots and Recent Trends, in: International Journal of Group Tensions, 28 (1/2), p. 187–215.

Thommen, J.-P. (1983): Die Lehre der Unternehmungsführung – Eine wissenschaftshistorische Betrachtung im deutschsprachigen Raum, Bern (1983).

Thomson, J./Gurowka, J. (2005): Sorting out the clutter, in: Strategic Finance, 87 (2), p. 27–33.

Tillema, S. (2005): Towards an integrated contingency framework for MAS sophistication: Case studies on the scope of accounting instruments in Dutch power and gas companies, in: Management Accounting Research, 16 (1), p. 101–129.

Timian, K. A./Fleming, M. M. K. (2000): Toward Diversified Cost Accounting Systems, in: The National Public Accountant, 45 (1), p. 24–46.

Tosi, H. L./Slocum, J. W. (1984): Contingency Theor:y Some Suggested Directions, in: Journal of Management, 10 (1), p. 9–26.

Traverso, E./Bayer, M. (2008): Im Bann der Gewalt: der europäische Bürgerkrieg 1914 – 1945, München (2008).

Triandis, H. C. (1982a): Dimensions of Cultural Variation as Parameters of Organizational Theories, in: International Studies of Management & Organization, 12 (4), p. 139–169.

Triandis, H. C. (1982b): Review of culture's consequences: International differences in work-related values, in: Human Organization, 41 (1), p. 86–90.

Triandis, H. C. (1994): Culture and social behavior, New York (1994).

Trompenaars, F./Hampden-Turner, C. (2005): Riding the waves of culture – Understanding cultural diversity in business, 2nd. edn., London (2005).

Tscheulin, D. K./Helmig, B. (1994): Aufbau einer Kostenträgerrechnung im Krankenhaus, in: Das Krankenhaus, 86 (11), p. 501–508.

Tsui, J. S. L. (2001): The Impact of Culture on the Relationship Between Budgetary Participation, Management Accounting Systems and Managerial Performance: An Analysis of Chinese and Western Managers, in: International Journal of Accounting, 36 (2), p. 125–146.

Tung, R. L./Verbeke, A. (2010): Beyond Hofstede and GLOBE: Improving the quality of cross-cultural research, in: Journal of International Business Studies, 41 (8), p. 1259–1274.

Tunnell, G. B. (1977): Three Dimensions of Naturalness: An Expanded Definition of Field Research, in: Psychological Bulletin, 84 (3), p. 426–437.

Türk, K. (1989): Neuere Entwicklungen in der Organisationsforschung – Ein Trend-Report, Stuttgart (1989).

U

Ueno, S. (2000): Culture and Budget Control Practices: A Study of Manufacturing Companies in U.S.A and Japan, in: Monden, Y. (ed.): Japanese cost management, London (2000), p. 461–482.

Ueno, S./Sekaran, U. (1992): The Influence of Culture on Budget Control Practices in the USA and Japan: An Empirical Study, in: Journal of International Business Studies, 23 (4), p. 659–674.

Ueno, S./Wu, F. H. (1993): The Comparative Influence of Culture on Budget Control Practices in the United States and Japan, in: International Journal of Accounting, 28 (1), p. 17–39.

Ulrich, H. (1970): Die Unternehmung als produktives soziales System, Bern et al. (1970).

Ulrich, H./Probst, G. J. B. (1995): Anleitung zum ganzheitlichen Denken und Handeln – Ein Brevier für Führungskräfte, 4th. edn., Bern (1995).

Ulrich, P./Hill, W. (1976a): Wissenschaftstheoretische Grundlagen der Betriebswirtschaftslehre (Teil I), in: Wirtschaftswissenschaftliches Studium, 5 (7), p. 304–309.

Ulrich, P./Hill, W. (1976b): Wissenschaftstheoretische Grundlagen der Betriebswirtschaftslehre (Teil II), in: Wirtschaftswissenschaftliches Studium, 5 (8), p. 345–350.

Ulrich, P./Hill, W. (1979): Wissenschaftstheoretische Grundlagen der Betriebswirtschaftslehre, in: Raffée, H./Abel, B. (eds.): Wissenschaftstheoretische Grundfragen der Wirtschaftswissenschaften, München (1979), p. 161–190.

United Nations (2011): ISIC Rev.4, available at: http://unstats.un.org/unsd/cr/registry/regcst.asp?Cl=27, last revised 16.09.2011.

Usunier, J.-C. (1998): International and cross-cultural management research, London (1998).

Uterreitmeier, A. (2003): Auswirkungen alternativer Skalierungsarten auf das Antwortverhalten von Befragten, in: Planung & Analyse, 30 (3), p. 65–71.

V

Vallabhaneni, S. R. (2008): Corporate management, governance, and ethics best practices, Hoboken, NJ (2008).

Vallance, S./Fellow, H. (1999): Performance Appraisal in Singapore, Thailand and the Philippines: A Cultural Perspective, in: Australian Journal of Public Administration, 58 (4), p. 78–95.

van der Stede, W. A. (2003): The effect of national culture on management control and incentive system design in multi-business firms: evidence of intracorporate isomorphism, in: European Accounting Review, 12 (2), p. 263–285.

Vance, C. M./McClaine, S. R./Boje, D. M./Stage, H. D. (1992): An Examination of the Transferability of Traditional Performance Appraisal Principles across Cultural Boundaries, in: Management International Review, 32 (4), p. 313–326.

VDMA (2010): Maschinenbau in Zahl und Bild 2010, Frankfurt am Main (2010).

Venkatraman, N. (1989): The Concept of Fit in Strategy Research: Toward Verbal and Statistical Correspondence, in: Academy of Management Review, 14 (3), p. 423–444.

Vikas, K. (2006): Relevance Lost: Relevance Confirmed – Die Renaissance des German Management Accounting, in: Seicht, G. (ed.): Jahrbuch für Controlling und Rechnungswesen, Wien (2006), p. 27–42.

Vogel, E. F. (1979): Japan as number one – Lessons for America, Cambridge (Mass.) (1979).

Vondran, R. (1985): Gemeinsamkeiten und Unterschiede im Management, in: Hanau, P./Kimoto Saburo/Markmann, H./Tezuka, K. (eds.): Die Arbeitswelt in Japan und in der Bundesrepublik Deutschland, Neuwied (1985), p. 39–46.

W

Wagenhofer, A. (1993): Kostenrechnung und Agency Theorie, in: Weber, J. (ed.): Zur Neuausrichtung der Kostenrechnung. Entwicklungsperspektiven für die 90er Jahre, Stuttgart (1993), p. 161–185.

Wagenhofer, A. (2006): Management Accounting Research in German-Speaking Countries, in: Journal of Management Accounting Research, 18, p. 1–19.

Währisch, M. (1998): Kostenrechnungspraxis in der deutschen Industrie – Eine empirische Studie, Wiesbaden (1998).

Währisch, M. (2000): Der Ansatz kalkulatorischer Kostenarten in der industriellen Praxis, in: Zeitschrift für betriebswirtschaftliche Forschung, 52 (11), p. 678–694.

Walgenbach, P./Kieser, A. (1995): Mittlere Manager in Deutschland und Großbritannien, in: Schreyögg, G./Sydow, J. (eds.): Empirische Studien, Berlin (1995), p. 259–309.

Wallace, O. R. S./Gernon, H. (1991): Frameworks for International Comparative Financial Accounting, in: Journal of Accounting Literature, 10, p. 209–264.

Waterhouse, J. H./Tiessen, P. (1978): A Contingency Framework for Management Accounting Systems Research, in: Accounting, Organizations & Society, 3 (1), p. 65–76.

Webb, W. B. (1961): The Choice of the Problem, in: American Psychologist, 16 (5), p. 223–227.

Webber, S./Clinton, D. (2004): Resource Consumption Accounting Applied: The Clopay Case, in: Management Accounting Quarterly, 6 (1), p. 1–14.

Weber, J. (1993): Stand der Kostenrechnung in deutschen Großunternehmen – Ergebnisse einer empirischen Erhebung, in: Weber, J. (ed.): Zur Neuausrichtung der Kostenrechnung. Entwicklungsperspektiven für die 90er Jahre, Stuttgart (1993), p. 257–278.

Weber, J. (1996): Selektives Rechnungswesen, in: Zeitschrift für Betriebswirtschaft, 66 (8), p. 925–946.

Weber, J. (2004): Controlling einfach gestalten, Vallendar (2004).

Weber, J. (2005): Gestaltung der Kostenrechnung – Notwendigkeit, Optionen und Konsequenzen, Wiesbaden (2005).

Weber, J. (2011): Kostenrechnung – Relevance lost again?, in: Controller-Magazin, 36 (2), p. 36–37.

Weber, J./Goretzki, L./Zubler, S. (2010a): Welche Erkenntnisse kann die empirische Controllingforschung zum Erfolg des Controllings beitragen?, in: Controlling, 22 (6), p. 322–329.

Weber, J./Hirsch, B./Rambusch, R./Schlüter, H./Sill, F./Spatz, A. C. (2006): Controlling 2006 – Stand und Perspektiven, Berlin (2006).

Weber, J./Preis, A./Boettger, U. (2010b): Neue Anforderungen an Controller – Ergebnisse aus der Unternehmenspraxis, Weinheim (2010).

Weber, J./Reitmeyer, T./Frank, S. (2000): Erfolgreich entscheiden – Der Managementleitfaden für den Mittelstand, Wiesbaden (2000).

Weber, J./Schäffer, U. (1998): Controlling-Entwicklung im Spiegel von Stellenanzeigen 1990-1994, in: Kostenrechnungspraxis, 42 (4), p. 227–233.

Weber, J./Weißenberger, B. E. (1997): Relative Einzelkosten- und Deckungsbeitragsrechnung – A critical evaluation of Riebel's approach, in: Management Accounting Research, 8 (3), p. 277–298.

Weber, J./Weißenberger, B. E. (2006): Einführung in das Rechnungswesen – Bilanzierung und Kostenrechnung, 7th. edn., Stuttgart (2006).

Weber, J./Weißenberger, B. E./Aust, R. (1997): Benchmarking von Kostenrechnungsprozessen: Ansatzpunkte für eine wirtschaftlichere Leistungserbringung, in: Kostenrechnungspraxis, 41 (1), p. 27–33.

Weißenberger, B. E. (2004): Integrierte Rechnungslegung und Unternehmenssteuerung: Bedarf an kalkulatorischen Erfolgsgrößen auch unter IFRS?, in: Zeitschrift für Controlling & Management, 48 (special edition no. 2), p. 72–77.

Welge, M. K. (1988): Unternehmensführung, Band 3: Controlling, Stuttgart (1988).

Welge, M. K./Fessmann, K.-D. (1980): Effizienz, organisatorische, in: Grochla, E. (ed.): Handwörterbuch der Organisation, 2nd edn., Stuttgart (1980), c. 577–592.

Welton, R. E./Davis, J. R. (1990): Accounting Implications of the Perception of Professional Ethics: A Comparative Analysis of American and New Zealand Students, in: The International Journal of Accounting, 25 (4), p. 268–283.

Wendel, V. (2004): Controlling in Nonprofit-Unternehmen des stationären Gesundheitssektors, Berlin (2004).

Werner, S./Brouthers, L. E. (2002): How International is Management?, in: Journal of International Business Studies, 33 (3), p. 583–591.

White, L. (2009): Resource consumption accounting: Manager-focused management accounting, in: Journal of Corporate Accounting & Finance, 20 (4), p. 63–77.

Whitehill, A. M. (1995): Japanese management – Tradition and transition, London (1995).

Whitley, R. (1992): Societies, Firms and Markets: the Social Structuring of Business Systems, in: Whitley, R. (ed.): European Business Systems. Firms and Markets in Their National Contexts, London (1992), p. 5–45.

Whitley, R. (1999): Firms, institutions and management control: the comparative analysis of coordination and control systems, in: Accounting, Organizations & Society, 24 (5/6), p. 507–524.

Whitt, J. D. (1979): Motivating Lower-Level Management of Mexican Affiliates, in: Management Accounting, 57 (6), p. 46–49.

Whorf, B. L. (1956): Language, thought, and reality, selected writings of Benjamin Lee Whorf, Cambridge Mass. et al. (1956).

Wiersema, W. H. (1996): Implementing Activity-Based Management: Overcoming the Data Barrier, in: Journal of Cost Management, 10 (2), p. 17–20.

Wijewardena, H./Cooray, S. (1995): Accounting education in Australia and Japan: a comparative examination, in: Accounting Education, 4 (4), p. 359–377.

Wijewardena, H./Zoysa, A. de (1999): A Comparative Analysis of Management Accounting Practices in Australia and Japan: An Empirical Investigation, in: International Journal of Accounting, 34 (1), p. 49–70.

Wild, J. (1966): Grundlagen und Probleme der betriebswirtschaftlichen Organisationslehre – Entwurf eines Wissenschaftsprogramms, Berlin (1966).

Wild, J. (1976): Theorienbildung, in: Grochla, E./Wittmann, W. (eds.): Handwörterbuch der Betriebswirtschaft, 4th edn., Stuttgart (1976), c. 3889–3910.

Wilkins, A. L./Ouchi, W. G. (1983): Efficient Cultures: Exploring the Relationship between Culture and Organizational Performance, in: Administrative Science Quarterly, 28 (3), p. 468–481.

Williams, J. J./Seaman, A. E. (2001): Predicting change in management accounting systems: national culture and industry effects, in: Accounting, Organizations & Society, 26 (4/5), p. 443–460.

Winston, R. J. (1968): The U.S. accountant goes to the orient, in: Management Accounting, 46 (12), p. 39–44.

Winter, P. (2005): Japanische Kostenrechnungssysteme. Analyse der Kostenrechnungssysteme nach dem japanischen Kostenrechnungsstandard, Working Paper (2005).

Witt, M. A. (2006): Changing Japanese Capitalism: Societal Coordination and Institutional Adjustment, Cambridge (2006).

Wold, H. (1980): Model construction and evaluation when theoretical knowledge is scarce: Theory and application of partial least squares, in: Kmenta, J./Ramsey, J. B. (eds.): Evaluation of econometric models, New York (1980), p. 47–74.

Wold, H. (1982): Systems under Indirect Observations Using PLS, in: Fornell, C. (ed.): A Second Generation of Multivariate Analysis, New York (1982), p. 325–347.

Wollnik, M. (1977): Die explorative Verwendung systematischen Erfahrungswissens – Plädoyer für einen aufgeklärten Empirismus in der Betriebswirtschaftslehre, in: Köhler, R. (ed.): Empirische und handlungstheoretische Forschungskonzeptionen in der Betriebswirtschaftslehre. Bericht über die Tagung in Aachen März 1976, Stuttgart (1977), p. 37–64.

Wömpener, A. (2010): The Globalisation of a Profession – Comparative Management Accounting in the Context of Emerging and Developed Countries, Working Paper (2010).

Woodward, J. (1958): Management and technology, London (1958).

Y

Yagi, R. (1990): Accounting education in firms: the case of Hitachi (in Japanese), in: Kigyo Kaikei, 42 (5), p. 68–73.

Yamada, T. (1991): The Regulation Approach, Tokyo (1991).

Yasunaga, H./Ide, H./Imamura, T./Ohe, K. (2006): Influence of Japan's New Diagnosis Procedure Combination-Based Payment System on the Surgical Sector: Does it Really Shorten the Hospital Stay?, in: Surgery Today, 36 , p. 577–585.

Yin, R. K. (2009): Case study research – Design and methods, 4th. edn., Thousand Oaks, Calif (2009).

Yoshikawa, T. (2000): ABC to ABM no riron oyobi jissen no kenkyuu, Yokohama (2000).

Yoshikawa, T. (1994a): A review of Japanese management accounting literature and bibliography, London (1994).

Yoshikawa, T. (1994b): Some aspects of the Japanese approach to management accounting, in: Management Accounting Research, 5 (3), p. 279–287.

Yoshikawa, T. (2001): Cost accounting standard and cost accounting systems in Japan. Lessons from the past – recovering lost traditions, in: Accounting, Business & Financial History, 11 (3), p. 269–281.

Yoshikawa, T./Innes, J./Mitchell, F. (1989): Japanese management accounting: a comparative survey, in: Management Accounting, 67 (11), p. 20–23.

Yoshikawa, T./Innes, J./Mitchell, F. (1990): Cost Tables: A Foundation of Japanese Cost Management, in: Journal of Cost Management, 4 (3), p. 30–36.

Yoshimori, M. (1995): Whose Company Is It? The Concept of the Corporation in Japan and the West, in: Long Range Planning, 28 (4), p. 33–44.

Yu, J./Zaheer, S. (2010): Building a process model of local adaptation of practices: A study of Six Sigma implementation in Korean and US firms, in: Journal of International Business Studies, 41 (3), p. 475–499.

Yuchtman, E./Seashore, S. E. (1967): A System Resource Approach to Organizational Effectiveness, in: American Sociological Review, 32 (6), p. 891–903.

Z

Zax, M./Takahashi/Shigeo (1967): Cultural Influences on Response Style: Comparisons of Japanese and American College Students, in: The Journal of Social Psychology, 71 (1), p. 3–10.

Zimmermann, C. (2001): Controlling in international tätigen mittelständischen Unternehmen, Wiesbaden (2001).

Zoysa, A. de/Herath, S. K. (2007): Standard costing in Japanese firms: Reexamination of its significance in the new manufacturing environment, in: Industrial Management & Data Systems, 107 (2), p. 271–283.

Zucker, L. G. (1977): The Role of Institutionalization in Cultural Persistence, in: American Sociological Review, 42 (5), p. 726–743.

Zucker, L. G. (1987): Institutional theories of organization, in: Annual Review of Sociology, 13, p. 443–464.

Zur, E. (1992): Kalkulation im öffentlichen Auftragswesen, in: Männel, W. (ed.): Handbuch der Kostenrechnung, Wiesbaden (1992), p. 605–617.

Zwirner, C. (2010): Kapitalmarktorientierung im Jahr 2010, in: Zeitschrift für internationale und kapitalmarktorientierte Rechnungslegung (11), p. 529–531.

Münsteraner Schriften zur Internationalen Unternehmensrechnung

Herausgegeben von Peter Kajüter

Band 1 Daniela Barth: Prognoseberichterstattung. Praxis, Determinanten und Kapitalmarktwirkungen bei deutschen börsennotierten Unternehmen. 2009.

Band 2 Tobias Dickmann: Controllingintegration nach M&A-Transaktionen. Eine empirische Analyse. 2010.

Band 3 Simon Esser: Produktorientiertes Kostenmanagement in der chemischen Industrie. Eine empirische Analyse. 2011.

Band 4 Christian Reisloh: Influence of National Culture on IFRS Practice. An Empirical Study in France, Germany and the United Kingdom. 2011.

Band 5 Matthias Moeschler: Cost Accounting in Germany and Japan. A Comparative Analysis. 2012.

www.peterlang.de

FSC
www.fsc.org
MIX
Papier | Fördert gute Waldnutzung
FSC® C083411

Kolibri 360 GmbH
Ferdinand-Jühlke-Straße 7
99095 Erfurt, Deutschland
produktsicherheit@kolibri360.de